D1354140

Corsica

Jean-Bernard Carillet
Miles Roddis

On the Road

JEAN-BERNARD CARILLET Coordinating Author
On the west coast, **Girolata** (p151) is a special place: this hamlet can only be reached by boat or on foot. In July and August, it gets very crowded – there's a flotilla of yachts and day-trippers. But I came in September, and I had the whole place to myself. I wandered amid the *ruelles* (lanes), marvelling at the unforgettable vistas over the bay. Then it was time for a *spuntinu* (light meal) at a *paillotte* (beachside restaurant) – something I take very seriously. I can still remember the fabulous *ambrucciata* (tart with *brocciu* cheese), which gave me enough energy to walk back up to the main road, about 1½ hours later.

MILES RODDIS The GR20 is a legendary walk through Corsica's high mountains encompassing an incredible diversity of landscapes including dense forests, glacial lakes, snowcapped peaks and rocky gullies. I'd completed the first two hours of the **GR20's Day 13** (p72), walking solo, the way I enjoy it most. It was tough going, a constant series of steep rises and dips, plus lots of four-limbed clambering over slabs of rock. Then I dropped into the deep, still coolness of a beech wood. At its heart was a clearing into which an icy stream gurgled, the perfect spot to rest against a boulder, breathe deeply and bask in the magnificent surrounds.

Corsica

It's no wonder that so many visitors fall in love with Corsica. Within the space of a day, you can journey from chic seaside towns to remote hilltop hamlets, from the sparkling turquoise waters of the coast to the towering mountainscapes of the interior. Whether your passion is the rustic delights of *cucina corsa*, wilderness adventures or beachside hedonism, this rugged little island is sure to charm you with its natural beauty, rich culture and fiery spirit.

Must-See Coastal Cities

A succession of cities strut down Corsica's coastline, like supermodels on a catwalk. Not only strikingly beautiful, each has a strong personality and soul. There's really nowhere better to sample *la dolce vita*.

❶ Bonifacio
Corsica's belle of the ball, Bonifacio (p196) can't be beaten for its breathtaking coastal scenery and for the buzzing atmosphere of its port and old town.

❷ Porto-Vecchio
With its ritzy, Riviera-like atmosphere and busy seafront, Porto-Vecchio (p203) is a typical picture-postcard town worth a visit. Don't forget your designer sunglasses.

❸ Calvi
Sprawl on Calvi's (p126) long sandy beach before retiring to a quayside restaurant, all under the watchful eye of the citadel.

❹ Ajaccio
Hedonistic, civilised and seductive, Ajaccio (p164) has charm in spades. Its relaxed pace of life is infectious. Shop 'til you drop in its palm-fringed avenues.

❺ Bastia
Who said that Bastia (p100) was rough around the edges? The city exudes an appealing Italian flavour, and its atmospheric Vieux Port is best enjoyed at dinner time, a glass of pastis in hand.

❻ Porto
A tiny seaside resort, Porto (p147) boasts the most sensational setting of the west coast, with the cliffs of Les Calanques and the Réserve Naturelle de Scandola in easy reach.

Sand, Sea & Rivers

This rugged island is bordered by dozens of Seychelles-like expanses of white sand, perfect for self-indulgent beach bumming. Each has a unique character, yet all are lapped by a soothing sea, that great antidote to the stress of modern living.

Author Tip
If you want to escape the summer crowds, the gin-clear, Jacuzzi-like *vasques* (natural rock pools) in the interior beckon.

❶ Île Lavezzi
Bliss out on the Archipel des Lavezzi (p201), a clutch of uninhabited islets. The arid Île Lavezzi, which gives its names to the whole archipelago, is a great place to cast yourself adrift.

❷ Réserve Naturelle de Scandola
The exceptional coastal wilderness of this reserve (p152), a Unesco World Heritage site, is a breeding ground for magnificent osprey, giant groupers and curious seaweeds. Only approachable by sea, consider renting a small motor boat to explore this unique environment.

❸ Plage de Saleccia
The setting for the film *The Longest Day* (1960), this 1km-long stretch of icing-sugar sand dissolves into beautiful turquoise waters (p122). Truly off the beaten track, you'll need to sail or pedal here.

❹ Plage de Rondinara
If you're looking for your island dream, then look no further than this sensational, horse-shoe-shaped beach (p203) lapped by waters like liquid glass.

❺ Vasques of the Vallée du Travo
The natural pools of the Travo River (p233) are made for those who love nothing better than a refreshing dip in crystal-clear waters, with mountains rising gloriously on all sides.

❻ Plage de Tra Licettu
Not yet overwhelmed by the crowds, this secluded beach (p193) is best approached by a small motor boat (with a Pietra in hand) or a sea kayak for maximum effect.

Corse Profonde

For a glimpse of a more traditional Corsica, take a trip to the mysterious hinterlands of the central mountains – the heart and soul of Corsica. In the countless valleys and spurs that slice up the dramatic scenery are scattered discreet hamlets that beg exploration.

❶ Villages Perchés

The Balagne Craft Trail (p139) makes for a very pleasant day's driving around the rustic hilltop villages of the Balagne interior (top left) through a landscape dotted with olive groves, deep ravines and dramatic granite outcrops. Too gentle for you? Tackle the rally roads that serve the splendidly isolated hamlets of Le Boziu (p242).

❷ Glacial Lakes

You could be forgiven for thinking you've hit Mongolia near the exquisite high-altitude lakes of the interior, especially after making the climb all the way up to Lac de Ninu (p67; bottom left). Other superb lakes include Lac de Melu (p243) and Lac de Capitellu (p243).

❸ L'Alta Rocca

Light years away from the coastal fleshpots, the Alta Rocca (p211) offers a real sense of wilderness, with deep forests and granite villages strung over rocky ledges. Towering above it all are the awesome Aiguilles de Bavella (p217).

❹ Sartène

The archetypal Corsican town, Sartène (p189), with its stalwart granite houses and narrow streets, retains a charming authenticity.

❺ La Castagniccia

Rippling hills, dense chestnut forests, lush valleys, majestic mountains, placid villages, Baroque churches and not a primary road in sight: it doesn't get more *Corse profonde* than La Castagniccia (p224).

❻ Corte & the Vallée du Tavignano

The bastion of Corsican culture, Corte (p237) attracts plenty of visitors to its renowned museum and bustling old town. Nearby, the car-free, lightly tramped Vallée du Tavignano (p243) is a gem.

Heritage & Tradition

The forces that have shaped Corsica's past still resonate today: the mystical prehistoric remains of Filitosa, the splendour of the Baroque churches and the powerful, spiralling harmonies of Corsican polyphony. Explore these ancient legacies for a taste of the rich cultural fabric of contemporary Corsica.

1 Genoese Towers
Around 60 Genoese towers dating from the 16th century still stand guard along the coast. The most impressive of these stunning fortified structures can be found in Cap Corse (p109). Towers in Porto (p147) or near Campomoro (p188) are also worth checking out.

2 Ancient Churches
Corsica's greatest architectural treasure is ecclesiastical. Don't miss the sumptuously decorated Baroque churches, such as Bastia's Église St-Jean Baptiste (p103; above) or the poignant Pisan Romanesque churches.

3 Prehistoric Sites
Take a giant stride back to the Torréens' times at Filitosa (p182) and explore the archaeological site's mysterious megalithic menhirs encircling the foot of a 1200-year-old olive tree.

4 Musée Fesch
A must for culture vultures, this Ajaccio museum (p165) has some outstanding 14th- to 19th-century Italian paintings, including works by Titian and Veronese.

5 Polyphonic Tunes
Be sure to catch a live performance of Corsican polyphony, preferably in an ancient church or at Calvi's festival of polyphonic singing (p257) held in the town's citadel in mid-September. The profound sonorities and the marvellous chants are sure to rouse your soul.

6 Festivals
Corsicans love to celebrate and there's nearly always something going on around the island. Don't miss the solemn, colourful processions during Easter, especially in Sartène (p189).

Outdoor Galore

Corsica's outstanding natural beauty will prompt even the most hard-core couch-potato to drag themselves outside. On land or sea there are plenty of ways to get active, and nonthrillseekers take heart – horse-riding excursions or Parcs Aventure are tailor-made for those who want to experience the island's wild side without the strain!

❶ Canyoning
Explore the iconic canyons of the interior, Canyon de la Vacca (p217) and Canyon du Baracci (p185), set in some of the most grandiose scenery in Corsica. Be prepared to get wet!

❷ Walking & Trekking
Need to push your limits? Embark on a sensational 15-day, 200km trekking odyssey along the legendary GR20 (p54; above). For a softer option, try one of the gentle paths through the valleys or along the coast.

❸ Diving
Hug a grouper the size of a small car in the crystal-clear waters off Îles Lavezzi! The quiet awe of a dive with these thick-lipped creatures is unforgettable (p81).

❹ Horse Riding
Saddling up is a fun and ecofriendly way to commune with the Corsican wilderness and enjoy the long sandy beaches (p193), glorious hinterlands and lush forests (p225). Donkey rides (p185 & p142) are also available for the little 'uns!

❺ Parcs Aventure
All the rage on the island, Parcs Aventure allow you to revive your childhood fantasies and swing Tarzan-style from tree to tree. The most atmospheric ones can be found near Bavella (p217), in Vizzavona (p248) and near Solenzara (p234).

❻ Kitesurfing & Windsurfing
It ain't Hawaii, but the wind-whipped Bonifacio area (p202 & p194) consistently ranks as one of the most thrilling spots in the Med for kitesurfing and windsurfing.

Culinary Temptations

Unlike the *haute cuisine* of the mainland, the *cucina corsa* (Corsican cuisine) is wholesome and comforting, using tried-and-true recipes and fresh local produce. Forget the diet for a few days and ease a belt hole for mouth-watering charcuterie, tantalising desserts, pungent cheeses, fresh fish and toothsome grilled meats, and wash it all down with a glass of Corsican wine or a cold beer.

❶ Hmm, Cheese!
Brocciu: a mantra in Corsica. This mild, crumbly white cheese (p90) can be found on practically every single menu, in a variety of guises. Perfect picnic fodder.

❷ Sweet Fix
Savour the sugar and flavour buzz of a *fiadone* (flan made with *brocciu* cheese, lemon and eggs) or a chestnut-flour cake, two iconic Corsican desserts (p91).

❺ Heaven in a Glass
Put some zing in your step with a glass of a full-bodied AOC Patrimonio (p92) or a treacherous *liqueur de myrte* (liqueur flavoured with myrtle, p91).

❻ Fish & Seafood
Oysters, mussels, sea bass, scorpion fish, lobster, red mullet... Corsica is *the* place to devour the bounteous offerings of the Mediterranean, all expertly cooked (p90).

❸ Charcuterie: Tempt the Devil in You
You won't be able to resist the temptation of a morsel of *prisuttu*, *coppa* or *salsiccia*, all made from herb-saturated pork (p89).

❹ Time for a Pietra
After a long day exploring the countryside, nothing can beat a fresh, chestnut-flavoured Pietra (p91), best enjoyed on a terrace with a view over the Med or the mountains.

Contents

Regional Map Contents

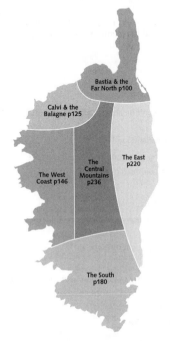

Bastia & the Far North p100

Calvi & the Balagne p125

The East p220

The Central Mountains p236

The West Coast p146

The South p180

Getting Started

Corsica is dubbed *L'île de beauté* (the island of beauty), and it's no wonder why. With everything from mountain ranges to idyllic beaches and secluded villages, Corsica offers a kaleidoscopic palette of options in a relatively small area. There's never a dull moment!

For outdoor enthusiasts, the range of scenery and activities is almost countless. From sea kayaking to trekking, canyoning to diving, there is barely a sport or activity, whether on land or on the sea, that isn't catered for here. But Corsica allows for far more than just hot-weather beach holidays and adrenaline rushes – there's a wealth of history, culture and tradition to explore, too. You could also set yourself a gastronomical route full of delectable surprises.

Although there are bus and train systems that cover the island, a rental car is definitely the order of the day for anyone who really wants to explore (delving into hidden valleys or hunting down hard-to-reach beaches). Although tourist trails are well trodden, it's easy to escape the crowds and tailor your itinerary to suit your own tastes.

WHEN TO GO

See climate charts (p254) for more information.

Hmmm…When the maquis is in full blossom in May and June, the scents are memorable and the vivid hues unforgettable. This is by far the best season to explore Corsica. The weather is sunny without being stifling, the countryside bursts with spring flowers, the locals are more hospitable and the flood of summer tourists, largely dictated by the French *vacances scolaires* (school holidays), has yet to crash over the island.

Most French people hit the road in July and August, so those two months – in which prices soar, tempers flare and the island broils – are best avoided.

DON'T LEAVE HOME WITHOUT...

- Patience – this is island time, after all
- Hiking boots – even if you're not a serious hiker, you won't be able to resist the temptation of a few walks
- Detailed road maps to tackle those nerve-racking hinterland roads
- Your driving licence and car documents if driving, along with appropriate car insurance
- An adaptator plug for electrical appliances (see the boxed text, p251)
- Lonely Planet's *French Phrasebook*
- An appetite for pungent cheese and artery-clogging charcuterie
- Your C-card if you're a diver, as well as a medical examination certificate from a doctor (mandatory for diving in France)
- A sleeping bag if you're planning on camping or staying at *gîtes d'étape*
- Snorkelling gear if you're anticipating heavy beach time
- A set of smart casual clothes: grimy T-shirts, shorts and dusty sandals don't cut the mustard in bars and restaurants in some chic coastal cities
- Maximum-protection sunscreen, sunglasses and a hat
- Some paperback books in English (poor availability in Corsica)

The core of the peak season is from mid-July to mid-August, when Corsica is chock-a-block with visitors. Flights and ferries are full to bursting, too. It's imperative to make reservations well in advance if you're planning to visit the island during this period.

Another good season is autumn, from September to mid-October. It's refreshingly peaceful and the weather is usually warm. Most places are open, without being overwhelmed by the crowds. It's generally comfortable for land-based outdoor activities such as walking, horse riding and canyoning. As for water sports, the water temperature is most favourable from June to October, and can reach 25°C in August.

Between late October and springtime, the island goes into snooze mode and most tourist facilities are closed, which is a bit of a shame since the climate is usually mild and sunny in winter, at least on the coast (it can be downright chilly inland). It's a good season for photographers, with perfect light and enchanting hues. Some *chambres d'hôtes* are open year-round, as are certain hotels in the main cities, which means that with some preplanning and your own wheels you can easily get around the island, and have the whole place to yourself! Winter is also the best season if you're hunting for that perfect charcuterie – believe us!

Walkers on the GR20 and other routes, the elderly and those travelling with children will surely prefer the less sweltering months of May, June and September, when roads and amenities are also less congested. Serious hikers should take note that the snow lingers until as late as mid-June on some sections of the GR20.

You may also prefer to organise your trip to coincide with one of the many festivals that fill the Corsican calendar – Easter is a particular highlight. For more details see p256.

COSTS & MONEY

Though travelling in Corsica may not be cheap, neither is it prohibitively expensive. As a general rule, you can expect to pay at least €70 to €200 for a decent double room in high season (often more in August). You will have to pay the same minimum rates if you are on your own, as there are very few single rooms. Camping, sleeping in off-the-beaten track *chambres d'hôtes* or renting a *gîte rural* for a week can be good-value accommodation options. Sites charge an average of €6/3/3 per person/tent/car. If you're solo, staying at *gîtes d'étape* can be another well-priced option (about €13 per night); most people think they are geared only to hikers, but all travellers are welcome.

The interior of the island is also significantly cheaper than the coast. While Bonifacio and Porto-Vecchio rank as the most expensive cities in Corsica, the Alta Rocca, about 30km to the north, is much more affordable and can be used as a convenient base.

Another key factor to consider is the wild difference in costs between the high season (July and August) and the rest of the year. During these peak months room prices on the coast can be jacked up by 100% in many cases. The good news though is that even the most popular tourist places, such as Porto-Vecchio and Bonifacio, drop their prices dramatically out of season. You'll find excellent deals, and fewer people, in the shoulder seasons either side of summer: in April, May, June, September and October, which can result in some real bargains in accommodation and transport. Not all tourist facilities are open, but you can easily get by.

The cost of eating out is variable, depending on the location. Most restaurants offer tourist menus for about €15. However, it is often better to choose a good restaurant and have one good course rather than a mediocre complete meal.

TOP FIVES

Vasques (Natural Pools)
Beat the heat! Take a refreshing dip in the gin-clear waters of the mountain rivers...

- Vallée du Travo (p233)
- Solenzara River (p234)
- Pont de Noceta (p247)
- Tavignano River (p243)
- Vallée de la Restonica (p241)

Walks
Corsica's abundance of well-marked hiking trails makes it a haven for walkers from around the globe. More walking options are detailed in the regional chapters and in the Walking & the GR20 chapter (p54).

- GR20 (p56)
- Sentier des Douaniers (p112)
- Col de la Croix to Girolata (p152)
- Vallée du Tavignano (p243)
- Pertusato Lighthouse (p198)
- Monte Cinto (p244)

Atmospheric Chambres d'Hôtes
Find heaven in one of those lovely cocoonlike B&Bs in a grandiose setting...

- La Diligence (p226), in Verdèse
- Littariccia (p211), near Porto-Vecchio
- Villa Clotilde (p232), in the Fiumorbu
- Châtelet de Campo (p177), in the Haut Taravo
- Carpe Diem (p170), near Ajaccio

Bus and train travel (often seasonal as well) is generally quite expensive if you consider the actual distances travelled. Hiring a car will cost you about €250 per week with unlimited mileage and comprehensive insurance.

Don't forget to leave room in your budget for activities such as diving (from €40), horse riding (from €17), canyoning (about €40) or *parc aventure* (about €15).

Realistically, a traveller wanting to stay in comfortable midrange hotels or *chambres d'hôtes*, eat two square meals per day, hire a car and not feel restricted to one or two outdoor activities per week should reckon on a minimum daily average of €100 to €120 per day based on two people sharing a room at €80, plus car hire.

TRAVEL LITERATURE

The Corsican visitor's bible, Dorothy Carrington's revered 1971 *Granite Island: a Portrait of Corsica*, also known as *Corsica: Portrait of a Granite Island*, is a travel book only in the sense that it is structured around the author's comings and goings around the island. Its learning and passion for Corsica is immense. Now out of print, you may find it in a library, second-hand bookshop or on the internet.

Scenic Roads
Clunk your seat belt, hold on to your hat and be prepared for heart-stopping drives along ribbon-thin roads...

- The D80, from Patrimonio to Pino (p109)
- The D81B, from Calvi to Galéria and Porto (p134)
- The D268, from Solenzara to Col de Bavella (p234)
- The D69, from Aullène to Col de la Vaccia (p214)
- The D146, from Piedicroce to Cervione (p226)

Corsica for Children
Fear not; if you're with the little ones, there are lots of sights and activities to keep them happy.

- The A Cupulatta Centre (p169)
- A donkey ride with Balagn'ane (p142)
- The Petit Train in Ajaccio (p169)
- A picnic by the Vecchio River (p247)
- A boat trip to the Réserve Naturelle de Scandola (p152) or Îles Lavezzi (p201)

Quintessentially Corsican Village
There are dozens of contenders for that title. Here's a (ruthless) selection:

- Fozzano (p187)
- Sant'Antonino (p143)
- Vescovato (p221)
- Zonza (p212)
- Morosaglia (p227)

How exotic Corsica must have seemed to continental writers when they began to discover it in the 19th century, perfect for the purposes of swash-buckler fiction. If you search hard, you may be able to find an old edition of Alexandre Dumas' *The Corsican Brothers*, Guy de Maupassant's Corsica stories or Honoré de Balzac's story *La Vendetta*. Unsurprisingly, they all deal with honour, murder, implacable hatreds and revenge.

For details on Corsican authors, see p41.

Travellers with a good reading knowledge of French will have access to much richer resources. Nicolas Giudici's *Le Crépuscule des Corses* is a brilliant and pessimistic analysis of Corsica's prospects in the world (*crépuscule* means 'twilight').

L'Art du Graffiti en Corse by Pierre Bertoncini is a fully illustrated coffee-table book presenting the history of this illicit art and subculture on the island.

There's something for travellers of all ages to enjoy in *Asterix in Corsica* by R Goscinny, translated into several languages. The subtle historical puns and references may be lost on younger readers, but they will no doubt enjoy this classic romp through the maquis as Asterix and chums fend off the Romans.

INTERNET RESOURCES

Aller en Corse (www.allerencorse.com) Accommodation listings and other practical information for visitors (French and English).

Clique Corse (www.cliquecorse.com, in French) Practical and cultural information site.

Corse Matin (www.corsematin.com, in French) Corsica's leading daily newspaper.

Corse Musique (www.corsemusique.com) A portal dedicated to Corsican music, with links to groups' websites and audio snippets.

Corsica Bus (www.corsicabus.org) Bus and train timetables.

Corsica Image Bank (www.corsica-imagebank.com) A photo library dedicated to Corsica, with zoom-in maps and more than 6500 shots – a good site to get a feel of the village, city or beach you're planning to visit.

Corsica Isula (www.corsica-isula.com) The most exhaustive English-language website about Corsica, with links to other useful sites.

Gîtes de Corse (www.gites-corsica.com) Has a wealth of information on *chambres d'hôtes* and *gîtes ruraux*, with online bookings.

L'Agence du Tourisme de la Corse (www.visit-corsica.com) The island's official tourist-board site.

Lonely Planet (www.lonelyplanet.com) Concise information, postcards from other travellers and the Thorn Tree bulletin board, where you can ask questions before you go, or dispense advice when you return.

Parc Naturel Régional (www.parc-naturel-corse.com) Here you'll find oodles of information on walking, the environment and microregions.

See also p261, p264 and p250 for other useful websites.

Snapshot

If there's one island that can be defined as schizoid, it must be Corsica. On the one hand, affable and respectful people, idyllic landscapes, a blossoming tourist industry, a unique culture, an infectious dolce vita, the best charcuterie and the most pungent cheeses in the world, and an unmatched tranquillity. On the other hand, a pervading sense of defiance and rebellion, as testified by the latest trend on the island, T-shirts bearing the words 'Che Corsica', or less light-hearted activities, such as fire-bombing and a host of internecine *règlements de compte* (settling of scores) among separatist groups.

Some of the more striking graffiti you'll find in Corsica points to the on-going issues of national identity and independence, with 'Terra Corsa ai Corsi' (Corsica for Corsicans) or 'Francesi Fora' (French Go Home) seeming to be the preferred slogans, along with the acronyms of nationalist movements scrawled on many public buildings on the island, like territorial markers. Not to mention the ubiquitous bullet-ridden roadsigns, with the French placename spray-painted out.

In terms of voting at the polls, Corsican nationalism has generally been a fringe phenomenon (pulling in about 10% to 15% of the vote at each election), but it extends far beyond net political results. Virtually all Corsicans recognise that the nationalists have helped protect the culture of the island and its landscape, preventing mass urbanisation of the coastline (there's no Riviera in Corsica) and fostering the revival of Corsu (the Corsican language), which forms the basis of the Corsican identity.

There's no denying that there's a Corsican malaise, which is palpable but hard to define. No French government has ever managed to reach a kind of permanent agreement with Corsican separatists, and all strategies have failed. There's a strong sense of insularity, which is certainly due to centuries of invasion and occupation, and a deep-seated feeling among Corsicans that their cultural identity is threatened by mainland France. For the *pinzutti* (the French mainlanders), the Corsicans are spoiled children who get a lot of funds from the EU and from Paris.

Autonomy and confrontation with the state are not the only issues. The main economic concern is the reliance on subsidies from the mainland and the tourist industry (the island's single biggest provider of employment). Late 2006 some intrepid Corsican politicians said that the very strict Loi Littorale, which prohibits all new building within 100m of the shoreline, should be loosened in order to foster economic growth. As the situation stands, certain elected deputies think that the island is 'frozen' and is unable to develop. The nationalists immediately reacted to this proposal, saying that these politicians should be *abattu et combattu* (literally, shot down and fought). Is this to be understood literally? Probably not, but this gives an idea of the very fervent way the island's future is debated.

Though these political undercurrents are palpable, fear not; tourists are never the target of nationalist activity and will always feel welcome by all Corsicans, who will greet you with a *pace i salute* (best wishes). They are keen to share their unique culture and the treasures of their island – its fabulous land- and seascapes, its unforgettable food, its wealth of activities, its diverse cultural sights and its poignant polyphonic chants.

FAST FACTS

Population: 262,000

Territory size: 8682 sq km

Brocciu season: November–June

Number of Corsican clubs in the French second-division soccer league: 2

Number of AOC-labelled wines: 9

Highest point: Monte Cinto (2710m)

Number of local beers: 4

Size of the biggest groupers encountered in the Archipel des Lavezzi: 1.50m

Network of waymarked paths: more than 2000km

History

World history is generally told without reference to Corsica at all, except, in passing, as the place that gave birth to Emperor Napoleon Bonaparte. Nevertheless, Corsica's history is a fascinating and turbulent one. Its strategic position long attracted the attentions of the major Mediterranean and European powers. Armies from Pisa, Genoa, France, Spain and Britain, not to mention the Moors and the armies of the Roman and Holy Roman Empires, have all fought on Corsican soil. This long history of conflict reflects another battle – the islanders' struggle to assert their identity while dominated by a succession of foreign rulers. Indeed, Corsicans have battled for their independence ever since the Romans occupied the island, beginning in 259 BC.

NEOLITHIC CORSICA

It is likely that the island was inhabited in the Palaeolithic era, but the earliest skeletal remains, of Bonifacio Woman, dating from 6570 BC, are from the early Neolithic era.

The first inhabitants of the island probably came from what is nowadays Tuscany, in Italy, and the nearest place on the European mainland. They survived by hunting, gathering and fishing. You can still see rock caves of the kind in which they lived at Filitosa (p182) in the south.

Around 4000 BC the inhabitants of the island, like so many early European societies, became captivated by big stones. At various sites, particularly in the southwestern corner of the island, they erected great standing slabs of stone (menhirs), and shelter-like constructions (dolmens), in which two or more standing stones support a huge, horizontal slab as a 'roof'. At some point they began to shape and carve their menhirs, which became simple statues with carved warrior faces.

Examples of these menhirs still stand at various places across the island, including Patrimonio (p119), where a pair flank the stage of the annual Nuits de la Guitare festival.

Dorothy Carrington's Granite Island: a Portrait of Corsica is possibly the finest book about Corsica in any language.

THE TORRÉENS

In about 1100 BC a new race, possibly originating from the eastern Mediterranean, came to the island. These new islanders have come to be known as Torréens, named after their seemingly indestructible signature edifices, the *torri*, or towers, which stand alongside or on the ruins of menhirs and dolmens. Some of the best examples of these towers dot the coastline of Cap Corse (p109).

Evidence suggests that the Torréens routed their predecessors, the menhir and dolmen builders who, with less sophisticated weapons, appear to have migrated or fled north. Many Torréens, it seems, then headed south to Sardinia, where they built some of the first conical stone edifices, now called *nuraghi*.

The island's architectural development continued, and early *castelli* (castles) are the most significant vestiges of the settled, more organised way of life that the island's inhabitants had begun to lead. The remains of three of these *castelli* can be visited in the mountains between Porto-Vecchio and Propriano (see p215).

60,000 BC	4000–1800 BC
First indications of human presence on Corsica	Monoliths and megalithic tombs constructed by the island's inhabitants

GREEKS & ROMANS

In the 6th century BC the Phocaean Greeks founded Alalia at what is today the conurbation of Aléria (p228) on Corsica's flat eastern plain. Alalia thrived on trade and Corsica soon rose to relative fame.

For the cosmopolitan, seafaring peoples of the Mediterranean, however, the island was primarily a place for brief port calls. Nobody before Rome actually undertook to invest in and dominate the island, and when Rome did step in, it was above all for strategic reasons: to prevent Corsica from falling into the hands of its enemies, the Carthaginians.

Rome conquered Alalia, renaming it Aléria, and set about imposing its way of life and government upon the islanders, exacting tribute, and even selling some of them into slavery. Rome, though, never went to any great pains to improve the island. In what was to become a recurrent pattern in Corsica, those islanders least willing to bend to invaders retired to the interior and the protection of the unconquerable mountains.

GOTHS, VANDALS & MOORS

After the collapse of the Western Roman Empire in AD 476, the distant Byzantine Empire (the Eastern Roman Empire, based in Constantinople) began to take an interest in former Roman territories such as Corsica. The collapse of Rome had initially left Corsica vulnerable to Rome's own despoilers – the Goths under Totila and the Vandals under Genseric. It's likely that the Vandals, having laid waste to Gaul, took to the water and sacked Aléria too. Byzantium's equally bloody conquest of the island in the first half of the 6th century ended the brief dominion of the Germanic tribes.

During the 8th century Corsica was also increasingly subject to attack by the Moors, Muslims from North Africa. Whether as organised navies or as free-booting pirates, the Moors raided for slaves, and from time to time they would take possession of a coastal village or a whole coastal region, even venturing deeper inland. Between the 8th and 18th centuries the islanders lived in perpetual fear of invasion from the south.

Of the few choices in English, www.corsica.net gives a reasonable overview of Corsican history while www.terra corsa.info/history.html is more skeletal.

PISAN SPELL

The 10th century saw the rise to power of the nobility. Important seignorial families, often immigrants of Tuscan or Ligurian origin, created fiefdoms on the island and ruled them with a rod of iron. Some historians argue that Corsica's close-knit clan system dates right back to this period. In 1077, at the request of a group of Tuscan feudal lords, the Pope appointed the bishop of Pisa to oversee his Corsican interests.

The then-powerful Italian city of Pisa, continually at odds with its rival, Genoa, put commerce ahead of all other values and its bishop effectively served as a front man for Pisan merchants. Corsica nevertheless also benefited from Pisan overlordship, and this period was one of peace, prosperity and development. Handsome Pisan-style churches were erected in the Balagne, the Nebbio and on and around the northeastern coast. Four prime examples are the Cathédrale du Nebbio (p116) in St-Florent, the Église de San Michele de Murato (p121), Aregno's Église de la Trinité (p143), and the Cathédrale de la Canonica (p108).

Pisa's good fortune in Corsica aroused the jealousy of Genoa, her perpetual rival, and Genoese ambitions took a turn for the better when in 1133 Pope

565 BC	**259 BC**
Alalia (Aléria) founded by the Phocaean Greeks	Rome seizes Corsica and holds on to it for more than five centuries

Innocent II divided the island between these two Italian republics. From then, Genoa set about gaining ground piecemeal, picking off villages and advancing little by little.

First Genoa undermined its rival's supremacy by fortifying the town of Bonifacio (p196) in the south. Genoese forces then ventured north, where they turned Calvi (p126) into a stronghold. By the 13th century, despite opposition from some island lords who remained loyal to Pisa, Genoa was top dog. Pisa's defeat in 1284 in the sea battle of Meloria, a small island near Livorno, marked the end of her domination of Corsica.

GENOESE OCCUPATION

Before Italian unification in the second half of the 19th century, Genoa was one of the great early modern merchant states and a powerful force in the Mediterranean. Indeed, if it had been more ambitious, Genoa rather than Spain might very well have been the first to discover and exploit the Americas; Columbus, after all, was Genoese, whether he was born in Genoa proper or, as some Corsicans would have it, in Calvi, which was controlled by Genoa at the time (see the boxed text, p129).

The site www.storiacorsa
.com gives a Corsican
slant to the history of
the island. Parts are
translated into English
with more promised.

Genoa occupied and dominated Corsica for five centuries, during which time the island was turned into a fortress. However, the Genoese had little sentiment for the Corsicans, who were made to pay taxes and often evicted or excluded from towns and put to work on the land to serve Genoa's commercial and economic interests. Those who disobeyed were punished severely.

The Genoese administration created towns and set the population to work cultivating olive and chestnut trees, with a view towards turning Corsica into Genoa's breadbasket (see the boxed texts, p245 and p154). By the mid-16th century, when the Genoese believed they at last had Corsica under control, the island's strategic importance in the Mediterranean basin and, more widely, in Europe as a whole, once again was a catalyst for major disruption.

SAMPIERO CORSO

In 1552 the people of Siena, another powerful city state, like Genoa, in what is now Tuscany on the Italian mainland, rose up against the Spanish garrison that was occupying the city and called on France for protection. The wily Henri II, king of France, saw his chance to gain territory and influence on the shores of the Mediterranean. Corsica, offshore and strategically located, got caught up in the struggle.

In 1553 an expeditionary corps reached Bastia under the command of the French Maréchal de Termes and his second in command, the Turkish privateer Dragut, a French ally. Bastia fell, followed swiftly by other towns, and within only a few days Corsica was declared French territory.

During this campaign, Sampiero Corso, a Corsican colonel in the French army, came to symbolise the fight against the Genoese. Popular though he was on the island, his unifying presence wasn't enough to safeguard the French victory. Playing off the Mediterranean superpowers, the Genoese appealed to Charles V, the king of Spain and holy Roman emperor, for support. Charles, smarting from France's attempt to dislodge his troops from Siena and always eager to cock a snook at his neighbour north of the Pyrenees, went on the attack and the French, after suffering a series

AD 774	1077
Moors from North Africa begin to raid Corsica	The Pope appoints the bishop of Pisa to oversee Corsican affairs

---

SAMPIERO CORSO 'THE FIERY'

Born in 1498 near Bastelica, Sampiero Corso became known as 'the most Corsican of Corsicans'. He rose to fame on the mainland as a soldier in the French army. Vehemently anti-Genoese, Sampiero fought with great courage alongside the French army in 1553 in a bid to reconquer his native island. Although the French were dislodged, he refused to give up hope. He returned to the island with a band of partisans in 1564, having failed to obtain European backing for his venture. He managed to destabilise the Genoese for a short while but never came near to vanquishing them. Three years later, Sampiero was ambushed and decapitated by rival Corsican mercenaries. His head was displayed in Ajaccio for all to see and thus, humiliatingly, ended the life of Corsica's first seeker of an independent existence for the island, murdered by his own compatriots.

---

of defeats, signed the Treaty of Cateau-Cambrésis, recognising Genoese supremacy on the island.

After this temporary respite under the French, the Corsicans found themselves again at the mercy of their familiar oppressor. Sampiero Corso made a brief, independent and abortive attempt to dislodge them in 1564 (see the boxed text, above) but despite a favourable start, his campaign was short-lived and the Genoese consolidated their control.

WARS OF INDEPENDENCE

What is known as Corsica's Forty Years' War began in 1729, when a determined old peasant in a mountain village near Corte refused to pay tax to a Genoese tax collector. The effects of his action snowballed, with more and more Corsicans refusing to pay their tribute to Genoa.

The rebels grew bolder and more organised, stealing weapons and, though disparate and uncoordinated, became a threat to Genoese rule.

Yet again, outsiders were to determine Corsica's destiny, this time in the form of the emperor of Austria and his forces, to whom the Genoese, with a revolt on their hands that threatened to spread more widely, successfully appealed for assistance.

St-Florent and Bastia, briefly held by the rebels, were recovered. After defeat at the Battle of Calenzana (1732), the Genoese forces regrouped and gradually regained control, but it was a transient success. The revolt recovered momentum and, at a meeting in Corte in 1735, the Corsicans drew up a constitution for a sovereign state, free and independent of European interference.

There followed a somewhat bizarre episode of the kind that seems to dog Corsican history. In 1736 an eloquent, opportunistic German aristocrat by the name of Theodore von Neuhoff (see the boxed text, p30) disembarked in Aléria. Seeing him as the leader for whom they had been looking, the rebels allowed this peculiar man to declare himself king of Corsica. His reign, however, lasted barely nine months.

Theodore's earlier, undignified flight notwithstanding, the Corsicans, many of them glad to be rid of this exotic interloper, pushed on and so rattled the Genoese that in 1738 they accepted France's self-interested offer of assistance. The French king, Louis XV, was delighted to be involved once more in the island's affairs, this time with Genoa's blessing instead of in the role of invader. He sent an expeditionary corps to Corsica – paid for by the Genoese – under the command of General de Boissieux.

Dr Julia Gasper of Oxford University is currently writing *A Biography of Theodore von Neuhoff*, the first in-depth study in English of the would-be king of Corsica.

Genoa defeats Pisa in the naval Battle of Melonia, marking the end of Pisan rule and beginning Genoese occupation

French troops land and capture Bastia, declaring Corsica French territory

---

THEODORE I, KING OF CORSICA

Born in Metz in 1694, on the border of France and present-day Germany, Theodore von Neuhoff was an adventurer with a talent for intrigue whose mercenary career took him to most of the major countries of Europe. He served first of all in the French army, then that of Sweden. Later he crossed the Pyrenees, where he was given the rank of colonel and made what was no doubt an advantageous marriage – to one of the ladies-in-waiting to the Queen of Spain. His meanderings through Europe continued: to Portugal, the Netherlands and Italy, where he fell in with a group of Corsican rebels and exiles and managed to convince them that he could help them shake off the Genoese yoke if they would crown him king of the island.

Ever the hustler, he managed to raise the money for his expedition from Greek and Jewish merchants in Tunis and secured modest military support from the Bey of Tunis, the Ottoman viceroy. Landing in Corsica in March 1736 with a motley bunch of rebels and mercenaries, he pulled on his crown, issued a series of edicts and promulgations, created a brief-lived order of knighthood and started campaigning against the Genoese, at first with some success. But his campaign soon began to stutter as a result of infighting among the rebels and his military strategy, based on classic, static siege warfare, whereas his Corsican troops were good for lightning strikes and guerrilla warfare, or nothing.

Disenchantment among his supporters was inevitable. The Genoese put a price on his head and, in an early example of war propaganda, published a lurid and tendentious account of his colourful life before ascending the throne.

When the hapless Baron Theodore von Neuhoff, King of all Corsica, sneaked from the island, reputedly disguised as a priest, he crisscrossed Europe in a largely abortive effort to raise cash and rally support. Arrested for debt in Amsterdam, he made three brief and equally unsuccessful return visits to the island, then made his way to London, where he languished for a while in a debtors' prison. He died, impoverished, in London 20 years after his short-lived Corsican campaign. You can see his tomb in St Anne's churchyard, just off London's Wardour St. In Corsica, a range of artefacts relating to his ill-fated rule are displayed at the Musée de L'Adecec (p223) in Cervione.

In 1753, when the last French regiments pulled out, over 1000 Corsicans had gone into exile abroad, the rebellion appeared to be over and Genoese rule seemed again consolidated.

PASCAL PAOLI & THE REVOLT

Tranquillity, as tends to happen in Corsica, was brief. In 1755, no more than two years after the last French soldier had sailed away, the charismatic Pascal Paoli led an insurrection that could so easily have changed the island's fortunes permanently. Educated in Naples, Paoli succeeded where everyone else before him had failed, uniting the factions and rival families as one against Genoa. What's more, he devised a constitutional state – unique in that still dynastic and absolutist age – which, given time, might have ensured Corsica a happy, self-regulating independence. But it was not to be.

James Boswell's 1768 *Journal of a Tour to Corsica and Memoirs of Pascal Paoli*, still very readable today, led to a Paoli and Corsica craze in Britain.

Genoa made several desperate, disastrous attempts to regain control of an island that had seemed hers for ever. Then France seized the opportunity it had been waiting for. In 1764 France, scarcely 30 years after her first intervention at Genoa's request, accepted the increasingly enfeebled Genoese city state's offer for her to take over the strongholds of Bastia, Ajaccio, Calvi and St-Florent, thus effectively guaranteeing control of the island.

1559	1729–69
The Treaty of Cateau-Cambrésis recognises Genoese supremacy once more	Corsica's War of Independence ends with the Battle of Ponte Novo, which marks the beginning of French rule proper

The Treaty of Compiègne, which sealed the agreement, was but a first stage: the Treaty of Versailles, four years later, formalised the Genoese cession of Corsica to France. Now France itself began acting less like a mediator and more like a ruler.

Pascal Paoli was the victim of decisions taken far away from his island. He mobilised his supporters but they and their resources just couldn't compete.

PASCAL PAOLI – PIONEER

Pascal Paoli, Corsica's revolutionary leader, was at the head of Corsica during its short period of independence between 1755 and 1769. On the island, Pascal, known to Corsicans as the 'father of the nation', is held in the same esteem as – and certainly with more affection than – Napoleon Bonaparte himself.

Son of Giacinto Paoli, a distinguished rebel leader in the struggle against Genoese occupation, Pascal was born in 1725 in Morosaglia, in the Castagniccia region, where since 1889 his ashes have been buried in the small chapel beneath his childhood family home (p227). When he was 14, he followed his father, who had gone into exile during the French occupation, to Naples. Here he received his education, reading the works of radical thinkers of the Enlightenment such as Montesquieu and corresponding with Jean-Jacques Rousseau. He was only 30 when he returned to the island and succeeded in uniting the disparate rebel forces. Three months later he was declared General of the Nation (the naming ceremony was held near La Porta p226) at the Couvent St-Antoine de Casabianca.

He managed to winkle out the Genoese from everywhere throughout the island except their six fortress towns, which they still controlled. But his short-lived military successes aren't his greatest claim to fame. Cultured and intellectually outstanding, as much political and social thinker as military commander, he developed agriculture, began the drainage of malaria-infested coastal marshes – and promulgated a democratic constitution well before the French revolution and more than three decades before America's revolutionary thinkers convened to work out something along similar lines in Philadelphia. In just 14 years, he founded Île Rousse (p135) as a rival to Genoese Calvi, established the Moor's head (see the boxed text, p32) as Corsica's symbol and set up a mint in the tiny town of Murato (p121). With his power base in Corte (p237), he's also remembered as the founder of Corsica's first university – an institution, like so many others that briefly flourished, then withered when his short rule ended (it wasn't until 1981, nearly two centuries later, that Corsica would again have its own university, established, as before, in Corte).

His efforts to root out criminality and Corsica's trademark murderous vendettas were heroic. The English writer James Boswell visited Paoli and was a voice for the Corsican cause in Britain. The later religious reformer John Wesley called him, with more than a measure of hyperbole, 'as great a lover of his country as Epaminondas and as great a general as Hannibal'. In America, patriots on the outskirts of Philadelphia met in the General Paoli Tavern, in what was later to become the town of Paoli. (There are in fact now four towns named Paoli in the US).

In 1769 his outnumbered and outgunned troops were routed by the vastly superior French forces and Paoli took refuge in England. In 1789 a very different post-revolutionary France made its peace with the erstwhile rebel commander and sent him back to France with the title of lieutenant-general. Flattering this must have been for Paoli but, soon alienated by the excesses of the revolution on the mainland, he summoned a regional assembly in Corte, declared himself president and formally seceded from France, later (in a bizarre gesture for a self-proclaimed nationalist) offering 'his' island to the British.

Retiring to a life of exile in London in 1796, he was granted a pension and, his glory days over, died there in February 1807. There's a cenotaph in his honour in Westminster Abbey.

1769	1794
Birth in Ajaccio of Napoleon Bonaparte, future emperor of France	British troops seize St-Florent, Bastia and Calvi; George III, king of England, proclaimed as sovereign in Corsica

---

THE MOOR'S HEAD

A black head swathed in a white bandana; you see it everywhere – on beer-bottle labels, on the Corsican coat of arms that adorns public buildings and fluttering on Corsica's traditional flag. It was Pascal Paoli who made the Moor's head the island's official emblem. Yet no-one really knows why. What deepens the mystery is that the Moors, in their incarnation as pirates from the Mediterranean's southern shores, were one of Corsica's traditional enemies. During the Crusades, any crusader who had a victory over the 'infidels' could add the Moor's head to his personal coat of arms, suggesting that the Moor's head was a symbol of Corsica's victory over its enemies.

Why, though, does the Corsican Moor wear his bandana around his forehead, whereas the four Moors on the coat of arms of Sardinia, just to the south, wear theirs as blindfolds (as did the Moors so plentifully represented in Corsica before Paoli's time)? Corsican General Ghjuvan Petru Gaffori, when he attacked the Genoese citadel in Bastia in 1745, was perhaps the first to reposition the cloth. 'Corsica at last has its eyes open,' Gaffori said. And Paoli commented, 'Corsicans want to see clearly. Freedom must walk by the torch of philosophy. Could we say that we seem to fear the light?' Both of these remarks suggest that Corsica had come to identify itself with its Moor's head.

Their defeat at the Battle of Ponte Novo on the River Golo, northeast of Ponte Leccia, on 8 May 1769, marked the beginning of French rule of Corsica in earnest, and Paoli fled to London.

CORSICA, FRANCE

Yet again Corsica had a military government of outsiders. In re-establishing law and order and taking control of the administration, the French followed the example of the Genoese, but more softly, softly. They promulgated a new set of laws, the Code Corse, particular to the island and taking into account its peculiarities, and they made earnest efforts to increase the yield of Corsican agriculture. Corsica increasingly adapted itself to a style of French governance – but one that would be blown apart, on the mainland and on the island, by the French Revolution.

Dorothy Carrington's Napoleon and His Parents: On the Threshold of History makes brilliant use of archival material available only on the island.

The revolution was initially applauded by many Corsicans. For the impoverished islanders, it gave new voice to popular dissatisfaction. In 1789 a decree proclaimed: 'Corsica belongs to the French Empire and its people shall be governed by the same constitution as the rest of France'. An amnesty was granted, and Paoli returned to the island. But reconciliation between Corsica and France was not complete. In 1793 Paoli was blamed for the failure of the French revolutionary government's expedition to Sardinia, just to the south of Corsica. He had, it was alleged, committed fewer troops than the government had expected. The extreme, irreconcilable Revolutionary Convention that had judged and executed Louis XIV and his queen, Marie-Antoinette, ordered Paoli's arrest for counter-revolutionary behaviour. He declared Corsica's secession, and requested help from Britain.

Spain, France, the Austro-Hungarian Empire and here, invited to the table, yet another imperial player. For Britain this was an opportunity of the same kind that Genoa's cry for help had been for France.

Ranging the Corsican coast in 1794, the British fleet easily captured St-Florent, Bastia and Calvi (it was during a battle for Calvi that Admiral Horatio Nelson lost the sight in his right eye; see p128). George III, king of

1794–96	1807
The brief Anglo-Corsican kingdom	Pascal Paoli, hero of the Corsican independence movement, dies in exile in London

England was proclaimed sovereign in Corsica. Yet the British soon proved a disappointment to Paoli. He had believed Britain to be liberal and enlightened but quickly understood that Britain was no more likely to benefit Corsicans than other alien rulers had been. Local hero Paoli was passed over for the vice-royalty and again went into exile in London, where he died in 1807, in receipt of a modest British government pension until his last day.

The Anglo-Corsican kingdom had lasted just over two years. As Jonathan Fenby drily observes in his excellent *On the Brink: The Trouble with France*, 'two years of nominal rule by George III, who was proclaimed "Anglo-Corsican King"… cannot have been much of a consolation for having lost America'.

Following the English departure in 1796, the island's affairs came once again under the jurisdiction of France and its post-revolutionary leader, Napoleon Bonaparte, a Corsican by birth.

Far from promoting the special interests of the island of his birth, the future emperor's single ambition for Corsica was to make it French, once and for all. Immediately, Napoleon's enforcers came into conflict with the clergy, resulting in an anti-French insurrection in 1798. Mistrustful of Corsica's own political class, Napoleon excluded Corsicans from island administrative posts and broke the island up into two *départements*.

19TH & 20TH CENTURIES

Corsica periodically asserted its individuality during the 19th and 20th centuries, rejecting some central government decisions from France. The clan structure endured and there was an upsurge in banditry. During this period levels of rural poverty endured, and attempts to develop infrastructure and agriculture achieved little.

Under France's second empire (1852–70; at its head, Napoleon III, son of Napoleon I's brother Louis) real investment was made in Corsica's infrastructure (such as the Corsican rail network that continues to trundle along

---

NAPOLEON BONAPARTE: SON OF CORSICA?

Paradoxically, the island's most famous son did more to Gallicise Corsica than any other individual. Despite his early expressions of Corsican patriotic feeling, Napoleon grew to be extremely ambivalent about his native island, if not hostile to it. In his final exile on the island of St-Helena in the southern Atlantic, someone asked him why he'd never done more to help develop Corsica's economy. His answer: '*Je n'en ai pas eu le temps*' (I never had the time). His policy towards Corsica, once installed as emperor of all France, was in fact altogether cold-blooded. Let the Corsicans keep their religion and their priests, he said, but let them love France and serve in her armies. A mere two roads, one between Ajaccio and Bastia, one between Bastia and St-Florent, should suffice, he said, for a people whose principal highway should be the sea. Native Corsicans, he decreed, were to be excluded from the administration of the island as they simply weren't trustworthy.

In 1814, the year of Napoleon's first definitive defeat, the people of Ajaccio threw a bust of the Emperor into the sea, while the citizens of Bastia actually welcomed British troops. Corsican resentment, however, seems to have passed with time and, by the mid-19th-century, the house in Ajaccio where Napoleon was born (p168) had become almost a place of pilgrimage. Ultimately Napoleon was lionised as the homeboy who'd made good in the wider world and brought the island fame. And there's no doubt about his contemporary economic value to the island as his name helps to boost the tourist trade…

1914–18	**1943**
In WWI 30,000 Corsicans die fighting for France	Corsica is the first region of France to be liberated by the Allied forces in WWII

today). Corsicans took advantage of the greater employment opportunities available in mainland France in enormous numbers, and they also filled a disproportionately high number of posts throughout the French Empire. The sword, though, has cut both ways: 30,000 Corsicans, a huge number compared to the island's slender population, died for France on the European battlefields of WWI.

WWII brought hostilities to the island itself. In 1940 Corsica was occupied by more than 90,000 Italian and German troops. Those who opposed the occupation forces took to the countryside, to the maquis, the tangled cloak of undergrowth that covers much of the island, and the term was coined to describe the whole of the French Resistance. Corsica was the first region of France to be liberated and, like its neighbouring islands in the Mediterranean, served as a forward base for the liberation of mainland Europe.

Stephen Wilson's academic monograph *Feuding, Conflict and Banditry in Nineteenth-Century Corsica* examines the reality behind what was so often glamorised by romantic novelists and short-story writers.

THE CORSICAN MALAISE

Corsica's latter-day difficulties date primarily from the 1960s, when a movement for Corsican autonomy was formed to combat what was perceived by some to be France's 'colonialist' policy in Corsica. One particular source of friction was France's use of Corsica for the resettlement of thousands of *pieds noirs*, French citizens living in North Africa who fled Algeria when that country achieved independence.

In 1975 tensions exploded when Corsican separatists, led by the Simeoni brothers, unearthed a scandal in the eastern coastal town of Aléria, involving fraudulent wine-making practices in a winery run by a *pied noir*. The protesters occupied a building used to store wine, and an attempt by the police to resolve the situation ended in two deaths.

The Front de Libération Nationale de la Corse (FLNC) was formed in 1976, and talk of autonomy increasingly turned to talk of full independence. That year averaged more than one bombing *per day* and the violence, usually against property and often settling arcane internal scores, continued at a reduced level for well over a decade.

Jonathan Fenby, in a chapter of his *On The Brink: The Trouble with France* exposes Corsica's clan rivalries, its violence and corruption.

In the early 1980s two measures were adopted to appease the nationalists. Firstly, a university was opened in Corte; for many years, after the French had closed down Pascal Paoli's university, young Corsicans had travelled to mainland France or Italy for their education. Secondly, the Assemblée de Corse was created; previously, the island had belonged to the Provence-Alpes-Côte d'Azur region. The détente arising from these measures was short-lived, however, and in 1983 the government tried unsuccessfully to proscribe the FLNC.

By the 1990s the FLNC had broken into multiple splinter groups, all armed and mostly violent, and other independent groups had come into existence. From 1993 to 1996 these groups warred against each other every bit as furiously as they had previously against the perceived coloniser. Long regarded as the caretakers of Corsica's environment against external depredations and indifference, the nationalist movements were increasingly regarded by many as gangs of hoods and thugs, who considered Rambo-like armed conflict and protection of their cronies' private interests as more important than political action.

The quarrel still continues in various arenas such as policies for economic development, the environment and language. Tourism is a particularly

1976	1981
Front de Libération Nationale de la Corse (FLNC) formed	Inauguration of the University of Corsica Pascal Paoli in Corte and creation of the Corsican regional assembly

sensitive area. For the central government, it brings wealth to an island with poor soil for agriculture, few resources and virtually no industry. For the nationalists, tourism is seen as a tool of assimilation. Much of their rage is reserved for concrete holiday developments (second homes are a favourite target of the bombers), which tend to be ghost communities, except for the two months of high summer (but let's stress once again that the separatists have maintained a strict hands-off policy regarding tourists themselves).

CORSICA TODAY

The assassination of the regional prefect, Claude Érignac, on 6 February 1998 upped the separatists' ante considerably. Érignac was the highest representative of the French state on the island, and his death sparked strong expressions of disgust among Corsicans themselves – as many as 40,000 of them took to the streets to demonstrate.

French President Lionel Jospin's government launched a 'Clean Hands' operation, aiming to reinforce law and order on the island, but his tough approach failed to win the hearts and minds of most Corsicans, who felt they had been demonised as terrorists.

The responses of successive French governments of left and right was alternatively muscular police enforcement and open or off-the-record talks with nationalist leaders. The cause of law and order wasn't helped by the torching of an illegal beachside shack by, it was soon revealed, undercover police working to instructions from no other than Bernard Bonnet, the hardline successor to the murdered Érignac as *préfet* (this was no set-up: Bonnet was tried, found guilty and sentenced to three years in prison for his abuse of power).

As a result of negotiations in 1999 within what came to be known as the Matignon Process, a law was passed granting greater autonomy to the island and retaining several of its preferential fiscal privileges. It also stipulated that the Corsican language should be taught as a subject in primary school – and approved a massive programme of yet more investment in the island amounting to €2000 million over 15 years.

In July 2003, after 30 years of nationalist violence and 200 years of French rule, Corsicans were invited to vote on their future status in a referendum linked to plans for decentralisation throughout France which would have united Corsica's two *départements* into a single administrative region. The vote was split virtually 50:50 right up to polling day, when those who rejected the proposal, which was supported by nationalist leaders, won by a small margin. The result was seen as a snub to both these local leaders and to Prime Minister Jean Pierre Raffarin's plans to decentralise power while keeping Corsica under French rule.

Meanwhile, Corsica's long legacy of terrorism, violence, significant graft and insularity to the outside world shows little sign of abating despite the desire of the vast majority of islanders to have a job, relative comfort and be able to get on with their lives as both Corsicans and French citizens.

Opinion polls on Corsica regularly indicate around 10% support for full independence. By contrast, 42% of those consulted in a recent sounding in mainland France would be content if the island drifted away.

1998	**2003**
France's top official on the island, Claude Érignac, is assassinated by nationalist extremists	The anti-independence lobby narrowly wins a referendum on autonomous rule for Corsica

The Culture

REGIONAL IDENTITY

Centuries of invasion and occupation have created a kind of siege mentality on the island of Corsica. While few could accuse Corsicans of being xenophobic, a deep-seated desire to protect their cultural identity can sometimes lead to an attitude of self-preservation and an acceptance of outsiders that on occasion borders on mere tolerance. The message behind bullet-ridden road signs, with the French placename spray-painted out will be lost on few. The tourist industry, the island's single biggest provider of employment, is, for some, a mixed blessing. According to more than a few nationalists, the steady stream of tourists (an estimated 2.3 million annually, bringing in a minimum of 1000 million euros) only serves to exploit the environment and denude the region's cultural fabric. Add to this a love-hate relationship with mainland France and what are perceived as its self-interested policies for the region, and you may begin to understand the Corsican psyche.

Corsicans are conservative, stoical, tradition-loving people with an integrity that doesn't suffer fools gladly. While their reputation for being hostile and unwelcoming is unjustified, there's a grain of truth in the stereotype. Don't expect to find arms wide open to greet you, particularly in some of the more remote mountain villages. That said, once you've earned the trust and respect of a Corsican, you won't find a more hospitable, generous host.

Corsicans refer to their mainland French compatriots, a trifle disparagingly, as *pinzutti*, the pointed ones – a distant reference to the three-cornered hats once worn by French troops.

LIFESTYLE

Family ties are strong in Corsica. Children often live in the family home until well into their 30s or until marriage, when they may then move out but remain within shuffling distance of the family roof. Outside the main towns life can be desperately quiet – especially in the mountain villages in winter, when there's a mass exodus of Corsica's young people to Marseille, Nice and Paris until the tourist season rolls around again. For many families who have moved to Ajaccio, Bastia or other coastal towns, the original family home back in the village still retains a powerful pull. Closed and shuttered for most of the year, it comes to life each major holiday, when family members return to their roots.

In early modern times privileged Corsicans pursued education at all levels in Italy. Pascal Paoli (see the boxed text, p31) opened the first university in Corsica in 1765, but when the French took over they closed Paoli's university, and for the next two centuries Corsicans seeking a higher education were obliged once again to leave the island for Italy or, as was increasingly the case, for the French mainland. The result was an epidemic brain drain. Corsica's best and brightest left the island to study and often did not return. The situation was only remedied in 1981 when the University of Corsica Pascal Paoli in Corte (p239) opened for business in response to nationalist demand.

A QUESTION OF IDENTITY *Miles Roddis*

I watched the 2006 football World Cup final in a *refuge* (mountain hut) high up on the GR20, to which the warden, God bless him, had hauled up a TV especially for the game. There were around 40 of us hikers, jostling for position and peering at the small screen. Also watching were his two young sons, the one cheering every successful Italian move, the other shouting just as volubly for France. Here at precisely 1880m, I thought in a brief moment when the action lapsed, is the Corsican paradigm: of France but not quite of France, leaning towards Italy when the occasion (and what an occasion!) demands, yet at the same time fiercely independent.

ROADSIGNS

Roadsigns in Corsica express much more than an indication of the next village or town. With the French version of the name spray-painted out by more ardent nationalists, they represent a modest, high-profile political statement. They're also targets in a more literal sense. You're bound to come across signs peppered with bullet holes to the point where some are illegible. Far from being the work of B-grade movie hoods, they're an expression of the jubilation of a group of hunters at the day's bag, or the result of a little sharpshooting practice in preparation for the next prowl through the maquis in search of warm-blooded prey.

Certain rules of inheritance have served to preserve Corsican family unity and continuity. The affiliation to a clan automatically provides an extended family, which also includes members of a village community in a structure that is protective of its influence and authority. However, Corsica isn't one big happy family; ties within families, clans and villages are matched by wariness of those on the outside – other families, clans and villages.

Corsica's traditions, marked by a code of obligatory hospitality and often wildly disproportionate rough justice, have never been universal on the island or without dissenters. However the response to the violent traditions has often itself been violent. Pascal Paoli, during the brief lifespan of independent republican Corsica in the mid-18th century, perhaps meant to help his countrymen rethink their antique and chilling concept of honour, when he razed the homes of vendetta murderers and put up signposts to publicise the occupants' crimes. Napoleon was even more extreme: if a murderer could not be arrested, he had four of the offender's close kinsmen arrested and executed instantly.

A sense of honour is a particularly important legacy of the island's turbulent past. A bloody vendetta might result from a land dispute, amorous

The theme of Alexandra Jaffe's *Ideologies in Action: Language Politics on Corsica* is self-explanatory. This book will be of interest not just to people on their way to Corsica but anyone with an interest in the survival of 'small' languages.

DOS & DON'TS

Corsicans are accustomed to foreigners and are, in general, friendly. You may, however, want to punctuate conversation with more than the usual number of 'monsieurs' and 'madames'. Instead of just a curt 'Merci', be generous. Say 'Merci, monsieur' or 'Merci, madame'. You'll gain points for showing patience and more points still for taking your time at things rather than rushing. When driving in towns, you may find the road obstructed by a truck whose driver is taking a break, or by two motorists having a chat. Restrain yourself and remember you're on holiday (unless you're racing to catch a flight). It is considered rude to beep or show impatience. The same goes for drivers practising 15-point turns on the road – a friendly wave rather than a 30-second honk will work wonders.

It's also considered polite to introduce yourself early in any conversation that goes beyond a mere exchange of niceties or simple commerce; Corsicans like to know who they are dealing with. In a similar vein, if you enter a bar with a local, it's considered rude if the stranger is not first introduced and their connection to the local person or place established. Remember, it's also more customary to buy rounds than to try to divide up a bill. Corsicans will also head straight for a bar stool rather than the lounge, which is typically the preserve of women, romantic couples, card players and tourists.

Should you happen to be invited into a Corsican home, there is no need to take your hosts a present. In Corsica, a bottle of wine extended as you cross the threshold may be thought to imply your uncertainty as to whether the house is able to provide.

Corsicans are as *au fait* with the stereotypical Mediterranean *mañana* philosophy as their mainland counterparts. Don't expect opening hours to be adhered to, schedules to be kept or plans to move at a northern European pace. Rather than get annoyed, slip into the rhythm and enjoy the easy-going pace.

DO AS I SAY, NOT AS I DO *Miles Roddis*

I'm not particularly proud of this one, but it happened. You quickly learn that lots of places in Corsica, including even midrange hotels and restaurants, don't accept credit cards. But petrol stations, where throughout the Western world you simply slap down your credit card and don't even think of reaching for your money?

I'd filled up at a fuel station outside Porto and handed over my piece of plastic. 'Don't take credit cards,' said the owner gruffly. 'Why ever not?' I asked. 'Costs me too much money.' 'Then you need to put up a sign telling drivers so,' I said, just a little bit assertively. 'Why the hell should I?' came the reply. And so things degenerated until I finally expostulated for all to hear, 'Am I still in France, for heaven's sake?'

It wasn't a clever thing to say but I was wound up. And for the rest of our days in Porto, I would go to sleep wondering if our car would be yet another victim of a Corsican bomb. Its tank full, it would have made a splendid blaze…

rivalry or nothing more than injured pride. Blow and counterblow, such tit-for-tat killings might continue for generations unless the parish priest managed to broker an accord that both families would accept.

The island has spawned a number of 'bandits of honour', outlawed and seeking refuge in the maquis, sometimes for years, after having avenged an offence by violent means. Even today, such cases rarely come to trial because of the silence of potential witnesses, even from the families of those gunned down, and the police's inability to assemble enough evidence to secure a conviction.

Weapons have always been an important part of Corsican culture – and not only for hunting. Today, though, visitors to the island need not fear getting caught in the crossfire of feuding families or protectionist mafia rackets; apart from the odd burnt-out shell of a building, you might never be aware of the internal machinations of the island's myriad factions.

For all the island's tradition of arson, bra-burning didn't make it to the agenda in Corsica. While mothers are held in almost reverential esteem by Corsican men, women's rights and gender equality issues are lagging well behind the rest of Europe. Only four out of 10 of the workforce is female and a mere seven out of 51 representatives in the Corsican assembly are female. Corsica's attitude to gays could also be seen as less progressive than

THE CORSICAN DIASPORA

Armenians, Parsees, Jews and Corsicans too; the 260,000 inhabitants of the island are way outnumbered by the number of émigré Corsicans. How many have left the island and sunk roots elsewhere can only be guessed at, especially since many have intermarried, choosing partners from their new society. Guestimates vary wildly between 800,000 and 1.5 million, worldwide. What's more verifiable are official statistics indicating that in mainland France there are around 60,000 Corsicans – a number that swells considerably each autumn, once the tourist season is over and the island's hotels and restaurants put up their shutters and dismiss their staff. Most Corsican residents on the mainland, whether seasonal or permanent, live in Marseille and around Provence.

This is no new phenomenon. In the 19th century as the French Empire expanded, particularly in Africa and Southeast Asia, Corsicans, escaping from an island with no industry to speak of and few prospects for employment, sought their fortune in faraway lands. From privates to senior officers, they were active in the army and were to be found – out of all proportion to the island's population – behind administrative desks as customs officers, governors, administrators and many more occupations that called for a suit or uniform. Two presidents of Venezuela can claim Corsican ancestry and it's estimated that around 4% of the population of Puerto Rico has a predominance of Corsican blood in its veins.

that of mainland France. Though gay relationships are tolerated, Corsica's traditional mores and society mean that open expressions of affection by same-sex couples might send conservative sensitivities into a spin, especially in rural areas.

POPULATION

Of Corsica's total population of 260,000, roughly 100,000 live in the two major towns of Ajaccio and Bastia. Although this island-wide figure represents an increase of almost 4% in the last decade (and a healthy figure compared to the all-time low of 170,000 inhabitants in 1955), depopulation remains a serious concern, especially in the mountain hamlets and villages. There, in many communes over a third of the villagers are over 60 and, according to official statistics, in more than half of Corsica's more than 350 communes, not a single birth is registered every other year.

Most Corsicans have Italianate surnames and French given, or first names.

SPORT

Several large sporting events are held in Corsica during summer, including the five-day adventure race Corsica Raid Adventure and other cycling, sailing and rally-driving events (see p256).

Football

The last two years have been fairly cataclysmic for Corsica's two professional football teams. In 2005, **Sporting Club de Bastia** (www.sc-bastia.com in French) was relegated to the French second division after many years among the big boys. The very next season, **AC Ajaccio** (www.ac-ajaccio.com in French), no doubt to the malicious glee of many an SC Bastia supporter, was demoted from the first division too. So Corsica now has two teams in the second division, each eager to struggle back to the top flight.

MULTICULTURALISM

One in 10 people living on Corsica is non-French. Moroccans account for just over a half of these, ahead of Portuguese, Italians and Tunisians. The largest concentration of Moroccans is in Bastia, while Tunisians tend to settle in Ajaccio. In a demographic blip, Calvi has a relatively high proportion of immigrants, many of them Eastern European, thanks in large part to the presence of a French Foreign Legion base on the outskirts of town (p128). In fact, outside l'Île de France (the Paris region), Corsica is the region with the highest proportion of foreigners in France. Of those who come to Corsica, most are, unsurprisingly, young men, seeking work in the agricultural, building and to a lesser degree tourism sectors. They are easily absorbed during 'the season' but with significant unemployment in the more spartan months and the annual brain drain of Corsica's youth to mainland France, resentments can run rife. It must be noted that some Corsicans are racist, especially against North Africans, who represent a relatively large community on the island.

BRUSHING WITH GREATNESS

If you enjoy snuggling up to the stars, albeit a pair of distant ones, here is a pair of enticing rural accommodation options.

The wonderful isolated *chambres d'hôtes* of A Flatta (p141) is run by the daughter of Jacques Anquetil, five times winner of the gruelling Tour de France cycle race. And Hôtel Dominique Colonna (p243), in the Vallée de la Restonica outside Corte, belongs to the eponymous Monsieur Colonna, football international and European Cup medallist.

CHEZ ROSSI Miles Roddis

The first Corsican I ever met was – improbably to me yet entirely logically to my French colleagues – running a restaurant on the main street of Vientiane, Laos. Rossi (no-one ever called him by his first name) was big and ebullient with a wide, letterbox smile, a Vietnamese wife and a daughter whom I used to covet (I was a very young teacher at the time). Each lunchtime, a group of us teachers would repair to Rossi's, together with a mixed bag of French NGO workers, entrepreneurs, ex-army personnel who'd stayed on after Laotian independence and the odd one or two whose profession you didn't ask about.

As I got to know them better, I was astounded at how many of my fellow-diners came from Corsica. This tiny restaurant in a distant country, had I but known it at the time, must have been typical of so many similar meeting places throughout former French colonies.

RELIGION

Corsica, its sizeable Muslim immigrant minority apart, is overwhelmingly Catholic, even if many Corsicans are only passively so. One source (a Corsican language-use survey) estimates that about 8% attend church regularly, 21% sometimes, 11% rarely, 44% only for social ceremonies and 16% never. There's certainly no lack of religious fervour evident, however, on each town's saint's day celebrations and during the lavish Holy Week processions of towns such as Bonifacio, Sartène, Cargèse, Calvi and Erbalunga.

Catholicism in Corsica coexists with vestiges of mystical and superstitious behaviours and beliefs, among them, for example, belief in the *spiritu* (the dead who return from beyond to revisit their terrestrial homes) and the malign power of the *occhju*, the evil eye. Two forces to fear are the *strega*, a witch who slips through the keyhole at night to prey upon young children and suck their blood, and the *lagramanti*, spirits of the mist who hover near lakes and rivers, their laments enticing passers-by to a watery doom. More positively, the *signatoru* is a medium with the power to cure illness and parry the force of the evil eye by incantations.

Sound out www.corse musique.com for the largest who's who of Corsican music on the net.

ARTS
Music
POLYPHONIC SINGING & FOLK MUSIC

'A voice from the depths of the earth, a song from the dawn of time.' So wrote Dorothy Carrington on first hearing Corsica's unique polyphonic singing. You're bound to hear it, wafting out of cafés and restaurants or played over the speakers sotto voce as you inspect supermarket shelves or sit waiting at a bus station. But for uninterrupted pleasure and time to appreciate its melodic intricacies and haunting refrains, you need to attend a recital, often as not held in the local parish church. In summer, several ensembles tour the island and any tourist office can give you details of upcoming events.

As emotional as flamenco, recalling ancient Gregorian chants and with strains that seem to have wafted over from the southern, Arab and Berber side of the Mediterranean, it speaks to the soul. It's singing for solidarity, typically in a trio or small chorus, where each participant takes a different melody, and it's sung a cappella, without musical accompaniment. The Corsican anthem, *Diu vi Salvi Regina*, at once hymn and battle cry, is often sung a cappella on public occasions.

The *paghjella*, for three or four male voices, is the form that you're most likely to hear. The men, usually dressed in black, stand with a hand over one ear so as to hear their own 'inner voice' without being distracted by the sounds of their neighbours. Often, they will put an arm around each other's shoulders, emphasising the collaborative, mutually supportive nature of what they are creating. Each voice contributes a different harmonic element: one provides the melody, another the bass, while the third, more high-pitched, improvises on the theme. The themes of the *paghjella* are usually secular and speak of powerful emotions – separation and parting, lament, loss and love, more often than not unrequited.

Sacred song, often to this day sung in Latin, tends to be more formal, though infused with elements of the *paghjella*. This is the genre of the Mass and accompanies religious festivals such as local saint's days or the elaborate Holy Week processions. Often the singing at such public celebrations is undertaken by members of the local *cunfraternita*, or lay brotherhood.

At funerals too, the *cunfraternita* normally sing. The *voceru*, a women's art, is sung, mournfully, at the wake that usually follows. The women sob and rock to and fro as if in a trance, and their singing is at once halting, riveting and usually improvised. In the old days, during vendettas, the *voceri* were typically accompanied by cries for vengeance. In the *lamentu*, a gentler expression of the same general tendency, a woman bemoans the absence of a loved one.

The *chjam'e rispondi* have a call and response form that recalls the conventions of some spiritual and blues music. As *chjam'e rispondi* are improvisational, they lend themselves to competitions.

Corsican vocal music is not always performed a cappella. It might be accompanied by wooden or horn flutes, percussion or the *cetera*, a 16-stringed instrument. Most Corsican folk instruments are typically wind-based, as you'd expect from a primarily pastoral society. Fifes and flutes such as *a caramusa*, *u liscarolu* and *a ciallamella* are fashioned from wood or bone. Rhythm is often provided by *chjoche* (castanets), while violins, the *cetera* or guitars supply the string accompaniment.

A e nozze e a l doli si cunosce i suoi (At weddings and funerals you acknowledge your own) – Corsican proverb.

Groups that have recorded the traditional Corsican forms include the hugely popular Canta U Populu Corsu, the Celtic-inspired I Muvrini, A Filetta and I Chjami Aghjalesi. Petru Guelfucci, who performs with the group Voce di Corsica, has become something of a household name throughout France as a soloist and has even developed a following beyond France.

One classic older recording is a set of three LPs, made between 1961 and 1963, under the title *Musique Corse de Tradition Orale*. This treasure, if you can find it, gives you an idea of how Corsican music must have sounded when it was still more expression than performance (some tracks feature the father of Jean-François Bernardini, the leader of I Muvrini). Another collectors item – a piece of social history even – is the *Canzone di i Prigiuneri Corsi in Alimania 1916–1917* (Songs of the Corsican Prisoners in Germany), distributed by the Corsican publisher La Marge; the recordings were made on wax rolls by German ethnomusicologists in WWI prisoner-of-war camps.

CONTEMPORARY MUSIC

In the field of popular music, Tino Rossi, a crooner and balladeer, simply was Corsica to mainland France and to much of the world beyond. In the course of his career, from his first recordings in the 1930s through to his death in 1983, he recorded precisely 1014 songs and sold over 300 million records.

A new breed of musicians has evolved a hybrid sound that stems from both traditional Corsican and contemporary music. Cinqui So, from Ajaccio, mixed polyphonic music with earthy world music beats in their 2002 album *Essenza and Isula*. It's probably the first Corsican band to produce a trip-hoppy, ambient music that mixes traditional spiritual songs with electronica.

Literature

Storytelling in the vernacular was for many centuries exclusively oral – indeed Corsican has only been a written language for something over a century. Like much oral literature, it wavered between fantastic folk imaginings *(fola)* – talking animals, human-to-animal metamorphoses ('Once upon a time there was a father and a mother who had as a child a little red pig', begins one typical story) – and the often artful rendering of incidents from daily life. Stories were told around firesides on winter evenings and passed on by shepherds on their journeys from summer to winter pasture or at fairs and markets. Like much oral literature, they were often rendered in poetry or in song – from lovers' serenades to bandits' ballads – in part because it made them easier to remember.

Much of this oral literary heritage has been adopted by modern Corsican polyphonic groups (see p40). There was never a great national epic, though collections have been assembled (for example, the 1979 French-language *Contes Populaires et Légendes de Corse* in the Richesse du Folklore de France series). These narratives resemble folk stories elsewhere: the Corsican Gendrillon, for example, is the French Cendrillon – Cinderella in the English version of this tale that crosses cultures and languages.

Dorothy Carrington's *Granite Island* (1947), the most literate and comprehensive account of Corsica, was originally published in French.

For some centuries literate Corsicans expressed themselves on paper in Italian. At the end of the 18th century they began to use French instead, and French is far and away the dominant language of literary expression today.

Scarcely any works by Corsican writers have been translated into English. You may, however, come across translations of some of France's 19th-century greats, who were captivated by Corsica – or at least the romantic vision of an island where first-hand experience was not necessarily deemed essential for writing with authority. Balzac wrote *La Vendetta*, while Alexandre Dumas penned his picaresque *Les Frères Corses* (The Corsican Brothers) and Guy de Maupassant, master of the short story, produced *Une Vendetta*, *Histoire Corse* (A Corsican Tale) and *Un Bandit Corse* (A Corsican Bandit; said to have been read avidly by the bandits themselves).

Corsica's two most prominent contemporary novelists, Angelo Rinaldi, writer, journalist, literary critic and member of the Académie Française, and Marie Susini, who vividly evokes the claustrophobia of rigid family life and an insular existence, are well worth a read if your French is good. Only Susini's *Les Yeux Fermés* has been translated into English as *With Closed Eyes* (1966) – and to track down even that will require a lot of diligent ferreting through secondhand bookshops.

L'Île sans Rivage (1989) by Marie Susini, an author with a love-hate relationship with her native island, looks sceptically at Corsican family structure and island insularity.

Rinaldi is an expatriate son of the island. Bastia-born in 1940, he has produced over 10 novels and meticulously describes postwar Corsican society in *Les Dames de France*, *La Dernière Fête de l'Empire*, *Les Jardins du Consulat* and *Les Roses de Pline*.

Archange Morelli wrote *La Moisson Ardente* (1997), a detective story set in Corsica at the beginning of the 16th century, while Marie Ferranti's *La Fuite aux Agriates* (2000) tells the story of a young woman drawn by love into the maelstrom of island politics.

Justice en Corse (2002), a novel by Corsican journalist and writer Jean-Claude Rogliano (1942–) recounts the true story of how he was stitched up by a neighbour and the neighbour's relative, the local magistrate, when he bought a 13th-century tower in the minuscule hamlet of Carcheto. Other works of his, which are generally steeped in Corsican culture, include *Visa pour un Miroir* (1998) and *Le Berger des Morts* (2001).

The most successful novel by a Corsican writer is *Terre des Seigneurs* (1986, revised 1996) by Gabriel Xavier Culioli. Tracing the life of a Corsican family over a full century, it's sold more than 35,000 copies.

Lastly, let's not overlook *Asterix in Corsica*, with a fresh paperback edition out in 2005. With the usual toe-curling puns and witty stereotypes in plenty, the pugnacious little warrior from Gaul and his portly pal Obelix help the Corsican chief Boneywasawarriorayayix to fight the might of Roman imperial power.

Architecture

Corsica's greatest architectural treasure is ecclesiastical. Small churches and rural chapels were built in the pre- and early Romanesque period (from the 9th to 11th centuries), but only about 10 survive, mostly in ruins. There are more extant examples of what's termed the Pisan Romanesque style. At the end of the 11th century, the Pope appointed the bishop of Pisa to oversee his interests on the island. The good bishop commissioned a team of architects from his home town with orders to place Pisa's stamp firmly on the island in the form of churches and small cathedrals. These delightful places of worship, with their distinctive polychrome walls and engagingly naive sculptures and friezes, are well worth a detour. Among the most impressive still standing are the Cathédrale de la Canonica (p108), south of Bastia, and the Église de San Michele de Murato (p121) in the mountains south of St-Florent. You'll come across others in the Nebbio, Castagniccia and Balagne regions.

Genoa, successor to Pisa as the power on the island, introduced the Baroque style of architecture of northern Italy to the island in the 17th and 18th centuries. These churches have façades featuring triangular or curvilinear pediments, splendid giant organs and sumptuously decorated interiors that make extensive use of trompe l'oeil, lashings of stucco and multicoloured marble. Many churches in the Balagne and Castagniccia were built in this style. Out of a total inventory of about 150, good examples include the churches and oratories of Bastia and La Porta's church of St-Jean Baptiste (p226) in Castagniccia. On a smaller scale, one common feature at the entry to villages and towns are freestanding mortuary chapels, Baroque or more restrained and classical, constructed by wealthy families on private land to sustain their presence, even beyond the grave.

The island's military and defence architecture is hard to miss. Most evident are the Genoese watchtowers that girdled the coast, of which around 60 remain standing today in various states of repair. Some were extended and maintained by the French once they took over control of the island. Dour, functional citadels dominate numerous coastal towns from Bastia and Calvi all the way down to Bonifacio.

Largely without ornament and fortresslike, traditional Corsican houses are usually constructed from granite (although shale was preferred in the chalky areas of Bonifacio and St-Florent) and often rise four or five storeys high. Small apertures in the façades keep the houses warmer in winter and cooler in summer. The large narrow slates on the roofs vary in colour according to where they are from: grey-blue in Corte, green in Bastia and silver-grey in Castagniccia.

Another distinctive feature of domestic architecture are the seasonal yet semipermanent *bergeries*. Here, in the high country, shepherds would

---

HOUSE FOR SALE?

As everywhere in France, inheritance in Corsica is determined according to strict proportions laid down by the Napoleonic Code, which is often regarded as an almost sacrosanct reference in legal matters. This can create problems, particularly when it comes to selling the family house, where ownership might be devolved to as many as 20 or more cousins, uncles, nieces and nephews, all of whom need to give their approval before a sale can take place and several of whom are probably part of the Corsican diaspora, living hundreds, if not thousands of kilometres away.

But many Corsicans are keen for a change. A proposed new law, which would be applicable only to Corsica, would simplify inheritance and make it easier for families to sell or renovate their property. With this initiative comes wariness; quite a few of the more extreme nationalist groups would like to see sales limited to fellow-Corsicans to prevent yet more houses, particularly in impoverished inland villages, being taken over by second-home owners from mainland Europe.

maintain a lonely vigil over their flocks as they cropped the sweet summer grasses. Typically, a settlement would have a modest, stone-built hut, an external oven, circular corral and a thick-walled stone shed where cheeses were kept cool and stored.

Corsica has some impressive 20th-century modernist architecture; the *préfecture* building and the Notre Dame des Victoires church in Bastia, the Lycée Laetitia in Ajaccio, the HLM (a low-cost public housing development) in Olmeto and numerous private villas at Pointe de Spérone all have their charm. A superb 38-page booklet, *Architectures Modernes en Corse*, will point enthusiasts in the right direction. It's available from some larger tourist offices, or contact **Le Service du Patrimoine, Collectivité Territoriale de Corse** (☎ 04 95 51 64 73; 22 cours Grandval, BP 215, 20187 Ajaccio).

Painting

As with architecture, Corsica has tended to import or imitate Pisan and Genoese painting rather than develop a school of its own. Ajaccio's Musée Fesch (p165), the biggest museum in Corsica, houses the largest collection of Italian paintings in France after the Louvre. Assembled by Napoleon's step-uncle, Cardinal Joseph Fesch (the Italian commissioner for war and later an astute businessman), it contains dozens of early Italian works, by and large looted from Italy during the Napoleonic wars.

'Ajaccio's Musée Fesch houses dozens of early Italian works, by and large looted from Italy during the Napoleonic wars'

In the 19th century a handful of Corsican artists such as Charles Fortuné Guasco and Louis Pelligriniles, now all but forgotten, gained a small measure of recognition by studying and working in mainland Europe and exhibiting in Paris.

In the late 19th and early 20th centuries the magnificent buckling mountains of Corsica, its fretted coastline, turquoise waters and the very special quality of its light were a source of inspiration to a number of innovative artists. Matisse confided: 'it was in Ajaccio that I had my first vision of the South'. Fernand Léger, early in his career, spent several summers on the Corsican coast, while Maurice Utrillo and his mother, the painter Suzanne Valadon, Paul Signac and the American James McNeill Whistler were also regular visitors.

Island painters such as Lucien Peri, François Corbellini, Pierre Dionisi and Jean-Baptiste Pekle are synonymous with Corsica's 20th-century artistic reawakening. More often than not they too have taken their inspiration from the island's stunning land- and seascapes.

Crafts

Riaquistu, recovery or reclaiming, is a term often applied to the revival of traditional Corsican culture, particularly its music and crafts. Ancient skills such as knife-making and leatherwork, briar pipe fashioning and basket weaving are again being practised. In a more modern idiom, potters throw and jewellers produce a range of exciting contemporary adornments.

In the Balagne region, where this craft movement is particularly active, you can follow the Route des Artisans de Balagne (The Balagne Craft trail; see p139).

Two good sources of more information are *L'Art des Artisans*, a free booklet, available from tourist offices, which gives details of artisans throughout the island, and the website www.corsica-isula.com, which has an excellent section on Corsican craftfolk.

Environment

'Le soleil a tant fait l'amour à la mer qu'ils ont fini par enfanter la Corse' (The sun made love to the sea so often that they finally gave birth to Corsica). So eloquently and fancifully, Antoine de St-Exupéry, author of *Le Petit Prince* (The Little Prince), described the genesis of the island.

THE LAND

Around 30 million years ago a lump of land broke away from mainland Europe, slowly spun around an axis somewhere in the middle of the Gulf of Genoa, and eventually came to a standstill 170km southeast of Nice (mainland France). Corsica was born.

The 8722-sq-km island, together with the neighbouring Italian island of Sardinia, a mere 12km to its south, form the Corso-Sardinian microcontinent. Spanning 183km from top to bottom and 85km at its widest point, Corsica is crowned at its northern end by the 40km-long peninsula of Cap Corse.

Mountains run riot. No sooner does the land rise above sea level than it soars into the clouds, climaxing with Monte Cinto (2706m). Plenty of peaks – Monte Ritondu (2622m), Paglia Orba (2525m), Monte Pedru (2393m) and Monte d'Oro (2389m) – give the island's highest summit a run for its money.

Along the western coast, pockets of flatness beside four gulfs – Golfe de Porto, Golfe de Sagone, Golfe d'Ajaccio and Golfe du Valinco – allow for human habitation at sea level. Crags lunge from the sea and centuries of erosion have sculpted the ancient magmatic rock base found here into *tafoni* (cavities), dramatic red-rock inlets and sculpted promontories such as the wildlife-rich Réserve Naturelle de Scandola.

Alongside the less dramatic eastern coast runs the lowland agricultural plain of Aléria. Complex sedimentary and metamorphic rocks, such as schist, make up the island's northeastern fringe, including the long, slender finger of Cap Corse. Firstly, a sedimentary platform built up on the sea floor over millennia, creating layer by compressed layer from grains of sand mixed with shell particles. Then came the metamorphosis of these earlier rocks as a result of the heat and pressure that was a by-product of the Alps rearing skywards in the Tertiary era. The island's central herringbone mountain range and numerous east–west valleys were the result of a rift zone that divides the island in half at Corte. Inland, the River Tavignano flows through Corte to Aléria; the 80km-long Golo, the island's fastest-moving river, links the Valdu Niellu forest with the Étang de Biguglia; and the Liamone, Rizzanese and Taravo Rivers all flow out to the west coast. Corsica has 43 glacial lakes.

With its stunning variety of ornamental rocks and rare orbicular diorite, the island is a geologist's dream. Diorite, an igneous rock recognisable by its grey honeycomb structure, is found in Ste-Lucie-de-Tallano in the Alta Rocca; and you may also see rocks of green ophite (a complex magmatic rock created during the major folding periods). Red rocks, the crystalline platform, are in evidence around Pianna and Scandola, while white chalk formations are found around the southern foot of the coastline near Bonifacio.

Col (French) and *bocca* (Corsican) mean the same thing – a mountain pass. The Col de Verghio (1467m), midway between Porto and Corte, is the island's highest road pass.

WILDLIFE

Corsica shelters a rich variety of flora and fauna, much of which is protected. Travellers who set so much as a little toe into the island's interior will come across a menagerie of free-roaming pigs, cows, goats, sheep, mules and other domesticated and feral land animals. Delve deeper into the mountainous

---

PROTECTING CORSICA'S COASTLINE

France's Loi Littoral of 1986 prohibits all new building within 100m of her shoreline. A sensible measure, you would think, protecting Corsica's splendid coast from damaging development (modest in its terms too, compared to the president of neighbouring Sardinia's call for an embargo on construction within 2km of the coast). But there are plenty of voices raised against this environmentally positive legislation. Currently in preparation is the Plan d'Aménagement et de Développement Durable de la Corse (PADDUC), which would loosen controls in the name of promoting tourism and sustainable development. Principal among the opponents of such relaxation is the Collectif pour la Loi Littoral, a consortium of local associations, political groupings and elected deputies. Rubbing their hands in the wings are vested interests in the often murky construction industry, keen to wrest further profit from yet more holiday housing, for which there's a ready, guaranteed market.

---

terrain (pack patience and a pair of binoculars in your rucksack) and you will be well rewarded.

Fauna

Corsica's mountain king, the mouflon, reigns in the Bavella and Asco areas. These hardy herbivores, a type of short-fleeced sheep, roamed in their thousands at the beginning of the 20th century but now number no more than 500. Hanging out in lower valleys between December and February, they retreat to higher altitudes to avoid the worst of the summer heat. If the one you spot (look for distinctive white facial markings) has huge 80cm-long coiled horns, it's a male.

It might be in French but www.parc-naturel-corse .fr, the website of Corsica's largest protected area, is crammed with useful, practical and fascinating facts about the island and its fauna and flora.

The maquis (p48) can bristle with animal activity. Wild boar snout out acorns, chestnuts, roots and fruit; the fist-sized Eurasian scops-owl fills the night with its shrill whistles; and weasels and foxes also slink. Dark-green snakes slither (they're not poisonous and won't attack unless threatened) and shiny back *malmignatte* spiders scuttle (look for red stripes on the abdomen); they're venomous but mercifully rare. Between mid-November and February Hermann's tortoise – in France, found in only one place on the mainland and in Corsica – hibernates in the maquis under piles of leaves. This land tortoise, about 19cm long with orange and black stripes, lives for up to 80 years. In the face of declining numbers, it's being specially bred in semicaptivity at the Village des Tortues de Moltifau in the Parc Naturel Régional de Corse. For more information, go www.parc-naturel-corse .fr/education/villagetor.html.

The last indigenous Corsican red deer, a native of the maquis ever since antiquity, died on the island in the 1960s, but was reintroduced in 1985 from Sardinian stock. Initially confined to protective enclosures in Quenza, Casabianda and Ania di Fiumorbu, the first deer were released into the wild in the late 1990s. These gentle creatures live on brambles, strawberry trees, acorns and chestnuts, and now number over 100. Wild boars, foxes, stray dogs and poachers continue to threaten their existence.

Birds of Corsica: an Annotated Checklist by Jean-Claude Thibault and Gilles Bonaccorsi makes an invaluable reference guide for any half-serious, Corsica-bound spotter.

BIRDS

Bird-watchers need to keep their eyes well-peeled to spot a bearded vulture or lammergeier with its soaring wingspan of up to 2.7m. To distinguish it, look for a black 'beard' under its beak and white or yellowish plumage covering the lower part of its body. The rarest of Europe's four vulture species, the bearded vulture nests in rocky niches at high altitude (around 1500m) but descends to lower altitudes in winter. You won't find this solitary bird joining the vulture feeding frenzy at a carcass. It waits for its moment, seizes

TREADING LIGHTLY

We've no wish to play nanny and much of this is commonsense. This said, you too, as a visitor, can play a modest role in helping to preserve Corsica's unique natural environment. By sticking to a few simple, unencumbering precepts, your impact will be all the less heavy.

- Buy a sturdy, heavy-duty plastic bag, locally endorsed, for all your purchases (they're great for lugging gear to the beach or tidying away camping equipment, too). See the boxed text, p53.

- Pack all your litter and dump it in an official container. Wildlife will grub it up in the hope of dinner if you bury it. While it can be messy, it's socially responsible to pack out the detritus of others, less responsible.

- Don't use detergents or toothpaste, even if they claim to be biodegradeable, anywhere near streams. The same rule applies to natural functions, it goes without saying…

- When hiking, stay on designated trails. Every footstep is a threat to the coastal foreshore and fragile, high-mountain plants, which use the brief summer to reproduce.

- Obey the 'no camping' restrictions when trekking.

- Never light a fire in the open air anywhere on the island, except in the rare places where it's allowed. Barbecues and camp-fire coffee are fun but forest and maquis fires are the scourge of Corsica.

- Be content to look at flowers and plants. Many struggle to survive.

a sizeable bone then drops it from a height onto a rocky surface to shatter the bone and release the marrow at its heart. Your best chance of seeing it is in the Monte Cinto massif. Birds of prey such as the golden eagle and red kite soar overhead in the Vallée de la Restonica near Corte.

The Corsican nuthatch, one of the few species endemic to the island, flutters in the Vallée de la Restonica. Discovered at the end of the 19th century, this ground-dwelling bird is recognisable by the white 'brow' across its head. Rarely exceeding 12cm in length, it flits around conifer forests, dining on insects and pine seeds. The Corsican finch, sparrowhawk, wren and spotted flycatcher are equally common in this neck of the woods.

The Corsican coastline also has rich pickings for twitchers. The audouin's gull, so rarely found on mainland Europe, nests among rocks on the protected Îles Finocchiarola off Cap Corse and is recognised by its dark-red, black-striped, yellow-tipped beak. The shag, a web-footed bird with black-green plumage, is another nesting species on the islands and in the nearby Réserve Naturelle de Scandola. The edge-of-the-world hamlet of Barcaggio (p113) on Cap Corse is prime bird-watching territory. Spring sees storks, herons, spotted crakes and dozens of other migratory birds pass by. The osprey, a formidable fisherman thanks to sharp eyesight and talons, can also be spotted around Cap Corse and on the rocky coasts and headlands of the Réserve Naturelle de Scandola, where it nests. The peregrine falcon is another known nester here.

'The Corsican coastline also has rich pickings for twitchers'

ENDANGERED SPECIES

Of France's seven endangered and eight critically endangered mammals, one tiny fellow is endemic to Corsica. Generally tucked inside a black and brown striped shell, the green-bodied Corsican snail *(helix ceratina)* faces extinction. Having not been seen since 1902, the molluscs were discovered near Ajaccio in 1995. Assailed by the airport, a military base, a large car park and a busy beach, these plucky molluscs had chosen a tough spot to make their last stand. The six hectares of coastal land they inhabit is now protected, and a captive breeding programme is underway.

BENEATH THE WAVES

Corsica's fish life will leave you goggle-eyed. Here's but a sample of what you might find if you scuba dive or snorkel.

Bogue This vegetarian species lives in shoals above Poseidonion beds, feeding on the leaves. It is silver in colour with horizontal golden markings. Born male, it grows into a female.

Brown meagre This predator (40cm to 80cm long) swims in shoals near the rocky sea floor or above Poseidonion beds. Look for silvery-grey markings and an arched back.

Cardinalfish This red 'king of the mullet', about 15cm long, lives near cave entrances or beneath overhangs.

Damselfish These fish congregate in compact, slow-moving schools near the water's surface and close to shallows. Look for grey and black markings and scissor-shaped tails.

Forkbeard Two forked barbels under the chin distinguish this shade-loving brown fish.

Grouper The thickset darling of scuba divers, sometimes growing to as long as 1.5m, is distinguished by its enormous thick-lipped mouth and the whitish flecks on its brownish scales. It spends most of its time in holes in the rock. Born female, specimens change sex when they get older.

John Dory This fish with superb stripes on its dorsal fin owes its French name, St-Pierre, to the tale that the black spot on its flank was left by St Peter after Jesus instructed him to catch the fish and remove the gold coin from its mouth.

Labridae This family's colourful representatives include the rainbow wrasse, the most 'tropical' fish in the Mediterranean. A maximum of 20cm long, it swims near the surface and has remarkable turquoise and red mottled markings.

Moray eel You won't want to get too close to this fierce predator, which waits in crevices, from which only its mouth is visible. Growing to 1.5m, it is distinguished by its speed, its sharp teeth and its dark, sometimes yellow-flecked markings.

Red scorpion fish Known locally as *capon*, the red scorpion fish lies in wait for its prey on the sea floor, using its camouflage skills to blend in with its surroundings. Its body is covered in poisonous spines and outgrowths. Again, best left well alone…

Swallow-tail sea perch This small, graceful, orange-red fish is usually found in the gloom at the entrances to caves or wrecks.

Two-banded seabream Extremely common, two-banded seabream swim alongside divers who descend to the rocky sea floor. The most widespread variety is the silvery white bream (around 40cm long), which has two characteristic black marks on its gills and tail.

For the best of Corsica's dive sites, see p79.

With fewer than 250 breeding pairs in Europe, the bearded vulture is also endangered. Hunger is one of the biggest threats to this carrion-eating bird. In the Parc Naturel Régional de Corse, park authorities monitor its dozen or so pairs of vultures and supplement their natural diet with additional food in the form of goat and sheep carcasses at sites in Ascu and the Forêt de Tartagine.

The Mediterranean monk seal, another European and North African creature facing extinction, has not been seen in the Réserve Naturelle de Scandola – once home to a small colony – since 1995.

Divers keen to know exactly what's what through that mask should get hold of Kurt Amsler's *Corsica Diving Guide*, a detailed look at 26 of the island's most thrilling dive sites and the 130-odd marine species divers could see.

Flora

The habitat of Corsican flora splits neatly into three zones: the legendary maquis and oak, olive and chestnut trees that grow in the so-called Mediterranean zone (up to altitudes of 1000m); the pine and beech forests in the mountain zone (1000m to 1800m); and, above the tree line, the ground hugging, sparse grasses and small mountain plants of the higher alpine zone (above 1800m). Just 15% of Corsican land is cultivated; forest and maquis carpet more than half of the island.

TREES

In Corsica's heavily scented maquis, covering around 2000 sq km, tree heather grows 2m tall and its white flowers exude a honey-like scent. Fruit

---

A PRICKLY CUSTOMER

The prickly pear, a member of the *Cactaceae* family, is another mountain-zone inhabitant, found anywhere between 800m and 1800m. It resembles a cactus, with bristly, pulpy, oval-shaped 'arms' and yellow flowers. Its sweet, juicy fruits are known as prickly pears or barbary figs. They're thirst-quenching but don't be tempted to grasp one with your bare hands; the soft skin is coated with hundreds of tiny, hair-like prickles that are the very devil to extract from your fingers.

---

trees include the mastic, the red fruits of which turn black to exude a resin-like fragrance.

Holm oak, cork oak (the bark of which is peeled off every 10 years or so to fashion stoppers for wine bottles) and olive trees all grow below 600m and are other maquis inhabitants. The cork oak is more common in the south of the island, around Porto-Vecchio, while the olive, its fruit pressed to extract the oil, thrives on sunny coastal slopes, particularly in the Balagne on the northwest coast.

Lemon, kiwi and avocado trees are cultivated in the eastern lowlands, as is the more widely distributed chestnut tree. Introduced to the island in the 16th century, the chestnut quickly lent its name – La Castagniccia – to the eastern plains on which it was cultivated. Its husks open in October to expose a flavourful brown fruit, which is used in local cuisine or ground into flour. See the boxed texts, p245 and p227 for more about chestnut trees.

In the higher mountain areas, the tough Corsican or laricio pine dominates. As it ages, the tree spreads its foliage horizontally like a parasol and lives for an age. Some island specimens (you'll come across some venerable examples in the Forêt de Vizzavona, see p248) are reckoned to be up to 800 years old.

Neither red nor grey squirrels, the curse of so much British woodland, scurry in Corsican forests.

SHRUBS & OTHER PLANTS

Precisely 2980 species of flora have been identified on Corsica. Since the island has been physically separated from the European mainland for millennia, a good number of plants have evolved separately from their cousins on the mainland and are unique to Corsica. There are 130 endemic plants, while a further 75 exist nowhere else except on Corsica and its neighbour, Sardinia. In the more remote Alpine zones, nearly half of the species that survive the harsh winters at this height are endemic.

The maquis positively bursts with sweet-smelling plants and herbs, most of which flower in spring and early summer. Typically scrubby and short, the maquis is tough enough to survive summer's intense heat, burns quickly, but grows rapidly too. It provides a safe-haven for most of Corsica's 40 kinds of orchid and pungent herbs such as rosemary, lavender and the tiny blue-violet flowering Corsican mint with its heady summertime aroma. Drier hillsides and the lower flanks of mountains flame with bright yellow broom throughout the summer.

THE ASPHODEL

This hardy plant with its white or delicate pinkish flowers grows at all altitudes and can survive in just about any kind of soil. Flowering in the springtime, it has three distinct names in Corsican (and several dialectal variants too), depending upon whether the speaker is referring to the living plant, its dried form or when it's burnt to give light. Traditionally, its stalks would be twisted to make torches, while the leaves would be used for stuffing mattresses and saddles. More symbolically, they would be woven into crosses which villagers believed would protect or enhance their harvests.

UNDERWATER PLANTS

Don a snorkel and mask, and get ready to be dazzled by the Corsican coastline's extravaganza of flora – as rich and as brilliant underwater as any on dry land.

■ Poseidonion – endemic to the Mediterranean, this green plant (named after Poseidon, the Greek god of the sea), forms vast grassy meadows on the sand creating a choice biotope, home to numerous species of fish seeking shelter or spawning in the foliage.

■ Seaweed – there are several forms: brown, green or red, hard or soft. Calcified varieties can have superb mineral formations. Certain species of red algae are recorded nowhere else in France.

Other common species that you're likely to come across:

Autumn crocus This late bloomer lives up high. The distinctive pink to lilac flower with its spear-shaped petals appears well before the scarcely visible leaves, which grasp it around its base.

Corsican hellebore This poisonous plant, a variant found only in Corsica and Sardinia, has frondy, toothed leaves (in which shepherds used to wrap their fresh cheeses) and a profusion of lovely, light-green flowers.

Corsican peony Once profuse, this local variant of peony has papery pink or red flowers with yellow stamens and likes to live beneath beech trees. A victim of its very prettiness, it's becoming rarer, mainly as a consequence of overpicking.

Corsican thyme Here's another variant upon a popular theme, found only in Corsica and Sardinia. Low growing, bushy, with delicate pink and white flowers and a powerful aroma, it thrives anywhere between 500m and 2000m.

Cyclamen The tiny wild cyclamen, an early flowerer, peeks out from rocks and crannies in pink clusters.

Myrtle A bushy evergreen shrub with aromatic leaves and lovely, fragrant white flowers that bloom in spring. Its blue-black berries make a wonderful flavouring for liqueurs.

Rock rose/cistus The most common maquis shrub, it thrives up to around 1200m. You'll recognise it by its five-petalled flowers, which are either white or pinkish-mauve with yellow stamens. Among several varieties of rock rose is the more diminutive Montpellier cistus with its dainty white flowers.

Strawberry tree Known in French as the *arbousier* and nothing to do with strawberries, this shrub thrives in thickets and woods and can grow to over 10m. It has small, white bell-shaped flowers that dangle in clusters. The fruit is small, crinkly surfaced orange or red balls.

The paperback edition of *Wild Flowers of the Mediterranean* by Marjorie Blamey and Christopher Grey-Wilson slips easily into a daypack.

NATURE RESERVES

The single most decisive step in the preservation of Corsica's unique wildlife was the creation of the Parc Naturel Régional de Corse (PNRC) in 1972. Protecting more than two-thirds (specifically, 3505 sq km) of the island, the reserve is the island's biggest promoter of environmental consciousness. Unlike national parks in France, which can only protect uninhabited areas, the PNRC, within whose boundaries over 25,000 people live, 'protects and stimulates the survival of natural, cultural and human heritage'. Positive measures include the creation of some 2000km of marked trails, not to mention costly measures taken to preserve endangered species and to educate and sensitise locals and visitors through, for example, guided nature walks and information centres.

On the island's west coast lies the astonishing Réserve Naturelle de Scandola, a 919-hectare pocket of land and 1000 hectares of sea that swims with 125 fish species and 450 types of seaweed. So rich in marine life is this reserve that it's inscribed on the Unesco World Heritage list. To its south, the Golfe de Porto, Golfe de Girolata and the plunging red cliffs of Les Calanques that stagger south along the coastline between Porto and Piana are also on the Unesco list. The coastline around Galéria, immediately north of the Scandola reserve, also enjoys international recognition as the Réserve de Biosphere de la Vallée du Fangu, 234 sq km dedicated to scientific research.

A good chunk of the remaining one-third of Corsican land falling outside the PNRC and/or Unesco orbit is protected by three other small reserves.

Off the northernmost tip of Cap Corse lie the Îles Finocchiarola, three pin-prick islands (four hectares in all), off limits to visitors between 1 March and 31 October to allow several rare birds to breed in peace.

South of Bastia, the Réserve Naturelle de Biguglia provides a safe haven for more than 100 bird species and serves as a vital stopover between Europe and Africa for migrating birds. Up to 20,000 birds winter around the shallow, 1450-hectare lagoon that forms Corsica's largest and most important wetland.

In the far south, more islands are protected by the Réserve Naturelle des Bouches de Bonifacio. Of the six islets in the Lavezzi archipelago, two – Île de Cavallo (nicknamed Millionaires' Island) and Îlot de San Baïnsu – have, bizarrely, escaped being included in this 800-sq-km protected zone. Here, the marine life is particularly rich and enjoys special protection; 120 sq km of water are strictly off limits to scuba divers. The reserve is best known for its revived brown grouper population – protected since 1993 after decades of unregulated fishing had practically wiped them out from the western shores of the Mediterranean.

At the lower end of the east coast, the Réserve Naturelle des Îles Cerbicale – a cluster of five islets northeast of Porto-Vecchio – also protects marine bird life, and some unique flora too.

RÉSERVES NATURELLES

There are almost 120 nature reserves in France, of which Corsica has five splendid examples.

Park	Features	Activities	Best time to visit
Réserve Naturelle de Biguglia	reed-bed wetland with all types of warblers, migratory herons, osprey, red-footed falcon, black- and white-winged terns	bird-watching, walking	spring, winter (migratory birds)
Réserve Naturelle de Scandola	natural treasures of world renown including osprey, peregrine falcon, brown grouper	diving, snorkelling, walking, bird-watching, botany in the periphery only	spring (walking & botany), summer (diving)
Réserve Naturelle des Bouches de Bonifacio	archipelago reserve with rich marine life including 68 fish species, including the grouper	scuba diving (restricted)	summer
Réserve Naturelle des Îles Cerbicale	five-islet reserve with 136 flora species packed into 36 hectares	botany, bird-watching, walking	spring
Réserve Naturelle des Îles Finocchiarola	protected nesting islets for audouin's gulls, cory's shearwater, scopoli's shearwater, cormorants	bird-watching	Nov to Feb (closed rest of year)

Visitors to these reserves must observe a number of regulations. In particular, it's forbidden to pick plants, remove rocks, leave rubbish behind or light fires. Pets are not encouraged and fishing, hunting and camping are prohibited.

ENVIRONMENTAL ISSUES

Most Corsicans are keen to promote the ecological wellbeing of their island and environmental issues figure large in the demands of many nationalist factions. The latter aren't averse to showing muscle too, if they believe the issue to be important enough. In 1973, for example, there was what almost amounted to a popular uprising against offshore toxic-waste disposal by an Italian multinational in what was termed the so-called *boues rouges* (literally 'red slicks') affair. Corsican eco-nationalism, as it is called (which, in 1973, manifested itself as Corsican terrorists bombing the waste-dumping Italian ships), still persists. And while bomb threats can't be defended, they do make property developers think twice about lining Corsica's coastline with mega-hotels and rows of holiday homes.

Fires pose by far the biggest threat to the island's sun-sizzled environment. The sweet-smelling scrubland of the Corsican maquis flares at the strike of a match. Of the thousands of fires reported each year, it's calculated that some 90% are started by campers, cigarette smokers, arsonists or irresponsible visitors on picnics. Other culprits include hunters setting fire to forests to drive out wild boar, property developers (who sometimes start fires wilfully), shepherds, who burn expanses of land to make meadows for grazing, and farmers, burning stubble to produce potash, which is used to improve soil quality.

Between 1973 and 2001 no fewer than 2830 sq km of land burnt. As many as 20 fires are reported on a single summer's day – an alarming trend that Mediterranean Europe's increasingly drier and hotter climate is only exacerbating. In the summer of 2003 unrelenting temperatures cost Corsica almost €11 million in fire-fighting expenses as fire swept across 270 sq km of land – the worst fires for 30-odd years. Severe drought, moreover, saw islandwide water restrictions.

Preventive measures taken by local government include a summertime islandwide ban (until 30 September) on camp fires, barbecues and other outdoor fires, and prohibiting smoking in forests and the maquis. Lighting up (anything) warrants a €750 fine. To protect fauna already ravaged by fires, the Corse-du-Sud prefect banned hunting game (popular targets of the hunters' rifles such as wild boar, pheasant, woodcock and hare) in fire-scarred areas in southern Corsica for the 2003–04 season.

Measures taken by the local offices of the **Office National des Forêts** (ONF; www .onf.fr/reg/corse in French), which manage the island's national forests, include making more fire breaks and educating the public through forest visits (the ONF provides seasonal guided visits to the national forests of Bavella, Bonifatu, Marmaro, Chiavari, Valdu Niellu, Aïtone, Pineta, Fangu, Vizzavona and

---

WATCH YOUR STEP

Foraging animals and careless hikers threaten Corsica's 40-odd fragile highland lakes. The Parc Naturel Régional de Corse (PNRC) has a programme whereby seasonal workers collect the rubbish that summer visitors leave behind at the most popular lakes – Melu, Ninu and Creno – and at the same time enforce the camping bans. As a further precaution, the GR20 has been diverted from the grassy areas around Lac de Ninu. Walkers should respect the rules: no fires, no rubbish and no off-piste tramping.

Summer grazing threatens *pozzines* (from the Corsican *pozzi*, meaning 'pits'). These small water holes are linked together by rivulets that flow over an impermeable substratum (like peat bogs). Lush, green and often squelchy, they're like little green oases amid more desiccated grasses. They feel like a carpet of cool moss – and do just feel them rather than walk over them. Most are fairly inaccessible. If you're walking the GR20, you'll come across them around Lac de Ninu and on the Plateau de Coscione.

BAGS OF ENVIRONMENTAL SUPPORT

After consulting citizens in a 2003 referendum, the Corsican legislature enacted a law, unique to the island, that should be emulated by many much larger communities. Appalled at the volume of tattered, drifting, disposable plastic bags polluting the island and threatening its marine life (dolphins and turtles, especially at risk, would swallow them, imagining they were gulping a tasty jellyfish), it decreed that supermarkets could no longer pack their produce in such free material. But this was more than a negative proscription. Nowadays, every supermarket sells, for the very modest outlay of €1, large bags – of plastic, yes, but stout, sturdy and infinitely re-useable. Bearing the words *On ne me jette pas, je ne pollue pas, je contribue à un meilleur environnement* (You don't throw me away, I don't pollute, and I play my part in bettering the environment), they're worth that euro for the colour photos of the Corsican countryside that bedeck each side. Do as the Corsicans do when they shop – and, hey, they also make a cheap, easily packed and original souvenir or present for the folks back home.

l'Ospédale; ask at local tourist offices for details). Other preventive measures include planting more fire-tolerant foliage such as subterranean clover *(trifolium subterraneum)*. For more inflammatory information – and for details of the independent initiative of a Corsican community action group to reduce the hazard of fire – see the boxed text, p111.

Corsican farmers continue, as they traditionally have, to allow their livestock to roam. Semidomestic pigs (see the boxed text, p246) in particular, ranging freely, also threaten forests as they snuffle and turn over the soil as they grub for food.

On the coast, environment protection is tackled head-on by the **Conservatoire du Littoral** (www.conservatoire-du-littoral.fr in French). This public body has built protective barriers around the Roccapina and Barcaggio dunes to prevent further erosion by tourists and over-grazing livestock trampling across the fragile sands, and so crushing the plants that help to stabilise these shifting sands. More significantly, the Conservatoire has bought 9084 hectares of threatened coastal sites – 21% of Corsica's roughly 1000km of coastline – in order to protect them. These include the 5300-hectare Désert des Agriates (being considered as a potential nuclear-testing site until the Conservatoire intervened back in 1989); southern Corsica's dune-rich Sartenais coastline (2500 hectares); the Bouches de Bonifacio; and the tip of Cap Corse.

TRAVEL WIDELY, TREAD LIGHTLY, GIVE SUSTAINABLY – THE LONELY PLANET FOUNDATION

The Lonely Planet Foundation proudly supports nimble nonprofit institutions working for change in the world. Each year the foundation donates 5% of Lonely Planet company profits to projects selected by staff and authors. Our partners range from Kabissa, which provides small nonprofits across Africa with access to technology, to the Foundation for Developing Cambodian Orphans, which supports girls at risk of falling victim to sex traffickers.

Our nonprofit partners are linked by a grass-roots approach to the areas of health, education or sustainable tourism. Many – such as Louis Sarno who works with BaAka (Pygmy) children in the forested areas of Central African Republic – choose to focus on women and children as one of the most effective ways to support the whole community. Louis is determined to give options to children who are discriminated against by the majority Bantu population.

Sometimes foundation assistance is as simple as restoring a local ruin like the Minaret of Jam in Afghanistan; this incredible monument now draws intrepid tourists to the area and its restoration has greatly improved options for local people.

Just as travel is often about learning to see with new eyes, so many of the groups we work with aim to change the way people see themselves and the future for their children and communities.

Walking & the GR20

Corsica is a walker's paradise. The number one reason to come to Corsica is to get off the roads and into nature – on foot. Some of the most inspirational and iconic hiking trails in Europe are here, passing through scenery of such bewildering beauty that all thoughts of aching legs will be forgotten.

And it's so simple to enjoy it. Corsica is necklaced with a good network of walking paths, mountain huts and *gîtes d'étape* (mountain lodges), allowing walkers the opportunity to explore the island's deeper recesses and its convoluted hinterland of enigmatic valleys.

'The number one reason to come to Corsica is to get off the roads and into nature – on foot'

Walking options range from the most challenging two- or three-week hike, such as the 200km-long GR20 to an easy afternoon stroll along the coast; there is something for all tastes and all abilities. Well-known and much enjoyed walks across the island include the Mare e Monti and Mare a Mare trails. Although less overhyped than the GR20, these routes take in some spectacular mountain and coastal scenery, with the added bonus of ending each day comfortably in a village. They also offer a shorter and less intimidating physical challenge than the GR20. There are also countless options for shorter walks, good if you only want to walk for a morning or an afternoon. Some of them are detailed in the destination chapters.

INFORMATION

The best source of information for walkers is the Parc Naturel Régional de Corse (PNRC). The PNRC includes more than 1500km of hiking and walking paths. The Golfe de Porto, the Réserve Naturelle de Scandola and the island's highest peaks, including the Aiguilles de Bavella, are all part of the PNRC.

The **Maison d'Information Randonnée du PNRC** (PNRC walking information office; ☎ 04 95 51 79 00; www.parc-naturel-corse.com; 2 rue Sergent Casalonga, Ajaccio) publishes a wealth of information about the park in English, Spanish and French, along with a number of walking guides (mostly in French). For more information on walking, the PNRC also runs a **Maison d'Information** (☎ 04 95 62 87 78; Calenzana; ☼ Apr-Oct) in Calenzana (see p140) or you can contact the **Comité Régional de la Randonnée Pédestre de Corse** (☎ 04 95 77 18 21; 6 rue du Capitaine Benedetti, 20100 Sartène).

TOURS

Several UK outdoor adventure outfits offer walking tours on Corsica, embracing both the GR20 and less challenging but still robust hikes. Established players include the following:

ATG Oxford (☎ 01865 315 678; www.atg-oxford.co.uk; 69-71 Banbury Rd, Oxford OX2 6PJ)

Explore (☎ 0870 333 4001; www.explore.co.uk; Nelson House, 55 Victoria Rd, Farnborough GU14 7PA)

Headwater (☎ 01606 720 033; www.headwater-holidays.co.uk; The Old School House, Chester Rd, Northwich CW8 1LE)

HF Holidays (☎ 020 8905 9558; www.hfholidays.co.uk; Imperial House, The Hyde, Edgeware Rd, London NW9 5AL)

Ramblers Holidays (☎ 01707 331 133; www.ramblersholidays.co.uk; Lemsford Mill, Lemsford Village, Welwyn Garden City AL8 7TR) An offshoot of the nonprofit Ramblers Association.

Sherpa Expeditions (☎ 020 8577 2717; www.sherpaexpeditions.com; 131a Heston Rd, Hounslow TW5 0RF)

Walks Worldwide (☎ 01524 242 000; www.walksworldwide.com; 12 The Square, Ingleton, Carnforth LA6 3EG)

World Walks (☎ 01242 254 353; www.worldwalks.com; 30 Imperial Square, Cheltenham GL50 1QZ)

RESPONSIBLE HIKING

To help preserve the ecology, beauty and wilderness of Corsica, consider the following tips when hiking.

Rubbish

- Carry out *all* your rubbish. Be careful not to overlook easily forgotten items, such as silver paper, orange peel, cigarette butts and plastic wrappers. All empty packaging should be stored in a dedicated rubbish bag. Make an effort to carry out any rubbish left behind by other hikers.
- Never bury your rubbish: digging disturbs soil and ground cover and encourages erosion. Buried rubbish will likely be dug up by animals, who may be injured or poisoned by it. It may also take years to decompose.
- Minimise waste by taking minimal packaging and no more food than you will need. Take reusable containers or stuff sacks.
- Sanitary napkins, tampons, condoms and toilet paper should be carried out despite the inconvenience. They burn and decompose poorly.

Human Waste Disposal

- Contamination of water sources by human faeces can lead to the transmission of all sorts of nasties. Where there is a toilet, please use it. Where there are no toilet facilities available, it's essential to bury your waste responsibly. Dig a small hole about 15cm deep and at least 100m from any watercourse. Cover the waste with soil and a rock. In snow, dig all the way down to the soil.

Washing

- Don't use detergents or toothpaste in or nearby any watercourses, even if you are using biodegradable products.
- For personal washing, always use biodegradable soap and a water container (or even a light-weight, portable basin might do the trick) a minimum of 50m away from any watercourse. Try to disperse the waste water and suds as widely as possible over the ground to allow the soil to filter it fully.
- Wash cooking utensils 50m away from watercourses using a scourer, sand or snow instead of detergent.

Erosion

- Hillsides and mountain slopes, especially at high altitudes, are prone to erosion. Stick to existing trails and avoid short cuts.
- If a well-used trail passes through a mud patch, walk through the mud so as not to increase the size of the patch.
- Avoid removing the plant life that keeps topsoils in place.

Wildlife Conservation

- Don't attempt to exterminate animals in huts. In wild places, they are likely to be protected native animals.
- Discourage the presence of wildlife by not leaving food scraps behind you.
- Do not feed the wildlife as this can lead to animals becoming dependent on hand-outs, to unbalanced populations and to diseases.

THE GR20

The GR20 has achieved cult status among walkers in Europe, and rightly so. Linking Calenzana, in the Balagne, with Conca, north of Porto-Vecchio, this fantastic high-level walk stretches diagonally from northwest to southeast, following the island's continental divide (hence its Corsican name, Fra Li Monti, which means 'Between the Mountains'). It is the most famous of the

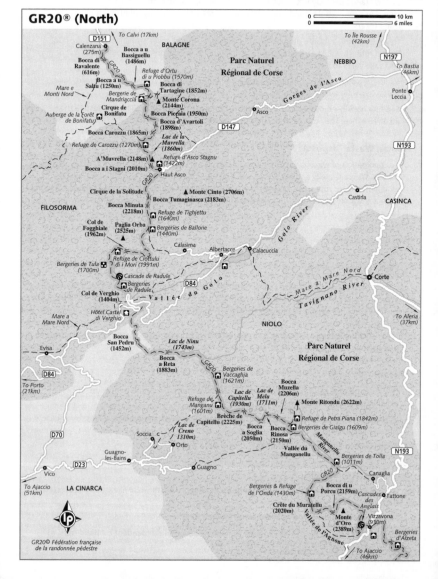

GR20® (North)

grandes randonnées (long-distance, waymarked walking routes), attracting more than 15,000 brave souls to take on its heights from all over Europe every year. It's usually covered in 15 *étapes* (stages), but you can tailor it to your own expectations and make it shorter if you wish, thanks to various access points along the way.

The diversity of landscapes makes this a memorable adventure, with forests, granite moonscapes, windswept craters, glacial lakes, torrents, peat bogs, maquis, snowcapped peaks and plains.

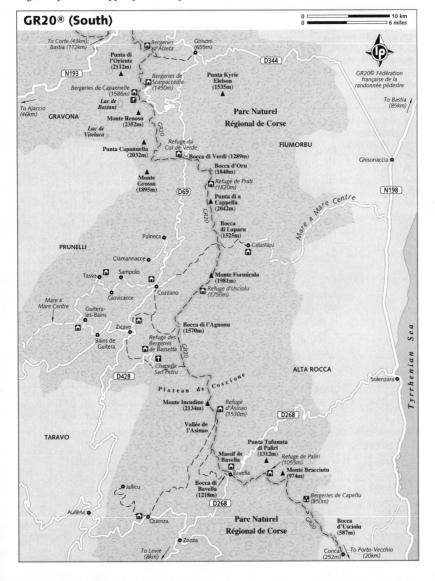

GR20® (South)

Although the mythical GR20 is a genuine mountain route that requires physical commitment, it's not beyond the abilities of an average walker. Sure, the changes in altitude are unrelenting, some stretches are tricky, the path is rocky and sometimes steep and the weather conditions can be difficult, but it can be undertaken by anyone reasonably fit and with a good deal of motivation. It's not as tough as it used to be. Meals are offered along the way (see p64) and there are plenty of opportunities to really *enjoy* the GR. Bear in mind that it's not a competition, not even a challenge; consider it as a superb route amid sensational landscapes.

PLANNING
When to Go
The GR20 can be comfortably walked any time between May and October, although some parts of the route remain snow-covered until June, making them tricky to negotiate. The peak-season months of July and August are best avoided if you have an aversion to crowds. From mid-August to the end of September, there are frequent storms, especially in the afternoon.

What to Bring
The GR20 is a long and challenging walk, and requires some preparation. Don't forget to carry a good supply of cash, as there are no ATMs on the GR20 and credit cards are only accepted in a few places. As a general rule, you'll need between €15 (if you bring your own food) and about €35 per day if you eat and sleep in *refuges*.

Good news: most *refuges* on the GR20 now offers *petit ravitaillement* (supplies), soft drinks, alcohol (beer and wine) and meals. Don't expect gastronomic ecstasy, though – it's normally satisfying, wholesome *soupe Corse*, spaghetti, stews, charcuterie and cheese. Plan on €10 to €15 for a meal. You'll find water at every *refuge*, but between stops there are very few sources of drinking water. These have been detailed in the walk description.

Camping gear is strongly recommended, as there is only a limited number of places available in *refuges* along the way, and they tend to fill up quickly in summer. Note that reservations can't be made at the PNRC-run *refuges*. When camping you have access to equipment inside the huts.

Refuges are usually manned from May to September. Some stay open until mid-October if the weather is fine.

Weather in the mountains can fluctuate quickly between extremes, so come prepared for all conditions. You can call ☎ 08 92 68 02 20 for the latest weather reports in French.

Books
The excellent Fédération Française de la Randonnée Pédestre (FFRP) Topo-Guide *À Travers la Montagne Corse* (No 67) details the GR20. The FFRP also

---

GR20 FACTS

Duration	15 days
Distance	168km
Difficulty	Demanding
Start	Calenzana
Finish	Conca

Nearest towns Calenzana (p140), Porto-Vecchio (p203)

Summary A legendary, if demanding, walk through the granite ranges of inland Corsica. Experience the isolation and grandeur of the mountains well away from the coastal crowds.

EQUIPMENT CHECKLIST

- boots
- fleece jacket
- hat (warm)
- headlamp
- high-energy snacks
- jacket (waterproof)
- maps
- mobile phone
- pocket knife
- runners, sandals or thongs
- sleeping bag
- socks and underwear

- sunglasses
- sunhat
- sunscreen
- survival bag
- tent
- thermal underwear
- toilet paper
- toiletries
- towel
- walking poles
- water container

---

publishes *Corse entre Mer et Montagne*. Albiana's *GR20 Le Grand Chemin* (in French) is also comprehensive. Cicerone's *Corsican High Level Route: GR20* is a handy English-language companion for the trail.

Maps
Waymarking *(balisage)* and signposting of the path is usually excellent (red and white paint stripes) but you might want to bring maps to get a more comprehensive and detailed view of the topography. For the GR20 route, choose the IGN 1:25,000 maps. You'll need six (Nos 4149OT, 4250OT, 4251OT 4252OT, 4253OT and 4253ET).

NEAREST TOWNS
Calenzana
Thirteen kilometres from Calvi, Calenzana (p140) is the northern starting point for the GR20 and is also on the route of the Mare e Monti Nord walk (p78).

Porto-Vecchio
Porto-Vecchio (p203) is the nearest town of a reasonable size to Conca, at the end of the walk. It makes a good base for exploring the surrounding areas, especially the Alta Rocca region, the Aiguilles de Bavella and the spectacular coast north and south of the town.

GETTING TO/FROM THE WALK
The trek starts at Calenzana. There is no public transport from Conca, at the end of the walk, to Porto-Vecchio. However, staff at La Tonnelle (p76) in Conca can arrange a shuttle service on request to Porto-Vecchio (€7). Some of the alternative access points to the GR20 are served by public transport.

Castel di Verghio (Day 5) Served by a daily bus between Corte and Porto via the D84.

Tattone (Reached via a side trip on Day 8) On the Bastia–Vizzavona–Ajaccio train line. It takes just seven minutes and €2.50 to get from Tattone to Vizzavona by train.

Vizzavona (Day 9) On the train route between Ajaccio and Bastia.

Zicavo (a detour on Day 13) Also served by daily buses (except Sunday) from Ajaccio.

Bavella (Day 14) Can be reached daily (except Sunday) in the peak season from Ajaccio or Porto-Vecchio (only Monday and Friday in the low season).

Quenza (Day 14) Can be a GR20 departure point. It's served by the Ajaccio–Porto-Vecchio buses.

SAFETY GUIDELINES FOR WALKING

Before embarking on a walking trip, consider the following points to ensure a safe and enjoyable experience:

- Be sure you are healthy and feel comfortable walking for a sustained period.
- Obtain reliable information about physical and environmental conditions along your intended route (eg from park authorities).
- Be aware of local laws, regulations and etiquette about wildlife and the environment.
- Walk only in regions, and on trails, within your realm of experience.
- Be aware that weather conditions and terrain vary significantly from one region, or even from one trail to another. Seasonal changes can significantly alter any trail. These differences influence the way walkers dress and the equipment they carry.
- Ask before you set out about the environmental characteristics that can affect your walk and how local, experienced walkers deal with these considerations.

THE WALK
Day 1: Calenzana (275m) to Refuge d'Ortu di u Piobbu (1570m)
7hr, 10km, demanding

Be prepared: this first stage is not for the faint-hearted. This day is one long ascent with a net altitude gain of about 1250m, with steep gradients, crossing a series of ridges, with hardly a downhill break and long stretches without shade. There's no guaranteed source of water, so bring at least the recommended 2L per person. Start very early (around 6am). If you want an easier start, you can bypass this gruelling stage by starting from Auberge de la Forêt in Bonifato (see p62).

The walk starts in Calenzana by winding up to the top of the village, then the path starts to climb steadily through ferns, with good views back to Calenzana and Moncale, another hillside village. At the well-signposted 'Carrefour de Sentiers' (550m), less than an hour from Calenzana, the Mare e Monti Nord route (p78) splits from the GR20. Soon after, the trail reaches the rocky **Bocca di Ravalente** at 616m.

From the pass, the trail skirts a wide terraced valley, staying fairly level and passing a few small babbling streams that usually dry up later in the season, before climbing relatively gently to 820m. After this easy stretch the trail becomes steeper, zigzagging uphill to another pass, **Bocca a u Saltu** (1250m). About 3½ hours from the start, this area makes the perfect spot for lunch. Over the other side of the ridge, on the northeastern face of Capu Ghiovu, the trail starts to climb even more steeply; you may have to use your hands to hoist yourself up some of the rocks. About halfway up this stretch is a stream that is a good source of drinking water if it hasn't dried up.

The wide grassy expanse at **Bocca a u Bassiguellu** (1486m), 5½ hours into the walk, is dotted with shady pine trees and makes another good place for a rest stop. From here the trail crosses a rather rocky and unsheltered stretch but stays fairly level along the way. The *refuge* comes into view across the valley, into which you descend before a final short climb brings the day to an end.

Refuge d'Ortu di u Piobbu (camping €4, dm €9.50; ⏱ May-Sep), at 1570m, has 30 beds and plenty of camping space. However, it has just one rather primitive toilet and shower; there is a water source about 200m beyond the *refuge* along the GR20. There are a few meals (€12) and drinks on offer as well as snacks.

GR20 – TOP TENS

Best Meals
Who said that it's not possible to eat well on the GR20? After a strenuous day, you'll never forget a hearty meal at the following places:

- Day 3: Chalet Haut Asco
- Day 4: Bergeries de Ballone
- Day 5: Refuge de Ciottulu di i Mori
- Day 5: Hôtel Castel di Verghio
- Day 8: Bergeries de Tolla
- Day 9: Bar Restaurant de la Gare (Vizzavona)
- Day 11: Refuge du Col de Verde
- Day 13: Refuge des Bergeries de Bassetta
- Day 14: Auberge du Col de Bavella
- Day 15: La Tonnelle

Best Refuges & Places to Stay
- Day 1: Refuge d'Ortu di u Piobbu
- Day 4: Refuge de Tighjettu
- Day 5: Refuge de Ciottulu di i Mori
- Day 5: Hôtel Castel di Verghio
- Day 6: Refuge de Manganu
- Day 7: Refuge de Petra Piana
- Day 9: Hôtel-Restaurant I Laricci
- Day 10: Gîte U Fugone
- Day 14: Refuge di Paliri

Best Mountain Scenery
Every day along the GR20 outdoes itself. The following landscapes will keep you rapt for days:

- Day 1: Refuge d'Ortu di u Piobbu
- Day 4: Bocca Tumasginesca
- Day 5: Col de Fogghiale
- Day 6: Bergeries de Vaccaghja
- Day 7: Lac de Melu & Lac de Capitellu seen from Brèche de Capitellu
- Day 9: Crête du Muratellu
- Day 11: Bocca d'Oru
- Day 13: Plateau de Coscione & Monte Incudine
- Day 14: Aiguilles de Bavella
- Day 15: Bocca d'Usciolu

Side Trip: Monte Corona
2½-3hr

Walkers who still feel strong may want to climb nearby Monte Corona (2144m). A trail, marked by cairns and flashes of paint, goes up the slope directly behind the *refuge* to **Bocca di Tartagine** (1852m). From there head south and climb the rocky ridge until you see the rounded summit, which is covered in loose stones and marked by a cairn. The spectacular view stretches from the *refuge* below to the north coast.

Day 2: Refuge d'Ortu di u Piobbu (1570m) to Refuge de Carozzu (1270m)
6½hr, 8km, demanding

Two routes exist for this day. The one fully described in this section is graded demanding and is the most direct route. It cuts across a range of mountains, with rocky and often spectacular scenery. The alternative low-level route skirts the mountain range crossed by the main route. It leads off to the west from the Refuge d'Ortu di u Piobbu meandering down the valley to the **Auberge de la Forêt de Bonifatu** (540m). From the auberge, it's a relatively easy two-hour uphill walk in the forest to reach the Refuge de Carozzu.

The day's walk starts with a gentle ascent through pine forest to a ridge (1630m). In front of you is a sharp drop to the valley bottom and then a long, steep ascent (500m) to an even higher ridge on the other side.

The trail descends quickly to the valley floor, passing the ruined **Bergerie de Mandriaccia** (1500m) shepherd's hut and the Mandriaccia stream, then starts the long climb up the other side. About halfway up this unrelenting ascent there's a good source of drinking water, probably the only one you'll come across all day.

Eventually, about three hours from the start, you'll come to **Bocca Piccaia** (1950m). There's very little shade.

The trail does not cross the ridge immediately but stays on the northern side, remaining at a fairly high altitude until it crosses to the other side and gently descends to **Bocca d'Avartoli** (1898m). Traversing the southern and western faces of the next ridge, the trail drops steeply before climbing sharply to cross the next pass. It then goes to the eastern side of the ridge, crossing back again to the western side at **Bocca Carozzu** (Inuminata; 1865m), about five hours into the walk.

From here the route begins the long and somewhat tedious descent to the *refuge*. At the start of the descent it's worth looking back at the wonderful views enjoyed in the last couple of hours of the walk. It's only towards the end of this descent that you'll find some shady trees. A short distance before the *refuge* the trail crosses a stream.

Refuge de Carozzu (camping €4, dm €9.50; ☽ May-Sep), at 1270m, is in a magnificent setting, hedged in by sheer rock faces on three sides, but with an open terrace looking down the valley. It sleeps 26 and there are plenty of camp sites in the surrounding woods. Corsican cheese omelettes (€7), a platter of charcuterie (€8), soup and a *menu* (€14) are on offer. Beer, wine, soft drinks and cakes are also sold, but no *ravitaillement* (supplies).

If you follow the path from the *refuge* towards Lac de la Muvrella for 10 minutes, past a passage of rocks with cables, you'll come to a stream with a series of delightful (albeit chilly) **swimming pools**. You might also spot some mouflon here.

WARNING

Take note of and observe Parc Naturel Régional de Corse (PNRC) rules and regulations; in particular, lighting fires at any point along a route in the park is strictly forbidden, as is camping outside the designated areas near *refuges*.

As far as drinking water from streams is concerned, safety is not guaranteed: do not use it unless strictly necessary, and then purify it.

Day 3: Refuge de Carozzu (1270m) to Haut Asco (1422m)

4½-5hr, 6km, moderate

The day starts with a short, rocky zigzagging path up through the forest to a ridge, then a slightly longer drop to the Spasimata River at 1220m. This is crossed on an atmospheric **suspension bridge**. At first the trail edges along above the river, crossing long sloping slabs of rock. At some points plastic-coated cables offer handholds, which are reassuring, but note that these rocks can be dangerously slippery when it rains.

Leaving the river with its tempting rock pools, the trail then starts a long, rocky ascent to **Lac de la Muvrella** (1860m), which is reached after 2½ hours. The lake water is not safe to drink. If you look back during the final stages of the ascent, you'll see Calvi on the north coast. From the lake it's a 20-minute scramble to the knife-edged ridge. After a short drop on the other side, the trail soon starts to climb again, skirting around the side of A'Muvrella to **Bocca a i Stagni** (2010m), from where the views over the Asco Valley are sensational. The total time of ascent from the Spasimata River is roughly three hours.

The day is less taxing than the previous two, ending with a long, tedious 600m descent to **Haut Asco**, visible far below, which you'll reach after 1½ hours. Haut Asco looks like any ski resort in the off-season – bare, dusty and forlorn – but it's a haven for walkers after the spartan conditions of the last couple of days.

Refuge d'Asco Stagnu (camping €4, dm €9.50; mid-May–mid-Oct), at 1422m, has 30 beds in rooms for two, four or six people. It also has hot showers, a huge kitchen and a dining area as well as a terrace. There's plenty of camping space on the grassy ski slopes and campers can use the showers at the *refuge*. The welcoming warden has a good selection of supplies, including fruits, energy bars, tinned food, chocolate and cheese.

You can also stay at the motel-like **Chalet Haut Asco** (☎ 04 95 47 81 08; Haut Asco; s/d €38/50, with half-board €55/90, dm €7-9, with half-board €28-30; May-Sep) at Haut Asco. It has three- and six-bed dorms as well as old-fashioned but clean rooms with private bathrooms (heaven!). You can feast on hearty Corsican specialities at the restaurant (mains €7 to €20, *menu* €16), and stock up on supplies at the bar. Good news: credit cards are accepted (minimum €15).

Day 4: Refuge d'Asco Stagnu (1422m) to Bergeries de Ballone (1440m)

7hr, 8km, demanding

This is generally held to be the most spectacular day on the GR20, crossing the sensational Cirque de la Solitude.

From Haut Asco the trail starts on the left (south) side of the ski run. It's easy to lose the trail at the start when it heads away from the ski slope into the trees. If you do wander off the trail, it's not a problem: you can rejoin the route when it climbs above the valley and the ski slopes to cross the glacial moraines. The views over the valley and Haut Asco are stunning.

Allow about two hours to reach the site of the old Refuge d'Altore at 2000m. From the small lake at the site, a steep 45-minute climb leads to **Bocca Tumasginesca**, or Col Perdu (Lost Pass), at 2183m. From the pass the **Cirque de la Solitude** falls dramatically away beneath your feet. For most walkers this is the highlight of the entire GR20, and one's first reaction is probably sheer amazement that its navigation is possible.

The descent and ascent of the Cirque de la Solitude is more of a rock climb than a walk. However, there are chains bolted into the rock face to make the climb easier. Since other walkers are often almost vertically below you, it's important to take great care not to dislodge rocks or stones as you climb.

'The Cirque de la Solitude falls dramatically away beneath your feet. For most walkers this is the highlight of the entire GR20'

THE GR20 FOR HEDONISTS *Jean-Bernard Carillet*

If, like me, you're as much of a hedonist as a keen walker, fear not: you can also enjoy the GR20 and combine it with seamless effort and pleasure. If you take a softer, more comfortable (and less masochistic) approach, without sacrificing the true spirit of the GR20, you'll find the route much less daunting, easier to complete and much more rewarding.

Here's what I did: I took the plane from Paris to Calvi where I arrived late morning. Rather than starting the walk in Calenzana (the usual starting point), I started from Bonifatu, which meant I would bypass the first two stages, which are considered very demanding if you're not properly prepared (and I wasn't!). I took a taxi to Auberge de la Forêt in Bonifatu (see p141), where, first thing first, I had a very good meal. I stored part of my luggage in the auberge (free service) and kept only 12kg in my backpack. From there, I headed to Refuge d'Ortu di u Piobbu, after a fairly easy two-hour uphill walk in the shade – a perfect warm-up after several months of inactivity. I was ready to tackle the later demanding stages in optimal conditions!

On Day 3, in Haut Asco, I chose to stay in the Chalet Haut Asco in a room with private bathroom and hot shower (bliss!). And had another mood-lifting meal at the adjoining restaurant.

It's a novelty on the GR20: the wardens prepare meals, and they're copious and pretty tasty (charcuterie, soups, pasta, omelettes). You don't need to bring your own supplies, which saves several kilograms in your backpack. And really, it was a joy to tuck into a good meal at the *refuges* each evening. On Day 5 I couldn't resist the temptation of another comfy room and a hot shower, in Hôtel Castel di Verghio (see p156). And, of course, a gargantuan meal at the restaurant.

On Day 8 I recommend to take the low-level route and to sample an invigorating meal at the lovely Bergeries de Tolla. On Day 9 I stayed at Hôtel Restaurant I Laricci (p248) in Vizzavona and enjoyed a delicious steak at the Bar Restaurant de la Gare, accompanied by a glass (or two) of wine. On Day 13 it was the low-level alternative again via the Refuge des Bergeries de Basseta, which is an oasis on the GR20.

Another hint: if you feel tired and need to recharge the batteries, it's possible to do *demi-étapes* (half-stages): Days 5, 13 and 14 can be broken down into two days each.

I took my time. A number of hardcore walkers set off at 6am, but I started no earlier than 8.30am after a good breakfast. And I stopped several times along the way to work on my sun tan and enjoy a refreshing dip in the streams followed by a siesta.

So, if you want to walk the GR20 without sacrificing comfort, here's the winning combination: splurge at the few hotels along the way, treat yourself to the hot meals prepared by the *refuges* (rather than carrying depressing freeze-dried food), buy fresh supplies at the *refuges* and don't hesitate to make pauses and enjoy the landscape! And don't feel compelled to walk the GR20 in its entirety; there is no shame in biting off just a small section, using the alternative access/exit points along the way. Why suffer? Why, indeed.

Typically it takes about 2½ hours to cross the cirque (a steep-sided basin formed by the erosive action of ice).

From Bocca Tumasginesca it's 200m down to the scree-covered valley floor, where many walkers stop for lunch. On the other side the route crosses rock slabs, often guided by fixed cables, and makes a series of steep, rocky, chain-assisted ascents before emerging into an equally steep gully (or couloir) filled with loose rocks and stones. Towards the top the climb becomes a little more gentle, before emerging 240m above the valley floor at **Bocca Minuta** (2218m), the second-highest point on the GR20.

Past the ridge the scenery is dramatically different: much wider and more open. The trail makes a long and at times steep descent down the Ravin de Stranccciacone before reaching the Refuge de Tighjettu about 1¼ hours after leaving Bocca Minuta.

Refuge de Tighjettu (camping €4, dm €9.50; ☽ mid-May–mid-Oct), at 1640m, has limited camping space, so many campers prefer to pitch their tents lower down, by the river. Note that the river rises rapidly when there are storms.

The warden sells food, such as Corsican cheese, charcuterie, biscuits and tinned food, and also prepares simple meals (from €6).

It's only another 30 minutes' walk down the valley to the **Bergeries de Ballone** (camping €4-6; ☺ Jun-Oct), at 1440m. There are plenty of good spots at which to pitch your tent around the *bergeries*. Beds are also available in small tents for €6.

At the *bergeries* there's also a popular restaurant and bar, with beer, wine, snacks and breakfast, and copious hot meals (*menu* €15).

Day 5: Bergeries de Ballone (1440m) to Castel di Verghio (1404m)
6½-7hr, 13km, moderate

Day 5 contains a half-day option, with the possibility of breaking the journey at the Refuge de Ciottulu di i Mori. From the Bergeries de Ballone, it's also possible to access to the villages of Calasima (about 1½ hours) and Albertacce (2¼ hours).

The day begins with a gently undulating ascent through pine forests where streams tumble down from the hills to the west to join the Viru River at the valley floor. Across the valley to the east you can see the road leading up from Albertacce to Calasima, at 1100m the highest village in Corsica. The trail turns west round the eastern slope of Paglia Orba and then emerges from the forest for the steep and rocky slog up to **Col de Fogghiale** (1962m) after about three hours.

On the other side of the pass a wide valley opens out to the south, but the route continues west, crossing the slopes of Paglia Orba and climbing slightly to reach the *refuge*.

Refuge de Ciottulu di i Mori (camping €4, dm €9.50; ☺ May-Sep), at 1991m, is the highest *refuge* in the entire GR20; it has 24 beds. Most hikers arrive here by midday and refuel here. The *gardien* (warden) prepares filling meals for €16 and simple dishes, such as omelettes, soup, charcuterie (€6 to €8) or sandwiches (€6). There's a lovely terrace from where you can sample your meal while soaking up the gorgeous views.

Along one side of the building there's a terrace looking out over the valley below. Directly behind the *refuge* is **Paglia Orba** (2525m), the third-highest peak in Corsica. Climbers may want to make the three-hour round trip to the summit of the mountain via the Col des Maures, but the final stretch includes some reasonably challenging rock climbing.

The route continues round to the western side of the Vallée du Golo, descending slightly to 1907m before dropping steeply down to the river at 1700m, just below the ruins of the Bergeries de Tula. For the next couple of hours the walk follows the impressively rocky ravine of the **Golo River**, passing a series of appealing rock pools. The path tracing the lower part of the valley was, for many centuries, a traditional route along which farmers took their livestock when migrating to summer pastures.

The valley narrows before the trail reaches the **Cascade de Radule** (1370m) and the **Bergeries de Radule**, after five to six hours. Cheese is sometimes sold at the *bergeries*. For the final hour you walk through the beech forests of the Valdu Niellu, crossing the Mare a Mare Nord trail (p76) before finally emerging on the D84 just 100m west of Castel di Verghio (1404m). The ski slopes are on the other side of the road.

For details on accommodation options, see p156.

Day 6: Castel di Verghio (1404m) to Refuge de Manganu (1601m)
5½hr, 14km, moderate

The GR20 runs gently through pine and beech forests, dropping gently to 1330m before making a sharp turn to the right (west) and climbing to the

'The path was once a traditional route along which farmers took their livestock when migrating to summer pastures'

small shrine at **Bocca San Pedru** (Col de Saint Pierre; 1452m), reached after about 1½ hours.

From the pass the route continues to climb, following the carefully laid stones of an ancient mule path and offering superb views to the east. The trail climbs to a ridge, drops off it, climbs back on to it and eventually reaches **Bocca a Reta** (1883m). It then descends to **Lac de Ninu** (1743m), about 3½ hours from the start. Surrounded by grassy meadows and *pozzines* (interlinked waterholes), the lake makes a wonderfully tranquil stop for lunch. Water is available at a spring just above Lac de Ninu.

The trail continues east, following the course of the Tavignano stream, which drains the lake, across meadows and then through patches of beech forest past the remains of an abandoned *refuge* to the **Bergeries de Vaccaghja** (1621m), one to 1½ hours from the lake. The *bergeries* usually sell cheese. From here you can see the Refuge de Manganu, less than an hour's walk across the valley. The trail drops gently from the *bergeries* to **Bocca d'Acqua Ciarnente** (1568m) and finally makes a short, sharp ascent, crossing a bridge over the Manganu stream to the Refuge de Manganu.

The pleasant **Refuge de Manganu** (camping €4, dm €9.50; ❤ Jun-Sep), at 1601m, has 26 beds and plenty of grassy camping space around the building, good showers and toilets and a selection of tempting swimming spots in the Manganu stream. Supplies, including chocolate, salads, pasta and biscuits are available, and simple meals are prepared for dinner (€9).

Day 7: Refuge de Manganu (1601m) to Refuge de Petra Piana (1842m)

6hr, 10km, demanding

'The route climbs to the highest point on the GR20 before teetering round a spectacular mountain face that drops down to glacial lakes'

This is a hard day, as the route climbs to the highest point on the GR20 before teetering round a spectacular mountain face that drops down to glacial lakes. Water is available from streams during the first ascent and from another stream on the final descent to the Refuge de Petra Piana.

After crossing the bridge from the Refuge de Manganu, the GR20 immediately begins to climb, emerging onto a small meadow after 30 minutes, climbing again to another brief, horizontal break at around 1970m and then ascending even more steeply up a rocky gully. This finally becomes a scramble to the **Brèche de Capitellu** (2225m), a spectacular small slot through the spiky ridge line of peaks. Around 2½ hours from the *refuge*, this crossing is the highest point on the GR20 and the view to the east is breathtaking.

The trail bends to the southeast and edges around the eastern face of the ridge, high above the lake. There's often snow on the path well into the walking season, so take great care; it's a long way down. Just before another small pass at 2000m, where the trail crosses to the southern side of the ridge, another trail diverges off to the east and drops down to **Lac de Capitellu** (1930m). It's possible to continue down from there to **Lac de Melu** (1711m).

The main route climbs slightly to reach **Bocca a Soglia** (2050m), about an hour's walk from the Brèche de Capitellu. Lots of day-trippers drive into the valley from Corte to walk up to the lakes.

The trail then bends to the northeast, high above Lac de Melu, climbing to the soft-edged little **Bocca Rinosa** (2150m) and passing Lac de Rinosa before reaching **Bocca Muzzella** (Col de la Haute Route; 2206m), about five hours from the start of the day. From here it's less than an hour, downhill all the way, to the Refuge de Pietra Piana.

The small, 28-bed **Refuge de Petra Piana** (camping €4, dm €9.50; ❤ May-Sep), at 1842m, is nicely situated right on the edge of the ridge, looking south down the Vallée du Manganellu. There's plenty of grassy camping space and good facilities. There are two toilets and two solar-heated showers. Dinner (€11)

HIGH-ALTITUDE LAKES & POZZINES

Corsica's 40-odd high-altitude lakes, formed from the glaciers that used to cover the mountains, were unknown to scientists until the 1980s but are now actively monitored by Parc Naturel Régional de Corse (PNRC) personnel. A number of different analyses have shown that some are endangered by the digging of pigs and the pollution caused by tourist overpopulation in the summer. The PNRC has implemented a protection programme for the most popular lakes – Melu, Ninu and Creno – in the summer. Seasonal workers collect the rubbish left by walkers and ensure that the camping bans are upheld. The GR20 has even been diverted so that it does not contribute to the destruction of the grassy areas around Lac de Ninu. Respect the rules: no fires, no rubbish and no walking at inappropriate places.

The *pozzines* (from the Corsican *pozzi*, meaning pits) are also a fragile environment, threatened by intensive farming. *Pozzines* are little water holes that are linked together by small streams and are on an impermeable substratum – they're like peat bogs. They feel like a carpet of cool moss to walkers. They are found near Lac de Ninu and on the Plateau de Coscione, between the GR20 and the Refuge des Bergeries de Bassetta.

comprises *spaghetti au pesto* (spaghetti with basil sauce) and homemade cakes. Snacks and supplies are also sold.

Side Trip: Monte Ritondu
5hr return

Keen walkers may consider climbing Monte Ritondu (2622m), the second-highest mountain in Corsica. This is not a technically demanding climb, although the 800m ascent is a bit taxing.

Cairns mark the route to a meadow and dried-up lake just above the *refuge*. The trail then zigzags uphill before crossing the ridge at 2260m, south of the peak. Don't descend from the ridge towards the small lakes below – continue north along the eastern side of the ridge, crossing patches of snow until the large **Lavu Bellebone** lake comes into view. The trail drops down to the lake's southern end and edges round the southeastern side before starting the steep climb up the slope of the rocky gully that leads to the spiky rock marking the Col du Fer de Lance. From here the trail turns west and climbs to a small metal-roofed shelter, huddled just below the summit. There are superb views in all directions from the summit.

Day 8: Refuge de Petra Piana (1842m) to Refuge de l'Onda (1430m)
5hr, 10km, easy

Good news: by the standards of the GR20, stage eight is an easy day (well, almost) – a chance to recover from the tribulation of the previous five *étapes*. There's plenty of opportunities to take refreshing dips in the Manganellu River, which flows through a succession of deep gin-clear **vasques** (pools), waterfalls and stands of majestic laricio pines.

As soon as the trail leaves the *refuge* there's a choice between following the main GR20 through the Vallée du Manganellu or taking an alternative high-altitude route (with double-yellow markings), which follows ridgetops to the Refuge de l'Onda. The high-altitude route is quicker but less interesting. It takes four hours, includes some technical and exposed stretches and has superb views over Ajaccio.

The main GR20 starts to plunge steeply downhill and soon reaches the **Bergeries de Gialgu** (1609m). The trail continues to drop, following an ancient mule track of neatly laid stones that winds down the hill to the Manganellu stream at 1440m. It then plunges through often dense forest to the delightful **Bergeries de Tolla** (mains €8-12, menu €19; ☺ mid-Jun–mid-Sep) at an altitude of 1011m, about 2½ hours from the start. Here you can feast on hearty Corsican staples, such as *omelette au fromage de brebis et à la menthe fraîche* (omelette with ewe's milk cheese and fresh mint). Ease a belt hole for the *bergeries'* signature dessert, the tempting *amandes et noisettes grillées au miel de châtaignier* (a mix of chestnut honey and grilled almonds and nuts), which is a fireworks of calories. It also sells lots of trekking supplies, as well as wines and liqueurs to accompany your meal.

Just below the *bergeries* a bridge crosses the Manganellu stream (940m). From here you can detour off the GR20 to the villages of Canaglia and Tattone (see below).

The GR20 turns upstream from the bridge and almost immediately passes over the Goltaccia, which flows into the Manganellu. Do not cross over this bridge but continue upstream and uphill beside the Goltaccia. Eventually the trail crosses the river and climbs away to the north side, reaching the **Bergeries de l'Onda** after one hour from Bergeries de Tolla. The *bergeries* sell cheese and charcuterie. The camp site is surrounded by fences to keep the many pigs and sheep from poking around the site.

Refuge de l'Onda (camping €4, dm €9.50; ☽ Jun-Sep) itself is higher up the hill, overlooking the *bergeries* and camp site from 1430m. It has 16 beds, one shower and one toilet, but is not as appealing as the *bergeries*.

Side Trip: Canaglia & Tattone
2hr or 4hr return

The walk is approximately one hour from the Manganellu bridge on the GR20 to the pretty village of Canaglia. The wide track running alongside the river and the string of little pools make this a popular route with walkers. From Canaglia it's 4km by road to Tattone, where you can stay at the **Bar Camping du Soleil** (☎ 04 95 47 21 16; Tattone; camping adult/tent/car €5.50/2.50/2.50; ☽ May-Sep), near the train station, which has a pizzeria and a bar that also sells snacks. It's 100m from the railway station.

Refuge Chez Pierrot (☎ 04 95 47 20 65, 06 14 66 42 20; RN193, Tattone; dm with/without half-board €30/14; ☽ Jun-Sep) has basic five- to eight-bed dorms and two bathrooms with hot showers. Pierrot is a real character and offers local specialities, including stews and soups, and sells cheese and charcuterie. Bookings are essential. Pierrot can pick you up in Canaglia or Vizzavona and will take you to your preferred departure point the following day. This is a good way to short-circuit the GR20 route between Petra Piana and Vizzavona.

Day 9: Refuge de l'Onda (1430m) to Vizzavona (910m)
5½hr, 10km, moderate

This is traditionally the midstage of the GR20, and ends in Vizzavona, the best-equipped stop along the GR20. Water is plentiful along this part of the trail.

This moderately graded route sets off northwards, following the high-altitude alternative route to the Refuge de Petra Piana, but soon doubles back to head south up the long climb to the **Crête du Muratellu** (2020m), reached after 2½ hours. From this windswept height the rest of the day's walk is a long descent.

An alternative route, marked only by stone cairns, continues up the Crête du Muratellu and turns east to **Bocca di u Porcu** (2159m), from where it veers southeast to climb to the summit of **Monte d'Oro** (2389m), the fifth-highest mountain in Corsica. There are stretches of difficult rock climbing on this route, which should not be attempted by inexperienced climbers. It rejoins the main GR20 route just before Vizzavona and adds about three hours to the day's walk.

'The wide track running alongside the river and the string of little pools make this a popular route'

The main GR20 route makes a steep and rocky descent (which can be slippery in the rain) from the Muratellu ridge into the upper heights of the Vallée de l'Agnone. The descent becomes less steep and the surroundings greener as the route drops below 1600m and passes the remains of an abandoned *refuge* at 1500m. The trail passes a high waterfall, the **Cascades des Anglais** (1150m), roughly four hours from the start, and continues through pine forests, sometimes high above the tumbling stream. Monte d'Oro broods over this scene from the northeast.

Head past a bridge over the Agnone; from here into Vizzavona the route makes the transition from walking path to a track quite suitable for cars. There are several turns, several bridges and what seems like an interminable trudge before the trail finally emerges onto the road right in the middle of the hamlet of **Vizzavona**, only a short distance from the train station.

For details on accommodation and eating options in Vizzavona, see p248.

Day 10: Vizzavona (910m) to Bergeries de Capannelle (1586m)
5-5½hr, 13.5km, moderate

Two hours steeply up, the same gently down, 30 minutes of abrupt uphill work, then a mild descent to the *refuge*. That's today's topography, punctuated by magnificent views as you approach Monte Renosu (2352m), standing out against a backdrop of laricio pine and beech trees.

From the station in Vizzavona, walk up the road that passes in front of Hôtel-Restaurant I Laricci, leaving the access path to the GR20 Nord on your right. After a little bridge, take the path on your right and cross the N193, reached in about 10 minutes, to continue along a wide track. Turn right again at a sign for Bergeries de Capannelle. After three minutes or so, the GR20 leaves this track to take a path on the left. This makes a steep, twisting ascent through a wood of beech, chestnut, laricio pine and holly to pass by a rusting pylon about an hour out.

Where the route meets a path with yellow markings, follow these to the right for no more than 100m to enjoy a wonderful view of Monte d'Oro.

Back on the GR20, you soon emerge into open terrain, from where you can see ahead to your next goal, the pass of Bocca Palmente. Be careful not to miss a right turn for the col. Ignore the first sign for an off-route *source*. Instead, drink deep from another, ice-cold **spring**, right beside the trail and just below **Bocca Palmente** (1647m) with its circular stone corral. The highest point of the day, it's reached about two hours after leaving Vizzavona.

ALTERNATIVE ACCESS POINTS ALONG THE ROUTE

Completing the GR20 will give you a sense of pride and achievement, and rightly so. But while the goal of many is to walk it end to end, even a couple of days on the traverse will allow you to experience the beauty of Corsica's mountain wilderness.

The obvious way to divide the GR20 is into two sections: from Calenzana to Vizzavona (over nine days), and south from Vizzavona to Conca (in six days). Vizzavona is the most convenient midway point, with train and road links to Ajaccio and Bastia.

Between Calenzana and Vizzavona, it's possible to join the trail at several villages along the way: Haut Asco (at the end of Day 3), Castel di Verghio (at the end of Day 5) and Tattone, a short side trip from the main trail (on Day 8). For just a small taste of the GR20, Days 4 and 5 take in some of the most spectacular scenery of the whole walk, across the Cirque de la Solitude.

In the southern section of the GR20, Zicavo (Day 13), and Quenza and Bavella (Day 14) are all popular access points for walkers. Reaching Zicavo and Quenza involves a detour from the GR20, but these traditional villages, tucked away in remote valleys, are the very soul of Corsica and well worth exploring in their own right.

The path drops to the **Bergeries d'Alzeta**, then continues level. After about 30 minutes a hairpin bend, from where a turn-off leads to Ghisoni, has a stunning view over the Monte Renosu massif, and makes an ideal picnic spot.

The GR20 follows the contour line along the hillside through a forest of laricio pines. About 1¼ hours beyond the Ghisoni turn-off, it descends gently to the gaily painted **Bergeries de Scarpaccedie** (1450m). Just before these shepherds' huts, there's a **waterfall** and clear pool, deep enough to dunk yourself in.

After a stream 10 minutes beyond the huts, turn sharp right to begin 20 to 30 minutes of hard, uphill slog. Turn right at a sealed road to enjoy, after around 100m, another spectacular view of Monte Renosu and the sweet anticipation aroused by a sign proclaiming the Gîte U Fugone's draft beer. From here, it's a 20-minute descent to the Bergeries de Capannelle, clustered around the single lift of this mini ski resort. The *bergeries*, all still owned by local families, now serve as cottages for holidaymakers and hunters.

Friendly **Gîte U Fugone** (☎ 04 95 56 39 34; www.gite-ufugone.com in French; dm with half-board €31; ⊙ May-Sep) accepts advance reservations. It has 62 beds in dorms for four or five and half-board is all but mandatory. The restaurant does particularly generous *menus* (€10 to €20) based on Corsican specialities and a little grocery store sells basic foodstuffs.

Gîte U Renosu, 300m away, is only open in winter.

Just before the Gîte U Fugone, the **PNRC refuge** (dm €5), a charming house of stone, is decidedly basic though it does have cooking facilities. The fee is collected by the owner of Gîte U Fugone.

You can camp for free near Gîte U Fugone. There are free external cold showers but better to treat yourself to the luxury of a hot one (€2.50) at the *gîte*.

Day 11: Bergeries de Capannelle (1586m) to Refuge de Prati (1820m)
6-7hr, 16km, moderate

The first five hours, hovering mostly around the 1500m contour line, are relatively easy as far as the Bocca di Verdi. Here, there's an attractive *refuge* within the forest, offering the option of stopping early, though it does leave you with a long following day that begins with a steep 1¾-hour ascent.

Follow the sign indicating Bocca di Verdi at the foot of the ski lift to plunge into beech forest. After 30 minutes, the trail passes near the **Bergeries de Traggette** (1520m) – don't be seduced by the more evident path to the right that leads to them. You then descend above and in parallel with a fast-flowing stream to meet the D169, which you'll probably reach well within the hour. Turn right along this blacktop road and, after 50m, right again to head uphill and enjoy stunning views over the Fiumorbu region and the Punta Kyrie Eleïson range before the path plunges into a thick forest of pine and beech.

Some 45 minutes later, the GR20 rounds a hairpin bend to the right. After snowmelt, the streams that gurgle from the mountain's flank may require the nimbleness of a mountain goat (we confess, we weren't agile enough and tumbled in). After a third hairpin bend, a further 45 minutes later and with the **Punta Capannella** (2032m) before you, the Lischetto stream cascades down in a profusion of small **waterfalls**.

Once over the Lischetto, it won't take more than 30 minutes to reach the **Plateau de Gialgone** (1591m) with **Monte Grossu** (1895m) rearing before it. Near the southern extremity of this lovely green plain, a wooden sign indicates a side trail to the *pozzines*, lush, outcrops of verdant grass, a two hour out-and-back detour.

The GR20 now begins a rocky, zigzagging descent (don't worry about a counter-current stretch that takes you briefly upstream and, seemingly, back uphill). This culminates some 30 minutes later at a little wooden bridge straddling the Marmanu stream with a **spring** around three minutes beyond it.

'Just before these shepherds' huts, there's a waterfall and clear pool, deep enough to dunk yourself in'

The path continues level or dropping gently and, just after a clearing on the right, widens to become a broad, rocky lane. At a picnic area, around 45 minutes beyond the bridge, the track to the left soon brings you to **Bocca di Verdi** (Col de Verde; 1289m) and the **Refuge du Col de Verde** (☎ 04 95 24 46 82; www.boccadiverdi.com; camping per person/tent €5/5.50, dm with/without half-board €33/12; ⊙ mid-May–mid-Oct). Also called the Relais San Petru di Verde, it enjoys a lush green setting beside the D69. With an attractive terrace, it serves meals (dinner *menu* €18) and has self-catering facilities, accepts reservations by phone or email and – joy of joys – has a couple of hot showers, free to overnighters.

Between the *relais* and Refuge de Prati, there's 550m of altitude gain in around 1¾ hours of walking. After 10 minutes of gentle ascent through pine forest along a former logging track, turn left. After a second left turn 10 minutes later, the real climbing begins. It takes 20 minutes of sustained effort to reach an intermediate plateau.

A stream marks the end of this gentle intermission as the path again twists steeply upwards, mercifully in the shade of a beech wood. After 15 minutes of climbing, a small clearing on the right gives a first glimpse southwards of the Haut Taravo Valley and the mountains to its east, to be attacked on Days 12 and 13, their folds and crests receding to the horizon in muted shades of grey.

After a little over 30 minutes of steep, unshaded ascent, a giant cairn marks the saddle of the **Bocca d'Oru** (1840m) with a precipitous view down over the eastern plains and the sea beyond.

From here, it's a delightful 20-minute lope along a flat plateau to the **Refuge de Prati** (camping €4, dm €9.50; ⊙ Jun-Sep), totally rebuilt after having been destroyed by lightning in 1997. This welcoming 32-bed PNRC *refuge* has self-catering facilities and enjoys a beautiful setting above a cropped green sward that's ideal for camping. There are home-cured cheeses and charcuterie for sale and in July and August it also does lunches, as well as dinner (€13). If the dorm is full, you're assured of a canvas roof over your head; it rents tents (€2 per person). It's worth rising with the dawn to see the sun slowly burst above the sea – and to be first in one of the only two toilets and, for the hardy, the single, icy shower.

Day 12: Refuge de Prati (1820m) to Refuge d'Usciolu (1750m)
5-5½hr, 9.5km, demanding

This is one of the GR20's most spectacular and challenging days with some very steep sections, plenty of rock clambering and the possibility of high winds on the exposed ridges.

From the *refuge*, a clear path leads southwest, straight on to the ridge. After 10 minutes of gentle ascent to warm the muscles comes about 20 minutes of steep, switchback ascent, then a long traverse of bare granite outcrop where you'll need to be aware of your every footfall. The ample reward for all this effort is the sensational vista, westwards over the villages of Palneca, Ciamannacce and Cozzano and embracing to the east Prunelli, perched atop its hillock, and Ghisonaccia, down on the plain.

NORTH TO SOUTH OR SOUTH TO NORTH?

From which direction should you tackle the GR20? Nearly two-thirds of walkers opt for the north–south route, as does this guide. There are various reasons for this – access to Calenzana is easier, the main guide to the route is in this direction, habit – but logic would dictate going from south to north. The southern section between Conca and Vizzavona is easier, giving your body a chance to get used to the effort. Going in this direction also means that you don't have to walk with the sun in your eyes (but you'll have to cope with your shadow…).

Fifteen minutes beyond the traverse, a steep, head-down ascent ends at a small notch, offering another spectacular view, followed by a gentle descent and easy ambling through thick mountain undergrowth. And so this soul-stirring ridge walk and clamber continues; rocky descents and boulder fields are relieved by moments of delightful striding where you can lift your head high and gaze all around.

Skirting the highest point of **Punta di a Cappella** (2042m), the trail rounds the Rocher de la Penta before moving off the ridge and into a little copse of stunted beeches that offer welcome shade. From here it's less than 30 minutes of easy descent to **Bocca di Laparu** (1525m), another shady spot about three hours out. Here the GR20 intersects with the Mare a Mare Centre trail (p76) coming up from Cozzano.

Continuing along the GR20, there's a **spring** 150m off-route that normally flows between June and early September. The trail continues along the ridge, dipping and climbing steadily for about 450m of altitude gain, up to **Monte Formicula** (1981m and the highest point of the day). Allow around 1¾ hours for the ascent, which mostly follows the eastern side of the ridge, sometimes hopping to the windier western side.

Once you're off the bare rock south of Monte Formicula, it's downhill all the way to day's end, and a mere stroll compared to your earlier exertions.

Leaning against the mountain, the **Refuge d'Usciolu** (camping €4, dm €9.50; ☺ mid-May–Sep), about 45 minutes beyond Monte Formicula, at 1750m, has a bird's-eye view over the whole valley. Like all PNRC *refuges*, it doesn't accept reservations but, as the Refuge de Prati, it has tents for hire, should the dorm's 36 places all be occupied. It's a friendly spot where the harnesses of the packhorses jangle. Dinner is served promptly at 6.30pm (dish of the day €8) so don't linger too long on the trail.

'Rocky descents and boulder fields are relieved by moments of delightful striding'

Day 13: Refuge d'Usciolu (1750m) to Refuge d'Asinao (1530m)
7½-8 hr, 14.5km, moderate

It's possible to do this section over two days, with a detour (not described here) to the village of Zicavo (p177) or an overnight camp at the Refuges des Berger-ies de Bassetta, attacking Monte Incudine (2134m) on the second day.

From the Refuge d'Usciolu, a short, steep path brings you back to the ridge after 10 minutes and a sign for Cozzano, 2½ hours' walking away. Here, it's possible, but not very practical, to leave the route (one bus a day, leaving at 7am, links the village with Ajaccio).

From the signpost, it's a tightrope walk along the steep ridge for a good 90 minutes. The altitude is an almost constant 1800m, but the trail goes up and down in a continual series of tiny ascents and descents, making the going very hard, particularly across large slabs of rock. There's no shade but the way is well signed and the views are sublime.

About 1¾ hours out, the path drops into a shady beech forest and broadens into a well-defined track. Some 15 minutes later, enjoy a break in a lovely grassy clearing – an ideal place for lunch with a nearby signed **spring**. The pastoral setting is in stark contrast to the barren austerity of the route along the crest.

Ten more minutes bring you to the crossroads at **Bocca di l'Agnonu** (1570m), where you turn sharp left (southeast). If you want to do a *demi-étape* (half stage), you can reach from Bocca di l'Agnonu the impeccably run **Refuge des Bergeries de Bassetta** (☎ 04 95 25 74 20, 06 87 44 04 08; dm with half-board in chalet per person €38), roughly 1½ hours' walk off the GR20 with only a slight change in altitude. This private *refuge*, a converted *bergerie*, is an attractive, picturesquely sited option if you would rather complete this section over two days. The *refuge* has 17 beds, some in the former *bergerie*, others in small, recently built chalets. Excellent Corsican meals (*menu* €17, daily special €10) are served in a big

---

REFUGE WARDENS

That ugly word 'warden' in English has overtones of prisons, men in uniform and overbearing authority. But the cheerful guardians of the GR20's Parc Naturel Régional de Corse (PNRC) *refuges* tend to be splendid company. Is it the job that makes them so congenial or are they made that way?

Francis, keeper of the Refuge d'Usciolu for over 15 summers, is typical, his whole family sharing in his tasks. Each day he descends with his four packhorses to bring up supplies for meals and to stock the veritable grocery store of provisions that he runs for passing hikers. Corsican to the marrow, he plays folk music of the island unintrusively over a pair of speakers. And after dinner, he passes round, offering a shot of delightful bilberry liqueur to diners. He's also a recognised postman with the right to stamp with the *refuge*'s own postmark the postcards he sells.

---

communal room with a fireplace. The next day you don't need to retrace your steps; you can rejoin the junction with the GR20 at the foot of the Monte Incudine via another path through the Coscione plateau.

Some 1¼ hours after leaving the Bocca di l'Agnonu, you emerge from the woods and drop to the undulating **Plateau de Coscione**, overlooked by Monte Incudine with its distinctive U-shaped notch, visible for most of the day and today's major challenge.

From here, it's easy walking all the way to the foot of Monte Incudine.

Continuing along the GR20, the trail soon crosses a rickety wooden footbridge over the Furcinchesu stream, where shady patches of grass beside the right bank make a wonderful picnic spot. Now the ascent of Monte Incudine begins. About 30 minutes of switchback ascent through beech wood, brings you to **Aire de Bivouac i Pedinieddi** (1625m), a little plateau with the scattered remains of the Refuge de Pedinieddi, also devastated by lightning. There's an icy-cold **spring** 10 minutes further along the trail.

About 20 minutes beyond the spring, you reach the long saddle of **Bocca di Luana** (1800m), where the route turns right (south) and begins a difficult climb to the ridge leading to the summit. A strenuous 1¼ hours from Bocca di Luana, you'll reach the cross on the summit of **Monte Incudine** (2134m), the highest point on the southern sector of the GR20, where snow may linger well into June.

All that remains is the descent to the *refuge*. But what a descent and what an assault upon kneecaps, joints and toes! After 20 minutes of relatively easy walking along the ridge, the path plummets down to the *refuge* with an altitude loss of 500m. It comes at the end of a long day so take special care; allow a good 1½ hours to descend from the summit to the Refuge d'Asinao unless you're particularly surefooted.

Refuge d'Asinao (camping €4, dm €9.50; ⊙ mid-May–Sep), at 1530m, has room for only 22 people. Meals are available (dinner €13). The small store sells basic refreshments such as charcuterie, honey, cheese, beer and wine.

Day 14: Refuge d'Asinao (1530m) to Refuge de Paliri (1055m) via the Alpine Route
5¾-6¼hr, 13km, moderate to demanding

This day offers a spectacular alpine alternative to the main trail not long after starting out. From the Refuge d'Asinao, head west before gradually turning south to reach the valley, where you ford the Asinao River after about 30 minutes' walk. On the way, you pass a sign indicating a turn-off to Quenza (p214), a jewel among villages on the Mare a Mare Sud trail (p76). It's three to four hours from the GR20 and boasts a *gîte d'étape*, hotels and a couple of grocery stores.

LE PLATEAU DE COSCIONE

For centuries, this undulating plateau with its hillocks, streams, incised valleys and prairies was the summer pasture for thousands of sheep, its grass cropped short as a buzz-cut by all those chomping ruminants. These days, however, only a few cattle roam this lovely expanse, where scrub and low, thorny undergrowth are gradually taking over now that its sweet grasses are no longer snuffled and chewed by hungry sheep.

Once over the Asinao River, the path climbs gently. Beyond a **spring**, about one hour from the *refuge*, it evens out, enabling you to walk at a steady clip along the mountain's flank, maintaining an average altitude of 1300m along a ledge above the River Asinao. Views – to the foothills of the Massif de Bavella and over the Asinao Valley – are impressive, glimpsed through the foliage of mixed wood (including, for the first time on the GR20 heading south, birch trees).

About 20 minutes beyond the spring, it's decision time. Straight ahead, the main GR20 route skirts the Bavella mountainside to the southwest of the massif. It's not so demanding but longer and lacks shade in its latter stages. Taking off to the left is the warmly recommended **Alpine Route.** Marked with double yellow stripes, it takes you to the heart of the Massif de Bavella and is one of the highlights of the GR20. The two routes converge shortly before Bocca di Bavella.

Deviating from the official GR20 trail, the Alpine Route is one of the most beautiful. However, it's also technically demanding, passing through fallen rocks and stones and requiring you to use your hands across a chained slab of rock at one point. If you suffer from vertigo, you'll be more at ease on the main route. It is also better to avoid this option in the wet, as there's a real risk of slipping.

The climb up the mountainside is very steep. There's a short respite for about 10 minutes, then the path emerges from the forest and continues to climb towards **Bocca di u Pargulu** (1662m), reached around 45 minutes after taking off from the main GR20 route. Towards the end, the rock faces, with their knife-edge points, can feel overwhelming but when you reach this col and see the panoramic views, all will seem worthwhile. In the jagged landscape, the eight peaks to left and right that look like giant chipped teeth are the Aiguilles de Bavella (Bavella Needles). At the northeastern end of this jagged range, is the **Punta Tafunata di i Paliri** (1312m), distinguished by the large hole through which the sky appears. The Refuge de Paliri, today's goal, lies out of sight, behind and below it.

From the col, the path descends steeply through a stony gully for about 30 minutes until it reaches the famous chain across a smooth, steep slab, about 10m in width. After another 30 minutes of tricky progress down, up and across rocky slopes, you reach a pass with wonderful views of the peaks and Bavella to the east. The route to Bavella plunges through a deep gully of pink granite, where the yellow blazes are sometimes scant and in places dangerously inadequate.

Roughly four hours after you set out, the trail rejoins the normal route of the GR20. It's then only a short stroll through a pine wood to **Bocca di Bavella** (1218m) and its seething car park.

Go past the Madone des Neiges (a statue of the Virgin Mary) and take the sealed road (one of the few concessions to civilisation on the GR20) to the left for about 300m to the busy little hamlet of **Bavella**, packed with visitors and sporting a handful of restaurants (where you can enjoy a cold drink and the rare luxury of a hot lunch), a grocery store and the opportunity to overnight at the **Auberge du Col de Bavella** (☎ 04 95 72 09 87; dm with/without half-board €32/15; ⟳ Easter-Oct). Some walkers choose to leave the GR20 here, although this is a shame as the last stage of the traverse has its own more gentle charm, its greenness, gentle woodland and easier striding in contrast to the rugged appeal of earlier stages. Meals are available (*menus* €15.50 to €22).

Pause to drink deep from the refreshingly cold **spring** that's opposite Auberge du Col de Bavella, then take the forest track to its right. After barely 10 minutes of level walking, look out for an unmarked left turn to take a path that descends through ferns to a stream bed; its banks make a pleasant picnic spot if you haven't explored the gastronomic delights of Bavella. About five minutes beyond the stream, follow a forest track to the right for 50m to cross the Volpajola stream by an Irish bridge.

To the east looms a long range of mountains, which you will cross via Bocca di Foce Finosa. A couple of minutes beyond the bridge, fork right to begin the ascent. It takes a strenuous 30 minutes to climb 200m in altitude to **Bocca di Foce Finosa** (1214m). Before beginning the last hour's descent, down the east face of the range, take a last look back at the sheer, grey bulk of the Massif de Bavella and the Aiguilles at its southwestern extremity. The descent starts sharply, then turns northeast and levels out, bringing this long stage to a pleasant conclusion (fill up your water bottles at the **spring**, 200m before the *refuge*, to save a brief backtracking).

Built from the stones of a former *bergerie*, the little **Refuge de Paliri** (camping €4, dm €9.50; ☷ mid-May–Sep), at 1055m, has a magnificent setting from where on a clear day you can see as far as Sardinia to the south. Jean-Baptiste, the dynamic new warden (pick up some of his home-cured cold meats and sausages for your final lunch on the trail), has injected new life into this spacious site, a welcome contrast to the huddled huts and handkerchief-sized camping pitches of the high-mountain *refuges*. Meals are available (dinner €13).

Day 15: Refuge de Paliri (1055m) to Conca (252m)
4½-5hr, 12km, moderate

To wind down, back where the world is again green, this last day offers scenery as lovely as anywhere on the GR20 for half the effort.

From the *refuge* the path descends briefly before coming to the heart of a superb forest of maritime pines and ferns. To your left rears the imposing spectre of **Anima Danata** (Damned Soul) with its distinctive sugar-loaf shape. From the first of the day's several rocky outcrops, reached after 45 minutes, you can see the **Monte Bracciutu** massif to the east and **Monte Sordu** to the southeast.

The path then curves northeast round a cirque, above which surge the peaks of the Massif du Bracciutu. After about 30 minutes you reach **Foce di u Bracciu** (917m), where the trail turns sharply south.

After following the contour line for about 10 minutes, it's 30 minutes of tough ascent before you haul yourself over **Bocca di Sordu** (1065m) with its distinctive masses of fallen rock and spectacular vistas as far as the sea.

Just after the pass you drop 50m across relatively steep granite slabs that could easily become a natural slide in the wet. These lead to a sandy path that slices through pine forest (about two hours from the start). Five to 10 minutes later the trail emerges onto a little plateau dotted with granite domes and strangely weathered rocks, at their feet maquis and a few maritime pines. About two hours out you come across the ruins of **Bergeries de Capellu** (850m), which would be a pleasant spot for a break, were it not strewn with the filth of irresponsible picnickers. There's a signed **spring** 300m off the piste.

The trail leads steadily down to the Punta Pinzuta stream, crossing to its left bank after about 2½ hours of walking. Here, you pick up a sandy forest track that runs above the stream. Some 15 minutes later, the route crosses back at a large bend with a pair of large, enticing **rock pools** where you can cool off.

A good 20-minute climb takes you out of this steep-sided valley and up to a pass. The path, level for the most part, continues along the mountainside for 45 minutes until it reaches **Bocca d'Usciolu** (587m), a narrow U-shaped passage through a wall of granite, beyond which the pink roofs of Conca beckon.

'The path descends briefly before coming to the heart of a superb forest of maritime pines and ferns'

CHEERS!

It's over, you've done it and you deserve some immediate gratification. Sink into a seat on the terrace of Bar GR20 and pour yourself a beer. Or if your thirst is greater, continue to La Tonnelle, whose bar offers, for €18.50, a splendid selection of the best of Corsican ales – two bottles each of Pietra, Colomba and Serena, plus one each of herb-flavoured Torra Myrte and Torra Arbouse.

The 30-minute descent into **Conca** in the valley below passes through thick undergrowth, emerging at a sealed road. Turn left and at a crossroads take the road leading downhill into the village.

La Tonnelle (☎ 04 95 71 46 55; http://monsite.wanadoo.fr/gitelatonnelleconca; camping €5, dm with/without half-board €37/18; ☾ Mar-Oct), with rooms for two, four or five, makes an attractive final-night option. Meals are available (*menu* €14). If you prefer to push on, it runs a minibus service to Porto-Vecchio (€7), where there's onward transport to Bastia and Ajaccio. Although it requires a minimum of four passengers, you rarely have to wait long for a quorum.

THE MARE A MARE ROUTES

Three Mare a Mare (Sea to Sea) paths link the west and east coasts via the central mountains.

Unlike the GR20, which stays high in the mountains away from settlements, the Mare a Mare routes pass through some of the prettiest villages on the island. The routes are generally less taxing and less crowded than the GR20 and offer considerable comfort with *gîtes d'étape* and hotels every night.

There are no ATMs on the trails and the *gîtes* don't take credit cards.

MARE A MARE NORD

The Mare a Mare Nord is said to be the prettiest of the Mare a Mare trails. It links Moriani (p222) on the east coast to Cargèse (p160) in the west, and passes through vastly different areas. It is split into 10 days, each lasting from four to six hours and reaching altitudes of up to 1600m. For the final section of the walk, between Évisa and Cargèse, the route merges with that of the Mare e Monti Nord. It is better to avoid the period between November and April, when parts of the route may be under snow.

MARE A MARE CENTRE

The Mare a Mare Centre provides an excellent opportunity to explore the more traditional, inland areas of Corsica. The route can be completed in seven days, each with three to seven hours' walking. Starting in Ghisonaccia (p230) on the east coast, and finishing in Porticcio (p174) on the west coast, it passes through the little-known microregions of the Fiumorbu and the Taravo before crossing the hinterland of Ajaccio.

The maximum altitude is 1525m at Bocca di Laparu, so the best time to do the walk is between April and November. Take a detailed map (as the markings are not very regular).

MARE A MARE SUD

This famous, easy walk links Porto-Vecchio (p203) in the southeast to Propriano (p183) in the southwest. The walk is divided into five days, each of which lasts an average of five hours, and reaches a maximum altitude of 1171m. With fine views to the Aiguilles de Bavella and Monte Incudine, it crosses through the magnificent region of Alta Rocca and many of the

THE MARE E MONTI & MARE A MARE
ROUTES & OTHER WALKS

0 ⎯⎯⎯⎯⎯⎯ 30 km
0 ⎯⎯⎯⎯⎯⎯ 20 miles

WALKS

1 The Sentier des Douaniers
2 Plage de la Roya to Ostriconi
3 Col de la Croix to Girolata
4 Col de Verghio to the Bergeries de Radule
5 Ponte Vecchju to Ponte Zaglia
6 Les Calanques: A Walk to the Château Fort
7 Capu Rossu
8 Soccia to Lac de Creno
9 The Ridge Road
10 Piscia di Gallo
11 Pertusato Lighthouse
12 Monte Cinto
13 Évisa to Cascades d'Aïtone
14 Around Vizzavona

Cap
Corse

D80

Bastia

St-Florent

D81

Île Rousse

HAUTE-
CORSE

Algajola

N193

Calvi

N197

D81

Calenzana

Ponte Leccia

D51

Bonifatu

GR20

Galéria

Moriani

Girolata

D84

Corte

Sermanu

Santa Reparata
di Moriani

Calacuccia

Pianellu

N198

Golfe de
Porto

Porto Ota

Évisa

12

13

4

3

N200

Tyrrhenian
Sea

6

D84

Piana

Marignana

Soccia

Alternative Route

Vivario

7

D70

Cargèse

Sagone

Vizzavona

Ghisoni

14

Aléria

MEDITERRANEAN
SEA

D81

N193

D344

Col de
Laparo

Ghisonaccia

Ajaccio

Col St-
Georges

Guitera

Cozzano

Serra di
Fiumorbu

San Gavinu
di Fiumorbu

9

Porticcio

Quasquara

Zicavo

Solenzara

Bisinao

D69

GR20

D268

Col de
Bavella

Coti-Chiavari

Aullène

Quenza

Zonza

Conca

Olmeto

Lévie

Porto Pollo

Burgo

Propriano

Ste-Lucie
de Tallano

10

D268

Sartène

L'Ospédale

Porto-Vecchio

CORSE-
DU-SUD

Îles Cerbicale

N196

D839

N198

Figari

Bonifacio

11

Archipel des Lavezzi

Îles Sanguinaires

THE MARE A MARE & MARE E MONTI

Ⓐ Mare e Monti Nord
(Calenzana to Cargèse, 10 stages)
Ⓑ Mare a Mare Nord (Moriani to Cargèse,
with southern variant, 10 stages)
Ⓒ Mare a Mare Centre (Ghisonaccia
to Porticcio, 7 stages)
Ⓓ Mare e Monti Sud
(Porticcio to Propriano, 5 stages)
Ⓔ Mare a Mare Sud (Porto-Vecchio
to Propriano, 5 stages)

island's most beautiful villages. The third day of the trail offers three options: a short version that skips the Plateau de Jallicu, a detour through the village of Aullène or a long version via Zonza, which adds a day to the itinerary. This route is passable year-round.

THE MARE E MONTI ROUTES

As the name suggests, these are paths between the sea *(mare)* and the mountains *(monti)*. Accommodation is offered by *gîtes d'étape* (see p251) in villages along the way.

MARE E MONTI NORD

The Mare e Monti Nord (literally 'Sea to the Northern Mountains') is a superb (and not very demanding) walk linking Calenzana (p140) in the Balagne to Cargèse (p160), south of the Golfe de Porto. It is divided into 10 days of four to seven hours each, and its highest point is 1153m. It passes through several exceptional natural sites, such as the Forêt de Bonifatu, the Réserve Naturelle de Scandola and the Gorges de Spelunca, and stops in some gorgeous villages, notably Galéria, Ota and Évisa.

The route is passable year-round, but the periods before and after the main season (May to June and September to October) are preferable to avoid the worst of the heat. The path crosses the Mare a Mare Nord in two places: Évisa and nearby Marignana.

MARE E MONTI SUD

'Highlights are the incredible views over the bays, the historic Genoese towers and superb beaches'

This path runs between the bays of two well-known seaside resorts in the southwest of Corsica – Porticcio (p174) and Propriano (p183). It's divided into five days of five to six hours and ascends to a maximum height of 870m. There are stops in Bisinao, Coti-Chiavari (which towers above the two bays), Porto Pollo and Olmeto. The walk ends in Burgo (7km north of Propriano).

The highlights are the incredible views over the bays, the historic Genoese towers and superb beaches (the Baie de Cupabia and Porto Pollo). Like its northern counterpart, this path is passable year-round and is not particularly difficult. Spring and autumn are the best times. The path meets the Mare a Mare Sud in Burgo.

There are only two *gîtes d'étape* on the route, one in Bisinao and one in Burgo. In the other villages you can stay in a hotel or at a camp site.

OTHER WALKS

Walking in Corsica is by no means limited to the GR20 and the Mare a Mare and Mare e Monti walks. There's every bit as much, and perhaps more, for those who prefer an easy walk of a single day, half a day or less. Details of some of the best short walks are in the regional chapters of this guide.

The PNRC can provide brochures on easy 'country walks' it has designed around the villages of Alta Rocca, Bozio, Fiumorbu, Niolo, Taravo, Vénachese and Giussani – all in interior parts of the island that visitors don't often see. These walks, all three to seven hours in length for the round trip, are perfectly suited to casual walkers and even to families.

The Great Outdoors

If you want it, Corsica's got it. The extraordinarily varied terrain of this little-populated island and the fretted coastline lapped by azure waters provide an incredible stage for the action seeker in search of anything from canyoning and Parc Aventure (the latest rage) to multiday horse-riding trips – not to mention superb Via Ferrata circuits and fantastic hiking trails (see p54). Seafaring types will appreciate the good kitesurfing and diving opportunities that abound on Corsica's coasts. If you don't do something in Corsica that you've never done before, you're missing the point!

The island's line-up of adrenaline-pumping activities obviously encompasses an element of risk, but the perception of danger is part of the thrill. Chances of a mishap are arguably minuscule, but reassure yourself that the company you choose takes adequate safety precautions.

And if you need to recharge the batteries after all that exertion, rest easy: snug restaurants serving platters of charcuterie or pungent cheeses are never far away. Ready? Now it's time to flex your physique, soothe your muscles, fill your eyes with more than you thought possible and allow the landscape to sweetly overwhelm you. Take your pick!

Make sure you have travel insurance that fully covers you for any planned activities.

WATER ACTIVITIES

DIVING

The Bahamas it ain't, but when it comes to providing enthralling diving for the experienced and novices alike, Corsica has no peers in the Mediterranean. Its appeal is due primarily to the unbeatable repertoire of diving adventures it offers. Shipwrecks, fish life in abundance and a dramatic seascape (as dramatic as on land, which is saying a lot) are the reality of diving here. You can mingle with big groupers, barracudas, dentex, rays and a host of technicolour critters that flutter around rock formations. Good news: you don't need to be a strong diver – there are sites for all levels. Added bonuses include professional dive centres, superb visibility, low pollution and warm waters in summer.

Diving Conditions

In winter water temperatures are usually between 13°C to 14°C. Summer water temperatures range from a balmy 21°C to 25°C. The best season for diving is from May to October. A 5mm wetsuit is recommended. Visibility varies a lot, from a low of 10m at certain sites to a maximum of 40m. The libeccio (southwesterly wind) can roil the waters in some of the less protected gulfs.

TOP FIVE ADVENTURES FOR KIDS

Not to worry if you're travelling with the wee ones, since most outfits accommodate children with special gear, pricing and activity options.

- Horse riding at Moriani-Plage (p223) or donkey riding near Propriano (p185)
- Canyoning at Bavella (p217)
- Taking an introductory dive with École de Plongée Île Rousse (p136), a dive centre specialising in children's diving
- Windsurfing or sailing in the Golfe du Valinco (p185)
- Swinging Tarzan-style through the trees at St-Pierre de Venaco (p247)

Dive Centres

There are about 35 dive centres in Corsica. Most are open from April to October. All of them are affiliated to one or more professional certifying agencies (usually CMAS and, less frequently, PADI). You can expect well-maintained equipment and qualified instructors. But like a hotel or a restaurant, each dive centre has its own style. Do your research and opt for the one that best suits your expectations.

They offer a whole range of services and products, such as introductory dives (*baptêmes*; for children aged eight years and over, and adults), night dives, exploratory dives, speciality dives (eg Nitrox dives) and certification programmes (usually CMAS or PADI).

See the regional chapters for dive-centre contacts.

A simple medical certificate is compulsory for diving in France. You can get one from your doctor in your home country or have it faxed or emailed to the dive centre. Otherwise, you can get one from any doctor in Corsica (€21 – the price of a consultancy).

COSTS & DOCUMENTS

The price of an introductory dive includes equipment hire, while the price of an exploratory dive varies according to how much equipment you need to rent. Most dive centres in Corsica have a price for *plongeurs équipés* (divers who have their own equipment) and *plongeurs non équipés* (divers who need to rent equipment). There are usually five- and 10-dive packages, which are much cheaper than single dives.

If you're a certified diver, don't forget to bring your C-card and your logbook with you. A medical certificate is also mandatory.

HOW MUCH?

Introductory Dive €38-55

Exploratory Dive €35-45

Open Water Certification €290-400

Top Dive Sites in Corsica

There are hundreds of dive sites scattered around the island. The following sites are just a selection.

AROUND PORTO-VECCHIO

A dozen or so dives can be taken in this area, mainly in the vicinity of the Îles Cerbicale. See p204 and p209 for local dive centres.

La Pinella (maximum depth 12m) A photogenic shipwreck, close to Porto-Vecchio's harbour. You can explore the inside.

RESPONSIBLE DIVING

Please consider the following tips when diving and help preserve the ecology and beauty of reefs.

- Never use anchors on the seabed, and take care not to ground boats on coral.

- Avoid touching or standing on living marine organisms or dragging equipment across the seabed.

- Be conscious of your fins. Even without contact, the surge from fin strokes near the seabed can damage delicate organisms. Take care not to kick up clouds of sand, which can smother organisms.

- Practise and maintain proper buoyancy control. Major damage can be done by divers descending too fast and colliding with the seabed.

- Take great care in underwater caves. Spend as little time within them as possible as your air bubbles may be caught within the roof and thereby leave organisms high and dry. Take turns to inspect the interior of a small cave.

- Resist the temptation to collect corals or shells or to loot marine archaeological sites (mainly shipwrecks).

- Ensure that you take home all your rubbish and any litter you may find as well. Plastics in particular are a serious threat to marine life.

- Do not feed fish.

BEGINNERS: TAKE THE PLUNGE!

You've always fancied venturing underwater on scuba? Now's your chance. What could be better? Corsica is a perfect starting point for new divers, as the warm water in the shallow coves is a forgiving training environment. Most dive centres offer courses for beginners and employ experienced instructors, many of them competent in English.

Just about anyone in reasonably good health can sign up for an introductory dive *(baptême)*, including children aged eight and over. It typically takes place in shallow (3m to 5m) water and lasts about 30 minutes. It's escorted by a divemaster.

If you choose to enrol in an Open Water course *(brevet Niveau 1)* while in Corsica, count on it taking about four days, including a few classroom lectures and open-water training. Once you're certified, your C-card is valid permanently and recognised all over the world.

Le Danger de La Vacca (maximum depth 40m) A series of seamounts. Very exposed, but draws lots of fish.
Le Danger du Toro (maximum depth 40m) Three seamounts that brush the surface. Canyons, seafans and lots of action.
Les Arches (maximum depth 37m) Dramatic underwater scenery with walls and arches. Abundant fish life.

BONIFACIO

Groupers, groupers, groupers! BIG thick-lipped groupers near the Îles Lavezzi, which draw divers like bees to a honey pot. See p198 for local dive centres.

La Tête de Cheval (maximum depth 30m) A drop-off festooned with seafans and broken up by caves and fissures. Atmospheric and fishy (dentex and barracudas en masse).
L'Écueil des Lavezzi (maximum depth 30m) A large plateau at about 5m that slopes gently to about 50m. Very fishy (rays, moray eels, dentex, groupers, barracudas).
Les Grottes (maximum depth 10m) A shallow dive at the exit of Goulet de Bonifacio. Good for beginners.
Mérouville (maximum depth 30m) Bonifacio's signature dive. Groupers galore! Groupers aside, it's pretty barren, though.

TIZZANO

No crowds and very few dive boats: this is diving near Tizzano. It's a real gem with a host of untouched sites for those willing to venture away from the tourist areas. Diving here is focused on the *secs* (seamounts) that lie off Cap Senetosa. It's got plenty of fish and it's atmospheric. The hitch? Most sites are exposed to the prevailing winds – expect agitated seas. See p193 for local dive centres.

GOLFE DU VALINCO

The highlight of this area is the stunning seascape, with numerous vertigo-inducing drop-offs, arches and caverns, giving the sites a peculiarly sculpted look. However, don't expect throngs of fish obscuring your vision. See p185, p181 and p188 for local dive centres.

La Grande Vallée & Le Colorado (maximum depth 30m) Same terrain as Les Cathédrales. Groupers and seafans.
La Vallée des Mérous (maximum depth 35m) Lots of fish action.
Le Sec du Belvédère (maximum depth 30m) A massive seamount with plenty of seafans and red coral.
Le Tonneau (maximum depth 35m) Big rocky seamount riddled with fissures and arches.
Les Cathédrales (maximum depth 35m) A long-standing favourite, which never fails to impress with its contoured terrain resembling a cathedral.

GOLFE D'AJACCIO

The Golfe d'Ajaccio is a diver's treat, with a good balance of scenic seascapes and dense marine life. The most spectacular dives in this area are found mainly in the southern section of the gulf, between the Tour de l'Isolella (also known as the Punta di Sette Nave) and Capo di Muro. There's also a handful of sites scattered along the Îles Sanguinaires in the north. See p168 and p175 for local dive centres.

La Meulière (maximum depth 15m) A shipwreck dating from WWII.

La Tête de Mort (maximum depth 30) This site has everything, from a plateau to arches, caves and gullies.

Le Tabernacle (maximum depth 22m) A well-regarded site, suitable for all levels. A plateau slopes gently to 22m.

Sette Nave (maximum depth 35m) Another killer site, with lots of nooks and crannies in the rock formations and a profusion of marine life.

GOLFE DE LAVA & GOLFE DE SAGONE

This area has a vibrant assemblage of dramatic rock formations that shelter a stunning variety of species. And there's the Banc Provençal, which ranks as one of the best dives in the Mediterranean. See p161 for local dive centres.

Castellaci (maximum depth 35m) A series of drop-offs, honeycombed with caves.

Le Banc Provençal (maximum depth 30m) *The* iconic dive site this side of the island. A phenomenal seamount that brushes the surface; a magnet for all kinds of species.

Le Canadair (maximum depth 30m) Wreck of an airplane that crashed in 1971. It lies upside down.

Pietra Piombata (maximum depth 35m) A bijou seamount, suitable for all levels. Seafans, red coral and barracudas.

Punta Capigliolo (Pointe de Locca; maximum depth 30m) A sheer drop-off, north of the gulf of Liscia.

Punta Paliagi (maximum depth 35m) A mix of drop-offs and plateaus.

GOLFE DE PORTO

Do you see the exceptional coastal wilderness of Golfe de Porto and the crags and cliffs of Les Calanques that fret the skyline? It's more or less the same story below the waterline. This gulf boasts an exceptional diversity of underwater wonders, with a jaw-dropping topography – just as on land – and masses of fish due to the proximity of the Réserve Naturelle de Scandola.

Sadly, it's very exposed to the libeccio, the prevailing wind. Too good to be true… See p148 for local dive centres.

GEORGES ANTONI'S UNDERWATER PARADISE

Georges Antoni is a well-known Corsican underwater photographer and the author of *Feux d'Artifice Sous la Mer* (Fireworks Under the Sea) and *Mes 50 Plus Belles Plongées en Corse* (My 50 Most Beautiful Dives in Corsica), both available in bookshops on the island. When we met him, he was shooting a film on diving for a French TV programme. After years spent taking pictures abroad, he still thinks Corsica is an unmatched haunt for divers. 'Corsica is a like an oasis in the Mediterranean. Conditions are optimal: there's no pollution, no industries, no sewage, no fertilisers. Another key factor is the topography: there's no continental shelf here, so you get fantastic drop-offs and a dramatic terrain. We also have two big marine parks, Scandola and Lavezzi, and marine life is abundant. We get lots of barracudas and rays, which you would normally only encounter in tropical seas. And groupers are so prolific!'.

What's your favourite dive site in Corsica, Monsieur Antoni? 'I can't give a definitive answer; each area in Corsica has its own riches. Take Porto-Vecchio: you'll feel like you're diving in the Seychelles. In the Cap Corse, the ambience is totally different. And near Bastia, you've got excellent wrecks. All the divers I've met in Corsica rave about the diving here, whatever the location.' So do we!

Capo Rosso (maximum depth 30m) This headland is exposed to the open sea, which means lots of marine life, including dentex, tuna and barracudas.

La Voûte à Corail (maximum depth 25m) Red coral in abundance – a feast for the eyes.

Punta Mucchilina (maximum depth 30m) Just outside Réserve Naturelle de Scandola. Tons of fish, a small shipwreck and a contoured terrain. Magical.

Senino (maximum depth 30m) A seamount festooned with healthy seafans and broken up by faults. Atmospheric and fishy.

Vardiola (maximum depth 30m) A sugarloaf-shaped rock formation brushing the surface, with a chimney you can explore.

AROUND CALVI

The many contrasts in the area around Calvi make it attractive to divers. While the southern part of the bay is nothing to write home about, the shoreline around the Pointe de la Revellata, to the west, is extraordinary. The wreck of a B-17 bomber in the Baie de Calvi is another draw. See p130 and p134 for local dive centres.

La Bibliothèque (maximum depth 20m) 'The Library' comprises a series of big boulders.

La Revellata (maximum depth 35m) The underwater scenery is grandiose, with lots of canyons, faults, valleys and boulders. Very fishy.

Le B-17 (maximum depth 27m) One of the most popular sites in Corsica. Wreck of a B-17 bomber, in a good state of preservation.

Le Danger d'Algajola (maximum depth 35m) A huge rocky plateau, with a variety of fish.

Le Sec du Clocher (maximum depth 35m) A big boulder with fissures and faults. Lots of seafans below 27m.

BAIE DE L'ÎLE ROUSSE & GOLFE DE ST-FLORENT

There are few sites in the Baie de L'Île Rousse, but the handful that do exist – rocks rising from a sandy sea bed and cloaked with magnificent seafans – are truly beautiful. The Golfe de St-Florent has a couple of good surprises up its sleeves too. See p136 and p118 for local dive centres.

L'Aventure & Çaira (maximum depth 18m) Two shipwrecks near the citadel in St-Florent.

Le Grand Tombant (maximum depth 35m) The aptly named 'big drop-off' tumbles from 20m to 39m and is sprinkled with colourful seafans and sponges. Lots of fish on the top, including octopuses.

Le Naso (maximum depth 32m) A huge rock formation tumbling from 13m to 32m. It's resplendent with fish life.

AROUND BASTIA

Corsica's eastern coast is usually overlooked by most divers, and it's a shame. True, this side of the island lacks the dramatic seamounts and contoured terrain that are so commonly encountered on the west coast, but the gently sloping sand-and-silt sea bed is strewn with rocky outcrops that provide shelter for a whole range of critters. And wreck fans will find nirvana here too, along the eastern coast of Cap Corse. See p110 and p112 for local dive centres.

Cinquini (maximum depth 35m) Various layers of rocks between 24m and 35m, with lots of invertebrates, crustaceans, groupers and moray eels.

Heinkel-111 (maximum depth 33m) Wreck of a German bomber. Divers can enter the fuselage.

La Canonnière (maximum depth 40m) This 45m-long wreck was sunk in 1943. Shelters groupers, lobster, corbs and conger eels.

Thunderbolt P-47 (maximum depth 22m) Small, well-preserved planewreck.

KITESURFING & WINDSURFING

Given the constant winds that bluster around the island, windsurfing and kitesurfing are popular pastimes here. Windsurfer rentals and lessons are available at virtually all *centres nautiques* (nautical centres) but the best spots are on the

'The gently sloping sand-and-silt sea bed is strewn with rocky outcrops that shelter a whole range of critters'

south coast, near Bonifacio, which has the best winds year-round. For those of us whose windsurfing dreams are more modest, lots of fun can be had in the main gulfs on the west coast, including Golfe du Valinco and Golfe d'Ajaccio.

Looking for a new high? Kitesurfing is one of the fastest-growing sports in Corsica and should be on every adrenaline junkie's 'must-do' list. Kitesurfing takes the best of board sports and combines it with incredible airborne action. While it may be impressive to watch, it's harder to master. Aficionados of surfing, skateboarding and windsurfing will recognise the moves – that'll help, but you'll need some lessons before hitting the water. First you learn how to fly the kite, then you practise body dragging (letting the kite pull you across the water) and finally you step on board.

The Corsican kitesurfing epicentre is on the southern coast at Bonifacio. Plage de la Tonnara (p194), Plage de Piantarella (p202) and Golfe de Sant' Amanza (p202) are the best spots, where you'll find major schools offering lessons and rental gear. In the north, Calvi and Algajola are good places to head to.

SEA KAYAKING

Sea kayaking is a great way of exploring the coast at a gentle pace, and the sheltered coves provide magnificent kayaking opportunities. Most *centres nautiques* have one- or two-person kayaks for hire at about €10 per hour. Some recommended spots include the Golfe de Pinarello (p208) near Porto-Vecchio, Tizzano (p193), Porto Pollo (p181), Calvi (p130) and Île Rousse (p136). See the destination chapters for contacts.

LAND ACTIVITIES

Corsica is a mecca for the skittish. The rugged terrain of this little-populated island really does beg to be biked, hiked, skied, climbed and otherwise actively pursued. Hiking is extraordinary and deserves its own chapter (p54). But you needn't be limited to your own two feet: try a four-legged creature or see it all from above from a rope slide!

CANYONING

A must-do for thrill seekers, canyoning is a mix of climbing, hiking, abseiling *(rappel)*, swimming and some serious jumping or plunging down water-polished chutes *(toboggans)* in natural pools, down a river gorge and waterfalls. It has a small but rapidly growing following in Corsica. The Massif de Bavella (p217) is the mother of all canyoning experiences on the island, with two iconic (though now heavily commercialised) canyons: La Vacca and La Purcaraccia, which are set in some of the most grandiose scenery in Corsica. Both are suitable for all levels. Another classic venue is the Canyon du Baracci near Propriano (see p185). In the Vallée du Niolo (p245), the Canyon de la Ruda and the Canyon de Frascaghju are the main hotspots.

Corsica's ultimate canyoning experience is the Canyon de Falcunaghja, a very aerial circuit with no less than 17 rappels.

Experience is not usually necessary. Water confidence and reasonable fitness are an advantage. Adventure centres that offer canyoning (see the destination chapters) provide wetsuits, helmets and harnesses. All canyoning trips are led by qualified instructors who intimately know every pool, slide, boulder and waterfall in any particular canyon. A half day's canyoning will set you back around €40. Bring a picnic and spare clothes.

CYCLING & MOUNTAIN BIKING

Ready to sweat out? There's no better way to immerse yourself in the vibrant colours, heady scents and rugged scenery of Corsica than cycle touring – as long as you're fit enough to handle the island's mountainous

TOP FIVE DESCENTS

After unremitting uphill work comes the joy of whooshing down without a single turn of the pedals... Here's a selection of screaming downhills (check your brakes first!) that are sure to be etched in your memories forever:

- The D268, between Col de Bavella and Solenzara (p234)
- The D69, between Vivario and Ghisoni, and on to Ghisonaccia (p247)
- The D84, from Col de Verghio to Porto (p153)
- The D420, from Aullène to Petreto-Bicchisano (p214)
- The D368, from Zonza to Porto-Vecchio (p211)

topography, that is. It has diverse terrain, tough ascents and swooping descents, an abundance of camping grounds and *gîtes d'étapes*, and countless country roads, most of which are gloriously free of noisy traffic. The Castagniccia, the Casinca, the Cap Corse, the Central Mountains, the Alta Rocca, the Balagne and the West Coast (especially between Porto and Calvi, and between Ajaccio and Propriano) are excellent cycling areas, all blessed with exceptionally scenic backroads.

The biggest bonus of all might be the opportunities to discover the 'real' Corsica, with its secretive villages and traditional culture, far from the maddening crowds and the glitz of the coastal cities.

If this gets your legs twitching, try to avoid July and August, which are unpleasant, for the heat and the enormous influx of tourists. Spring and autumn, with their moderate temperatures, are the best seasons.

Bike hire is available in the main seaside cities, but if you're going to be doing extensive cycling, consider bringing your own wheels. Bike shops are thin on the ground, so it's essential to carry spare parts. Mountain-bike (*vélo tout-terrain;* VTT) hire is widespread and costs around €15 per day. Most outlets require a deposit (cash, signed travellers cheques or credit card) of anything from €30 to €250. Rental shops are listed under the Getting Around sections of this guide; several places arrange guides, plan itineraries and run biking tours.

Mixing cycling with public transport works pretty well. Bikes can be carried on the train and some bus services carry bikes too. Cyclists keen to see Corsica's mountainous interior usually begin by taking the train to Corte, Vizzavona or some other starting point high in the mountains. (See p273 for information on travelling by train with your bike.)

HORSE RIDING

Feel like seeing the land from horseback instead of a car seat? Saddling up is a fun and ecofriendly way to commune with the Corsican wilderness and enjoy the long sandy beaches, glorious hinterlands and lush forests. Horse riding is commonplace on the island, and opportunities can be found just about everywhere. You don't need any riding experience, as riding schools *(centres équestres)* cater to all levels of proficiency. Unlike many parts of the world where beginners only get led by the nose around a paddock, here you really can get out into the countryside on maquis, forest and beach rides.

Rides range from one-hour jaunts (from around €17) to week-long, fully catered treks. The best thing about horse riding in Corsica is that you can access terrain you can't get to otherwise – a wise way to escape the crowds. The best time to trek is in spring or autumn, when it's a bit cooler, though summer excursions usually explore the cooler mountain areas. Particularly good areas include the Alta Rocca (p211), the Castagniccia (p224), Sartène (p189), Solenzara (p232), the Vallée de l'Ortolo (p192) and Tizzano (p193).

Donkey rides are also available near Propriano (see p185) and in the Balagne (p142) – children love it!

See the destination chapters for more details of individual riding centres.

PARAPENTING

Parapenting involves jumping off the edge of a hill or mountain with a parachute. Altore (see p117) organises parapenting in St-Florent. It has five takeoff points in the Balagne region, depending on your level. Landing is on the beach.

PARC AVENTURE

This is the latest craze in Corsica, and we recommend that you to try it at least once during your stay. Fancy swinging through the forest à la *George of the Jungle*? Well, a Parc Aventure (adventure park) allows you to revive your childhood fantasies. Don't be confused, though: it's *not* a theme park.

Various companies have built a network of fixtures into the trees, at heights varying from a few metres to about 25m above ground. They usually include aerial platforms, walkways, 'Tarzan' swings, suspension bridges, cable bridges, vertical nets and steel-rope lines (also known as tyrolean slides), which are all connected. Visitors are strapped into harnesses and hooked onto a cable-and-pulley system that allows them to move safely from tree to tree. Some circuits include several tyrolean slides that gain progressively in height and length, with the longest spanning over 250m.

It's another great and thrilling way to see nature, and it's amazingly safe. Children are welcome provided they are over 1m in height. For kiddies, special 'baby parcs' have been installed. Depending on the circuit, the tour lasts anything from 30 minutes to two hours. All you need is shorts or long pants, a T-shirt and trainers. You are provided with a harness and helmet, and the circuit usually begins with a crash course on how to use the equipment. Qualified instructors are positioned at designated areas on the circuit and can provide tips or assistance.

The most reputable Parcs Aventure are found in Bavella (p217), Calvi (p130), L'Ospédale (p211), Propriano (p185), Solenzara (p234), St-Pierre de Venaco (p247) and Vizzavona (p248). Other good playgrounds include Vallée de l'Asco and Vallée du Niolo.

PARC AVENTURE MADNESS

There was only one Parc Aventure in Corsica in 2000. At the time of writing there were 22 Parcs scattered across the island. This speaks volumes. Isabelle Giacobbi-Lamy lives in St-Pierre de Venaco and runs the Grandeur Nature Parc Aventure (p247), the second one to be opened in Corsica (in 2001). 'True, Parcs Aventure are springing up like mushrooms on the island. This activity is very popular because it's accessible to anybody. You don't need training, and the whole family can enjoy it at the same time. Children and youngsters adore it!' The fun factor is another clincher, with a variety of fixtures. 'The fixtures that are the most popular are the tyrolean slides. Most customers ask about the length of the slide – the longer, the better. It's an easy way to get a buzz.' The scenery is another draw. Corsican forests are fantastic. 'All that greenery, the scents, these are stimulating too.' What about the impact on the environment? 'We brief our customers before they set off. They are asked to respect the trees, and our instructors supervise the circuit.'

Now it's your turn!

ROCK CLIMBING

As the most mountainous of the Mediterranean islands, Corsica is something of a holy grail for any would-be Spiderman or Spiderwoman. The majority of climbing options are concentrated in central or southern Corsica. The most famous spot is around Aiguilles de Bavella (p217), with superb cliffs and granite spires. Other hotspots include the Vallée du Niolo, the Vallée de la Restonica, the Vallée de l'Asco and the Gorges du Prunelli. For super-climbers, the Paglia Orba (p65) is the ultimate face.

Adventure centres around the island run courses and organise climbing trips. Plan on €90 for a half day. Reputable agencies:

Altipiani (☎ 06 86 16 67 91; www.altipiani-corse.com; Ponte Leccia)
Altore (☎ 04 95 37 19 30; www.altore.com; St-Florent)
AS Niolu (☎ 04 95 48 05 22; www.asniolu.com; Calacuccia)
Grandeur Nature (☎ 06 03 83 68 36; www.grandeurnature-corse.com; St-Pierre de Venaco)
In Terra Corsa (☎ 04 95 47 69 48; www.interracorsa.fr in French; Ponte Leccia)
Jean-Paul Quilici (☎ 04 95 78 64 33; www.jpquilicimontagne.com; Quenza)

SKIING

Strange as it may seem, Corsica has three winter ski resorts: Bastelica-Ese in the Vallée du Prunelli, about 30km east of Ajaccio (see p178), Ghisoni (p247) and Verghio (p153). The season normally runs from December to March. They have limited infrastructure: a few *refuges* that rent out equipment, a couple of ski lifts and a few downhill runs. Frankly said, it's nothing thrilling, but where else in the world can you ski with the azure waters of the Mediterranean in the background?

Cross-country skiing is also popular in the Forêt de Valdu Niellu (p153), high in the Vallée du Niolo, and on the Coscione plateau (p72).

The website www.ski -corse.com (in French) should give you a rough idea of the skiing options in Corsica.

VIA FERRATA

Another fun and dizzying approach to Corsica's mountains, Via Ferrata (literally, 'Iron Path' in Italian) is increasingly popular on the island. It uses intriguing and often ingenious combinations of ladders, metal brackets, chiselled footholds and even bridges to allow progress on steep or vertical cliffs. Steel cable, acting as both a handhold and security, is bolted to the rock at waist level, with walkers clipping onto it with a lanyard (dynamic rope) and karabiner system. In short, it's a mix of rock climbing and walking. More recent circuits also include tyrolean slides (rope slides) for added thrills.

There are varying degrees of difficulty. Novices start on easy routes and progress on to more challenging and exposed routes with vertical ladders and sections along narrow ledges. Children over 12 are welcome.

The first Via Ferrata that was installed in Corsica is the 400m Via Ferrata di a Manicella in the Vallée de l'Asco. It ranks as one of the most atmospheric circuits in France. Other superb playgrounds include the Via Ferrata A Buccarona (p234) near Solenzara and the difficult Via Ferrata U Calanconi (p233) in Chisà.

Food & Drink

First things first: don't mistake Corsica for, say, Provence. Sophisticated *haute cuisine* prepared by superstar chefs? Virtually nonexistent. If you're in search of überchic restaurants, silver cutlery and unflappable service, you've come to the wrong place. The *cucina corsa* (Corsican cuisine) is what the French call a *cuisine du terroir,* which would translate as 'country cuisine'. It's more traditional family cooking than creative concoctions, typically hearty and wholesome fare made using tried-and-true recipes and fresh, local produce. And what produce!

It's important to bear in mind that Corsican food has evolved historically from the agrarian peasant diet of the mountains. In the 18th century most Corsicans, under threat from would-be colonisers, retreated to the safety of the mountains, a terrain that lent itself well to pig, sheep and goat rearing. The carpet of maquis covering the peaks yielded an abundance of aromatic herbs – wild mint, fennel, catmint, rosemary and laurel – and natural produce such as honey and the versatile chestnut. Little has changed in the intervening years. It wasn't until the 20th century when people began reclaiming the coast that the island's wealth of fish and seafood began to find its way to the table.

Of course there are several elements of French gastronomy evident in Corsican cuisine, notably the cooking methods, such as the stewing of meat *en daube,* in red wine and garlic. But Corsican cuisine owes its distinct characteristics to a host of factors. Firstly, its location in the Mediterranean provides a wealth of raw materials: fragrant olive oils, sun-loving fruits and vegetables, and mouth-watering cured meats, easily and economically preserved in the Mediterranean heat. Some staples from the Italian kitchen have crossed the short passage of water to the island and, especially on the east coast, it's common to see a regional variation of polenta, cannelloni and lasagna on the menu.

Despite the influence of Italian and French cuisine on its menus, however, Corsican cuisine remains relatively untouched by exterior trends, so while you gladly won't see a chipper or McDonald's on its streets, neither are you likely to see a juice bar or sushi restaurant. The endurance of this wonderful earthy style of cooking that takes full advantage of the fruits of the land is refreshing.

All we can say is *buon appititu*!

> Corsicans began relying on the chestnut tree to produce flour as early as the 16th century when the Genoese began taking the island's grain crop back home.

STAPLES & SPECIALITIES

The ingredients that make Corsican cuisine distinctive are above all the regional charcuterie (cured meats), the chestnut, the local seafood and *brocciu* (fresh sheep or goat cheese, also spelled *bruccio* and *brucciu*).

CORSICA'S BEST PRODUCE SHOPS

This is a quick selection of our favourites places to stock up on high-quality Corsican *produits corses* (Corsican products), including charcuterie, cheese, jams, honey, terrines, biscuits and wines. Just mentioning them initiates salivation…

- U Stazzu (p172), Ajaccio
- U Muntagnolu (p214), Zonza
- L'Orriu (p208), Porto-Vecchio
- Bocca Fina (p187), Propriano
- Cap Corse Mattei (p106), Bastia

'CORSICAN' CHARCUTERIE?

Prisuttu, lonzu, coppa, figatellu, salsiccia…Corsican charcuterie (cured meats) has achieved cult status among connoisseurs. But standards do vary a lot. Some unscrupulous producers in Corsica import (legally) pigs from the Netherlands, Sardinia, Brittany or Spain, let them feed only a week or two on chestnuts, slaughter them, transform the meat into charcuterie, label it *'charcuterie corse traditionnelle'* (traditional Corsican charcuterie) and sell it to gullible visitors.

As long as there's no official certification label (there's talk about establishing an Appellation d'Origine Contrôlée (AOC) for charcuterie, similar to the one used for wines and olive oil), your best bet is to stock up in reputable produce shops.

Paul-Antoine Lanfranchi owns a *gîte d'étape* and a well-regarded restaurant in the Haut Taravo Valley (see p177), which is famous for its home-cured meats. 'We are the fourth generation of butchers, and our cured meats are 100% organic and natural. I use secret, family recipes that were imparted by my grandmother. We rear free-range our own Corsican pigs. They feed only on chestnuts and acorns, which gives the meat a distinct flavour.' Does homemade charcuterie taste really different from industrial charcuterie, Monsieur Lanfranchi? 'The texture and the flavours are totally different. Try the two kinds of charcuterie, and you'll see what I mean. But *charcuterie artisanale* has a cost: you'll be looking at €30 for a kilogram of *coppa*.' For charcuterie-lovers, what's the best recommendation to source the best products? 'Go in the mountain villages, and buy charcuterie direct from the producer. And follow the seasons: an authentic *figatellu* is never made in summer. If you find *figatellu* on a market or in a restaurant in summer, just skip it!' For an idea of Paul-Antoine's products, check out the website www.chez-paul-antoine.com.

Charcuterie & other Meats

Carnivores will have found their spiritual home in Corsica. Meat of every species, shape and genesis dominates the local diet. The Corsicans' taste for charcuterie is well known, and it's evident in their sausages and hams, whose particular flavour is derived from *cochons coureurs* (free-ranging pigs), which traditionally feed on chestnuts, acorns, and plants imbued with the fragrance of the maquis. From these herb-saturated porcines comes the *figatellu,* a thin liver sausage, and Corsica's pride, but also the prosciutto-like *lonzu* and *coppa,* as well as *salciccia* and *prisuttu.*

The *assiette de charcuterie* (charcuterie platter) you will see as a starter on many a *menu Corse* will consist of a sampling of thin slices of four or five of these meats. If you want to know which is which, ask your server. Most of the pork-based charcuterie are made during winter. Unlike some of the other meats, which may cure over anything from six months to a couple of years, *figatelli* are generally eaten soon after production. If you're offered *figatelli* in summer, it's probably the frozen variety, which may have less flavour.

Main courses, generally speaking, will answer to your idea of French cookery, but look out for the local speciality of veal with olives (rarely made using Corsican veal), and *sanglier* (wild boar), especially in long-simmering stews called *civets* or *daubes* in French or *tiani* (*tianu* in the singular) in *menu Corse. Sanglier* is best eaten during the hunting seasons of autumn and winter. *Stuffatu* and *ghialadicciu* are slow-braised mutton and pig's stomach stews respectively (popular in winter), *premonata* is beef stewed with juniper berries and *cabri* is kid, which is typically roasted with rosemary and garlic. Most of these dishes will be served with *pulenta,* a Corsican variation of Italian polenta, made with chestnut flour.

Recipes for blackbird and other wild birds, roasted with sage or cooked as a salmis (partially roasted, then gently simmered in wine, shallots and onions) or prepared in terrines, also attest to the ingenuity of an isolated people.

'Free-ranging pigs traditionally feed on chestnuts, acorns, and plants imbued with the fragrance of the maquis'

Fish & Seafood

Growing weary of artery-clogging cured meats? It's time to give your taste-buds something different to sing about. The warm waters of the Mediterranean provide an ample and varied net of produce: sea bream, sea bass, squid, sardines, scorpion fish, lobster and red mullet. Oysters and mussels are a speciality around the east coast, and *langoustes* (lobster) appear on menus all around the coast both in *ziminu* (or *aziminu*), the Corsican version of the soup bouillabaisse (normally only served for two people) and served with pasta, simply cooked in a little olive oil and garlic. Sardines stuffed with *brocciu* are generally delicious, and inland you'll come across plenty of farmed trout, stuffed with either almonds or a selection of herbs from the maquis. *Rougets à la bonifacienne* is a southern speciality featuring mullet cooked with anchovies, tomatoes and garlic.

Say Cheese!

It's impossible to visit Corsica without coming across *brocciu*, which can be found on practically every single menu, in a variety of guises. This mild, crumbly, white cheese, not a million miles from ricotta, is made from the *petit-lait* (whey) of either goat's or ewe's milk, and is the only cheese accredited with an AOC (Appellation d'Origine Contrôlée). True *brocciu*, as opposed to the inferior-tasting *brousse* (made from imported or powdered milk), should be available only from about November to June, when the lactating goats or sheep provide their characteristic milk. Corsicans take this distinction seriously; a restaurant caught passing off *brousse* as *brocciu* can be closed down. *Brocciu* can be eaten fresh, as a creamy *fromage frais,* baked with the zest of oranges or *cédrat* (a sweeter type of lemon) in a *fiadone* cheesecake, or drained, salted and aged for use in savoury dishes. Be sure to try an omelette of *brocciu*. The cheese combines particularly harmoniously with mint, with which it will almost always be paired in an omelette. You can also enjoy *brocciu* in pasta dishes, such as cannelloni and lasagne, or stuffed into vegetables.

Brébis and chèvre are the overall names given to a range of ewe's and goat's milk cheese. *Bastelicaccia* is a soft creamy ewe's milk cheese with a natural crust, and *sartinesi* is a raw, hard-pressed, sharper tasting ewe's milk cheese. *Tomme Corse* is a semi-hard, granular, raw, ewe's milk cheese. *Niolincu* from the south and *Vénacu* from the Alta-Rocca are both popular soft cheeses. Hard cheeses are often served as a starter or instead of a dessert (or even as a bar snack), with a basket of crusty bread and a dollop of sweet fig jam, which acts as a delicious relish against the sharp flavour of the cheese. The *buglidicci* (pancakes with ewe's milk cheese) are also tasty. Pregnant women should check whether certain cheeses have been made with pasteurised milk, and should avoid raw-milk varieties altogether.

For everything you ever wanted to know about Corsican cheese but were afraid to ask, see www.fromages-corse.org.

Olive Oil

Corsican olive oil *(oliu di Corsica)* is extremely aromatic and is a staple of the Corsican kitchen. For quality-control purposes an AOC was introduced in 2004. There are six varieties of olives on the island. The principal olive oil–producing regions are the Balagne, the Alta Rocca and the Casinca.

Snacks

The 'sandwich Corse' seen on many café menus, is a *panino* (grilled sandwich, an Italian term) of charcuterie and cheeses. Varieties include the Libecciu, the Stellu (according to the menu, 'the most Corsican of panini'), the Velacu and the Astu.

Traditional Corsican soups are served in winter and are a meal in themselves. Vegetarians beware. The vegetable soup, made with butter beans and garden vegetables, will often be made with meat stock, or even contain *lardons* of pork or sausage. Check before you order.

Dessert

For dessert, try the wonderful *fiadone* (a light flan made with *brocciu*, lemon and eggs), the calorie-loaded *beignets au brocciu* (*brocciu* fritters), the toothsome *ambrucciata* (tart with *brocciu*) or the high-energy *canistrelli* (biscuits made with almonds, walnuts, lemon or aniseed). Corsican homemade jams (made with clementines, figs, chestnuts and so on) are also delicious.

You'll see a variety of cakes, tarts, biscuits and *beignets* (a type of doughnut), especially inland, made from the subtle-tasting chestnut flour. Chestnutty delights include *falculelli* (pressed and frittered *brocciu* cheese served on a chestnut leaf) and *gâteau à la farine de châtaigne* (chestnut-flour cake).

There are six official varieties of Corsican honey *(mele di Corsica)* produced at different times of the year, mostly scented with chestnut, aromatic herbs from the maquis or fruits.

The Tribbiera microbrewery in Ghisonaccia (see p231) uses mountain spring water to make Dea, Prima, Apa (with Corsican honey), Ambria and Mora (a dark beer). These beers are only available at the brewery-bar.

DRINKS

No matter what your poison, you're in the right place if you're after a drink.

Alcoholic Drinks

BEER

Two breweries on the island produce four different beers. Pietra is an amber beer whose ingredients include chestnut flour from the Castagniccia. Enthusiasts contend that even though the beer doesn't taste of chestnuts, its flour is nevertheless largely responsible for the beer's unique characteristics. Serena is a lighter product of the same brewery; the label bears a Corsican Moor's head. The pale Colomba beer, launched in 1999, is flavoured with maquis herbs, principally myrtle. In 2002 the Torra, called *bière du maquis* (maquis beer), was launched by another brewery based near Ajaccio. The pale Torra is flavoured with arbutus while the amber Torra is flavoured with myrtle.

WINE

Corsica has nine AOC-labelled wines produced mainly from the original rootstocks of the country, using varieties of grape such as Vermentinu, Sciaccarellu and Niellucciu. There are now roughly 7000 hectares of vineyards on the island, notably in the Nebbio and on the eastern coast, and these vineyards can be visited. Corsican wines (red, white and rosé) can be bought in produce shops for as little as €5 a bottle, and the mark-up in restaurants is not scandalous. These are not necessarily the most distinguished of wines but they're increasing in quality and some of them have gained national recognition.

The official Corsican wine site, www.vinsdecorse .com, has good links to other gastronomy-related sites.

BRANDY & LIQUEUR

Cap Corse Mattei, invented by Louis Napoléon Mattei in 1872, is a local wine-based aperitif, comparable to red martini, made from muscat wine. Casanis is a *pastis,* and although not strictly from Corsica (it's from Marseille), it was developed by a Corsican with the good Corsican name of Casabianca, and the label still has the Corsican Moor's head on it. You won't be shot for asking for a Ricard or a 51, but ask for a Casa anyway and pronounce it ca-*zah*. Other excellent aperitifs include liqueurs, which are usually flavoured with myrtle *(liqueur de myrte)* or chestnut *(liqueur de châtaigne)*, and sweet *muscat du Cap Corse.*

The *eaux de vie* (brandies or *acquavita* in Corsican) for consumption after dinner are particularly good when based on a citrus fruit the Corsicans call *cédrat* (for all practical purposes, a lemon) or on myrtle or other maquis

Liqueur de myrte and *liqueur de châtaigne* are sweet and go down a treat, but go easy on it if you've had a long day in the sun!

plants. These are generally homemade and at 45% alcohol by volume are like rocket fuel. If at the end of dinner your server puts down a little plate with a couple of sugar cubes on it and an unlabelled bottle, you are to pour a little of the contents of the bottle over the sugar cubes and suck them. This is a very old custom and a very good one.

Le Vin Corse from Edition du Journal de la Corse is an excellent coffee-table book specialising in Corsican wines.

Whisky lovers should try the P&M, which is the only Corsican whisky, blended and distilled in Corsica.

Nonalcoholic Drinks
WATER
Although tap water is drinkable throughout the island, most locals prefer to drink bottled mineral water. Corsican mineral waters are excellent.

Orezza High-quality sparkling water from the Castagniccia (see p225). Very carbonated and rich in iron. It's served in the chicest restaurants in Paris. Check out the website www.orezza.fr.

CORSICAN WINES – HEAVEN IN A GLASS

Except in the Nebbio no proper 'wine route' has been established yet but you can tailor your own tour and drive between many of these estates since most wineries welcome visitors and offer *dégustation* (tastings).

AOC Ajaccio
Area: from Golfe de Porto to Golfe d'Ajaccio
Most famous Domaines: Comte Peraldi, Clos Ornasca, Domaine Abbatucci, Clos Capitoro

AOC Coteaux du Cap Corse & AOC Muscat du Cap Corse
Area: Cap Corse
Most famous Domaines: Clos Nicrosi, Domaine Pieretti, Domaine Gioielli, Domaine de Pietri

AOC Sartène
Area: Vallée de l'Ortolo, Propriano area, Tizzano area
Most famous Domaines: Domaine Fiumiccicoli, Domaine Saparale, Domaine Sant' Armettu, Domaine Mosconi

AOC Calvi
Area: the Balagne interior
Most famous Domaines: Clos Landry, Domaine Alzipratu, Domaine Renucci

AOC Figari
Area: around Figari and Pianottoli-Caldarello
Most famous Domaines: Clos Canarelli, Domaine de la Murta

AOC Porto-Vecchio
Area: around Porto-Vecchio
Most famous Domaines: Domaine de Torraccia, Domaine de Granajolo

AOC Patrimonio
Area: around Patrimonio and St-Florent
Most famous Domaines: Domaine Gentile, Domaine Orenga de Gaffory, Clos de Bernardi, Domaine Leccia, Domaine Lazzarini

AOC Vin de Corse
Area: Eastern plain, from Bastia to Solenzara
Most famous Domaines: Domaine de Musoleu, Clos d'Orléa, Clos Fornelli, Clos Poggiale

St-Georges Well-known still water from Col St-Georges. The bottles are designed by famous French designer Philippe Starck. Check out the website www.eauxstgeorges.fr.
Zilia Spring water from the Balagne.

SODAS

There's a Corsican variation of Coca Cola, called Corsica Cola, with a Corsican Moor's head on the label. Let's face it: it's too sweet and does not equal Coca Cola.

CELEBRATIONS

Food and wine are celebrated throughout Corsica, with many microregions and towns holding *foires agricoles et rurales* (agriculture and rural fairs). It's generally a great day out, offering the visitor a chance to mingle with the locals and to sip and savour some of the best food, wine and hospitality that particular part of the island has to offer.

The most renowned festivals include A Tumbera in February, Fête de l'Olive in March, A Fiera di u Casgiu in May, the Foire du Vin de Luri in July and the Foire à la Châtaigne in December. See p256 for a run-down of festivals.

WHERE TO EAT & DRINK

As in mainland France you can take your pick of where to eat, anywhere from a bar to a restaurant, a café, a *ferme auberge* and the lovely *paillottes* (beach restaurants). Corsicans take their meals seriously. You could set your watch by the exodus from offices and businesses at midday for lunch, so to avoid queues it might be better to wait till at least after 1pm. For Corsicans, dinner at home is normally eaten between 8pm and 9pm (many people don't knock off work until 7pm or after), but in restaurants it can be later.

You can pick up a snack such as a sandwich, panini or salad in a bar theoretically at any time of the day. Bars normally open around 7am and many serve until 2am or 3am, though the kitchen will probably close at about 10pm, and you may not get a salad or hot dish before midday. Restaurants usually open from midday (almost never before) to 2pm, and any time after 6.30pm until 11pm. Cafés will normally open for breakfast and close just before dinner. Their menus (somewhere between those of a bar and restaurant) usually provide a choice of hot meals and a good selection of desserts and pastries. A *ferme auberge* is usually a working farm that serves diners traditional dishes made from ingredients produced on the farm itself. Some places double up as accommodation, but the restaurant is open to non-guests and will offer good-value meals of an excellent standard. Unlike in restaurants, bookings are mandatory in most *fermes auberges*

AOC (Appellation d'Origine Contrôlée) wines have met stringent regulations governing where, how and under what conditions they are grown, fermented and bottled. Red wines account roughly for 40% of the total production of AOC wines in Corsica; white wines 11%; and rosés 49%.

A BRIGHT FUTURE FOR CORSICAN WINES

A passionate wine-maker, Philippe Farinelli is the owner of Domaine Saparale in the Vallée de l'Ortolo, near Sartène. He's optimistic about the future of Corsican wines. 'It's true that Corsican wines did not have a good reputation on the French market until 10 years ago. Corsican wine-makers used to favour quantity, not quality. But now it's a very different story. The younger generation of Corsican wine-makers has managed to foster a new mindset among professionals and now the mantra is quality. And it pays off. Corsican wines are now well rated by connoisseurs on the island, on the mainland and abroad – we get orders from Brazil, the USA, northern Europe and Canada.' What is the next step, Monsieur Farinelli? 'We want to get closer to the public; we want to develop wine-touring, with signs, leaflets and proper cellar doors. It will be ready for the next edition of your guidebook!'

and the food is served table d'hôte (literally 'host's table'), meaning in set courses with little or no choice. *Paillottes* are set on beaches and are open in summer; they major in fish dishes and pizzas.

Around the coast and in busier towns, you'll find that most restaurants close outside the tourist season between November and April; during the season they open for both lunch and dinner, seven days a week. Prices must be indicated outside the restaurant, but you may need to ask if restrictions apply to *menus* (they might, for example, serve between certain hours or on certain days).

Since Corsicans are well used to catering to visitors' needs during the season, nothing is too much trouble – children are accepted at any hour, and solo or female travellers are made to feel comfortable. In some of the mountain villages, however, solo women might feel like a local curiosity in the small, male-dominated bars.

The most famous *paillotte* is Chez Francis (www.chez -francis.com in French), south of Ajaccio. It hit the headlines when it was destroyed by French *gendarmes* acting under direct orders from the state's representative. Since then it has been restored and now it's one of the west coast's trendiest seafood eateries!

Tipping

French law requires that restaurant, café and hotel bills include the service charge (usually 10% to 15%), so a *pourboire* (tip) is neither necessary nor expected. If you want to leave something extra, that's up to you. A cover charge (for bread and tap water) is also included in the price of the meal.

Quick Eats

Except for stalls selling caramelised nuts and fish stalls on the beach, you won't come across many street vendors. Many of the bigger villages and most towns will have at least one day of the week when they hold a market, which will include food stalls. Check with the local tourist office, as this is where you'll find a wealth of fresh local produce for picnics (fruit and cheeses, olive oils, wine and charcuterie). The quality is invariably good and the price is often a fraction of that in a supermarket.

VEGETARIANS & VEGANS

Corsica is a nation of meat lovers, and though vegetarians won't go hungry, it has to be said that they will inevitably find menus limited and repetitive. There are only so many omelettes and *lasagnas au brocciu* a person can eat in one holiday.

OUR TOP FIVE

This is a quick selection of some of our favourite places to move mandibles, chosen for their high-quality Corsican cuisine and their lovely surrounds. Polish off your meal with a well-chosen Corsican wine.

A Flatta (☎ 04 95 62 80 38; www.aflatta.com in French; mains €19-26, menu €30; ☽ dinner Mon-Fri, lunch & dinner Sat & Sun Apr-Jul, Sep & Oct, lunch & dinner daily Aug) The end of the Earth! Fresh fish dishes and unparalleled views down the valley. See p141.

Auberge Santa Barbara (☎ 04 95 77 09 06; www.santabarbara.fr; Sartène; mains €17-28, menu €29; ☽ Tue & Wed Apr-Oct) One of Corsica's leading chefs tickles your tastebuds. See p191.

Aux Coquillages de Diane (☎ 04 95 57 04 55; Étang de Diane, Aléria; mains €12-22; ☽ lunch & dinner Jun-Sep, lunch Oct-May, dinner Fri & Sat Oct-May, closed Jan) Hmm, will it be fresh oysters, a pot of mussels or a *loup de mer* (sea bass)? See p229.

Hôtel des Roches Rouges (☎ 04 95 27 81 81; Piana; mains €22-25, menus €32-40) Savour gourmet nouvelle cuisine (a rarity in Corsica) in magnificent surrounds. See p158.

Le Moulin Farellacci (☎ 04 95 74 62 28; http://lemoulinfarellacci.free.fr in French; Calvese; ☽ mid-Jun–mid-Sep) Fast the day before… A six-course dinner awaits! We could hardly lift ourselves off our chairs at the end. Musical accompaniment too. See p183.

DOS & DON'TS

▪ Tips are built into the price of your meal, so don't tip unless you really want to.

▪ It's not unusual to see (mainly French) diners feed their pooch scraps from their plate at the table.

▪ You may find nonsmoking sections in restaurants nonexistent or so small that the air is taken over by the billow of blue haze. Sit on the terrace if there is one.

Staples will be salads, soups, crepes, omelettes, cheeses, bread products and, if you are not averse, fish. On the east coast, especially, you're more likely to find restaurants serving pizza and pasta. There are no vegetarian restaurants in Corsica per se, so you'll have to shop around to get away from the charcuterie and meat stew on practically every menu. Dishes such as stuffed aubergines and tomatoes *(farcies)* are common, and though a vegetable platter might strike some Corsican restaurateurs as a novelty, they do serve vegetables as side dishes and might be willing to assemble a plate of several vegetable side dishes for you. You'll have to rely on those eggs and *brocciu,* though, for your protein. Certainly don't be afraid to ask.

Beware of dishes that ostensibly look like vegetarian options, only to reveal a 'healthy hint' of meat beneath the surface. Many Corsicans innocently consider it no harm to add a piece of meat to a mainly vegetable dish, so if in doubt, ask. Corsican vegetable soup often contains meat stock, if not meat pieces, and *aubergine à la bonifacienne* is stuffed with minced meat and breadcrumbs.

In the bigger towns you may find an Indian or Chinese restaurant, which will add some spice to your otherwise homogenous diet.

EATING WITH KIDS

Corsicans welcome children with open arms. Most restaurants have high chairs and all, with few exceptions, will allow accompanied juniors to dine at any hour. Most places that do welcome children have separate kids' menus. Where restaurants offer a special children's menu, it will usually consist of a simplified, mostly meat-based version of the adults', sometimes with chips. Depending on how cultivated your little ones' palates are, you may find yourself resorting to savoury crepes, pizza, pasta or omelettes. A picnic might give you the opportunity to make up a few healthy and nourishing favourites for at least one meal of the day.

If travelling with a baby, you should consider bringing enough formula (especially if it's soy-based) for the whole journey. Brands differ and though many of the more common types are available in supermarkets and pharmacies, you may not find your particular brand. There is a limited selection of baby food in jars, so either carry a few for emergencies or mix up a small portion from your own meal in a restaurant; servers will generally oblige you by mincing meat or fish if necessary. Be careful if adding soup, which may have salt already added.

HABITS & CUSTOMS

Corsican food is not eaten on the run, and is generally eaten at certain specified hours of the day. Between noon and 2pm or 3pm, many businesses shut their doors so that employees can eat a proper lunch. Portions are smaller than in many other countries, but courses are more numerous. Lunch and dinner are usually accompanied with wine.

But start with breakfast. Corsican *petit déjeuner* consists of croissants, *pain au chocolat* (bread with chocolate filling) or *tartines* (pieces of French bread smothered with butter). Coffee is generally *café créme* or *café au lait* (coffee with lots of hot milk).

At *déjeuner* (lunch) and *dîner* (dinner), you generally begin with an entrée or hors d'oeuvre (starter or appetiser), followed by a main dish, and finish with a dessert or cheese and finally coffee. You can, to be sure, short-circuit this ritual by ordering just a main dish à la carte or by eating at a café.

EAT YOUR WORDS

To discover the difference between a *ghialadicciu* and a *fiadone* (and we suggest you do), here are some handy phrases for you to digest.

Useful Phrases

I'd like the set menu.
zher pron ler mer·new | *Je prends le menu.*

Could you recommend something?
es·ker voo poo·vay re·ko·mon·day | *Est-ce que vous pouvez recommender*
kel·ker shoz | *quelque chose?*

I'd like to reserve a table.
zhay·mer·ray ray·zair·vay ewn ta·bler | *J'aimerais resérver une table.*

Do you have a menu in English?
es·ker voo a·vay la kart on ong·glay | *Est-ce que vous avez la carte en anglais?*

I'd like a local speciality.
zhay·mer·ray ewn spay·sya·lee·tay | *J'aimerais une spécialité*
ray·zhyo·nal | *régionale.*

Please bring the bill.
la dee·syon seel voo play | *L'addition, s'il vous plaît.*

Is service included in the bill?
es·ker ler sair·vees et un·klew | *Est-ce que le service est inclu?*

Where is the bathroom?
oo son lay twa·let | *Où sont les toilettes?*

I'm a vegetarian.
zher swee vay·zhay·ta·ryun/ | *Je suis végétarien/*
vay·zhay·ta·ryen | *végétarienne.*(m/f)

I don't eat...
zher ner monzh pa de... | *Je ne mange pas de...*
> **meat**
> vyond | *viande*
> **fish**
> pwa·son | *poisson*
> **seafood**
> frwee der mair | *fruits de mer*

Menu Decoder

STARTERS & SOUP

bouillabaisse	bwee·ya·bes	Mediterranean-style fish soup, made with several kinds of fish, including rascasse (spiny scorpion fish); often eaten as a main course
croûtons	kroo·ton	fried or roasted bread cubes, often added to soups
soupe de poisson	soop der pwa·son	fish soup

COMMON MEAT & POULTRY DISHES

civet	see·vay	game stew
grillade	gree·yad	grilled meats
marcassin	mar·ka·sun	young wild boar

DESSERTS & SWEETS

beignet	ben·yay	doughnut
canistrelli	ka·nee·stre·lee	dry biscuits
figatone	fee·ga·to·nay	chestnut flan
flan	flun	egg-custard dessert
gâteau	ga·to	cake

French-English Glossary
BASICS

de la bière	de la bee·yair	beer
du café	doo·ka·fay	coffee
du lait	doo lay	milk
du sel	doo sel	salt
du thé	doo tay	tea
la boulangerie	la boo·lon·zhree	bakery
la climatisation	la klee·ma·tee·za·syon	air-conditioning
l'addition	la·dee·syon	bill
le déjeuner	ler day·zher·nay	lunch
le dîner	ler dee·nay	dinner
le petit déjeuner	ler per·tee day·zher·nay	breakfast
l'épicerie	lay·pee·sree	grocery store
(non) fumeur	non·foo·mer	(non) smoking
riz	ree	rice

MEAT, CHICKEN & POULTRY

agneau	a·nyo	lamb
bifteck, steak	beef·tek, stek	steak
bœuf	berf	beef
bœuf haché	berf ha·shay	minced beef
cervelle	sair·vel	brains
charcuterie	shar·kew·tree	cured or prepared meats (usually pork)
chèvre	she·vrer	goat (can also refer to goat's cheese)
coppa	kop·pa	spare pig's rib
côte	kot	chop (of pork, lamb or mutton)
côtelette	kot·let	cutlet
dinde	dund	turkey
figatellu	fee·ga·te·loo	liver sausage
foie	fwa	liver
ghialadicciu	gya·la·dee·choo	braised pig's stomach
jambon	zhom·bon	ham
lapin	la·pun	rabbit
lard	lar	bacon
lonzu	lon·dzoo	pork fillet
mouton	moo·ton	mutton
oie	wa	goose
pieds de porc	pyay der por	pigs' trotters
porc	por	pork
poulet	poo·lay	chicken
prizuttu	pri·tsu·tu	cured ham
rognons	ron·yon	kidneys
sanglier	song·glee·yay	wild boar
saucisson	soo·see·son	large sausage

saucisson fumé	soo·see·son foo·may	smoked sausage
tripe	treep	tripes
viande	vyond	meat
volaille	vo·lai	poultry

FISH & SEAFOOD

calmar	kal·mar	squid
crabe	krab	crab
chaudrée	sho·dray	fish stew
coquille St-Jacques	ko·kee·yer sun·zhak	scallop
crevette grise	krer·vet greez	shrimp
crevette rose	krer·vet roz	prawn
fruits de mer	frwee der mair	seafood
gambas	gom·ba	king prawns
huître	wee·trer	mussels
langouste	long·goost	lobster
moules	mool	mussels
palourde	pa·loord	clam
poisson	pwa·son	fish
sardine	sar·deen	sardine
saumon	so·mon	salmon
thon	ton	tuna
truite	trweet	trout

VEGETABLES, HERBS & SPICES

ail	ai	garlic
anis	a·nees	aniseed
artichaut	ar·tee·sho	artichoke
asperge	a·spairzh	asparagus
aubergine	o·bair·zheen	aubergine (eggplant)
avocat	a·vo·ka	avocado
betterave	be·trav	beetroot
carotte	ka·rot	carrot
champignon	shom·pee·nyon	mushroom
courgette	koor·zhet	courgette (zucchini)
concombre	kon·kon·brer	cucumber
crudités	krew·dee·tay	chopped raw vegetables
épice	ay·pee·say	spice
haricots	a·ree·ko	beans
haricots blancs	a·ree·ko blong	white beans
haricots verts	a·ree·ko vair	French (string) beans
herbe	airb	herb
légumes	lay·gewm	vegetables
maïs	ma·ees	sweet corn
poivron	pwa·vron	green pepper
poireau	pwa·ro	leek
laitue	lay·tew	lettuce
lentilles	lon·tee	lentils
oignon	wa·nyon	onion
olive	o·leev	olive
peas petits pois	per·tee·pwa	
persil	pair·seel	parsley
pomme de terre	pom der tair	potato
salade	sa·lad	salad or lettuce
tomate	to·mat	tomato

Bastia & the Far North

For many, Bastia is their first port of call, whether they arrive by air or tumble off a ferry from mainland Europe. But so many visitors pass through, on and out, scarcely giving her a glance. She deserves more. For centuries, the town was the de facto capital of Corsica until Napoleon snatched away that honour and bestowed it upon Ajaccio. Her roots still show through in the characterful old port (nowadays given over to pleasure craft), the narrow alleys that nuzzle up to the quayside and the citadel, with its commanding views of town and sea.

To the city's north lies the long finger of Cap Corse. Along the promontory's eastern shore are a succession of small resorts and harbours, ideal for families. Should the summer crowds begin to oppress, simply cross over the sierra that extends along the interior and drop to the west coast – wilder, less trafficked, bucking and rumpled.

St-Florent, the only other town of consequence (if a settlement of only 1500 can be called a town) sits at the base of the cape's west coast. It's a chic little resort (see the luxury yachts moored alongside quai d'Honneur) that has some tempting dining options. It's also a great base for radiating out to explore the Nebbio region's inland villages and, to the west, the haunting wilderness of the Désert des Agriates and its lovely beaches of fine sand.

HIGHLIGHTS

- **Wraparound View**
  Haul your way up to the Tour de Sénèque (p114)

- **Walking & Waves**
  Hike a section of the Sentier des Douaniers (p112) around
  Cap Corse's northern tip

- **Dining**
  Enjoy a total gastronomic experience at Ferme-Auberge
  Campo di Monte (p121) near Murato

- **Wining**
  Visit a vineyard and sample some of the
  famous AOC wines of Patrimonio (p119)

- **Funky Festival**
  Take your pick of folk, jazz or salsa at the
  international Nuits de la Guitare (p121) in
  Patrimonio

- **Boat & Beach**
  Take a boat trip from St-Florent (p116) and spend
  the day on the fine white sand of Plage du Loto (p121) or Plage de Saleccia (p121)

- **The Open Road**
  Drive down the less-explored west coast (p113) of rugged Cap Corse

Sentier des ★
Douaniers

★ Tour de
Sénèque
Western Cape ★

Plage du Loto
Plage de Saleccia ★   ★   ★ Patrimonio

★
Ferme-Auberge
de Campo
di Monte

BASTIA

pop 38,000

Most visitors drive off the teeming ferries from mainland Europe (in terms of passenger traffic through its port, Bastia ranks second in France only to the Channel port of Calais), then head straight out of town for Cap Corse or the beaches around St-Florent. But Bastia warrants more than a fleeting glance. Economically Corsica's most dynamic city and capital of the *département* of Haute-Corse, this thriving city has a rough-round-the-edges appeal that accepts but doesn't pander to tourism. Linger a little and you won't be disappointed.

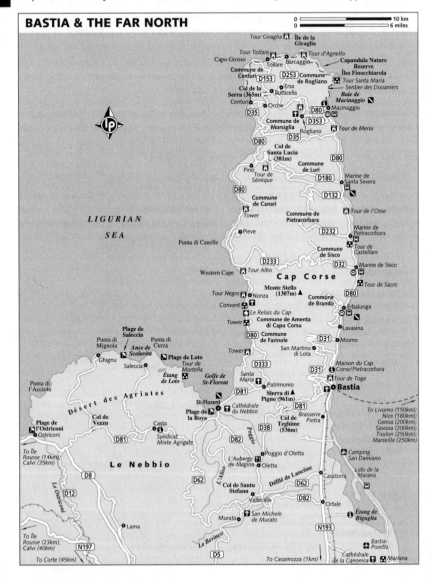

BASTIA & THE FAR NORTH

HISTORY

The city of Bastia was officially founded in 1372, although there were settlements in the area as far back as Roman times. The Genoese governor of the time, residing in the poorly defended Château de Biguglia in a malaria-infested area several kilometres away, understandably decided to go up-market and build himself a fortress (or *bastiglia* – hence Bastia) on the only really significant rocky headland on this stretch of coastline. This fortress was a strategically important element in protecting the island from seaborne incursions.

But not everyone saw things that way. Many freedom-minded Corsicans saw the fortress, or citadel, as the prime symbol of Genoese oppression. Indeed, on several occasions villagers came down from the mountains and sacked the town in protest over Genoese taxes. But despite the periodic instability, Bastia would always lick its wounds and continue to expand.

Napoleon (a son of Corsica, remember) would stand for no such nonsense from his compatriots and revolts in the town were brutally suppressed. More damaging for the town in the long term was his 1811 diktat that Ajaccio should supplant Bastia as capital of Corsica.

In 1943, in one of the cruellest errors of WWII, US Air Force bombers raided the town, just after the last Axis troops had withdrawn. Several people, joyously celebrating their liberation in the streets, were killed and many buildings destroyed.

In the postwar period the strength of Bastia's port has contributed to the town's resurgence as the island's most dynamic economic pole.

ORIENTATION

Place St-Nicolas, a long, traffic-free rectangle, is at the heart of Bastia. At the square's northern end, av Maréchal Sébastiani, links the southern ferry terminal with the train station. West of the square, parallel blvd Paoli and rue César Campinchi, each running north–south, are the main shopping streets.

INFORMATION
Bookshops

Le Point de Rencontre (☎ 04 95 31 23 10; cnr blvd Général Giraud & la Montée Ste-Claire) Bookshop-cum–arts centre with a range of local-interest texts. Stages regular exhibitions and readings by local authors.

Cultural Centres

Una Volta (☎ 04 95 32 12 81; www.una-volta.org in French; ☺ Sep-Jun) Bastia's cultural home stages exhibitions and literary events.

Emergency

Police station (☎ 04 95 54 50 22; rue du Commandant Luce de Casabianca)

Internet Access

Café Albert I (11 blvd Général de Gaulle; per hr €3; ☺ noon-2am)
Cyber Oxy (1 rue Salvatore Viale; per hr €3.10; ☺ 10am-2am Mon-Fri, 1pm-2am Sat)

Laundry

Lavoir du Port (25 rue du Commandant Luce de Casabianca; ☺ 7am-9pm)

Left Luggage

Objectif Nature (☎ 04 95 32 54 34, 06 12 02 32 02; www.objectif-nature-corse.com in French; 3 rue Notre-Dame de Lourdes; ☺ 8am-7pm Mon-Sat, 8.30am-noon Sun) Will store your pack during working hours for €3 per day.

Medical Services

Bastia hospital (☎ 04 95 59 11 11; Furiani) Bus 1, which leaves from opposite the bus station on blvd Général Graziani, terminates at the hospital.

Post

Post office (av Maréchal Sébastiani)

Tourist Information

Tourist office (☎ 04 95 54 20 40; www.bastia-tourisme .com; place St-Nicolas; ☺ 8am-8pm daily Apr-Sep, 9am-noon & 2-5pm Mon-Sat Oct-Mar) Has leaflets in English for two town walking tours and two drives around the environs of the town.

SIGHTS
Place St-Nicolas

This vast square, nearly 300m long and one of France's largest, overlooks the commercial harbour. Shaded by palms and viciously pollarded plane trees, it's bordered by a string of attractive terrace cafés along its western edge. At night rollerbladers race and twirl, taking advantage of this traffic-free space. There's a lively flea market on Sunday mornings and throughout summer it's enlivened by free concerts. On 14 July fireworks spurt and crack above it to mark Bastille Day.

At the square's northern end is Bastia's **War Memorial**, a striking bronze statue of a mother

BASTIA

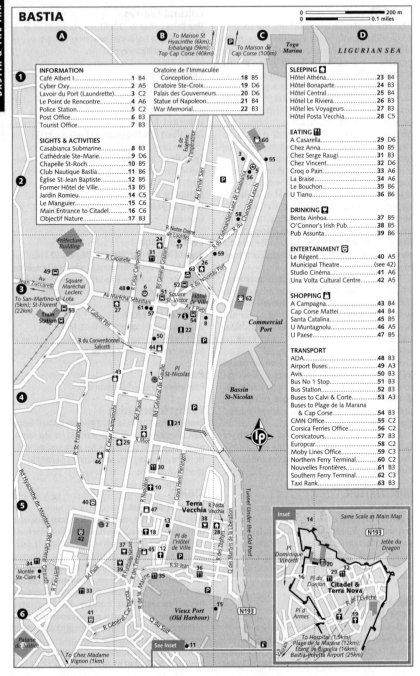

0 — 200 m
0 — 0.1 miles

To Maison St
Hyacinthe (6km);
Erbalunga (9km);
Top Cap Corse (40km)

To Maison de
Cap Corse (100m)

*Toga
Marina*

LIGURIAN SEA

INFORMATION

Café Albert I	1	B4
Cyber Oxy	2	A5
Lavoir du Port (Laundrette)	3	C2
Le Point de Rencontre	4	A6
Police Station	5	C2
Post Office	6	B3
Tourist Office	7	B3

SIGHTS & ACTIVITIES

Casabianca Submarine	8	B3
Cathèdrale Ste-Marie	9	D6
Chapelle St-Roch	10	B5
Club Nautique Bastia	11	B6
Église St-Jean Baptiste	12	B5
Former Hôtel de Ville	13	C5
Jardin Romieu	14	C5
Le Manguier	15	C6
Main Entrance to Citadel	16	C6
Objectif Nature	17	B3

Oratoire de l'Immaculée Conception	18	B5
Oratoire Ste-Croix	19	D6
Palais des Gouverneurs	20	D6
Statue of Napoleon	21	B4
War Memorial	22	B3

SLEEPING

Hôtel Athéna	23	B4
Hôtel Bonaparte	24	B3
Hôtel Central	25	B4
Hôtel Le Riviera	26	B3
Hôtel les Voyageurs	27	B3
Hôtel Posta Vecchia	28	C5

EATING

A Casarella	29	D6
Chez Anna	30	B5
Chez Serge Raugi	31	B3
Chez Vincent	32	D6
Croq o Pain	33	A6
La Braise	34	A6
Le Bouchon	35	B6
U Tianu	36	B6

DRINKING

Benta Ainhoa	37	B5
O'Connor's Irish Pub	38	B5
Pub Assunta	39	B6

ENTERTAINMENT

Le Régent	40	A5
Municipal Theatre	(see 42)	
Studio Cinéma	41	A6
Una Volta Cultural Centre	42	A5

SHOPPING

A Campagna	43	B4
Cap Corse Mattei	44	B4
Santa Catalina	45	B5
U Muntagnolu	46	A5
U Paese	47	B5

TRANSPORT

ADA	48	B3
Airport Buses	49	A3
Avis	50	B3
Bus No 1 Stop	51	B3
Bus Station	52	B3
Buses to Calvi & Corte	53	A3
Buses to Plage de la Marana & Cap Corse	54	B3
CMN Office	55	C2
Corsica Ferries Office	56	C2
Corsicatours	57	B3
Europcar	58	C2
Moby Lines Office	59	C3
Northern Ferry Terminal	60	C2
Nouvelles Frontières	61	B3
Southern Ferry Terminal	62	C3
Taxi Rank	63	B3

BASTIA & THE FAR NORTH

Préfecture
Building

R Capanelle

Square
Maréchal
Leclerc

Av
Jean Zuccarelli

To San-Martino-di-Lota
(5km); St-Florent
(22km)

Train
Station

R Gabriel Péri

R du Conventionnel
Salicetti

Av Maréchal Sébastiani

Square
St-Victor

Hôtel
de Ville

Av F Pietri

Pl
St-Nicolas

*Bassin
St-Nicolas*

*Commercial
Port*

Bd Général de Gaulle

Bd Paoli

Bd Paoli

R César Campinchi

R César Campinchi

R Miot

R St-François

Bd Hyacinthe de Montera

Bd Général Graziani

Montée
Ste-Claire

R Favalelli

R Napoléon

Cours Henri Pierangeli

*Terra
Vecchia*

R Posta
Vecchia

Pl de
l'Hôtel
de Ville

R Fontaine Neuve

R des Terrasses

R du Palais de Justice

R de la Marine

R St-Jean

Q des Martyrs de la Libération

*Tunnel
Under the Old Port*

*Vieux Port
(Old Harbour)*

Q du Sud

R Général Ch-hucca

*Palaise
de Justice*

To Chez Madame
Vignon (1km)

See Inset

N193

R de
Eugénie
Impératrice

R Émile Sari

Av Commandant Luce de Casabianca

R Notre Dame
de Lourdes

R du Chanoine Leschi

R du Nouveau Port

Inset

Same Scale as Main Map

N193

*Jetée du
Dragon*

Pl
Dominique
Vincetti

Pl du
Donjon

Pl d'
Armes

*Citadel &
Terra Nova*

R de l'Evêché

Pl de
l'Eglise

To Hospital (1.5km);
Plage de la Marana (12km);
Étang de Biguglia (16km);
Bastia-Poretta Airport (25km)

giving her youngest son to the motherland, a bombastic theme executed with great sensitivity. Even more evocative for Corsicans is the black conning tower of the **Casabianca submarine**. It's preserved in honour of Jean L'Herminier, the captain, and his crew who, in the months leading up to the recapture of the island from Axis forces in 1943, landed agents, arms, radios and supplies in support of the Corsican resistance.

The square also boasts a **statue of Napoleon**. Nancy Napoleon, you might say, his naked torso draped in a camp Roman emperor's tunic as he peers out to sea towards Elba, place of his first exile and so few kilometres eastwards across the waters.

Terra Vecchia

This, the oldest part of town, was traditionally where Corsicans lived, while the Genoese occupiers looked down upon them from Terra Nova. From place St-Nicolas, rue Napoléon passes two Baroque chapels. The smaller **Chapelle St-Roch** has a fine 18th-century walnut organ gallery while the **Oratoire de l'Immaculée Conception**, with its rich wooden panelling and elaborately painted barrel-vaulted ceiling, briefly served as the seat of the Anglo-Corsican parliament in 1795. Its throne was meant for King George III and *God Save The King* was played on the organ at the opening and closing of each session.

Behind the chapel stretches **place de l'Hôtel de Ville**, also known as place du Marché – as for centuries, there's a small produce market, Tuesday to Friday, and a much larger one on Saturday and Sunday. Around the square are some handsome four-storey buildings and, in one corner, the former town hall. In the southwest corner is the 17th-century ochre **Église St-Jean Baptiste**, Corsica's largest church, with twin bell-towers and a tall classical façade.

From the square, narrow side streets wind their way between tall houses down to the **Vieux Port** (old harbour) and **quai des Martyrs de la Libération**. The buildings nearest the harbour took a battering during WWII bombing missions designed to drive out Axis occupiers. Today, tempting terrace restaurants ring the harbour.

Citadel & Terra Nova

From the south side of the Vieux Port, steps lead up to the **Jardin Romieu** (8am-8pm summer, 8am-5pm winter), a pleasant expanse of green that clings to the hillside for dear life. The even steeper steps and tunnel of the **rampe St-Charles**

bring you through the defensive walls of the citadel to **place du Donjon**, at its heart. Overlooking this cobbled square is the **Palais des Gouverneurs** (Governors' Palace), long closed to the public and earmarked – as it has been for many years – as the venue for the Musée d'Ethnographie Corse, so long in gestation. This citadel fortress, built in 1530, was the seat of the Genoese governor of Corsica for over two centuries. The Terra Nova quarter, many of its buildings recently refurbished in attractive ochres, reds, yellows and greens, grew up around its flanks.

Inside the late-15th-century **Cathédrale Ste-Marie**, with its imposing yellow and white façade, drop a €0.20 coin into the box to illuminate the glass-encased silver Virgin Mary for two minutes. Admire too its Italian organ, one of the finest on the island, and the finely painted trompe l'oeil ceiling. Behind the cathedral, the rococo **Oratoire Ste-Croix** has a fine ceiling and, in one of the side chapels, a much-venerated black-oak crucifix, reputedly hauled from the sea by fishermen in the 14th century. Above the altar, an unusual sculpture depicting God the Father looks down benevolently.

ACTIVITIES

Friendly **Objectif Nature** (04 95 32 54 34, 06 12 02 32 02; www.objectif-nature-corse.com in French; 3 rue Notre-Dame de Lourdes; 8am-7pm Mon-Sat, 8.30am-noon Sun) is a long-standing pioneer of adventure sports in Corsica. Guided activities include canyoning (€40 to €50), sea kayaking along the Désert des Agriates (€35 to €45), horse riding (€30 for two hours) and parapente (€60). It also runs night-fishing trips out of Bastia harbour with buffet dinner on board (€80) and rents bicycles (€18/40 per day/three days). The owners speak impressive English.

Between June and September, **Le Manguier** (06 73 52 48 05, 06 89 37 50 66; www.navirelemanguier .com), a former French navy tug boat moored in the Vieux Port, does day trips (€95 including breakfast and lunch), visits to the Italian islands of Capraia and Elba and a six-day sortie around Cap Corse.

Also in the Vieux Port, **Club Nautique Bastia** (04 95 32 67 33, 06 11 83 09 14; www.club-nautique -bastia.fr in French) runs sailing and windsurfing courses from its headquarters. Between mid-June and mid-September, it also mounts courses and rents catamarans, windsurfs and kayaks from its base at the northern end of the Étang de Biguglia (p108).

From April to October, **Via Corsica** (☎ 06 24 26 59 66) runs two-hour guided walking tours (adult/child €8/free) in French around the themes of Baroque Bastia, Genoese Bastia and Bastia and its Confréries (lay religious brotherhoods). Ask the tourist office for dates and program details.

WALKING TOUR

WALK FACTS
Start/finish tourist office
Distance 2.75km
Duration One to 1¼hr

This easy walking tour takes in Bastia's major areas of interest.

From the **tourist office (1)** on place St-Nicolas, walk south past the **statue of Napoleon (2**; p101). The tall 17th- and 18th-century buildings flanking the square on its southern and western sides could have been transplanted from any number of smaller Italian cities, with their steep interior stairs visible from the street.

From the main square, cours Henri Pierangeli runs into Terra Vecchia, Bastia's oldest quarter, where **place de l'Hôtel de Ville (3**; p103) is home to the former town hall building (now used primarily for weddings) and the Église St-Jean Baptiste.

From the church, cross rue St-Jean and go down the steps that lead to the **Vieux Port (4**; p103) today mainly a marina. As Bastia grew into a major port, a new commercial harbour was built to the northeast, leaving this sunny strip to pleasure boats, restaurants and cafés.

Hugging the curve of the port, quai du Sud leads, via rampe St-Charles, to **Jardin Romieu (5**; p103), a shady little garden. At its extremity, take the flight of steep stone steps that lead through the citadel's battlements via a tunnel and up to rue St-Michel, where you turn right for **place du Donjon (6**; p103) with the Palais des Gouverneurs on its northern flank.

From the square, head southeast along narrow rue Notre Dame to reach **Cathédrale Ste-Marie (7**; p103). A plaque on a house to its right affirms that Victor Hugo lived here briefly as a toddler when his father was a general in the town's garrison. Skirting the side of the church, you come to the **Oratoire Ste-Croix (8**; p103).

Drop down a flight of steps and turn left into Chemin des Turquines, then left again up

the steps of rue de L'Évêché and right into rue de la Paroisse. **A Cava (9)** at No 6 sells traditional Corsican products; the *patron* will be happy to proffer a taste of his favourite house liqueur: a 40% *eau de vie* infused with local maquis.

Rue de la Paroisse brings you back to place du Donjon where you can stop for a drink on the terrace of **Bar la Citadelle (10)**. Cross the

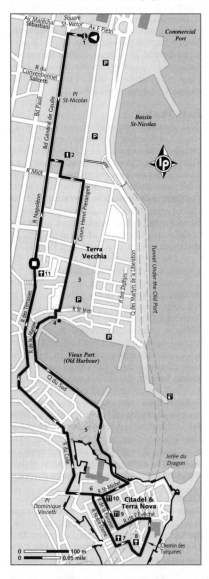

square and exit via the main entrance to the citadel. Follow rue du Colle northwards and skirt the Vieux Port to join rue des Terrasses, which has several worthwhile craft shops. Once you've passed the imposing façade of the **Oratoire de l'Immaculée Conception (11**; p103), place St-Nicolas is again back in sight.

FESTIVALS & EVENTS

Processions de la Semaine Sainte Holy Week is celebrated fervently with colourful processions; late March to early April.

Feux de la St-Jean A giant bonfire in the Vieux Port celebrates the year's longest day (23 June) and honours Bastia's patron saint.

A Notte di a Memoria A historical re-enactment of the changing of the governors ceremony amid much pomp and ceremony; one Saturday in July.

Musicales de Bastia (☎ 04 95 32 75 91) Five days of Baroque music, polyphonic singing, blues and popular song in October.

Festival Arte-Mare A celebration of Mediterranean cinema and cultures for 10 days in mid-November.

SLEEPING

Given the huge amount of traffic passing through the port during high season, it's wise to book ahead in summer. Off-season, rates fall and some places simply close down.

Gîtes

Le Manguier (☎ 06 73 52 48 05, 06 89 37 50 66; www.navire lemanguier.com; per person with half-board €50; ☼ Oct-May) Here's a truly unique option. If you fancy a night afloat in the Vieux Port, this ex-navy tug boat operates as a *bateau gîte* outside the summer season and has five simple doubles. Do ring in advance; the owners, a pair of free souls, may have weighed anchor and set sail for new seas by the time you read this.

Hotels

Hôtel Athéna (☎ 04 95 34 88 40; 2 rue Miot; s/d €50/60; ☒) The Posta Vecchia runs this less-expensive sister hotel, which has spick-and-span modern rooms in a quiet location. Contact Hôtel Posta Vecchia if no-one's in.

Hôtel Posta Vecchia (☎ 04 95 32 32 38; www.hotel -postavecchia.com in French; 8 quai des Martyrs de la Libération; d €53-75, tr €70-95, q €80-105; ☒) But a well-cast pebble from the old port, this is the only hotel in Bastia that faces the sea. Its entrance is on rue Posta Vecchia. Rooms vary considerably in size. Most have a bright, colourful décor and some are equipped with a fridge.

Hôtel Le Riviera (☎ 04 95 31 07 16; www.corsehotel riviera.com; 1bis rue Adolphe Landry; s/d €55/60; ☒) The 20 rooms at this cheerful, value-for-money hotel extend over three floors (and, yes, there's a lift!). It's a rare example of a place where you're better off with a street-facing room, since the air-con throbs and echoes around the interior patio.

Hôtel Central (☎ 04 95 31 71 12; www.centralhotel .fr; 3 rue Miot; s €55-65, d €65-90) Living up to its name and conveniently positioned for both old and new ports, this comfortable option has 18 bright, whitewashed rooms with timber floors, check curtains and maritime prints. Rooms overlooking the courtyard garden are quieter than those facing the street and there are a handful of studio apartments equipped with a kitchenette.

Hôtel Les Voyageurs (☎ 04 95 34 90 80; www.hotel -lesvoyageurs.com; 9 av Maréchal Sébastiani; s €63, d €73-83, tr €83-93; ☒☒☒☒) Run with panache by the same family for over a century yet thoroughly modern and comprehensively renovated (with wi-fi) in recent years, Hôtel Les Voyageurs is justifiably popular with business visitors. The pleasing lounge and reception area streams with light. Its 24 rooms have soothing pale yellow walls, glass- and wrought-iron furniture and sparkling bathrooms. The best of the doubles are cavernous and come with a cosy sofa and bathtub. Parking €6.

Hôtel Bonaparte (☎ 04 95 34 07 10; www.hotel -bonaparte-bastia.com; 45 blvd Général Graziani; s €65-80, d €70-90; ☒☒) Close to place St-Nicolas and ideal for an early ferry departure or late arrival, this smart 23-room family-run hotel has well-appointed, sound-proofed rooms, five of them with balcony. The two vast junior suites have a separate lounge, screened by curtains. Parking €8.

Camping

Camping San Damiano (☎ 04 95 33 68 02; www.camp ingsandamiano.com; camp sites per person €5-7; ☼ Apr-Oct) Served by the airport bus, this large camping ground amid the pines, 8km south of Bastia, is right beside the beach. It also has furnished bungalows, rented by the week.

EATING
Cafés

There's plenty of scope for people-watching from the terrace of one of the many cafés that line the western side of place St-Nicolas.

Chez Serge Raugi (☎ 04 95 31 22 31; 2bis rue Capanelle) The terrace is usually packed on summer nights with customers who come to sample its scrummy ice-creams.

Restaurants

Chez Vincent (☎ 04 95 31 62 50; 12 rue St-Michel; mains €8-15; ☉ Mon-Fri, dinner Sat) Up in the citadel and with a small terrace overlooking the Vieux Port, Chez Vincent is a friendly, informal spot where you can snack on pizzas or select from the chalkboard. Go wild and opt for the *assiette du bandit Corse* (Corsican bandit platter, €16), a selection of island favourites including wild boar pâté and chestnut fondant.

La Braise (☎ 04 95 31 36 97; 7 blvd Hyacinthe de Montera; mains €8-20; ☉ Mon-Fri, lunch Sat) This Bastia classic has recently changed hands. Gone, some will lament, is Jo, the ebullient former *patron*, into well-earned retirement. The place might have had a thorough spring clean but what remains constant is the simple, well-prepared cuisine such as prawns *flambés* in pastis and red mullet with *pistou* (pesto).

A Casarella (☎ 04 95 32 02 32; rue St-Michel; mains €10-16, menu €28; ☉ Mon-Fri, dinner Sat Dec-Oct) A Casarella, a near neighbour of Chez Vincent, also has a small attractive terrace. Inside, it's tastefully decorated with artefacts and contemporary canvases. The innovative cuisine has a strong Corsican bias and includes dishes such as fillet of veal rolled in herbs from the maquis and *casciate* (fresh cheese baked in chestnut leaves). Be adventurous and try the 'discovery' dégustation platter, featuring the chef's most recent creations. Reservations are normally essential.

Chez Anna (☎ 04 95 31 83 84; 3 rue Jean Casale; mains €13.50-16, fish menu €24.50; ☉ Mon-Sat) This nice little spot has a plant-covered façade, a streetside terrace and a pleasant 1st-floor brick-ceilinged dining room. Portions are generous and they also throw a mean pizza.

Le Bouchon (☎ 04 95 58 14 22; 4bis rue St-Jean; mains €14.50-23.50; ☉ closed Sun & Wed) Portions are smallish but tastefully presented at this quayside restaurant-cum-wine bar. They include goat, a variety of locally caught fish dishes and pigeon with figs and polenta. There's a good selection of wines by the glass (€4.50), both local and from the mainland, and service is affable, if on the slow side. It doesn't accept credit cards.

U Tianu (☎ 04 95 31 36 67; 4 rue Rigo; ☉ 7pm-1am Mon-Sat Sep-Jul) A local favourite that has hardly changed in a quarter of a century, this informal, family-run place is tucked away down a side street and up a flight of rickety stairs behind the Vieux Port. You'll stagger out after indulging in its superb-value five-course *menu* of traditional Corsican favourites (€19, including an aperitif, coffee and a *digestif*).

Quick Eats

Croq o Pain (☎ 04 95 58 80 95; 2 blvd Paoli; ☉ 10am-10pm) A friendly snack joint with a variety of sandwiches (€4.20) and salads (€4.70).

DRINKING & ENTERTAINMENT

You'll find the most life around the Vieux Port and on place St-Nicolas.

There are two attractive bars on rue Fontaine Neuve. **Pub Assunta** (☎ 04 95 34 11 40) has a pool table and local bands play on Thursday and most weekends. **Benta Ainhoa** (☎ 04 95 30 88 81; ☉ 5.30pm-2am) is run by two engaging young Basque couples. It serves tapas, prepared from fresh produce bought in daily, has a good selection of Corsican, Basque and Rioja wines and plays eclectic world music – everything from Irish jigs to South American Indian songs.

O'Connor's Irish Pub (☎ 04 95 32 04 97; 1 rue St-Érasme; ☉ 6pm-2am), is your standard turnkey Emerald Isle watering hole.

Bastia has two cinemas: **Le Régent** (☎ 04 95 31 30 31; www.leregent.fr in French; rue César Campinchi), a multiscreen cinema with the latest releases; and **Studio Cinéma** (☎ 04 95 31 12 94; www.studio-cinema.com in French; rue Miséricorde), which screens both French and international releases.

L'Apocalypse (☎ 04 95 33 36 83; ☉ Wed-Sun) at Lido de la Marana, 11km south of Bastia, is a lively summertime dance venue that attracts a mainly teenage crowd.

SHOPPING

Cap Corse Mattei (☎ 04 95 32 44 38; 15 blvd Général de Gaulle; Mon-Sat) is a Bastia institution. The interior of this gloriously retro shop with its Art Deco façade has hardly changed since the day Louis-Napoléon Mattei first open for business in 1872. During over a century of service it has continued to sell not only its celebrated brand-name Cap Corse apéritif, but various spin-off products that make ideal souvenirs and local specialities such as fig jam, olive oil and fruit liqueurs.

Several tempting shops sell quality Corsican products such as charcuterie, cheese, honey, wine and liqueur.

A Campagna (☎ 04 95 34 00 78; 25 rue César Campinchi)
Santa Catalina (☎ 04 95 32 30 69; 8 rue des Terrasses)
U Muntagnolu (☎ 04 95 32 78 04; 15 rue César Campinchi)
U Paese (☎ 04 95 32 33 18; 4 rue Napoléon)

GETTING THERE & AWAY

Two reliable travel agents:
Corsicatours (☎ 04 95 31 03 79; rue Maréchal Sébastiani)
Nouvelles Frontières (☎ 04 95 32 01 62; rue Maréchal Sébastiani)

Air

Bastia-Poretta airport (☎ 04 95 54 54 54; www.bastia
.aeroport.fr) is 24km south of downtown Bastia.
There are at least five daily Air France flights
to/from Nice, Marseilles and Paris (Orly).
CCM-Air Corsica has at least three flights
daily to/from Marseilles, Nice and Paris (Orly
Ouest) and also does a daily run to/from Lyon.
British Airways operates three times weekly
to/from London (Gatwick).

Boat

Bastia has two ferry terminals. The northern
one has showers, toilets and an **information
point** (⏱ 7am-9pm). The main, southern terminal has a ticket office for same-day and
advance travel for SNCM, Corsica Ferries
and Moby Lines (the ticket office for CMN is
opposite the northern terminal in a separate
building). Fares fluctuate substantially with
the seasons and bookings are recommended
at peak times. For more information on ferry
services see p267.

Four companies sail between Corsica and
mainland Europe. CMN and SNCM operate
joint ticketing and services.
CMN (☎ 08 10 20 13 20; www.cmn.fr) Overnight services
to Marseilles.
Corsica Ferries (☎ 08 25 09 50 95; www.corsicaférries
.com) Services to Nice and Toulon in France, and to Savona
and Livorno in Italy.
Moby Lines (☎ 04 95 34 84 94; www.mobylines.fr)
Boats to Genoa and Livorno in Italy.
SNCM (☎ 04 95 54 66 90; www.sncm.fr) Services to
Marseilles.

Bus

Most buses for the Bastia area leave from the
bus station (a grand term for a little parking
area with no ticket office), just north of place
St-Nicolas.

The tourist office has a comprehensive list
of buses serving the town. Main operators
and destinations:

Autocars Cortenais (☎ 04 95 46 02 12) Leaves from
the train station for Corte (€10, three times weekly).
Autocars Santini (☎ 04 95 37 04 01) Leaves from the
bus station for St-Florent (€5, twice daily).
Les Beaux Voyages (☎ 04 95 65 15 02; www.lesbeaux
voyagesencorse.com in French) Leaves from the train station
for Calvi (€15, once or twice daily) via Île Rousse (€10).
Eurocorse (☎ 04 95 21 06 31) Leaves from route du
Nouveau Port for Ajaccio (€19, twice daily) and Corte (€10,
twice daily).
Rapides Bleus (☎ 04 95 31 03 79) Leaves from in front
of post office for Porto-Vecchio (€20, once daily).

Car & Motorcycle

Most car-hire firms have branches both in
Bastia and at the airport. Advance booking is
essential in high season. For car-hire outlets
in town, see p270.

The following all have offices at the airport.
ADA (☎ 04 95 54 55 44)
Avis (☎ 04 95 54 55 46)
Budget (☎ 04 95 30 05 04)
Europcar (☎ 04 95 30 09 50)
Hertz (☎ 04 95 30 05 16)
National Citer (☎ 04 95 36 07 85)
Sixt Location (☎ 04 95 54 54 70)

Train

The **train station** (☎ 04 95 32 80 61) is at the western end of av Maréchal Sébastiani, beside
square Maréchal Leclerc. There are four trains
daily to Ajaccio (€20.70, four hours), via Corte
(€9.70, two hours, five daily) and Casamozza
(€3.40, 30 minutes, five daily). Two trains
daily run between Bastia and Calvi (€15.70,
three hours) via Île Rousse (€13, 2½ hours)
and requiring a change at Ponte Leccia.

GETTING AROUND
To/From the Airport

The airport bus (€8, 30 minutes, seven to nine
daily) leaves from in front of the Préfecture
building beside square Maréchal Leclerc. The
tourist office has schedules, and timetables are
also posted at the bus stop. **Airport taxis** (☎ 04 95
36 04 05) cost €35/48 day/night or Sundays.

Bicycle

Objectif Nature (p103) rents out bikes.

Car & Motorcycle

Driving in town can be a nightmare. Head
straight for the car parks beside and beneath
place St-Nicolas and forget about your vehicle
until you leave town.

Public Transport

Urban bus services are run by the **Société des Transports Interurbains Bastiais** (☎ 04 95 31 06 65).

Taxi

Ring **Taxis Oranges Bastiais** (☎ 04 95 32 24 24) or **Taxis Bleus** (☎ 04 95 32 70 70).

AROUND BASTIA

LA CORNICHE

It's not Bastia. No more is it quite of Cap Corse. But gosh, it makes a wonderful drive, easily accomplished in a couple of hours. The D31 snakes its way around the steep mountain slopes that lour over the city from the north. Here (such an agreeable surprise and so close to Corsica's second-largest city) you'll be tempted to pause and explore a trio of little villages – **Ville di Pietrabugno**, **San Martino di Lota** and **Santa Maria di Lota**, each with its own outriding hamlets – before dropping to **Miomo** and, once more, the coast. Again and again, you'll enjoy stunning views of the shore and, far out to sea, the Italian islands of the Tuscan archipelago.

If, understandably, you have lingered too long, there are several wonderful spots in which you can make an overnight halt, including **Maison St Hyacinthe** (☎ 04 95 33 28 29; mshcorse@aol.com; Commune de Santa Maria di Lota, Miomo; r incl breakfast per person Jun-Sep €26.50-39, Oct-May €25.50), a peaceful convent run by Polish nuns, which lies deep in the hills behind Bastia. Accommodation, in single or double rooms, is in several buildings, spread over a large compound. Of its 47 simple, impeccably maintained rooms, 13 have their own bathroom. It's well signed from the D80; in Miomo, take the D31 westwards for 2.5km.

The peaceful hamlet of San Martino di Lota, 6km from Bastia along the D31 Corniche road northwest of town, also has a couple of attractive choices. **Hôtel-Restaurant La Corniche** (☎ 04 95 31 40 98; www.hotel-lacorniche.com; r 40-88; ☑ Feb-Dec; P ☒ ☒) is a 19-room hotel with sweeping views of the coastline and surrounding mountains. Its gourmet restaurant (menus €26 to €45), has a magnificent panoramic terrace and is strong on local produce.

The **Château Cagninacci** (☎ 04 95 31 69 30; www .chateaucagninacci.com in French; r incl breakfast €85-110; P ☒) is another tempting option. Originally a 17th-century Capuchin convent, later converted into a Tuscan-style villa, it's perched high on a hillside with spectacular views out to Elba from the terrace. Of its four spacious rooms, one has a balcony and two have air-con.

ÉTANG ET RÉSERVE NATURELLE DE BIGUGLIA

Along the coast running south from Bastia stretches a vast 11km lagoon, separated from the sea by a long sandy beach. With a total surface area of 1450 hectares, it's the largest closed body of water in Corsica.

Declared a nature reserve in 1994, it's an important area for Corsican flora and migrating birds. Well over 100 species call by or live here, while eel and mullet are farmed in the waters. Though sailing and bathing are prohibited, a **footpath** follows the northern and eastern shore for about 2km with an observation post near the halfway point. There's a small **information centre** (☎ 04 95 33 55 73; ☑ 8am-noon & 1-5pm Mon-Fri) on the western side of the lagoon.

Driving south from Bastia towards Lido de la Marana, you pass **Brasserie Pietra** (☎ 04 95 30 14 70), the brewery that produces Corsica's favourite dark beer, as well as the lighter malt beer Serena and the maquis-scented blonde beer Colomba. During July and August, it arranges free 30- to 45-minute **brewery tours** (☑ 9am-noon & 2-5.30pm Mon-Fri).

Lido de la Marana is a narrow spit of sand more than 10km long. Separating the Étang de Biguglia from the sea, it's increasingly occupied by tourist developments. The beach is nothing special, but there's plenty of space to spread your towel. If you're feeling more active, a track bordering the eastern fringe of the lake is popular with rollerbladers and cyclists and there's windsurfing from the beach.

At the southern end of the Étang de Biguglia, 25km south of Bastia, the Pisan **Cathédrale de la Canonica**, consecrated at the beginning of the 12th century, rises above the coastal plain. On the decorative arched moulding over its western entrance, there's a charming, if much-weathered, frieze of exotic animals. The site was a place of worship even earlier; beside the Pisan building is the small archaeological site of **Mariana**, with its remains of a late-4th-century Christian church.

Getting There & Away

In summer, **Autocars Antoniotti** (☎ 04 95 36 08 21) buses leave Bastia's bus station twice daily at 11.30am and 6pm (Sundays once daily at

11.30am). Signed Marana, they call by Camping San Damiano (€2.50) and run alongside Lido de la Marana and Étang de Biguglia (€3.50).

CAP CORSE

The maquis-covered Cap Corse peninsula, 40km long and around 10km wide, stands out from the rest of Corsica, giving a giant geographical finger to the French Riviera. A wild and rugged region, it's often called an 'island within an island'.

For many years, the peninsula was ruled by important noble families from the city and republic of Genoa and surrounding Liguria, the coastal region of Italy closest to the border with France. These families prospered from trading in wine and oil and the Genoese and Ligurians regarded Cap Corse an ally. History rarely proved them wrong.

This northern tip of Corsica, the nearest to mainland Europe, was an important centre for merchants and trading. It has a long maritime tradition and was, apart from Bonifacio, the only area within Corsica whose people made a living from fishing. Indeed, the inhabitants of Cap Corse were the first islanders to broaden their horizons overseas, emigrating to the French colonies in North Africa and the Americas. Then, once they had made their fortune, many returned home. The most successful commissioned a colonial-style house, known as a *maison d'Américain,* immediately recognisable and standing out from its more modest neighbours.

Today, punctuated by watchtowers built under the Genoese to protect the vulnerable peninsula from Berber raiders, the cape is dotted with charming coastal fishing villages and small communities perched precariously up in the hills.

The west coast, with wilder scenery and narrow switchback roads, contrasts with the gentler eastern coastal strip. It's possible to dash around the cape's perimeter in one hectic day of driving. It's much better, however, to radiate out from Bastia or St-Florent over two or more days. Alternatively, spend the night en route at one of the accommodation options that we recommend (being sure to reserve in advance from mid-July to the end of August).

Information

The **Maison de Cap Corse** (☎ 04 95 31 02 32; www .destination-cap-corse.com; ☺ 9am-noon & 2-6pm Mon-Fri), immediately north of Toga Marina and 800m from place St-Nicolas, while not a tourist office, responds to email and phone inquiries. Its *Le Cap à Pied* is a useful practical guide with a freestanding map (both in French) that outlines 21 walking trails around the peninsula. Both the Bastia and Macinaggio tourist offices carry copies.

Getting There & Away

The D80 snakes its way all around Cap Corse, in the main clinging close to the spectacular coastline. Build in plenty of extra time; progress, especially on the west coast, will be slow as you negotiate the tight bends and pass oncoming traffic warily.

Buses of the **Société des Transports Interurbains Bastiais** (☎ 04 95 31 06 65) run to Erbalunga (€2, six to eight daily), Pietracorbara (€2.60) and Macinaggio (€6.40, two daily except Sunday) leaving from the stop opposite Bastia's tourist office.

GENOESE TOWERS

Around 60 of the 85 Genoese towers that the Banco di San Giorgio built in Corsica in the 16th century remain standing today in various states of preservation. Mostly round but occasionally square, these fortified structures are about 15m high and are particularly common around Cap Corse.

The avowed motive for constructing the towers was to protect the island from Berber raiders, but you can't help thinking that in building them Genoa also sought to protect its strategic and commercial interests in Corsica from European challengers. Sited all around the coastline so that each was visible from the next, the towers formed a vast surveillance network. A system of signals enabled a message to circle the island in one hour.

On Cap Corse, Pino (p114), Erbalunga (p110) and the Sentier des Douaniers (p112) all have fine examples of these structures, which are such a feature of the island.

ERBALUNGA

Though you're only 9km out of Bastia, it would be a shame not to make a brief stop to visit Erbalunga's little harbour, one of the cape's prettiest. It's difficult to imagine the time when the port, where today only a handful of inshore fishing boats bob alongside a crumbling Genoese tower, was a thriving entrepôt. Then more important than either Ajaccio or Bastia, it exported wine and olive oil by the hectolitre to Genoa. Leave your vehicle in the free car park beside Hôtel Demeure Castel Brando.

Each August, the two-week **Festival d'Erbalunga** (☎ 04 95 33 20 84) promotes open-air concerts in the village's central square.

Pozzo, 3km inland from Erbalunga, is the trailhead for climbing Monte Stello (1307m). In its main square, a sign 'Monte Stello 3 hours' indicates the path that takes off through the maquis.

Sleeping & Eating

Hôtel Demeure Castel Brando (☎ 04 95 30 10 30; www.castelbrando.com; d €99-199; ☺ mid-Jan–mid-Nov; P ☒ ☐ ☒) Stay in the elegant main building, originally a mid-19th century mansion, or opt for a superior-grade room in one of the three annexes within the mature garden, shaded by tall palms. Its 45 rooms are tastefully furnished in cream and peach with elegant antiques. It has wi-fi access, there are a couple of heated pools and a spa too. The particularly rich breakfast (€12) is served on the patio. You can hire a kayak (per day €25) or a bike (€15). Last but not least, you won't find a more welcoming hotel anywhere on the island.

A Piazzetta (☎ 04 95 33 28 69; pizzas around €7.50, mains €12-16) Delightfully placed on Erbalunga's small, shady square with the harbour just in view, A Piazzetta offers pizzas and a regularly changing menu (consult the blackboard for its specials), with most choices pulled from the sea.

L'Esquinade (☎ 04 95 33 22 73; mains €14.50-18) With the port at your feet, shaded by a frondy tamarisk tree and cooled by a soft sea breeze, dining is a delight on the small terrace of L'Esquinade, where the food competes favourably with the view. It doesn't accept credit cards.

Le Pirate (☎ 04 95 33 24 20; www.restaurantlepirate.com in French; mains €18-38, menus €59-90; ☺ Wed-Sun, dinner Tue, daily in summer) Le Pirate, where a life-size Long John Silver greets you as you enter, almost dips its toes in the water. Renowned throughout and beyond Corsica for both its cuisine and service, it's popular year-round with discriminating Bastiais.

SISCO

pop 750

The *commune* of Sisco embraces a scattering of mountainside hamlets, which trace a trail down through the maquis to a small **marina** and none-too-sandy beach.

At Marine de Sisco, the **Dollfin Dive School** (☎ 04 95 58 26 16, 06 07 08 95 92; www.dollfin-plongee.com in French; ☺ year-round), beside restaurant A Casaïola, runs diving courses and arranges dives (€36). It also rents kayaks and bikes. For more information on diving see p79.

Sleeping & Eating

A Casaïola (☎ 04 95 35 20 10; camp sites per adult/tent/car €5.50/2.50/3.50) A good camping ground, shady and set for the most part amid natural woodland, it also rents out kayaks (€8 per day).

Hôtel-Restaurant A Stalla Sischese (☎ 04 95 35 26 34; r €55-103; P ☒ ☒) Some 400m inland along the D32, this is the peninsula's newest hotel. Rooms are on the small side but all have a balcony, bathtub and separate bathroom and toilet cubicle. It's grafted onto a longstanding and recommended restaurant (mains €16, *menus* €20 to €26) that serves well-regarded Corsican favourites (its *menu dégustation* consists of seven local specialities). There's a

---

A CERCA

On Good Friday, the people of Erbalunga, Pozzo and a couple of nearby hamlets take part in A Cerca – literally 'The Search' – a unique procession said to go back to pagan times, reflecting an ancient fertility rite. At dawn, men, women and children set out from their village on a 14km circular pilgrimage walk along the paths that link their communities. Each procession is often within sight of the other three, yet they never intersect or overlap.

Erbalunga's pilgrims, once back in the village, wind into a spiral, the Granitola (Snail), that gradually unfolds as the participants continue their way while another element of the procession forms itself into the four arms of the cross.

CORSICA'S TWISTED FIRESTARTERS

Napoleon Bonaparte, Corsica's most famous son, once famously remarked that he could smell the island of his birth from his exile on Elba, across the water. He was probably referring to the maquis, a dense undergrowth of sage, juniper, myrtle and other hardy plants and shrubs that covers thousands of square hectares all across the island. Indeed, each spring when the maquis explodes into a carpet of pink and yellow flowers, it releases a uniquely pervasive fragrance.

But every year, as Mediterranean temperatures nudge the mid-30s, thousands of hectares of the spiny network turn into death-trap towering infernos. Indeed, tales of firefighters risking everything to tackle huge bush blazes dominate the summer news bulletins, and reports of walkers caught unawares amid burning scrubland are the high-season mainstay of *Corse Matin*'s front-page splash.

Corsicans suspect that a large number of the fires are started quite deliberately. Some locals blame the shepherds, accusing them of burning the ground to force new shoots to sprout through the parched ground; others cite dastardly real-estate agents seeking to commandeer grazing land for yet more holiday homes. Other possible culprits include careless tourists and deliberate troublemakers. Everyone is alleged to have a vested interest in Corsica's pyromania problem.

But not everyone is prepared to sit back while the island goes up in flames. 'The truth is that fires generate a lot of money and keep a lot of people in work. The fires benefit everyone except the island itself and its people,' says Roger Filippe, president of **L'Amichi di u Rughjone** (☎ 04 95 35 05 04; www.amichidiurughjone.org in French), a community action group set up out of frustration with the local administration's inability to resolve the fire issue.

The 250-odd members, all volunteers, work to repair damage to the local environment, maintain safe hiking trails and lobby to raise awareness of the way bureaucracy keeps the fires burning.

---

young couple in charge; Raphaël rules in the kitchen, while Muriel ('If I did the cooking we'd be out of your guidebook in a flash,' she confesses with commendable honesty) handles reception.

A Casaïola (☎ 04 95 35 21 50; pizzas €9) A popular place run by the same family who run the camping ground just down the hill. Dine on its shady terrace opposite a small chapel or on a wooden deck overlooking the waves.

PIETRACORBARA

pop 450

The 4km between Sisco and Pietracorbara offer spectacular vistas with scarcely a house in sight. From **Marine de Pietracorbara** (also called the Marine d'Ampuglia), a long strand of fine white sand, the best on the cape's eastern coast, stretches northwards.

At **Santa Servara**, 8km further north, you have a choice: to continue along the D80 or to head westwards and inland along the D180 towards Pino via the village of Luri (p114) and the Col de Santa Lucia (p114).

Camping La Pietra (☎ 04 95 35 27 49; www.la-pietra .com; Marine de Pietracorbara; camp sites person €6.30-8, tent €3.70-4.50, car €3.30-3.60; ☾ Apr–mid-Oct) is a superior, shaded camping ground with large plots, each protected by a high mature hedge, and plenty

of could-be-at-home facilities, immaculately maintained. A pleasant walk of around 400m through fields and woodland brings you to the beach.

New owners have comprehensively worked over **Hôtel-Restaurant Macchia e Mare** (☎ 04 95 35 21 36; www.macchia-e-mare.com in French; s €60-90, d €65-105), which enjoys a prime site on a hillock at the southern entrance to the marina. Four of its eight rooms have large balconies and coastal views and all have brand new furnishings and decoration, some of it smacking of kitsch. The restaurant (mains €16 to €19, *menus* €27) also has coastal views through its picture windows

MACINAGGIO (MACINAGHJU)

Macinaggio, hub of the eastern cape, has a pleasant little harbour that offers the island's best moorings; everything from small sailing boats to sleek luxury yachts are berthed here. With a good range of activities, the town makes a good base for exploring the northern reaches of the promontory.

A port ever since Roman times, it was used by the Genoese to export wine and olive oil to the mainland. And Corsicans remember it as the place where Pascal Paoli landed in 1790 after his enforced exile in Britain.

SENTIER DES DOUANIERS (CUSTOMS OFFICERS' TRAIL)

Hikers will love this rugged coastal path that leads away from the beach at Macinaggio and, winding its way through the fragrant maquis of the Capandula Nature Reserve, hugs the protected shoreline. Views are spectacular, with various sections grazing the coastline, looking out to the **Îles Finocchiarola** and passing the Genoese **Tour de Santa Maria** and **Tour d'Agnello** en route.

The trail leads on to complete the first stage at Barcaggio; allow up to three hours. From here, and if you're not already flagging in the sun, the path you continue for another 45 minutes to Tollare. From Tollare it's a hefty but spectacular four-hour trek to the harbour at **Centuri** (opposite). It's not a particularly strenuous walk but be sure to take a hat and plenty of water; there are no springs en route. Avoid the midday sun, which can be especially ruthless along this strip of coast.

It's possible to do only the first section. It's also possible to spread the whole walk over two days, breaking in Barcaggio, thanks to the San Paulu boat (below).

Information

The cape's only **tourist office** (☎ 04 95 35 40 34; www.ot-rogliano-macinaggio.com in French; port de plaisance de Macinaggio; 🕙 9am-noon & 3-7.30pm Mon-Sat, 9am-noon Sun Jul & Aug, 9am-noon & 3-6pm Mon-Fri, 9am-noon Sat May, Jun & Sep, 9am-noon & 2-5pm Oct-Apr) is at the southern end of the marina.

Laverie Clean Up (🕙 9am-noon & 3-6pm Mon-Sat), a laundrette, is beside the post office.

Activities

For a taste of the trail the way those customs officers would have travelled it in the past, the **Centre Équestre** (Riding Centre; ☎ 04 95 35 43 76) does accompanied horse treks (1½ hours €24, 2½ hours €35) year-round along a stretch of the Sentier des Douaniers.

Families may prefer a boat trip along the protected coastline with the **San Paulu** (☎ 04 95 35 07 09; www.lebateau.fr.st in French; adult/child €20/10), moored opposite the tourist office. The two-hour round-trip follows the stunning coastline as far as Barcaggio (on whose beach, if you take the morning boat, you can linger, returning with the 4.30pm sailing). Sailings are at 11am and 3.30pm from Macinaggio, leaving Barcaggio at noon and 4.30pm.

The promontory's most spectacular beach is **Plage de Tamarone**, 2km north of the marina, just past Camping U Stazzu (right), with its long expanse of fine sand. There's a kiosk for snacks but no showers or toilets.

Cap Corse Immersion (☎ 04 95 35 31 70, 06 85 75 17 06; http://capcorseimmersion.free.fr in French) offers diving outings and a range of courses. For more information on diving see p79.

Leave space in the car boot/trunk for a bottle or two of the local Clos Nicrosi, one of Corsica's finest *crus*. Its sales outlet is opposite the U Ricordu hotel .

Sleeping & Eating

Camping U Stazzu (☎ 04 95 35 43 76; camp sites €14; 🕙 mid-May–Sep) A 1km signed drive from the post office, this shady spot with large pitches is convenient for both Tamarone beach and the port.

U Ricordu (☎ 04 95 35 40 20; www.hotel-uricordu.com in French; r per person incl breakfast €37.50-82.50; 🕙 Apr-Oct; P 🔀 🖳) Just north of the post office, U Ricordu, popular with tour groups, has 53 well-appointed rooms, most with air-con and some overlooking the garden and heated pool. Half-board (per person €77.50 to €92.50) and a minimum stay of five nights are required between mid-July and mid-August only.

Hôtel Les Îles (☎ 04 95 35 43 02; d €50-60, tr €70; 🕙 year-round) This small hotel, separately run from the neighbouring restaurant of the same name, also overlooks the marina. Rooms are smallish but quite adequate. Choose either sea views or one of the quieter rooms facing the rear.

U Libecciu (☎ 04 95 35 43 22; www.u-libecciu.com in French; s €68-92, d €96-130; 🕙 Apr-Oct; P) Enjoying a quiet location away from the marina's social hub, this hotel has 30 spacious, unexceptional rooms, nearly all with balcony. Those on the top floor have larger balconies but, in the absence of air-con, can be torrid in high summer.

Osteria di U Portu (☎ 04 95 35 40 49; mains €9-17, menus €15-22; 🕙 Feb-Nov) Enjoying a superb location overlooking the marina, this friendly restaurant, with its appealing red and yellow décor, is run by a dynamic young team. It serves the freshest of fish and seafood and it's a minor agony, dithering between their five course *menu découverte* (€17) of Corsican dishes and the *menu de la mer* (€22). It also rents out four attractive *chambres d'hôtes* (rooms €50 to €70 from April to October).

THE NORTHERN TIP ✕

Just over 10km west of Macinaggio along the D80, you can make a 15km round-rip detour to visit **Barcaggio (Barcaghju)**, Corsica's northernmost village, and its spectacular beach. Otherwise accessible only by boat or by walking in along the Sentier des Douaniers, it has a magnificent beach with great views of the protected islet of Giraglia. To get there, turn right at **Ersa** onto the narrow D253, which winds its way through the maquis to reach this remote spot.

The hamlet's only accommodation, **Hôtel La Giraglia** (☎ 04 95 35 60 54; s/d incl breakfast €63/71, with bathroom €71/80; ✆ Apr-Sep) enjoys a pretty location though its rates are on the high side for its simple, rather gloomy rooms, some of which overlook the sea and have a balcony. It doesn't accept credit cards.

Capo Grosso, west of Barcaggio and the even smaller settlement of Tollare, has stunning views – if you can handle following the unmarked and heavily rutted road off the D153 for 2.5km.

Back on the D80, your first view of the altogether wilder, steeper and more rugged western coast will linger long on the retina.

CENTURI

pop 230

Pause at the **Col de Serra**, overlooking Centuri, for the briefest of walks up to the **Moulin Mattei**, with its distinctive pink witch's hat. From the base of this former windmill, 'restored' by the Mattei company, producers of Cap Corse apéritif, there's one of the promontory's finest seascapes. Nowadays the sails are purely decorative By contrast, the nearby battery of modern windmills twirl and capture the winds that howl over the saddle of the mountain.

Leave the D80 briefly to take the D35, which drops steeply to the port of Centuri, which has a free car park beside it. Marking the end of **Le Sentier des Douaniers**, Centuri is a particularly welcome sight for walkers. It's a pretty setting with yachts moored in the aquamarine stretch of sea between the village and the small slab of island just offshore. But the focal point of this tiny hamlet is its attractive stone-built harbour, from where boats still put out to lay their pots for rock-lobster, a prominent item on the menus of the several tempting eating choices on its perimeter.

Sleeping & Eating

Hôtel-Restaurant du Pêcheur (☎ 04 95 35 60 14; r €50-65; ✆ Easter-Oct) You can't miss this restaurant on the north side of the harbour with its pink brickwork and blue shutters. Its six simple rooms with thick stone walls are cool and some offer a great vista across the harbour at sunset. They're on the small side, but it's a cheerful place and Centuri's cheapest overnight option. Choose a rear room; those at the front get the noise from the bar opposite, active until 2am. In July and August, you're obliged to eat dinner in the restaurant downstairs – no great imposition since the cuisine is just fine.

Hôtel-Restaurant de la Jetée (☎ 04 95 35 64 46; www.la-jetee.net in French; r €55-75; ✆ Apr-Sep; ⚇) This hotel, well priced for a resort such as Centuri, has 14 comfortable rooms, some with sea views, and a pleasant, shaded terrace overlooking the port. The fresh fish that features

---

THE AUTHOR'S CHOICE ✗

The area's cosiest and most welcoming choice sits up in the hills, a mere 5km west of Macinaggio yet a world away from the crowded coast. At **Hôtel-Restaurant U Sant'Agnellu** (☎ 04 95 35 40 59; www.hotel-usantagnellu.com in French; r per person with half-board €55-80; ☎ mid-Apr–mid-Oct), you'll eat particularly well (this recommended restaurant with its panoramic terrace is open to all-comers) and sleep cosseted and in comfort. Choose one of the seven rooms that face the sea, retire early and set your alarm to enjoy the sunrise as it streaks across the bay. The cheerful Albertinis, your hosts, have a particular affinity with the place – not surprising, since they were married in room 8, when the hotel still functioned as public offices. The *menu* (€17 to €20) is creative, with delightful desserts such as its signature *mousse de brousse au miel* (fresh white cheese whipped to a mousse into which honey is stirred), and features mainly local products (when the octopods come close to shore, Monsieur Albertini takes his boat and hauls them in).

From Macinaggio, take the D80 westwards and turn left onto the D53, signed Rogliano. Next morning, you can continue through the hamlet to rejoin the D80.

prominently on the restaurant menu (mains €10.50 to €18.50, *menu* €16.50) may well have been caught by the owner himself.

Hôtel-Restaurant Le Vieux Moulin (☎ 04 95 35 60 15; www.le-vieux-moulin.net in French; r hotel €50-80, annexe €90-130, per person with half-board hotel €80-100, annexe €90-125; ☺ Mar-Oct; (P) (꙳)) Perched above the harbourside competition, Centuri's most prestigious lodging is really two places – the original building, which is a converted 19th-century *maison d'Américain,* and two more recently constructed annexes with deep balconies that offer more comfort but less character. This said, all rooms are furnished tastefully and with attractive period furniture. Its restaurant (mains €12 to €36, *menus* €30 to €60) has a lovely, deep shaded terrace.

Cavallu di Mare (☎ 06 16 20 14 19; daily specials around €10, giant salads €8-9, menu €15; ☺ noon-10pm Jul & Aug, lunch Easter-Jun & Sep) On the south side of the harbour, this simple eatery with its attractive stone terrace is the best budget option, offering generous portions and friendly service. It offers a free welcoming apéritif.

A Macciotta (☎ 04 95 35 64 12; menus €16.50-21) The slim terraces of this enticing gourmet option, with its fisherman's cottage interior, occupy both sides of the lane leading inland from the northern end of the port. It serves the best in seafood, including mussels with *brocciu*, squid salad and sea urchins, and a mean bouillabaisse. And they know their fish – here's another restaurant owner who casts his own nets.

PINO
pop 150

Should you pass through Pino around meal-time, **La Tour Génoise** (☎ 04 95 35 12 29; pizzas €8-10, mains €13-15, menus €18-30; ☺ lunch & dinner Jul & Aug,

lunch mid-Mar–Jun & Sep–mid-Oct) enjoys a pleasant setting amid a grove of mature trees. Reserve a table on its small terrace to enjoy superb sea views.

INLAND CHARMS

From Pino, you can continue to follow the coast southwards along the D80 as far as St-Florent. Alternatively, it's possible to hop eastwards, back over the mountains along the D180. This leads, via Luri, across the cape and down to the eastern shore at Santa Severa marina.

Even if you don't take this latter option, it's well worth making a 10km round-trip diversion along the D180 as far as the **Col de Santa Lucia** (381m). From it, a little vigorous leg stretching, mostly through mixed woodland, brings you to the **Tour de Sénèque** and perhaps the finest of the cape's many superlative-inducing panoramas.

Leave your car beside the dilapidated chapel at the col and follow the red flashes as far as a complex of abandoned buildings. Here the gradient becomes stiffer and you'll be using all four limbs to negotiate one brief stretch. But oh, the vista from the crumbling tower, embracing both Cap Corse's eastern and western shorelines and the Monte Stello range, the cape's north–south dorsal spine. Allow one hour for this fairly strenuous, hugely rewarding round-trip walk.

Around 5km beyond the col, **Luri** hosts a **wine fair** on the first or second weekend of July. Its small wine museum, **A Mimoria di u Vinu** (☎ 04 95 35 06 44; www.acunfraternita.com in French; adult/child €3/free; ☺ 10am-noon & 4-7pm Wed-Sat Jul & Aug, 10am-4.30pm Tue-Fri Jun & Sep) presents the history of Corsica's wine industry through a range of

---

MAISONS DES AMÉRICAINS

In the 19th century, many Corsicans emigrated to mainland France or to her colonies to escape poverty. Others headed to the Americas, especially the US, Venezuela, Puerto Rico and Peru to seek their fortune. In many hamlets of Cap Corse, only the eldest son of his generation remained behind. Just like contemporary migrants to Europe and America from the Indian subcontinent, some, having made their pile, returned to the villages of their birth and built themselves a fine residence, a *maison des américains.* In striking contrast to the more modest local rural architecture, these proud structures, often with a nod towards the Italian *palazzo* or colonial architecture, proudly asserted 'I have made it. Look at me and mine.'

Around Cap Corse, you can identify these extravagances by their sheer size, their generally rectangular shape and steep four-sided roofs. Adornment often includes a monumental staircase, a pillared balcony above the main entrance, the use of wrought iron for decoration and gardens planted with palms and exotic trees.

implements and a short video and offers an introduction to wine tasting.

Les Jardins Traditionnels du Cap Corse (☎ 04 95 35 05 07; admission €4; ☷ 10am-noon & 3-6.30pm Mon-Fri mid-Apr–mid-Oct), also in the *commune* of Luri, reserves and displays the indigenous plants and flora of the peninsula. After a wander through the gardens, visit the exhibition room and round off with time in the *maison du goût,* the tasting house, where you can sample and buy a range of products, all organic, grown by the voluntary association that runs the gardens.

CANARI

Gîte i Fioretti (☎ 04 95 37 13 90; www.ifioretti.com in French; d incl breakfast €60-70; ☷ year-round) Engage in an overnight retreat in one of the six rustically furnished cells, nowadays painted in soothing yellow, of this tastefully restored 16th-century Franciscan monastery. Each room overlooks either the sea or the vast internal courtyard.

✕ Au Bon Clocher (☎ 04 95 37 80 15; meals €30; ☷ Apr-Oct) Facing the village lighthouse, which later served as a bell tower *(le clocher)*, this impressive choice, in itself worth the detour into the village, engages its own private fisherman. About 100m below Gîte i Fioretti, it has a gorgeous terrace, where you'll be tempted to linger. The cuisine is subtle and innovative, with dishes such as *feuilleté de fruits de mer,* lightly seasoned with saffron and generous in its seafood quotient.

NONZA
pop 70

This charming hamlet is quite the most attractive on the cape's western coast. Presided over by a fortified tower, its stone houses seem about to tumble down the steep hillside and into the bay below. Enjoy a brief wander

through the meandering lanes, so tight and precipitous that no vehicle will ever negotiate them.

Nonza's social hub is **Café de la Tour**, with the village fountain topped by a squat bust of the ubiquitous Pascal Paoli beside it.

The ochre and oxblood façade of its 16th-century **Église Ste-Julie** rises from the roadside. Just to its north, a path descends to **Fontaine Ste-Julie**, a spring dedicated to Corsica's patron saint. A memorial plaque on the small shrine recalls that, in AD 303, 'St Julie was martyred and crucified for her Christian beliefs. After her death, her breasts were cut off and hurled against the rock, whence this miraculous spring arose'. From its twin outlets, the water flows cool on even the hottest day.

Below the fountain, the path drops sharply down to the long stripe of black shingle beach, little frequented at this end and great for Robinson Crusoe loneliness. To reach it by car, head 2km northwards along the D80, then cut along a narrow paved road that leads to the shore. Do take a sun umbrella, as there's no shade.

Opposite the church, take the steep streets that lead up to the 16th-century **tower** (admission free; ☷ 8am-sunset) for superb views across the village and the gulf beyond.

Sleeping & Eating
Casa Lisa (☎ 04 95 37 83 52; d €50-65) Casa Lisa has five simple rooms, a lovely garden overlooking the gulf and a fine flagstone staircase. It's well signed, down a set of winding paths opposite and just south of the church.

Casa Maria (☎ 04 95 37 80 95; www.casamaria-corse .com in French; d incl breakfast €80-140; ☷) This tastefully restored, warmly recommended 18th-century mansion sits beside the lane that ascends to the tower. Four of its five rooms

---

THE AUTHORS' CHOICE

Le Relais du Cap (☎ 04 95 37 86 52; www.relaisducap.com; d €40-65; ☷ Apr-Oct; ▣) Four kilometres south of Nonza hides the ultimate getaway. Take a track off the D80 to drop to the shoreline and this lone house perched on the rock at the end of the tiny hamlet of Olmeta du Cap.

It has four doubles with shared bathroom that offer staggering sea views and one self-contained apartment that can accommodate up to four people (doubles €80 to €100 plus per person €15). It's rented on a weekly basis (doubles €310 to €720 plus per person €50) in July and August. The genial, welcoming owners run their own boat, moored to the rocks, from where you can plunge straight into the sea. Alternatively, ease yourself in gently from the pebble beach, close at hand and overlooked by an intact Genoese tower.

The terrace with its spectacular vista as far as La Balagne has a barbecue and self-catering facilities. Here you take the copious buffet breakfast (€6).

BASTIA & THE FAR NORTH

CON MAN AND HERO

It was the year 1768 and French troops, invited to the island by Genoa, were firming their grip upon the island. Holed up in Nonza's tower as the French closed in was a lone Corsican officer, Captain Jacques Casella, and his soldiers. As the siege continued, his men prudently deserted him, slinking away one dark night and leaving behind most of their weapons.

Captain Casella, alone in the tower, prepared to take on the might of the French army. With a single cannon and a line of muskets abandoned by his soldiers, he managed to maintain a constant barrage and, incredibly, convinced his adversaries that there was a whole battalion holed up in the tower. The doughty captain finally surrendered, but not before he had negotiated that his force might march out with dignity. To the astonishment of the French troops, out hobbled the old warrior, alone and head held high.

have sea views and three sit harmoniously beneath the sloping roof. There's a large vine-shaded garden into which banks of purple bougainvillea cascade. Ask the friendly owners about the love letters, found in a crack of the wall, penned over a century ago by the village teacher to their distant relative Marie.

U Franghju (☎ 04 95 37 82 16; mains €8.50-13, menu €21; ◷ May–mid-Oct) Beside the church, this small restaurant has a lovely little terrace, shaded by a lone plane tree, with panoramic views over the sea. It has a short, creative and regularly changing à la carte selection, chalked on a slate.

LE NEBBIO

The Nebbio, relatively lightly travelled, is something of a buffer zone, squeezed between Bastia and Cap Corse to its north and La Balagne with its coastal fleshpots and rugged interior beauty extending to the south.

West of the fashionable St-Florent stretch the little-visited expanses of the Désert des Agriates, desiccated, perhaps a little forbidding but rewarding for those who enjoy solitude and make the effort to penetrate its emptiness. The Nebbio's also one of the island's prime wine-producing areas. There are over 30 vineyards, still in the hands of small-scale producers in and around Patrimonio. This, the first Corsican region to be granted AOC status, still produces some of the island's finest vintages.

ST-FLORENT (SAN FIURENZU)
pop 1500

St-Florent, the Nebbio's main town – in fact its only place of any size – is a chic resort, a kind of St-Tropez in miniature locals would have you believe. Indeed if you stroll along

the quayside overlooking the marina, where luxury yachts the size of a your house are moored, you see what they're driving at. The town compensates for the absence of major monuments (the cathedral, the one building of historical interest, requires a measure of tenacity if you're to gain access) with delightful nearby beaches. And, for a place of its size, St-Florent has some first-class dining options.

Orientation
St-Florent is little more than a village and is easily navigable on foot. The main D81 road from Bastia and Patrimonio skirts the eastern side of the town and leads into place des Portes, the main square. The narrow streets of the small old town stretch northwards towards place Doria. Crossing the River Poggio, the D81 continues south towards Oletta, while sandy Plage de la Roya stretches westwards.

Information
Casa Lav' (◷ 9am-9pm) Not what you might think but a laundrette.

Conca Micro (rte de la Cathédrale; per hr €4.50; ◷ 9am-11pm Mon-Sat, 9am-noon & 5.30-8pm Sun Jul & Aug, 9am-noon & 2-7pm Mon-Sat Sep-Jun) Has eight computers for internet access.

Post office Shares the Centre Administratif with the tourist office and town hall.

Presse Centrale (place des Portes) Sells foreign newspapers, maps and film.

Tourist office (☎ 04 95 37 06 04; ◷ core hours 9am-noon & 2-5pm Mon-Fri, 9am-noon Sat)

Sights
An easy, not even 10-minute ascent from the harbour brings you to the rather forlorn tumbledown outer bulwarks of the **citadel**. Built under the Genoese, its much-restored interior is closed to the public. What makes the climb

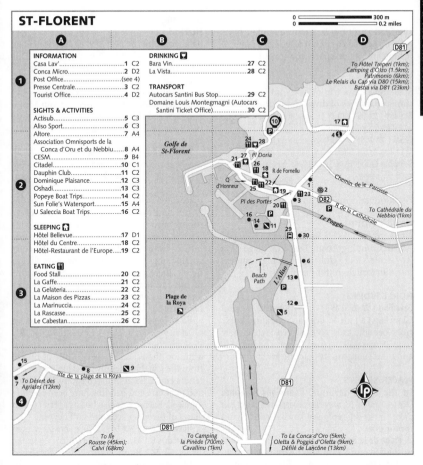

ST-FLORENT

INFORMATION	
Casa Lav'.....................................**1**	C2
Conca Micro...............................**2**	D2
Post Office..............................(see 4)	
Presse Centrale.........................**3**	C2
Tourist Office............................**4**	D2

SIGHTS & ACTIVITIES	
Actisub.......................................**5**	C3
Aliso Sport.................................**6**	C3
Altore..**7**	A4
Association Omnisports de la	
Conca d'Oru et du Nebbiu.....**8**	A4
CESM...**9**	B4
Citadel.....................................**10**	C1
Dauphin Club...........................**11**	C2
Dominique Plaisance................**12**	C3
Oshadi.....................................**13**	C3
Popeye Boat Trips...................**14**	C2
Sun Folie's Watersport............**15**	A4
U Saleccia Boat Trips..............**16**	C2

SLEEPING	
Hôtel Bellevue..........................**17**	D1
Hôtel du Centre........................**18**	C2
Hôtel-Restaurant de l'Europe.....**19**	C2

EATING	
Food Stall.................................**20**	C2
La Gaffe...................................**21**	C2
La Gelateria.............................**22**	C2
La Maison des Pizzas................**23**	C2
La Marinuccia..........................**24**	C2
La Rascasse.............................**25**	C2
Le Cabestan............................**26**	C2

DRINKING	
Bara Vin..................................**27**	C2
La Vista...................................**28**	C2

TRANSPORT	
Autocars Santini Bus Stop.........**29**	C2
Domaine Louis Montegmagni (Autocars	
Santini Ticket Office)................**30**	C2

worthwhile is the eagle's eye panorama from the ample terrace that extends beneath it.

Absurdly, the one historical sight of real interest in St-Florent isn't easy to visit. The **Cathédrale du Nebbio** (Église Santa-Maria-Assunta; admission €1), a fine example of 12th-century Pisan religious architecture, is about 1km east of the town centre on the site of an ancient Roman settlement. Even the tourist office couldn't tell us its short and arbitrary opening hours. Try your luck and ask there in the first instance.

Activities
BOAT TRIPS

From June to mid-September two companies organise boat trips to the superb **Plage du Loto** (also called Plage du Lodo, du Lodu and, to complete the confusion, du Lotu), on the edge of the Désert des Agriates, in turn an easy 30 minutes' walk from the equally superb **Plage de Saleccia**. En route, boats cruise past the ruined Genoese Tour de la Mortella.

The **Popeye** (☎ 04 95 37 19 07; adult/child €11/6) is an old fishing boat that sets sail six times daily from 8.45am to 3.15pm. The journey to Plage du Loto takes around 30 minutes and the last return sailing is at 7.30pm.

The launch **U Saleccia** (☎ 06 17 50 65 58; adult/child €11/6) departs from just along the quay a similar six times daily between 8.15am and 2.30pm. The last return boat for the day sails at 6.45pm.

BASTIA & THE FAR NORTH

CYCLING

Aliso Sport (☎ 04 95 37 03 50) rents mountain bikes (€18/85 per day/week). It also sells a range of fishing and water-sports equipment.

DIVING

St-Florent has a trio of dive outfits, offering similar packages of dives and courses.

Actisub (☎ 06 12 10 29 71; www.actisub.com in French; quai d'Aliso; ☺ Jun-Sep)

CESM (☎ 04 95 37 00 61; www.cesm.net; ☺ Apr-Oct) At La Roya beach. Offers sailing and windsurfing courses.

Dauphin Club (☎ 06 14 62 84 46; ☺ year-round) In the main marina.

For more information on diving see p79.

HANG GLIDING

Altore (☎ 06 88 21 49 16; www.altore.com; ☺ Apr-Oct), within Camping Acqua Dolce on Plage de la Roya, offers hang gliding, including a tandem introductory flight for beginners.

HORSE RIDING

Cavallinu (☎ 06 82 45 93 11; ☺ year-round), behind Camping La Pinède, does accompanied horse rides (per hour €15), plus a signed circular route (one hour at walking pace), where children ride and indulgent parents hold the lead.

WATER SPORTS

In the main harbour, **Dominique Plaisance** (☎ 04 95 37 07 08; www.dominiqueplaisance.com; quai d'Aliso; ☺ Apr-Oct) rents sea kayaks, canoes and motor boats.

Plage de la Roya is a gorgeous long ribbon of sand around 2km southwest of the town centre. Here, a couple of outfits seek to sever you from your beach towel:

Association Omnisports de la Conca d'Oru et du Nebbiu (☎ 06 12 10 23 27; www.corskayak.com in French; ☺ Apr–mid-Oct) Offers rental, courses and accompanied outings in kayaks, catamarans and windsurf.

Sun Folie's Watersport (☎ 06 13 07 39 83; www.sun folies.com in French; ☺ mid-May–Sep) Rents everything from pedalos to sleek motor boats. Also does water skiing (per 10 minutes €25), banana rides (€10) and flyfishing (€20) from its beachside base.

RELAXEZ-VOUS

Oshadi (☎ 04 95 37 00 21; quai de l'Aliso) is a shop and café that peddles healthy eating supplements and organic produce. It's one of the few such places on the island, has a *hammam* (€10) and does massages (€45).

Sleeping
HOTELS

Hôtel du Centre (☎ 04 95 37 00 68, fax 04 95 37 41 01; rue de Fornellu; d €45-70, tr €60-75; ☺ year-round) This attractive option in the heart of the action has been run by the same dynamic proprietress for nearly 40 years. Most of its 12 simple but well-maintained rooms offer harbour views. Families should ask for No 9, a large suite (€80) on the 1st floor with two interconnecting doubles.

Hôtel-Restaurant de l'Europe (☎ 04 95 37 00 03; www.hotel-europe2.com in French; place des Portes; r €48-88, tr €62-110; ☺ mid-Jan–Oct; ⚡) Run by a local family – two brothers and their sister – this place has a prime location right on place des Portes and overlooking the harbour. All 17 rooms have high ceilings and most have attractive, if on occasion careworn, antique furniture. Rooms 7 and 24, each with a balcony overlooking the harbour, are the plum choice. Below, there's a great café terrace and recommended restaurant (*menus* €22) that sources local producers for most of its supplies and regularly changes its *menus*.

Hôtel Treperi (☎ 04 95 37 40 20; www.treperi.com in French; d €59-89, tr €81-111; ☺ Easter-Oct; P ⚡) Peeking above the vineyards and perched on a hilltop that catches every whiff of breeze from the sea, this friendly hotel has a pool and tennis court. Each of its 18 rooms has a safe, and furniture and bedding have been recently renewed. Each room also boasts a terrace with views of the vineyards and gulf beyond.

Hôtel Bellevue (☎ 04 95 37 00 06; www.bellevue.com .fr in French; s €65-139, d €71-147, q €80-155; ☺ Apr-Oct; P ⚡ ⚡ ⚡) Rooms, attractively furnished in blue and white and some with twin wash-basins, have wrought-iron bedsteads and a large fridge. Eight in a separate ground-floor wing have a terrace and overlook the extensive garden. There's direct access to a small pebble beach and wi-fi.

CAMPING

Camping d'Olzo (☎ 04 95 37 03 34; www.campingolzo.com; camp sites per adult/tent/car €6/4.50/4; ☺ Apr-Oct) This smallish camping ground has shady pitches and decent facilities. It's 2km northeast along the D81, in the direction of Patrimonio. The friendly Italian owner fires up pizzas nightly in a wood oven and cooks lasagne to order.

Camping La Pinède (☎ 04 95 37 07 26; www.camping -la-pinede.com; camp sites €18-25; ☺ May-Sep; ⚡) Beside the River Aliso it has its own pool. It's a quiet spot, shaded by mature pines, willows and eucalyptus. For an extra €7 per night, you can enjoy a choice riverside pitch. It hires out camping fridges (per night €4) too.

Eating
RESTAURANTS
Quai d'Honneur and its continuation towards the harbour bar is one long line of restaurants, each of which merits more than a glance.

Le Cabestan (☎ 04 95 37 05 70; rue de Fornello; mains €11-18; ☺ mid-Apr–Oct) This barrel-vaulted tunnel of a place with a small mezzanine floor is very much of the island. There's polyphonic singing sotto voce in the background and it does a great value *menu Corse* (€17). The *daurade* (sea bream), peppered and stuffed with tomato, lemon and herbs from the maquis, is grilled to perfection.

La Gaffe (☎ 04 95 37 0012; Marina; mains €12-27, menu €28; ☺ Wed-Sun, dinner Mon & Tue) Here's a tempting if rather different quayside terrace restaurant, in business for over 30 years. Chantal Bourneuf, the chef (and a woman in this male-dominated profession), offers superb fish and seafood, prime ingredients plucked from the sea, cooked simply and with care. Her *menu*, sampled slowly on the quayside terrace, accompanied by a bottle of local Domaine Gentile white will linger long on the palate.

La Maison des Pizzas (☎ 04 95 37 08 52; pizzas €7-11, mains €14-22) Recognisable by its signature red and white linen and right on place des Portes, this attractive choice offers much more than your standard pizzas and prepares quality meat and fish dishes. It's also the only restaurant in town that stays open year-round. Eat on the terrace, in the low-beamed interior or, for a picnic pizza, order at the little serving hatch for takeaways.

La Rascasse (☎ 04 95 37 06 99; quai d'Honneur; mains €15-29, menu €38; ☺ mid-Mar–Oct) You can dine in the brick-arched interior or at its harbourside terrace, where the giant yachts moor. It offers the finest fish and seafood, served in tempting, attractively presented morsels and with a smile. All in all, a delightful gastronomic experience.

La Marinuccia (☎ 04 95 37 04 36; mains €20.50-28, menu €20.60; ☺ Wed-Mon, dinner Tue May-Oct) La Marinuccia, feet in the water and the citadel's ramparts looming above, sits beside a quiet little cove that you never even knew existed. You can dine in the vaulted interior or on the

wooden terrace with the sea lapping below. To get here take the signed lane off place Doria. Mains are expensive, its wine even more so, but the *menu touristique* represents great value.

QUICK EATS
La Gelateria (rue de Fornellu) You'll probably have to wait a while in line at this popular ice-cream stall, which offers over 50 different flavours. All the usual favourites are there to be scooped plus more original ones such as ginger, maquis herbs, lemon liqueur and liquorice.

For a quick snack, there's a simple wooden food stall just south of place des Portes that does good, giant salads (€8) and panini (€6) to take away.

Drinking & Entertainment
Bara Vin (place Doria; ☺ 6pm-late May-Sep) With its impressive range of AOC Patrimonio wines (€3.50 to €6.30) and a terrace spilling onto place Doria, this is the place for an early evening apéritif. You can snack or turn the experience into a full dinner; it does a large selection of tapas (€3 to €6), a cheese platter and a meze plate (€13).

La Vista (☎ 04 95 37 10 83; place Doria; ☺ from 10pm Jun-Sep) This piano bar metamorphoses into a discothèque at weekends.

La Conca d'Oro (☎ 04 95 39 00 46; www.concaclub.com in French; rte d'Oletta) In high summer this open-air discothèque, 5km southeast of town on the Oletta road, pounds until dawn.

Getting There & Around
Autocars Santini (☎ 04 95 37 02 98) runs a twice-daily bus service (€5, one hour, 6.45am and 2pm Monday to Saturday) to Bastia. In July and August, it also operates a twice-daily service to Île Rousse (€10, one hour, 11am and 6pm Monday to Saturday). The bus stops opposite the shop of Domaine Louis Montemagni, about 200m south of place des Portes.

There are two paying car parks where the River Aliso meets the marina and another free one beside rte de la Cathédrale.

PATRIMONIO
pop 650
Patrimonio, 6km from St-Florent, has two principal claims to fame: its vineyards and its annual guitar festival. You'll recognise the

Osteria di San Martinu (☎ 04 95 37 11 93; mains €13-15; ☽ May-Sep) This Osteria specialises in plentiful meat dishes, grilled over vine wood and served on its large, open terrace (we savoured the lamb chops, juicy, tender and still pink in the middle). It does a magnificent four-course *menu Corse* (€20). Here too, portions are large and choosing a starter – should it be a giant platter of local charcuterie, or the vegetable soup with pasta that you're more eating than drinking? – is particularly agonising. The house carafe red and rosé wines (supplied by Domaine Lazzarini, just up the road and run by the owner's brother) are exceptional value.

village from a distance by its 16th-century Église St-Martin, a stout stone construction of granite and brown schist watching over the village that's become an informal icon for the Corsican wine industry.

The wines – crisp dry whites, rosés more golden than pink and robust, opaque reds – well merit your attention. The sweet fruity muscat dessert wine, once exported in quantity by the Genoese, now rarely gets beyond the island.

The chalk and clay soil has been used for growing vines ever since Roman times and the Patrimonio area was the first in all Corsica to be granted an Appellation d'Origine Contrôlée (AOC) seal of quality. Today a signed *route des vins* (ask at the St-Florent tourist office for its slender *AOC Patrimonio: La Route des Vins* brochure) leads from St-Florent through the vineyards of Patrimonio and around nearly 500 hectares of land cultivated for wine by over 30 small growers. Most of the wineries welcome passing visitors for tastings without appointment.

Wine Cellar Visits

Among the recommended *caves*:
Domaine Gentile (☎ 04 95 37 01 54) Perhaps the most exclusive *cru*.
Domaine Lazzarini (☎ 04 95 37 18 60) Primarily muscat and reds.
Domaine Leccia (☎ 04 95 37 11 35) Excellent reds that regularly win awards.
Domaine Orenga de Gaffory (☎ 04 95 37 45 00) The pick of the full-bodied reds.

INLAND NEBBIO

We describe a tour of around 70km that takes in the Nebbio's inland villages, possible in half a day but better taken at a more leisurely pace, perhaps with an overnight stop en route.

From St-Florent, take the D81 northwards and drop into Patrimonio if you haven't already visited it (should you be off to a late start, Osteria di San Martinu there makes a great lunch stop).

Otherwise, continue to the **Col de Teghime** (536m), high up on the island's spine and straddling the mountains between Bastia and St-Florent. Less than a kilometre beyond the pass, take a narrow tarred road left for the steep 4.5km ascent to the summit of the **Sierra di Pigno** (961m), bristling with radio and telephone antennae. From its windy top, there are soul-stirring views in all directions: eastwards as far as the Italian island of Elba on a clear day, west to the bay of St-Florent and Désert des Agriates, north over the snaggle-toothed peaks of Cap Corse, while below sprawls Bastia, extending almost to the shimmering waters of the Étang de Biguglia.

(Just below the pass, on its eastern side, descending towards Bastia – and mercifully not on today's route – is a less compelling site: a massive open-air rubbish tip where flocks of birds wheel and scavenge.)

Return to the col and take the signed D38 left to pass through the straggling hamlets of **Poggio d'Oletta** and **Oletta**, dominated by its 18th-century Église de San Cervone. At the northern entrance to Oletta, just off the D38, **L'Auberge A Magina** (☎ 04 95 39 01 01; menu €15, mains €15-20; ☽ Tue-Sun Apr-Oct) has great views across the Nebbio from its terrace.

At the roundabout marking the **Col de Santu Stefanu**, 4km beyond Oletta, we suggest a branching programme. But first pause at the second of two monuments honouring the Moroccan troops and their French officers who, at this strategic spot and at the Col de Teghime, battled their way in 1943 to take Bastia, the first French town to be liberated from Axis rule.

From the roundabout, two roads, the D62 and the D82, snake around the deep gash of the **Défilé de Lancône**, then drop to the N193 and the coast. For a switchback thrill, follow the more spectacular D62 for a kilometre or two, as it creeps along the contours of this narrow gorge, then return to the roundabout, to take the exit signed **Murato**.

You can't miss the gorgeous Pisan Romanesque **Église de San Michele de Murato** with its distinctive green and white stripes and checkerboard patterning. The white blocks (of chalk) came from St-Florent and the green (ophite) was quarried from the bed of the nearby River Bevincu. Naive figurines in basalt peer down from the upper reaches. It dates from around 1140, and local legend has it that the church was built in just one night by angels.

During Corsica's brief independence in the 18th century, the village, a kilometre or so further along the road, was the seat of the mint where the coins of the new state were struck.

If night's approaching by now, there's a restaurant and a warmly recommended *chambres d'hôtes* just a short drive away. For both, you'll need to pre-plan and reserve in advance.

Around 4km outside Murato, **Ferme-Auberge Campo di Monte** (☎ 04 95 37 64 39; menu €45; 🕑 dinner daily mid-Jun–mid-Sep, dinner Thu-Sat, lunch Sun mid-Sep–mid-Jun) is a truly exceptional restaurant in a glorious setting within its own grounds. After sipping an apéritif on the terrace, you progress to the restaurant and one of the tastefully furnished small rooms – almost niches – within a lovely slate roofed stone building. And the *menu*? Well, it's according to the whim of the *patronne*. But, as thousands of satisfied clients will attest, be assured that you're in for a great gastronomic experience. She doesn't accept credit cards so pack your wallet. To get there, turn left beside Victor Bar in Murato, direction Rutali, then take a signed dirt track on the right.

From Murato, retrace your route to the by now familiar roundabout at Col de Santu Stefanu.

A left turn down the D62 will bring you, after 2km, to the hamlet of **Vallecalle** and, 500m below the church, **Chambres d'Hôtes Gaucher** (☎ 04 95 37 60 60; http://hotescorses.free.fr; s €41-51, d €53-63, tr €73-93, q €83-103; 🕑 year-round; P). This delightful, rambling 18th-century mansion has been comprehensively and tastefully renovated by the Gaucher family (Mme Gaucher, an architect, contributing the design and her husband, who speaks excellent English and is knowledgeable about the island, the heavy manual labour). There are only three bedrooms, each vast and minimally furnished with crisp sheets and cream bedspreads. Outside, you can enjoy the lovely garden and terrace with striking views. If you'd like dinner (a bargain €17 including wine and coffee), you'll need to order in advance.

To return to St-Florent from Col de Santu Stefanu, lock onto the D82 and follow it back through Oletta and on to the coast.

DÉSERT DES AGRIATES

Between St-Florent and the mouth of the Ostriconi River lies an arid landscape known as the Désert des Agriates, an area of low chalky mountains and a maquis so sun-scorched that even the plants seem rocklike.

It's hard to believe this area was once Genoa's breadbasket. Indeed, right up until the 20th century, life in the area was governed alternately by the rhythms of seasonal livestock grazing and sowing. In October, shepherds from the Nebbio highlands and the Vallée d'Asco would bring their goats and sheep down for the winter. In June, farmers arriving by boat from Cap Corse would take over the area. At one time, the region was as famous for its olive groves as those of the Balagne villages (p139). The widespread use

NUITS DE LA GUITARE

The **Association Les Nuits de la Guitare** (☎ 04 95 37 12 15; www.festival-guitare-patrimonio.com) organises Guitar Nights, one of the highlights of Corsica's summer calendar. From humble beginnings and for a week each year in July, the festival, which will be celebrating its 20th anniversary in 2008, puts the tiny Nebbio village of Patrimonio on the map for something other than its excellent wines.

The programme is eclectic and in any one year might include Corsican, classical and flamenco guitar and styles as diverse as rock, salsa, blues and jazz. The 2006 lineup, for example, included artistes as diverse as Joe Satriani, the Ron Carter jazz trio, flamenco maestro Vicente Amigo and Led Zeppelin front man Robert Plant.

Events take place in the open-air Théâtre de Verdure de Patrimonio on an outdoor stage flanked by a couple of menhir statues.

Tickets (€30 to €35) are available from selected music and bookshops across Corsica.

of *écobuage* (cultivation on burnt stubble) and fires fanned by the prevailing winds are mainly to blame for transforming its once-fertile soil into a stony, barren desert.

The 35km of coastline, by contrast, offer spectacular back-to-nature scenery. The outstanding **Plage de Saleccia** – setting for the film *The Longest Day* (1960) – stretches for nearly 1km, its shimmering white sand and turquoise waters comparing favourably with any tropical island paradise.

The smaller but equally stunning **Plage du Loto** and **Plage de l'Ostriconi**, at the eastern and western edges of the Agriates region respectively, are also superb. Some claim the latter has the finest-grained sand in all of Europe.

Various harebrained schemes were proposed to transform the desert in the 1970s – including building a Club Med–style holiday complex. All were resisted and nowadays the full 5000-odd hectares of the Désert des Agriates enjoy protected status.

There's a small **information office** (☎ 04 95 37 09 86; year-round) on the D81 towards the hamlet of Casta.

Sleeping & Eating

Relais de Saleccia (☎ 04 95 37 14 60; www.hotel-corse -saleccia.com in French; d €43-68; mid-Apr–Sep) Beside the D81 in Casta, 12km west of St-Florent, this is a friendly place whose café-restaurant (mains €8 to €13) has a terrace with sweeping views over the Désert, as do the most appealing of its 11 simple rooms. It rents mountain bikes (see right).

The following are your overnight options along the Plage de la Roya to Ostriconi Walk (opposite), otherwise accessible only by boat, bike or 4WD.

Camping-Restaurant U Paradisu (☎ 04 95 37 82 51; Plage de la Saleccia; camp sites per adult/tent €5/2.50, bungalows per person €15; year-round) Slumber in one of the bungalows (it's wise to book in advance) or just roll up and camp. Either way, you'll enjoy a wonderful site, where you can almost dip your feet in the waters of the Plage de la Saleccia. Pitches are shady and there's a small grocery store, where you can stock up on provisions for the next day. Meals are available (mains €15 to €20).

Les Paillers de Ghignu (reserve through the Désert des Agriates information office ☎ 04 95 37 09 86; per person €10; Apr-Oct) These restored huts were once occupied by shepherds during the winter transhumance. Conveniently located just near the Plage de Ghignu, the huts offer basic shelter (bring your own sleeping bag). There are hot showers and a spring that flows past nearby where you can replenish your water bottles.

Camping de l'Ostriconi (☎ 04 95 60 10 05; www .village-ostriconi.com in French; camp sites per adult/tent/car €7/3/3; Easter-Sep;) Just off the D81 and close to Plage de l'Ostriconi with its soft sand, this well-equipped camping ground also rents bungalows (€35 to €90 according to size and season), should you fancy a little cosseting after your trek.

Getting There & Away

BICYCLE

The most fulfilling, if the most taxing, way. Relais de Saleccia (left) rents mountain bikes (€17 per day). A sandy track takes off from the D81, 500m west of this small hotel, and snakes down to the Plage de Saleccia. Allow three to 3½ hours for the ride and build in time to explore and laze on the beach.

THE PRESIDENT & THE TERRORIST

At the age of 58 Raúl Leoni was voted president of Venezuela in the December 1963 elections. His Murato-born father, Clément Leoni, had left Bastia for Caracas at the age of 22 to try his luck in the South American republic about a decade before the future president was born there. Raúl Leoni made his first and only visit to Corsica in 1970, but father and son are both now heralded as symbols of successful Corsican migration. Leoni's opponent in the 1963 election, Arturo Uslar Pietri, a distinguished man of letters, was also of Corsican descent.

Born in Murato in 1790, Giuseppe Fieschi was yet another kind of émigré. A sometime shepherd, sometime solider, he organised an attempt on the life of the Orleanist citizen king of France, Louis-Philippe, and the royal family, during the fifth-anniversary celebration of the July 1830 revolution that overthrew the last Bourbon monarch, held in Paris. The daring assassination attempt failed but 19 people were killed and many more injured. Fieschi and his accomplices were condemned to death and executed a year later.

PLAGE DE LA ROYA TO OSTRICONI WALK

A fairly long but hugely fulfilling two-day trek takes you along the coastal path that starts at St-Florent's **Plage de la Roya** and threads westwards as far as the estuary of the River Ostriconi. The Désert des Agriates information office in Costa and St-Florent's tourist office both carry a slim leaflet that gives a skeletal description of the route. For the few sleeping possibilities along the way, see p122.

A 5½-hour walk from Plage de la Roya brings you to **Saleccia**; it's immensely tempting to linger on the magnificent stretch of sand and overnight here. This is quite possible since there are two sleeping options, but it will leave you with a long second day.

Otherwise, push on for another 2¾ hours to **Ghignu** and its basic accommodation, then set out fresh next morning for the 6½-hour final leg as far as **Ostriconi**.

In high summer, the midday sun sears and reflects from the water. Take a hat and plenty of water, hit the trail early and perhaps hole up for a couple of hours when the sun's at its zenith.

BOAT

The most pleasant and effortless way of getting to the Plage du Loto jetty is by boat in an easy day trip from St-Florent (p117).

CAR

The D81 skirts the Désert des Agriates' southern fringe. Two roads branch off from the D81 into the desert proper. Both about 12km long, one leads to Saleccia while the other terminates at Ghignu. Each is suitable only for 4WDs and is rough and very stony. The two tracks are even more difficult to negotiate when the rain has dug deep ruts in the ground that are then baked hard by the sun.

Calvi & La Balagne

Two of Corsica's finest seaside towns, each with a gorgeous beach, an interior with scenery that's gentler on the eye than the starkness of so much of inland Corsica, rural hamlets that ooze character and a southern coastal fringe with a hold-on-to-your-hat coastal drive: the Balagne is almost a microcosm of the island.

Calvi, landing point for the tens of thousands who pour off the ferries from mainland France and Italy and one of the first Corsican towns to embrace tourism, contrasts with its quieter northern neighbour, Île Rousse. Linking them is the dinkiest train you've ever bucked and swayed on, a great ride for its own sake and sole means of access to lots of getaway beaches and coves.

Inland is another, more tranquil world where low hills unfurl eastwards from the coastal plain to the Monte Cinto massif. Man has left his stamp upon the interior, often called the 'garden' or 'orchard' of Corsica, reflecting its fertile soil and mild microclimate. Citrus orchards and ancient olive groves abound despite recurrent and devastating fires, the latest and among the most disastrous as recently as 2005. The craft hamlets of Pigna and Lama; the fortress villages of Speloncato and Sant'Antonino, each perched atop a knoll with heartstopping 360-degree views; Calenzana, starting point of two major long-distance trails and bustling with walkers – these and others each tempt you to linger.

Too gentle for you? Need a little adrenalin pumping? Then take the coastal drive from Calvi to Galéria. Both the scenery and thrill of the drive are heartstopping in equal measure.

HIGHLIGHTS

- **Scents of the Maquis**
  Linger in the Parc de Saleccia (p136), savouring the trees, shrubs and flowers of the island

- **Seek Your Fortune**
  Explore the abandoned silver mine at Argentella (p135)

- **Shopping**
  Snoop out local specialities along the Balagne craft trail (p139)

- **Music Maestro**
  Bop with the best at the renowned jazz festival in Calvi (p130) or hum to Corsican choral singing at Festivoce in Pigna (p144)

- **Bump & Sway**
  Jump aboard the Tramways de Balagne (p133) for an unforgettable trip along the coastline

★ Parc de Saleccia
★ Tramways de Balagne
★ Pigna   ★ Balagne Craft Trail
★ Calvi
★ Argentella

LA BALAGNE

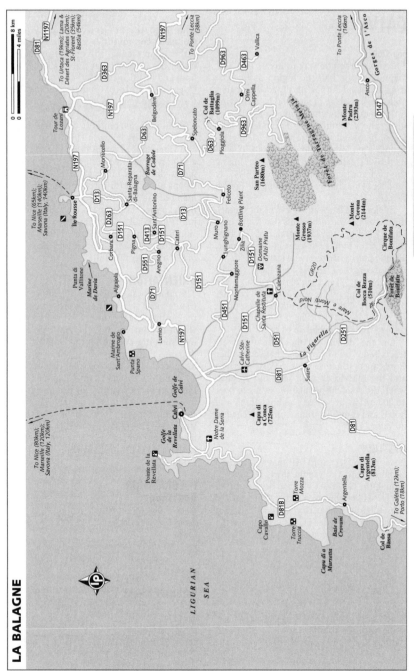

CALVI

pop 5200

The most dramatic way to arrive in Calvi, 'capital' of the Balagne region, is by boat from mainland Europe, ideally as dawn bursts above its backdrop of mountains. A thriving little town, it stretches lazily along the bay under the watchful eye of its citadel. It's the Corsican town that's closest to the Mediterranean coast of metropolitan France and, with its thriving café culture, restaurants ringing the port and sandy beach, it resembles any number of the smaller towns along the French Riviera.

Explore the lanes and alleys of the citadel, dine at one of the restaurants that fringe quai Landry, loll on the long strand of beach to the south or indulge in some more strenuous aquatic activity. Do reserve at least half a day to jump aboard the Tramways de Balagne (see the boxed text, p133) and trundle to Île Rousse and back, stopping off at some delightful beaches on the way. Calvi is also a major access point for the villages of the Balagne interior (see the driving route described on p139).

On the downside, the little town attracts more holidaymakers than any other Corsican destination except Porto-Vecchio and the Ajaccio area. In July and August, when the resident population swells to over 40,000, prices are correspondingly high and hotels and camping grounds are stretched to bursting.

HISTORY

It was in the 1st century AD that the Romans laid the foundations of the town of Calvi, although the Golfe de Calvi had been a port of call for sailors from even earlier times. Sacked subsequently by Barbary raiders, Calvi got back on its feet under the Pisans between the 11th and the 13th centuries. Rivalries between local lords, especially those from Cap Corse, finally led the population to turn to Genoa for protection in 1278. The then-powerful republic on the Italian mainland could not have asked for better luck and wasted no time in turning the inhabitants of Calvi into good Genoese citizens. Using Calvi as a base, along with the southern town of Bonifacio (which it already controlled), Genoa was able to exert its power over the rest of the island.

Calvi came to be so totally identified with its loyalty to Genoa that many other Corsican communities considered Calvi, rather than Genoa, the oppressor. It was under the Genoese that Calvi's citadel was built and fortified against the outside world. Over the centuries of Genoese overlordship, Calvi would nevertheless be put sorely to the test.

In the mid-16th century Corsica was caught up in the rivalry between Henri II of France and Charles V of Spain (king of Spain and also holy Roman emperor). In 1553 France dispatched a squadron made up of French troops and Turkish forces under the command of the Turkish privateer Dragut. This fleet captured Bastia, St-Florent and Bonifacio but failed to take Calvi. It was on this occasion that Genoa gave the town its motto in recognition: *Civitas Calvi Semper Fidelis* (City of Calvi forever faithful).

ORIENTATION

The citadel – also known as the upper town *(haute ville)* – is built on a promontory to the northeast of the lower town *(basse ville)*, which is home to most of the town's eating, sleeping and shopping options. The hub of activity by day is centred around the long beach that stretches southeast of town. By night it transfers to quai Landry (along the front of the marina) for bars, beers and brasseries. Blvd Wilson is the main shopping street and the place to find banks and shops. Rue Alsace Lorraine, part of the small cobbled pedestrianised area, is worth a browse for its handful of artisan workshops and craft studios.

INFORMATION
Bookshops

Black 'n' Blue (20 blvd Wilson) French and a few foreign-language books, guides, maps and a selection of Corsican CDs.

Press'Info (av de la République) A good range of French-language and foreign newspapers, magazines and guidebooks.

Internet Access

Café de l'Orient (16 quai Landry; €1 connection plus per min €0.10; ☺ 10am-midnight) Quayside café with a set of computer terminals.

Corsica 2B Informatique (av Santa Maria; per hr €3; ☺ 9.15am-9pm Mon-Sat, 3.30-9pm Sun) Half the price and twice as fast.

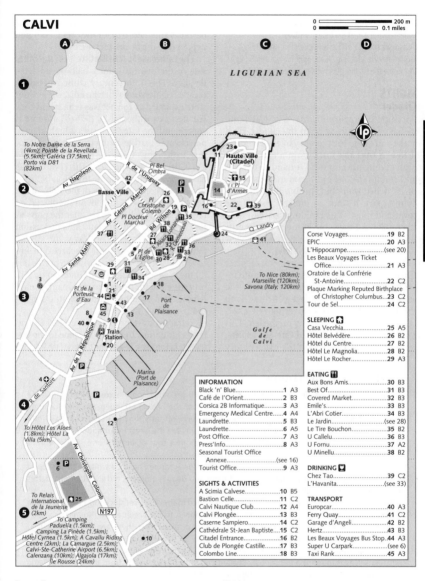

CALVI

LIGURIAN SEA

Haute Ville
(Citadel)

To Notre Dame de la Serra
(4km); Pointe de la Revellata
(5.5km); Galéria (37.5km);
Porto via D81
(82km)

Pl d'Armes

Basse Ville

Pl
Christophe
Colomb

Pl Docteur
Marchal

Q Landry

To Nice (80km);
Marseille (120km);
Savona (Italy, 120km)

Pl de
l'Église

Pl de la
Porteuse
d'Eau

Port
de
Plaisance

**Golfe
de
Calvi**

Train
Station

Marina
(Port de
Plaisance)

To Hôtel Les Aloes
(1.8km); Hôtel La
Villa (5km)

To Relais
International
de la Jeunesse
(2km)

N197

To Camping
Paduella (1.5km);
Camping La Pinède (1.5km);
Hôtel Cyrnea (1.5km); A Cavallu Riding
Centre (2km); La Camargue (2.5km);
Calvi-Ste-Catherine Airport (6.5km);
Calenzana (10km); Algajola (17km);
Île Rousse (24km)

INFORMATION	
Black 'n' Blue	**1** A3
Café de l'Orient	**2** B3
Corsica 2B Informatique	**3** A3
Emergency Medical Centre	**4** A4
Laundrette	**5** B3
Laundrette	**6** A5
Post Office	**7** A3
Press'Info	**8** A3
Seasonal Tourist Office Annexe	(see 16)
Tourist Office	**9** A3

SIGHTS & ACTIVITIES	
A Scimia Calvese	**10** B5
Bastion Celle	**11** C2
Calvi Nautique Club	**12** A4
Calvi Plongée	**13** B3
Caserne Sampiero	**14** C2
Cathédrale St-Jean Baptiste	**15** C2
Citadel Entrance	**16** B2
Club de Plongée Castille	**17** B3
Colombo Line	**18** B3

Corse Voyages	**19** B2
EPIC	**20** A3
L'Hippocampe	(see 20)
Les Beaux Voyages Ticket Office	**21** A3
Oratoire de la Confrérie St-Antoine	**22** C2
Plaque Marking Reputed Birthplace of Christopher Columbus	**23** C2
Tour de Sel	**24** C2

SLEEPING	
Casa Vecchia	**25** A5
Hôtel Belvédère	**26** B2
Hôtel du Centre	**27** B2
Hôtel Le Magnolia	**28** B2
Hôtel Le Rocher	**29** A3

EATING	
Aux Bons Amis	**30** B3
Best Of	**31** B3
Covered Market	**32** B3
Emile's	**33** B3
L'Abri Cotier	**34** B3
Le Jardin	(see 28)
Le Tire Bouchon	**35** B3
U Callelu	**36** B3
U Fornu	**37** A2
U Minellu	**38** B2

DRINKING	
Chez Tao	**39** C2
L'Havanita	(see 33)

TRANSPORT	
Europcar	**40** A3
Ferry Quay	**41** C2
Garage d'Angeli	**42** B2
Hertz	**43** B3
Les Beaux Voyages Bus Stop	**44** A3
Super U Carpark	(see 6)
Taxi Rank	**45** A3

Laundry

Laundrette (10 blvd Wilson; 7am-10pm)
Laundrette (av Christophe Colomb; 7.30am-10.30pm)
Above Super U car park.

Medical Services

Emergency Medical Centre (04 95 65 11 22; rte
du Stade; 24hr) Off rte de Santore.

Post

Post office (cnr blvd Wilson & av de la République)

Tourist Information

Tourist office (04 95 65 16 67; www.balagne-corsica
.com in French; port de plaisance; 9am-12.30pm &
3-6.30pm daily Jul & Aug; 9am-noon & 2-6pm Mon-Sat
May, Jun, Sep & Oct; 9am-noon & 2-6pm Mon-Fri Nov-Apr)

Covers Calvi and all La Balagne. English-language website under construction at the time of writing.

Seasonal tourist office annexe (☺ 10am-1pm & 3-6pm Tue-Sat Jul & Aug, 11am-6pm Tue-Sat Jun & Sep) Just inside the citadel; offers audio-guided tours (€7).

SIGHTS
Citadel

For superb wraparound views of Calvi and its bay, haul yourself up to the citadel. Built at the end of the 15th century by the Genoese, it towers over the town from atop its 80m-high granite promontory. A handful of cafés and restaurants set out tables in the shadow of its ochre walls but, unlike its Bonifacio counterpart, it's not an integral part of the town and most of its buildings are closed to the public. All the same, it more than merits the climb, not least for the spectacular view it offers across the Golfe de Calvi.

Pass through the entrance arch, just off place Christophe Colomb, with the town's motto inscribed above it. From here little alleyways lead steeply upwards to the place d'Armes, with the former Palais des Gouverneurs Génois (Genoese Governors' Palace) on the left. This imposing building, renamed **Caserne Sampiero**, was built by the Genoese in the 13th century and extended during the 16th. It serves as the barracks and mess hall for the French Foreign Legion (see the boxed text, below).

The **Cathédrale St-Jean Baptiste** is on the other side of the place d'Armes, halfway up a little alley. This 13th-century church narrowly escaped obliteration when an adjacent powder store exploded in 1567; it was rebuilt and consecrated as a cathedral in 1576. The dome is superb and the interior boasts a high altar of polychrome marble dating from the 17th century, to the right of which is the *Christ des Miracles* (Christ of The Miracles). This ebony statue has been venerated since the town was besieged in 1553. According to legend, the ships of the besieging Franco-Turkish forces simply turned tail and sailed back out to sea after the population of Calvi carried the statue in a procession through their streets. The *Vierge du Rosaire* (Virgin of the Rosary) statue has three different robes: a black one for Good Friday, a purple one for the Wednesday after Palm Sunday and a rich brocade cloth for use in processions. The nave is now often used to host polyphonic singing (p40) evenings in summer.

Retrace your steps to the place d'Armes and take a little street to the left to come to the **Oratoire de la Confrérie St-Antoine** (Oratory of the St Antoine

---

THE FRENCH FOREIGN LEGION

In the lanes of the citadel or around the port, you'll probably come across members of the Deuxième Régiment Étranger de Parachutistes (REP) of the Légion Étrangère (Foreign Legion), cutting a swathe through the tourists and enjoying some off-duty time from Camp Raffali, their military base out near Calvi's airport. These burly recruits are the latest incarnation of the French Foreign Legion, an elite body of crack troops for whom a tour of duty in one of the world's danger spots is second nature.

You'll spot them by their distinctive garb: on their close-cropped heads, a white pillbox-shaped *képi* or green beret with the Legion's winged-hand-and-dagger emblem, red shoulder epaulettes and a green tie (implausibly, the symbol of celibacy!).

The Legion is a career choice that has been shrouded in mystery ever since King Louis Philippe founded the force in 1831, principally to add extra punch to the conquest of Algeria.

Many of the myths of the Legion now look rather outdated but there are two maxims that still hold true: anonymity is guaranteed and, in return for five years of service, soldiers can earn French citizenship – not to mention a decent wage. That's why many of today's recruits who put themselves through the notoriously challenging entrance exam hail from the war-torn Baltic States and disparate fragments of the former Soviet Republic.

The secretive nature of the force still persists, although since troops have recently seen action in Kosovo and Sierra Leone, these days it's trying to be more transparent to a public still fascinated by the romance of the Legion's legacy. Calvi's Camp Raffali opens its doors to the public twice yearly – on 30 April and 29 September – giving a rare glimpse of the daily life of the 1000-odd legionnaires based here.

The April opening coincides with a major procession of the regiment through the streets of Calvi with recruits dressed in all their finery (including a blue belt a full 4.2m long).

A CALVIAN CALLED COLUMBUS?

Place Christophe Colomb, ave Christophe Colomb, a commemorative plaque to mark the 500th anniversary of the discovery of the Americas... Calvi latches on to the memory of Columbus, discoverer of the New World, as Ajaccio venerates Napoleon and Île Rousse celebrates Pascal Paoli. Why, there's even a plaque in Calvi's citadel that claims to mark the explorer's birthplace. A little 72-page book, *Christophe Colomb, Corse*, written by Joseph Chiara and available from the Calvi tourist office (but only in French, regrettably), makes the case for Columbus' Calvian birth.

Roger Caratini, however, in his masterly *Histoire du Peuple Corse* (1995), mocks the Corsican 'amateur historians' who have made 'dogma' of Columbus' Calvian origins. All serious scholars and documents agree, Caratini asserts, that Columbus was the son of a Genoese weaver; the first person to argue the case for Columbus' birth in Calvi, in the mid-19th century, was a 'credulous churchman'.

But Chiara believes that Columbus' birth in Genoa (distinct from his undisputed Genoese 'citizenship') will itself never be more than a hypothesis. He suggests that when Columbus went looking for underwriting at the Spanish court, he would have blown his chances by admitting to being of Calvian origin since the Calvians had massacred a Spanish garrison, thus putting an end to Spanish ambitions in Corsica. Chiara's arguments, supported by reference to Columbus' name and own recorded use of language, have irresistible romantic appeal.

There's something more at stake for Corsica in the dispute. If Corsica gave the world Napoleon but not Columbus, well, maybe it was just chance. If Corsica gave the world both Napoleon *and* Columbus, then there begins to be a pattern, which could be seen to indicate an inherent Corsican desire to dream more boldly and travel further than other ethnic groups. What's certain is that, wherever Columbus himself might have been born, there were a lot of Calvians among his crews, and by the mid-16th century Calvians were living in the New World in numbers out of all proportion to the Corsican population.

Brotherhood; 10am-6pm), a charitable institution that has been active in Corsica since the 14th century. Behind the façade, which features a primitive slate lintel depicting the abbot St Antoine, are walls painted with 15th- and 16th-century frescoes (some, alas, severely time-worn) and, on the north wall, an ivory Christ attributed to the Florentine sculptor Jacopo d'Antonio Tati, known as *Le Sansevino*.

The citadel has five **bastions**, each offering wonderful seascapes. One of the most famous attacks on the citadel came in 1794 when the town, which Genoa had ceded to France 30 years earlier, came under attack from the British army and Corsican separatist forces led by Pascal Paoli. It was heavily bombarded and largely destroyed during the battle, which cost Admiral Horatio Nelson his right eye. Following the onslaught, Calvi eventually capitulated and ceded to the combined forces. The Anglo-Corsican kingdom was short-lived, however, and Calvi returned to French control no more than two years later.

Near **Bastion Celle** in the northwest corner is a marble plaque marking the alleged birthplace of Christopher Columbus (see the boxed text, above).

At the far end of the ferry quay, and standing in the shadow of the citadel, is the **Tour de Sel**, built for defence and subsequently used as the town's salt store.

ACTIVITIES
Beaches
Calvi's lovely sandy beach stretches around the bay southeastwards for 4km from the marina.

The Tramways de Balagne railway (p133) links Calvi to a series of charming smaller beaches that punctuate the coast all the way to Algajola and beyond to Île Rousse.

Boat Trips
Between April and October **Colombo Line** (04 95 65 32 10; www.colombo-line.com in French) organises excursions in glass-bottomed boats from its kiosk-style office right on the harbour. There are three tours to choose from, each taking in the magnificent Réserve Naturelle de Scandola (p152).

Tour 1 (adult/child €55/28; 9.15am-3pm daily May-Sep) Sails via the Réserve Naturelle de Scandola to Girolata, where it makes a two-hour stop.

Tour 2 (adult/child €44/22; 2.30-5.15pm daily Apr-Oct) To explore the Réserve Naturelle de Scandola.

CALVI & LA BALAGNE

Tour 3 (adult/child €70/35; ☺ 9am-5.30pm once or twice weekly April–mid-Oct) Sails via the Réserve Naturelle de Scandola to Ajaccio, with a three-hour stopover.

Adventure Trail

Beside the coast among the pines, **A Scimia Calvese** (adult/child €18/15; ☺ 9.30am-7.30pm daily Jul & Aug, 3-7.30pm Wed Easter-Jun, Sep & Oct) is an exhilarating, elevated, 700m-long climbing structure of bridges, ladders, beams, logs, pulleys and cables. It's run by the adventure sports company **Altore** (☎ 06 83 39 69 06; www.altore.com in French). To the east of Calvi along the D151 between Montemaggiore and Cateri, Altore (it's the Corsican word for 'bearded vulture') also offers introductory flights and paragliding courses.

Diving

The waters off Calvi offer plenty of scope for diving (including the chance to explore the wreck of a WWII B-17 bomber), whatever your level. Typical prices including equipment hire: introductory dive (€40), beginner's course (€230 to €280), open-water course (€380). The following are all based at the marina.
Calvi Plongée (☎ 04 95 65 33 87; www.calviplongee .com in French) Based on a boat moored to the quayside.
Club de Plongée Castille (☎ 04 95 65 33 67; www .plongeecastille.com)
EPIC (École de Plongée Internationale de Calvi; ☎ 06 13 38 61 26; ☺ year-round)
L'Hippocampe (☎ 04 95 60 57 74; www.hippocampe2b .fr) Visit their great website for a virtual dive.

Also see p79 for more information about diving.

Windsurfing & Sailing

Calvi Nautique Club (☎ 04 95 65 10 65; www.calvinc .org in French; ☺ May-Oct), at the northern tip of the beach, rents windsurfers (€15 per hour), funboards (€21 per hour) and single or double kayaks (€10/15 per hour).

In July and August it runs courses (Monday to Friday, two hours per day) in sailing (Optimist; €157), windsurfing (€157) and catamaraning (€197).

Horse Riding

A Cavallu Riding Centre (☎ 04 95 65 22 22; www.a -cavallu.com in French; ☺ year-round) offers trail rides (€20 per hour) and lessons. Confirmed cowboys and cowgirls should consider its carnet (€160), which entitles you to 10 hours (you

can mix and pick) of guided rides, lessons or (for experienced riders) bareback riding through the surf. The centre is 500m down a dusty track, left of the N197 about 2km from the centre of town in the direction of the airport.

TOURS

Between April and September, **Corse Voyages** (☎ 04 95 65 00 47; blvd Wilson), in conjunction with Autocars Mariani, offers coach trips from Calvi. Destinations, in order of their day of departure, include the following:
Forêt de Bonifatu (half-day €15; ☺ departs 1.45pm Mon)
Maquis circuit (full-day tour of the interior €27; ☺ departs 7am Tue)
Villages of the Balagne (half-day €16.50; ☺ departs 1.45pm Wed)
Cap Corse (full-day €27; departs 7.30am Thu)

Les Beaux Voyages (☎ 04 95 65 11 35; www.lesbeaux voyagesencorse.com in French; résidence le Vieux Chalet) organises a similar set of excursions with almost identical prices. Both companies offer reduced fares for children.

FESTIVALS & EVENTS

Calvi is big on festivals, mostly held during summer months.
Processions de la Semaine Sainte Fervent Holy Week celebrations; late March early April.
St-Érasme The blessing of the fishing boats every 2 June.
Rencontres d'Art Contemporain Works by contemporary painters and sculptors are exhibited in the citadel throughout the summer between mid-June and mid-September.
Calvi Jazz Festival (☎ 04 95 65 16 67; www.calvi-jazz -festival.com in French) Open-air and indoor concerts plus a range of jam sessions featuring big names from the international jazz scene; held on the June long weekend.
Calvi on the Rocks Three days of electronic and experimental music in mid-July that pull in international acts (Neny Cherry, for example, in 2005).
Rencontres de Chants Polyphoniques (☎ 04 95 65 16 67) Festival of polyphonic singing held at various venues in the citadel in mid-September.
Festival du Vent (☎ 01 53 20 93 00; www.lefestivaldu vent.com) An annual festival celebrating the role of the wind in the arts, science and sport; held in late October.

SLEEPING

In high season, be sure to book a room in advance or you risk finding yourself on the beach. At this time, hotels are expensive compared to mainland France. Camping grounds, by contrast are mostly spacious with broad pitches and excellent facilities.

Hotels

Hôtel du Centre (☎ 04 95 65 02 01; 14 rue Alsace Lorraine; d €29-46, tr €36-55; ☺ Jun-Sep) Built in the 19th century as a police station and barracks, this simple option is the best budget place in the heart of town. Its whitewashed rooms have basic furniture, shower and washbasin; toilets are in the corridor. The welcome's friendly despite the handwritten exhortations that plaster reception. It doesn't take credit cards. There's also a two-person studio (€235 to €330 per week). Reception's open all day but closes promptly at 9pm.

Hôtel Cyrnea (☎ 04 95 65 03 35; www.hotelcyrnea .com; rte de Bastia; s €48-55, d €54-74, tr €72-92, q €86-112; ☺ year-round; ⓟ ⊠ ⓧ ⓡ) Most of the 41 rooms at this great-value hotel beside Camping Paduella have a spacious balcony and all have double-glazing. Those facing the rear, towards the mountains, have the best views. Reception staff are welcoming and speak good English.

Hôtel Belvédère (☎ 04 95 65 01 25; place Christophe Colomb; d €45-115, tr €70-130; ☺ year-round ⓧ) Overlooking place Christophe Colomb at the foot of the citadel, and looking fresh after a recent refit, the Belvédère has 27 smallish but comfortable rooms, some with magnificent views of the bay. It's a particular bargain out of season, when prices fall as low as €45.

Casa Vecchia (☎ 04 95 65 09 33; www.hotel-casa-vec chia.com in French; rte de Santore; s €50-60, d €55-85; ☺ year-round; ⓟ) Near the centre of town, Casa Vecchia is really several houses, set in and around a dusty mature compound with an almost colonial feel. The two-storey hotel building at its heart has large rooms. Two other houses consist of apartments that can be rented by the week while the Maison Corse (minimum stay one week in July and August) has rooms with corridor facilities (single/double €40/45).

Hôtel Le Magnolia (☎ 04 95 65 19 16; www.hotel-le -magnolia.com in French; rue Alsace Lorraine; r €60-120; ⓟ ⓧ) Converted from a 19th-century mansion and overlooking a vine-shaded garden, Le Magnolia is a charming spot with 12 rooms, each decorated in a different style, which are comfortable and well furnished.

Hôtel Le Rocher (☎ 04 95 65 20 04; www.hotel-le -rocher.com in French; blvd Wilson; r €70-170; ☺ mid-Apr–mid-Oct; ⓟ ⓧ) The 20 spacious rooms of this central, recently made-over hotel all have

fresh furniture, attractive fabrics, marble bathrooms, flat-screen televisions and balconies. Its three mezzanine rooms (€105 to €200) have views of the gulf and can accommodate up to four people.

Hôtel La Villa (☎ 04 95 65 10 10; www.hotel-lavilla .com; chemin de Notre Damede la Serra; 2-person villas €200-450; ⓟ ⓧ ⓠ ⓡ) In a secluded location in the hills overlooking Calvi and set in gorgeous gardens, its raft of inhouse facilities includes four pools, a fitness centre, a beach club with water-sports equipment and a Michelin-starred restaurant. There are also suites and apartments – even a helipad, should you prefer to leave the car at home.

Hostels

Relais International de la Jeunesse (☎ 04 95 65 14 16; dm incl breakfast €15, with half-board €25; ☺ Apr–mid-Nov; ⓟ) Unless you're driving (if so, leave your car at the last bend and continue on foot), it's a good 45-minute uphill walk from the port to this hostel – but it's worth every step. Here, way above the town, the panorama is unbeatable, bar drinks, soft, long and shorts, are all €1 and the place is friendliness itself. A couple of dorms sleep 11 but there are also smaller rooms for two, three and five, some with en suite facilities.

Camping

Camping Paduella (☎ 04 95 65 06 16; www.camping paduella.com; rte de Bastia; camp sites per adult/tent/car €7/2.70/2.70; ☺ mid-May–mid-Oct) This friendly, well-maintained camping ground is a 300m walk from the beach. Shaded by mature trees, it has impeccable washrooms, scrubbed several times daily, with some individual cubicles. It also has fully equipped tents for hire (€46 to €72 for two to six persons, high season minimum rental one week).

Camping La Pinède (☎ 04 95 65 17 80; www.camping -calvi.com; rte de Bastia; camp sites per adult/tent/car €8.50/3/3; ☺ Apr-Oct) At the heart of a pine and eucalyptus wood and a short stroll from the beach, this attractive choice has a pool and a couple of tennis courts. It also rents caravans (€27.50 to €70.50 for two to four persons) and chalets (€60 to €172 for two to six persons).

EATING

Restaurants

Le Tire Bouchon (☎ 04 95 65 24 41; rue Clemenceau; mains €9-16; ☺ Apr-Oct) This cheerful, animated option, as much wine bar as restaurant, is a delight.

Order from the dishes of the day, posted on the chalkboard, and treat yourself to a glass of the finest AOC wine, available by the glass.

U Fornu (☎ 04 95 65 27 60; impasse Bertoni; mains €16-21, menu €16; ☙ Mon-Sat, dinner Sun Apr-Dec) Raised above blvd Wilson on a shady terrace with candles set into the wall, this little eatery offers mainly Corsican dishes. Its dining room is in what was once a small, pleasantly vaulted bakery. It doesn't accept credit cards.

U Minellu (☎ 04 95 65 05 52; traverse de l'Église; mains €17-19, menu Corse €17; ☙ mid-Mar–mid-Oct, closed Mon except Jul & Aug) This small family-run place with its vaulted ceiling and exterior tables beneath a lantern-lit wooden canopy is down a tight alley, just off rue Alsace Lorraine. It offers a good-value *menu* and a decent range of AOC Corsican wines. The *menu Corse* includes specialities such as *brocciu* cannelloni, Corsican cooked pork, and chestnut and apple cake.

L'Abri Cotier (☎ 04 95 65 12 76; rue Joffre; mains €17-25, menus €21-35; ☙ Apr–mid-Nov; Ⓥ) It's safer to reserve at this popular spot, just off the quayside; ask for one of the coveted tables beside the panoramic window, one floor up and lording it over the restaurant terraces below. The cuisine is imaginative (try, for example the sea bass accompanied by a basil flan) and the house desserts are a dream (save a corner for their chestnut ice cream with toffee sauce). It also does a vegetarian platter.

Aux Bons Amis (☎ 04 95 65 05 01; rue Clemenceau; mains €18-22, menus €17-26; ☙ Apr-Sep, closed Wed except Jul & Aug) With its nautically themed décor, Aux Bons Amis has a short, select à la carte choice and serves up the best of fresh fish and seafood. Two downsides: the flickering TV is an intrusion, even though the sound's turned off; and the house white is best avoided…

Le Jardin (☎ 04 95 65 08 02; rue Alsace Lorraine; mains €18-24, menus €21) This restaurant, which adjoins the Hôtel Le Magnolia, serves good, wholesome Corsican food with a nod towards *haute cuisine.*

U Callelu (☎ 04 95 65 22 18; quai Landry; mains around €25, menus €20; ☙ Mar-Oct, closed Mon except Jul & Aug) This quayside restaurant has an attractive beige interior with a floral theme. Renowned for the quality and variety of its fresh fish dishes, it also offers attentive service.

Émile's (☎ 04 95 65 09 60; quai Landry; mains €20-40, menus €40-60; ☙ Mar–mid-Nov) Keep your eyes open for Emile's, up an easily overlooked flight of steps that leads from the quayside to its

1st-floor panoramic terrace. Here at Calvi's choicest restaurant you'll enjoy a sophisticated gastronomic experience; why, even the menu reads like a book of poetry.

Quick Eats & Self-Catering

Best Of (1 rue Clemenceau; sandwiches €4-7; ☙ 11.30am-10pm) If you're looking for a snack on the move, call by here to pick up some original sandwiches, paninis and wood-fired bread topped with local specialties.

Covered market (☙ 8am-noon Mon-Sat) Calvi's small market has plenty of pickings for self-caterers with its richly scented local sausages and tempting desserts.

DRINKING & ENTERTAINMENT

L'Havanita (quai Landry; ☙ from 6pm) This tiny shack of a place is down by the waterfront, squashed between a couple of restaurant terraces. It's a pleasant place to enjoy a drink and savour a background drift of Latino music.

Chez Tao (☎ 04 95 65 00 73; rue St-Antoine; ☙ 9pm-5am May-Oct) Within the citadel walls and occupying what was once the palace of the bishops of Sagone, Chez Tao is a hip piano bar that's a Corsican institution. The lavishly decorated venue was conceived in 1935 by Tao Kanbey de Kerekoff, who served in a White Cavalry regiment during the Russian revolution, then, defeated in battle, headed west, winding up on the island. Nowadays, it's run in the same opulent, flamboyant style by his son, Tao-By, who tickles the ivories, playing a mix of French and Corsican songs and melodies plus international favourites. Drinks are from €10.

La Camargue (☎ 04 95 65 08 70; rte de Bastia; ☙ Apr-Sep) About 2.7km from town heading towards Île Rousse and just before the airport turnoff, La Camargue has a pool, piano-bar and open-air dance floor. In high summer there's a free shuttle bus from town.

GETTING THERE & AWAY
Air

Calvi-Ste-Catherine airport (☎ 04 95 65 88 88; www .calvi.aeroport.fr) is 7km southeast of town. There are at least four flights daily to Nice, Marseille and Paris (Orly). Since the runway is so close to the mountains, flights are sometimes redirected to Bastia when winds are exceptionally high. There is no bus service from Calvi to the airport. A **taxi** (☎ 04 95 65 03 10) to/from town costs around €20.

TRAMWAYS DE BALAGNE

Every year the spectacular beaches and hidden coves of the Balagne coastline suddenly come to life with the first beach towel of summer. The lifeline that connects these isolated coves is the Tramways de Balagne, an offshoot of Chemins de Fer de la Corse (p272).

This bone-shaking little train trundles between Calvi and Île Rousse up to nine times daily between April and October, calling at 15 stations en route. All stops are request-only with bronzed groups of bathers and hikers popping out from behind a rock to hail the iron horse as she chugs slowly by. Someone will come around during the trip to collect the fare and make a note of where you want to get off.

There has been talk for years of improving the rolling stock but so far little has changed. All to the good; it's the train's uniquely lo-fi quality that is the main source of its charm. Indeed, rail enthusiasts from all over the world now converge on Calvi to ride the Tramways de Balagne before she is finally put out to pasture.

The one-way/return fare from Calvi to Île Rousse (50 minutes) is €4.50/8. If you're likely to be making multiple journeys, such as return day trips from Calvi to the Balagne beaches, consider buying a carnet of six tickets (€8). The line is divided into three sectors and you peel off one ticket per sector.

Boat

Corsica Ferries (☎ 08 25 09 50 95; www.corsicaférries .com) has services to Nice (at least three times weekly May to August) and to Savona in Italy (once weekly July and August).

The ferry terminal is below the southern side of the citadel. You can buy tickets at the port two hours before departure or from **Les Beaux Voyages** (☎ 04 95 65 11 35; www.lesbeauxvoyages encorse.com in French; place de la Porteuse d'Eau).

For more information on ferry crossings, see the Transport chapter (p267).

Bus

Les Beaux Voyages runs a regular bus service, Monday to Saturday, from Calvi to Bastia (€15, 1½ hours), Île Rousse (€3.50, 30 minutes) and Ponte Leccia (€9, one hour). Between Monday and Saturday in July and August it also has a once daily service to Galéria (€6.50, 1¼ hours) and twice daily to Calenzana (€6, 20 minutes). Buses leave across the road from their offices on place de la Porteuse d'Eau.

From mid-May to mid-October, **Autocars Ceccaldi** (☎ 04 95 22 41 99) runs one bus daily (€17, 2½ hours) to/from Porto via Col de la Croix, start of the footpath for Girolata (see the boxed text, p152). It leaves from beside the Super U car park at 1.30pm.

Except in July and August, there are no buses on Sunday.

Car

For car rental, see p270.

Train

From Calvi's **train station** (☎ 04 95 65 00 61) there are two departures daily to Bastia (€15.70, three hours) and Ajaccio (€24.10, five hours) via Corte (€13.10, three hours); all journeys require a change at Ponte Leccia. For Île Rousse, take the Tramways de Balagne (see the boxed text, above).

GETTING AROUND
Bicycle

Garage d'Angeli (☎ 04 95 65 02 13; www.garagedangeli .com in French; place Christophe Colomb) rents mountain bikes (€13/36/73 for one/three/seven days).

Taxi

There's a **taxi rank** (☎ 04 95 65 30 36) on place de la Porteuse d'Eau. Taxis run excursions for two to four people to the Forêt de Bonifatu (€35), Galéria (€55) and Calenzana (€23).

AROUND CALVI

Three kilometres west of Calvi along the D81B (direction Galéria and Porto), you have a tempting choice of two splendid panoramas.

POINTE DE LA REVELLATA

This outcrop of land, across the Golfe de la Revellata from Calvi's citadel quarter, offers a foretaste of the still wilder and more beautiful coastline that lies beyond along the D81B (see the boxed text, p134).

You can risk your car's suspension and drive as far as you can along the sandy track. Better though to park at the bend in the road and continue along the track on foot. Along the way to the tip of the promontory, views become ever better as you pass a sandy beach and tiny, fretted coves lapped by turquoise waters.

NOTRE DAME DE LA SERRA

Signed from the same bend, a blacktop road runs for 1.5km up to this tiny chapel, five centuries old and perched on a wild and windswept hill, offering a magnificent panorama of Calvi and its citadel.

A statue of a shrouded Virgin Mary can be seen here gazing out over the Golfe de Calvi in silent contemplation. The chapel makes for an easy afternoon hike and a welcome escape from the tourist throng crowding the streets of Calvi.

GALÉRIA

pop 300

Galéria, a tiny, sleepy little fishing village with a smattering of hotels and places to eat, is the only settlement of any size on the wild coastline between Calvi and Porto. There are reasons for so few dwellings. For centuries the coast was exposed to the depredations of Barbary pirates. Later malaria took root and was only eradicated in the mid-20th century. You can stretch out on its beach of coarse-grained sand or head 500m north to Plage de Ricinccia, a stretch of red shingle watched over by a Genoese tower.

L'Incantu (☎ 04 95 62 03 65; www.incantu.com; rte de Calca), about 300m from the parish church, is one of Corsica's prime diving operators. See p79 for more information about diving.

If you're fairly fit, you can do a day of the Mare e Monti route, following the signed trail across the peninsula to Girolata (p151), that other jewel of this wild coastline.

Galéria is 40km from Calvi and 55km north of Porto by the magnificent coastal D81B.

ALGAJOLA

pop 215

From tiny Algajola, 15km from Calvi and 7km west of Île Rousse, a splendid crescent of sandy beach, coveted by surfers for its waves, curves northwards. Much quieter than its larger neighbours (though it too receives plenty of visitors in July and August), it has a couple of good hotels and a handful of rewarding places to eat. It also makes for a fun day trip from either resort by the clanking Tramways de Balagne.

There's an appropriately minuscule **tourist office** (☎ 04 95 62 78 32; ☿ 9am-noon) in a room at the back of the station.

Between April and October, **Sport et Nature** (☎ 06 08 21 09 51; www.algajola-sportetnature.com), located on the beach, rents gear and offers courses in surfing, diving, sea kayaking, windsurfing and other watery sports.

Sleeping & Eating

L'Esquinade (☎ 04 95 60 70 19; www.esquinade.com in French; s €30-60, d €38-75; ☿ May–mid-Oct) This simple, clean little place, next to the post office, is a good option. Ask for a room overlooking the garden for the best views and you'll wake up to church bells and a superb Mediterranean vista. The bar downstairs is a friendly spot for a snack.

Hôtel-Restaurant Stella Mare (☎ 04 95 60 71 18; stellamare2@wanadoo.fr; r €49-85; ☿ mid-Apr–Oct;

DRIVING FROM CALVI TO PORTO

You *could* play safe and take the main D81 that runs between Calvi and Porto. Much more satisfying yet slower is the D81B, which snakes along the coast from Calvi as far as Galéria, traversing awesome coastal scenery before turning inland, where dun-coloured meadows lap against sheer granite cliffs, plunging into the Parc Naturel Régional de Corse (PNRC).

The tight, switchback bends will have you wrestling with the steering wheel and the sheer drops to the waves send butterflies fluttering around the stomach. There are no guard rails, rock falls are frequent and the patched and repatched tarmac is still riddled with unexpected potholes. Oh, and watch out for stray mountain goats!

The narrowness of the road makes passing other vehicles – not those in your own lane but those coming *at* you – a nerve-racking game of chicken. It's not a road trip for the faint hearted but be prudent, take your time and you'll enjoy one of Corsica's most spectacular drives.

ARGENTELLA

This detour is a must for those with a penchant for industrial archaeology. Around 20km along the D81B south of Calvi, direction Galéria, park your car opposite Camping Morsetta and its friendly bar. Take the track beside the car park to discover, after no more than 100m, the entrance to the long-abandoned silver mine complex of Argentella, nestling in the foothills of Capu di Argentella with the waters of the Baie de Crovani before it.

Several hopeful companies have extracted silver and profit from the lead-bearing rock. First exploited by the French, the mine was sold in the 19th century to the British, who installed steam engines in the factory at the base of the hill and constructed a weir and dam to collect water for cooling, then in their turn sold it on.

Root around the crumbling administrative quarters and explore the furnaces (taking care; the structures really are tottering) with their still-intact brick chimney standing proud. Then walk up to the old dam, which still holds back the waters that drain from Capu di Argentella. Here, frogs croak and plop, baby turtles bask, and fish swim and gulp. Gaze back upon the factory and its roofless outbuildings, all of warm brick and looking for all the world like some abandoned monastic settlement.

If you've the energy and time, you can continue up the track for around 45 minutes to the minehead itself and more abandoned buildings.

P ⚅) Each of the 16 rooms (all recently renovated) has a splendid panorama of either the mountains or the coast. Ask for No 10, which has views of both and a balcony too. There are great sea views from the terrace where a buffet breakfast (€9) and evening sundowners are served. The owners can advise on local activities and walking trails and staff speak excellent English.

Bar Brasserie Le Chariot (☎ 04 95 60 70 49; place d'Algajola; menu €17.50) A popular bar (there's draft Pietra) and restaurant with a pleasant terrace. It does good grills (€14 to €18), pizzas and pastas (€5.80 to €8) and, at weekends, paellas (€19).

La Veille Cave (☎ 04 95 60 70 09; mains €14-17, menus €16.50-25; ☾ Apr-Oct, closed Mon lunch) On the attractive terrace of this friendly establishment, you really ought to indulge in one of their *pierrades* – meat, fish or seafood sizzled on a hot stone. Alternatively, opt for the *agneau Corse de lait*, local baby lamb, roasted to perfection.

U Castellu (☎ 04 95 60 78 75; mains €14-17, menu €20; ☾ Apr-Oct) Facing Algajola's small, privately owned citadel, U Castellu has a pretty shaded terrace. The cuisine is creative, including its own foie gras with sweet onion garnishing, marinated octopus and skewers of succulent *lotte* (angler fish).

Getting There & Away

In summer up to nine Tramways de Balagne (p133) trains daily link Algajola with Île

Rousse (€3.30, 20 minutes) and Calvi (€3.75, 30 minutes).

ÎLE ROUSSE (ISULA ROSSA)

pop 2800

Île Rousse these days touts itself as the St-Tropez of Corsica, and with good reason. It pulls in media luvvies such as Elton John, Jean-Paul Gaultier and Jean-Paul Belmondo, whose gin palaces moor at what the town has sycophantically named the quai d'Honneur. Like Calvi, it makes an excellent base both for exploring the rich hinterland of La Balagne and for indulging in seaside pleasures, as active or as passive as you care to make them.

Turquoise and lapis lazuli waters, over which shimmers an intense light, contrast with the porphyry coloured rocks from which the town (The Pink Island) takes its name (it was originally and more prosaically called Paolina after its founder; see p136).

Steep yourself in its shallow waters and sprawl on its long sandy beach. Once the heat of the day begins to abate, retire barely a metre or two to A Marinella, the town's promenade that invites an evening stroll. Punctuate the day at least once with a coffee or something stronger beneath the shady plane trees of place Paoli, to the click and thud of lobbed *pétanque* balls.

HISTORY

It's ironic that this appealing holiday resort, through whose port pour tens of thousands of holidaymakers from mainland Europe, was originally founded very much as a Corsican political statement. In 1758 the nationalist leader Pascal Paoli (p30; see the bust of Babbu di a Patria, the Father of the Nation, staring proud in – you've guessed it – place Paoli) established the town, thumbing his nose at Genoa-controlled Calvi, barely 25km along the coast. Soon, this quiet fishing hamlet became a serious commercial rival to its larger neighbour and remained so until it fell into decline after WWI. Nowadays, it again enjoys prosperity as a passenger port and coastal resort.

ORIENTATION

The four narrow cobbled streets of the small old quarter, where many of the shops and restaurants are concentrated, rise northwards from central place Paoli (leave your vehicle in the paying car park just to its east). From here the town's long beach stretches eastwards. The ferry quay is at the limit of the Pietra peninsula, 500m north of the train station, which marks the western limit of the town.

INFORMATION

Bookshops

Maison de la Presse (av Piccioni) Books, maps and foreign-language publications.

Internet Access

Movie Stores Cyber (rte de Calvi; per hr €5; ☿ 10am-midnight Mon-Sat, 3pm-midnight Sun)

Laundry

Self-service laundrette (rue Napoléon; ☿ 7am-midnight)

Post

Post office (rte de Monticello)

Internet Access

Tourist office (☎ 04 95 60 04 35; www.balagne-corsica.com; place Paoli; ☿ 9am-7pm daily Jul & Aug, 9am-noon & 2-6pm Mon-Fri Sep-Jun)

SIGHTS & ACTIVITIES

Parc de Saleccia

These recently established **landscaped gardens** (☎ 04 95 36 88 33; rte de Bastia; adult/child €7/5; ☿ 9.30am-1pm & 3-8pm Mon-Sat, 10am-8pm Sun Jul & Aug, 9.30am-12.30pm & 2.30pm-dusk Wed-Mon Apr-Jun, Sep & Oct), 4.5km from town on the Bastia road, are the single-handed creation of a passionate Corsican, Bruno Demoustier, who fought off a proposed development of 200 holiday villas. They showcase the plants, trees and shrubs of the island – the tough plants of the maquis scrubland, pines, myrtles, fig trees, over 100 varieties of olive tree and banks of azaleas and oleanders bursting with colour. The entry may seem a little steep but you have the satisfaction of knowing that you're helping to preserve Corsica's rich botanical heritage.

Diving

Île Rousse has two diving centres, both in the port area.

Beluga Diving (☎ 04 95 60 17 36; www.beluga-diving.com; rte du Phare; ☿ mid-May–mid-Oct) Behind Hôtel La Pietra. Introductory dive €43, courses from €265. Offers Nitrox (oxygen enhanced) dives and also does packages including accommodation.

École de Plongée Île Rousse (☎ 04 95 60 36 85; www.plongee-ilerousse.com in French; ☿ Mar-Oct) Dives including equipment are €38 to €40, courses €300 to €460.

Also see p79 for more information on diving.

Canoeing, Sailing & Windsurfing

Club Nautique d'Île Rousse (☎ 04 95 60 22 55; www.cnir.org in French; ☿ Mar-Christmas) Rents kayaks, windsurfing boards, funboards and catamarans and runs courses. Organises sea-kayak tours.

Nautimarine (☎ 04 95 60 00 73; www.nautimarine.com in French; rte de Calvi; ☿ year-round) Rents motor boats (from €200 per day) – a wonderful way to explore the coastline of the Désert des Agriates (p121).

Walking

It's an easy stroll over the short umbilical causeway that links rocky **Île de la Pietra** to the mainland, past a small **Genoese watchtower** and up to the **lighthouse**, from where there's a spectacular seascape. Allow 20 to 30 minutes for the round trip from the port.

The tourist office sells a wallet file (€12) that details 13 short, easy, signed country walks in the immediate vicinity, none of them longer than 4km.

Cycling

La Passion en Action (☎ 04 95 60 15 76; av Paul Doumer) rents bikes (from €18/45/85 per day/three days/week).

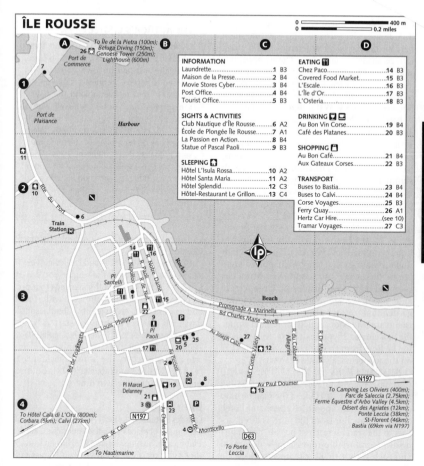

ÎLE ROUSSE

INFORMATION
Laundrette	1 B3
Maison de la Presse	2 B4
Movie Stores Cyber	3 B4
Post Office	4 B4
Tourist Office	5 B3

SIGHTS & ACTIVITIES
Club Nautique d'Île Rousse	6 A2
École de Plongée Île Rousse	7 A1
La Passion en Action	8 B4
Statue of Pascal Paoli	9 B3

SLEEPING
Hôtel L'Isula Rossa	10 A2
Hôtel Santa Maria	11 A2
Hôtel Splendid	12 C3
Hôtel-Restaurant Le Grillon	13 C4

EATING
Chez Paco	14 B3
Covered Food Market	15 B3
L'Escale	16 B3
L'Île d'Or	17 B3
L'Osteria	18 B3

DRINKING
Au Bon Vin Corse	19 B4
Café des Platanes	20 B3

SHOPPING
Au Bon Café	21 B4
Aux Gateaux Corses	22 B3

TRANSPORT
Buses to Bastia	23 B4
Buses to Calvi	24 B4
Corse Voyages	25 B3
Ferry Quay	26 A1
Hertz Car Hire	(see 10)
Tramar Voyages	27 C3

CALVI & LA BALAGNE

Horse Riding

Ferme Équestre d'Arbo Valley (☎ 06 16 72 53 12; arbovalley@yahoo.fr; off rte de Bastia; 1/2hr rides €17/27; ☼ Apr–Oct) does full- and half-day rides (€70 including lunch) to nearby villages or the Désert des Agriates (p121). Turn right 100m beyond the Parc de Saleccia to take a bumpy, dusty track for 1.75km.

FESTIVALS & EVENTS

Oursinade A celebration of, believe it or not, the sea urchin. Street stalls offer the rich roe-like flesh at the heart of these spiky sea-dwellers with a variety of accompaniments. Held on a variable Sunday in March or April.
Festimare Celebrates the sea, with plenty of fish and seafood specials on offer and activities for children and adults alike; held over a weekend in early June.

SLEEPING
Hotels

Hôtel-Restaurant Le Grillon (☎ 04 95 60 00 49, fax 04 95 60 43 69; 10 av Paul Doumer; s €39-50, d €44-54, tr €52-60; ☼ mid-Feb–mid-Nov; P ✕) With simple, well-maintained rooms (eight of them with balcony) and a popular, warmly recommended ground-floor restaurant (*menus* €13 to €16), this friendly place offers excellent value. The hotel is at the rear and its informal reception is in the public bar.

Hôtel Splendid (☎ 04 95 60 00 24; www.le-splendid -hotel.com; blvd Comte Valéry; s €50-70, d €54-95, tr €74-130, all with buffet breakfast; ☼ Apr–Oct; P ✕ ⊠ ⊠) An engaging young couple are the third generation of the same family to run this two-star hotel, which is altogether more exciting than its dull concrete façade might suggest. There's a neat little kidney-shaped pool with bar (the main bar, inside, has a billiard table) and a small terrace, shaded by tall palms. There's been considerable investment recently and its 50 rooms are well-priced except during the peak month of August. Wi-fi's available. Interesting fact: the hotel served as a WWII military hospital.

Hôtel L'Isula Rossa (☎ 04 95 60 01 32; www.isularossa.com in French; rte du Port; d €45-105, tr €55-110; P ✖ ; ✆ mid-Apr–mid-Oct) This place, handy for the harbour, has 21 neat if unspectacular rooms, some with sea-facing balconies. Except in high summer, they represent very good value. The two interconnecting attic level rooms (€65 to €115) are particularly suitable for families.

Hôtel Cala di L'Oru (☎ 04 95 60 14 75; www.hotel-caladiloru.com; blvd Pierre Pasquini; r €59-116; ✆ Mar-Oct; P ✖ ✈) Here's a friendly, family-run hotel with loads of character. The very creditable paintings and photos in public areas are by the owner's sons and even Mum has a canvas or two on display. A large terrace and most of the 26 rooms overlook a tranquil garden that features plants and shrubs of the island and the pool's much more than a puddle in a corner. If you're driving, follow signs for Le Port from the junction with the N197 on the western, Calvi side of town.

Hôtel Santa Maria (☎ 04 95 63 05 05; www.hotelsantamaria.com in French; rte du Port; s €74-156, d €85-167; ✆ year-round; P ✖ ✈) One of the many trump cards of this well-appointed three-star hotel, a well-cast anchor from the port, is direct access to the small scratch of private beach just below. Comfortable rooms, gaily decorated and each with a small balcony, overlook Île de la Pietra.

Camping

Camping Les Oliviers (☎ 04 95 60 19 92, fax 04 95 60 30 91; rte de Bastia; camp sites per adult/tent/car €6/3.50/2.50; ✆ Apr-Sep) This pleasant, flowery camping ground is 2km east of town and a 200m walk from a small pebble beach.

EATING

Covered food market (✆ 8am-1pm) With its 21 classical columns like a Greek temple implanted beside place Paoli, this 19th-century market is the spot for self-caterers.

L'Osteria (☎ 04 95 60 08 39; place Santelli; menus €12-19; ✆ Apr-Oct) Overlooking a quiet square away from the quayside crowds, L'Osteria is a welcoming spot with rustic dining room

THE AUTHOR'S CHOICE

L'Escale (☎ 04 95 60 10 53; rue Notre Dame; mains €10.50-13.50) At this big, bustling place, surely the best value in town, you'd be well advised to reserve (request a table on the glassed-in terrace overlooking the bay) – the secret's out. Content yourself with a pizza (€9.50 to €13.50), take it relatively light with one of their vast, frondy salads or perhaps go for a plate of steaming mussels, prepared seven different ways. Whatever, save an extra large cranny for one of their giant desserts, eased down with a nip of 65% proof firewater, proffered free with the bill.

and small terrace, offering reliable, primarily Corsican cuisine.

L'Île d'Or (☎ 04 95 60 12 05; place Paoli; mains €13.50-17, menus €15-18) Here across the square, you can eat inside or in the shade of the awnings that protect its vast terrace. The choice is wide, for all budgets and often creative (how about a soufflé flavoured with sea urchins for starters?).

Chez Paco (☎ 04 95 60 03 76; rue Paoli; menus €15-28; ✆ mid-Feb–Oct) They're strong on seafood and rice dishes here; try the house-special paella (€18 to €21) or bouillabaisse (€28). Both require a minimum of two diners.

DRINKING

Café des Platanes (place Paoli) Among the cafés on the fringes of place Paoli, the venerable Café des Platanes, in business since 1928, has an interior that's all varnished woodwork and brass rails and a terrace with comfy wicker chairs.

Au Bon Vin Corse (☎ 04 95 60 15 14; place Marcel Delanney) Head here to pick up your stash of local liqueurs, honeys, olive oil and wine from the barrel or to sip on the spot from their range of local *crus*. For supplementary vitamin C, choose the fruity *vin aux fruits* (€2.20).

SHOPPING

Au Bon Café (place Marcel Delanney) You'll smell the aroma of freshly roasted beans before you even see this small temple to the divine brew, which boasts a giant roasting pan (approaching its 100th anniversary), beans from around the world, jute sacks piled high and coffee makers of all shapes and complexities.

Aux Gateaux Corses (rue de Nuit) This is the spot to pick up a range of freshly baked Corsican specialities such as *canistrelli*, confected from lemons, aniseed, flecks of chocolate and raisins, and others sweetmeats based on chestnuts.

GETTING THERE & AROUND

Air
Île Rousse is 25km from Calvi-Ste-Catherine airport (around €40 by taxi). There is no public transport connection.

Boat
From the ferry terminal, **SNCM** (www.sncm.fr) runs boats to Nice and Marseilles. **Corsica Ferries** (☎ 08 25 09 50 95; www.corsicaferries.com) sails to/from Nice, Toulon (express service) and Savona, Italy. For more details, see the Transport chapter (p267).

Tramar Voyages (☎ 04 95 60 08 56; av Joseph Calizi) and **Corse Voyages** (☎ 04 95 60 11 19; place Paoli) both sell tickets.

Bus
Buses of Les Beaux Voyages pass through Île Rousse, running between Calvi (€3.50, 30 minutes) and Bastia (€10, two hours) via Ponte Leccia (€7, one hour). Bus stops are unmarked.

In July and August **Autocars Santini** (☎ 04 95 37 02 98) runs buses twice daily Monday to Saturday between Île Rousse and St-Florent (€10, one hour).

Car
For car rental, see p270.

Train
The **train station** (☎ 04 95 60 00 50) is at the western edge of town. There are two departures daily from Île Rousse to both Bastia (€13, 2½ hours) and Ajaccio (€21.40, four hours) via Corte (€10.40, 2¼ hours). All require a change in Ponte Leccia.

Tramways de la Balagne links Île Rousse with Algajola (€3.30, 15 minutes) and Calvi (€4.50, 50 minutes) up to nine times daily between Easter and September.

LA BALAGNE INTERIOR

Freshly signed in both French and English, the scattered hilltop villages of La Balagne are a world away from the coastal fleshpots and merit at least a few days of your time to soak up their charm.

History has it that most were established way back in the 9th century, when the pope of the time sent Ugo Colonna to liberate the island from Muslim control. He and a handful of stalwart companions built a series of *castras* (fortified mini-chateaus) at strategic points to control both the inland valleys and the coastline.

These ancient hilltop villages are matched by an equally dramatic landscape. Looming granite outcrops, their colours changing by the hour and angle of the sun, are sliced by ravines, gulleys and sheer incisions. Hugging the villages, olive groves, once so prolific, struggle to survive the twin onslaughts of man's neglect and forest fire, competing against cherry, walnut and chestnut.

We've outlined a couple of round-trip day outings (spread them over two days if you enjoy lingering) that take in all the major sites. One's based upon Calvi while the other heads out from Île Rousse. So clunk your safety belt, hold on to your hat and brave the twisting switchback D roads that thread to these inland treasures.

INLAND FROM CALVI (67KM)
Head eastwards out of Calvi along the N197. After 4.5km, turn right onto the D151, then left at the first roundabout to take the D451.

Montemaggiore
After 8km, you will reach Montemaggiore, perched high above the plain. From the terrace in front of the 17th-century Baroque **Église de St-Augustin**, there's a splendid panorama, extending as far as Calvi and the coast. The village was formerly a major centre for olive oil production before fires devastated the area in the 1940s. Today its small population (maybe 100 souls in winter – if that) celebrates

---

THE BALAGNE CRAFT TRAIL

Pick up a copy of the free leaflet *Strada di l'Artigiani* from the Île Rousse or Calvi tourist office. Called the Route des Artisans de Balagne in French, the trail's clearly marked signposts indicate a range of traditional crafts and artisans such as potters, cutlers, stringed-instrument makers, binders and beekeepers. Many of these artisans' workshops are open to the public and visits are free.

its former halcyon days with an **olive oil fair** each July (see p256).

Lunghignano

In Lunghignano, 1.5km further on, you'll smell the sweet aromas of **U Fragnu** (☎ 04 95 62 75 51; 9am-noon & 2-6pm Apr-Oct), an old olive press that still squeezes its own oil, despite a fire that swept through the valley in 2005, destroying around 80% of the trees. In addition to olive products in many guises, it sells delicious homemade cakes and pickles. As you leave, spare a pat for Georges, the ever-patient donkey who turns the grindstone.

After 3km, you pass on the left the bottling plant of **Zilia** (☎ 04 95 65 90 70), one of Corsica's most popular mineral waters, which can be visited by appointment.

Drop off after a further 3.75km for a wine tasting at reputed **Domaine d'Alzi Pratu** (☎ 04 95 62 75 47; 8am-noon & 1.30-7pm Mon-Sat), near the former convent of the same name, and perhaps to pick up a bottle or two.

Chapelle de Santa Restituta

Two kilometres beyond this small winery is the Romanesque Chapelle de Santa Restituta, dedicated to the martyred patron saint of nearby Calenzana who was beheaded in the village square in the early 4th century. The townspeople originally planned for the chapel to be in a different spot but changed their plans when, so goes the story, their building materials were mysteriously and repeatedly moved at dead of night. The spirit of Restituta herself, they concluded, must have been communicating with them to indicate where she wanted her chapel. To visit the interior, ask for the key at the nearby tobacconist. The adjacent olive grove, equipped with picnic tables (one of them an old millstone), makes a pleasant, shaded picnic spot.

Calenzana

pop 1700 / elevation 300m

A further 1.5km bring you to Calenzana, largest of the villages in the Balagne and trailhead for both the GR20 (p56) and the Mare e Monti Nord walking trails (p78). Next to the Gîte Municipal is the Parc Naturel Régional de Corse's (PNRC) **Maison du GR20** (☎ 04 95 62 87 78; 10am-noon & 3-6pm May–mid-Oct), good for information about the GR20 and other trails.

The construction of Calenzana's **Église St-Blaise**, located in the village square, began in 1691, though it took 16 years to complete. Its acanthus-leaf capitals were added in 1722 and the high altar in polychrome marble (based on drawings by Florentine architect Pierre Cortesi) in 1750. The splendid freestanding Baroque bell tower was completed in 1875.

The village, once a major pocket of opposition to Genoese occupation, was the site of a major battle during the Corsican uprising against Genoese troops and their Austrian mercenary allies. The area beneath and around the bell tower was the last resting place of some 500 Austrians, killed in a bloody conflict on 14 June 1732.

Given its regular through-traffic of hungry and thirsty hikers, Calenzana is well blessed with services and shops.

SLEEPING & EATING

Gîte Municipal (☎ 04 95 62 77 13; gite-calenzana@wanadoo .fr; dm/tent €5.60/4; Apr-Oct; **P**) Recently renovated, it's a few hundred metres along the D51 in the direction of Calvi, just past the service station on the right. This favourite spot for hikers has one double and seven rooms sleeping four. There are hot showers and self-catering facilities and outside there's shady ground to pitch a tent. If you're attacking one of the long-distance trails, you can leave your vehicle for up to two weeks. Next door is the PNRC's Maison du GR20 (see left), a source of info about the GR20 and other trails.

Hôtel Bel Horizon (☎ 04 95 62 71 72; s/d/tr €45/55/60) Opposite the church, this hotel has rooms with showers and shared toilets. Its strong point is the breakfast terrace overlooking the mountains. Book ahead as this is also popular with walkers seeking a level of comfort above the *gîte*.

L'Atelier du Village (place Commune) Follow the sweet smell of lemons wafting from the door to discover this store's fine selection of homemade honeys, jams, marmalades, cakes and almond-based goodies.

Chez Michel (☎ 04 95 62 70 25; 7 cours St-Blaise; mains €13-19, menu €16, pizza & pasta €6-7.50; Apr-Dec) On the main road just below the church, Chez Michel (also called Le Calenzana) is renowned for its tasty *menu Corse* (€16) and portions large enough to satisfy the most voracious hiker. We trust that this will remain true; the nephew of the longstanding owner was about to take over when we last visited.

A Stazzona (☎ 06 82 69 65 35; 17 rue du Fondu; mains €14-18, menu €16; Wed-Mon May-Oct) About 200m

---

THE AUTHOR'S CHOICE

A Flatta (☎ 04 95 62 80 38; www.aflatta.com in French; d €75–105; 🕙 Apr-Oct; 🅿 🐾 🔲) Here's the ultimate getaway, just a gorgeous, 3km solitary drive away from Calenzana, from where it's signed. At the head of a tight valley, it snuggles beneath sheer, jagged peaks, while in front the valley widens towards the open sea. Its five rooms, though on the smallish side, are a delight with beamed ceilings, rustic furnishings and tiled bathrooms with kidney-shaped baths. For even greater comfort, opt for the suite (€110 to €190) with its huge four-poster bed and bathroom with double washbasins and separate toilet. Wi-fi is available.

There's a cosy bar, its walls bedecked with cycling photos – notably of Jacques Anquetil, the legendary French racing cyclist, father of A Flatta's owner.

The restaurant (mains €19 to €26; menu €30; open dinner Monday to Friday, lunch and dinner Saturday and Sunday April to July, September and October, lunch and dinner daily August) merits a trip up the valley for its own sake. Eat on the terrace with its unparalleled views down the valley. Fish and lobster are of the freshest, brought up by a local fisherman.

---

north of the church, this place has a short, simple menu (try the *magret* of duck in honey) and enjoys a choice setting. Either dine inside in what was once a blacksmith's forge or in the shady rear garden.

Forêt & Cirque de Bonifatu

On the Calvi side of Calenzana, take a left turn onto the D51, signed Forêt de Bonifatu. The road continues over the first flat plain of the day, where, probably for the first time, you'll hit dizzying speeds in excess of 60km per hour. At a T-junction after 9km, turn left onto the D251. In its lower reaches, the forest of Bonifatu is dense and all but impenetrable. Higher up, outcrops of granite, pink, beige or grey according to the light, poke through. At the **Col de Bocca Rezza** (510m), it's well worth making a pause to take in the rocky landscape, sometimes called the Chaos de Rezza, that extends before you. Continue to the **car park** (mid-Jun–Aug €3.50, Sep–mid-Jun free) and road's end below Auberge de la Forêt.

The word Bonifatu means 'place of good life', and in the early years of the 20th century, this area was frequented by convalescents who came to take advantage of its pure air. The purity of the local ecosystem sustains a variety of Corsican fauna, including foxes, bearded vultures, Corsican nuthatches and wild boars. The forest, spreading over 3000 hectares and ranging in elevation from 300m to 2000m, is a mix of maritime and laricio pines, green oaks and other broad-leafed trees.

Until the last century, the forest was traversed by shepherds taking their flocks between winter and summer grazing grounds. These days the area is mainly frequented by walkers and a number of trails of various levels of difficulty lead from the car park. Easiest and most popular is the **Sentier du Mouflon** (Mouflon Path), which takes you on a forest circuit of about 2½ hours. But you needn't press on for the full *montée*; simply follow it downstream for a while to discover several secluded rock pools that invite a dip. About 20 minutes from the car park, tracks diverge to take you to the **Refuge de Carozzu** (two hours away) or the **Refuge d'Ortu di u Piobbu** (about three hours beyond), each on the GR20 route.

Auberge de la Forêt (☎ 04 95 65 09 98; camping €7.50, dm with/without half-board €33/15, d/tr 64/51, d or tr per person with half-board €43) is a veritable institution. Here, the GR20 originally started before it was decided to let Calenzana in on the act. The auberge also lies astride the Mare e Monti Nord trail. It's a cosy, inviting, walker-friendly if spartan option with a more than decent restaurant (mains €10 to €12; menu €18). Doubles have showers and corridor toilets and the four dorms accommodate four or six sleepers.

Heading back to Calvi, retrace your steps as far as the junction with the D51, then continue straight (the road becomes the D81). On the left, 2km before the Calvi-Ste-Catherine airport, a signed sandy track leads, after 600m, to a winery whose fruity Cuvée Prestige white, pressed from grapes picked early in the harvesting season, will delight your palate.

Continue to the roundabout at the junction with the N197 and turn left to return to Calvi.

INLAND FROM ÎLE ROUSSE (122KM)

There's a lot to pack in and, as everywhere on the island, you won't be averaging more than 50km per hour. One option is to break the journey in Feliceto and return to Île Rousse by the D13, then head for the hills again next day. Alternatively, we recommend several other accommodation options where you can overnight.

Take the N197 eastwards from Île Rousse and, after 7km, turn right, signed Belgodère.

Belgodère (Belgudè)
pop 370
This tiny village, 15km from Île Rousse, sits high above the olive groves of the Vallée du Prato. In the main square, the church, its façade spruce and freshly painted has a fine Baroque altarpiece.

West of the square are the remains of an old fort, from where there's a wonderful panorama. Go through an archway between the two cafés behind the war memorial and continue steeply uphill, following the *point de vue* sign.

Hôtel-Restaurant Le Niobel (☎ 04 95 61 34 00; www .hotel-niobel.com in French; s/d/tr €40/60/75; ⊙ Easter-Oct; ℗), 400m from the square, in the direction of Ponte Leccia, was originally the boarding house for the village school. It has 11 well-maintained rooms, three with balconies overlooking the valley. The new owners, a cheerful young couple from La Balagne, have overhauled the bedrooms and introduced a tempting restaurant *menu* (€25) of Corsican specialities. Dine inside or, for fine views, on the terrace.

Continuing along the N197, turn right after 7km onto the D963, which will bring you to Olmi-Cappella.

Olmi-Cappella
This hamlet, scarcely bigger than its name, is at the heart of the Giussani region and is renowned for its high mountain walking. You can't miss the **tourist office** (☎ 04 95 47 22 06; ⊙ 9am-12.30pm & 4.30-6.30pm Apr-Oct). Above the village, it shares with the town hall and post office the substantial building that was La Balagne's first school. It has seven sheets (€1 each) describing walks of three to 11km, each with an explicit 1:25,000 map. For more detail, arm yourself with the Top 25 sheets *Île-Rousse* (4249OT) and *Corte & Monte Cinto* (4250OT).

You like to hike light? Opposite the church, **Balagn'ane** (☎ 04 95 61 80 88; www.rando-ane-corse.com in French) hires out donkeys (€44 per day) and can provide a wealth of information about walks in the area.

For nibbles en route, call by **Maison Casanova**, 200m below the church, which turns out 13 varieties of biscuit using traditional Corsican recipes.

At first sight, you'd swear **U Chiosu di a Petra** (☎ 04 95 61 91 01; r incl breakfast €60) had been there for centuries. In fact the owner hauled up over 50 tonnes of stone and scoured the region for old doors, window frames, beams – anything abandoned yet recyclable. The result is a simply delightful *chambres d'hôtes* with three rooms – the hunter's, the shepherd's and the country cottage – each with its distinctive character, and a lovely shared living room. Not least of the charms is the copious buffet breakfast with 12 varieties of homemade jam. You'll find it on the main road above the village.

Forêt de Tartagine Melaja & Pioggiola
Continue along the D963 until it peters out after 18km beside a forestry lodge. The drive is a stunning one and not for those who fear heights. Tame at first and running through deciduous woodland, it then snakes along a narrow, lightly trafficked corniche, where even a cow is an event. The forest – oak and chestnut in the tight gorges, primarily pine on the upper slopes – occupies a massive 2700 hectares.

Cross the bridge beyond the lodge and head upstream to a tiny silted-up dam bordered by boulders that makes a great picnic spot. Easiest among several walking options is the marked trail that follows the valley downstream.

Retrace your tracks for 15km, then 3km before Olmi-Cappella turn sharp left onto the D63, signed **Pioggiola**.

In the village, **Auberge Aghjola** (☎ 04 95 61 90 48; www.auberge-aghjola.com in French; r with half-board €52-62; ⊙ Easter-mid-Oct; ℗ ⊠ ☺), a pretty, ivy-covered house, has nine comfortable rooms and a broad terrace shaded by a pair of venerable lime trees. The welcome's particularly warm and you'll eat very well indeed (they cure and salt their own cold meats).

Park and pause for a moment at the Col de Battaglia (1099m), 2.5km above Pioggiola. Here, as you leave the Parc Naturel Régional de Corse, there's a spectacular view of Speloncato, huddled tight atop a spur of Monte Tolo, the reservoir that backs up behind the Barrage de Codole and the coastline beyond.

Speloncato (Spiluncatu)
elevation 600m

A steep, twisting 7km descent brings you to one of the most beautiful villages in the Balagne. Perched above the site of an ancient Roman encampment, it owes its name to the nearby caves (*e spelunche* in Corsican) and its charm to its little streets with their densely packed stone houses. At this altitude, Speloncato is often shrouded in mist and even in high summer it can feel pleasantly cool.

Église St-Michel, Romanesque in style, has a handsome 18th-century Baroque choir and a magnificent Tuscan organ (1810). The incongruous bell tower with its phallic dome was grafted on in 1913.

Hôtel A Spelunca (☎ 04 95 61 50 38; hotel.a.spelunca@wanadoo.fr; d €55-75; ⊙ Apr-Oct; P), your only overnight choice here, is a fine building, constructed in 1850 by Cardinal Savelli, director-general of police in Rome and a native son of Speloncato. Run by a delightful old lady, its 18 comfortable rooms, built around a central staircase, are furnished with pieces of the era.

Continue through the village, towards Île Rousse and at a T-junction after 4km, turn left onto the D71.

Feliceto

If it's getting late, **Hôtel Mare e Monti** (☎ 04 95 63 02 00; www.maremonti.c.la; d €68-124, tr €104-126, q €120-140; ⊙ Apr–mid-Oct; P ⊠ ⊠) makes a charming overnight stop. Originally constructed by a Corsican family who made good in South America and returned home with their riches, its 16 recently renovated rooms have terracotta floor tiles and great mountain views. There's a mosaic-lined swimming pool, a more-than-creditable restaurant and a pretty rear garden.

Right next door is the sales outlet of **Domaine Renucci** (⊙ 10am-noon & 3-6.30pm Mon-Sat), a well-respected winery producing a range of good-quality AOC wines and top-quality olive oil.

In the valley, just 500m below the church, **Verrerie Corse** (⊙ 10am-noon & 3-6.30pm) is a glass-blowing workshop, run by two brothers.

Continuing along the D71, fork right after 8km onto the D151, then, very soon after, take a signed right turn up to the hilltop village of Sant'Antonino.

Sant'Antonino
elevation 550m

One of the highest and certainly one of the prettiest villages in the Balagne, Sant'Antonino also offers a superb 360-degree panorama. To this impregnable fastness the people of the plains below would retreat before the threat of Muslim invasion. Nowadays, however, it risks killing itself with its cuteness, exploited to the point of extortion.

Park your car (€1) in the square beside **Église St-Annunziata**. From here, donkey rides around the village (€10 – see what we mean?) leave every 20 minutes from 3.30pm. Climb the attractive cobbled streets, bordered by shops selling everything from quality goods to gewgaws (it's not only the tourists who get milked; you can even buy asses' milk soap), for ever more impressive views.

At **La Taverne Corse** (☎ 04 95 61 70 15; mains €8-15, menu Corse €20; ⊙ mid-Apr–mid-Oct) you can pick up a sandwich or panini. For something more substantial, go for a grill or the *menu Corse*. Nearby **La Voûte** (☎ 04 95 61 74 71; mains 9.50-18; ⊙ Easter-Sep) is an agreeable, airy place with great views from its panoramic terrace. It offers well-prepared standard Corsican specialities and pizzas (€7 to €9.50).

Back at the car park, stop by **Cave Antonini** (⊙ Apr-Oct), famous more for its lemons than its wines, to enjoy a refreshing glass of freshly squeezed juice poured over ice, to which you add water and sugar according to taste.

Return to the D151 and turn right.

Aregno

Aregno, barely 1km beyond the junction and surrounded by citrus and almond orchards, merits a brief stop to view its 12th-century **Église de la Trinité**, within the village cemetery. Built in the two-tone Pisan Romanesque style, it's a reminder of the distant days when Pisa, not Genoa or Paris, controlled the island's destiny. Note the naive basalt figurine beneath the pediment of the façade picking a thorn from his foot.

Continue along the D151 about 3km beyond Aregno to the craft village of Pigna.

Pigna

Just off the D151 and 7km from Île Rousse, the craft village of Pigna is, like Lama (p144), a fine example of how a hamlet, victim of depopulation and falling into terminal decline, can forge itself a new identity and viability – thanks to a dynamic mayor, committed villagers and an influx of newcomers with a variety of talents. Poke around its steep cobbled alleys to find the workshops of a potter, sculptor,

---

DETOUR: LAMA

Clinging to a rocky spur, with Monte Astu (1535m) rearing above it, the cutesy hamlet of Lama (pop 130) demands a detour from the main N1197 simply to browse its lanes and sense its vitality. Lama, like Pigna (p143), is an impressive example of how a village with the skids under it can redefine and revitalise itself. Nowadays confident and prosperous-looking, its almost every building, from humble cottage to fine bourgeois mansions and Italianate *palazzi*, seems to have been painted and pointed.

Bright flowers are everywhere and people too are taken into account. There's an open-air swimming pool, the village supports a multipurpose shop, there's a mobile grocery van, the baker calls by every day except Monday and the greengrocer and butcher drop in twice a week. And here's a nice, welcoming touch: on its door, the **tourist office** (☎ 04 95 48 23 90; www.ot-lama.com; ⏱ 9am-noon & 2-6pm Mon-Fri year round, plus 2-6pm Sat, 11am-noon & 2-6pm Sun Jul-Aug) posts the names of new visitors and the families they're staying with. The office covers the whole of the Ostriconi Valley and has a lengthy list of *chambres d'hôtes* and *gîtes*.

A couple of signed walking trails lead from Lama. For a full-day challenge, a route leads to the summit of Monte Astu (1535m; 3½ hours) via the Refuge de Prunincu (1048m; two hours). Less strenuously, a 2km route leads to Urtaca, the next village northwards.

For a week in late July or early August, Lama hosts the **Festival Européen du cinéma et du monde rural** (European Festival of Film & Rural Life; www.festilama.org), with an intensive programme of feature films and documentaries.

---

engraver, painter and makers of candles, musical boxes, lutes, flutes and more. And pick up some small work of gastronomic art from **Casa Savelli**, a richly endowed delicatessen.

Pigna's other claim to artistic fame is its year-round musical events, especially **Festivoce** (☎ 04 95 61 73 13; www.festivoce.casa-musicale .org in French), held over 10 days in July in its bijou auditorium.

Casa Musicale (☎ 04 95 61 76 57; www.casa-musicale.org in French; r €49-92) is a warmly recommended place with oodles of character. Its seven rooms (two with balcony) have magnificent views and wall frescoes. The restaurant, converted from an old olive press, serves excellent fare (mains €15 to €18) and the hotel promotes regular traditional Corsican music concerts and recitals.

U Palazzu (☎ 04 95 47 32 78; www.hotel-palazzu.com; r €100-140) is a bright, modern *chambre d'hôte* with three huge rooms and a couple of even bigger suites in an 18th-century mansion. Eat on the terrace of its stylish, separately run restaurant (*menus* €39 to €48, lunchtime salads and cold cuts €14 to €18) and savour the magnificent view or dine inside in this converted olive mill. Equally attractive is its stone flagged interior with its heavy wooden beams. It's open mid-April to mid-October (closed Monday except July and August).

At the bottom of the village, **A Casarella** (⏱ mid-Apr–mid-Oct, closed Mon except Jul & Aug) with its lovely little vine-shrouded terrace serves tapas

(€3.50 to €4.70), fresh organic fruit juices (€2.30) and homemade ice cream (€4.50).

Continue along the D151 just a few kilometres beyond Pigna to Corbara.

Corbara

Five kilometres from Île Rousse in the tiny village of Corbara, the **Musée de Corbara** (☎ 04 95 60 06 65; place de l'Église; admission free but donations welcome; ⏱ 3-6pm Jun–mid-Oct) is a delightful treasure-trove of Corsican historical artefacts, sprawling over several rooms. Assembled by its art historian owner, Guy Savelli, exhibits include a book of Corsican history written in 1594, an original *Account of Corsica* by James Boswell (recounting his journey to Corsica and meeting with Pascal Paoli), and a fascinating set of early-20th-century postcards. Alongside his collection of pistols and small arms, Monsieur Savelli treasures a set of fighting knives. 'In the old days, even the women used to carry these knives – it was for protection,' he says ominously.

Abutting the village church with its over-the-top Baroque altar, the two rooms of the **Musée du Trésor** (☎ 04 95 46 15 53; adult/child €3/2; ⏱ 10am-1pm & 4-7pm Apr-Oct), in the former sacristy, has a charming small collection of religious art, its highlight an 18th-century statue in marble of the Virgin crushing a snake, representing evil.

Continue to the junction with the main N197 and turn right to return to Île Rousse.

The West Coast

Three huge bites have been chomped from the crumpled coastline of Corsica's west coast with its plunging cliffs, staggering views and glorious coastal driving. The gulfs of Porto, Sagone and Ajaccio, more sheltered than the wilder promontories that separate them, are edged by golden beaches whose shallow turquoise and aquamarine waters offer some of the island's best scuba diving and water sports.

Chief among the coastal resorts after Ajaccio (allow yourself at least a night in Corsica's biggest and most bustling town to explore its Napoleonic heritage) is Porto. This pretty little port makes a great base for enjoying two Unesco World Heritage sites to its north and south: the protected Réserve Naturelle de Scandola, with its unique range of flora and fauna and, on its fringes, remote little Girolata, accessible only by boat or on foot. Nearer to Porto and more accessible are the teetering columns, pillars and giant boulders of Les Calanques, fashioned over millennia by wind and water. Explore, too, smaller coastal pleasure grounds such as Cargèse, with its Greek heritage, and Sagone or make your way down to one of the charming little walk-in-only creeks that fret the coastline.

It's easy to retreat from the summertime crowds of the coast to immerse yourself in the green hinterland among cool inland pines, beech and chestnut trees in the Forêt d'Aïtone and lightly travelled Liamone Valley. But for the truly getaway experience, head for the Haut Taravo, deep inland, with its mountain hamlets that still offer a taste of authentic, unhurried village life.

THE WEST COAST

HIGHLIGHTS

▪ **Day's End**
Watch the sun set from the 'chateau fort' overlooking the plunging cliffs of Les Calanques (p156)

▪ **Seen from the Sea**
Take a boat trip to view the spectacular protected Réserve Naturelle de Scandola (p152)

▪ **Belle Époque**
Sip a sundowner on the terrace of Piana's Hôtel les Roches Rouges (p158), then dine in the frescoed splendour of its restaurant

▪ **Rustic & Rural**
Explore the unspoilt inland hamlets of the Haut Taravo (p177)

▪ **Spread Your Towel**
Sprawl on the fine sand of Plage d'Arone (p159) or the golden beaches of Golfe de Sagone (p160)

▪ **Boots On!**
Hike between Genoese bridges along the towering Gorges de Spelunca (p153), then on and up to the charming mountain village of Évisa (p154)

★ Réserve Naturelle de Scandola

Gorges de Spelunca ★   ★ Évisa
★ Les Calanques
★ Piana

★ Plage d'Arone

Golfe de ★
Sagone

Haut Taravo ★

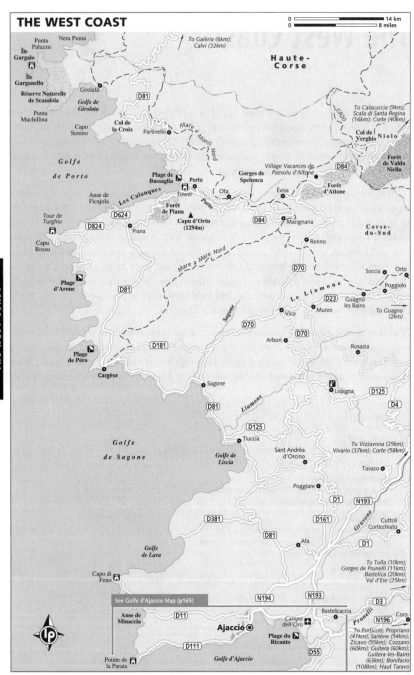

THE WEST COAST

0 — 14 km
0 — 8 miles

Punta Palazzu
Nera Punta
Punta
Île Gargalo
Île Garganellu
Réserve Naturelle de Scandola
Punta Muchillina
Girolata
Golfe de Girolata
D81
Capo Senino
Col de la Croix
Partinello
To Galéria (6km); Calvi (32km)
Haute-Corse
To Calacuccia (9km); Scala di Santa Regina (16km); Corte (40km)
Col de Verghio
Niolo
Forêt de Valdu Niellu
Golfe de Porto
Mare e Monti Nord
Village Vacances de Paesolu d'Aïtone
D84
Plage de Bussaglia
Porto
Gorges de Spelunca
Forêt d'Aïtone
Anse de Ficajola
Les Calanques
Tower
Ota
Évisa
Forêt de Piana
Porto
Marignana
Corse-du-Sud
Tour de Turghiu
D624
Capu d'Ortu (1294m)
D84
Piana
D824
Capu Rossu
Mare a Mare Nord
Renno
Soccia
Orto
Poggiolo
Plage d'Arone
D81
Le Liamone
D23
Guagno les Bains
To Guagno (2km)
Sagone
D70
Vico
Murzo
Plage de Péro
D181
Arbori
D70
Rosazia
Cargèse
Sagone
Liamone
Lopigna
D125
D4
Golfe de Sagone
D81
Golfe de Liscia
D125
Tiuccia
Sant'Andréa d'Orcino
To Vizzavona (25km); Vivario (37km); Corte (58km)
Tavaco
Poggiare
D1
N193
Gravona
Cuttoli Corticchiato
D381
D161
D1
D81
Afa
To Tolla (10km); Gorges de Prunelli (11km); Bastelica (20km); Val d'Ese (25km)
Golfe de Lava
Capo di Feno
N194
N193
D3
See Golfe d'Ajaccio Map (p165)
Anse de Minaccia
D11
Campo dell'Oro
Bastelicaccia
Prunelli
N196
Coro
Pointe de la Parata
Ajaccio
Plage du Ricanto
D55
To Porticcio; Propriano (41km); Sartène (54km); Zicavo (55km); Cozzano (60km); Guitera (60km); Guitera-les-Bains (63km); Bonifacio (108km); Haut Taravo
D111
Golfe d'Ajaccio

THE WEST COAST

GOLFE DE PORTO

PORTO

pop 350

This tiny seaside resort has the west coast's biggest buzz after Ajaccio. The setting is superb; inland, sheer pink cliffs tumble into a turquoise sea while over the Golfe de Porto the crags and cliffs of Les Calanques (p156) and the exceptional coastal wilderness of the Scandola nature reserve (p152) fret the skyline.

Packed in summer but deserted in winter, Porto makes a good base for exploring both sites, and the mountainous back country too.

The village is split by a promontory, topped by a restored Genoese square tower, erected in the 16th century to protect the gulf from Barbary incursions.

Orientation

Porto's pharmacy, beside the D81, the main road through this stretch of coast, makes a useful landmark, standing at the intersection with the road that leads 1.5km down to the harbour. East of it is the quarter known as Vaïta, or Porto le Haut.

If you're driving and aiming for the beach or the best place to park (see p150), take the road signposted 'Porto rive gauche', off the D81, direction Piana.

Information

L'Aiglon Sells French and foreign newspapers.
Laverie 2000 (9am-8.30pm) Laundrette.
Le Moulin (per hr €8; 2pm-2am Apr-Sep, 2-10pm Oct-Mar) Internet access. Expensive but Porto's sole option.
Post office Beside Hôtel Lonza in Vaïta.
Tourist office (☎ 04 95 26 10 55; www.porto-tourisme .com; place de la Marine; 9am-7pm Mon-Sat, 9am-1pm Sun Jun-Sep, 9am-6pm Mon-Sat Apr & May, 9am-7pm Mon-Fri Oct-Mar) Sells the excellent *Hikes & Walks in the Area of Porto.*

Sights & Activities

You can buy a combined ticket (adult €6.50) that gives admission to both the Genoese Tower and aquarium.

GENOESE TOWER

Standing guard over the entrance to the harbour, the **Genoese tower** (adult/child €2.50/free; 9am-9pm Jul & Aug, 11am-7pm Apr-Jun & Sep) was built in 1549, at a time when most of the other 85 towers around the Corsican coast were being

constructed. Restored in 1993, it has a wealth of interesting information (in French and English) about their financing, construction and functioning – and about the tough existence of the tower watchman. You reach the tower via a series of steps starting next to La Tour Génoise restaurant. From the top, in fine weather, you can see the tower on Capu Rossu at the southern tip of the Golfe de Porto.

AQUARIUM DE LA POUDRIÈRE

Within the town's former gunpowder magazine, this little **aquarium** (☎ 04 95 26 19 24; adult/child €5.50/3; 8am-9pm Jul & Aug, 8am-7pm Sep-Jun) has about 500 fish and plenty of information (in French) on the flora and fauna of the gulf. See if you can spot the cannily camouflaged octopus.

BOAT TRIPS

Between April and October, four companies with very similar tariffs do 3½-hour daytime cruises to the Réserve Naturelle de Scandola (€36 to €40) and two-hour evening boat trips to Les Calanques (around €20). For Scandola, opt for the slightly more expensive option that allows you time ashore in Girolata (p151). The smaller boats can nudge into some of the tiny inlets that are denied to the larger models.
Nave Va (☎ 04 95 26 15 16; www.naveva.com) Biggest of the operators with the largest boat. Also offers a five-hour cruise embracing both Scandola and Les Calanques (adult/child €45/37). Info from Hôtel Le Cyrnée.
Pass'Partout (☎ 06 79 99 13 15) A new player with an attractive small boat. Info from Glacier-Snack Les Flots Bleus.
Porto Linea (☎ 04 95 26 11 50, 06 08 16 89 71) *Mare Nostrum,* a bright yellow 12-seater offers (we quote) 'an appropriately poetical commentary by the captain'. Info from Hôtel Monte Rosso.
Via Mare (☎ 06 07 28 72 72) With Porto Linea, the most experienced of the operators. Info from Le Golfe.

BOAT & CANOE HIRE

If you prefer independence and setting your own pace, consider exploring Scandola and Les Calanques in your own boat. Smaller models don't require a special licence.
Le Goéland (☎ 06 81 06 88 08; mid-May–Sep) On the river's left bank; rents motor boats (per half-/full day from €75/115).
Patrick & Toussaint (☎ 06 81 41 70 03; Jun–mid-Sep) A jolly pair who rent both motor boats (per half-/full day from €75/115) and canoes (per hour/half-day/full day from €10/25/40).

THE WEST COAST

THE WEST COAST

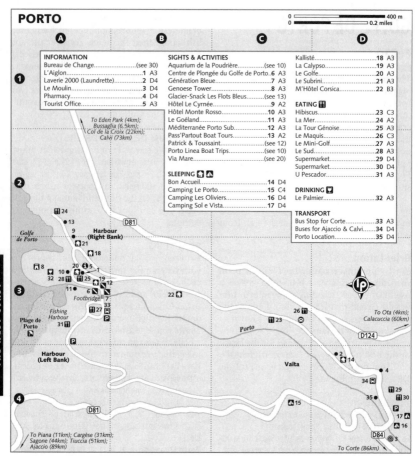

PORTO

INFORMATION	
Bureau de Change.....................(see 30)	
L'Aiglon..................................1 A3	
Laverie 2000 (Laundrette)............2 D4	
Le Moulin..............................3 D4	
Pharmacy................................4 D4	
Tourist Office..........................5 A3	

SIGHTS & ACTIVITIES	
Aquarium de la Poudrière..............(see 10)	
Centre de Plongée du Golfe de Porto.6 A3	
Génération Bleue........................7 A3	
Genoese Tower..........................8 A3	
Glacier-Snack Les Flots Bleus.........(see 13)	
Hôtel Le Cyrnée.........................9 A2	
Hôtel Monte Rosso.....................10 A3	
Le Goéland.............................11 A3	
Méditerranée Porto Sub...............12 A3	
Pass'Partout Boat Tours...............13 A2	
Patrick & Toussaint.....................(see 12)	
Porto Linea Boat Trips.................(see 10)	
Via Mare................................(see 20)	

SLEEPING	
Bon Accueil............................14 D4	
Camping Le Porto......................15 C4	
Camping Les Oliviers..................16 D4	
Camping Sol e Vista...................17 D4	

Kallisté..................................18 A3	
La Calypso..............................19 A3	
Le Golfe.................................20 A3	
Le Subrini...............................21 A3	
M'Hôtel Corsica.......................22 B3	

EATING	
Hibiscus................................23 C3	
La Mer..................................24 A2	
La Tour Génoise........................25 A3	
Le Maquis...............................26 C3	
Le Mini-Golf............................27 A3	
Le Sud..................................28 A3	
Supermarket...........................29 D4	
Supermarket...........................30 D4	
U Pescador.............................31 A3	

DRINKING	
Le Palmier.............................32 A3	

TRANSPORT	
Bus Stop for Corte.....................33 A3	
Buses for Ajaccio & Calvi..............34 D4	
Porto Location..........................35 D4	

WALKING

Pick up a copy of the tourist office's *Hikes & Walks in the Area of Porto* (€2.50), which details 28 signed walks at all levels of difficulty around Porto, Les Calanques and other villages such as Évisa and Ota. For longer hikes, you'll need to supplement this with the IGN Top 25 sheet 4150 OT, *Porto & Calanche de Piana*.

BEACH

It's not the most stunning beach in Corsica but the partly sandy, mostly pebbly **Plage de Porto** is a reasonable spot for a dip and a sunbathe. This said, it can be dirty with seaborne plastic and general dross and there's no sign of a regular maintenance programme.

DIVING

You can enjoy some of Corsica's finest scuba diving around the Golfe de Porto, which drops to 800m at its deepest. Diving is forbidden within the Scandola reserve but Porto's three outfits can take you to the best spots just outside the protected area and there are plenty of other enticing options. Each runs diving courses (starting at around €300). Single dives start from €25 without equipment and €35 including gear rental while a pack of 10 dives starts at €320/230 with/without gear.

Centre de Plongée du Golfe de Porto (☎ 04 95 26 10 29, 06 84 24 49 20; www.plongeeporto.com in French; ☼ Easter-Oct)

Génération Bleue (☎ 04 95 26 24 88, 06 07 43 21 28; www.generation-bleue.com; ☼ May-Oct)

Méditerranée Porto Sub (☎ 04 95 26 10 27, 06 14 94 08 44; www.le-mediterranee.com; ☉ mid-Apr–Sep)

See also p79 for more on diving.

Sleeping

Prices go sky-high in July and August. In other months, the canny traveller is the winner of the keen price war between hotels, which post their prices of the day, as changeable and as in tune with the market of the moment as any bookmaker's odds.

HOTELS

Bon Accueil (☎ 04 95 26 19 50; ba20150@aol.com; d €35-46, tr €46-51; ☉ year-round; P ⓧ) In Vaïta and above a cheerful café-cum-souvenir shop, this friendly option has 23 modern rooms, some of which can accommodate up to six. Simply but immaculately furnished, most have balconies. Front-facing ones have views through the eucalyptus trees to the river.

Le Golfe (☎ 04 95 26 13 33; r €38-60; ☉ mid-Mar–Oct) With their clashing colours, winsome artwork and plastic flowers, the rooms here might not be your ideal honeymoon destination. But you haven't come here for the aesthetic experience and you can't beat the welcome or the harbour location. The 10 rooms are generous in size, eight have bathrooms and balconies, and the majority have sea views. The two cheapest rooms have a shower and washbasin, with corridor toilet.

Kallisté (☎ 04 95 26 10 30; www.hotel-kalliste.com in French; s €42-56, d €57-76, tr €70-86; ☉ Apr–Oct; P ⓧ ⓧ) This three-star place occupies two buildings that are set back from the road and passing traffic. Its 59 spick-and-span rooms have large bathrooms and ample cupboard space; nearly all have a balcony with sea views, too. Except for the first two weeks of August, when prices rocket, the Kallisté represents great value. There's a supplement of €8 for air-con.

M'Hotel Corsica (☎ 04 95 26 10 89; www.hotel-corsica -porto.com; d €50-76; ☉ Apr–Oct; P ⓧ ⓧ) The un-missable pink M'Hotel Corsica, in Vaïta, sits amid eucalyptus forest, well apart from the bustle of the marina. Its 30 simply furnished rooms all have a balcony and the toilet cubicle is independent of the bathroom. Room 5 is the largest and best furnished. Some bedrooms have air-con (€10 supplement) and others have an optional kitchenette (€4 supplement, minimum three nights).

La Calypso (☎ 04 95 26 11 54; www.hotel-la-calypso .com in French; d €54-104; ☉ Apr–Oct; P ⓧ ⓧ) Down by the harbour, the Calypso is in an attrac-tive stone building, its façade enlivened by awnings and window boxes bursting with fresh flowers. It has eight large, well-furnished rooms and a terrace that lords it over the portside action below. Outside high season, it offers excellent value.

Eden Park (☎ 04 95 26 10 60; www.hotels-porto.com in French; r per person incl breakfast €57-107; ☉ Apr–mid-Oct; P ⓧ ⓧ) Eden Park, 5km north of Porto on the D81, is a delightfully tranquil retreat. Five rooms are in the main building while the remaining 30 are disposed in bungalows within the hotel's large leafy grounds. There's a tennis court, a children's playground and, in July and August, a piano bar. The large, at-tractive terrace of its gastronomic restaurant L'Acropole (p150) overlooks the landscaped, palm-shaded swimming pool. It lends bikes for free – an offer worth taking up since the beach is a good 800m walk away.

Le Subrini (☎ 04 95 26 14 94; www.hotels-porto.com in French; d €60-120; ☉ Apr–Oct; P ⓧ) With its mar-ble floors, chintz and wicker furniture, the comfy three-star Subrini, in the harbour area, feels like it hasn't left the 1980s. All of its 24 spacious, well-equipped rooms overlook the harbour and have full frontal views of the Genoese tower. Those on the lower floors have a balcony, while upper-level ones have a broad loggia.

CAMPING

Camping Le Porto (☎ 04 95 26 13 67; www.camping -le-porto.com in French; camp sites per adult/tent/car €5.30/2.50/2.50; ☉ mid-Jun–Sep) This smaller, wel-coming camping ground enjoys a lovely site in a mature mixed forest, part of which was once terraced orchards. It accepts reservations.

Camping Sol e Vista (☎ 04 95 26 15 71; www.camping -sole-e-vista.com; camp sites per adult/tent/car €6/2.50/2.50; ☉ Apr-Oct) Above the Spar supermarket beside the D81, this large attractive camping ground with its shady terraces climbs steeply up the mountainside. Facilities include washing ma-chines, children's playground and a small café at the upper end. There are great views of the mountains and the toilet blocks (a pity there are no separate male and female facilities) are cleaned regularly.

Camping Les Oliviers (☎ 04 95 26 14 49; www.camping -oliviers-porto.com in French; camp sites per person €6.50-8.50, tent €2.50-6, car €2.50-3.50, chalets per week per 4 people

THE WEST COAST

€300-640, 5 people €370-640, 6 people €440-745, 7 people €470-835; ☺ Apr-Oct; ☜) Amid olive groves, this welcoming, well-maintained camping ground has a rock-lined swimming pool – for an even more back to nature experience, you can dunk yourself in the pools of the river that flows below – and a restaurant plus pizzeria. Why, there's even a fitness centre if you've still energy to burn after a day of swimming or mountain walking. Timber chalets, all with air-con, kitchen and bathroom, sleep up to seven people. Like Porto's other camping options, it can be desperately crowded in high season but it accepts reservations (minimum stay four nights).

Eating
RESTAURANTS

Lots of restaurants and hotels along the seafront serve pizzas and inexpensive, unsurprising menus.

U Pescador (☎ 04 95 26 15 19; mains €7-15, menus €13-16.50; ☺ May-Sep) Near the beach and sandwiched between the car park and a recently planted grove of trees (with the sea just out of sight, alas), the Fisherman does a quite magnificent fish soup. Rub a clove of garlic into the toasted bread, sprinkle on some grated cheese, pour on the rich broth, add a dollop of rich *rouille*, sip and sigh with pleasure. To follow, both the fish and seafood are delightfully fresh.

Le Mini-Golf (☎ 04 95 26 17 55; menus €16-25; ☺ mid-Apr–Sep) You'll get particularly generous pizzas (€8.50 to €12) at this restaurant, in a little green area on the left bank; it also does full meals. After dining, work off the calories with a round of minigolf, owned by the same charming *patronne*.

La Tour Génoise (☎ 04 95 26 17 11; mains €12.20-17.50, menus €17-21.70; ☺ Apr–mid-Oct) With its 'surf' or 'turf' menus and shady terrace, this place, just above the marina and overlooking the Genoese tower, is a pleasant option. A half-litre pitcher of local wine costs €6.

Le Sud (☎ 04 95 26 14 11; mains €20-22, menu €29, noon special €19; Ⓥ) With its hippy chic–inspired décor, terracotta urns, sun mirrors and whitewashed walls, Le Sud affects Mediterranean cool. From its sweeping terrace you can enjoy some of Porto's finest and most imaginative dishes in a relaxed atmosphere and with a great panorama of the marina to boot. The refreshingly simple meat- or fish-based à la carte selection offers dishes such as *lapin*

de la garrigue au romarin (wild rabbit with rosemary). Vegetarians will relish the *assiette du sud* (€14) with minted cucumber, tapenade, roasted peppers and chickpea purée.

La Mer (☎ 04 95 26 11 27; mains €18-27, menus €29; ☺ mid-Mar–mid-Nov) At Porto's northern extremity, La Mer has the finest views of all from its terrace overlooking the gulf and the Genoese tower, which is illuminated at night. It, too, serves good fish dishes, which, according to the catch of the day, may include grilled snapper and fresh sardines.

Le Maquis (☎ 04 95 26 12 19; mains €20-29, menus €19-32) There's a cosy all-wood interior but, for preference, reserve a table on the balcony with magnificent views of the bay, comfortable wicker chairs and candles flickering all around. Service is friendly and attentive and the food a delight. Save a cranny for the cheeseboard with around a dozen different varieties, mostly without name and all bought directly from the producer.

L'Acropole (☎ 04 95 26 10 60; dinner menus €19-31) The restaurant of Eden Park hotel (p149) has a gorgeous setting and is renowned for its gourmet cuisine. The *menus*, based on French and Corsican traditional cooking, include steaks, charcuterie, local fish and seafood, all presented with style.

SELF-CATERING

Hibiscus (rte de la Marine) A great little delicatessen that specialises in richly scented sausages, charcuterie and other Corsican gastronomic delights.

A couple of supermarkets on the D81, not far from the pharmacy, provide for self-caterers.

Drinking

Le Palmier is a small bar, opposite Hôtel Monte Rosso, with a tight little terrace and a delightful view of the harbour and Genoese tower. It's the ideal spot to sip a pastis as the sun creeps below the horizon.

Getting There & Around

Autocars Ceccaldi (☎ 04 95 22 41 99) run two buses between Porto and Ajaccio (€11, two hours), calling by Piana and Golfe de Sagone coastal towns. It also connects Porto and Calvi (€17, 2½ hours), via Col de la Croix, once daily from 15 May to 10 October. Buses stop at the pharmacy.

Between July and mid-September, **Autocars Mordiconi** (☎ 04 95 48 00 04) runs one bus daily along the spectacular route between Porto and Corte (€20, 2¾ hours) via Évisa (€8, 45 minutes) and Calacuccia (€15, 1¾ hours). Buses start from the left bank, beside Le Mini-Golf.

Porto Location (☎ 04 95 26 10 13; 8.30am-9pm Apr-Oct) hires out cars (per day from €51), scooters (from €33) and mountain bikes (from €9).

Driving through Porto can be a slow shuffle. Better to leave your car in the parking areas behind the beach and walk over the footbridge.

AROUND PORTO
Bussaglia

Bussaglia is 7km northwest of town. From the D81 take a sharp left turn 400m beyond the Eden Park hotel to follow a narrow road that runs parallel to a streambed, ending at the gently curving Bussaglia beach, facing the dramatic backdrop of Les Calanques. The coarsely pebbled beach is satisfyingly quiet, given its proximity to Porto. The loose pebble bed makes it difficult to enter the water without footwear and this, combined with a relatively steep shelf and strong drag, makes swimming here unsuitable for small children. On the plus side, it's one of Corsica's very few beaches with a freshwater shower, albeit paying.

On the beach, you can hire motor boats (per half-/full day €70/110 plus fuel), pedalos and kayaks (both per hour/half-day/full day €15/30/50).

SLEEPING & EATING

Hotel L'Aiglon (☎ 04 95 26 10 65; hotelaiglon@tiscali.fr; s €48, with bathroom €47-58, d €70, with bathroom €62-80, per person with half-board €53-77; Apr–mid-Oct) Not much has changed here since the 1950s, and charmingly so. This pretty stone house with its wide terrace overlooking the maquis still feels like a family home. The 18 sparse rooms are bright and simply decorated with colourful, museum-quality fabrics and quaint country furnishings. You can browse a dusty copy of a French *policier* novel or play chess in the cool shade of the foyer. Half-board (compulsory in August) features a rustic Corsican *menu* that might include *terrine de sanglier* and delicious roast pork in port. The beach is 700m away.

Résidence Marina Livia (☎ 04 95 26 12 60; chalets per week per 2 people €320-600, 3 people €350-650, 4 people €380-700; Apr–mid-Oct) The nicest thing about this small compound is its location – 200m from the beach in a former olive grove and orchard, bursting with colourful flowers. The wooden chalets are simply equipped with kitchenettes and bathrooms, all have verandas and the location is peaceful. Prices vary according to season.

Bussaglia has only two beachside restaurants, both tempting and each with a terrace that catches the sea breezes. Friendly **Mare Chiare** (☎ 04 95 26 11 86; pizzas €7-9, salads €8.20-12, panini €4-6.50) serves filling snacks as well as full meals. At its neighbour, **Les Galets** (☎ 04 95 26 10 49), you could also settle for a tasty pizza or select from its extensive selection of fresh fish dishes (€14 to €24).

GIROLATA

Although not officially part of the Scandola nature reserve, Girolata and the bay on which it sits are outstanding. You can spot this hamlet from many points on the drive between Calvi and Porto but you can only reach it by boat or on foot.

Despite its inaccessibility, Girolata, between the Scandola peninsula and Capo Senino, gets quite busy in July and August. Private yachts carrying the kind of people who frequent end-of-the-world beaches pull in at the superb harbour, as do a whole flotilla of sightseeing boats from Porto and other coastal resorts.

On 19 March locals from the region descend on the village in small boats for the **feast of St Joseph**.

Sleeping

Girolata lies on the Mare e Monti Nord trail and has two *gîtes d'étape* (mountain lodges).

La Cabane du Berger (☎ 04 95 20 16 98; camp sites per person €8, dm/cabins with half-board €40/60; Jun-Oct) The Shepherd's Cabin, beside the landing stage, is primarily a bar and restaurant, but it has *gîte d'étape* facilities and simple wooden cabins.

Le Cormoran Voyageur (☎ 04 95 20 15 55; dm with half-board €34; Apr-Sep) This red stone house, where the village meets the beach, is lovingly tended by Joseph Teillet Ceccaldi (a fisherman and one of Girolata's leading citizens). It has 20 beds divided among three reasonably comfortable rooms sleeping six or eight. Half-board, with an emphasis on fish dishes, is obligatory and there are no self-catering facilities.

THE WEST COAST

COL DE LA CROIX TO GIROLATA WALK

The trail from the Col de la Croix (Bocca a Croce; 22km north of Porto on the D81) sets off on a clear path down a gentle slope through dense maquis to pass a pretty pebbled fountain after about 15 minutes. At a fork, reached after a further fifteen minutes, take the left path, which leads down to the **Tuara cove**. It should be idyllic, but the charm can sometimes be spoiled when the tide carries in gravel and rubbish. Don't spend too much time here; instead walk around to the northern end of the beach. Two paths thread through the maquis; the one on the left follows the line of the coast while a second, to the right, heads up the hill. Take the path to the right; there's a 20-minute climb to the junction with the **Mare e Monti Nord** (p78; orange markings).

Once at this crossroads, you have a stunning view over Girolata and the Baie de Girolata, guarded by a small Genoese fort. To the southwest is Capo Senino. On the other side, to the northeast, Punta Muchillina, at the limit of the Réserve Naturelle de Scandola, pokes out. Descending to Girolata from here takes about 30 minutes.

Girolata tends to get overcrowded in summer and its beach is disappointing. There are a few good restaurants on the seafront, though (see below).

You can return by a slightly different route. Cross back over the beach in Girolata and follow the path you came on for about 20m. Then, instead of continuing upwards, take the path to the right, which follows a ledge around the coast as far as the Tuara cove. Allow about three hours for the round-trip.

Eating

There are several restaurants, nicely situated above the beach and beneath the Genoese fortress. All offer good fish-based menus.

Le Bel Ombra (☎ 04 95 20 15 67; menus €20-25; ☻ May-Oct) Just above Le Cormoran Voyageur, you can enjoy an unrestricted view over the cove from the teak armchairs on its terrace. Next door, **Le Bon Espoir** (☎ 04 95 10 04 55) offers the same great view, fish dishes and a *menu Corse*.

GUY LE FACTEUR

As you walk the mule track that leads to Girolata from Col de la Croix, the silence may be broken by the putt-putt of a yellow post office motorbike, wrestled over the bumps and ruts by a man with a flowing white beard beneath an ancient army crash helmet. It's Guy the Postman, a national celebrity since he was the subject of a French TV documentary. Guy Ceccaldi, a strapping ex-legionnaire, now over 65 years old, used to walk to Girolata and back six times a week, bringing not only the mail but news of the outside world. Nowadays motorised, he burns up the energy he saves in his favourite pastime – prowling the maquis and hunting wild boar.

RÉSERVE NATURELLE DE SCANDOLA

Created in 1975, the Scandola nature reserve at the northern end of the Golfe de Porto occupies 920 hectares of land and approximately 1000 hectares of sea. Owing its exceptional ecological richness to a varied geology as well as a particularly favourable climate and regular sunshine, it is home to a large variety of plant and animal species, including osprey, cormorant, puffin, coral and various types of seaweed. Scientists come in droves to study this flora and fauna.

Although the reserve was established too late to save the last colonies of monk seal and Corsican deer (now reintroduced around Quenza in the Alta Rocca), Scandola is a unique breeding ground for grouper and osprey. Another of its curiosities is a type of calcareous seaweed, so hard that it can form a thin pavement on the water's surface.

Scandola is bound in the north by Punta Palazzu and in the south by Punta Muchillina. **Île Gargalo** with its tower and **Île Garganellu**, at the western edge of the reserve, have won renown both for their wildlife and for their volcanic caves and faults. Bird-watchers are usually in luck until around the end of June.

The reserve, a Unesco World Heritage site in recognition of its unique marine environment, is managed by the Parc Naturel Régional de Corse (PNRC).

THE WEST COAST

THE KING OF THE SCANDOLA NATURE RESERVE

The Scandola peninsula was home to just three osprey pairs in 1973. Today there are about 20 pairs, which is more than one-third of the entire osprey population in the whole of the Mediterranean. A large bird of prey with a white body and brown wings, the osprey is a magnificent sight, especially when hunting. It soars in wide circles until it spots a fish moving just below the water's surface, then dives towards the waves, extending its claws at the very last moment to grab the fish.

Getting There & Away

There's no motor-vehicle access or footpath into the Scandola nature reserve, so the only way to get up close is by water. Companies organising boat trips operate out of Porto (p147), Cargèse (p161), Sagone (p162), Ajaccio (p168), Porticcio (p175) and Calvi (p129).

PORTO TO COL DE VERGHIO

Leave Porto by the D124 in order to take in Ota, renowned for its pair of superb Genoese bridges. This minor road then crosses the river to connect with the main D84, which continues the climb through the mountains to the plunging Gorges de Spelunca near Évisa, the Forêt d'Aïtone and Col de Verghio (Bocca di Verghju), beyond which lies the Niolo (Niulu) region (p244). From here you can continue down the valley and on to the Forêt de Valdu Niellu, Calacuccia, the Scala di Santa Regina and Corte.

Ota

pop 150 / elevation 335m

Sleepy Ota, 5km east of Porto, perches above its cemetery. The terracotta-topped granite houses teeter in rows that follow the contours of the mountain. Many still preserve their characteristic external steps that lead to the upper floors. A great pair of *gîtes d'étape* with accompanying restaurants, open to all, offer shelter to hikers undertaking the Mare e Monti Nord trail, which passes through the hamlet.

From Ota, there's a popular undemanding walk (see p154). Suitable for both casual and serious hikers, it takes you into the spectacular **Gorges de Spelunca**. It's fine for families, who can combine a leisurely stroll with a dip in

one of the many rocky pools. To stretch the legs further, you can prolong the experience by trekking steeply upwards to Évisa.

SLEEPING & EATING

Chez Félix (☎ 04 95 26 12 92, fax 04 95 26 18 25; place de la Fontaine; dm with/without half-board €32/13; ☺ year-round) Rooms of the *gîte* (in a separate building; check in at the restaurant) accommodate between four and eight sleepers and there are also two basic doubles (€45) and two with bathroom (€50). There's a communal kitchen but, unless every penny counts, go for half-board. The restaurant is open to all. Its attractive *menu* (€20) changes daily and it also serves omelettes and snacks (€5 to €10). Chez Félix also operates the village taxi service.

Chez Marie & Bar des Chasseurs (☎ 04 95 26 11 37; dm with/without half-board €33/16) A friendly place, just down the road, with spotless dorms and one double room, all with shared bathrooms. It has a well-equipped kitchen for self-caterers – if you can resist the restaurant's local dishes (mains €8 to €13), such as kid with butter beans (€13) and *cannelloni au brocciu* (€9), or the four-course *menu* (€22). The terrace has glorious views of the valley below.

U Fragnu (☎ 04 95 26 15 60; mains €15-23, menus €20-22; ☺ year-round) Sadly, the cook at this wonderfully situated restaurant had suffered a serious motorbike accident at the time of research. But the food remained wonderful and, whoever they may need to recruit, the ambience is very special. You're dining in a former olive mill, beneath a lovely vaulted ceiling; beside you the original granite wheel that executed the first crushing, before you the wooden press that squeezed the berries to release their oil.

Marignana

pop 100 / elevation 750m

This hamlet, on a mountainside between Ota and Évisa, was famous in the 19th century as the scene of a prolonged and bloody vendetta and, later, as the hideout of the partisans of *le maquis* during WWII. Nowadays, in addition to its reputation as a producer of rich charcuterie, it's an R&R stop for hikers on the Mare a Mare Nord and Mare e Monti trails.

At the convivial bar and restaurant of **Ustaria di a Rota** (☎ 04 95 26 21 21; dm with/without half-board €33/15, d €35), you can indulge in fine Corsican specialities (*menu* €15). In addition to its large dorms, Ustaria di a Rota also has a few doubles with washbasin in a nearby building.

PONTE VECCHJU TO PONTE ZAGLIA WALK

The route, punctuated by interpretive panels in French, starts at the edge of the double-arched road bridge, 2km east of Ota. Until the D84 was hacked out of the mountain, this former mule track, partly cobbled, was the only link between the villages of Ota and Évisa. It's a spectacular trail, running along the plunging valley of the River Porto and through the Spelunca canyon, beneath huge, humbling cliffs, some more than 1000m high. These days it's part of the Mare e Monti Nord long-distance walk (p78), running between Calenzana and Cargèse and signed with orange markers.

Before setting out, backtrack about 300m downstream from the road bridge to take in the Ponte Vecchju (old bridge), the first of two outstanding Genoese bridges.

Once en route, the rocky path soon begins to climb fairly steeply up the western flank of the valley, but green oaks provide substantial shade. After 30 minutes you come to Ponte Zaglia, the second Genoese bridge, all but hidden in the depths of the vegetation. Close by the bridge, you can refresh yourself in any number of pools. It takes between an hour and 1½ hours to complete this easy there-and-back walk.

For a more extensive outing, you can start this walk in Ota (a path drops to the valley bottom just past the Chez Félix restaurant). More stimulating but more demanding, you can continue along the Mare e Monti trail beyond Ponte Zaglia as far as Évisa. The shaded path ascends the steep hillside by a series of switchbacks, emerging onto the D84 beside the village cemetery. For this variant, count on around five hours' round-trip from the double bridge.

ÉVISA

pop 200 / elevation 830m

The lively little village of Évisa, between the Gorges de Spelunca and the Forêt d'Aïtone, is popular with walkers because of its location at the junction of the Mare a Mare Nord and Mare e Monti Nord trails and the chance to stock up on provisions.

The village's more general fame arises from its annual chestnut harvests, mere gleanings compared to the bumper years of the 19th century but still pulling in about 1200 tonnes of chestnuts each year, of which a good 1000 tonnes are ground into chestnut flour. Évisa chestnuts even have their own appellation, and the village holds **La Fête du Marron**, a chestnut festival celebrated every November.

Sleeping & Eating

Gîte d'Étape U Poghju (☎ 04 95 26 21 88; gite-etape -upoghju@club-internet.com; dm with/without half-board €32/13; Apr–mid-Oct) This *gîte* is justifiably talked about along the trails for the warmth of its reception. Dormitories sleep four or eight and there are a couple of doubles too. It's in the lower part of Évisa. By car, take the signed turn-off from the main road at the western end of the village; on foot, take the lane between the post office and the school and drop down a flight of steps.

L'Aïtone (☎ 04 95 26 20 04; www.hotel-aitone.com in French; d with shower €35-40, with bathroom €50-110; Feb-Oct; P) Opposite U Pozzu (the two hotels are run by a pair of brothers), L'Aïtone's 32 rooms, all overlooking the valley, are comfortable if a little old-fashioned. The more

THAT OLD CHESTNUT

Since the 16th century, Corsicans have planted *châtaigniers* (chestnut trees), known as *l'arbre à pain* (the bread tree) because it was a staple of so many Corsicans' diet.

Nothing was wasted. The wood was fashioned into furniture and whittled into stakes for fencing. The leaves and branches were fed to the goats and what remained would be used for winter heating.

Tasty dishes made with chestnuts include *beignets au brocciu à la farine de châtaigne* (*brocciu* cheese frittered in chestnut flour), *délice à la châtaigne* (chestnut cake), *castagnacciu* (a moister chestnut cake) and *falculelli* (pressed, frittered *brocciu* served on a chestnut leaf). And let's not forget Pietra, Corsica's wonderfully rich amber ale flavoured with chestnuts, or the delightful ham from free-range pigs raised on chestnuts with its distinctive flavour.

ÉVISA TO CASCADES D'AÏTONE WALK

This easy two- to 2½-hour 7km out-and-back walk follows a section of the Mare a Mare Nord long-distance trail (p76) to a series of clear natural pools. It begins beside Modern' Bar towards the eastern end of Évisa. Follow the orange markings.

Called the Chemin des Châtaigniers (The Chestnut Grove Route), it's punctuated by 13 interpretive panels (in French) that explain chestnut farming, once a mainstay of the local economy and principal item in the villagers' diet. For the first 45 minutes it follows a sandy lane between chestnut groves, where Mediterranean and laricio pine are gradually reasserting themselves. After intersecting with the D84, take the wide path that drops gently to the pools and waterfalls that mark your destination. Like so many others at this popular spot, disregard the monolingual notice forbidding bathing, placed there by a backside-covering local authority, and paddle or plunge into their cooling waters.

---

expensive ones have balconies and the bathroom is separate from the toilet. Families will enjoy the pool, tennis court and children's playground. The restaurant (mains €14 to €24, *menus* €16 to €20) has truly spectacular views from its broad terrace.

La Châtaigneraie (☎ 04 95 26 24 47; www.hotel-la -chataigneraie.com in French; d €36-49, tr €55-63; Apr-Oct;) La Châtaigneraie (Chestnut Grove), a stout building of grey granite on the western side of the village, is run by a friendly Corsican and his Californian wife. It's a welcoming, homely place – their young children are sure to address you in solemn conversation – with vast grounds. The 12 no-frills bedrooms are impeccably clean. The restaurant (mains €16 to €18) merits a visit in its own right. For a not-so-light lunch, opt for its mixed platter of Corsican meats (€15). Portions throughout are ample. Among the tempting mains, you'll enjoyed the *filet de porc aux cèpes, girolles et châtaignes* (tenderest fillet of pork with chestnuts and two kinds of mushroom). And whatever you select from their list of homemade desserts (€7 to €9), should you still have a spare cranny to fill, is bound to be a winner.

U Pozzu (☎ 04 95 21 11 45; www.hotel-gites-u-pozzu .com in French; d €36-50, q €50-70, apt per week with 2 beds €250-320, with 4 beds €310-450; May-Sep) At the eastern limit of Évisa, U Pozzu has comfortable, well-priced doubles and fully equipped apartments with simple rustic furnishings. It's a child-friendly place with table tennis and board games. Not so plastic-friendly, however; credit cards are taboo.

Mathieu & Patricia Ceccaldi (☎ 04 95 26 25 13; mid-Apr–Oct) Sells its own potted meats, charcuterie and chestnut flour and lots of other Corsican specialities, bought from small producers in the area. Opposite Modern' Bar.

Getting There & Away

Between July and mid-September, there's one bus, daily except Sunday, to/from both Porto (€8, 45 minutes) and Corte (€17, two hours).

AROUND ÉVISA
Forêt d'Aïtone

The Forêt d'Aïtone – all 1670 hectares of it, rising from 800m to 2000m – begins a few kilometres east of Évisa and stretches as far as the Col de Verghio. In the 17th century the Genoese forged a path through this beautiful forest to Sagone, from where timber from the forest was transported to the shipyards of Genoa. There, the tall straight laricio pine trunks, some 60m in height, were fashioned into beams, masts and crosspieces for the powerful Genoese navy, for long masters of the Mediterranean. The laricio pine, covering around 800 hectares, is still the dominant species. Beech accounts for around 200 hectares and you'll also come across maritime pine, fir and larch. The forest has also long been famous for its wealth of plant extracts and essences.

As you rise ever higher from Évisa, look out on the left after about 4km for a sign to the Cascades de Aïtone, a tumble of waterfalls and naturally scooped out basins that serve as miniature swimming pools. They're only about 10 minutes off-road along a pleasant footpath. Also see above.

A few hundred metres away, the short **Sentier de la Sittelle** (Nuthatch Path) – look out for the image of the nuthatch on signposts – offers an opportunity to explore the forest close up. The path follows for the first part the former Piste des Condamnés (Trail of the Condemned), named in memory of the prisoners who did forced labour in the forest in the 19th century.

Col de Verghio

The Col de Verghio (1467m), Corsica's highest driveable pass, marks the boundary between Haute-Corse and Corse-du-Sud. There's a statue by the sculptor Bonardi representing Jesus in a long cloak, his arm outstretched, his palm turned upwards towards the heavens. In summer, a vendor of Corsican produce and drinks in the car park is his constant companion.

Several **walking paths** take off from the col, which has unobstructed views over the Forêt d'Aïtone on one side and the Forêt de Valdu Niellu on the other. See below for details on the walk to the Bergeries de Radule, which lies on the GR20.

The Niolo region and the Forêt de Valdu Niellu stretch eastwards from Col de Verghio. A few parcels of forestry land are used to study the longevity of the Corsican laricio pine. Some trees here are 300 years old and have grown to a height of 30m.

SLEEPING & EATING

Hôtel Castel di Verghio (☎ 04 95 48 00 01; camp sites per person €6, s/d/tr €42/51/65, with half-board €65/90/123; ☯ Apr-Sep) Catering mainly for walkers, the Hôtel Castel di Verghio has 29 simple but more than adequate rooms. In the evening, the hotel's restaurant offers a €17 *menu* that attracts hordes of hungry hikers. The hotel bar also sells a range of basic foodstuffs. Extensive renovations were planned for early 2007 so prices may change to reflect this upgrading.

Accommodation is also available in Calacuccia (p245), about 20km from Col de Verghio.

GETTING THERE & AWAY

During summer, a bus service linking Corte and Porto passes by Hôtel Castel di Verghio once daily in each direction.

LES CALANQUES (LES CALANCHES)

The phantasmagorical rock formations known as Les Calanques rear up more than 400m above the sea in teetering columns, towers and irregularly shaped boulders. Truly awe-inspiring, they're a highlight of any visit to Corsica.

As you sway around switchback after switchback along the D81, one breathtaking vista follows another. Gargantuan granite shapes, naturally coloured with iridescent shades of pink grapefruit, ochre and ginger, resemble a Dali painting. Guy de Maupassant, who visited Corsica in 1880, likened these strange geological formations to 'some fantastic fairy-tale race, petrified by an unknown supernatural force'. In fact, this amazing stone garden, a Unesco World Heritage site, was formed by the erosion of wind and sea.

The D81 winds its way through Les Calanques from west of Porto almost as far as Piana, twisting and turning for several kilometres.

Walks

For the full technicolour experience, Les Calanques need to be savoured on foot – ideally in the relative coolness of early morning, before the crowds arrive, or at sunset, when the rocks almost glow with muted copper tones. The first three of the routes described following starts at the **Pont de Mezzanu**, approximately 1.5km from Piana towards Porto (halfway between the Chalet des Roches Bleues souvenir shop and Piana). The tourist office in

---

COL DE VERGHIO TO THE BERGERIES DE RADULE WALK

This easy out-and-back walk (allow about 1½ hours comfortably) threads through the forest with glorious views peeking through. The path, waymarked in yellow, takes off from behind the statue of Jesus that stands guard over the Col de Verghio, marking the border between Haute-Corse and Corse-du-Sud.

The *bergeries*, difficult to make out from a distance against their barren background, are on the GR20 (to return to the Col de Verghio, don't be seduced into erring along its route, which is blazed in red and white). During the summer months, a shepherd lives in this cluster of stone shepherds' huts and sheep pens clinging to the side of the mountain. A few minutes' walk away, where a natural stone basin catches water flowing over some small falls, you might think you've stumbled across heaven on earth.

Piana (right) has a free brochure and map detailing each.

La Forêt de Piana Has two alternative routes (round-trip 2½ and three hours respectively) that pass through the pine forests and chestnut groves above Les Calanques.

Le Capu d'Ortu Starts from the same point as the Forêt de Piana walk, then ascends to a rocky spur. The walk takes six hours (round-trip) and rises to the Capu d'Ortu plateau (1294m).

Le Château Fort Leads to a rocky promontory overlooking the Golfe de Porto and Les Calanques. Takes 45 minutes to one hour round-trip.

Le Sentier Muletier Takes about an hour and follows the mule track that linked Piana and Ota before the D81 was built in 1850. It's signposted in blue.

Sentier du Coeur The name refers to the heart-shaped indentation in the rock to which it leads. The walk takes no more than 15 minutes and starts from Le Moulin des Calanques.

Getting There & Away

If you're driving, there's very limited roadside parking; the early car gets the space. Les Calanques are an easy walk from Piana, which has more ample parking facilities, but do be wary of traffic, both in front and behind, on the tight bends.

Alternatively, Autocars Ceccaldi buses running between Ajaccio and Porto can drop you off at the Chalet des Roches Bleues souvenir shop.

PIANA

pop 425 / elevation 438m

Piana, 68km from Ajaccio, peers down over the Golfe de Porto from the small plateau on which it squats. Inland and poised between the rival attractions of Les Calanques and Capu Rossu, it makes a seductive alternative to overcrowded Porto, 12km southwest. If you're after quietness (guaranteed, even in high summer, once the day's through-traffic has rumbled on) and a little beach inactivity

(Plage d'Arone – p159 – the area's finest, is a spectacular 12km drive away), it offers some tempting sleeping and eating options.

In the 15th century Piana was ruled by the hot-headed *seigneurs de Leca,* who governed a vast area on the west coast of the island. Rebelling against Genoa, they and all the male population were massacred. The Genoese then banned anyone from living in Piana, which came to life again only in the 18th century, once Genoese influence on the island was on the wane. **Église Ste-Marie**, built between 1765 and 1772, dates from this renaissance.

To enjoy the village, walk north, towards the coast, and explore the streets behind the church, bordered by attractive stone houses, several of them renovated. On the façades of too many others, however, the lovely original stonework is masked by a patina of cement.

The **tourist office** (☎ 04 95 27 84 42; www.sipiana .com; 9am-6pm Mon-Fri, 9am-1pm Sat & Sun Jun-Sep, 8.30-11.30am & 1.30-4pm Mon-Fri Oct-May) is set back from the main road, beside the post office. It carries a useful leaflet, *Piana: Sentiers de Randonnées,* which describes and maps six walks in or starting from Les Calanques.

Sleeping

All the sleeping options we recommend (except for Gîte Giargalo) are on the D81, the main road that cuts through the village.

Gîte du Belvédère (☎ 04 95 27 80 52; camp sites per person €8, dm €12, d €40-50) This place is definitely recommended for well-priced budget accommodation. On the Ajaccio side of the village near Le Scandola, it's the only camping opportunity in the village (bivouacs only) and has sweeping views over the gulf. Dorms are for six and it has a dozen or so doubles.

Gîte Giargalo (☎ 04 95 27 82 05; www.gite-giargalo .com; ancien chemin Piana à Ota; dm €15, s/d/tr incl breakfast €55/67/89, r per person with half-board €35-46; year-round; **P**) Signed from the main square and

---

LES CALANQUES: A WALK TO THE CHÂTEAU FORT

This short walk leads from the Tête de Chien (Dog's Head), a distinctively shaped rock that's signposted on a large bend in the D81, 3.5km east of Piana (if you're approaching from Porto, you'll see why the rock's so named). The path divides now and again but all options lead in the same direction. Set out early to avoid the crowds that throng this popular, accessible trail and avoid wearing sandals; the route, although undemanding, is rocky and steep in places.

After 20 to 30 minutes, you reach a broad natural platform known as the Château Fort (Fortress), from where the view over the Golfe de Porto and deep rocky inlets of Les Calanques is stunning, particularly at sunset. Allow an hour at most for this out-and-back walk.

THE WEST COAST

THE AUTHOR'S CHOICE

Hôtel les Roches Rouges (☎ 04 95 27 81 81; www.lesrochesrouges.com in French; d €76-80, tr €110, qd €125-135; ♈ mid-Mar–mid-Nov; **P**) At the entrance to Piana on the Porto side, the terrace of the Red Rocks, looking over Les Calanques at sunset, must offer one of the finest views on earth. Even if you don't stay here, stop in for a drink or, even better, a meal at its superb gourmet restaurant and savour the vista.

Les Roches Rouges was established as a prestige hotel in 1912, since when little seems to have changed, except for the addition of a telephone or two and wi-fi access. The place oozes faded turn-of-the-century elegance with its magnificent dining room and sweeping foyer, where guests play chess and backgammon. Rooms are huge and sparsely furnished and one of the hotel's many charms is its lived-in, just slightly dog-eared condition. Ask for a room with a sea view – and what a view! – a mere €5 per person more expensive.

300m up the road behind the tourist office, this is a most attractive option, whether you slumber in one of the six charmingly decorated rooms with bathroom or on a bed in one of the four dormitories that sleep four to six. The cuisine on offer draws upon Corsican specialities and, wherever possible, organic produce, while Madame's bread, pasta and an impressive assortment of jams are all homemade.

Le Scandola (☎ 04 95 27 80 07; www.hotelscan dola.com; s & d €38-75, tr €48-85, q €58-95; ♈ Mar-Nov; **P** ✕ ♈) Just up the road from Hôtel Continental, friendly Le Scandola has 12 rooms, all with balconies offering superb views of the gulf, and showerheads the size of dinner plates. Ask for one of the recently and tastefully renovated bedrooms. There's also a first-rate restaurant (mains €14 to €26) and wi-fi access.

Antoine Casanova (☎ 04 95 27 84 20, 06 76 89 16 60; 1-/2-room studios off-season €40/60) Antoine, owner of Le Casanova restaurant, rents out rustic studios with sea views at the end of the village. In high season prices are €400/500 per week for the one-/two-room studios.

Hôtel Continental (☎ 04 95 27 89 00; www.continen talpiana.com; s/d/tr €44/52/62, d with bathroom €65-74, all incl breakfast; ♈ Apr-Oct; **P**) We're really talking of two interconnected hotels, separated by an extensive garden, where breakfast (you'll beg for more of Madame's delightful homemade croissants) is served. The main building, in an imposing blue-shuttered townhouse just south of the main square on the Ajaccio side of the village, has 12 basic but pleasant rooms with rustic wooden floorboards. The five rooms of the more modern annexe, each with bathroom and balcony, offer views of the village and mountains.

Hôtel Mare e Monti (☎ 04 95 27 82 14; www.mare-e -monti.com; d €55-78, tr €69-85, all incl breakfast; ♈ Apr-Sep; **P**) This hotel, on the Porto side of the village and run by the same family for three generations, has 12 immaculate, comfortable, if somewhat fusty, rooms, all with bathtub and small balcony. The six with sea views come at no extra cost.

Eating

Le Phocea (☎ 04 95 27 80 98) The name of this place refers to the type of Brazilian tree, imported and planted before this tiny *tabac-bar* almost 100 years ago. It's a shady pit stop for a coffee and sandwich or panini (€4 to €5.50).

Le Casanova (☎ 04 95 27 84 20; pizzas €8.20-10, mains €12-19, menus around €15; ♈ Apr-Oct) No, not a philandering patron but the name of the friendly family (Mum, Dad, one brother as maître, the other powering the kitchen) who run this bustling restaurant. In an attractive stone house whose terrace occupies most of the square, Le Casanova serves large wood-fired pizzas and a *menu Corse* (€15) with specialities such as *figatellu* (pork liver sausage), prepared, like all their charcuterie, by the village butcher. Or go à la carte and indulge in the house speciality – *coquille St-Jacques au myrte* (scallops cooked in myrtle liqueur).

Hôtel des Roches Rouges (☎ 04 95 27 81 81; mains €22-25, menus €32-40) At the restaurant here, settle into a comfortable cane armchair and savour gourmet nouvelle cuisine, the magnificent décor (the frescoes are a Unesco-recognised monument) and an exceptional panoramic view of the gulf through the vast picture windows. The menu is inventive though portions are small and there's a good selection of local wines, also available by the half-bottle.

WALK TO CAPU ROSSU

From the road you can clearly make out the silhouette of the **Tour de Turghiu** (331m), your goal, as it rises above Capu Rossu to the west. The rocky path, lined initially with low stone walls, descends steadily through the maquis to pass above the first of several ruined *bergeries* on the left after around 20 minutes.

The trail skirts south of the rocky escarpment with its variegated shades of grey and pink. In front of a restored *bergerie* with a pink-tiled roof, about an hour out, you can make out the remains of a circular threshing floor. Here, take a turn right (northwards) to tackle the steep climb up to the tower, at first via a series of tight zigzags, then following the cairns that mark the trail's upward progress. After about 30 minutes' walk, you reach the Tour de Turghiu with an impressive sheer 300m drop to the sea beneath and heartstopping views of the Golfe de Porto and Golfe de Sagone (near its head curls the white crescent of the Plage d'Arone, ideal for a subsequent swim to cool off). Give yourself about three hours for the round-trip, set out early, take plenty of water and be sure to wear a hat since there's scarcely a square centimetre of shade along the way.

AROUND PIANA
Marine de Ficajola

From the church in Piana, follow the D824 towards the Plage d'Arone for 1km, then turn right onto the narrow D624 for a white-knuckle-steep, twisting 4km descent through rocky red mountains, offering marvellous views over the extraordinary rock formations of Les Calanques. Leave your vehicle at the end of the road and walk for about 10 minutes down a path to this tiny cove, where lobster-fishing boats once used to take shelter. Really you're here for the splendour of the ride to get here; the secret's out and the pocket of beach can get very crowded in high summer.

Plage d'Arone

To reach this gorgeous stretch of fine sand, the best on this section of coast, follow the D824 for 12km from the church in Piana until

---

THE AUTHOR'S CHOICE

You come here as much for the site as for the cuisine. **Café de la Plage** (☎ 04 95 20 17 27; pizzas €9-11.50, mains €17-23; Apr-Sep) has a delightful vine-shaded terrace with the beach just beyond. For the freshest of fish, check out that day's catch, chalked up on the blackboard. For a little midday indulgence, tuck into its brimming *assiette de fruits de mer* (seafood platter; €28). If you do, you'll probably need to work off lunch. Conveniently, it also hires out kayaks (per hour/day €7/30).

---

it peters out at the beach. The drive takes you along a ridge offering wonderful views over the Golfe de Porto as it cuts through wild mountain scenery and maquis to end up south of Capu Rossu.

This crescent-shaped beach has a special place in Corsican history; it was here that the first weapons for the Corsican resistance arrived on the submarine *Casabianca* in 1943, under the command of Captain L'Herminier (after whom several quays in Corsican harbours are named).

Camping de la Plage d'Arone (☎ 04 95 20 64 54; camp sites per adult/tent/car from €5/2/2; May-Sep) is a lovely little camping ground (but with little shade), a mere 600m from the beach.

The camping ground apart, there's no accommodation but you do have two splendid dining options, Le Casablanca and Café de la Plage.

Le Casablanca (☎ 04 95 20 70 40; mains €10-24; mid-Apr–Sep), with its pleasant shady terrace overlooking the west end of the beach, comes highly recommended by locals for its tasty wood-fired pizzas and seafood specials such as turbot and prawn kebab.

Capu Rossu (Capo Rosso)

Between the Golfe de Porto and the Golfe de Sagone, this scrub-covered headland of pink-grey rock stands 300m high. Crowned by the **Tour de Turghiu**, it offers splendid views over each. To get there, take the D824 out of Piana, as for Plage d'Arone, follow it for 6km and park below a snack bar at a bend where the road begins its descent to Plage d'Arone.

GOLFE DE SAGONE

Getting There & Away

Buses of **Autocars Ceccaldi** (☎ 04 95 22 41 99) running between Ajaccio and Porto call by coastal towns twice daily.

CARGÈSE (CARGHJESE)

pop 980

The original settlement that led to the creation of this sleepy little town was founded in 1676 to house a community of 730 Greeks, who had appealed to Genoa for refuge from the conquering Turks. There is no longer much to mark the town as Greek, however, other than the Greek Orthodox religious festivals celebrated in the Eastern Rite church (Église Catholique de Rite Grec), and the immigrants' distant descendants are no longer in any significant way distinguishable from other Corsicans. Nowadays the charm of Cargèse, sitting on a promontory overlooking the sea, lies simply in its quiet streets and the gleaming white façades of its houses. With five beaches in the vicinity, it's a great base for sun-worshippers. The best, Plage du Péro, is a long strand of pure white sand 1.5km north of Cargèse. At its extremities, Pointe d'Omigna and Pointe de Cargèse, a pair of handsome Genoese towers keep watch.

Information

Laverie Cargésienne (rue Colonel Fieschi; ⏰ 8am-8pm) Laundrette.

Post office (rue de la République)

Tourist office (☎ 04 95 26 41 31; www.cargese.net; ⏰ 9am-7pm daily Jun-Sep, 9am-12.30pm & 2.30-6pm Mon-Sat Oct-May) Has an internet point (per hour €5).

Sights

ÉGLISE CATHOLIQUE DE RITE GREC

This white-fronted church, facing the Église Latine Ste-Marie, has several fine icons (some of which were brought from Greece in 1676) and an impressive interior staircase. The present church dates from 1852, when it replaced the original building, which was no longer large enough to accommodate the entire congregation. The new church took 20 years to build and the parishioners were themselves frequently enlisted to help. Like all Greek churches, it's above all distinguished by the richness of its ornamentation and the delicacy of the portraits of the iconostasis, the traditional painted wooden partition separating the altar from the nave. More modern is the mural at the western end depicting in visual form the fate of this tiny Greek community.

ÉGLISE LATINE STE-MARIE

In 1817 the town's non-Greek families, no doubt after eyeing a trifle enviously the Greek

---

FROM THE PELOPONNESE TO CARGÈSE

In 1663 some 800 Greeks from the southern Peloponnese fled their Ottoman-Turk conquerors and entered into talks with the Genoese authorities to find a new homeland. Twelve years later the Genoese granted them the territory of Paomia, just above what is now Cargèse, at a distance of about 50km north of Ajaccio. In March 1676 the surviving 730 émigrés – those who had not perished en route – set foot on Corsican soil for the first time. Their colony flourished. Some even gave up the 'akis' with which Greek names characteristically end and replaced it with a more Corsican-Italianate 'acci'. But then came the hitch. When the Corsicans rebelled against the Genoese in 1729, the Greeks, true to their pledge to their Genoese benefactors, sided with Genoa, and the Corsicans sacked Paomia. The Greek community moved to Ajaccio, where it then lived unobtrusively for about 40 years.

Relations between Greeks and Corsicans improved during the brief period of Corsican independence but it was only in the first decade of French rule that Cargèse itself was granted to them and they began to build new homes there. This time they were set upon by inhabitants of the neighbouring village of Vico and by Niolo shepherds who traditionally wintered their flocks in the Cargèse area. Until around 1830 the Greeks shifted back and forth between Cargèse and relatively friendly Ajaccio but by then tempers had at last cooled and hostilities had gradually ceased. The Greeks installed themselves in Cargèse and for most of the past two centuries they and their Corsican neighbours have lived together in exemplary harmony – to the point that nothing in particular distinguishes the two communities except the continuing allegiance of most of the Greeks to the Greek Orthodox church.

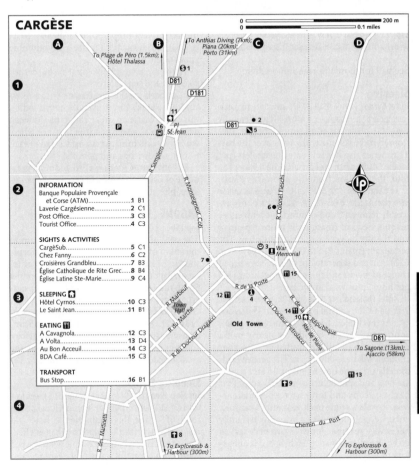

CARGÈSE

THE WEST COAST

community's extravagant church, decided that it was high time to build a Roman-Catholic sanctuary of their own. Work on the neo-classical building began eight years later and continued until 1828. Seven years after completion, God let them down and wind blew the roof off. There's an intriguing trompe l'oeil ceiling but at the end of the day the church's best feature is the view over the gulf from the square at its west end.

Activities
BOAT TRIPS
Nave Va (☎ 04 95 28 02 66; www.naveva.com; adult/child €48/22; ☺ May-Sep) organises boat trips to the Scandola nature reserve, passing by Capu Rossu and Les Calanques. Boats leave the harbour at 9.30am and return around 4.30pm.

The fare includes a two-hour stop at Girolata and a half-hour swim in an inlet. **Chez Fanny** (☎ 04 95 26 44 43; rue Colonel Fieschi) a souvenir shop, sells tickets.

Croisières Grand Bleu (☎ 04 95 26 40 24; http://croisiere .grandbleu.free.fr in French; rue Marbeuf; adult/child €40/20), a local company, offers the same programme with two departures daily, at 8.45am (returning 3.30pm) and 3.30pm (returning 8.45pm).

DIVING
Cargèse has three diving outfits, each offering similar courses and dives.
Anthias Diving (☎ 06 16 84 34 11; www.anthiasdiving.fr; Plage de Chiuni) On a beach 10 minutes north of Cargèse on the D81. Also offers snorkelling and flipper outings (€15).
CargèSub (☎ 06 86 13 38 96; www.cargesub.com in French; rue Colonel Fieschi)

Explorasub (☎ 06 11 01 19 54; www.explorasub.fr in French; rte du Port) For info, visit Bar-Restaurant U Rasaghiu in the port.

See p79 for more information on diving.

Sleeping

Hôtel Cyrnos (☎ 04 95 26 49 47; www.torraccia.com in French; rue de la République; d €40-60) This friendly two-star place has nine simple, bright, tile-floored rooms, some with views over the bay. The owner also has self-catering chalets (per week €400) with deep balconies. Sleeping four, they're 3km from town towards Piana.

Le Saint Jean (☎ 04 95 26 46 68; www.lesaintjean.com; place St-Jean; d €45-78; P 🕸 🖥) Rooms are freshly renovated and comfortable with either maquis views or (marginally more expensive and slightly bigger) overlooking the bay. The restaurant (mains €11 to €15, *menus* €17.50 to €22), run as a separate operation, has a broad choice of *menus* and there's internet access (€5 per hour) plus wi-fi at the bar.

Hôtel Thalassa (☎ 04 95 26 40 08; www.thalassalura.com; s/d €80/90, with half-board €100/144; May-Sep; P) At this hugely friendly, family-run place, constructed by the Garidaccis nearly half a century ago and fully renovated in 2004, your children will be spoilt rotten. The garden leads directly onto the beach and its 26 airy rooms are neat and simply furnished. All except four have a balcony and three have wheelchair access. Regulars come back year after year (one guest we spoke to has been bringing his family here every summer for over two decades) so do book well in advance. Half-board is obligatory in July and August.

Eating

Cargèse is no great gastronomic destination but there are several more than adequate restaurants along the main road and more choice beside the harbour.

BDA Café (☎ 04 95 26 43 37; rue de la République) A funky, modern café with a low vaulted ceiling and sunny terrace. The friendly young brother-owners serve salads and panini all day.

Au Bon Acceuil (☎ 04 95 26 42 03; rue de la République) This bar in the centre of town is a traditional place with panelled walls and a lively terrace that serves good-value, hot snacks all day. Walk through to the minute terrace with its glorious sea views.

A Volta (☎ 04 95 26 41 96; mains €8-30) At the end of rue du Docteur Petrolacci in the old town, A Volta serves fine fare. Opt for the fresh

fish, creatively prepared, or a hearty pasta (€9.50), taken on the terrace with stunning views of the bay.

There are a couple of great resources for snackers and self-caterers.

A Cavagnola (rue du Docteur Dragacci; 9am-7.30pm May-Sep) A stone's throw from the tourist office, this place carries a great range of Corsican delicacies and also has a small terrace where you can tuck into pizzas and salads (each €7.60), sandwiches and paninis.

Au Petit Marché (rte du Pero) Also does a great range of Corsican wines, cheeses and charcuterie, plus dishes to take away.

SAGONE (SAONE)
pop 250

The coastal resort of Sagone, a thin strip to the south of Cargèse, has a beautiful, steeply shelving beach. Originally a Roman settlement, Sagone had a bishop's palace from the 6th to the 16th century, one of Corsica's oldest, but no trace remains today.

Nave Va (☎ 06 07 71 28 57; www.naveva.com; adult/child €48/22; May-Sep)) does boat trips to Scandola and Girolata from Sagone, leaving at 9am and returning around 5pm. Reserve at the kiosk beside the port or at La Marine.

Sleeping & Eating

Les Flots Bleus (☎ 04 95 52 21 65; s/d €51/63, with half-board €77.50/114.50; Apr-Oct; P) In Tiuccia, 5km south of Sagone, this small, friendly hotel and restaurant sits on the edge of what is effectively its own beach. It has simple whitewashed rooms with tasteful, rustic furnishings and terracotta floors. The busy restaurant (mains €7.50 to €17.50, *menus* €14.50 to €26), which serves Corsican dishes, seafood and salads, is particularly good value. There's a garden and all rooms, the bar and especially the restaurant have a magnificent panorama of the bay.

THE AUTHOR'S CHOICE

L'Ancura (☎ 04 95 28 04 93; pizzas €8-11, mains €16-20; May-Sep) is simply a shack beside the port with a small, shaded terrace just opposite. Fresh fish, hauled in by a local fisherman, arrives daily at the Anchor and its delightful desserts are all made on the spot. Capacity's limited – unlike L'Ancura's reputation – and dinner reservations in particular are essential.

Hôtel-Restaurant La Marine (☎ 04 95 28 00 03; hotellamarinesagone@wanadoo.fr; d €60-70; ⏰ Apr-Oct; P) Once a family house, this friendly hotel is in a great location right on the beach as you enter town from Ajaccio. Rooms are cheerily decorated in bright colours, and those with sea views (€10 extra) have breezy balconies from which to take in the glorious views of the gulf. Its busy terrace restaurant (pizzas €7.50 to €8.50, mains €10 to €14) overlooking the beach serves excellent fresh salads and outstanding seafood.

A Stonda (☎ 04 95 28 01 66; pizzas €9-12, mains €17-20; ⏰ Tue-Sun Dec-Oct) Locals travel for miles to get a table at A Stonda (located opposite Hôtel-Restaurant La Marine). Under tiki paper lampshades and hanging baskets, in what looks no more than an open stone shed that catches every sea breeze, you'll find some of the best food around. The simple menu of grilled meat, seafood and wood-fired pizza changes daily and uses organic and seasonal local produce. The only negative is its location, right beside the busy D81.

LE LIAMONE

This mountainous green microregion, also known as Les Deux Sorru, takes its name from the river that flows through it to the Golfe de Sagone. Largely forested, it offers ample scope for walking. Extending between Sagone and Col de Verghio, its largest villages are Renno (Rennu) and Vico (Vicu). The ones we describe lie along the Mare a Mare Nord route.

Vico

pop 900

Nestling in the mountains 14km from Sagone, Vico, with its narrow, tree-lined streets and tall townhouses, offers welcome respite from the heat of the coast. Peaceful after dark, it's busy during the day with local trade, ramblers stocking up on fresh produce and men playing *boules* on place Padrona.

Overlooking the village on the south side, the **church** of the 17th-century **Couvent de St François**, a still-active monastery, merits a stop. The striking wooden crucifixion in the south aisle predates the monastery and is reputed to be Corsica's oldest. Penetrate, too, into the sacristy, which has a wonderful carved chestnut cope chest.

There's singing in place principale on Thursday evenings.

SLEEPING & EATING

Ferme-Auberge Pippa Minicale (☎ 04 95 26 61 51; d €50, per person with half-board €39; ⏰ Jun-Oct) The hostess of this *gîte*, on the outskirts of the village, offers five cosy rooms, but the main reason to stay here is her hearty home cooking, based around the family farm's own seasonal vegetables and home-cured meats such as herb-stuffed pork or *figatellu* cooked on a wood fire.

Café National (☎ 04 95 26 60 25; place Principale; pizzas €7-9.50, mains €14-22) This bar is well situated in an old stone building in the corner of a small square. At a terrace table under shady chestnut and lime trees, you can sample fine crusty sandwiches with local charcuterie and cheeses, frondy salads, omelettes or wood-fired, generously topped pizzas. One negative: in a village where the tap water's of the purest quality, don't let them force bottled mineral water upon you.

Soccia & Orto

The road that winds its way up beyond Vico leads to a picturesque cluster of villages perched on the mountainside. Clinging on at an elevation of 700m, the pretty village of Soccia (population 120) is set amid mountainside terraces. A great place to escape from the GR20, it's also the starting point for the pleasant Lac de Creno walk (p164). Within the **village church** (⏰ 10am-noon & 4-7pm), constructed in 1875, there's a fine 15th-century triptych. The war memorial in the picturesque village square with its litany of almost 50 victims from one tiny hamlet is, like so many such monuments in France, testimony to the devastating impact of WWI upon rural life.

Orto (population 55) is just over the mountain from Soccia as the Mare a Mare walker walks yet a 10km roundabout drive. At the end of the road, smaller and even more remote, its few houses, each seeming to overhang the one below, are dominated by the bare, brooding cliffs of Monte Sant'Eliseo.

Guagno

pop 140 / elevation 800m

A twisting road leads up the valley for 8.5km to Guagno, a four- to five-hour walk from the GR20. Several trails lead from Guagno to this celebrated long-distance trail, which you can join either at Col de Soglia or just to the south of the Pietra Piana *refuge*. The village hosts a *gîte d'étape* and a small grocery shop.

THE WEST COAST

SOCCIA TO LAC DE CRENO: HIKE OR HORSEBACK

Drive from Soccia, following signs for the lake (Lavu di Crenu in Corsican) for 3km and leave your vehicle beside the small summertime café at the end of the road. In July and August you can hire a donkey or pony (per hour/half-day €10/25) to clipclop up the rocky trail. Otherwise, follow the path that clings to the southern flank of the valley as it mounts the northern slopes of Monte Sant'Eliseo (1511m). You can't go wrong – just look out for the yellow blazes and donkey droppings. There's no shade until you enter a pine wood, where after around 45 minutes a welcome spring flows. The lake (1310m), five minutes or so beyond the spring, is a lovely green oasis. Fringed by spongey sphagnum and encircled by laricio pines, it's the perfect picnic spot – though you may find that too many others think likewise. In spring, you'll have the added delight of water lilies in flower. Since it's a particularly sensitive protected area (among other rarities, the *drosera*, a rare carnivorous plant, grows here so keep your boots on!), there's no swimming. Allow 2¼ to 2½ hours for the round-trip.

GOLFE D'AJACCIO

AJACCIO (AJACCIU)

pop 52,900

Ajaccio, Corsica's largest town, is the capital of the *département* of Corse-du-Sud, site of the Assemblée Territoriale de la Corse – and famous as the birthplace of Napoleon Bonaparte. Commanding the lovely sweep of bay that extends from the red rocks of Pointe de la Parata to Porticcio and beaches beyond, it's a city that breathes confidence. Yes, tourism matters to the city's economy but this major commercial and passenger port goes about its business almost oblivious to the stream of summertime visitors.

With its mellow-toned buildings, large marina and café terraces, it has more than a whiff of the Côte d'Azur, over the water. Its museums range from the splendid Musée Fesch via enough Napoleonic memorabilia to last you a lifetime to the delightfully idiosyncratic little family collection of the Musée du Capitellu.

History

One legend attributes the town's origins to the mythical Greek hero Ajax. Another has it that its name derives, more prosaically, from that of a Roman encampment. In fact, modern Ajaccio probably dates from no earlier than 1492, when Genoese families first began moving here from other less healthy spots on the island. Indigenous Corsicans were banned from living in the town until 1553, when it was seized by Sampiero Corso and his French allies, assisted by the Turkish privateer Dragut. Shortly afterwards a citadel was built on the foundations of a pre-existing Genoese castle. Recaptured in 1559 by the army of the Republic of Genoa, the town was not truly open to Corsicans until 1592.

The birth of Napoleon on 15 August 1769 was a turning point in the town's history. In accordance with the emperor's decree of 1811, Ajaccio replaced Bastia as the island's capital (see the boxed text, p165); since then it has remained Corsica's principal town.

Orientation

The main artery, cours Napoléon, runs between place de Gaulle (place du Diamant) and the train station. The old town is bounded by place de Gaulle, place Foch and the citadel. Rte des Sanguinaires (D111), which leads to Pointe de la Parata, heads westwards out of town, following the coast.

Information

BOOKSHOPS

Album (2 place Foch) Good selection of foreign-language books and some international newspapers.

EMERGENCY

Police (☎ 04 95 11 17 17; rue Général Fiorella)

INTERNET ACCESS

Bistrot du Cours (10 cours Napoléon; ☽ 8am-10pm Mon-Thu, 8am-2am Fri & Sat) Twenty minutes' free internet access with each drink, 30 minutes' wi-fi.

Cyber Espace (1 rue Docteur Versini; per hr €3; ☽ 10.30am-2am Mon-Sat Jul & Aug, 9.30am-12.30am Mon-Sat Sep-Jun)

LAUNDRY

Lavomatic (1 rue du Maréchal Ornano; ☽ 8am-10pm)
Quick Wash (51 cours Napoléon; ☽ 1-8pm)

THE WEST COAST

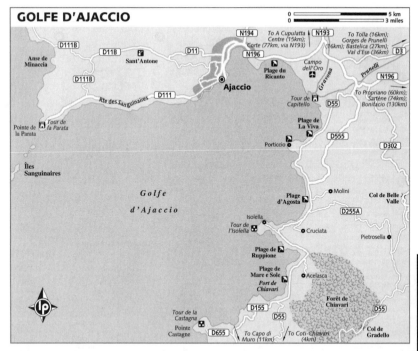

GOLFE D'AJACCIO

THE WEST COAST

MEDICAL SERVICES
Hospital (☎ 04 95 29 90 90; 27 av de l'Impératrice Eugénie) Has 24-hour emergency department.

POST
Main post office (13 cours Napoléon)

TOURIST INFORMATION
Parc Naturel Régional de la Corse (PNRC) information office (☎ 04 95 51 79 00; www.parc -naturel-corse.com in French; 2 rue Sergent Casalonga; ☷ 8am-6pm Mon-Sat Jun-Sep, 9am-noon & 2-5pm Mon-Sat Oct-May) Information on the park and its hiking trails.
Tourist office (☎ 04 95 51 53 03; 3 blvd du Roi Jérôme; www.ajaccio-tourisme.com; ☷ 8am-8.30pm Mon-Sat, 9am-1pm & 4-7pm Sun Jul & Aug, 8am-7pm Mon-Sat, 9am-1pm Sun Apr-Jun, Sep & Oct, 8am-12.30pm Mon-Fri, 8am-noon & 2-5pm Sat Nov-Mar; ▣) Also has one free internet point.

Sights
MUSÉE FESCH
Cardinal Fesch (see the boxed text, p167), whose bronze statue stares proprietorially over the courtyard, amassed over 16,000 paintings and *objets d'art*. The museum was

built at his instigation to house the vast collection that he donated to the town in 1839.
Musée Fesch (☎ 04 95 21 48 17; www.musee-fesch. com; 50 rue du Cardinal Fesch; adult/child €5.35/3.80; ☷ 2-6pm Mon, 10.30am-6pm Tue-Thu, Sat & Sun, 2-9.30pm Fri Jul & Aug, 9.30am-noon & 2-6pm Tue-Sun Apr-Jun & Sep, 9.30am-noon & 2-5.30pm Tue-Sat Oct-Mar) has France's largest collection of Italian paintings outside the Louvre. Mostly the works of minor or

---

NAPOLEON'S CAPITAL

Ajaccio rose to fame under Napoleon, its most illustrious native son. In 1811 an imperial decree made Corsica a single *département* with Ajaccio as its capital. There was an outcry in Bastia, which lost its status as the island's main town, but Napoleon justified his decision by asserting that Ajaccio 'should be the capital…since it is a natural harbour that lies across the water from Toulon and is thus the closest to France after St-Florent'. In accordance with the emperor's wishes, Ajaccio went on to spearhead the campaign to Gallicise the island.

THE WEST COAST

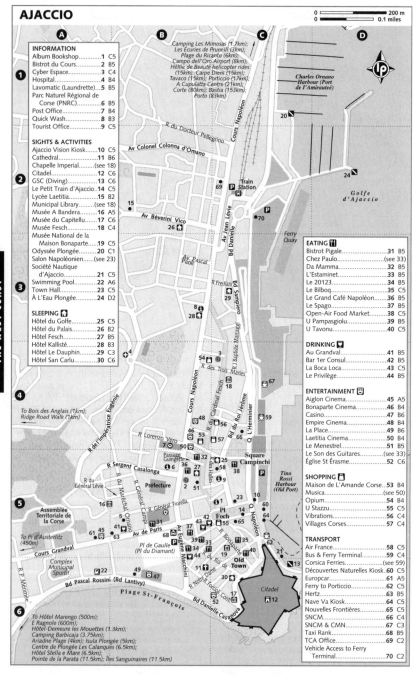

AJACCIO

0 ———— 200 m
0 ———— 0.1 miles

INFORMATION
Album Bookshop	**1** C5
Bistrot du Cours	**2** B5
Cyber Espace	**3** C4
Hospital	**4** B4
Lavomatic (Laundrette)	**5** B5
Parc Naturel Régional de Corse (PNRC)	**6** B5
Post Office	**7** B4
Quick Wash	**8** B3
Tourist Office	**9** C5

SIGHTS & ACTIVITIES
Ajaccio Vision Kiosk	**10** C5
Cathedral	**11** B6
Chapelle Imperial	(see 18)
Citadel	**12** C6
GSC (Diving)	**13** C6
Le Petit Train d'Ajaccio	**14** C5
Lycée Laetitia	**15** B2
Municipal Library	(see 18)
Musée A Bandera	**16** A5
Musée du Capitellu	**17** C6
Musée Fesch	**18** C4
Musée National de la Maison Bonaparte	**19** C5
Odyssée Plongée	**20** C1
Salon Napoléonien	(see 23)
Société Nautique d'Ajaccio	**21** C5
Swimming Pool	**22** A6
Town Hall	**23** B3
À L'Eau Plongée	**24** D2

SLEEPING
Hôtel du Golfe	**25** C5
Hôtel du Palais	**26** B2
Hôtel Fesch	**27** B5
Hôtel Kallisté	**28** B3
Hôtel Le Dauphin	**29** C3
Hôtel San Carlu	**30** C6

EATING
Bistrot Pigale	**31** B5
Chez Paulo	(see 33)
Da Mamma	**32** B5
L'Estaminet	**33** B5
Le 20123	**34** B5
Le Bilboq	**35** C5
Le Grand Café Napoléon	**36** B5
Le Spago	**37** B5
Open-Air Food Market	**38** B5
U Pampasgiolu	**39** C5
U Tavonu	**40** C5

DRINKING
Au Grandval	**41** B5
Bar 1er Consul	**42** B5
La Boca Loca	**43** B5
Le Privilège	**44** B5

ENTERTAINMENT
Aiglon Cinema	**45** A5
Bonaparte Cinema	**46** B4
Casino	**47** B6
Empire Cinema	**48** B4
La Place	**49** B6
Laetitia Cinema	**50** B4
Le Menestrel	**51** B5
Le Son des Guitares	(see 33)
Église St Érasme	**52** C6

SHOPPING
Maison de L'Amande Corse	**53** B4
Musica	(see 50)
Opium	**54** B5
U Stazzu	**55** C5
Vibrations	**56** C4
Villages Corses	**57** C4

TRANSPORT
Air France	**58** C5
Bus & Ferry Terminal	**59** C4
Corsica Ferries	(see 59)
Découvertes Naturelles Kiosk	**60** A5
Europcar	**61** A5
Ferry to Porticcio	**62** C5
Hertz	**63** B5
Nave Va Kiosk	**64** C5
Nouvelles Frontières	**65** C5
SNCM	**66** B5
SNCM & CMN	**67** C2
Taxi Rank	**68** B5
TCA Office	**69** C2
Vehicle Access to Ferry Terminal	**70** C2

Camping Les Mimosas (1.7km);
Les Écuries de Prunelli (3km);
Plage du Ricanto (6km);
Campo dell'Oro-Airport (8km);
Hélie de Beauté helicopter rides (15km); Carpe Diem (15km);
Tavaco (15km); Porticcio (17km);
A Cupulatta Centre (21km);
Corte (80km); Bastia (153km);
Porto (83km)

Charles Ornano
Harbour (Port
de l'Amirautée)

Golfe
d'Ajaccio

Ferry
Quay

Tino
Rossi
Harbour
(Old Port)

Square
Campinchi

Old
Town

Citadel

To Bois des Anglais (1km);
Ridge Road Walk (1km)

To Pl
d'Austerlitz
(450m)

Assemblée
Territoriale de
la Corse

Prefecture

Pl
Foch

Pl de Gaulle
(Pl du Diamant)

Complex
Municipal
Sportif

Plage St-François

To Hôtel Marengo (500m);
E Ragnole (600m);
Hôtel-Demeure les Mouettes (1.3km);
Camping Barbicaja (3.75km);
Ariadne Plage (4km); Isula Plongée (5km);
Centre de Plongée Les Calanques (6.5km);
Hôtel Stella e Mare (6.5km);
Pointe de la Parata (11.5km); Îles Sanguinaires (11.5km);

CARDINAL FESCH

Joseph Fesch (1763–1839) was Napoleon's mother's half-brother; his father, a military man in the service of Genoa, was Swiss – which explains Joseph's un-Corsican name. His religious vocation was apparently genuine (he studied in the seminary at Aix and served as archdeacon of Ajaccio), but not his only interest. He left the church for a time to make himself rich and accompanied his warrior nephew to Italy as a super-glorified quartermaster. By 1800 Fesch was nevertheless back in clerical garb. In 1802 he was archbishop of Lyon. The following year he was promoted to cardinal and Napoleon appointed him ambassador to Rome with the leading French Romantic literary figure François-Auguste-René Chateaubriand as his first secretary.

In Rome, Fesch's great achievement was to persuade the Pope to travel to Paris for the purpose of personally crowning Napoleon emperor – not that Napoleon allowed him to do so. Napoleon, the paradigm of the self-made man, took the crown from the Pope's hands and crowned himself. All of this, though, is only to scratch the surface of Fesch's complex career that moved alternately between the ecclesiastical and the secular. Fesch's substantial responsibilities did not, moreover, preclude his finding time to amass the enormous collection of paintings and books that enrich and form the basis of the museum that bears his name.

anonymous 14th- to 19th-century artists, there are also canvases by Titian, Fra Bartolomeo, Veronese, Botticelli and Bellini. On level one look out for *La Vierge à l'Enfant Soutenu par un Ange* (Mother and Child Supported by an Angel), one of Botticelli's masterpieces. *Portrait de l'Homme au Gant* (Portrait of the Gloved Man) by Titian matches another in the Louvre. Level two displays mainly 17th- and 18th-century Italian works, while items in the basement will please those who enjoy Napoleon collectibles, others less so.

Within the **Imperial Chapel** (adult/child €1.50/0.75), constructed in 1860 and leading into the courtyard, several members of the imperial family lie entombed in the crypt. But don't expect to find Napoleon's own remains here – he's buried in Les Invalides in Paris.

MUNICIPAL LIBRARY

In the left wing of the Musée Fesch and entered via rue du Cardinal Fesch, Ajaccio's **municipal library** (☎ 04 95 51 13 00; admission free; ⏰ 10am-5pm or 6pm Mon-Fri), built in 1868, merits a browse. The two lions guarding the entrance (yet another donation by Cardinal Fesch) are modelled on the beasts that stand watch over the tomb of Pope Clement XIII at St Peter's in Rome. Inside, within the 30m-long reading room, uniform leather-bound volumes stretching to the ceiling, wooden ladders and an 18m-long central table speak of serious-minded research.

Napoleon's brother, Lucien Bonaparte, commissioned the library as early as 1801 to house the thousands of works piled pell-

mell under the museum's gables. He added an additional 12,000 volumes, confiscated during the French Revolution from *émigré* aristocrats and members of the religious orders and Cardinal Fesch made yet further contributions.

MUSÉE A BANDERA

Tucked away on a little side street, the **Musée A Bandera** (Flag Museum; ☎ 04 95 51 07 34; 1 rue du Général Lévie; adult/child/student €4/free/2.60; ⏰ 9am-7pm Mon-Sat, 9am-noon Sun Jul–mid-Sep, 9am-noon & 2-6pm Mon-Sat mid-Sep–Jun) provides an overview of Corsican history from its origins until WWII. Among the highlights are a diorama of the 1769 battle of Ponte Novo that confirmed French conquest of the island, a model of Ajaccio port as it was in the same period, a proclamation by Gilbert Elliot, viceroy of the shortlived Anglo-Corsican kingdom (1794–96) and some yellowing 19th-century pages from the *Petit Journal* and *L'Illustré*, recounting the arrest of famous Corsican bandits. There are also a few worthy panels describing the role of women in Corsican society and the considerable power that they have sometimes wielded.

MUSEUM PASS

The tourist office and participating museums sell a pass (€10), valid for a week, that gives access to the Musée Fesch and Imperial Chapel, Musée A Bandera, Maison Bonaparte and Salon Napoléonien.

THE WEST COAST

MUSÉE NATIONAL DE LA MAISON BONAPARTE

This **museum** (☎ 04 95 21 43 89; rue St-Charles; adult/18-25/under-18 €5/3.50/free; ☯ 9-11.30am & 2-5.30pm Apr-Sep, 10-11.30am & 2-4.15pm Oct-Mar, closed Mon mornings year-round), the house in which Napoleon was born, got off to a bad start. Ransacked by Corsican nationalists in 1793, then requisitioned by the English from 1794 to 1796, it was later rebuilt by the emperor's mother. In the 19th century it became a place almost of cult worship, where the more ardent devotees would tear off a strip of wallpaper or prize away a tile as a relic. Even today, visitors are asked to dress in a respectful manner, as though entering a hallowed place. Here, in the parental house where Napoleon lived until he was packed off to school on the mainland, aged nine, are yet more memorabilia of the emperor and his siblings, whom he planted around the thrones of Europe.

SALON NAPOLÉONIEN

There the emperor sits, enthroned like Christ in Majesty and surrounded by troops, clergy and courtiers, high on the ceiling fresco of this **ceremonial room** (☎ 04 95 51 52 62; place Foch; adult/under-15 €2.30/free; ☯ 9-11.45am & 2-5.45pm daily mid-Jun–mid-Sep, Mon-Fri mid-Sep–mid-Jun) within the town hall. Here, too, are sculptures and paintings of the imperial family, furniture from the 'return from Egypt' period, a Bohemian crystal light and a veritable mint of medals and coins struck in the emperor's honour.

OTHER SIGHTS

The **Musée du Capitellu** (☎ 04 95 21 50 57; 18 blvd Danielle Casanova; adult/under-10 €4/2; ☯ 10am-noon & 2-6pm Mon-Sat, 10am-noon Sun Mar-Oct) is a delightful little museum assembled by Paul Ottavi-Sampolo, its owner and curator. It provides a fascinating glimpse into the town's history through the eclectic paintings, porcelain, silverware and *objets d'art*, assembled over the years by one prominent Ajaccio family.

The 15th-century **citadel**, an imposing military fortress overlooking the sea that was a prison during WWII, is normally closed to the public but the tourist office organises guided visits (€6) at 10am Monday and Wednesday May to September.

The Venetian-style **Cathédrale de Ste-Marie** (☯ 9-11.30am & 3-6pm Mon-Sat, 9-11.30am Sun), with its ochre façade, was built in the second half of the 16th century. Beside the west door is the font where a very small Napoleon was bap-

tised. In the north aisle is Delacroix's painting of the *Vierge au Sacré Coeur*.

An immense statue of Napoleon atop a huge stone plinth that's inscribed with his battles and other achievements lords it over **place d'Austerlitz**, about 1km west of place de Gaulle.

Activities

BEACHES

The large **Plage du Ricanto**, bordered by a popular jogging trail, lies about 6km northeast of the town towards the airport. You can reach it on bus 1. Smaller beaches and tiny coves, reached by bus 5, stretch beside rte des Sanguinaires all the way to Pointe de la Parata. The sprawling seaside resort of Porticcio (p174), south of the airport, prides itself on its long strand of golden sand and there are yet more beaches to its south.

BOAT TRIPS

Nave Va (☎ 04 95 25 94 14; www.naveva.com; ☯ May-Sep) does daily boat trips to the Scandola nature reserve (€48 with a stop in Girolata), Bonifacio (€57 with a four-hour stopover) and the Îles Sanguinaires (€22 with a halt for an offshore swim and snorkel and one-hour layover on Mezzu Mare, largest of the four islets). Children aged between four and 10 pay a reduced price.

Découvertes Naturelles (☎ 06 24 69 48 80, 06 24 69 48 81; ☯ May-Sep) offers the same trips to the Scandola reserve (Wednesday and Thursday) in a glass-bottomed boat and to the Îles Sanguinaires (daily, plus a sunset run on Tuesday, Thursday and Sunday) at the same rates.

DIVING

You're spoilt for choice of diving outfits in and around Ajaccio. Reliable centres include the following:

À L'Eau Plongée (☎ 06 09 60 14 09; http://monsite.wanadoo.fr/aleauplongee in French) At the end of the south jetty, Port Charles Ornano.

Centre de Plongée Les Calanques (☎ 04 95 52 09 37; www.corse-plongee.com; rte des Sanguinaires) Beneath Hôtel Stella di Mare.

E Ragnole (☎ 04 95 21 53 55; www.eragnole.com; rte des Sanguinaires) Just west of the Champion supermarket. One of the few centres to remain open year-round.

GSC (Groupement Subaquatique de Corse; ☎ 06 30 35 77 59) In Port Tino Rossi.

Isula Plongée (☎ 04 95 52 06 39; www.isula-plongee.com in French; Cala di Sole) Beside rte des Sanguinaires.

HIKING THE RIDGE ROAD

The walk starts just opposite the **Bois des Anglais** (English Woods) bus stop near Ajaccio. To get there from town (15 minutes on foot), follow cours Grandval and av du Général Leclerc to the Grotte Napoléon, from where you veer right onto av Piétri. There's a sign indicating that the path is marked by blue arrows – but you'll have to peer for them since they're very faded.

The dirt track quickly narrows and winds its way through an arid landscape of cactus and aloe. The markings are almost nonexistent and there are numerous crossroads, but simply keep on climbing until you reach a wide forest track. Depending on how you go, this will take anywhere between 15 and 40 minutes.

This forest track is known as the **chemin des Crêtes** (Ridge road); it looks down over the town of Ajaccio and the Golfe d'Ajaccio and also gives a great view of Monte d'Oro, which begins to take shape inland at the bottom of the Vallée du Gravone. Follow this path away from the town centre as it snakes through the maquis and eucalyptus bushes and alongside large, eroded rock formations. You'll have wonderful views all the way, looking down over a string of beaches and inlets. After you've walked for about two hours, you'll clearly make out the Îles Sanguinaires.

Follow the route as it descends to the sunny resort of Vignola (about 30 minutes), where you meet the rte des Sanguinaires beside the No 5 bus stop opposite the Hôtel Week-End.

At the end of this walk (allow three to four hours), the beaches, snack bars and restaurants are plentiful, and you can return to Ajaccio on bus 5 (every 30 minutes to 7.30pm, then 8.30pm).

Odyssée Plongée (☎ 06 62 07 53 51; www.odyssee -plongee.fr in French) In Port Charles Ornano.

See p79 for more information on diving.

SAILING & BOAT HIRE
Société Nautique d'Ajaccio (☎ 04 95 21 40 43; www .snajaccio.asso.fr in French; Fossé de la Citadelle) in Port Tino Rossi, puts on sailing courses for children (from €61) and adults (from €122).

Several competing outfits around Port Charles Ornano offer motor boat hire.

Ajaccio for Children
With its fairly compact centre, Ajaccio is easily navigable on little legs (or big ones pushing buggies). Most hotels will provide cots on request, but few offer a babysitting service. Restaurants, unlike many in northern Europe, will accommodate children at any hour. On summer nights there are market stalls and funfair rides around the port area just south of place Foch.

Le Petit Train d'Ajaccio (☎ 04 95 51 13 69; www .petit-train-ajaccio.com in French) is a tourist 'train' that makes two circuits along Ajaccio's streets: one through the old town (adult/child €7/3, 45 minutes) and a longer one through the old town and on to Pointe de la Parata (adult/child €10/4, 1½ hours). Each leaves on the hour from the kiosk opposite the town hall on place Foch.

There are a several beaches to go for a picnic or swim but on cooler days young ones may prefer to splash about in the municipal **swimming pool** (Piscine Municipale; ☎ 04 95 50 41 50; blvd Pascal Rossini; adult/child €2/1; ⏲ 9am-noon & 2-6pm). It's closed in July and August, when everyone heads for the beaches.

The A Cupulatta Centre (p174), a breeding centre for turtles, has over 3000 hardbacks on view.

Tours
Ajaccio Vision (☎ 06 20 17 50 33; adult/child 5-12/child under 5 €10/5/free; ⏲ 4 trips daily, 10am-4.30pm Apr-Oct) runs tours of the city's main sights in double-decker open-top buses with multilingual commentary, stopping for a break at Pointe de la Parata. Tours depart from opposite the town hall on place Foch.

Hél'île de Beauté (☎ 04 95 52 97 12) runs helicopter tours of the Sanguinaire islands, Ajaccio bay and the beaches to the south (10/30 minutes from €57/150 per person), departing from its base in Tavaco, about 15km from Ajaccio on the Bastia road. Discounts for groups of five or more apply.

Between May and September, the tourist office organises daily 1½-hour walking tours (€6 to €9, in French) of the old town and Ajaccio's main sights.

Festivals & Events
A Madunuccia A major religious procession files through town on 18 March, honouring Our Lady of Misericorde, protecting Ajaccians from plague ever since 1656.

Festival of Saint-Érasme Nautically themed festivities, food stalls, boat rides and amusements in the harbour celebrate the patron saint of fishermen on 2 June.

Fêtes Napoléoniennes Napoleon's birthday (15 August) is marked by a parade, music, fireworks and amusements.

Sleeping

Cheap accommodation in high season is thin on the ground in Ajaccio.

HOTELS

Hôtel Kallisté (☎ 04 95 51 34 45; www.hotel-kalliste -ajaccio.com in French; 51 cours Napoléon; s €45-56, d €52-76, tr €69-89; P ✕ ✖ ▣) With 30 contemporary rooms in an attractive 19th-century wi-fi–capable building and a new wing under construction, this stylish city hotel – complete with a glass lift, terracotta-tiled floors and exposed brickwork – is a great deal. Staff speak good English and reception also serves, incongruously, as a car rental outlet. Parking costs €12.

Hôtel Le Dauphin (☎ 04 95 21 12 94; www.ledauphin hotel.com; 11 blvd Sampiero; s €52-59, d €56-69, tr €69-85, all incl breakfast; P ✖) Le Dauphin, opposite the ferry terminal, is a good economical choice. Above a popular bar, its 39 clean, modern rooms, some with balcony, are decorated in shades of blue.

Hôtel du Palais (☎ 04 95 22 73 68; www.hoteldupal aisajaccio.com in French; 5 av Béverini Vico; s €45-60, d €60-95; ☽ Mar-Jan; ✖) This two-star hotel, handy for the port, offers eight simple, comfortable, well-priced rooms with air-con. It also has roomy apartments sleeping from two to six (€250 to €640 per week).

Hôtel Fesch (☎ 04 95 51 62 62; www.hotel-fesch.com; 7 rue Cardinal Fesch; s €56-79, d €61-89; ☽ mid-Jan–mid-Dec; ✖) The venerable Hôtel Fesch, quiet and overlooking a pedestrian street, has 77 attractive, cheerful rooms, decorated with rustic wooden furniture and featuring free wi-fi. The lift, bizarrely, is on the 1st-floor landing, which won't do wheelchair-users or those toting heavy bags any favours, and there's a warren of corridors.

Hôtel Marengo (☎ 04 95 21 43 66; www.hotel-marengo .com in French; 2 rue Marengo; d with shower €55-59, with bathroom €69-79, tr €85-105; ☽ Apr–mid-Nov; ✖) This charmingly eccentric small hotel is down a cul-de-sac off blvd Madame Mère. Once a private villa, it's been run with panache by the same owner for over 20 years. Its 17 rooms all have a balcony, there's a flowery terrace and reception is an agreeable clutter of tasteful

prints and personal objects. 'Cet hôtel a une âme,' (This hotel has a soul), she told us, and we knew what she meant.

Hôtel San Carlu (☎ 04 95 21 13 84; www.hotel-san carlu.com; 8 blvd Danielle Casanova; s €65-105, d €80-115; ☽ Feb–mid-Dec; ✖ ▣) Overlooking the citadel, this place, with its pastel and chrome décor, will make 1980s aficionados feel at home. Its 40 soundproofed rooms, half of which have sea views, are spacious and clean, the service is friendly and you can't beat its central old-town location.

Hôtel du Golfe (☎ 04 95 21 47 64; www.hoteldugolfe .com; 5 blvd du Roi Jérôme; s incl breakfast €78-120, d incl breakfast €88-130; ☽ mid-Mar–Oct; ✖) This friendly hotel, constructed in 1806 and Ajaccio's oldest, is a stone's throw from the old port and offers views over the bay. Rooms are rather small for the price and some bathrooms so tiny that you nearly have to leave your washbag outside. It's well worth paying €10 extra for a balcony and sea view.

Carpe Diem (☎ 04 95 10 96 10; www.carpediem-pal azzu.com in French; Eccica Suarella; ste €200-350; P ✖ ✖) Some 15km east of Ajaccio along the N196, near the village of Eccica Suarella, this majestic 18th-century stone-built mansion has been elegantly and authentically restored. Its six suites, huge, individually styled and furnished with period pieces, retain their attractive original wooden beamed ceilings. There are changing art exhibitions in public areas, wi-fi access and a glorious terrace that leads on to the extensive garden.

CAMPING

Campers will find more attractive options in and around Porticcio (p176), an easy drive or ferry trip away.

Camping Les Mimosas (☎ 04 95 20 99 85; www.camping -lesmimosas.com in French; rte d'Alata; camp sites per adult/ tent/car €5/2.20/2.20; ☽ Apr-Oct) Significantly the better of Ajaccio's only two camping choices, Les Mimosas, tranquil and only 3km from the town centre, has 70 large, well-designated pitches in the deep shade of eucalyptus trees. There's a small shop, a bar serving snacks and a children's play area. Driving, take the D61 (rte d'Alata) on the north side of Ajaccio, from where it's signed. Otherwise, take bus 4 and get off at the Brasilia stop.

Camping Barbicaja (☎ /fax 04 95 52 01 17; rte des Sanguinaires; camp sites per adult/tent/car €6/3/3; ☽ Apr-Oct) Reasonably shaded and with a couple of lovely sandy coves an easy walk away, this camping

THE AUTHOR'S CHOICE

Hôtel-Demeure les Mouettes (☎ 04 95 50 40 40; wwwhotellesmouettes.com; 6 cours Lucien Bonaparte; s/d €99-229; ☒ Mar-Dec; ℗ ☒ ☒ ☒ ☒) Occupying a lovely 19th-century mansion that has served in its time as both convent and cinema studios, Les Mouettes, has operated as a hotel for over half a century. Under its dynamic new management, it was extensively and tastefully renovated in late 2006 and has wi-fi access. Laze on the deep, shaded terrace, lounge by the pool beneath a pair of century-old palms within the delightful garden or step down to the secluded beach just below. More energetically, hire one of its kayaks or bicycles. Of its 28 rooms, 22 have sea views (the superior grade ones have particularly large balconies). Service is attentive and discreet and breakfast (€15) is copious and varied. You'll be sleeping in illustrious company; among its many celebrity guests feature a couple of ex-prime ministers, Eric Cantona, Nina Simone and Michael Schumacher. Free parking.

ground could have so much going for it, but it needs some serious investment; facilities are run-down and ill maintained, while feral cats – and a handsome tortoise – prowl through the night.

Eating
CAFÉS
Bistrot Pigale (☎ 04 95 21 20 46; 6 av de Paris; mains €6-10; ☒ Mon-Sat; ☒) This busy, friendly bar serves hearty salads (€9), omelettes (€6 to €9) and a plate of cheeses and crusty bread (€4). There's outside seating.

RESTAURANTS
Chez Paulo (☎ 04 95 51 16 47; 7 rue du Roi de Rome; mains €6.50-11, menus €14-19; ☒ Mon-Fri, dinner Sat & Sun) There's always a crowd at Chez Paulo and for good reason. Visitors and locals alike watch life go by from its busy terrace and it has a good selection of fresh pasta and pizza (€6.50 to €8.50). There's live Corsican music each night after 10.30pm at the adjoining Le Son des Guitares.

Ariadne Plage (☎ 04 95 52 09 63; rte des Sanguinaires; pizzas €9-11, mains €14.50-22, fish menu €25.50; ☒ Apr–mid-Oct) With several imitators along this coastal strip, Ariadne Plage was the first of Ajaccio's *paillotes* (beach restaurants). African rhythms playing, planks underfoot, a reed roof above and, below, a sandy beach with bright red umbrellas: blink and you could be beside the Caribbean. The cuisine is equally exotic.

Da Mamma (☎ 04 95 21 39 44; passage Guingette; mains €12-20, menus €11-26; ☒ Mon-Sat, closed lunch Mon Jul & Aug) Tucked away down a steep alley and shaded by a magnificent rubber tree, Mama's Place is another hugely popular place that offers very reasonably priced fare and a variety of *menus*. The one at €23 includes cannelloni with *brocciu* and roast goat.

U Pampasgiolu (☎ 04 95 50 71 52; 15 rue de la Porta; mains €13-20; ☒ Mon-Fri, dinner Sat; ☒) At the Poppy, welcoming and much-garlanded by just about every French gastronomic guide, you'll dine very well indeed on the small terrace or within the cool, brick-vaulted interior. Go à la carte or choose the *planche spuntinu* (snack taster; €22) or *planche de la mer* (fish and seafood selection) for a great selection of Corsican specialities, served on wooden platters.

L'Estaminet (☎ 04 95 50 10 42; 5-7 rue du Roi de Rome; mains €15.50-20, menus €18.50-25; ☒ dinner daily, lunch Sun Jul & Aug, lunch & dinner Thu-Tue Sep-Jun) The glorious bar of dark stained wood could almost be a pulpit while you could play chess on the jazzy black-and-white floor tiles. The food is delightful, there's a well-chosen wine cellar and the cheeses are organic.

Le Spago (☎ 04 95 21 15 71; rue Emmanuel Arène; mains €15-22, dinner menu €20; ☒ Mon-Fri, dinner Sat) At this cool designer restaurant, decked out in marine and lime-green, the oil and vinegar dispensers squirt just the right amount, like aerosol deodorants; and His and Hers toilets are designated by the creative use of a pair of green apples – exactly how, we leave you to discover. You won't find a single Corsican speciality on the menu; just great salads and tasty, inventive dishes such as chicken and mango fricasse.

Le Bilboq (☎ 04 95 51 35 40; 2 rue des Glacis; 3-course menu €21) This colourful little place on a bustling lane specialises in inventive fish and seafood dishes, as well as finely prepared regulars such as bouillabaisse and grilled sea bream.

Grand Café Napoléon (☎ 04 95 21 42 54; 10 cours Napoléon; mains €23-30, menus €28-45; ☒ Mon-Sat) Behind the street-front café, itself rich in atmosphere, hides Ajaccio's most extravagant dining room, with potted plants, soaring cream arches, black-and-white terrazzo floors and red tablecloths, all recalling *belle époque* style and splendour. Despite the classical surroundings, the menu is surprisingly modern, featuring elegantly presented dishes such as monkfish on wild rice with marinated butter beans.

Le 20123 (☎ 04 95 21 50 05; 2 rue Roi de Rome; menu €32) These days an Ajaccio institution, this Corsican bistro started life in the village of Pila Canale (postcode 20123 – hence the name). When the Habani family came to the big city, they decided to re-create their old restaurant – village square, water pump, a washing line sagging with pantaloons, a classic Vespa, life-sized dolls in traditional dress and a hotchpotch of grandad's era country paraphernalia. But diners flock here primarily for its well-prepared country cooking, rich in local produce, especially the meats and charcuterie. Reservations are all but essential.

Drinking

You'll find yourself spoilt for choice around rue du Roi de Rome, place de Gaulle, av de Paris and blvd Pascal Rossini.

Au Grandval (2 cours Grandval) Opened in 1892, Monsieur Fleschi's bar has changed little, except for the addition of a formica counter 30 years ago. Archive photographs of Ajaccio streets cover the walls and outside you can sit by the palm tree, planted by the owner's grandfather on the 100th anniversary of Napoléon's death and listen to the chatter of the resident parakeet.

Bar 1er Consul (2 rue Bonaparte) This bar is a good spot for a morning coffee on the terrace overlooking busy place Foch. Inside, brown leather banquettes, smoke-stained walls and giant mirrors add to the period atmosphere.

La Boca Loca (rue de la Porta; ☺ Tue-Sat) A small grungy cave-like place with a strong Spanish flavour that stays open late. Its cocktails, tapas and live music (most evenings) are the main draw.

Le Privilège (place de Gaulle) A smart piano bar, this is a place to retreat from the heat and sip something subtle.

Entertainment

Le Menestrel (5 rue Cardinal Fesch) Live local musicians play most evenings though if you're under 40 you may find the repertoire on the staid side.

Le Son des Guitares (7 rue Roi de Rome; ☺ from 10.30pm Wed-Sun) Puts on local guitar soloists and ensembles. Admission is free and drinks ('renouvables tous les 45 minutes' – fresh purchase required every 45 minutes – says the churlish sign) cost €5.

La Place (☎ 04 95 51 09 10; blvd Lantivy; ☺ 11pm-3am) Beside the casino and the only disco in Ajaccio proper, this is an older person's pick-up joint where the music's mainly techno. Expect to pay in excess of €7 for drinks.

Casino Municipal (blvd Lantivy; ☺ 1pm-4am) The plush casino is fine for a flutter. The more serious gaming room, with roulette and black-jack, opens at 9.30pm. Visitors are expected to dress 'appropriately' and the two heavies at the door will eye you for appropriacy.

Throughout the summer, the tourist office runs a summer **concert programme** (adult/child €8/5) of traditional polyphonic singing at 7pm Wednesday evenings in Église St-Érasme.

Ariadne Plage (p171), right on the seafront, has live world music daily in July and August and twice-weekly in May, June and September. According to the evening, you can enjoy Gypsy, salsa, zouk and more.

The Empire, Laeticia and Bonaparte cinemas on cours Napoléon all screen new releases, while **Aiglon** (14 cours Grandval) shows independent French and foreign films.

Shopping

On Fridays in July and August, shops stay open until midnight and there's live music and street entertainment.

There's a **farmer's market** (☺ 8am-noon Tue-Sun) in square Campinchi. On weekends stalls of clothing and crafts join those of fruit, vegetables, and Corsican cheeses and meat products.

U Stazzu (rue Bonaparte) is *the* place for the very best of Corsican charcuterie. For five generations, the family have been rearing pigs in the high mountains, feeding them on acorns and chestnuts and despatching them when they're still tender and barely two years old. **Villages Corses** (44 rue du Cardinal Fesch) is another specialist delicatessen, also packed with Corsican delicacies, including charcuterie, cheeses, liqueurs, wine, chestnut flour and honey.

Maison de L'Amande Corse (2 rue Sébastiani; ☺ Tue-Sat, 4-8pm Mon) is a delightfully obsessive, single-product shop that offers almonds from Corsica (the island grows around 60% of the total French production), prepared in every

THE WEST COAST

possible way: almond oil, almond powder, cream of almond, almond soap, grilled, salted almonds – and wickedly tempting, delightfully sweet *nougatine d'amande*.

By contrast, **Opium** (6 rue des Trois Maries), with shops on both sides of the street, offers not a single Corsican product. The owner, herself a victim of the travel bug, instead sells original and striking jewellery and crafts, for the most part from Africa and Asia.

Vibrations (48 rue du Cardinal Fesch) carries a decent range of Corsican music and singing. **Musica** (26 cours Napoléon) has a smaller selection of Corsican music and film on DVD.

Getting There & Away

For additional details, see the Transport chapter's sections on Air (p264) and Sea (p267).

AIR

Campo dell'Oro airport (☎ 04 95 23 56 56; www.ajaccio .aeroport.fr in French) is 8km east of town. With mountains and sea on either side, touching down can be an experience to remember.
Air France (☎ 08 20 82 08 20; www.airfrance.com; 3 blvd du Roi Jérôme) Other airlines have offices at the airport.
Nouvelles Frontières (☎ 04 95 21 55 55; www.nouvelles -frontieres.com; 12 place Foch; ◷ 9am-noon Mon-Sat, 2-6pm Mon-Fri) A general travel agent.

BOAT

Mainland France

Ferries leave from the modern **terminal building** (☎ 04 95 51 55 45; quai L'Herminier), which also houses the ticket windows for intercity buses. Three companies sail between Corsica and mainland Europe. CMN and SNCM operate joint ticketing and services.
CMN (☎ 04 95 11 01 00; www.cmn.fr; blvd Sampiero; ◷ 8am-7.30pm Mon-Fri, 9am-noon Sat) Also runs crossings and shares routes and timetable with SNCM.
Corsica Ferries (☎ 08 25 09 50 95; www.corsicaférrries.fr; Gare Maritime) Has its office within the terminal building.
SNCM (☎ 04 95 29 66 99; www.sncm.fr; ◷ 8am-8pm Mon-Fri, 8am-noon Sat) Has two offices in the harbour, one next to the Compagnie Méridionale de Navigation (CMN) and the other, opposite the terminal building.

Porticcio

From May to September, both Découvertes Naturelles and Nave Va run a ferry service between Port Tino Rossi in Ajaccio and Porticcio (one-way/return €5/8, 20 minutes, each six or seven times daily). The first departure is at 8am and the last at 7pm.

BUS

Most bus companies have offices in the terminal building. Together, they provide service from Ajaccio to most other parts of the island.
Autocars Casanova (☎ 04 95 25 40 37) Runs five buses daily between Ajaccio and Porticcio (€3.20, 20 minutes).
Autocars Ceccaldi (☎ 04 95 22 41 99) Runs two buses between Porto and Ajaccio (€11, two hours), calling by Golfe de Sagone coastal towns.
Eurocorse Voyages (☎ 04 95 21 06 30) Runs twice-daily to Bonifacio (€20, four hours) and Porto-Vecchio (€20, 3½ hours), calling by Propriano (€10.50, 1½ hours) and Sartène (€11.50, 1¾ hours). Also serves Bastia (€19, three hours) via Vizzavona (€7.50, one hour), Corte (€11, 1¾ hours) and Ponte Leccia (€15, 2¼ hours) twice daily, Monday to Saturday.

TRAIN

Four trains daily leave **Ajaccio station** (☎ 04 95 23 11 03) for Bastia (€20.70, four hours) via Vizzavona (€7.40, 1¼ hours) and Corte (€11, two hours).

There are two departures daily for Calvi (€24.10, five hours) via Île Rousse (€21.40, four hours). Both require a change in Ponte Leccia.

Getting Around
TO/FROM THE AIRPORT

TCA bus 8 (€4.50, 20 minutes, 14 daily) runs between the airport, 8km from the town centre, and Ajaccio's bus and ferry terminal building. At the airport, the bus stop is 50m to the right as you leave the arrivals area.

A taxi from the airport to the town centre during the day costs around €20 in the daytime and nearer €25 at night and on Sunday. Ask whether the €2 airport tax is included or supplementary.

CAR

Finding parking in the centre of Ajaccio is a nightmare and few hotels have their own facilities. There are large paying car parks at the train station, beside the entrance to the ferry terminal, beneath place de Gaulle and northeast of place Foch.

At the airport, there are car hire firms in the car park across from the terminal. Major operators also have a branch in town.
Ada (☎ 04 95 23 56 57; www.ada-en-corse.com in French)
Avis (☎ 04 95 23 56 90; www.avis.fr in French)

THE WEST COAST

Budget (☎ 04 95 23 57 21; www.budget-en-corse.com in French)
Citer (☎ 04 95 23 57 15; www.corse-auto-rent.fr in French)
Europcar (☎ 04 95 23 57 01; www.europcar.fr in French)
Hertz (☎ 04 95 23 57 04/05; www.hertz-en-corse.com)
Rent a Car (☎ 04 95 23 56 26, www.rent-car-corsica.com)
Sixt Castellani (☎ 04 95 23 57 00)

PUBLIC TRANSPORT
TCA (☎ 04 95 23 29 41; 75 cours Napoléon) runs buses within Ajaccio. A single ticket, which you can buy on the bus, costs €1.20 and a carnet, valid for 10 journeys, is €9. Main lines:
No 4 Budiccione–town centre–Hôpital de la Miséricorde
No 5 Town centre–Pointe de la Parata (rte des Sanguinaires)
No 8 Transport terminal–airport

AROUND AJACCIO
Pointe de la Parata & Îles Sanguinaires
The four small islets with their jagged coastlines that constitute the Îles Sanguinaires take their name – meaning 'bloody' – from their distinctive red rock. Tantalisingly close to Pointe de la Parata at the northern limit of the Golfe d'Ajaccio, they can be visited by boat from both Ajaccio and Porticcio.

Bus 5 from Ajaccio terminates at Pointe de la Parata, from whose car park an easy, much-trodden trail leads around the promontory, giving impressive views of the islets. The largest of them, Mezzu Mare, was last inhabited in 1985, when the lighthouse was automated and its keeper pulled away for the last time. The ruins you see were once a quarantine point for coral fishermen upon their return from the coasts of West Africa, for fear that tropical diseases might rampage through town.

Tiny as they are, the islands support over 150 different plant species and, since there are no terrestrial predators, they're a haven for seabirds with resident colonies of crested cormorants, yellow-legged gulls and Cory's shearwater.

Both Découvertes Naturelles and Nave Va (p168) do boat trips to the islands, including the chance for an offshore swim and snorkel, from Ajaccio's Port Tino Rossi.

A Cupulatta Centre
A Cupulatta (☎ 04 95 52 82 34; www.acupulatta.com in French; Vignola, Vero; adult/child 4-11/under 4 €8/4.50/free), 21km from Ajaccio towards Corte on the N193, is Europe's largest centre dedicated to the breeding and preservation of tortoises. Opened in 1998 thanks to the enthusiasm of Philippe Magnan and his team of volunteers, it today shelters approximately 3000 hardbacks, representing more than 150 species from all over the world, some of them in danger of extinction. Signed in four languages, it's well documented, although you'll have to look around carefully to find some – not that they're likely to sprint away. Interesting tortoise fact: if the temperature of the ground in which a mother lays her eggs is more than 28°C, there's a greater probability of the young ones being female. Under 28°C, they're more likely to hatch out male (to our knowledge, this only applies to tortoises so don't worry about any side effects of the air-con!).

PORTICCIO (PURTICHJU)
pop 2250
Porticcio's best asset is its long sandy beach. The principal disadvantage of this parvenu of a seaside resort, which recalls the worst of the Italian Riviera and crowded Spanish Costa resorts, is its proximity to Ajaccio, 18km away by road and much nearer if you hop on the ferry and cross the bay. In summer Porticcio's main street is bumper to bumper with holiday traffic, mostly Ajaccians in search of a quick fix of sun, sand and surf. But let's not be too churlish; there's a jolly seaside atmosphere, a couple of great camping grounds, a superb top-end hotel and plenty of scope for watersports enthusiasts. And what a beach – among Corsica's finest…

Orientation
Porticcio extends thinly along the length of its beach. A series of uninspiring modern commercial developments – La Viva, Les Marines and Les Marines 2 – on either side of the D55 are its focal points. Shoreside Les Marines has the tourist office and the landing stage.

Information
Laundrette Behind the shops at Les Marines, rear of Maeva Plongée.
Post office Behind the Total petrol station in Les Marines 2.
Tourist office (☎ 04 95 25 01 01; www.porticcio.org in French; ☷ 8.30am-12.30pm & 2-8pm daily Jun-Sep, 9am-noon & 2-6pm Mon-Sat Oct-May) A blue kiosk in Les Marines beside the landing stage. A notice asks visitors to dress respectably and refrain from bringing in sand. Don't say we didn't warn you!

THE WEST COAST

Activities

You don't come to Porticcio for its sights; its beautiful **Plage de La Viva** fringing the town is the real draw and it has enough bars and restaurants, as well as stalls that hire out sailboards and deckchairs, to keep most punters happy.

Along the Golfe d'Ajaccio south of Porticcio stretch three smaller, less crowded and almost as inviting beaches: **Plage d'Agosta**, **Plage de Ruppione** and **Plage de Mare e Sole**.

BOAT TRIPS

Nave Va (☎ 04 95 25 94 14; www.naveva.com; ☼ May-Sep) does daily boat trips to the Scandola nature reserve with a stop in Girolata (€48), Bonifacio (€57 with a four-hour stopover) and the Îles Sanguinaires (€22 with a halt for an offshore swim and snorkel and one-hour layover on Mezzu Mare, largest of the four islets). Children between the age of five and 10 are half-price. Its kiosk is beside the landing stage.

Découvertes Naturelles (☎ 06 24 69 48 80, 06 24 69 48 81; ☼ May-Sep), with its kiosk beside Nave Va's, also offers the same trips to the Scandola reserve (Wednesday and Thursday) in a glass-bottomed boat and to the Îles Sanguinaires (daily plus a sunset run on Tuesday, Thursday and Sunday) at the same rates.

CYCLING

Between April and September, the **Shell station** (☎ 04 95 25 06 64), on the north side of town, rents out mountain bikes (€13/60 per day/week) against a €150 deposit (cash or credit card).

Au Royaume du Pêcheur (☎ 04 95 25 00 40; ☼ year-round), beside Camping Benista (p176), also hires out mountain bikes (per half-day/full day/week €10/13/60).

DIVING

Maeva Plongée (☎ 04 95 25 02 40; www.maeva-plongee.com in French; Marines de Porticcio; ☼ Apr-Sep) is right on the beach, 50m south of the tourist office. You'll pay €38 for an introductory dive on the beach, €47 for a boat dive, €33 to €45 for an exploratory dive or €155 to €215 for five dives, depending on whether you use your own equipment or not.

Corse Plongée (☎ 04 95 25 50 08, 06 07 55 67 25; www.corseplongee.fr.st in French; ☼ Mar-Nov) is the first building you come to on the Isolella peninsula, 6km south of Porticcio. Its standard offerings include the wreck of the *Meulière*, the Tête de Mort and the Grotte à Corail – but Nicolas Caprili, director, diver and skipper, prides himself on having several other secret sites up his sleeve.

See p79 for more information on diving.

WATER SPORTS

Centre Nautique de Porticcio (☎ 04 95 25 01 06; Plage de la Viva; ☼ Apr-Sep) rents windsurfers (per hour €15 to €21), kayaks (€10 to €15) and catamarans (€32 to €42).

Loca-Nautic (☎ 04 95 25 17 85, 06 09 57 12 50; www.loca-nautic.com in French; Plage de La Viva; ☼ Jul & Aug), beside the landing stage, hires out inflatable motor boats (no permit required), dinghies and water skis.

HORSE RIDING

In July and August, **Les Écuries de Molini** (☎ 06 22 87 61 15, 06 13 50 32 20; Molini), 2.4km off the D55 (the last 800m along a deeply pitted sandy track), does a couple of three-hour treks (€35) through the maquis or along the crests, returning via the beach. Guides speak English and these gentle outings are suitable even for beginners. Year-round they also organise treks of two days (€200) and three days (€300) with meals and overnight camp included in the price.

Centre Équestre de Porticcio (☎ 04 95 22 75 59), signed from the roundabout east of Les Marines 2, also does guided rides of the interior or beach (per hour €20).

Sleeping
HOTELS

Acqua Dolce (☎ 04 95 25 19 62; www.hotel-acquadolce.com; s €48-92, d €60-119, tr €78-162, 2-/4-/5-bed studios €45/70/80, per week Jul & Aug €532/826/980; Pisciatello; Ⓟ Ⓡ) Beside the River Prunelli, 3km from town in a lovely oak grove, Acqua Dolce is a good place to get away from the hustle and bustle of Porticcio. Rooms are simply furnished but clean and there are some lovely walks in the area. The studios have rustic wood-panelled walls, kitchenettes, showers and terraces. It's signed and set back on the left of the N196, direction Propriano, just beyond the Pisciatello turn-off. There's a minimum stay of three nights from September to June.

Le Maquis (☎ 04 95 25 05 55; www.lemaquis.com; r €175-550; ☼ closed variable 6 weeks Jan & Feb; Ⓟ Ⓧ 💻 Ⓡ) This delightful wi-fi–capable hideaway with its own private beach sits amid beautifully maintained grounds. Of its two pools, one is internal, heated and open year-round. The 27 bedrooms are spacious and, like public areas, individually and exquisitely furnished with antique pieces. L'Arbousier, its restaurant, offers gourmet cuisine (*menus* €36 to €42) in an equally tasteful environment.

CAMPING

Camping Mare e Machja (☎ 04 95 25 10 58; www .ifrance.com/maremachja; camp sites per adult/tent/car €6.90/2.80/2.80; ☺ mid-May–Sep; ☟) On a plateau overlooking the gulf, this spacious, peaceful camping ground seemingly occupies half a hillside. Pitches are large and well separated and the tiled washrooms and toilets are well maintained. Both the pool and the terrace of the restaurant, pizzeria and bar have great views of Porticcio, barely 2km below.

Camping Benista (☎ 04 95 25 19 30; www.benista .com in French; camp sites per double with car low/high season €19.50/24.10; ☺ Apr–Oct; ℗ ☟) This shaded four-star camping ground is beside the River Prunelli, 1.8km north of Plage de la Viva. Mature privet hedges demarcate each ample pitch, there's a pool and a bar-restaurant too. Often full in high season, it accepts reservations until 30 June, even for a single night.

Eating

Porticcio isn't one of Corsica's great eating destinations. On the plus side, nearly all restaurants have wide terraces overlooking Plage de la Viva and offer a feast for the eyes, perhaps less fulfillingly for the stomach.

If you're after something light, a couple of tempting *crêperies*, open throughout the day, each offering a huge range of toppings.

A Merendella (☎ 04 95 25 08 27; crepes €3.50-10) This place, whose fame extends all over the island, specialises in sweet fillings.

L'Alba Nova (☎ 04 95 53 41 47; crepes €3.50-10) You could devour a pancake a day for over a month and still not exhaust its repertoire, which includes crepes sizzled from chestnut flour.

La Saladerie (☎ 04 95 25 08 77; salads €8-23, menus €15.50-19; ☺ year-round, closed Thu Nov-Mar; Ⓥ) The view of the beach from here is only oblique but you dine on a pleasant vine-shaded terrace with a wooden deck. As you'd anticipate from its name, lavish, creative salads, are the signature dish. It also offers avocados prepared 10 different ways, fresh pasta dishes (€10 to €20) and a range of omelettes.

Le Club (☎ 04 95 25 00 42; mains €20-26, menus €28-32; ☺) For fine dining, this place stands head and shoulders above the competing beachside restaurants. There's a comfortable, pleasing dining room, decked in shades of ochre, if you can tear yourself away from its lovely terrace. The fish on offer is determined by what's in the nets of the previous day's catch and the house desserts are a dream. For a snack, call by Délices Club, its bakery, in the same building, which turns out tasty sandwiches, quiches, pizzas – and meringues the size of giant snowballs.

Getting There & Around

BUS

From July to mid-September, **Autocars Casanova** (☎ 04 95 25 40 37) runs five buses daily between Ajaccio and Porticcio (€3.20, 20 minutes), continuing to Plage de Verghia via Isolella. During the rest of the year, there's a morning and evening shuttle only.

CAR

To quit the slow, stop-start crawl through Porticcio, Marines 2 has two large car parks, one in front of the post office and the other beside the Champion supermarket.

FERRY

From May to September, both Découvertes Naturelles and Nave Va (p175) run a ferry service between Porticcio and Port Tino Rossi in Ajaccio (one-way/return €5/8, 20 minutes, each six or seven times daily). The first departure is at 8.30am and the last at 7.30pm.

TAXI

Call ☎ 06 15 30 54 24.

AROUND PORTICCIO

Forêt de Chiavari

The cork and eucalyptus groves of the Forêt de Chiavari are a peaceful place for a picnic and offer welcome respite from the heat. Taking off from the D55 near the Plage de Verghia, a winding road with stunning views of the bay leads ever upwards towards the mountaintop village of Coti-Chiavari. The huge, dilapidated buildings you pass on the left are all that remains of a 19th-century prison that saw action again during WWII.

Capo di Muro

The reward for a walk to the cliff-top tower of Capo di Muro, marking the southernmost tip of the Golfe d'Ajaccio, is an outstanding panoramic view of the bay. You can climb a small metal staircase to the 1st floor of the solid watchtower for even better viewing. Follow the D155 south, then take a small road to the right, just after the village of Acqua Doria. From the point where it peters out, it's an 800m-or-so walk to the tower.

HAUT TARAVO

High up in the furthest reaches of the Taravo Valley, which rises over 60km to the very heart of the island, are a cluster of tiny, austere one-bus-a-day hamlets, connected by a network of little trafficked by-roads. Nowhere guards the secrets of traditional Corsica better or more discreetly than this lush, remote valley, whose pure upland air is ideal for a little tramping, as gentle or as vigorous and lung-opening as you care to make it.

Zicavo (750m) lazily spreads itself along the flank of the mountain, its main street bordered by attractive houses, built to last in grey granite. Take a 1km detour, direction Aullène, (to the left beside the bridge) for a lovely little waterfall and a refreshing dip. From the village, a three hour round-trip walk brings you to **Bocca di l'Agnonu** (1570m) and the splendid **Coscione plateau** (p72), crossed by a rare flat stretch of the GR20.

Cozzano (725m), a few kilometres beyond Zicavo and equally charming, is another spot where you'll probably come across a few hikers, fresh down from the heights. From here a three-hour round-trip signed walk, following a stretch of the Mare a Mare Centre long-distance trail, brings you to the **Bocca di Laparu** (1525m) and another intersection with the GR20 as it snakes along the peaks that rise from the valley's eastern flank.

To the west of the main D83, signed roads lead you to **Giovicacce**, **Tasso**, **Sampolo**, **Guitera-les-Bains** and **Quasquara**, places so small they don't even feature on many a map.

Beyond Cozzano, the D83 climbs to the top of the valley and the Bocca di Verdi (Col de Verde; 1289m), a col that marks the Taravo Valley's highest point. Here, you can overnight at the splendid Refuge du Col de Verde (p70), right beside the GR20. Driving on beyond the pass, brings you to Ghisoni (p247), well worth a brief stop before dropping to the main N193 that links Ajaccio and Corte.

Sleeping & Eating

The Haut Taravo Valley is well endowed with modest, attractive places to stay and eat.

Gîte d'Étape Bella Vista (☎ 04 95 24 41 59; Cozzano; camp sites per person €6, dm €11, d €32; Apr-Sep) The building may be unexceptional but what a splendid panorama over the valley from this *gîte*! The dorms here sleep six, the three doubles have en suite bathrooms and there are facilities for self-caterers. Meals are also available (dinner €15). The owner, the former warden of the nearby Usciolu GR20 *refuge*, is a mine of information about local walking opportunities.

Chambres d'Hôtes Le Paradis (☎ 04 95 24 41 20; Zicavo; camping per person €5, dm incl breakfast €15, d with/without half-board €80/50) 'Paradise' may be pushing it a bit but the four bright, modern rooms, in an annexe grafted on to the main house, that Madame Pirany maintains with the help of her daughter are at least halfway there. Three can accommodate up to four sleepers and there are self-catering facilities. Bring your tent and you can pitch in the shade of an apple orchard. Dinners are based upon what her kitchen garden has in season, supplemented with charcuterie prepared by her son. A wonderful, family experience.

Châtelet de Campo (☎ 04 95 53 74 18; www .chatelet-de-campo.com; Campo; d incl breakfast €90-115; P X) This delightful granite-built mansion, tucked away in the woods overlooking Campo (which, with scarcely 50 souls, lays claim to be Corsica's tiniest hamlet) is far from modest. Views are inspiring and there's a gorgeous garden, complete with shady gazebo, and pool. Its four rooms (be sure to reserve) are light, airy and furnished with taste. The only impediment: it normally insists upon a minimum of two nights' stay. Meals are available (dinner €30).

Le Pacific Sud (☎ 04 95 24 41 37; mains €6-15; Apr-Sep) In Zicavo's main street this bar-restaurant and pizzeria serves generously topped pizzas and grills inside or on its terrace, just across the road.

Auberge & Gîte d'Étape Lanfranchi (☎ 04 95 24 44 40; www.chez-paul-antoine.com; Guitera; meals €18-23; closed Nov) This place, renowned throughout the valley for its rich cooking and ample portions, demands a detour for its home-cured meats, pâtés, sausages – everything that can be salvaged, scented and spiced from the pig (sink your teeth into the *côtelettes de sanglier avec de la sauce aux arbouse*, baby wild boar

THE WEST COAST

chops with arbutus berry sauce). Rooms accommodate four to 12 people (dormitory with/without half-board €33/13) or you can pitch your tent (€5 per person). To get to the hamlet of Guitera, follow the D28 for 3.5km from where it leaves the D83 at Guitera-les-Bains.

VALLÉE DU PRUNELLI

If you've had a temporary surfeit of mountain vistas and superb seascapes, take the D3 northeastwards up the Prunelli Valley. Wide, lush and cultivated in its lower reaches, it's green and gentle on the eye. This lightly travelled alternative (non-Corsican numberplates are a rarity) winds its way up into the mountains for about 25km as far as the village of **Tolla**, perched above a lake, man-made but no less attractive for that. At water level, the **Centre Nautique** (☎ 04 95 27 00 48) rents out kayaks, canoes and sailing boats. Beside it, **Restaurant La Ferme** (☎ 04 95 27 01 89) does horse rides in the surrounding countryside.

Both up- and downstream from the lake, the road runs above the **Gorges du Prunelli**, always present but more rarely visible, as it snakes its way through mixed wood as far as Bastelica.

Bastelica
pop 460

This mountain village is famous for its charcuterie, made from local *cochons coureurs* (p246). Among several producers who sell directly to the customer are Salaisons Sampiero and L'Aziana. Bastelica is also the home town of Sampiero Corso (p28), whose statue stands proud. A curious plaque, contributed by one William Bonaparte Wyse (an Irish grand-nephew of Napoleon), on the site of the house in which Corso was born, proclaims the hero to be 'the most Corsican of all Corsicans'.

The **Val d'Ese** ski resort is 16km from Bastelica along a road that runs through beautiful mountain scenery. At 1700m, this tiny resort has little impact on the environment: there are only two buildings and no hotel or restaurant. You can hire ski equipment in Bastelica and at the foot of the slopes.

Restaurant-Pension Chez Paul (☎ 04 95 28 71 59; r €45, s/d incl dinner €45/69; ☼ year-round), in the upper part of the village, has a wonderful picture window overlooking the valley. The welcome is warm from your bluff host with his foghorn voice and waggish chat. *Menus* cost from €12 to €24, according to the number of courses you select (the portions of hearty Corsican fare are gargantuan). Apartments with self-catering facilities are also available just up the road.

Interesting

The South

If you could visit only one region after the sensational Golfe de Porto, it would have to be the south. Cap Corse or Balagne fans can cry foul, but the south blends history, culture and beach, with a dash of Corsican pride and Mediterranean glam sealing the deal.

The south is blessed with an embarrassment of riches. For starters, you can't help but be dazzled by Bonifacio and Porto-Vecchio, the two Corsican supermodels. Then come the beaches. And what beaches! Take Plage de Palombaggia or the Îles Lavezzi; you could easily be forgiven for thinking you've hit the Seychelles. For those for whom beachside lounging spells death by boredom, there's an abundance of activities on land and sea. Have you ever galloped across a sandy beach on a moonlit night? Got up close and personal with big groupers? Or swung through pine forests the way Tarzan of the Jungle does it? Just as stimulating is the journey back into history. Drink it in as you linger in the alleyways of Sartène, or visit the megalithic sites at Filitosa or Cauria. Sense the still-resonating forces that have shaped this island for centuries.

You could spend weeks here and still have treasures to unearth. Who has heard of Tizzano, a hidden gem at the dead end of the southwest? Or the wild Vallée de l'Ortolo? And of course, the south is also a region of fine wining and dining. Now it's your turn to enjoy.

HIGHLIGHTS

- **Supermodel Show**
  Get the best views of wonderful Bonifacio (p196) from a boat

- **No Holds Barred**
  Lose your inhibitions and party the night away in chic Porto-Vecchio (p203)

- **Time Machine**
  Ponder Corsica's bizarre (pre)history at Filitosa (p182) and Cauria (p193)

- **Adrenaline Fix**
  Try kitesurfing or windsurfing (p194) at Plage de Piantarella or Plage de la Tonnara

- **Life's a Beach**
  Sun and splash on the idyllic beaches of Palombaggia (p209), Cupabia (p181) or Tra Licettu (p193)

- **True-blue Corsican**
  Explore the cobbled alleyways of mysterious Sartène (p189)

- **Outdoor Galore**
  Hike to the Piscia di Gallo waterfall (p212) in the cool Forêt de L'Ospédale or explore the canyon of La Vacca (p217) near Bavella

THE SOUTH

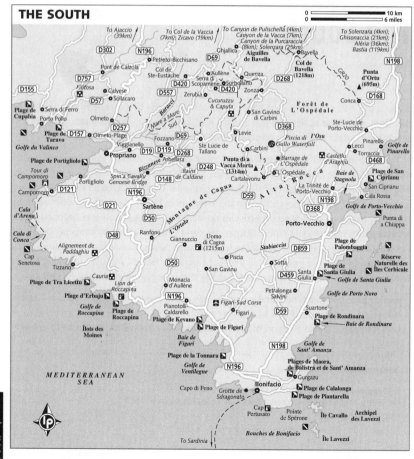

THE SOUTH

GOLFE DU VALINCO

Another huge bite chomped out of the fretted coastline of Corsica's west coast, the Golfe du Valinco resembles a giant mouth about to gobble up its prey. This gulf offers some of the wildest and most rugged coastal scenery of the island. At the eastern end of the bay, Propriano is a pivotal town and a buzzing holiday centre in summer. There are two smaller coastal pleasures on each side of its open mouth – on the north side is Porto Pollo, and on the south is Campomoro, both blessed with magnetic beaches and lapped with lapis lazuli waters.

The Golfe du Valinco has also its fair share of the mundane. Some of the beaches here are fantastically popular in summer, and it often looks like a busy day at Brighton beach: families crowded together with cool boxes and sun umbrellas, and lots of little kiddies splashing in the water and having great fun.

However, you don't have to go far from Propriano to find an air of authenticity. Propriano's surrounding countryside offers adventurers and hedonists the great escape they've been yearning for. It's best to have your own transport to explore this region.

NORTH OF GOLFE DU VALINCO
Porto Pollo & Around

What's not to love about Porto Pollo? There's great diving, superb beaches and good accommodation, not to mention a wonderfully unfussy ambience and nearby Filitosa. And this is all set in an area full of rolling hills and fragrant maquis pushing up against the Mediterranean, about 18km from Propriano. Its small size and the accessibility of water sports make it popular with young people and families who flock to it in high season for laid-back holidays.

Despite its popularity Porto Pollo retains the atmosphere of a small fishing village and is a great base from which to explore the surrounding countryside, including the tiny hilltop village of **Serra di Ferro**, perched 4km above Porto Pollo. From Serra di Ferro, press on to **Plage de Cupabia**, a crescent-shaped beach of adjective-defying beauty, accessed by a sealed road off the D155. East of Porto Pollo, **Plage de Taravo** is a choice stretch of sand for families and kitesurfers.

ACTIVITIES

Want to dive? Then Porto Pollo is the place to be. In fact, you shouldn't come to Porto Pollo without trying a dive – the best dive sites of the gulf are within easy reach. **Porto Pollo Plongée** (☎ 04 95 74 07 46; http://perso.orange.fr/portopolloplongee in French) is one of the best diving operations in the area. **AST Porto-Pollo** (☎ 04 95 74 01 67, 06 09 06 00 30; http://geocities.com/club_plongee_ast in French) is another well-established outfit. See p80 for information on sites.

On the road to Serra di Ferro (take the D155), the reputable riding centre **Fil di Rosa** (☎ 04 95 74 08 08) runs horse-riding trips. The possibilities start with one-hour rides (€19), in the morning and late afternoon. Recommended is the three-hour ride (€40), which takes in Serra di Ferro and the fantastic Plage de Cupabia. Children (aged over 10) are welcome.

If you're new to windsurfing and sailing, the calm waters off Porto Pollo are a good place for your initiation. **Centre Nautique** (☎ 06 09 40 37 65; ✆ May-Sep), near the harbour, handles rentals (from €35/15 per hour for a catamaran/surfboard) and also lessons. Seakayaking is available too (€15 per hour, €40 for a full day).

Bartoli Marine (☎ 06 86 93 16 33; Porto Pollo), in a Portakabin next to Porto Pollo Plongée, hires small boats equipped with 9hp outboard motors (no licence is required) for €90/60 per day/half-day. They're the perfect way to explore the inlets west of Porto Pollo.

SLEEPING & EATING

Camping U Turracconu (☎ 04 95 74 00 57; www.propriano.net/turracconu in French; Serra di Ferro; camp sites per adult/tent €7/6; ✆) Much better than its competitors in nearby Porto Pollo, U Turracconu is perched on a hill on the outskirts of Serra di Ferro, which means lots of breeze. And lots of tranquillity. And lots of shade. The lovely pool is an added bonus. From here it's a 20-minute, cross-country walk down to Plage de Cupabia. Recommended.

Les Eucalyptus (☎ 04 95 74 01 52; www.hoteleucalyptus.com; d €42-105; ✆ Apr-Oct; P ✆ ▣) Perched above the main strip, this is one of the best places for miles around, with neat common areas, a façade dripping with bougainvillea, quiet gardens and an assortment of well-designed rooms with all mod cons. We plumped for the *grand confort* rooms, which feature fine curtains, old-style tiles, pleasant fabrics, generous proportions and rewarding sea views. There's easy access to the beach and breakfast is included during July and August. Free wi-fi.

Hôtel-Restaurant L'Escale (☎ 04 95 74 01 54; hotel-skie@wanadoo.fr; s/d incl breakfast €46-65; ✆ Apr-Sep; P) L'Escale enjoys an advantageous location right by the beach in the heart of town. Alas, it's a bit long in the tooth, and it shows. Rooms in the concrete structure are none too inspiring and don't feature sea views (bar one), but on the plus side, it's one of the few economy places in the Golfe du Valinco.

Hôtel Kallisté (☎ 04 95 74 02 38; lekalliste@free.fr; d €57-64, with half-board mid-Jul–Aug €63-68; ✆ Apr-Oct; P ✆) This sharp-edged, concrete lump right in the centre was certainly not conceived by the most inspired architect on the island, but inside it's much more welcoming, with fresh, gleaming and well-equipped rooms and spotless bathrooms. Try for a room with a sea view. The beach is just across the street.

U San Petru (☎ 06 19 94 79 95; Serra di Ferro; mains €9-15; ✆ closed dinner Wed & Sun in low season) Not for dieters or vegetarians, the menu offers sinfully rich piles of artery thickeners – try the charcuterie (from the Taravo Valley), the macaroni and the *côte de porc* (pork chop), served indoors or alfresco on the shady terrace. Don't miss the *soirée guitare* (guitar night) on Wednesday and Friday in summer.

La Cantine du Golfe (☎ 04 95 74 01 66; mains €11-16; ✆ May-Oct) Sweet mercy, this restaurant with an edgy feel is a far cry from the trademark modernish or classical dining room, with contemporary furnishings (read: no plastic chairs), a sexy atmosphere and elegantly presented dishes, which might include *denti en* *tranche* (dentex), *pavé de thon* (tuna steak) and even an 'Assiette Fitness' (a low-calorie platter – no, really?). The lovely terrace overlooking the marina is another drawcard. A three-star hotel was under construction above the dining room when we visited.

GETTING THERE & AWAY
In July and August, **Alta Rocca Voyages – Ricci** (☎ 04 95 78 86 30) runs a daily bus service between Ajaccio and Bavella via Porto Pollo, Olmeto-Plage, Propriano and Sartène. Porto Pollo–Zonza costs €9; Porto Pollo–Ajaccio is €8.50.

Olmeto & Olmeto-Plage
pop 1150
From Propriano, a 9km sprint along the N196 brings you to Olmeto, which sits well behind the front lines of coastal tourism. Dramatically clinging to a rocky spur, Olmeto is a miniaturised version of Sartène, and exudes a similar eerie sense of austerity, with its stalwart stone houses overlooking the valley.

Olmeto-Plage is a cluster of restaurants, hotels and camping grounds down on the coast (but it's part of Olmeto), on the northern shore of Golfe du Valinco and along the D157, which leads to Porto Pollo. You'll find excellent beaches here, but don't expect perfect isolation in summer.

Hôtel-Restaurant Abbartello (☎ 04 95 74 04 73; www.hotelabbartello.com in French; Olmeto-Plage; d €31-60; May-Sep) is hands down one of the best-value hotels in the gulf, even in high season. Sure, there are much better places in the area if you want some serious cosseting, but the rooms are neat and the location is ace – the sea almost licks the walls of the rooms at the rear. Another plus is the restaurant (*menus* €15 to €27), which is considered a seafood mecca by local cognoscenti. It's run with verve and style, although the décor is a bit too virginal white.

L'Aiglon (☎ 04 95 74 66 04; N196; d €42-52, d with bathroom €55-57;) is a well-preserved, 19th-century mansion, which has endearingly old-fashioned rooms with sturdy old furniture, high ceilings and a time-warpish atmosphere. A more modern wing has rooms with private bathrooms and better facilities, but without the traditional veneer. Our main quibble is that it's right on the busy main road, but double-glazed windows should seal you off from the outside world.

Hôtel Santa Maria (☎ 04 95 74 65 59; www.hotel-restaurant-santa-maria.com; place de l'Église; d €45-60, s/d with half-board Aug €95/112; Jan-Feb & Apr-Oct;), a friendly family-run hotel in a well-maintained stone house, has retained quite a lot of its antiquated charm without sacrificing comfort. Rooms have been spruced up with a vibrant paint job and are smartly furnished. Just be mindful of the steep staircase. And if that ain't enough, this is also a bargain in low season. The attached restaurant, Chez Mimi, has limited choice but a constantly changing menu (mains €10 to €12, *menu* €16), which means fresh ingredients. Eat in the cool, vaulted room or nab a seat on the terrace.

Of the cluster of eateries that line the shore in Olmeto-Plage, **La Crique** (☎ 04 95 74 04 57; mains €10-14; May-Sep) was the flavour of the month when we visited. No plastic chairs, but teak furnishings and an agreeable terrace by the sea. It focuses on Mediterranean cuisine with a twist, such as *salade de crabe aux agrumes* (crab salad with citrus fruits). The waiters are snazzy in their white trousers and black shirts, too.

Filitosa & Around
The archaeological site of **Filitosa** (☎ 04 95 74 00 91; admission €5; 8am-8pm Apr-Oct) is sure to pique your curiosity. There are still many unsolved mysteries connected with this famous site that was discovered in 1946 by the owner of the land.

The oldest findings on the site suggest a human population living in caves. There are remnants of pottery, arrow heads and farming tools that point to fixed settlements beginning as early as 3300 BC.

The menhir statues of the megalithic period are even more impressive; the fact that they were erected at all marks a major human advance. The purpose of these granite monoliths, 2m to 3m high and carved to represent human faces or entire human figures armed with weapons, is not clear.

You'll first come to the menhir statue known as Filitosa V. This has a distinctive, rectangular head, and is the largest and 'best-armed' statue in Corsica; a sword and a dagger are both clearly visible.

If you continue along the path you come to some caves and the foundations of several huts before you get to the central *torre* (circular structure) with its six little statues, including the one known as Filitosa IX, the face of which is considered one of the masterpieces of megalithic art.

Another highlight includes five menhir statues lined up in an arc around the foot of a 1200-year-old olive tree.

There's a small **museum** at the entrance, with information about the Torréens-Shardanes (see the boxed text, right).

The Filitosa **tourist office** (9.30am-6pm May-Oct), 100m from the entrance to the site, is particularly helpful.

From Filitosa, you can drive a few kilometres east to **Calvese** and **Sollacaro**, two undiscovered hamlets blessed with lovely surroundings.

Sleeping & Eating

You can base yourself in nearby Porto Pollo, but you would miss out on a couple of lovely options in the countryside.

Domaine Comte Abbatucci (☎ 04 95 74 04 55; www .domaine-comte-abbatucci.com; Pont de Calzola; camp sites per adult/tent/car €4/2/2; Jun-Sep) This *ferme-auberge* (farm inn) is as remote as it gets while being only a short drive from Propriano. You'd be hard pressed to find a more atmospheric setting to pitch your tent, with a verdant four-acre property. Dinner (mains €6 to €15, *menu* €25) is a treat here; expect big portions of Corsican specialities using fresh produce from the farm. And joy of joys, it's also a famous vineyard, with excellent reds and whites.

U Mulinu di Calzola (☎ 04 95 24 32 14; www.umulinu .com in French; Pont de Calzola; d €44-53) An intimate riverside inn, surrounded by fragrant eucalypt and fig trees and a garden that leads down to the river. Stop for a filling lunch in the rustic dining room (mains €11 to €18, *menus* €15 to €29) with its whitewashed walls and beamed

THE AUTHOR'S CHOICE

Le Moulin Farellacci (☎ 04 95 74 62 28; http://lemoulinfarellacci.free.fr in French; Calvese; mid-June–mid-Sep) The full monty! A brilliantly converted olive mill, an impossibly copious six-course dinner, lovely views from the terrace and the cheeriest *soirées chants et guitares* (songs and guitars evenings) for miles around – if you're after the typical Corsican experience, this place is hard to beat. You might fear it's a tad folksy, but we guarantee it's authentic and the lads who sing and play the guitar know their stuff. Bookings are essential.

MYSTERIOUS PEOPLE OF THE SEA

Who were the Torréens, those people who appeared on Corsican shores around 1100 BC, drove out the settled inhabitants of Filitosa, destroyed many of their statues and built the *torri* (circular monuments) in their place? The traces they left are very faint indeed.

According to Roger Grosjean, the archaeological authority on Filitosa, they could actually have been Shardanes, the people enigmatically known to historians as 'sea people', who battled with the pharaoh Ramses III. They probably originated from Anatolia, from Crete or from along the coast of the Aegean Sea. It's said that after having been defeated by Ramses III, the Shardanes made their way to Corsica and then to Sardinia, before slipping back into obscurity.

ceiling or on the breezy terrace. Take a dip once you've digested your meal – this is the life! The 14 rooms are nothing flash but are fresh and airy, with tiled floors and exposed beams in some of them. It's 8km north of Filitosa. Head to Sollacaro and follow the scenic D302.

Chambres d'Hôtes Claude & Anita Tardif (☎ 04 95 74 29 48, 06 62 43 13 69; Sollacaro; d €70) An atmosphere of dreamlike tranquillity wafts over this appealing house in a tremendous setting. The neatly tended garden has places to lounge, the three rooms are not luxurious but fresh and spruce, and the views over the Golfe du Valinco are just stupendous. Residents may use the excellent, outdoor cooking facilities or order a *spuntinu* (light meal), which is served in the garden and will assuage any hunger pangs (€15). A good place to dawdle in and soak up the restful charm. It is 2.5km east of Filitosa along a small side road (it's signposted).

U Paese (☎ 04 95 74 29 06; Sollacaro; mains €8-12) In Sollacaro, this cute *restaurant de village* is worth considering for its tasty traditional dishes and unfussy ambience.

PROPRIANO (PRUPRIÀ)
pop 3500

Tourism is king in Propriano. If you don't mind a homogenised, vacation-community ambience, you'll likely enjoy this self-contained resort town at the eastern end of the Golfe du

THE SOUTH

Valinco. The waterfront bustles in summer, and a kind of sterility hangs in the air. If it's robust charm you're after, don't linger here but head to Sartène. There are no museums or sights as such, but a gentle wander along the marina makes a pleasant prelude to a seaside apéritif and a fine meal at one of the town's good restaurants. And, of course, there are enticing beaches and lots of water sports available.

Information

Banque Populaire (☎ 04 95 76 04 63; rue du Général de Gaulle; ✆ 9am-12.30pm & 1.45-5.15pm Mon-Fri) Has an ATM.

Laverie 2000 (av Napoléon; €5; ✆ 8.30am-6.30pm Mon-Sat) Laundrette.

Post office (☎ 04 95 76 73 00; quartier de la Plaine)

Société Générale (☎ 04 95 76 05 44; rue du Général de Gaulle; ✆ 8.15am-noon & 1.45-5pm Mon-Fri) Has an ATM.

Tourist office (☎ 04 95 76 01 49; www.propriano.net; ✆ 8am-8pm Mon-Sat, 9am-1pm & 4-8pm Sun Jul & Aug, 8am-12.30pm & 2.30-7pm Mon-Sat Sep & Oct, 9am-noon & 2-6pm Mon-Fri Nov-Apr) At the marina.

Virtual Suspects (rue du 9 Septembre; per hr €5; ✆ noon-1am) Internet café.

Sights & Activities

Propriano's prime attraction is the range of water-based activities on offer.

BEACHES

The best of the little beaches in town are **Plage du Lido**, west of the lighthouse, and its extension, **Plage du Corsaire**. There are better places to swim in the Golfe du Valinco, especially at the fantastic Plage de Portigliolo (p187), 7km south of town.

BOAT TRIPS

The most obvious way to explore the Golfe du Valinco and the lovely bays that grace the coast further south is to take a boat excursion. **I Paesi di u Valincu** (☎ 04 95 76 16 78, 06 03 77 42 56; www.corsica.net/promenade; marina; ✆ May-Sep) has various trips, including a 2½-hour excursion (€22) inside the gulf as well as a day trip embracing the idyllic coves south of the gulf, with swimming stops (€42). Children pay half-price. Sunset cruises are also available.

Promenade en Mer Valinco (☎ 06 12 54 99 28; www.xn--promenade-en-mer-propriano-khc.com in French; ✆ May–mid-Oct) offers perhaps the most original

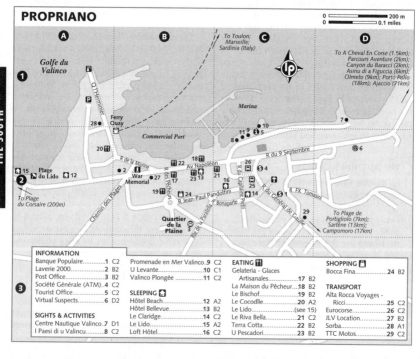

PROPRIANO

0 ——— 200 m
0 ——— 0.1 miles

To Toulon; Marseille; Sardinia (Italy)

Golfe du Valinco

Marina

To A Cheval En Corse (1.5km); Parcours Aventure (2km); Canyon du Baracci (2km); Asinu di a Figuccia (6km); Olmeto (9km); Porto Pollo (18km); Ajaccio (71km)

Ferry Quay

Commercial Port

R de la Marine

Av Napoléon

R du 9 Septembre

Plage du Lido

War Memorial

R des Pêcheurs

R Jean-Paul Pandolfini

Bonaparte

R du Capitaine Pietri

R du Général de Caulle

R FX Tomasini

To Plage du Corsaire (200m)

Chemin des Plages

R de la Parata

Quartier de la Plaine

To Plage de Portigliolo (7km); Sartène (13km); Campomoro (17km)

(and ecofriendly) cruise. The *Pique-Nique Convivial* is a delightful 3½-hour excursion (adult/child €35/15) on a catamaran (maximum 12 people), which includes snorkelling stops. Bring a picnic. It also runs regular tours with an outboard powered 12-seater (adult/child €16/11 for 1½ hours). The *Mer et Maquis* cruise includes a 3km-to-10km walk along the coastline.

Both operators have a kiosk on the harbour, near the tourist office.

DIVING

The Golfe du Valinco is a mecca for both experienced and novice divers. The best sites are near the southern and northern tips of the gulf. For beginners there are sheltered inlets closer to Propriano. See p81 for more details.

Reputable dive operators:

U Levante (☎ 04 95 76 23 83, 06 22 44 75 99; www .plonger-en-corse.com; marina)

Valinco Plongée (☎ 04 95 76 31 01, 06 07 11 80 48; www.valinco-plongee.com; marina)

HORSE RIDING

The riding centre **A Cheval En Corse** (☎ 04 95 76 08 02, 06 13 09 25 10; rte de Baracci) offers scenic *promenades à cheval* (horse riding) on the beach and in the maquis for around €50 for three hours. The stables are on the D257, about 2km north of Propriano, off the junction with the N196. Week-long treks are also available.

DONKEY RIDING

If you're with the little ones, nothing can beat a donkey ride on mule paths in the maquis, high in the hills overlooking the Golfe du Valinco. The children ride the donkey, while the parents walk and lead the animal. Contact **Asinu di a Figuccia** (☎ 06 03 28 92 00, 06 03 28 81 85; Olmeto; Apr-Aug), on the D257, between Propriano and Olmeto (it's signposted). An itinerary is provided. It costs €60 per donkey.

PARCOURS AVENTURE & CANYON DU BARACCI

There's an excellent **Parcours Aventure** (☎ 06 20 95 45 34; rte de Baracci; admission €15-17; Jul & Aug) in a forest of cork oak trees, about 3km from Propriano, off the D257. Two circuits are available. The *Découverte* is suitable for children over six, while the *Sensation* is equipped with tyrolean slides, Nepalese bridges, swings, platforms and other fixtures that will send shivers down your spine.

Further along the valley, canyoning is available in the Canyon du Baracci. It's an enjoyable circuit, with one 25m tyrolean slide, various jumps in natural pools and three *toboggans* (plunging down water-polished chutes). Another plus is that it's also easily accessible – it's a five-minute walk from the road. Contact **Tra I Monti & Canyon** (☎ 06 81 51 41 28, 04 95 76 33 93; Baracci; Apr–mid-Oct) or **Olivier Chapon-Seigneur** (☎ 06 12 41 19 74; ochaponghm@free .fr; May-Oct), who speaks English. A half-day will set you back €35.

WATER SPORTS

The waters off Propriano are usually mirror-calm – ideal for all kinds of water sports and best suited to beginners and children. The **Centre Nautique de Propriano** (☎ 06 12 54 99 28; www.centre-nautique-valinco.com; mid-May–Sep) is on the beach, 100m beyond the tourist office. It rents out windsurfers (€15 per hour), sailboats (from €15 per hour) and kayaks (from €10 per hour). The centre organises private and group lessons. It also hires out small 9hp motor boats (€55 per hour).

Sleeping

Hôtel Bellevue (☎ 04 95 76 01 86; www.hotels-propriano .com; marina; s €40-76, d €46-89; P) See the façade daubed with a camp shade of pink and with blue shutters on the seething waterfront? It's the Bellevue. Rest assured, the rooms are soundproofed and even if they're fairly standard in appearance, they're fresh and well tended. Those facing the sea have enticing views – well worth the extra fiscal effort. High-season prices include breakfast.

Le Claridge (☎ 04 95 76 05 54; www.hotels-propriano .com; rue Bonaparte; s €42-75, d €46-90; Apr-Oct; P) The well-managed Claridge won't get you writing home but the rooms are discreetly decorated and comfortable, with newish curtains and bedspreads, beige faux-wood floors and prim bathrooms. The weak point? Many rooms overlook a grim parking lot – not really the Corsica of your dreams.

Loft Hôtel (☎ 04 95 76 17 48; fax 04 95 76 22 04; rue Jean-Paul Pandolfi; r €45-70; Apr-Oct; P) For many years, the Loft Hôtel was a wine warehouse. Hard to believe it now as you step inside this modernised option with hospital-white rooms and spotless bathrooms. True, it's not designed for honeymooners, but most rooms have plenty of space to really strew your stuff around, and some of the upstairs doubles have sloping ceilings. You're in a fairly peaceful spot but no more than a few espadrille steps from the cafés and restaurants and mayhem of the waterfront. Wi-fi.

Hôtel Beach (☎ 04 95 76 17 74; beach.hotel@wanadoo .fr; av Napoléon; d €52-80; [P] Apr-Oct; [P]) The Hôtel Beach really is right on the beach. This is its biggest lure as the utilitarian building won't feature in the pages of *Condé Nast Traveler*. In its defence, the staff are helpful and all beach-facing rooms are serviceable, tidy and have balconies – just throw the windows wide, let in the fresh sea breeze and drink in the views.

Le Lido (☎ 04 95 76 06 37; le.lido@wanadoo.fr; av Napoléon; r €75-200; [P] May-Sep; [P] [X]) Bump it up a notch in this effortlessly chic little charmer, which boasts an irresistible location at the western edge of town, between two beaches. The 14 hacienda-like rooms are set around a leaf-dappled courtyard and have rear terraces that open onto the beach. Nothing glam, just a good balance of sleekness and warmth, with colourful tiles, rich textiles and bedding and earth-toned furniture to offset the white walls. Oh, and the attached restaurant is pure joy (lobster, anyone?). Shame that it's a tad compact and ludicrously overpriced in high season.

Eating

The main drag is almost wall-to-wall with restaurants. Most eateries boast a terrace overlooking the sea. If you enjoy fish, you've come to the right place.

RESTAURANTS

Le Cocodîle (☎ 04 95 73 27 85; quai L'Herminier; mains €8-17, menus €16-34; [P] closed Wed in low season) Le Cocodîle is a zinging place to eat, with colour-washed walls, a loungey feel and a breezy terrace. The menu will linger long on the palate, with a toothsome *salade de la mer* (seafood salad), squid medallions and a scrumptious chocolate pie with ice cream, all elegantly presented. Smart staff too. We'll be back.

Le Bischof (☎ 04 95 76 30 00; rue des Pêcheurs; mains €9-25, menus €15-17; [P] closed Dec & Mon Oct-Apr) In a city where fish dishes reign supreme, this den of carnivores is a happy exception. Hoe into succulent *brochettes* (skewered meat) or great clumps of meat grilled to perfection. The 600g *côte à l'os* (rib steak), Bischof's signature dish, will have you walk out belly-first. Bounteous wood-fired pizzas are also available. It's on the ground floor of an unremarkable building, off the main drag.

Le Riva Bella (☎ 04 95 76 24 69; av Napoléon; mains €9-25, menus €15-29; [P] Apr-Oct) One of our favourites in Propriano. This snazzy spot with elegant furniture offers a mix of savoury Mediterranean dishes with a creative twist, presented with great panache on amusing plates. Pounce on the brilliant-value *suggestions* (one main and one dessert) and wash it all down with a glass of Saparale (€2). Trendy waiters waft about the place, which is frequently full.

Terra Cotta (☎ 04 95 74 23 80; av Napoléon; mains €11-16, menus €16-27; [P] Mon-Sat Apr-Nov) In the contest for the mantle of the town's best restaurant, the Terra Cotta is a solid candidate, with a colourful indoor dining room and an agreeable terrace overlooking the sea – both are exceedingly comfortable and provide the perfect setting in which to sample lip-smacking Mediterranean specialities, such as *filet d'agneau poêlé aux herbes* (lamb with aromatic herbs). The *glace vanille et soupe de fraises* (vanilla ice cream with strawberry cream) is a perfect coda to a delightful meal.

U Pescadori (☎ 04 95 76 42 95; av Napoléon; mains €14-23, menus €16-48; [P] Mar-Nov) 'The Fisherman' is true to its name with a wide assortment of fish and seafood delivered daily from the harbour. Depending on your mood, you'll find the seafaring paraphernalia hanging on the walls a bit tarted up for tourists or a welcome change from the typical ho-hum décor you might find elsewhere. There is outdoor seating on the pavement, but no sea views to speak of.

La Maison du Pêcheur (☎ 04 95 76 23 10; av Napoléon; mains €17-24, menu €20; [P] Apr-Oct) With its doesn't-get-more-central location and good repertoire of fish dishes, this well-regarded eatery is one of the essential culinary stops while in town.

Le Lido (☎ 04 95 76 06 37; av Napoléon; mains €18-30; [P] May-Sep) In business since 1932, this Propriano icon is famous for one thing and one thing only: *langouste au four* (lobster; €18 per 100g), best enjoyed at dinner on the oh-so-romantic little terrace behind the veranda, with the waves almost lapping your toes. Wash it all down with a well-chosen Corsican wine, and you'll be in seventh heaven. There's also a more affordable *formule Bistrot* at lunchtime (mains from €10).

QUICK EATS

Gelateria – Glaces Artisanales (☎ 06 74 52 79 26; av Napoléon; ice creams €1.50-3; [P] Mar-Sep) Generous scoops and 30 fruit flavours are the trademarks of this little ice-cream parlour on the main strip. We start salivating just thinking of the *châtaigne* (chestnut); you don't want to know what happens when we recall the fig or the *myrte sauvage* (wild myrtle).

Shopping

Bocca Fina (☎ 04 95 76 28 10; rue des Pêcheurs; ☻ 9am-1pm & 3.30-9pm Mon-Sat) A little speciality shop that stocks excellent jams, fruit-flavoured liqueurs, *canistrelli* (dry biscuits), charcuterie, artisanal cheeses and Corsican wines.

Getting There & Around

BICYCLE

JLV Location (☎ 04 95 76 11 84; av Napoléon; ☻ 9am-noon & 3-7pm, closed Sun Oct-Apr) Hires mountain bikes (€14 per day) and scooters (€60 per day).

TTC Motos (☎ 04 95 76 15 32; www.ttcmoto.fr; rue du Général de Gaulle; ☻ 9am-noon & 5-7pm, closed Sun in winter) Rents mountain bikes (€15 per day) and scooters (€37 per day).

BOAT

Ferries link Propriano with Toulon and Marseille. You can buy tickets at **Sorba** (☎ 04 95 76 04 36; quai L'Herminier; ☻ 8-11.30am & 2-5.30pm Mon-Thu, 8-11.30am & 2-4.30pm Fri), a shipping agency representing all the lines. There are also connections with Porto Torres in Sardinia. See also the Transport chapter (p267).

BUS

Alta Rocca Voyages – Ricci (☎ 04 95 76 25 59; rue du Général de Gaulle) runs one daily bus (twice daily in July and August) between Ajaccio and Zonza via Olmeto, Propriano, Sartène and Ste-Lucie de Tallano. The Ajaccio–Propriano leg costs €7.50.

In summer, **Eurocorse** (☎ 04 95 76 13 50; rue du Général de Gaulle) has four daily services (two services in low season) between Ajaccio and Bonifacio via Olmeto, Propriano, Sartène and Porto-Vecchio. The Propriano–Porto-Vecchio leg costs €11.50.

INLAND FROM PROPRIANO

If all these beaches start to overwhelm, a 30-minute drive from Propriano transports you to yet another undiscovered world. From Propriano, take the D19 to **Viggianello** and **Arbellara**, about 10km from the coast. A further 4km or so will bring you to **Fozzano**, the quintessential Corsican village, with lofty granite houses and sweeping views over the gulf. Foz-

zano's notoriety stems from the bloody feuds that divided the village in the 19th century. It's now a peaceful settlement, with a couple of eye-catching buildings, including the 14th-century **Torra Vecchia** and the 16th-century **Torra Nova**. Feeling peckish on your travels? Head to **Chez Charlot** (☎ 04 95 76 00 06; Viggianello; mains €10-13, menu €18; ☻ mid-Apr–Sep), which specialises in traditional Corsican fare at very reasonable prices. There's a breezy terrace with mind-boggling views over the gulf.

After all that sightseeing, you might want to take a soothing dip in the **Bains de Caldane** (Caldane Baths; ☎ 04 95 77 00 34; Caldane; admission €4; ☻ 9.30am-8pm in summer, weekends in low season), in the Fiumicicoli River valley (from Arbellara, follow the D119 until the junction with the D268, then follow the signs). These sulphur hot springs have therapeutic properties. For the ultimate indulgence, order a glass of Champagne and drink it while lounging in the pool (€12).

Heading back to Propriano (or Sartène) along the D268, you'll go past the **Spin'a Cavallu Genoese bridge**, hidden down the road.

SOUTH OF THE GOLFE DU VALINCO
Plage de Portigliolo

Seven kilometres south of Propriano, Plage de Portigliolo (not to be confused with another Portigliolo further north in the Golfe d'Ajaccio) stretches out on either side of a little airfield that manages not to spoil the coastline. What a beach! It's an incredible 4km long and, with its fine, white sand and lack of development, is by far the nicest in the area. There's little or no shade so bring your own, as well as plenty of water.

There's a sailing school on the beach, **Club Vela e Ventu** (☎ 06 09 52 24 20; Plage de Portigliolo; ☻ Jun-Sep), which offers tuition to beginners and hires catamarans, surfboards and kayaks. The same company runs **Locanautic** (☎ 06 09 52 24 20; www.locanautic.com in French; Plage de Portigliolo; ☻ Jun-Sep), which rents small motor boats (no licence required) for €60/90 per half/full day.

South of Portigliolo, the road climbs a little before reaching a lookout. The coast is magnificent and the views back to the beach at Portigliolo are breathtaking. At the end of the road is the cute-as-can-be seaside resort of Campomoro.

If you fancy lingering a little longer by the Plage de Portigliolo, head to **Camping Lecci e Murta** (☎ 04 95 76 02 67; www.camping-lecciemurta.com;

THE SOUTH

Portigliolo; camp sites per adult/tent/car €9/5/5; ☷ Apr-Sep; ☏) – if only all camp sites in Corsica were as smart as the Lecci e Murta! Picture this: a 5-hectare property about 300m off Plage de Portigliolo, solid amenities, a nifty pool to cool off, a smart restaurant and the scents of the maquis thrown in for free. A winning formula.

Campomoro

pop 150

Picturesquely surrounded by striking, undulating mountains carpeted by maquis, and blessed with idyllic beaches, Campomoro is a gem. At the southern tip of the gulf, it really feels like the end of the line. Though there is only a handful of accommodation options and restaurants dotted around its large sandy beach, its popularity as a diving location gives it an attractive holiday atmosphere. Be warned: the place becomes packed in high season. During this period you'll have trouble finding both a bed for the night and a parking space in town.

A major landmark in the gulf, the stately **Tour di Campomoro** is at the end of the beach. Built in the 16th century by the Genoese, the tower is one of Corsica's largest, and it is also the only one on the island to have been fortified with a star-shaped surrounding wall. It was lovingly restored in 1986.

It's unnervingly easy to spend your entire day on the luscious ribbon of white sand **beach**, which curves gently for 1km, but there's also excellent diving to be had in the area (see p81 for details). **Campomoro Plongée** (☎ 06 09 95 44 43; www.campomoro-plongee.com in French; Campomoro) and **Torra Plongée** (☎ 06 83 58 81 81, 06 85 41 93 94; www.torra-plongee.com in French; Campomoro) both welcome beginners and experienced divers.

SLEEPING & EATING

Hôtel-Restaurant Le Ressac (☎ 04 95 74 22 25; www.hotel-ressac.fr in French; Campomoro; s €44-62, with half-board Jun-Sep €82-118, d €47-62, with half-board Jun-Sep €96-126; ☷) The modernish Ressac scores low on the charisma front but what the place lacks in character is counterbalanced by decent prices off-season. The rooms are comfortable and spacious but hardly inspiring. The view, however, is, so be sure to book a room *côté mer* (facing the sea).

Hôtel Campomoro (☎ /fax 04 95 74 20 89; www.hotelcampomoro.com; Campomoro; d €70, with half-board mid-Jun–mid-Sep €117; ☷ mid-May–mid-Sep) The Campomoro suffers from a dearth of character with rooms warranting neither complaint nor exultation, but it's neat and tidy and is not far away when you decide to take a soothing soak on the beach. The upstairs rooms have a balcony (view!).

La Mouette (☎ 04 95 74 22; Campomoro; mains €7-13; ☷ May-Sep) The bobbing boats on the bay outside are La Mouette's biggest drawcard. The menu covers a range of pasta dishes and salads that won't win prizes for imagination. But hey, it's the location you're paying for here.

Bar des Amis (☎ 04 95 74 20 89; Campomoro; mains €10-17, menus €16-27; ☷ May-Sep) Across the road from Hôtel Campomoro (same management), this little eatery boasts a spiffing location, with a veranda overlooking the beach. Foodwise, the emphasis is on fish and seafood, but salads and pasta are also available. If you're after something unusual, try *cigale de mer* (squill fish).

EXPLORING THE COASTLINE ROBINSON CRUSOE STYLE

Weary of those big, crammed tourist boats and whistle-stop 'cruises' along the coast? It's high time for a DIY trip. If, like us, you prefer independence and setting your own pace, consider exploring the gulfs and the wildest coastlines of Corsica in your own boat. Various outfits rent small 6hp or 9hp four- or five-seater motor boats that are easy to drive; no licence is required. The smaller boats can nudge into some of the tiny inlets that are denied to the larger models and that are not accessible by road. A map outlining the coast is provided, as well as life jackets. Plan on €100 per day. Bring a picnic and your snorkelling gear.

If you've got energy to burn, you could consider exploring the coast by kayak – it's even more ecofriendly.

Our favourites? Plage d'Erbaju, Plage de Tra Licettu, Cala di Conca and Cala d'Arena, between Tizzano (p193) and Campomoro, as well as a string of tiny inlets that are scattered along the southern shore of the Golfe du Valinco.

Hint: it's best enjoyed with your family, your friends…or your sweetheart! It can be downright romantic out there, we swear – what about a picnic on a secluded beach, honey?

THE SOUTH

LE SARTENAIS

So traditional. So proud. Quintessentially Corsican. The Sartenais has attitude to boot. While only 13km separate Propriano from Sartène (the 'most Corsican of all Corsican towns' according to French novelist Prosper Mérimée), a gulf divides them. The fast-paced coastal life seems light years away. Disconnected from the trappings of mass tourism, the Sartenais is different in spirit from the rest of the island – more inward-looking, more secretive, adamantly steeped in tradition. Tourism has had little impact on the area's character. And the Sartenais is a reminder of what the whole of Corsica used to be like.

SARTÈNE (SARTÈ)

pop 2500

Sartène does enchant on sight. With its narrow alleyways that twirl you unexpectedly into quaint nooks and crannies, its high granite walls and its tall townhouses, the old city will make you feel you're floating through another time and space. Indeed, the elegant architecture combines with the natural setting – it's perched high over the Rizzanese Valley – to create an unrivalled ambience.

Some travellers think Sartène is a bit austere and introverted, others regard it as a veiled, self-contained city that doesn't easily bare its soul. Sure, Sartène is less hedonistic than, say, Bonifacio or Propriano – its commercially minded counterparts down the mountain – but it's indisputably filled with character, soul and authenticity. If you want to see a slice of real Corsica, be sure to squeeze it into your sojourn.

And if you plan a visit in spring, try to make it coincide with the Catenacciu procession (right), a tradition dating from the Middle Ages and a definite must-see.

History

The town was subject to repeated Saracen raids during the 15th and 16th centuries, and pirates from Algiers took 400 of its inhabitants into slavery in 1583.

Danger for Sartène didn't always come from the outside, either. The town enjoys pride of place in the chronicles of Corsica's long tradition of vendetta. In the course of the Colomba Carabelli vendetta, a curate protagonist is said to have remained shut

---

THE PROCESSION DU CATENACCIU

On the eve of Good Friday, Sartène is the setting for one of the oldest religious traditions on the island – the Procession du Catenacciu. In a colourful re-enactment of the Passion, the Catenacciu (literally, 'the chained one'), an anonymous, barefoot penitent, covered from head to foot in a red robe and cowl, carries a huge cross through the town, dragging heavy chains at his feet. The Catenacciu is followed by a procession of other penitents (eight dressed in black, one in white), members of the clergy and local notables.

When they are not in use, the chains and cross of the Catenacciu can be seen in the Église Ste-Marie.

---

up for nine years in his home in the Borgo quarter for fear of reprisals. Another famous 19th-century rivalry pitted one family from the Borgo quarter against another from Santa Anna. What was in effect a small-scale civil war ended only with the ratification of a peace treaty in the Église Ste-Marie.

Undoubtedly, it was the tradition of the vendetta and other related exotica that has contributed to Sartène's reputation as a classically Corsican town.

Orientation

Sartène is built around place Porta, from which cours Sœur Amélie and cours Général de Gaulle, the town's main streets, lead off.

The old quarter of Santa Anna stretches out to the north of place Porta.

Information

LCL Crédit Lyonnais (☎ 04 95 77 71 00; place Porta; 🕑 8.30-12.30pm & 1.30-5pm Mon-Fri) Has an ATM.

Le Cyrnos (☎ 04 95 73 28 70; place Porta; per 15/30min €2/3; 🕑 6.30am-2am Mon-Sat) Internet café, at the back of the bar.

Post office (☎ 04 95 77 70 72; rue du Marché) Has an ATM.

Tourist office (☎ 04 95 77 15 40; ot-sartene@ wanadoo.fr; cours Soeur Amélie; 🕑 9am-7pm daily Jun-Sep, 9am-noon & 2-6pm Mon-Fri Oct-May)

Sights

It's pleasant ambling around the town centre with its café-lined square and fortresslike houses. The old town is a labyrinth of stone

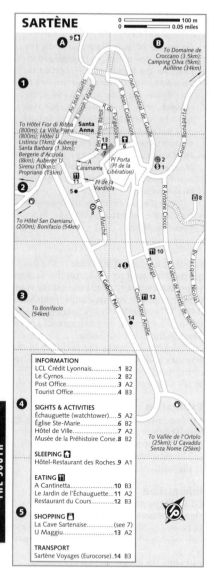

SARTÈNE

0 ——— 100 m
0 ——— 0.05 miles

INFORMATION
LCL Crédit Lyonnais...............1 B2
Le Cyrnos............................2 B2
Post Office.........................3 A2
Tourist Office......................4 B3

SIGHTS & ACTIVITIES
Échauguette (watchtower).....5 A2
Église Ste-Marie..................6 B2
Hôtel de Ville.....................7 A2
Musée de la Préhistoire Corse.8 B2

SLEEPING
Hôtel-Restaurant des Roches.9 A1

EATING
A Cantinetta.......................10 B3
Le Jardin de l'Échauguette...11 A2
Restaurant du Cours............12 B3

SHOPPING
La Cave Sartenaise.............(see 7)
U Maggiu..........................13 A2

TRANSPORT
Sartène Voyages (Eurocorse)..14 B3

Stations of the Cross dating from 1843. The chains and cross used during the Catenacciu procession are also on display.

Next to Église Ste-Marie is the building that now houses the **Hôtel de Ville** (town hall), but which, in the 16th century, was the palace of the Genoese lieutenants. If you go through the gateway below this former palace, you will come out on the narrow streets of the **Santa Anna district**, which is the real jewel of the old town. Try to find the delightful **impasse Carababa**.

An **échauguette**, or watchtower, to the northwest of the post office, bears witness to the importance the people of Sartène gave to keeping a lookout around the city. It is not open to visitors.

At the time of writing, the **Musée de la Préhistoire Corse** (Museum of Corsican Prehistory; ☎ 04 95 77 01 09; rue Antoine Crocce) was undergoing a major extension and was set to reopen by 2008.

Activities

The friendly, multilingual Claudine and Christian Perrier at **Domaine de Croccano** (☎ 04 95 77 11 37; www.corsenature.com; D148, rte de Granace) offer various horse-riding programmes starting from €21 per hour. The 'Promenade-Découverte du Sartenais' (three hours) is a enjoyable ramble amid the maquis, with fine views over Sartène and the sea. Kids will enjoy pony rides on the property (€6). It's 3.5km out of town on the road to Granace.

Sleeping

CHAMBRES D'HÔTES

Domaine de Croccano (☎ 04 95 77 11 37; www.corse nature.com; D148, rte de Granace; d €70-87; ☺ Jan-Nov) Come to unwind in this charming B&B and you may never want to leave. The three rooms, with exposed stone walls and period furniture, occupy a granite cottage nestled within a 10-acre property planted with olive trees, about 3.5km from Sartène. Neiiigh! Yes, there are stables here (see above). A beautifully presented breakfast is served on a breezy terrace, with an eagle's-eye panorama. In July and August, rooms are preferably rented by the week.

HOTELS

Hôtel U Listincu (☎ 04 95 77 17 51; fax 04 95 77 71 50; rte de Propriano; s €43-51, d €49-60; ☺ Apr-Sep; ⓟ ⓧ) This low-slung pad is not a stylish choice by any means, but its prices don't skyrocket in

stairways and little streets and alleyways, some of them so narrow that two people can barely pass through.

The bell tower of **Église Ste-Marie** (1766) rises above place Porta, which is still sometimes called place de la Libération. It boasts a superb altarpiece of polychrome marble (formerly in the Couvent St-François) and canvasses of the

the height of the peak season (a rarity in Corsica). It offers 14 rooms that are mundanely decorated but represent excellent value. Angle for a room at the rear, with views over the Rizzanese Valley. It's on the Propriano road, about 1km from town.

Hôtel Fior di Ribba (☎ 04 95 77 01 80; www.hotel fiordiribba.com in French; rte de Propriano; d €49-77; ☷ mid-Mar–Oct; **P** **✗** **⬛**) How can you not like a hotel that has a swimming pool so close to the sky you could use the clouds to towel yourself down? It's set in a large, plant-filled property, on the Propriano road, about 800m from town. Accommodation-wise, the Fior di Ribba is a tad less overwhelming, with fairly anodyne but clean rooms and pathogen-free bathrooms. Hint: pony up for the more expensive rooms that overlook the pool.

La Villa Piana (☎ 04 95 77 07 04; www.lavillapiana.com in French; rte de Propriano; r €50-150; ☷ Apr–Oct; **P** **⬛**) Almost a carbon copy of the Fior di Ribba, next door. Here, too, we were blown away by the shaded property, the gleaming pool and the fantastic view over town – you can swim while eyeing up the jagged peaks of the Alta Rocca. The 31 rooms are a mix of snugness and rustic charm, with carpeted floors, dark-wood furnishings, exposed beams, well-scrubbed bathrooms, sloping ceilings in the upstairs rooms and fans. There's also a tennis court for guests' use. For the price you'd expect air-conditioning, though.

Hôtel-Restaurant des Roches (☎ 04 95 77 07 61; www.sartenehotel.fr in French; 20 rue Jean Jaurès; s €53-87, d €61-96; **P** **✗**) The only venture in the centre of town, which means it's in high demand during summer. With a regal setting overlooking the valley and the Golfe du Valinco, it offers 60 modernised rooms with spotless bathrooms and air-conditioning. Nab a room with a view – the other ones look onto the parking lot. There's an attached restaurant. The only downside is that it feels a bit impersonal.

Hôtel San Damianu (☎ 04 95 70 55 41; www.sanda mianu.fr; s €76-125, d €96-150; ☷ Apr–Oct; **P** **✗** **⬛** **⬛**) The new kid on the block, the San Damianu has everything in spades: a perfect location just staggering distance from the *vieille ville* (old town), sleek rooms with all mod cons, a soothing yellow colour scheme, million-dollar views over the Rizzanese Valley and the mandatory sparkling swimming pool. It's just below Couvent San Damiano – clearly a solid choice if you need to confess your sins.

CAMPING

Camping Olva (☎ 04 95 77 11 58; rte de la Castagna; camp sites per adult €4-7, per tent/car €3/3; ☷ Apr–Sep; **⬛**) On the other side of town, 5km out on the D69 towards Aullène, is a sprawling eight-hectare park shaded by eucalyptus trees. Its amenities include a good tennis court, a swimming pool, a restaurant and a little supermarket.

Eating

A Cantinetta (☎ 04 95 77 08 74; rue Borgo; ☷ 10am-8pm Apr-Oct) In this minuscule cellar dating from the 19th century, you'll be welcomed by Marie-Dominique Bartoli. A fireplace, a couple of chunky wooden tables and old photographs on the walls – it's button-cute and high on atmosphere. Try the homemade chestnut-flour cakes (€4) or the platter of local cheeses with fig jam – sinfully good. And wash it all down with a glass of Fiumicicoli or a *vin de myrte* (myrtle wine).

Restaurant du Cours (☎ 04 95 77 19 07; cours Soeur Amélie; mains €6-15, menus €14-22; ☷ closed dinner Wed in low season) You'll be hard-pressed to find a cheaper place for a sit-down meal in the centre of town. Long on character and short on frills, this welcoming eatery set in a pokey vaulted room whips up pizzas (from €6), salads, meat dishes and seven varieties of tagliatelle.

Bergerie d'Acciola (☎ 04 95 77 14 00; rte de Bonifacio, Acciola; mains €6.50-10; ☷ Jun-Sep) A mandatory

---

THE AUTHOR'S CHOICE

Auberge Santa Barbara (☎ 04 95 77 09 06; www.santabarbara.fr; mains €17-28, menu €29; ☷ Tue & Wed Apr-Oct) Send your tastebuds into a tailspin at this iconic restaurant serving authentic dishes with a creative twist (joy of joys, not an *omelette au brocciu* in sight!). Award-winning chef Gisèle Lovichi is a true alchemist, with such delectable concoctions as *pigeon au myrte* (pigeon with myrtle sauce) or *côte de veau châtaignes confites* (veal cutlet with preserved chestnuts). Another draw is the bucolic setting, with elegant tables set around a well-manicured flower garden. A respectable wine list and exemplary service complete the perfect picture. Coming from Propriano, it's about 1.3km from the centre (follow the signs). Book ahead.

THE SOUTH

DETOUR: VALLÉE DE L'ORTOLO

Promise you won't tell *too* many people about this timeless valley that feels like the end of the world. From Sartène, take the D50 (direction Mola) to the southeast. The narrow road plunges downhill amid spectacular scenery – mountains, vineyards, forests and fields – you didn't know existed. Soak up the atmosphere until you reach the floor of the valley. In the middle of nowhere, like an apparition, the camp site and equestrian centre **U Cavaddu Senza Nome** (☎ 04 95 77 18 47, 06 21 16 39 35; www.ucavaddu.fr; Ranfonu, Ortolo; camp sites per adult/tent/car €7/4/3; ☷ Feb-Nov) welcomes campers in an angelic property. Bikes are available for hire (a perfect way to find your own slice of paradise in the valley) and there's even a stream nearby where you can splash. Children will feel at ease, with farm animals pottering about. Your hosts, a German-Austrian couple (fluent in English), organise horse-riding trips in the area for experienced riders (€17 per hour). The Domaine Saparale, a rising star on the Corsican wine scene, is a short stroll away. From the camp site, you can rejoin the N196 at Pont de l'Ortolo, about 2.5km further south – if you can tear yourself away from this enchanting valley.

---

stop for cheese lovers (and we know what we're talking about), this produce shop set in a lovely granite house on the Bonifacio road doubles as a restaurant in summer. We'll never forget the *terrine de fromage aux herbes* (cheese terrine with aromatic herbs) and the *crêpe à la farine de châtaigne* (chestnut-flour pancake). Don't leave without buying a pungent *casgiu casanu* (*fromage fermier* in French; farm cheese) at the shop. Local wines are available too. It's 8km from Sartène.

Auberge U Sirenu (☎ 04 95 77 21 85; www.usirenu .com in French; rte de Bonifacio, Orasi; mains €7-13, menus €13-16) Punters are drawn to the family-run U Sirenu for its choice grilled meats – go for the *sanglier et ses pâtes* (wild boar and pasta), best accompanied by a bottle of Saparale (€16). If you're counting the coins, opt for the pasta (from €7). The platter of charcuterie deserves a special mention: it's served on a wooden plate in the shape of the island. The dining room is certainly not sassy, but the terrace is much more enjoyable. Post-*repas*, you can bask lizardlike by the pool. It's on the road to Bonifacio, about 10km from Sartène.

Le Jardin de l'Échauguette (☎ 04 95 77 12 86; place de la Vardiola; mains €10-18, menus €18-26; ☷ May-Sep) No matter how hectic the day, as soon as you step inside this oasis of calm, stress evaporates as fast as light drizzle on asphalt in summer. Soak up the cool karma on the shady terrace while savouring well-executed classics, such as *légumes farcis au brocciu* (vegetables stuffed with sheep or goat cheese). A toothsome *crème brûlée à la banane* (banana-flavoured cream pie with a caramelised topping) will finish you off sweetly. Yum.

Shopping

Leaving Sartène without stocking up on delicious gourmet foodstuffs would simply be a crime. Go on, check out the following places and buy something – it's impossible not to.

La Cave Sartenaise (☎ 04 95 77 10 08; place Porta; ☷ Apr-Oct) Its exceptional selection of local wine makes La Cave Sartenaise an excellent stop for tipplers. If it's not crowded, the staff will be happy to give advice (in French) on the best Sartène wines to add to your cellar – we recommend a Saparale or a Fiumicicoli. Plenty of other Corsican goodies too (charcuterie, olive oil, cheese). It's right below the town hall.

U Maggiu (☎ 04 95 77 21 36; Vieille Ville; ☷ Apr-mid-Oct) The wonderful stalls positioned in front of the cute granite façade are designed to tempt the devil in you. And they do. Especially if you add the rows of lovingly homemade jams displayed on the shelves. And honey. And charcuterie. And liqueurs. You can see the problem.

Getting There & Away

Alta Rocca Voyages–Ricci (☎ 04 95 51 08 19) runs one daily bus (twice daily in July and August) between Ajaccio and Zonza via Olmeto, Propriano, Sartène and Sainte Lucie de Tallano (and also to Bavella in summer). Buses stop on place Porta.

In summer, **Eurocorse** (☎ 04 95 77 18 41) has four daily services (two services in low season) between Ajaccio and Bonifacio via Olmeto, Propriano, Sartène and Porto-Vecchio. **Sartène Voyages** (rue Gabriel Péri) is the agent for Eurocorse.

PREHISTORIC SITES OF THE SARTENAIS

Corsica's dolmens and menhirs remain shrouded in considerable mystery. Archaeologists and historians seem to agree at least that the dolmens mark burial sites. But what of the menhirs?

Some of the menhirs are extremely crude, but on others, human faces and weapons can clearly be made out. Yet there are others, as at Filitosa, so phallic that they're thought to have been fertility symbols for the land. Whatever their origins, they form a mystical backdrop to a walk in the area.

The sites of Cauria and Paddaghiu, south of Sartène, rank among the most interesting on the island. No admission is charged for any of these sites, and there are no facilities.

Cauria

The desolate and beautiful Cauria Plateau, about 15km south of Sartène, is home to three megalithic curiosities: the *alignements* (lines) of menhirs of Stantari and Renaju, and the Fontanaccia dolmen.

From Sartène, follow the road to Bonifacio for 2km before turning off onto the winding D48, on the right. The megalithic site at Cauria is signposted off to the left after another 8km. The next leg, 4.5km along a road that is only casually maintained, leads to a sign riddled with bullet holes. The sign points to the menhirs and the dolmens, along a driveable track to the right, but you can leave your car in the shade here and undertake the last 700m to the Alignement de Stantari on foot.

The **Alignement de Stantari** consists of nine stones: the fourth from the left represents a sword, and its next two neighbours represent faces with their mouths open in muted cry. The **Alignement de Renaju** is larger, slightly less orderly and 300m further on, at the edge of a little wood.

If you retrace your steps to the Alignement de Stantari, you can climb over a barrier made from the two main branches of a cork oak, then follow the path another 350m to the **Fontanaccia dolmen**. This megalithic monument is the largest of its type in Corsica.

Alignement de Paddaghiu

With nearly 260 menhirs, some standing, others lying, the Alignement de Paddaghiu is the largest collection of megalithic statuary in the Mediterranean. Four distinct *alignements*, each of them four to eight menhirs long, are the highlight.

To get there by car from Cauria, drive the 4.5km back to the D48 and turn left towards Tizzano. The entrance to the site is on the right, 1.3km beyond the Mosconi vintners' wine-tasting facility.

TIZZANO

Ah, Tizzano. At the end of the D48, which peels off the N196 about 17km to the north, another world awaits, and Tizzano appears like a mirage. This charming little cove is an enchanted place that has thankfully escaped development due its relative isolation and the staunch opposition of the landowners. It won't be long before you're smitten by the region's mellow tranquillity and laid-back lifestyle. There's a small **tourist office** (☎ 04 95 76 01 49; ☼ 10am-1pm & 3.30-7pm Jul & Aug) on the harbour.

Along the shore is a succession of secluded beaches. Hint: head to the 2km-long golden-sand **Plage de Tra Licettu**, accessible via a dirt track, about 6km to the southeast – a stunner. Sadly, the word has got out a bit since a well-known French magazine raved about it a couple of years ago (still, it's far less crowded than other beaches in the south, because access is difficult).

Very few visitors know that diving is available at Tizzano. And what diving! Friendly Fabrice Nermond, the owner of the only dive shop in Tizzano, **Altramanera** (☎ 06 60 74 87 19; http://altramanera.free.fr in French), takes only small groups. The sites are almost untouched, and you'll marvel at the chaotic aquatic life near Cap Senetosa (see p81).

Sea kayaking is a heavenly way to explore coves and inlets inaccessible from land, including **Cala di Conca** or **Plage d'Erbaju**, where you can laze in idyllic surrounds – bliss! **Stintu Marinu** (☎ 04 95 77 00 26, 06 10 61 35 10; www.stintu -marinu.com in French; ☼ May-Sep) rents kayaks for €35 per half-day. It also rents small five-seater motor boats for €60/90 per half-/full day. Bring your snorkelling gear and a picnic.

For horseback trail rides, you can't do better than the well-regarded equestrian centre **Cavadda di Santu Pultru** (☎ 04 95 77 23 15, 06 88 70 42 05; www.randochevalcorse.com in French; rte de Tizzano). Emmanuel Lucchini leads excursions (€40 for two hours, from €80 for a full day) into the maquis (taking in the prehistoric site of Cauria) as well as beach rides, during which you and your horse splash straight into the turquoise sea. The stables are on the D48, near the junction with the road that leads to Cauria.

In theory there is a **coastal path** from Tizzano to Campomoro but the section between Tizzano and Cap Senetosa is poorly marked. Inquire at the tourist office.

Sleeping & Eating

L'Avena (☎ 04 95 77 02 18; www.camping-corse.info in French; Tizzano; camp sites for 2 people €13-20; ⏲ Jun-Sep) An excellent camping ground, about 400m from the beach, with a host of amenities, including children's playgrounds and a restaurant. It also rents *gîtes toilés* (safari tents) by the night in June and September (€25; minimum two nights).

Hôtel Lilium Maris (☎ 04 95 77 12 20; www.lilium-maris.com; Plage de Tizzano; d €70-158, ste €125-235; ⏲ Apr-Oct; P 🍴 🐶) The fact that its position right on the beach is sensational means that this ambitious newcomer is destined for a long and prosperous life. Step inside and let the tranquillity envelop you. Rooms are gleamingly clean, stylishly furnished and have plenty of natural light. And did we mention the well-sprung mattresses, which are so bouncy you could use them as trampolines? If your credit card has leverage book a sea-facing room or a suite. The attached restaurant (mains €8 to €17) won't win any Michelin awards but is a perfect place to recharge the batteries after an afternoon spent in the waves.

Hôtel du Golfe (☎ 04 95 22 02 51; www.hoteldu golfetizzano.com; Tizzano; d €80-130; ⏲ May-Oct; P 🍴) Rooms here are comfortable but hardly fuel the imagination. Never mind, not even the hardest of hearts can deny the location is impeccable – this place is *les pieds dans l'eau* (right by the water). The adjoining restaurant (mains €10 to €20) focuses on seafood but lacks character.

Chez Antoine (☎ 04 95 77 07 25; Tizzano; mains €12-20; ⏲ May-Sep) Brothers Julien and Flo are at the controls of this immutable seafood favourite (it has been around since 1960). Feast on fish and seafood on the terrace overlooking a beach. Grilled fish (sea bass, corb, red mullet or weever, depending on the daily catch) is a snip at €5 per 100g – the best deal we came across in Corsica. Put some zing in your step with a glass of San Armetto, a local Sartène wine. Great stuff.

LE SARTENAIS TO BONIFACIO

About 20km from Sartène and 30km from Bonifacio, you can't miss the landmark **Roccapina** site, a Dali-esque rock formation that is (vaguely) reminiscent of a lion. Two enormous rocks on top of a ridge crowned by a Genoese tower define the basic shape; a few standing rocks suggest the mane.

The view down to the shimmering waters of **Plage de Roccapina** from the R196 is seductive. To get to the beach, take the potholed track, leading off the main road next to Auberge Coralli, and follow it downhill for 2.5km. A handful of boats moor in the calm, aquamarine water and the beach itself is fine and sandy, making it particularly suitable for children. There aren't any facilities or much shade on the beach itself though, so you will need to bring your own supplies and umbrella.

The coastline between Roccapina and Bonifacio is extremely alluring: a string of hidden beaches lapped by crystalline waters and backed by rolling hills carpeted with fragrant maquis.

Some 20km from Bonifacio on the N196, the village of **Pianottoli-Caldarello** is a good base if all the hotels are full in Bonifacio, with no fewer than 10 *chambres d'hôtes* in the area. From there, a narrow road leads down to the tranquil **Plage de Kevano**.

Too gentle for you? Head to **Plage de la Tonnara**, about halfway between Pianottoli-Caldarello and Bonifacio. This windswept beach makes windsurfing and kitesurfing hounds go gaga – it easily rivals Plage de Piantarella (p202), west of Bonifacio, and we can't get enough of the spectacular aerials performed by windsurfers and kitesurfers here. Want to give it a try? Contact **Paradiz Fun & Kite** (☎ 06 99 04 82 93; www.paradizkite.com in French; Plage de la Tonnara; ⏲ Jul-Oct), a kitesurfing and windsurfing school that runs lessons (€170 for four hours). Another up-and-coming kitesurfing and windsurfing spot is **Plage de Figari**, in Baie de Figari, a few kilometres to the northwest. The competent **Fun Eole Figari** (☎ 06 11 48 13 92; www.eolefigari.com in French; Baie de Figari) also offers lessons and courses (from €100 for five hours). English is spoken at both outfits.

SLEEPING

Camping Kevano Plage (☎ 04 95 71 83 22, fax 04 95 71 83 83; camp sites per adult/tent/car €8.50/4/4; Pianottoli; ✆ May-Sep) A solid three-star, with good facilities. It's about 400m from Plage de Kevano.

Auberge Coralli (☎ 04 95 77 05 94; rte de Bonifacio; d €44-59; ✆ Apr-Nov) This auberge, located right by the N196, features good rooms, which are rented by the week in July and August. The restaurant (mains €14 to €19) is famed for its hearty dishes, such as *agneau de lait rôti* (roasted milk-fed lamb) and *côte de veau sauce aux myrtes* (veal cutlet with myrtle sauce).

Chambres d'Hôtes L'Orca di San Gavinu (☎ 04 95 71 01 29, 06 76 58 18 89; San Gavinu; d €68, ste €95) Find heaven in this doll's house of a B&B run with grace and panache by Madame Bartoli. The façade of the entrancing mansion from the 19th century is festooned with a blistering array of flowers, and it's right in the heart of San Gavinu. It features seductively old-fashioned rooms that are embellished with various artistic touches, oak furnishings, robust parquet, fat pillows, well-chosen fabrics and soothing pastels. The atmospheric garden at the front is a delightful place to chill out with a *pastis* (liquorice-flavoured apéritif) in hand. Fancy a dip? The *vasques* (pools) of the nearby Vivaggio River beckon. A lovely nest.

Chambres d'Hôtes Sheranee (☎ 06 82 58 17 32, 06 82 58 25 31; www.sheranee.com; hameau de Vallicella; d €70) Although it lacks the charm and patina of the L'Orca di San Gavinu, this B&B, run by Renée and Irène, has a lot in its favour. It's well situated if you want to explore the far south and there's not a speck of dust to be found in the five spotlessly clean rooms. And if you need some hush and seclusion amid a field of olive trees, this retreat is hard to beat. It's gay-friendly.

Bergeries de Piscia (☎ 04 95 71 06 71; http://corse-chambres-hotes.com in French; d with half-board €160; ✆ May-Oct) Find bucolic bliss at these converted *bergeries* (shepherd's huts). We were bowled over by the faaabulous location and the glorious views over the coast. Rooms are quirkily laid out (but a bit poky), with a subtle combination of wood and other natural materials, offset with lots of white plaster and a few muted tones, as well as mosaics in the bathrooms. For the little 'uns, there are various animals to see on the property, including

mouflons and wild boars. The frosting on the cake is that you can loll by the sensational pool. Food (*menu* €35) here is a plus: feast on hearty Corsican fare served in an atmospheric room. Animals, greenery, peace – a delight for urbanites seeking a 'rustic chic' getaway.

Other *chambres d'hôtes* worth considering in the area:

Chambres d'Hôtes Berquez (☎ 04 95 71 83 82; jberquez@wanadoo.fr; Pianottoli-Caldarello; d €60; ✆ Jan-Oct) Three comfy rooms that can be noisy – it's just on the main road.

Chambres d'Hôtes Felicita (☎ 04 95 71 82 80; paule .tomasi@wanadoo.fr; Pianottoli-Caldarello; d €70) Six well-kept rooms in a stern stone house smack dab in the village.

EATING

Le Goéland Beach (☎ 04 95 73 02 51; Plage de la Tonnara; mains €8-20, menu €20; ✆ closed Mon in low season) An eatery well worth bookmarking, a pebble's throw from Chez Marco, with a menu featuring salads, pizzas and grilled meat dishes. There's live music at weekends in summer.

Le Golfe (☎ 04 95 24 39 11; Baie de Figari; mains €15-25, menu €25; ✆ closed Wed) If you can't stretch to dine at Chez Marco, Le Golfe is an excellent plan B, with ultrafresh fish served in simple surrounds.

Poggio di Mastri (☎ 04 95 71 02 65; Figari; menu €38; ✆ May-Oct) Bring an empty tum: the five-course *menu* is a culinary feast revolving around choice pieces of meat (wild boar, lamb) the size of doorstops, organic vegetables and prepared-to-perfection desserts. The dining room does impress, with a huge fireplace, hefty beams and wooden furniture. Location is the main disadvantage – it's close to the main road.

Chez Marco (☎ 04 95 73 02 24; Baie de Figari; menus €55-99; ✆ Apr-Oct) Lobster is king of the castle here. Although this classic temple of seafood runs the danger of pricing itself out of the market, it's still the place towards which all heads turn when it comes to tasting a range of bounteous marine offerings. The location is ace and there's a large dining area with exposed wood beams, stone walls and lobster pots hanging from the ceiling, as well as a terrace overlooking the sea.

GETTING THERE & AWAY

Eurocorse (☎ 04 95 21 06 30) buses stop at Roccapina on the route between Ajaccio and Bonifacio.

THE SOUTH

BONIFACIO (BUNIFAZIU)

pop 2700

Bonifacio is indisputably Corsica's belle of the ball. No doubt you'll be awestruck by its magnificent setting and breathtaking layout. The citadel, which is a compact mesh of narrow, twisting streets, hemmed in by ancient buildings, is dramatically perched on a thin peninsula. Down below, an inlet, or fjord, about 100m wide, plunges in behind the great cliffs to form the town's fine natural harbour, home to a buzzing port. And the shimmering blue seas of the Îles Lavezzi are a short boat ride away.

Bonifacio is also the maverick of Corsica. There's a distinctly Italian flavour, courtesy of the proximity of Sardinia, which adds to the appeal.

The flipside is that Bonifacio is horrendously crowded in summer, which can be a chore.

HISTORY

The town as we know it today was probably founded by the Marquis de Toscane Boniface in 828 AD. A few hundred years later, in 1187, the town was taken by Genoa, whose colonists prospered and, true to form, drove out the previous inhabitants.

Genoese Bonifacio had to fight for its life twice. The first occasion was in 1420, when Alphonse V of Aragon laid siege to the town for five months, on the grounds that Pope Boniface VIII had given Corsica to Spain; according to legend, the Escalier du Roi d'Aragon (King of Aragon's Stairway) was carved at this point. Ultimately, a Genoese squadron was dispatched to assist the colony and Alphonse was forced to retreat.

The second siege took place in 1553. This time it was an alliance between French troops, followers of Sampiero Corso and the Turkish pirate Dragut, who aimed to liberate the town. Bonifacio resisted the attack for 18 days. Together with the rest of the island, it was returned to the Genoese in 1559.

ORIENTATION

Bonifacio can be separated into two main sections: the marina at the end of the Goulet de Bonifacio, and the Genoese-built citadel – also known as the *vieille ville* (old town) or *haute ville* (upper town) – perched on the clifftop between the inlet and the sea.

INFORMATION

Boniboom (☎ 04 95 73 05 89; quai Jérôme Comparetti; per hr €5; ☽ 8am-2am) Internet café.

Bonifacio Hospital (☎ 04 95 73 95 73) On the marina; 24-hour emergency unit.

Harbour Master's office (☎ 04 95 73 10 07; marina; ☽ 8.30am-8pm in summer, 8am-noon & 2-6pm in low season)

Post office (☎ 04 95 73 73 73; Haute Ville) Has an ATM.

Société Générale (☎ 04 95 73 02 49; rue St-Érasme; ☽ 8.15am-noon & 2-4.50pm Mon-Fri) The only bank in town. Has an ATM.

Tourist office (☎ 04 95 73 11 88; www.bonifacio.fr; rue Fred Scamaroni; ☽ 9am-8pm daily May–mid-Oct, 9am-noon & 2-6pm Mon-Fri mid-Oct–Apr)

SIGHTS
Citadel & Upper Town

From the marina, the atmospheric **Montée St-Roch** leads to the citadel via **Porte de Gênes** (Genoa Gate; pedestrian access only). This gate was the only way of getting into the citadel until the Porte de France was built in 1854. To the north is the **Bastion de l'Étendard** (admission €2.50), a remnant of the fortifications built in the aftermath of the siege in 1553. It is home to the **Mémorial du Passé Bonifacien** (Memorial to Bonifacio's Past; admission €2.50), where various episodes in the town's history have been re-created. To the south of the bastion are **place du Marché** and **place de la Manichella**, with their jaw-dropping views over the Bouches de Bonifacio and Sardinia.

The street that now bears the name **rue des Deux Empereurs** was the citadel's main thoroughfare during Genoese supremacy. The two emperors are Charles V and Napoleon I; both lodged in the town, the former on his way to Algiers in 1541, the latter in 1793 on his way to conquer Sardinia. Commemorative plaques at Nos 4 and 7 indicate the houses the two men stayed in, but neither is open to the public.

The unmissable **Église Ste-Marie Majeure** was built by the Pisans and was completed in the 14th century. Although it has been modified on numerous occasions and has gradually lost its original style, it retains its main feature, the loggia, under the arches of which the notables of the town used to gather. Opposite it is the old cistern, in which the town formerly collected rainwater from the many aqueducts running above the streets of the *vieille ville*.

Even the **Escalier du Roi d'Aragon** (admission €2.50) is thought to have been connected with water provision. Legend has it that the 187 steps

BONIFACIO

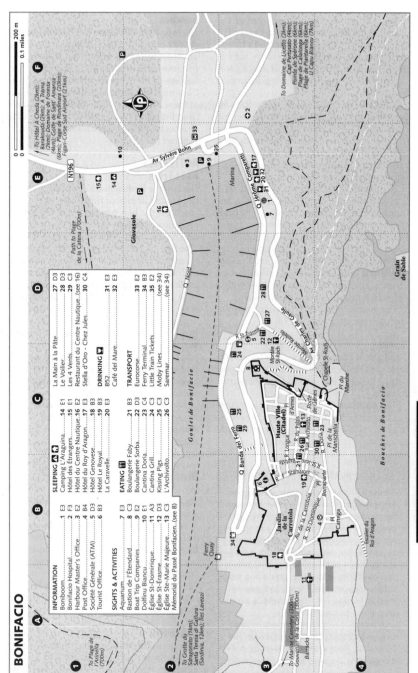

INFORMATION
Boniboom..............................1	E3
Bonifacio Hospital..................2	F3
Harbour Master's Office.........3	E2
Post Office...........................4	B4
Société Générale (ATM)..........5	D3
Tourist Office........................6	B3

SIGHTS & ACTIVITIES
Aquarium..............................7	E3
Bastion de l'Étendard.............8	C3
Boat Trip Companies..............9	E2
Dolfinu Biancu.....................10	E1
Église St-Dominique.............11	A3
Église St-Erasme..................12	D3
Église Ste-Marie Majeure......13	C3
Mémorial du Passé Bonifacien..(see 8)

SLEEPING
Camping L'Araguina.............14	E1
Hôtel des Etrangers..............15	E1
Hôtel du Centre Nautique.....16	E2
Hôtel du Roy d'Aragon........17	E3
Hôtel Genovese....................18	B3
Hôtel Le Royal.....................19	B3
La Caravelle........................20	E3

EATING
Boulangerie Faby................21	B3
Boulangerie Sorba...............22	D3
Cantina Doria......................23	C4
Cantina Grill.......................24	C3
Kissing Pigs........................25	C3
L'Archivolto.......................26	C3
La Main à la Pâte................27	D3
Le Voilier...........................28	D3
Les 4 Vents........................29	C3
Restaurant du Centre Nautique..(see 16)
Stella d'Oro - Chez Jules......30	C4

DRINKING
B52...................................31	E3
Café del Mare.....................32	E3

TRANSPORT
Eurocorse...........................33	E2
Ferry Terminal.....................34	B3
Little Train Tickets...............35	E2
Moby Lines.......................(see 34)
Saremar...........................(see 34)

down from the southwestern corner of the citadel to the sea, 60m below, were carved in a single night by the King of Aragon's troops during the 1420 siege. It is more likely that this impressive scar down the side of the cliff was carved to allow access to a spring discovered by monks.

To the west of the citadel is the **Église St-Dominique** (admission €2.50), one of the few Gothic churches in Corsica. It houses an altarpiece made of polychrome marble that dates back to the mid-18th century, as well as reliquaries carried in processions through the town during a number of religious festivals.

The **marine cemetery**, with its immaculate lines of tombs, stretches out to the sea a few hundred metres farther to the west. Although the surroundings are far from seductive, there is a spectacular view over the Sardinian coast, about 12km away. An underground passage dug by hand during WWII leads to the **Gouvernail de la Corse** (Rudder of Corsica), a rock about a dozen metres from the shore with a shape reminiscent of the rudder of a ship.

The tourist office offers a pass, allowing entry to four attractions for €6.

Marina

The **Église St-Érasme**, dedicated to the patron saint of fishermen, was built in the 13th century. The church is at the foot of montée Rastello.

The **Aquarium** (☎ 04 95 73 03 69; quai Jérôme Comparetti; adult/child €3.80/1.90; ☼ 9am-midnight Apr-Oct) is in a natural cave and features the marine flora and fauna of the Bouches de Bonifacio.

WALK TO PERTUSATO LIGHTHOUSE

There's a fantastic breezy walk you can take along the cliffs of Bonifacio to the Pertusato lighthouse, east of town. From the signposted starting point, which is just to the left of the sharp bend on the hill up to the *haute ville*, turn left and a ramp of paving stones climbs to the top of the cliffs. When you get there, follow the path along the cliffs to the southeast. There is low-growing maquis on your left; to the right, a sheer drop down to the sea.

After about 30 minutes the path joins the D260, which leads to the signal station and lighthouse, from where the views are nail-biting. Allow 2½ hours for the return walk.

Beaches

The little **Plage de la Catena** and **Plage de l'Arinella** stretch out at the back of the coves of the same name, on the north side of the *goulet* (narrow harbour entrance). There is a path leading to them on av Sylvère Bohn, near Camping L'Araguina. Unfortunately, both of these beaches tend to collect the rubbish from the *goulet*. With a car you can reach the beaches at Piantarella, Calalonga and Sant' Amanza (p202).

ACTIVITIES
Boat Trips

Don't leave Bonifacio without taking a boat trip around its extraordinary coastline, where you'll get the best perspective of the town's precarious position on top of the magnificent chalky cliffs. Two itineraries are offered. The first includes the *goulet*, the *calanques* (deep rocky inlets; *calanche* in Corsican), with their clear aquamarine waters, and the magical **Grotte du Sdragonato** (Little Dragon Cave) with its gloriously multicoloured sea bed. A 50-minute tour costs about €14. The second (around €25) focuses on the Îles Lavezzi (p201) and boats are operated shuttle fashion, so you can linger on the islands. But, if you do, take your own food and drink since you won't find any there. On the way back, the boats pass close to Île Cavallo, Pointe de Spérone, the *calanche* and the cliffs.

Numerous companies vie for customers in summer. Their booths are based on the marina. They offer more or less the same deal, but it's worth shopping around in search of special offers.

Diving

Whatever your level of expertise, you'll find your slice of underwater heaven in Bonifacio. Due to their proximity to the coast, the Îles Lavezzi are very popular among divers. See p81 for more details. Two dive centres:

Barakouda (☎ 04 95 73 13 02; http://club.barakouda .free.fr in French; rte de Porto-Vecchio) On the road to Porto-Vecchio, about 2km from the centre.

Dolfinu Biancu (☎ 04 95 72 01 33, 06 14 24 51 88; http://perso.wanadoo.fr/dolfinu.biancu; av Sylvère Bohn) On the harbour.

SLEEPING

Accommodation options are relatively scarce in Bonifacio and get fully booked well in advance. It's also slim pickings for those watching their money. Hint: if you want to avoid financial hari-kari, base yourself in the Pianottoli-Caldarello area (p194), which is a mere 20-minute drive from Bonifacio.

Hotels

Hôtel des Étrangers (☎ 04 95 73 01 09; fax 04 95 73 16 97; av Sylvère Bohn; d €38-68; ✆ Apr–mid-Oct; P ✗) The Foreigners Hotel deserves a pat on the back for quoting reasonable rates even in high season. Rooms are clean, double-glazed, modern and, if not especially aesthetically appealing, comfortable. The more expensive ones have air-conditioning. Of course, this value-for-money place is no secret – bookings are essential in season. It's on the main road, north of the harbour. Free parking.

Hôtel Le Royal (☎ 04 95 73 00 51; fax 04 95 73 04 68; rue Fred Scamaroni; s €40-95, d €45-100; P ✗) Although Le Royal scores low on the hipness scale, its fair prices and central location – it's right in the *haute ville* – make it a worthwhile option. Rooms are well organised, even if the décor plays it fairly safe. Angle for a room with a view.

Hôtel du Roi d'Aragon (☎ 04 95 73 03 99; www .royaragon.com; quai Jérôme Comparetti; d €52-197; P ✗) Functional rooms with TV and telephone ensure a decent, if unmemorable, night's sleep for guests keen to roll out of bed and into the *haute ville*. Ask for the more light-filled and airy *vue port avec terrasse* (front rooms with a terrace overlooking the harbour). A touch-up in the *standard* and the *latérale* (side) rooms wouldn't do any harm.

Domaine de Foresta (☎ 04 95 73 08 04; foresta1@ wanadoo.fr; rte de Sant' Amanza; s €55-70, d €60-90; P ✆) In a pinkish building set in a verdant property, the six rooms won't win any design awards but are tidy and the staff friendly. There's a pool, too. A good port of call if you don't want to deplete your accommodation budget. It's about 4km from Bonifacio on the road to Sant' Amanza, 300m off the road to Porto-Vecchio.

Hôtel A Cheda (☎ 04 95 73 03 82; www.acheda-hotel .com; Cavallo Morto; d €60-300, with half-board Aug €317-437; P ✗ ✆) If you have a car, consider this tasteful, intimate complex, on the eastern outskirts of Bonifacio. It features 13 rooms that occupy little private bungalows dotted around an exuberant garden. All are individually decorated in a Mediterranean style using natural materials. And did we mention the heavenly pool? The attached restaurant is held in high esteem, too.

Hôtel du Centre Nautique (☎ 04 95 73 02 11; www .centre-nautique.com; quai Nord; d €75-195; ✆ Mar-Oct; P ✗) This well-established abode occupies the former *capitainerie* (harbour master's office) on the waterfront. It's a smart place to rest your head, with a nautical theme that graces the communal areas, spick-and-span bathrooms and generously sized rooms with a mezzanine and L-shaped sofa bed. However, it's disappointing to find the bedrooms furnished in more or less standard hotel clobber.

A Trama (☎ 04 95 73 17 17; www.a-trama.com; rte de Sant' Amanza; d €85-185; P ✗ ✆) We're suckers for the relaxing atmosphere that prevails in this oasis of calm, on the road to Sant' Amanza. The 25 rooms are nothing too out of the ordinary but are set in a leafy park where you can mooch around and the well-tended pool is an instant elixir when it's sweltering hot. The attached restaurant has won accolade for its tasty dishes (dinner only).

La Caravelle (☎ 04 95 73 00 03; www.hotel-caravelle -corse.com; quai Jérôme Comparetti; d €100-225, ste €190-300; ✆ Apr–mid-Oct; P ✗) Though the rooms aren't huge, they're comfy enough to receive a tired body after a full day of exploring the town. If you want a room with million-dollar views over the harbour, snaffle one of the suites on the upper floors.

Hôtel Genovese (☎ 04 95 73 12 34; www.hotel-geno vese.com; haute ville; d €115-265, ste €150-535; ✆ Oct-Mar; P ✗ ✆) This nearly-but-not-quite boutique hotel will appeal to design-savvy travellers, with stylish furniture, soothing tones and a lovely swimming pool with teak deck built on the ramparts. Be sure to score an exterior-facing room, rather than a darker courtyard-facing room.

Camping

Camping L'Araguina (☎ 04 95 73 02 96; www.camping araguina.fr; av Sylvère Bohn; camp sites per adult/tent/car €6/2.50/2.50; ✆ Apr–mid-Oct) In summer, you'll feel like sardines in a tin in this tightly packed camp site, and facilities are just average, but it's the closest one to town. Tents can be rented.

EATING

Cantina Doria (☎ 04 95 73 50 49; rue Doria; mains €8-12, menus €12-15; ✆ Apr-Sep) Success has done nothing to dull the buzz at Cantina, an unpretentious, cavernous little joint in the *haute ville*. The menu, chalked up on a blackboard, contains invigorating dishes such as *spaghettis aux aubergines* (spaghetti with eggplant)

THE SOUTH

and *lasagnes au fromage Corse* (lasagne with Corsican cheese) at surprisingly honest prices. There are some streetside tables.

Kissing Pigs (☎ 04 95 73 56 09; quai Banda del Ferro; mains €8-15; closed Wed & Sun in low season) Get in early here as this zany fave, right by the harbour, teems with punters from far and wide anxious to wrap their mandibles around some of the best charcuterie and cheese platters in town. Go for the *moitié-moitié* (half-and-half), which is a combination of the two. Since wines also feature highly here, let things rip with the list of well chosen Corsican tipples. Fiumicicoli, anyone?

Cantina Grill (☎ 04 95 70 49 86; quai Banda del Ferro; mains €9-15, menus €15-17; Mar-Dec) The Cantina Doria has become so popular it has spawned a second outlet on the harbour with an emphasis on fresh fish. The three-course set menu (€17) is a bargain.

Le Voilier (☎ 04 95 73 07 06; quai Jérôme Comparetti; mains €10-17, menus €19-25; Apr-Oct) A bastion of *haute cuisine* on the marina, Le Voilier attracts serious gourmets keen to enjoy elaborate fish and meat dishes. The *carré de denti et pistou de coquillages* (dentex steak with a Provençal sauce) certainly won our hearts. Save room for desserts – the *crème brûlée au basilic* (cream pie with a caramelised topping and basil) is a victory for humanity.

Les 4 Vents (☎ 04 95 73 07 50; quai Banda del Ferro; mains €12-22; closed Mon & Tue in low season) The setting is eye-catching, with seafaring paraphernalia adorning the dining room and a terrace soothingly positioned on the waterfront. Les 4 Vents serves good Corsican dishes made with salutary attention to detail. Push the boat out with the *brochette d'espadon* (skewered cubes of swordfish) and *salade de seiches et crevettes* (shrimps and cuttlefish salad). Deadly.

La Main à La Pâte (☎ 04 95 73 04 50; montée Rastello; mains €12-26, menu €17; Apr-Oct) A long-standing restaurant serving nothing but high-quality pasta dishes at eminently affordable prices. You choose the colour (white, orange, green or black), the form (tagliatelle, fettuccine, rigatoni) and the accompanying sauce. Good fun and tasty.

L'Archivolto (☎ 04 95 73 17 58; rue Archivolto; mains €13-18; Apr-Sep & dinner Jul-Aug) This one-of-a-kind Bonifacio institution scores a perfect 10 on our 'charm-meter' for its mind-blowing décor, mellow atmosphere and imaginative cuisine. It feels like an antique shop, with an onslaught of quirky collectables from floor to ceiling. Foodwise, it's no less impressive, with *salade de poulpe à la coriandre* (octopus salad with coriander) or *spaghetti à la poutargue de thon* (spaghetti with tuna roe). In summer the tables spill out onto the lovely piazza outside.

Stella d'Oro – Chez Jules (☎ 04 95 73 03 63; rue Doria; mains €15-26, menu €23; Apr-Sep) This characterful eatery set in a former oil mill is held in high regard by locals and tourists alike. There's nothing unorthodox on the menu, just the usual Bonifacien suspects cooked to perfection: *aubergines à la bonifacienne* (eggplants cooked with cheese) and pasta. A *dessert du chef* (homemade dessert of the day) will finish you off sweetly.

Restaurant du Centre Nautique (☎ 04 95 73 02 11; quai Nord; mains €16-30) With its loosely nautical décor, this sleek venue attracts the glitterati (and the parvenu) for its first-rate pasta dishes and fresh fish grilled to crispy perfection. There's a limited but well-selected wine list, and the Domaine Torraccia goes down a treat. Nab yourself a seat on the restaurant's terrace and perve on the boats you wish you owned.

THE AUTHOR'S CHOICE

If, like us, you have a soft spot for pastries, you should make a beeline for the two *boulangeries* mentioned below. Both serve *uga seccata* or *pain des morts* (buns with raisins and walnuts) and *fugazzi* (flat cakes flavoured with aniseed and orange), two Bonifacien specialities. If you can resist these damn calorie-busting things, you're not human!

Boulangerie Faby (☎ 04 95 73 14 73; haute ville) There's something delightfully timeless about this old-fashioned *boulangerie* in the *haute ville*. The *patronne* can be grumpy, but that's part of the fun. Ah, its *uga seccata* (€2)! Sinful.

Boulangerie Sorba (☎ 04 95 73 03 64; rue St-Érasme) Another endearing outfit, near the harbour. Hmm! We can still smell the aroma of freshly baked *uga seccata* wafting from the door. It's been in business for more than 80 years, so it knows its stuff.

DRINKING & ENTERTAINMENT

Don't expect all-night carousing; Bonifacio is not Corsica's best destination for Dionysian revelry. The only place you'll find any action is the port area where a handful of bars stay open until the small hours in summer.

B52 (quai Jérôme Comparetti) It has a buzzing balcony area and terrace, and plays a good blend of hip-hop, soul and indie music but only really gets going around midnight.

Café del Mare (quai Jérôme Comparetti) 'Fiesta Latina, so Caliente' is the mantra here.

GETTING THERE & AWAY
Air

Figari-Sud Corse airport (☎ 04 95 71 10 10; www.figari .aeroport.fr) is in the middle of the maquis, 21km north of Bonifacio, near the village of Figari. Daily flights from mainland France, plus charter flights in summer from other European countries serve both Bonifacio and Porto-Vecchio. See also p264.

Like most airports in Corsica, this one has neither an ATM nor a *bureau de change*.

Boat

Bonifacio is the main jumping-off point for Santa Teresa di Gallura (Sardinia). Two companies run car ferries on this one-hour crossing. Tickets can be bought at the ferry terminal.

Saremar (☎ 04 95 73 00 96; www.saremar.it in Italian) has two to three daily departures depending on the season. Adult one-way fares are up to €16.50 (including port tax). A small-car fare is up to €41.

Moby Lines (☎ 04 95 73 00 29; www.mobylines.it) has up to four daily crossings each way from April to September. Prices are virtually the same as for Saremar.

See also p267.

Bus

Eurocorse (☎ 04 95 70 13 83) has services between Bonifacio and Porto-Vecchio, Roccapina, Sartène, Propriano, Olmeto and Ajaccio. There are two departures daily except Sunday. The journey to Ajaccio takes about 3½ hours and costs €21. For Bastia, you'll have to change in Porto-Vecchio.

GETTING AROUND

Bonifacio is such a popular destination that it does to cars what a spider's web does to flies. In summer, traffic sometimes backs up all the way from the town centre to the roundabout on the main road. Nor are matters helped by the scarcity of car parks. Your best bet, particularly in the high season, is to find a hotel that provides a parking space.

There's a little 'tourist' **train** (☎ 04 95 73 15 07) that runs from the port up to the *haute ville* (every half-hour from 9am to midnight in high season). The price (€5) is as steep as the route, but you may be doing your legs a favour by hopping on.

To/From the Airport

Transports Rossi (☎ 04 95 71 00 11) provides a shuttle service between the airport and Bonifacio in July and August (€9, 30 minutes, five services a day).

By taxi, the trip from the airport to Bonifacio centre costs about €45.

AROUND BONIFACIO

ARCHIPEL DES LAVEZZI

Paradise! Part of a protected area (known as Les Réserves Naturelles des Bouches de Bonifacio), the Archipel des Lavezzi (Lavezzi Archipelago), or Îles Lavezzi, is a clutch of uninhabited islets that are made for those who love nothing better than splashing in tranquil lapis lazuli waters or strolling across powder-soft beaches.

The 65-hectare **Île Lavezzi**, which gives its name to the whole archipelago, is the most accessible of the islands and the southernmost point of Corsica. The island's savage beauty aside, its superb natural pools make good swimming holes, and there is also a cemetery for the victims who perished on board the *Sémillante*, a three-mast frigate that ran aground on Île Lavezzi in February 1855.

In summer, various companies organise **boat excursions** to the island, either from Bonifacio (p198) or Porto-Vecchio (p204). You will need to bring your own lunch and drinks, as there is nowhere on the islands to buy anything.

Île de Cavallo, just north of the archipelago, is frequented by the very rich and is protected from outsiders; it's inaccessible except by private boat.

CAP PERTUSATO

If you're after that perfect picture, Cap Pertusato is the best vantage point in the area.

THE SOUTH

There's a **lighthouse** at the end of the road. It's an easy walk from Bonifacio (see p198). By car, take the D58, by the hospital (it's sign-posted). The seamless view of the cliffs, the Îles Lavezzi, Bonifacio and Sardinia is absolutely memorable.

Domaine de Licetto (☎ 04 95 73 03 59; www.licetto .com in French; rte du Phare; menu €33; ☒ Apr–mid-Oct), right in the maquis, has won plaudits for its gargantuan set menu: apéritif, starters, two main courses, cheese platter, dessert, *digestif* and wine. Menu stalwarts include *agneau de lait* (suckling lamb) and *aubergines à la bonifacienne*. Bring an empty tum! The setting is fairly unexciting but the food is fresh and delicious, and the restaurant strives to use only local ingredients. It also has seven tidy rooms (doubles €40 to €80) in a separate building.

POINTE DE SPÉRONE

Pointe de Spérone is famous for its golf course, which draws celebs from all over Europe.

More accessible to the simple mortals that we are, **Plage du Petit Spérone** is a tiny turquoise bay with a brochure-esque appeal – perfect for working on your tan.

PLAGE DE PIANTARELLA

Say 'Plage de Piantarella' to windsurfing and kayaking fiends and you'll see an ecstatic smile on their faces. With its shallow lagoon, this lovely bay ranks among the best spots in southern Corsica for water sports. With a kayak, you can navigate to Spérone and Pertusato; if you're fit, you could go as far as Île Lavezzi on a calm day.

Two ventures offer courses and rent gear: **Bonifacio Windsurf** (☎ 04 95 73 52 04; www .bonifacio-windsurf.com; Plage de Piantarella; ☒ May-Sep) Kayak/funboard rental is €12/20 an hour. Courses cost €130 to €150 (seven hours) and private lessons cost €60 an hour. Also runs courses for children aged over six (€150, six hours).
Club de Voile de Bonifacio (☎ 04 95 73 04 89; Plage de Piantarella; ☒ May-Sep) Kayak/funboard rental is €10/16 an hour. Courses cost about €80 (three hours).

Accommodation options include **Camping des Îles** (☎ 04 95 73 11 89; rte de Piantarella; www.camping -desiles.com; camp sites per adult/tent/car €7.50/3.20/3.20; ☒ Apr–mid-Oct; P ☒), 5.5km from Bonifacio. This camping ground is in a glorious setting and has enough amenities to make some hotels envious. Plage de Piantarella is about 1km away.

PLAGE DE CALALONGA

The little shale-covered Plage de Calalonga doesn't get too crowded and is popular with snorkellers. To get there follow the D58 east of Bonifacio for 6km, from where you'll need to walk a further 200m down a sandy track to the beach.

GOLFE DE SANT' AMANZA

Just 7km east of Bonifacio, the Golfe de Sant' Amanza is a hot windsurfing and kitesurfing spot and draws a crowd when the wind is right. Here you'll find the windswept **Plage de Maora, Plage de Balistra** and **Plage de Sant' Amanza**. All around the gulf you can stop and make your way down to the many little rocky coves or rough sandy inlets, with – if you're lucky – only stray wild goats (and a bunch of windsurfers) for company. To get there follow the D60, just off the main Bonifacio–Porto-Vecchio road.

The kitesurfing and windsurfing action centres on Plage de Balistra and Plage de Sant' Amanza. **Corsica Kiteboarding** (☎ 06 75 01 50 04; www .corsica-kiteboarding.com in French; ☒ Apr–Oct) is a 'travelling' kitesurfing school that offers introductory kitesurfing classes (from €140 for four hours) and rents equipment (from €80 per day). It uses Plage de Balistra, Plage de Piantarella and Plage de la Tonnara (see p194).

For a DIY tour of the gulf, your best bet is to hire a six-seater, 6hp motor boat (no licence required) for half a day. There are lots of coves and beaches that are not accessible by car (no crowds!) and that beg exploration. Contact **Pouss Vagues** (☎ 06 74 41 36 62, 06 07 94 25 82; www .poussevague.com in French; Sant' Amanza; ☒ mid-Apr–mid-Oct). It will cost you €80/110 per half-/full day. Petrol is included. It also rents kayaks (from €10 per hour).

The low-key **Grand Bleu Plongée** (☎ 06 60 65 84 39; Plage de Maora) is based on Plage de Maora and organises dive trips to Îles Cerbicale and Îles Lavezzi. See p81 for more information on diving.

After all that exertion, you might want to re-energise. **L'Épave** (☎ 04 95 73 05 81; Sant' Amanza; mains €11-35; ☒ May-Sep) is a good deal. Don't believe the humble menu. It underplays the spoils at this unpretentious, yet well-regarded, fish restaurant overlooking the sea. The seafood is fresh and cooked with élan. Think *salade du pêcheur* (fisherman's salad), *calamars aux fines herbes* (squid with aromatic herbs) or fish soup.

THE SOUTH

THE AUTHOR'S CHOICE

U Capu Biancu (☎ 04 95 73 05 58; www.ucapubiancu.com; Domaine de Pozzoniello; d €190-390, ste €505-665; ✆ Apr-Oct; Ⓟ ✗ 🖳 ◩) A bumpy, partly unsurfaced road leads to this unconventional four-star seducer perched on a cliff near the Golfe de Sant' Amanza, about 5km from the N198. A place of casual sophistication and unfussy ambience, this deluxe hideaway is brimming with cool vibes. We know of few properties that put more emphasis on customising guest services. Tomorrow is your birthday? They'll organise a party on the beach for you. Rooms are colour-saturated and of a healthy size and certainly qualify as 'rustic chic'. Oh, and there's a glorious pool, too. If, like us, you haven't graduated to luxury class yet, you can still soak up the ambience in the gourmet restaurant.

GOLFE DE SANT' AMANZA TO PORTO-VECCHIO

The stretch of road between Bonifacio and Porto-Vecchio is one of the best, and noticeably straightest, in the country! Between the Golfe de Sant' Amanza and the Golfe de Pinarello the jagged coastline is regularly punctuated by stretches of gorgeous, white-sand beach. Sadly, these beaches are no longer a secret; at the peak of the summer tourist season, they are frequently very crowded.

Be prepared to fall to your knees in awe when you first see the phenomenal horseshoe-shaped **Baie de Rondinara**, preferably on a sunny day. It is home to the fine sandy **Plage de Rondinara**, a salt-white strip of sand lapped by turquoise waters. Flanked by pines on one side, it's a gorgeous place to sun yourself. To find it from Bonifacio, take the Porto-Vecchio road for about 16km where you'll see a small turn to the right, in the direction of Suartone.

SLEEPING & EATING

Chambres d'Hôtes L'Hôte Antique (☎ 04 95 71 20 17, 06 22 24 85 73; www.lhote-antique.com in French; Petralonga Salvini; d €80-90; ✗ 🖳) An ideal base from where you can easily reach Porto-Vecchio, Rondinara, Santa Giulia and Bonifacio. This lovely B&B is run with care and efficiency by Jean-Luc and Françoise Pietri. The five rooms are very spacious and well appointed, with air-con and firm bedding as well as exposed beams and balconies in some rooms; they certainly qualify for 'modern chic'. *Table d'hôtes* (set menu) is available twice weekly (€25) and can be served in a lovely vaulted room, down-stairs. There's free wi-fi. It's in Petralonga Salvini, about 14km south of Porto-Vecchio, off the N198 (take the D459 to the right and follow the signs).

PORTO-VECCHIO (PORTIVECCHJU)

pop 10,600

Shamelessly sexy, seductive and fashionable, Porto-Vecchio is usually dubbed the Corsican St-Tropez, and it's no wonder. Sitting in a marvellous bay, it's the kind of place that lures French A-listers and wealthy tourists with its potent potion of ostentatious hipness. If you're looking to seriously indulge, Porto-Vecchio has lots of chic hotels and exclusive *résidences de tourisme* where you can pamper yourself. Night owls will be pleased to know that the city has a well-established party reputation during the season.

We'll be honest, though. Porto-Vecchio is the vortex around which southern Corsica's fun-in-the-sun vacation life whirls, which translates into a purgatory traffic gridlock in summer. The beaches, overrun by sunseekers, lose much of their appeal. The city has also succumbed to haphazard development, especially on the outskirts (think ugly shopping malls and incongruous roundabouts), which has sullied some of its gloss. And there's no doubt that Porto-Vecchio is overpriced – accommodation and food cost more here than anywhere else in Corsica, bar Bonifacio, which plays in the same league. Some say it's overdeveloped and overhyped. Others argue that the area is worth every penny of the *très cher* entrance fee.

Whatever your verdict, Porto-Vecchio is a definite must-see. Try to come during

THE SOUTH

shoulder seasons if you can, when it reverts to a charming, relatively low-key coastal town. And if all that bling and bustle overwhelms, the authentic, rustic Alta Rocca is never far away.

HISTORY
In a bid to establish itself on the eastern coast of the island, Genoa set its sights on Porto-Vecchio in the 15th century. The Genoese settled on the heights over the bay, where they created what is now called the *haute ville* (upper town), which they fortified with thick ramparts. The settlers were soon decimated by malaria, then prevalent along the coast.

Porto-Vecchio was essentially abandoned before re-emerging in 1564, when Sampiero Corso chose it as a base for his renewed efforts to liberate the island. The town was besieged and forced to capitulate a few months later. It did not really begin to thrive until the malaria-infested swamps around it were transformed into salt marshes. With the health hazard removed, the town blossomed.

ORIENTATION
Porto-Vecchio is quite spread out and divided into two parts. There is the *haute ville* with its little streets and the ruins of the citadel, and below this the more modern harbour, which stretches along av Georges Pompidou.

INFORMATION
Clinique de L'Ospédale (☎ 04 95 73 80 03; rte de L'Ospédale) Has a 24-hour emergency medical service.
Cyberlink (rue Jean Jaurès; per hr €6; ☑ 9am-midnight Mon-Sat, 10.30am-midnight Sun)
LCL Crédit Lyonnais (☎ 04 95 26 82 80; rue du Général Leclerc; ☑ 8.30am-12.30pm & 1.30-5pm) Has an ATM.
Post office (☎ 04 95 70 95 00; rue du Général Leclerc) Has an ATM.
Tourist office (☎ 04 95 70 09 58; www.destination -sudcorse.com; rue Camille de Rocca Serra; ☑ 9am-8pm Mon-Sat, 9am-1pm Sun May-Sep, 9am-12.30pm & 2-6.30pm Mon-Fri, 9am-12.30pm Sat Oct-Apr)

SIGHTS & ACTIVITIES
There are still a few vestiges of the old Genoese citadel here, notably the **Porte Génoise** and the **Bastion de France** (closed to the public). The beautiful rue Borgo gives a glimpse of what the city was like in earlier days.

Although there is no beach by the town proper, some of the island's best, and most famous, beaches are close by (see p209).

Boat Trips
Various operators offer *promenades en mer* (boat excursions) to Îles Lavezzi (p201) and Bonifacio. The full-day excursion passes along the Réserve Naturelle des Îles Cerbicale and the beaches to the south of Porto-Vecchio, including Plage de Rondinara, before reaching Îles Lavezzi, Île Cavallo, Pointe de Spérone and Bonifacio (weather permitting). There is a stop for a swim in a lovely little cove. It costs €55/30 for adults/children and includes lunch.

The following operators have a booth at the marina.
Monte Cristo (☎ 04 95 72 01 04; www.croisieres-monte cristo.com in French; ☑ May-Sep)
Ruscana (☎ 04 95 70 33 67; www.amour-des-iles.com; ☑ May-Sep)
San Antonio – Maria Serena (☎ 04 95 72 04 95; www.promenadesanantonio.com in French; ☑ May-Sep)

Diving
The following outfits organise dive trips to Îles Cerbicale. See p80 for more details.
CIP La Palanquée (☎ 04 95 70 16 53, 06 07 49 46 04; www.cip-lapalanquee.com in French; rue du 9 Septembre 1943)
Plongée Nature (☎ 06 64 43 26 04, 06 19 26 26 51; www.plongee-nature.com; rte de L'Ancienne Douane)

SLEEPING
The nearest budget option is the *gîte d'étape* La Tonnelle, in Conca (see p76).

Hotels
Hôtel Holzer (☎ 04 95 70 05 93; www.corse-eternelle .com; rue Jean Jaurès; s €45-53, d €58-75, s/d with half-board Aug €100/195; ☑ Feb-Nov; P ⊠) Bang in the thick of things, the well-respected Holzer rightly prides itself on its high level of service and amenities. Its well-equipped rooms deliver good value for money, except in August. Just two grumbles: rooms are a tad compact and parking costs a whopping €10 per day.

Hôtel Panorama (☎ 04 95 70 07 96; fax 04 95 70 46 78; rue Jean Nicoli; d €50-70; ☑ Apr-Sep; P) A mere hop and a skip from the old town, this concrete lump isn't much to brag about but at least it's serviceable and tidy and has good views over the gulf. Rooms 9, 10 and 11 on the top floor (no lift), with exposed beams, are the cosiest. Bathroom-wise, don't ever think of gesticulating in the tiny cubicles. Cheaper rooms have shared bathrooms. Free parking.

Hôtel Da Mama (☎ 04 95 70 56 64; www.damama .com in French; rte de Bonifacio; d €52-88; ☑ Apr-Sep; P)

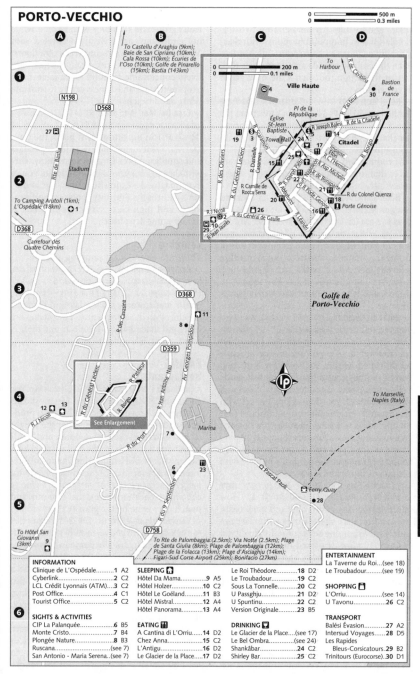

PORTO-VECCHIO

INFORMATION
Clinique de L'Ospédale........**1**	A2
Cyberlink........................**2**	C2
LCL Crédit Lyonnais (ATM)...**3**	C2
Post Office.......................**4**	C1
Tourist Office....................**5**	C2

SIGHTS & ACTIVITIES
CIP La Palanquée...............**6**	B5
Monte Cristo.....................**7**	B4
Plongée Nature..................**8**	B3
Ruscana........................(see 7)	
San Antonio - Maria Serena..(see 7)	

SLEEPING
Hôtel Da Mama..................**9**	A5
Hôtel Holzer....................**10**	C2
Hôtel Le Goéland...............**11**	B3
Hôtel Mistral...................**12**	A4
Hôtel Panorama.................**13**	A4

EATING
A Cantina di L'Orriu......**14**	D2
Chez Anna.....................**15**	C2
L'Antigu.......................**16**	D2
Le Glacier de la Place.....**17**	D2

Le Roi Théodore............**18**	D2
Le Troubadour...............**19**	D2
Sous La Tonnelle............**20**	C2
U Passghju....................**21**	D2
U Spuntinu....................**22**	C2
Version Originale...........**23**	B5

DRINKING
Le Glacier de la Place....(see 17)	
Le Bel Ombra..............(see 24)	
Shankâbar....................**24**	C2
Shirley Bar....................**25**	C2

ENTERTAINMENT
La Taverne du Roi...(see 18)	
Le Troubadour......(see 19)	

SHOPPING
L'Orriu....................(see 14)	
U Tavonu....................**26**	C2

TRANSPORT
Balési Évasion............**27**	A2
Intersud Voyages......**28**	D5
Les Rapides	
Bleus-Corsicatours.**29**	B2
Trinitours (Eurocorse).**30**	D1

For the price, this friendly, family-run place offers good value. An unassuming two-star hotel, it has well-appointed rooms with reassuringly deodorised bathrooms, all at prices even the cash-strapped can afford. It's a flick out of the action, but that's the only gripe. Free parking.

Hôtel Mistral (☎ 04 95 70 08 53; fax 04 95 70 51 60; rue Jean Nicoli; d €55-110; P 🔀) A coin's toss from the Panorama, this jolly good hotel wins no prizes for character but sports a façade dripping with bougainvillea and has well-equipped (if smallish) rooms with clean bathrooms. Some are nicer than others and have balconies, so ask to see a few. Rejoice: parking is free.

Hôtel San Giovanni (☎ 04 95 70 22 25; www.hotel -san-giovanni.com in French; rte d'Arca; s €55-65, with half-board Jul & Aug €88-98, d €60-75, with half-board Jul & Aug €125-145; 🕑 Mar-Nov; 🔀) The 1.25-hectare landscaped gardens are a visual treat, with lots of flowers, ponds and palm trees, not to mention a lovely pool. Added perks include bike hire, a Jacuzzi and a tennis court. The rooms are impeccable. It's on the southwestern outskirts of town.

Hôtel Le Goéland (☎ 04 95 70 14 15; www.hotel goeland.com; La Marine; d incl breakfast €75-105, with half-board Jun-Aug €135-260; 🕑 Apr-Oct; P) Talk about schizophrenic, this venture on the beach is all dolled-up with a stylish lobby and crisp rooms on the ground floor (think soft sandy yellow and pastel tones, terracotta floors and dark furniture), but then drops the act with its instantly forgettable rooms upstairs (but an upgrading was scheduled when we passed by). Just as you've abandoned hope, you plop into a sun-lounger and forget the hardships in the well-manicured garden complete with oleanders, pines and eucalypts.

E Casette (Map p210; ☎ 04 95 70 13 66; www.casette .com; rte de Palombaggia; d €150-650; 🔀 🖳 🏊) How 'suite' it is to stay at this chic and quiet oasis, the kind of place that dazzles with class not glitz. Offering a fine sense of individuality, it features 10 villas scattered in a lush garden. They boast all mod cons and are decorated with an eye for detail. The hotel's ultimate trump card, though, is its nifty swimming pool, with glorious views over the gulf. For wooers wanting their loved ones to say 'yes', this could be the place!

Grand Hôtel de Cala Rossa (Map p210; ☎ 04 95 71 61 51; www.hotel-calarossa.com; Cala Rossa; d with half-board €260-980; 🕑 Apr-Jan; 🔀 🖳 🏊) Situated 6km north of Porto-Vecchio, this upmarket establishment is part of the Relais & Chateaux group. Its 48 rooms with terrace, while not enormous, are stylishly decorated with Mediterranean colours and terracotta floors, whitewashed walls and ethnic furnishings. Every conceivable amenity is available, from a top-notch spa-and-fitness centre to a private white-sand beach.

Casa Del Mar (Map p210; ☎ 04 95 72 34 34; www .casadelmar.fr; rte de Palombaggia; d €350-900; 🕑 Apr-Oct; 🔀 🖳 🏊) So hip and ritzy it hurts, the Casa Del Mar is the secret hideaway for superstars and squillionnaires (not so secret now, eh?) with the most luxurious interior design you've ever imagined – exquisite furnishings, indulgent bathrooms, 'infinity' pool, magnificent views and high-class service proliferate. A dream-come-true hotel.

Camping

There are several local camping grounds.

Camping Arutoli (☎ 04 95 70 12 73; www.arutoli.com; rte de L'Ospédale; camp sites per adult/tent/car €6.50/3.50/3.50; 🕑 Apr-Oct; P 🔀 🖳 🏊) This three-star place, on the road towards L'Ospédale and Zonza, is the closest to the town centre. The pitches are quiet and shaded, the site is clean, and there is a restaurant, a laundrette and a pool.

EATING
Restaurants

A Cantina di L'Orriu (☎ 04 95 70 26 21; cours Napoléon; mains €5-19; 🕑 May-Sep) First and foremost, this is a treasure-trove of regional Corsican products, with shelves groaning under the weight of bottles and packets of goodies, and hams hanging enticingly from the ceiling (see p208). Better still, it has a tempting menu of bite-sized dishes (from €5), such as *assiette du berger* (cheese platter) or *gâteau à la farine de châtaigne* (chestnut cake), that you mix and match over wine by the glass (€3).

Version Originale (☎ 04 95 70 38 75; marina; mains €6-13; 🕑 Apr-Oct) Inventive, mouth-watering salads are the name of the game in this kooky den right by the harbour. They are all named after film stars and directors. Will it be a Merryl Streep or a Marlon Brando? It also churns out crispy paninis. With its brightly coloured chairs, steel tables and wooden deck, it's almost trendy.

U Spuntinu (☎ 04 95 72 28 33; place de la République; mains €12-15; 🕑 Apr-Oct) We found the prices inflated and the servings fairly skimpy, at least by Corsican standards. But the tough-to-beat location, right in front of the church St-Jean Baptiste, the cute terrace, complete with dark wooden tables and fine cutlery, and the well-presented dishes – salads, omelettes, charcuterie – call for magnanimity.

Sous La Tonnelle (☎ 04 95 70 02 17; rue Abbatucci; mains €12-25, menu €25; closed Sun & Mon in low season) It would be easy to stride past this cosy little eatery, but that would be one of life's sad mistakes. Consistently rated as one of the old town's best restaurants, it offers a fine selection of fish and meat dishes served in a narrow interior or on a vine-clad pavement terrace. We'll be back.

U Passaghju (☎ 04 95 20 15 66; rue du Colonel Quenza; mains €14-23; Apr-Nov) This discreet number offers a mix of traditional dishes with a creative twist. The chequered tablecloths and tiny vaulted room upstairs set the tone for, say, some *blinis de châtaignes au saumon fumé* (chestnut-flour pancakes with smoked salmon) or a *filet de bœuf aux gambas et bananes* (beef tenderloin with prawns and bananas).

Chez Anna (☎ 04 95 70 19 97; rue Camille de Rocca Serra; mains €15-19; dinner Mar–mid-Oct) This bright, straightforward trattorialike venue specialises in pasta. It does a good job: even the most demanding pasta cognoscenti give this spot the thumbs up. Overlook ravioli in favour of the lip-smacking *dollari* (pasta cooked with cream, parmesan cheese and meat), the restaurant's signature dish for more than two decades.

Le Roi Théodore (☎ 04 95 70 47 98; Porte Génoise; mains €15-24, menus €38-73) Expensive and elegant, the much-lauded Le Roi Théodore is one of Porto-Vecchio's top restaurants. Tucked away in the Porte Génoise, it provides a memorable dining experience with unobtrusive service and fabulous food. Those feeling particularly capricious might go for the *tartine de loup à la tapenade* (sea bass with a purée of olives). Needless to say the accompanying wine list is top class.

L'Auberg'in (Map p210; ☎ 04 95 72 21 07; rte de Palombaggia; mains €16-20; Jun-Sep) If you think the time has come to give your tastebuds something new to sing about, this is the place. This auberge is set in a lovingly restored *bergerie*, about 300m off the road to Palombaggia (follow the signs). Sit down at a low round table amid cushions for an array of *tajines* (try the vegetable one at €15), expertly cooked by the affable Hajiba, in a strange-looking ceramic bowl and funnel. Stone walls and warm colours create a tranquil and cosy atmosphere. Feeling conservative? Traditional Corsican dishes also feature on the menu. Don't forget to finish with a refreshing mint tea, made the Moroccan way with lots of leaves and sugar. A nice crosscultural change.

L'Antigu (☎ 04 95 70 39 33; rue Borgo; mains €17-22, menus €18-22) The sun drenches the rooftop terrace overlooking the gulf while you sink your teeth into a juicy *grillade* (grilled meat dish) or a succulent *pastilla de filets de rougets* (red mullet fillet terrine).

Le Troubadour (☎ 04 95 70 08 62; rue du Général Leclerc; mains €20-26, menu €29; Mon-Sat) Le Troubadour has a rustic feel with wood floors, low ceilings and lots of elbow room. The menu majors in fish and meat renditions of Corsican staples that sing in the mouth.

Quick Eats

Le Glacier de la Place (☎ 04 95 70 21 42; place de la République) Yes, you can stumble across excellent ice cream in Porto-Vecchio. Creamy chocolate and wavy banana…and myriad other flavours scream 'try me' from behind the glass in this buzzing bar and ice-cream parlour, smack dab in the centre. You can take away your plunder or grab a seat on the terrace while watching the world strutting by.

DRINKING & ENTERTAINMENT

Shirley Bar (☎ 04 95 71 27 59; rue Joseph Pietri) It's Hawaii forever in this funky little bar in a lane behind the church with an eccentric, Day-Glow tiki décor and killer cocktails. It's a gay-friendly place that draws an up-for-it young crowd to its tiny terrace. It also serves up exotic salads and tasty snacks throughout the day.

Le Glacier de la Place (☎ 04 95 70 21 42; place de la République) This long-standing institution serves the best and most wonderful hot choc in the history of time (from €2). It also boasts the largest selection of beers (180 varieties), liqueurs and spirits available on the island.

La Taverne du Roi (☎ 04 95 70 41 31; Porte Génoise) Most nights this intimate, inviting place features traditional Corsican singing with guitar accompaniment. The show starts at 9pm and costs €10.

Le Troubadour (☎ 04 95 70 08 62; rue du Général Leclerc) If Corsican singing is not your thing, this renowned restaurant features jazz sessions at weekends. A cool venue.

THE SOUTH

Shankâbar (☎ 04 95 70 06 53; place de la République) This colourful and imaginative bar is typically what the French call an *'avant-boîte'* (pre-club bar). Very popular and hip.

Le Bel Ombra (☎ 04 95 70 52 21; place de l'Église) In a similar vein to the adjoining Shankâbar, this busy bar becomes a popular stop-off for the preclubbing crowd in summer. It has a wide terrace from which to nurse a beer and watch life on the square go by.

Via Notte (Map p210; ☎ 04 95 72 02 12; www.vianotte .com; rte de Porra; ◷ Jun-Sep) *The* hottest club in Corsica. In summer nimble DJs get your heart pumping with eclectic tunes – pop, electro, funk etc. With more than 3000 revellers each night in summer, it's a place to party, not to whisper sweet nothings into your sweetheart's ear. It's in the open air and there's even a swimming pool. On the road out of Porto-Vecchio in the direction of Bonifacio.

SHOPPING

L'Orriu (☎ 04 95 70 26 21; cours Napoléon; ◷ May-Sep) This Porto-Vecchio favourite is fragrant with hams hanging from the ceiling, cheeses sitting on the shelves amidst wines, jams and terrines.

Another place to check out is **U Tavonu** (☎ 04 95 72 14 03; rue du Général de Gaulle).

GETTING THERE & AWAY
Air

Figari-Sud Corse airport is about 25km from Porto-Vecchio. For details see p264.

Boat

SNCM (www.sncm.fr) runs ferries from Marseille to Porto-Vecchio three times a week (up to four times a week in summer). In July and August, the Italian line **Medmar** (www.medmar group.it in Italian) connects Porto-Vecchio with Naples (Italy) via Palau (Sardinia) on a once-weekly basis.

You can purchase tickets from **Intersud Voyages** (☎ 04 95 70 06 03; quai Pascal Paoli; ◷ 8.45-11.45am & 2.30-6pm Mon-Sat). For more information on ferry crossings, see the Transport chapter (p267).

Bus

Les Rapides Bleus–Corsicatours (☎ 04 95 70 10 36; rue Jean Jaurès) operates a service twice a day (daily except Sunday and public holidays in winter) to Bastia via Solenzara, Ghisonaccia, Aléria and Moriani (€19, three hours). It also operates a shuttle service to Plage de Palom-

baggia and Plage de Santa Giulia in summer (€7 return, four shuttles daily).

Balési Évasion (☎ 04 95 70 15 55; rte de Bastia) has buses to Ajaccio via the Alta Rocca (L'Ospédale, Zonza, Bavella, Aullène). Buses depart daily in July and August, and on Monday and Friday only in winter (€20 to Ajaccio, €7 to Zonza).

Eurocorse operates a service to Ajaccio (€21, 3½ hours) via Sartène and Propriano. In summer there are four departures daily Monday to Saturday (two on Sunday and public holidays). There are also two departures daily in winter. In the other direction, buses run twice daily to Bonifacio (€7, 30 minutes). You can purchase tickets from **Trinitours** (☎ 04 95 71 24 64; rue Pasteur) or directly on the bus. Buses depart from in front of the office.

GETTING AROUND
To/From the Airport

Transports Rossi (☎ 04 95 71 00 11) operates a shuttle service between Figari-Sud Corse airport and Porto-Vecchio (€9, 30 minutes, five daily services) in July and August.

For a taxi, allow about €45.

NORTH OF PORTO-VECCHIO

To the north, the coast (Map p210) has plenty to set your camera's flash popping: it is liberally sprinkled with perfect coves and grandiose bays, studded with heart-palpitatingly gorgeous beaches.

Take the N198 to the north (direction Bastia). After a few kilometres, turn east onto the D468 towards the beaches at **Cala Rossa** and **Baie de San Ciprianu**. Further to the north is the stunning **Golfe de Pinarello** (Pinaraddu) with its Genoese tower and yet more beautiful stretches of sand.

SIGHTS & ACTIVITIES

If playing at sardines on the strand is not your thing, try horse riding with **Écuries de l'Oso** (☎ 04 95 70 69 81; rte de San Cipri_anu), on the road to Baie de San Cipriu. It offers guided excursions on the nearby beaches (from €18 per hour) and, for kiddies, pony rides in the maquis (€8 for 30 minutes).

The **École de Voile San Ciprianu** (☎ 04 95 71 00 48, 06 14 67 91 55; Plage de San Cipriani), 10km north of

Porto-Vecchio right on San Ciprianu beach, is an excellent place for all water sports, including windsurfing, sailing and kayaking. You can rent windsurfing equipment (€14 per hour, €18 for a funboard), catamarans (from €17), kayaks (€10 per hour) and pedal boats (€15). If you're reasonably fit, it's easy to paddle up to Golfe de Pinarello. Private and group sailing and windsurfing lessons are also available.

For some cultural sustenance, make a beeline for the prehistoric site of **Castellu d'Araghju**, about 3km off the N198, to the west, high in the hills. It is less visited than the sites of Cucuruzzu and Capula (see p215), but it is better preserved. It takes about 25 minutes to get up there from the village of Araghju. Climb to the top of the thick walls for a magnificent view over the Golfe de Porto-Vecchio and the mountains. Admission is free.

SLEEPING & EATING

Motel des Amandiers (Map p210; ☎ 04 95 71 43 64; Pinarello; d €40-56; ☺ May-Sep) If you love the überchic Hôtel Le Pinarello but can't afford it, the Motel des Amandiers is more than an acceptable fallback, with seven adjoining rooms set in verdant surroundings, behind Le Rouf restaurant.

Hôtel Le Pinarello (Map p210; ☎ 04 95 71 44 39; www.lepinarello.com; Pinarello; d €242-400, ste €380-590; ☺ mid-Apr–Oct) Take an ageing hotel, gut it, apply vision and money and end up with a modern-design abode for fashion-forward travellers without a trust fund. It didn't take long to make its mark, and for three good reasons: location, service and design. Rooms have all been stylishly decorated with rich designer fabrics and are coordinated in cooling creams and earthy hues, and the views over the sea are unforgettable.

37°2 (Map p210; ☎ 04 95 71 70 24; Plage de Cala Rossa; mains €7-20; ☺ May-Sep) A thong's throw from the Ranch'o, this *paillotte* (beach restaurant) is a casual hang-out with a light satisfying menu.

Ranch'o Plage (Map p210; ☎ 04 95 71 62 67; Plage de Cala Rossa; mains €15-26, menus €24-32; ☺ May-Sep) This upmarket *paillotte* occupies a privileged spot on the beach – if the wooden terrace was any nearer the water you'd have to swim to dinner. It has a long and steady good reputation for fresh seafood, particularly lobster, *chapon* (scorpion fish) and *daurade* (sea bream). Finish with the dreamy *carpaccio d'ananas frais*,

glace au brocciu (sliced pineapple with *brocciu*-flavoured ice cream).

Le Rouf (Map p210; ☎ 04 95 71 50 48; Pinarello; mains €16-29; ☺ May-Sep) Feast on ultrafresh *pêche du jour* (catch of the day, sold by weight) or drool over the *chapon rôti au four* (oven-baked scorpion fish) in this attractive restaurant overlooking the beach. The menu is limited, which is not necessarily a bad sign, and dishes are not too savagely priced.

SOUTH OF PORTO-VECCHIO

Wow! This is the Corsican paradise you've been daydreaming about: stylish accommodation, fragrant maquis, gin-clear waters, long stretches of sand edged with pine trees and splendiferous views over the **Îles Cerbicale**. Prepare yourself for soggy fingers and toes: here you'll probably spend as much time in the water as out of it. Alas, don't expect a Robinson Crusoe experience in summer – this area is chock-full of cars and sunseekers of all nationalities.

From Porto-Vecchio, follow the N198 to the south (Map p210) and turn left onto rte de Palombaggia (it's signposted), which winds around the coast and leads to the immense **Plage de Palombaggia**, one of the most iconic beaches in southern Corsica. South of Plage de Palombaggia, **Plage de la Folacca** (also known as Plage de Tamaricciu) is no less idyllic and claims one of the hippest beach restaurants in the area (see p210). Then **Plage d'Asciaghju**, which is also very popular for swimming and sunbathing, comes into view.

Continue a few kilometres further south over a pass called Bocca di L'Oru and you'll come across another gem of a beach, the gently curving **Plage de Santa Giulia**, lapped by shallow, azure waters and fringed by maquis.

ACTIVITIES
Diving
If just splashing around in turquoise waters ceases to do it for you, there are excellent diving options near the Îles Cerbicale (see p80), a short distance offshore from Plage de Palombaggia. Contact the following dive centres:

Aztech Marine (Map p210; ☎ 04 95 70 22 67; www .divecorsica.com; Plage de Santa Giulia)

THE SOUTH

AROUND PORTO-VECCHIO

SIGHTS & ACTIVITIES	
Aztech Marine......(see 2)	
Castellu d'Araghju...**1** A3	
Club Nautique Santa	
Marina..............**2** A5	
Dolfinu Biancu........**3** A4	
École de Voile de San	
Ciprianu.............**4** B3	
Écuries de l'Oso......**5** A3	
Hippocampe...........**6** B4	
Kallisté Plongée......**7** A4	
Locorsa................(see 2)	
Poney-Club A Staffa..**8** A4	

Grand Hôtel de Cala	
Rossa...............**12** B3	
Hôtel Le Pinarello..**13** B2	
Littaricia............**14** A4	
Motel des	
Amandiers......(see 18)	

EATING	
37°2...............**15** B3	
Costa Marina.......**16** A4	
L'Auberg'in........**17** A4	
Le Rouf............**18** B2	
Ranch'o Plage....(see 15)	
Tamaricciu.........**19** A4	
U Santa Marina.....**20** A5	

SLEEPING	
Camping U Pirellu..**9** A4	
Casa Del Mar......**10** A4	
E Casette...........**11** A4	

ENTERTAINMENT	
Via Notte..........**21** A4	

Horse Riding

If horse riding is more to your liking, the **Poney-Club A Staffa** (Map p210; ☎ 06 16 56 73 60; http://astaffa.ifrance.com in French; rte de Palombaggia) offers initiation rides in the maquis (with superb vistas on the gulf of Porto-Vecchio). A guided ride costs about €20 per hour. The company's *pièce de résistance* is its 3½-hour (early) morning ride (€55) to Plage de Palombaggia – the thrill of cantering or galloping along the beach when it is deserted is truly unforgettable.

Water Sports

The Plage de Santa Giulia is a fantastic playground for windsurfing, sailing and kayaking, especially for beginners and children. **Club Nautique Santa Giulia** (Map p210; ☎ 04 95 70 58 62; www.club-nautique.fr in French; Plage de Santa Giulia; ⏰ May-Sep), right on the beach at Santa Giulia, offers surfboard (€15 per hour), funboard (€18 per hour) and catamaran (from €30) rentals as well as surfboard and sailing lessons. Kayaks are also available (from €10 per hour).

You can also hire a four-seater motor boat (6hp; no licence required) to explore at your leisure the coves and beaches that are inaccessible by road. Contact **Locorsa** (Map p210; ☎ 04 95 70 64 43; www.locorsa.com in French; Plage de Santa Giulia; ⏰ May-Sep). A full day's rental will set you back €110 in July and August (€80 in low season).

SLEEPING & EATING

Camping U Pirellu (Map p210; ☎ 04 95 70 23 44; www.u-pirellu.com; rte de Palombaggia; camp sites per adult/tent/car €8/3.50/3.50; ⏰ Apr-Oct; P ⏰) An excellent camping ground, with loads of amenities, including a supermarket, pizzeria, tennis court and a swimming pool. The nearest beach, Plage de Palombaggia, is 4km away.

Costa Marina (Map p210; ☎ 04 95 70 36 57; rte de Palombaggia; mains €8-20; ⏰ dinner Apr–mid-Oct) Brimming with good cheer, this hip eatery overlooking the coastal road features excellent grilled meat and fish dishes. Top marks go to the wooden furniture (not a plastic chair in sight) and the breezy terrace. Smart service too.

Tamaricciu (Map p210; ☎ 04 95 70 49 89; www.tamaricciu.com in French; rte de Palombaggia; mains €13-25; ⏰ May-Sep) Everyone goes ga-ga for this furiously fashionable *paillotte* awash with teak fittings and right on the beach. The point is to be seen here and in summer getting a table on the terrace can be a titanic struggle. And how about the food? Feast on well-presented

---

Dolfinu Biancu (Map p210; ☎ 04 95 72 01 33, 06 21 46 71 49; http://perso.wanadoo.fr/dolfinu.biancu; Plage de la Folacca) Also represented in Bonifacio.

Hippocampe (Map p210; ☎ 04 95 70 56 54; www.hippocampe.de in French; La Chiappa) Inside the nudist camp of La Chiappa, off the road to Plage de Palombaggia.

Kallisté Plongée (Map p210; ☎ 04 95 70 44 59, 06 09 84 91 51; www.corsicadiving.com in French; Plage de Palombaggia)

THE AUTHOR'S CHOICE

Littariccia (Map p210; ☎ 04 95 70 41 33; www.littariccia.com; rte de Palombaggia; d incl breakfast €55-180; ☒) Looking for a night at some place extra-special? This lovely *maison d'hôtes* just cries out to be visited. Set in the hills overlooking the Plage de Palombaggia, it offers a mix of comfort, style and ambience, with 10 tastefully decorated rooms – lovely tiles, rich fabrics, soothing colours, sparkling bathrooms. The *coup de grâce* is the pool, which looks like a photo shoot out of *Vogue*, and the small spa. Not all rooms come with a seaview, though. Littariccia would be a 'find' just on the strength of its character, but when you factor in the affordable rates, this luxurious B&B is a 'discovery'. Why move from here? Why, indeed.

---

fish dishes or tuck into a pizza served bubbling hot from the oven. Service is brisk and sparkles with brio.

U Santa Marina (Map p210; ☎ 04 95 70 45 00; Santa Giulia; mains €20-40, menus €37-85; ☒ Mar-Oct) This food temple has garnered high praise these last years. The young chef treats his demanding patrons to such culinary (and poetic) delights as *filet de Saint-Pierre rôti aux artichauts avec tranche de fenouil* (red scorpion fish roasted with artichokes and flavoured with fennel). For the full survey of his skills, order the *menu gastronomique* (€85). The setting is more classic than hip and the dining room looks onto the sea and a swimming-pool.

GETTING THERE & AWAY

Les Rapides Bleus–Corsicatour (see p208) operates a shuttle service to Plage de Palombaggia and Plage de Santa Giulia in summer (€7 return, four shuttles daily).

L'ALTA ROCCA

The Alta Rocca is pure magic. Like an addictive drug, once you've had a hit of its bountiful offerings you'll crave a hell of a lot more. At the south of the long dorsal spine that traverses the island, the Alta Rocca is a bewildering combination of spectacular scenery, dense, mixed evergreen-deciduous forests and granite villages strung over rocky ledges. Here you can really feel a sense of wilderness, a world away from the bling and bustle of the coast. And there's the *pièce de résistance*: the iconic Aiguilles de Bavella. These serrated rock towers form one of Corsica's most enduring images.

What about culture? The region musters up a handful of well-preserved megalithic remains that are must-sees for anyone with an interest in Corsica's ancient civilisations.

Outdoorsy types will also find plenty of options to let their adrenaline go wild, with hiking, canyoning, horse riding and climbing all readily available – an additional incentive to spend time in the area. If you're more inclined to ecotourism than mass tourism, this region will prove your Shangri-la.

Information

Grab some information and brochures at the **tourist office** (☎ 04 95 78 56 33; alta-rocca@wanadoo .fr; ☒ 8.30am-noon & 2-5.30pm Mon-Fri in summer) in Zonza. You can also check out the website www.alta-rocca.com (in French).

Drivers take note: petrol stations are scarce in the Alta Rocca. There's one in Aullène and one in Levie, but their opening hours are erratic. There's only one ATM, in San Gavinu di Carbini.

Getting There & Away

Alta Rocca Voyages – Ricci (☎ 04 95 78 86 30) Ajaccio–Zonza (€16, daily, three hours) via Levie, Ste-Lucie de Tallano, Sartène, Propriano and Olmeto. Also serves the Col de Bavella in July and August.

Balési Évasion (☎ 04 95 70 15 55) Ajaccio–Porto-Vecchio via Aullène, Serra di Scopamène, Sorbollano, Quenza, Zonza and L'Ospédale (daily in July and August; Mondays and Fridays the rest of the year). Also serves the Col de Bavella in July and August.

Eurocorse (☎ 04 95 51 08 19) Ajaccio–Zonza (€17.50, daily except Sunday) via Olmeto, Propriano, Sartène, Ste-Lucie de Tallano and Levie.

L'OSPÉDALE

Lucky L'Ospédale! The village itself has few charms of its own but it's blessed with a fabulous location with sweeping views over the Golfe de Porto-Vecchio, about 20km to the south via the winding D368. Its appeal lies also in its proximity to the **Forêt de L'Ospédale**, about 1km up from the village. This extensive forest comprises majestic laricio pines.

WALK TO PISCIA DI GALLO

If the heat and crowds of Porto-Vecchio get too much for you, escape to the cool, calm surroundings of the Forêt de L'Ospédale, 25km above town, where you can take a 90-minute walk to the Piscia di Gallo waterfall and back. The start of the walk, marked by a signpost, is near a couple of snack bars beside the D368, 1km on from the Barrage de L'Ospédale. It's an easy walk through pine forests and maquis.

A short way into the forest on the D368 from L'Ospédale, a road peels off left to the hamlet of **Cartalavonu**. There's excellent hiking in the area, including an easy walk on Sentier des Rochers (Rocks Path), also known as the Sentier des Tafoni. The path is marked and is mainly flat among the laricio pines and the *tafoni* (cavities) formed in the rocks by erosion. After about 30 minutes you come to a little grassy plain studded with rocks. The Mare a Mare Sud trail (p76) crosses here, too, and the view is breathtaking.

Feeling energetic? From the *refuge* (see right) you can tackle the spellbinding **Punta di a Vacca Morta** (1314m), a relatively easy two-hour hike. At the top the 360-degree view over the far south is truly sensational.

Back on the D368, continue north until you pass the pretty chocolate-box lake formed by the **Barrage de L'Ospédale**, a reservoir supplying Porto-Vecchio with water. Keep your eye out to the left of the road, from where, through a thin curtain of pine trees, you will come upon a most bizarre vista – a vast lunar landscape of scorched earth studded with the burnt remains of pine-tree trunks leading to a shimmering lake. Swimming is not allowed, but for a bracing dip, nothing can beat the **Piscia di Gallo waterfall** (above), about one kilometre further up. The trailhead leading to the waterfall is clearly signposted.

Why not see this beautiful forest from a Tarzan perspective? **Xtrem Sud** (☎ 04 95 72 12 31; www .xtremsud.com in French; Forêt de L'Ospédale; ☿ May–mid-Sep) has set up a wonderful Parc Aventure, just after the Barrage de L'Ospédale when you come from Porto-Vecchio. There are three levels of ability. For the little 'uns (from the age of three), there's a separate 'baby parc'. A slice of the action costs €22/12 for adults/children. The Parc Aventure also features a

lovely Via Ferrata circuit, which is included in the price.

Sleeping & Eating

Le Refuge (☎ 04 95 70 00 39; Cartalavonu; dm with half-board €35, d incl breakfast €65; ☿ Apr-Nov) This well-kept inn is nestled in the Forêt de L'Ospédale at the end of the hamlet of Cartalavonu. You are brilliantly placed for exploring the area and for climbing the Punta di a Vacca Morta. For budgeteers, there's a *gîte d'étape* with six-bed dorms, each with its own bathroom. If privacy is a priority, opt for the no-frills but OK doubles. The restaurant (mains €9 to €19, *menu* €49) focuses on Corsican staples, such as veal tripe and grilled pork.

Chambres d'Hôtes U Spitaghju (☎ 04 95 26 77 53, 06 12 51 01 25; L'Ospédale; d €65-75) A home away from home, this pert little B&B is run with care by Nad and Dom and occupies a lovingly restored stone house on the main drag. The three rooms are muted and tasteful, with crisp linen and glistening bathrooms. Warm hues enhance the sense of comfort. Curl up with a book in the cosy lounge or flake out in the flower garden at the back while soaking up the eye-boggling views over the Golfe de Porto-Vecchio.

U Funtanonu (☎ 04 95 70 47 11; L'Ospédale; mains €14-20, menu €20; ☿ May-Sep) On the main drag this unexpected gem of a place prepares delectable fare served in snug décor that mixes wooden furniture, beamed ceilings, exposed stone walls and more contemporary fixtures, such as elegant cutlery and virginal white tablecloths. It's fronted by a cute vine-covered pergola. If you have ever wondered what wild boar stews *ought* to taste like, try its *civet de sanglier* – delicious. Vegetarians will plump for the tart with *brocciu*. If you want to blow your tastebuds (and your arteries), save room for the *flanc à la farine de châtaigne* (chestnut-flour cake). A respectable wine list and exemplary service complete the perfect equation.

ZONZA
pop 1800

Relax, recuperate and pile on the pounds – there are some good restaurants, the accommodation options are surprisingly diverse and the town isn't bad either! Zonza, in fact, is a peach of a place; you can't help but be dazzled by the fabulous backdrop – the soaring Aiguilles de Bavella.

Sleeping
CHAMBRES D'HÔTES
Chambres d'Hôtes de Cavanello (☎ 04 95 78 66 82; www.locationzonza.com in French; hameau de Cavanello; d €65-85; ⓡ) Feel like rejuvenating mind and body? This is a pretty pocket of Corsica, rural and pleasing on the eyes: several hectares of meadows and forests insulate you from all but wildlife, and the whole place could scarcely be more peaceful. It features five well-proportioned, individually decorated rooms. Room 5 carries a nautical theme, with blue and white hues, while room 4 verges on the rosy; No 3 is suitable for families. There's also a lovely half moon–shaped pool, so you may be reluctant to leave this place of easy bliss, about 2km from Zonza.

HOTELS
L'Aiglon (☎ 04 95 78 67 79; www.aiglonhotel.com in French; d €51-71; ⓨ Apr-Oct) We're suckers for the retro charm that wraps around this inviting place. Madame Quilichini has gone to great lengths to create a gently stylish atmosphere, with fine fabrics, in checks and stripes, Empire-style furniture, colourful bedspreads and gentle feminine touches. There are only 10 rooms, which ensures intimacy. The cheaper rooms share bathrooms. The only downside is the lack of views.

L'Incudine (☎ 04 95 78 67 71; d €54, with half-board Aug €136; ⓨ Apr-Oct) This old pile of a mansion has regained its panache since Parsilia, the owner's daughter, has spiffed the place up and renovated it with an eye for detail. Guests slumber in gracious rooms that are decorated in plain, warm tones and furnished with elegant fixtures. If you don't want to budge by evening, there's an adjoining quality restaurant.

Hôtel Clair de Lune (☎ 04 95 78 56 79; www.hotel clairdelune.com in French; rte de Levie; d €55-76; ⓨ Apr-Oct; ⓧ) A good bet for picky travellers. What sets it apart are the lashings of vivid colours that grace the rooms and the communal areas, with an effective yellow-, green- and blue-tinged colour scheme that contrasts sharply with the more austere façade. Amenities are solid too and include telephone, TV and air-conditioning. Read, doze or scribble a postcard or two by the fireplace in the cosy lounge or on the sun-dappled veranda. Guests are entitled to a 10% discount on any activity at Corsica Madness (p217).

Le Mouflon d'Or (☎ 04 95 78 72 72; www.lemou flondor.com in French; rte de Levie; d €60; ⓟ ⓡ) There

are 24 fully equipped, capacious concrete-and-wood bungalows scattered around an extensive park, about 700m from the centre of town. Furnishings are not the latest but it's tidy and welcoming. The glacé cherry on the pretty cake is the heavenly 25-metre pool and the two tennis courts. It's quite spread out so you get a decent dose of privacy. From mid-July to the end of August, it's usually rented by the week (and on a nightly basis during the rest of the year), but it can also be rented by the night if there are vacancies – cross fingers.

Hôtel Le Tourisme (☎ 04 95 78 67 72; www.hoteldu tourisme.fr; rte de Quenza; d €90-150; ⓟ ⓧ ⓡ) From the outside it's a bit underwhelming, but inside, this discreet number has good surprises up its sleeves. The 20 rooms are bright, light-filled and attractive; be sure to ask for a valley-facing room and you'll start your day with a smile on your face. Breakfasts are served in an atmospheric veranda. The *pièce de résistance* is the spiffing pool (heated) with a teak deck at the back, which invites splashing about or daydreaming.

CAMPING
Camping La Rivière (☎ 04 95 78 66 33; camp sites per adult/tent/car €4/2.50/2.50; ⓨ May-Sep) Another camping ground with an enviable location, about 2km from Zonza on the road to Quenza.

Camping Municipal de Zonza (☎ 04 95 78 62 74; camp sites per adult/tent/car €5.50/2.50/2.50; ⓨ May-Sep) This place is a haven of tranquillity in the depths of the forest, 3km east of the village on the D368.

Eating
Auberge du Sanglier (☎ 04 95 78 67 18; mains €8-15, menus €10-20) Its best asset is the all-wood terrace with addictive views over the mountain ranges. Foodwise, it's a bit patchy and the portions are far from formidable.

Le Randonneur (☎ 04 95 78 69 97; mains €8-15) Don't expect new-fangled concoctions in this no-nonsense eatery, just the usual pizzas and grilled meats flawlessly cooked. Prices are very reasonable too. The terrace is generally throbbing with a gleeful crowd of walkers, day-trippers and locals.

Restaurant de l'Incudine (☎ 04 95 78 67 71; mains €14-20, menu €20; ⓨ Apr-Oct) Ease a belt hole at this elegant venture sporting colourwashed walls and a large fireplace, and feast on palate-blowing Corsican dishes, such as *souris*

THE SOUTH

d'agneau au romarin (lamb with rosemary) or *échine de cochon grillée au miel de Bavella* (pork loin with local honey). Do keep space for one of the delightful homemade desserts and sluice it all down with a glass of Patrimonio – the perfect salve after a long day's driving on twisty roads.

Restaurant de L'Aiglon (☎ 04 95 78 67 79; www .aiglonhotel.com in French; mains €14-28, menu €19; ☒ Apr-Oct) Style meets substance at this well-regarded eatery. The menu here has been thoughtfully and creatively designed and the food is well prepared. The *bergerie d'Asinau* platter, comprising goat's milk cheese, roasted veal and a homemade cake, all served on a wooden plate, is pure indulgence. The interior is delightfully timeless, with old books, pictures, sturdy tables, a fireplace and low ceilings. Same location as the L'Aiglon hotel.

Shopping

U Muntagnolu (☎ 04 95 78 54 10, 06 10 75 78 88; ☒ May–mid-Oct) A great place to stock up on fabulous and well-presented Corsican goodies, such as *canistrelli* (dry biscuits), cheese, charcuterie, local wines, homemade jams and liqueurs. If you can't distinguish between *prisuttu* and a *lonzu*, the owner, Cathy Santoni, is ready to help.

QUENZA
pop 220

Heaven! Like nearby Zonza (and most other villages in the Alta Rocca), Quenza has a truly photogenic setting. It's cradled by thickly wooded mountains and the Aiguilles de Bavella loom on the horizon. At an altitude of 813m, the air is intoxicatingly crisp. This little charmer is more discreet than Zonza and is popular with walkers and outdoorsy types.

Sleeping & Eating

Gîte Corse Odyssée (☎ 04 95 78 64 05; corseodyssee@ aol.com; dm/d with half-board €38/82; ☒ Apr-Sep) So soothing! A backpacker's bonanza, this *gîte d'étape* in a modern building on a forested site boasts a sensational location, about 1km from Quenza. Beds are in two- to seven-person dorms. Not your average *gîte*, rooms here are all individually decorated in warm tones (ochre, earth-red, yellow). The whole place is very neat, your hosts are very helpful and the cosy dining room is a good place to share your Corsican experiences. To top it off, meals are copious and wholesome.

Relais-Équestre Chez Pierrot (☎ /fax 04 95 78 63 21; Ghjallicu; dm with half-board €35, d incl breakfast €60) It's hard not to be impressed by the end-of-the-world feeling that emanates from this place, on Plateau de Ghjallicu, about 5km uphill from Quenza (it's signposted). This remote location does mean a multitude of stars in the night sky and quiet, quiet nights. Rest your head in one of the five fully equipped, well-kept rooms in a granite building or bunk down in a spartan dorm. The *table d'hôtes* (dinner €23) has an unwaveringly authentic menu, with *tripettes* (tripe), *haricots à la Corse* (Corsican beans), soups and charcuterie, all prepared by Pierrot, your affable host, and served in intimate surroundings.

Auberge Sole e Monti (☎ 04 95 78 62 53; www.sole monti.com; r per person with half-board €70-125; ☒ May-Sep) With its fairly unexciting modern exterior, this typical middling auberge won't set hearts aflutter, but inside, it features smart and fresh rooms, some with balcony (Nos 5 and 16 are the most enticing). The restaurant (mains €12 to €28, *menus* €15 to €36; closed Monday and Tuesday lunch) has won plaudits for its mouthwatering Corsican specialities, with an emphasis on grilled meat and stews (beef, lamb, veal and wild boar). Nab a seat on the vine-covered terrace or enjoy the rustic-style dining room complete with an imposing fireplace and pink tablecloths. At lunch, you can have your meal served in the lovely garden across the street.

Ferme-Auberge Funtana Bianca (☎ 04 95 78 52 84; Ghjallicu; mains €12-18; ☒ Jun-Sep) As of 2006, Pierrot is no longer alone on Plateau de Ghjallicu. This delightful *ferme-auberge* is about 500m further up from Chez Pierrot. What an amazing location! As the owners put it, you've reached *le bout du monde* (the end of the earth) here, at an altitude of 1298m. The agreeably rustic décor is easy on the eye, with exposed beams, sturdy furnishings and stone walls, as well as a superb terrace. Foodwise, the menu has a pronounced regional flavour, with charcuterie, pork chop, roasted veal, chestnut fritters and *fiadone* (flan made with *brocciu*, lemon and eggs).

AULLÈNE (AUDDÈ)
pop 150

'Auddè' means crossroads in Corsican. It's clear how the place got its name: a major gateway, it's at a crossroads of four major inland routes, including the wonderfully scenic

D420, which heads west towards Petreto-Bicchisano for about 20km (and on to Ajaccio or Propriano) via the **Col de St-Eustache** (995m), and the D69, which winds due north for 26km to Zicavo and the Haut Taravo (p177) via the **Col de la Vaccia** (1193m). Both routes offer sublime views and bob and weave through dramatic landscapes – some sections are reminiscent of the American Wild West.

You can rest your head at the **Auberge du Col de la Vaccia** (☎ 06 84 75 70 27, 06 72 55 54 05; Col de la Vaccia; d incl breakfast €55; ⏱ May–mid-Oct), which must rank as one of the most secluded lodgings in Corsica – if you're in search of peace and solitude, this is the place! The four rooms are fresh and airy, but only one room comes with a view. There is also a restaurant (mains €8 to €15, *menus* €20 to €30).

In Aullène, you can stay at the excellent **Chambre d'Hôtes San Laurenzu** (☎ 04 95 78 63 12, 06 60 11 11 99; rue de la Poste; d €55; ⏱ Apr–Oct), the only splash of colour (yellow, that is) on the main street. There are three welcoming rooms, with laminate floors and wood-panelled ceilings. The owner and cook, Mireille Chiaroni, works her magic at **Le Chalet** (☎ 04 95 74 24 83; rue de la Poste; mains €8-15, menus €18-22; ⏱ Apr–Oct), next door. Don't come here for elaborate food, just classic Corsican dishes (suckling pig, anyone?) grandma-style, prepared from simple fresh ingredients.

SERRA DI SCOPAMÈNE
pop 125

Another quiet yet typical Alta Rocca hill village, Serra di Scopamène affords lovely views over the Rizzanese Valley. Penny-counting visitors and hikers following the Mare a Mare Sud trail will find heaven at the **Gîte d'Étape** (☎ 04 95 78 64 90; dm with half-board €38; ⏱ Apr–Sep), blessed with terrific views over the valley. The dorms are as neat as a pin and can sleep six people. Meals are copious and the chicken with honey and myrtle is a winner. It's closed from 8.30am to 4pm.

For more privacy, head to the hamlet of Zerubia, about 2km from Serra di Scopamène, where you'll find the excellent **Chambres d'Hôtes U Rughjonu** (☎ 04 95 78 73 64, 06 85 33 44 88; d €50; ⏱ mid-Apr–mid-Oct), a haven of a B&B run by affable Madame Comiti. The five rooms are neat and cosy and the views terrific. A *table d'hôtes* is available (€20).

All horse lovers should make a beeline for **A Staffa Corsa** (☎ 04 95 27 05 36, 06 21 22 56 18; www

.astaffacorsa.com in French), in Serra di Scopamène. This well-regarded riding centre offers scenic trail rides in the Alta Rocca – the perfect way to soak up the atmosphere of the lovely countryside.

LEVIE (LIVIA)
pop 720

For culture vultures, Levie is a definite must-see. Expand your knowledge of Corsican history at the **Musée de l'Alta Rocca** (☎ 04 95 78 46 34; admission €3; ⏱ 9am-6pm daily mid-May–mid-Sep, 9am-noon & 1.30-5pm Tue-Sat mid-Sep–mid-May), which has been upgraded and modernised. The museum does a good job of explaining Corsican geology, climate, flora and fauna. It also features an ethnology and an archaeology section.

After a visit to the museum, it's time to go out in the field. From Levie, head to **Pianu di Levie** (☎ 04 95 78 48 21; adult/child €5.50/3; ⏱ 9am-6pm Apr, May & Oct, 9am-7pm Jun & Sep, 9am-8pm Jul & Aug), about 7km to the north (it's signposted). Here you can get a feel for what life was like in ancient times in Corsica. The area comprises two archaeological sites, **Cucuruzzu** and **Capula**, both featuring well-preserved megalithic remains. The Cucuruzzu site was discovered in 1963 and is an interesting example of Bronze Age monumental architecture. Set in a granite wilderness, the ruins indicate that this was the site of an organised community whose activities were originally based on agriculture and animal husbandry but then broadened during the later Bronze Age (1200 to 900 BC) to include milling, pottery and weaving. The Castellu de Capula is somewhat more recent, although it is likely that Cucuruzzu was still in business when it was founded; Capula, it is believed, continued to be inhabited into the Middle Ages. The admission price includes the use of an individual audioguide (in English).

Allow at least a good 1½ hours. Even if your interest in ruins is slight, the enchanting setting and the lofty views are reason enough to come here.

In the mood for horse riding? The respected **Ferme Équestre A Pignata** (☎ 06 03 99 16 33, 04 95 78 41 90; www.apignata.com; ⏱ Jul & Aug) offers fantastic rides (half-day €40) to rarely visited points around Pianu di Levie with stunning views.

Sleeping & Eating

Camping Municipal d'Ora (☎ 04 95 78 48 17; www .campingora.com in French; San Gavinu di Carbini; camp sites per adult/tent/car €3/2.50/2.50; ⏱ Jun-Sep) 'Here people sleep well', the warden told us. And it's easy to see why: there's a profusion of shade, with laricio pines en masse, the property is huge, and it's cool, even in summer.

Gîte d'Étape de Levie (☎ 04 95 78 46 41; dm with half-board €35; ☺ Apr-Oct) Not the most thrilling *gîte d'étape* in Corsica, this place is a bit bland but it's a convenient staging post if you're suffering from wallet stress. It's near the police station.

Ferme-Auberge A Pignata (☎ 04 95 78 41 90; www .apignata.com; rte du Pianu; d with half-board €63-69; ☺ Mar-Oct) Hidden in the foothills of the Alta Rocca, this place has a haunting but beautiful remoteness. The air is clean, the views suggestive, the peace tangible. The highlight is the restaurant (*menu* €33), with a gargantuan *menu* that you enjoy in a vast, rustic-style room with a huge fireplace. All ingredients come from the farm or the garden. In summer, the terrace has million-dollar views over the rolling hills of the Alta Rocca. By comparison the six rooms feel a tad impersonal.

Chambres d'Hôtes Aravina (☎ 04 95 72 21 63, 06 33 87 04 14; rte du Pianu; d €80) It's a haven of tranquillity here, utterly secluded off the road to the Pianu di Levie archaeological sites. Its newish owners have already worked wonders in transforming this traditional dwelling into a sweet B&B. Welcoming, character-laden rooms heal well-travelled bones. No two rooms are the same – some have exotic touches, some are furnished with antiques. There's also a *table d'hôtes* (set menu €25). Oh, and the craggy Aiguilles de Bavella loom on the horizon.

La Sorba (☎ 04 95 78 41 62; mains €7-17; ☺ Apr-Sep) The indoor dining room is as atmospheric as a dentist's waiting room but the leaf-dappled pergola is a great place to loll after a day's sightseeing. Nosh on melt-in-your-mouth pizzas or well-executed grilled meats, including *brochettes de bœuf* (skewered beef). If only desserts were a bit cheaper, life would be perfect.

Bar-Restaurant La Pergola (☎ 04 95 78 41 62; rue de Sorba; mains €8, menu €16; ☺ Apr-Oct) Levie's little secret debunks the myth that small towns don't have culinary delights. This place is a rustic, hanky-sized Corsican eatery where you can eat nudged up with the locals at the indoor tables (only four) or out on the microscopic terrace. The food is authentic and home-style.

Pâtisserie A Tasciana (☺ Mon-Sat) Try their girth-expanding *sciacce di patati*, which is a potato pie with melted cheese. On the main drag.

CARBINI

pop 100

From Levie, the D59 drops down to a valley – a sensational descent through the woods – before winding uphill to Carbini. This tiny village is well worth a detour for the splendid Romanesque **Église St-Jean Baptiste**. Next to the church, there's an imposing **bell tower**, too.

From Carbini, you can follow the D59 due south; after 24km, it rejoins the Porto-Vecchio–Bonifacio road.

STE-LUCIE DE TALLANO (SANTA LUCIA DI TALLA)

pop 400

Another contender for the title of the prettiest village in Alta Rocca, Ste-Lucie de Tallano is perched on a ledge above the Rizzanese Valley. With its web of quiet streets, its higgledy-piggledy stone houses with reddish-orange tiled roofs and the *pétanque* players who take centre stage on the main square, this immediately likable place couldn't be more *Corse profonde*.

After having guzzled a Pietra on the main square, mosey around the village and head to the **moulin à huile** (oil mill; adult/child €2/1; ☺ 9am-noon & 3-6pm Mon-Sat May-Oct), the village's premier sight. Ste-Lucie is famous for its quality olive oil, and this mill illustrates the importance of olive cultivation in the area. The **Église Ste-Lucie** is also worth a visit, as is the Renaissance-style **Couvent St-François**, an imposing building, at the edge of the village on the road to Levie.

Sleeping & Eating

Gîte d'Étape U Fragnonu (☎ 04 95 78 82 56; www .alta-roc.fr; dm with half-board €38; ☺ Apr-Oct) A far cry from your usual *gîte d'étape*, U Fragnonu occupies a converted oil mill about 300m from the main square. It's efficiently run by Palma and Carlos, who pride themselves on the clinical cleanliness of the four-bed dorms and the congenial communal areas. Meals are copious and tasty. Carlos is a canyoning and climbing guide and organises day trips to Bavella.

Chambres d'Hôtes Palazzo (☎ 04 95 78 82 40, 06 79 07 93 77; d €62; ☺ Apr-Oct) If you have a soft spot for romantic getaways, you need look no further – this place in a characterful town house has charm in spades. Curl up with your beloved in one of the three thoughtfully decorated rooms complete with period furniture, four-poster beds (in two rooms), ancient tiles and pastel-coloured walls. It's elegant without being pretentious – the overall style is best described as 'rustic chic'. Bask in the sunny garden with a glass of Corsican wine in hand. Warmly recommended.

Restaurant Santa Lucia (☎ 04 95 78 81 28; mains €12-14, menus €17-23; ⊙ Feb-Nov) Lip-smackingly fresh produce underpins a menu ranging from pizzas to meat dishes to a few lighter snack options. It's smack dab in the centre.

Chez Dumé (☎ 04 95 78 80 67; mains €6-15, menus €22-25; ⊙ May-Oct) Stuff yourself for minimal coinage at this no-nonsense eatery, about 100m from the main junction. The terrace is a good vantage point to watch the *pétanque* players on the square.

COL & AIGUILLES DE BAVELLA

Stop for a moment and say 'aaah!' The Aiguilles de Bavella (Bavella Needles), about 8km northeast of Zonza, is one of those dreamlike places that make you question whether something so visually overwhelming could actually exist – no less than that. These granite pinnacles, which jab the skyline at an altitude of more than 1600m, are best observed from the Col de Bavella (Bavella Pass; 1218m). The colour that ranges from ochre to golden as the day progresses will ignite the imagination of photographers. Behind these stone 'needles' looms the profile of Monte Incudine (2134m). From the col, you can drop down to Solenzara following the D268 – an astonishing 30km descent (see p234).

On the flipside, don't expect to have the whole place to yourself. Within easy reach from the coastal cities of the south, the Col de Bavella is a tourist magnet in season. Come in spring or early autumn to indulge your imagination a little; in summer you'll spend your time dodging fellow visitors and struggling for parking.

The Bavella area is also a magnet for outdoor enthusiasts. Walking, Parc Aventure, rock climbing, canyoning, eating, drinking... it can all be done in the vicinity of the col.

Activities
CANYONING

Of the stellar spots for canyoning in Corsica, the Bavella area tops the list, with two major canyons that draw adrenaline junkies like bees to a honey pot: Canyon de la Vacca and Canyon de la Purcaraccia. Both are very atmospheric; you can expect various jumps, leaps in natural pools (yeah!), rappelling and

tyrolean slides. But access to both canyons involves a preliminary 30- to 50-minute hike. The time spent in the canyon is about three hours. In total, the outing lasts about five hours, more if you take a picnic. There's also the Canyon de la Pulischella, which is easier and perfectly suitable for families (no jumps and no tyrolean slides). All canyoning outings are guided by a qualified instructor (see below). Plan on €55 per person.

ROCK CLIMBING

Blessed with supreme granite monoliths, sheer spires, near-vertical walls and fantastic scenery, the Bavella area has long been a climber's utopia, home to dozens of mind-boggling ascents, graded 3 to 8 (easy to difficult). For novices, there's also a *falaise-école* (a training cliff specially equipped for beginners).

PARC AVENTURE

In search of new sensations? Try **Bavellaventure** (☎ 06 13 22 95 06, 06 22 29 38 84; www.jpquilicimontagne .com in French; ⊙ mid-Jun–mid-Sep), about 2km from Col de Bavella (direction Zonza; look for the kiosk on the roadside). This Parc Aventure boasts a sensational setting, with the Aiguilles de Bavella forming a perfect backdrop, as well as the Golfe du Valinco to the west. It comprises three different circuits, of varying levels of difficulty. Yes, there are tyrolean slides, including a thrilling 110m-long one! Prices range from €15 to €25 per person.

HIKING

There are excellent hiking options in the vicinity of the Col de Bavella, with well-marked trails suitable for all levels of fitness. The most popular walk goes to the Trou de la Bombe, a hole in a ridge southeast of the col (about two hours return).

OPERATORS

The major operators, each able to arrange most activities, include the following:

Aqa-Canyon (☎ 06 20 61 76 81, 04 95 78 58 25; www .aqa-canyon.com; Levie) Canyoning.

Corse Odyssée (☎ 04 95 78 64 05; corseodyssee@aol .com; Quenza) Based in the *gîte d'étape* in Quenza (see p214). Canyoning.

Corsica Canyon (☎ 06 22 91 61 44; www.corsica -canyon.com)

Corsica Madness (☎ 06 13 22 95 06, 04 95 78 61 76; www.corsicamadness.com in French; Zonza) Canyoning. Also rents mountain bikes (€15 per day).

In Terra Corsa (☎ 04 95 47 69 48; www.interracorsa.fr in French; Ponte Leccia) Canyoning, rock climbing, hiking.
Jean-Paul Quilici (☎ 04 95 78 64 33, 06 16 41 18 53; www.jpquilicimontagne.com in French) Canyoning, rock climbing, hiking.
Olivier Chapon-Seigneur (☎ 06 12 41 19 74; ocha ponghm@free.fr) Canyoning.
Xtrem Sud (☎ 04 95 72 12 31; www.xtremsud.com in French; Forêt de L'Ospédale) Canyoning.

Sleeping & Eating

Les Aiguilles de Bavella (☎ 04 95 72 01 88; mains €8-15, menus €15-21) The indoor dining room doesn't contain a whit of soul or character but there's outdoor seating and the food has more zest than the décor – think hearty meat dishes, pancakes and salads. The whopping pork chop with Bavella honey will really satisfy a post-walk hunger. The *gîte* has itty-bitty four-bed dorms (€15, with half-board €30), but it's reasonably clean and provides a great opportunity to meet like-minded travellers.

Auberge du Col de Bavella (☎ 04 95 72 09 87; www .auberge-bavella.com in French; mains €9-17, menus €16-22; ☽ Apr-Oct) In summer this inn gets positively packed to the rafters with a mixed bag of customers (aaargh, coach parties). Regardless of this, the food doesn't disappoint, with an emphasis on traditional Corsican fare (goat kid meat, veal cutlet with honey) as well as copious salads and pasta. The *gîte* is fairly basic, with six-bunk dorms (€15, with half-board €32).

Le Refuge (☎ 04 95 72 08 84; mains €9-15, menus €15-20; ☽ May-Sep) If you're after a cheap and filling meal, you could do worse than sample the salads, pizzas and meat dishes served at this simple yet snug inn.

The East

Eastern Corsica isn't as well travelled as its western counterpart and tourists tend to ignore it en route to more *soi-disant* magnetic destinations. It's a shame (or a blessing, depending on your perspective), as there's plenty to capture the imagination. Sure, the coastal plains that stretch from Bastia to Solenzara can seem numbingly monotonous to some, with a series of toy-town-like beach developments, but it's definitely not to be sneezed at. There are cities that are steeped in history, such as Aléria, a former Roman capital, and miles of beach-luscious coastline.

And the coastal plains are the best launching pad for exploring the mystifying hinterlands: the Morianincu, the Casinca, the Fiumorbu and the Castagniccia. Anyone wanting to get an intimate peek at a more traditional Corsica should visit these dauntingly beautiful microregions where the landscapes remain largely untouched and the people unaffected by the trappings of a fast lifestyle. In the countless valleys and spurs that slice up the spectacular scenery are discreet hamlets that retain a rough-diamond rural edge. This land is crisscrossed with tortuous roads that snake around mountain ridges, dramatically descending into thickly forested chestnut valleys and offering soul-stirring views. If that's not enough, there are always epicurean indulgences: a robust cuisine scene and attractive *chambres d'hôtes*, all amazingly low-priced.

HIGHLIGHTS

▪ **Playing Indiana Jones**
  Pump the adrenaline on the Via Ferrata A Buccarona or
  Corsica Forest Parc Aventure (p234)

▪ **Oysters & Mussels**
  Feast on fresh seafood at Étang de Diane (p229) or
  Étang d'Urbino (p231)

▪ **Cooling Off**
  Lounge on Solenzara's beaches (p232) or in the gin-clear
  waters of the Solenzara River (p234)

▪ **Experiencing the Past**
  Peek behind the Paoli legend at La Maison Natale de
  Pascal Paoli (p227) in Morosaglia

▪ **Rally Roads**
  Clunk your safety belt and bounce around the
  mountain roads in the Morianincu (p222) or
  the Rustinu (p227)

▪ **Geddy Up!**
  Explore the mysterious Castagniccia on horseback
  (p225) or gallop along a deserted beach by moonlight (p232)

▪ **Corse Profonde**
  Take a drive through the villages of little-known Fiumorbu (p231) or drive up to end-of-the-world Chisà (p233) in the Vallée du Travo

Le Rustinu ★
Morosaglia ★ ★ La Castagniccia
★ Le Morianincu

★ Étang de Diane
Le Fiumorbu ★ ★ Étang d'Urbino
★ Chisà
Solenzara River, ★
Via Ferrata A Buccarona &
Corsica Forest Parc Aventure ★ Solenzara

THE EAST

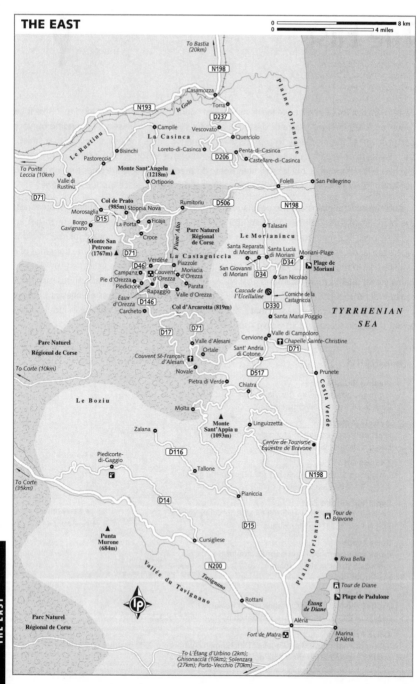

THE EAST

LA CASINCA

Never heard of this *micro-région*? You may be forgiven, because this must be one of the least travelled areas on the island – a blessing if you want to get away on your own. Falling between the Golo River to the north and the Castagniccia to the south, the Casinca is a remarkably well-kept secret, less than an hour's drive from Bastia. It comprises a necklace of tiny, hillside villages set among forests of chestnut and olive trees, with tall stone houses looking out over the eastern plains. Time seems to have stood still in this part of the island. There are no primary roads, only secondary roads that creep through beguiling settlements, offering gratifying scenic drives and smashing views over the plains and the Tyrrhenian sea. A good road map is essential – the IGN *Bastia Corte* (1:100 000) is fine.

Heading west along the D237 from Torra, the road climbs steeply to hilltop **Vescovato**. Formerly a fortified town, it was the site of the bishop's palace in the 15th century. With its little alleyways, its flights of steps, its lively central square shaded by a row of plane trees and its modest but authentic cafés, Vescovato has charm in spades. Be sure to have a look at the Baroque **church of San Martino**, built on a small terrace. A further 3km will bring you to **Venzolasca**, another picturesque village where you can marvel at the Baroque **church Ste-Lucie**, whose slender spire is a major landmark for miles around.

It's hard not to fall under the spell of **Loreto-di-Casinca**, another village featuring a dramatic setting on ridge overlooking the whole area. Aside from the superlative views over the plain and the sea, the focal point of the village is the lovely square surrounded by plane trees.

Backtrack to Venzolasca then head to **Penta-di-Casinca**, with another superb Baroque church and stunning schist buildings. From Penta-di-Casinca the D206 will lead you down to the N198 in the plain via **Castellare-di-Casinca**, which has a beautiful 10th-century church, **San Pancrazio**, famous for its triple apse.

Sleeping

Chambres d'Hôtes A Stella Serena (☎ /fax 04 95 36 65 29; Torra; d €50) A make-yourself-at-home informality is the order of the day at this quirky B&B situated about 300m off the Torra roundabout. Jacques and Sharon, a French-American couple, are very knowledgeable about the area and have decorated their house with books, woodcarvings, hats and other knick-knacks. There are three compact rooms with a shared bathroom and a shady patio terrace. It's definitely more convivial than intimate, but at this price we're not complaining. Call ahead for a pick-up from Casamozza train station.

Chambres d'Hôtes Domaine de Valle (☎ 04 95 38 93 03; domaine.valle@wanadoo.fr; Querciolo; d €60) Though recently built, this handsome house is not bereft of charm. It is nestled in a vast property replete with olive and clementine trees. The four rooms are impeccable and come equipped with ancient tiles and pristine bathrooms. The amiable owners sell some excellent homemade olive oil. Location-wise, it's in Querciolo, about 100m from the N198 (but there's no noise to speak of), and the nearest beach is 4km away.

Eating

L'Ortu (☎ 04 95 36 64 69; rte de Venzolasca, Vescovato; mains €7-17, menu €18; ✷ Wed-Sun Jun-Sep; **V**) Did you know? L'Ortu is a self-proclaimed altar to *'bio-végétarienne'* (organic-vegetarian) cuisine. Carrots, cheese, pancakes with tofu, spaghetti and other goodies rule the roost, including veal cutlet. With its all-wood, barnlike surrounds, this offbeat auberge resembling a Swiss chalet boasts a kind of ramshackle charm. Bookings are essential.

Chez Mathieu (☎ 04 95 36 53 76; Venzolasca beach; mains €9-20; ✷ May-Sep) Corsica's got dozens of *paillottes* (beach restaurants), what's so special about this one on Venzolasca beach? The *loup grillé* (grilled sea bream), my friends, the *loup grillé* (€15). Well-executed pizzas, salads and meat dishes are also available.

U Rataghju (☎ 04 95 36 30 66; Loreto di Casinca; menu €23; ✷ Apr-Oct) This place screams Corsica of yore. The dining room occupies an ancient chestnut drier and is endearingly old-fashioned, with sturdy tables, beamed ceilings, antique furniture and granite walls adorned with weapons, ancient tools and various artefacts. Food-wise, expect hearty Corsican dishes such as charcuterie, cornucopian stews and *beignets au brocciu* (*brocciu* fritters). There's a second dining room across the street, which is less characterful but offers smashing views over the plains.

Ferme-Auberge U Fragnu (☎ 04 95 36 62 33; Venzolasca; menu €37; ✷ dinner Jul & Aug, dinner Thu-Sat,

THE EAST

lunch Sun Sep & mid-Nov–Jun) This reputable *ferme-auberge* scores high on atmosphere and décor. But is it worth the trek? Hell yes. The snug, traditional dining room that is built around a huge olive press is a delicious relic from another era. It focuses on traditional Corsican fare: a thick soup, veal with olives, charcuterie, cheese and – you guessed it – chestnut-flour cake. Bring an empty tum, since you'll leave belly first. Bookings are mandatory.

LA COSTA VERDE

The Costa Verde has lopsided charm, which can be attributed to its schizoid nature. While the coastal section of this microregion is nothing to write home about, the hinterland is dizzyingly beautiful, with stupendous landscapes, a collection of *villages perchés* strung over mountain ridges and a fistful of religious buildings steeped in history. Although it's less than half an hour's drive from Bastia, this unknown corner of Corsica falls below many travellers' radars (we're not complaining). Another pull is the smattering of well-priced hotels, quality restaurants and cute *chambres d'hôtes*. Bring a good map – now it's your turn to dive in.

Information

The **Costa Verde tourist office** (☎ 04 95 38 41 73; www .otcostaverde.com; N198, Moriani-Plage; ☉ 9am-8pm in high season), on the main drag in Moriani-Plage, is a fountain of useful information on the area.

You'll find ATMs in Moriani-Plage.

Getting There & Away

Buses plying the route Bastia–Porto-Vecchio stop in Moriani-Plage (see p208). The Bastia–Moriani-Plage ride costs €7.

MORIANI-PLAGE

About 40km south of Bastia, this rather non-descript resort town will probably be your first glimpse of the Costa Verde. It consists of modern buildings, souvenir shops, super-markets and cafés that are scattered along the N198. Although it won't set a heart aflutter, Moriani-Plage has decent beaches if you want to splash about and offers useful services, including a tourist office and banks with ATMs. It's also the most obvious launching pad for exploring the Morianincu. Ah, the Morianincu…

Sleeping & Eating

Merendella (☎ 04 95 38 53 47; www.merendella.com; Moriani-Plage; camp sites per adult/car/tent €7.50/3/3; ☉ mid-May–Sep) This is by far the best camping ground for miles around, with lots of ameni-ties and a spiffing location, in a vast park right by the beach. Lots of shade, too.

Casa Corsa – Chambres d'Hôtes Doumens (☎ /fax 04 95 38 01 40, 06 25 89 89 32; www.casa-corsa.net; Casa Corsa, Acqua Nera Prunete; d €56-62) What a find! This ochre-coloured modern house has a stylish Provençal feel. The six cocoon-like rooms are embellished with lots of decorative touches, such as terracotta tiles, chestnut beams, col-ourwashed walls and colourful bedspreads. There's a lovely garden where you can mooch around. Breakfasts are copious and are served under a lovely vine-covered pergola. Should you want to take a dip, the Prunete beach is a five minutes' jog away. If only the Doumens could speak a few words of English! It's 6km south of Moriani-Plage, about 100m off the N198, accessible via a dirt track.

U Lampione (☎ 04 95 59 08 87; rte du Village, Moriani-Plage; mains €15-22, menu €18; ☉ closed Sun in low season) One of Moriani's best eating options, U Lam-pione has an attractive, vine-shaded terrace and a stylish dining room with wood furnish-ings; both provide the perfect setting in which to sample well-prepared meat and fish dishes. Try the *escalope* or *filet de bœuf* (beef scallop or fillet) – very tender. You can celebrate your good fortune at being here by ordering a bot-tle of local wine (from €15). No, it's not on the beach – it's on the road to San Nicolao, about 400m from the main crossroads.

LE MORIANINCU

In the mood for a green realm, a land of lush-ness, of verdant forests and muscular hills? The Morianincu offers all this, plus a won-derfully laid-back atmosphere. This micro-region might be a mere blip on the map, but it has bags of character and aesthetic appeal. It is studded with a succession of villages that crown the curving hills west of Moriani-Plage. Their austere façades and higgledy-piggledy schist rooftops and bell towers preside over an arresting landscape of dense forests and rip-pling hills, with the sapphire-blue sea forming a perfect backdrop.

From Moriani-Plage, the D34 wiggles up to **San Nicolao**, where the main highlight is its Baroque church. From there, you can easily reach **Santa Lucia di Moriani**, which is precariously perched on a ridge. Continue further to **San Giovanni di Moriani**, whose chief attraction is the slender 33m-high campanile of the church St-Jean. At the end of the D34, **Santa Reparata di Moriani** has an end-of-the-world feeling that will appeal to those in search of peace and solitude. Backtrack to San Nicolao, then follow the Corniche de la Castagniccia (see right) to Cervione.

The Morianincu is a hiker's haven, with a network of **hiking** trails linking most villages and sights. The leaflet *Randonnées dans le Morianincu* is available at the tourist office in Moriani-Plage or at the *gîte d'étape* Luna Piena in Santa Reparata di Moriani (see below).

Feel like cantering through dense chestnut forests? The riding centre **Les écuries de la Costa Verde** (☎ 04 95 30 64 39, 06 14 55 89 01; Moriani-Plage; http://ecuriescostaverde.free.fr in French), at the northern approach to Moriani-Plage, offers guided rides taking in the villages of the Morianincu (€25 for two hours). It also has exhilarating gallops on the beach at Moriani-Plage. For the little 'uns, pony rides are also available (€10 per hour).

Sleeping & Eating

Gîte d'Étape Luna Piena (☎ 04 95 38 59 48; Santa Reparata di Moriani; dm with/without half-board €30/11; ☽ Apr-Oct) If you are looking for some hush and seclusion, this wonderful *gîte d'étape* occupying a stone house at the end of the D34 is the perfect place to unwind. The two- to four-bed dorms are kept tickety-boo, the shared bathrooms are spotless and meals are available (*menus* €14 to €23). And did we mention the enchanting setting, along with plenty of greenery? Order a glass of something sweet and local and relax in the shade of a chestnut tree. Hiking in the area is spectacular.

Hôtel-Restaurant Le Belvédère d'E Catarelle (☎ 04 95 38 51 64; www.corsica-catarelle.com; San Giovanni di Moriani; r €60-120, per person with half-board €65; ☽ Jul & Aug; P) When it comes to Corsican specialities, Maddy, your chirpy host, knows her stuff: she has written a cookbook featuring tried-and-true recipes. Don't know what *buglidicci* are? It's time to get a hands-on education. Or you could plump for the *canette farcie au magret et clémentine Corse confite* (duckling with candied clementine). Another draw is the terrace (pity about the plastic chairs, though), with ravishing views

over the Morianincu and the sea. The hotel section is equally enticing. All the rooms are pleasing but you need to climb some steep stairs to reach the crowning glory – the suite called 'Anne', which features sloping beamed ceilings, warm fabrics and a terrace. It's gay-friendly. Bikers are welcome. Follow the signs from San Giovanni di Moriani.

Cava (☎ 04 95 38 51 14; San Giovanni di Moriani; mains €9-17, menu €23; ☽ Tue-Sun Jun-Sep) Blink and you'll miss the tiny entrance of this typical Corsican eatery. This is the place that guidebook authors hesitate to include in a book for fear that they can't get a table next time they visit. It has no pretensions for luxury, but everything is made from local produce. If you want a recommendation, go for the *terrine de foie gras aux figues* (terrine of foie gras and figs). The terrace at the rear affords unimpeded views of the coast.

CORNICHE DE LA CASTAGNICCIA

The corniche road (D330) that threads for 5km across the mountainsides from San Nicolao to Cervione deserves special mention. At times, the D330 clutches at the mountainsides as if in desperation, providing vista-point junkies with a steady fix. You can also dunk yourself in the **Cascade de l'Ucelluline** (Ucelluline Waterfalls), about 1.5km from San Nicolao (before the tunnel). Take the steep path on the right that leads to a series of tempting pools. Then the D330 crosses **Santa Maria Poggio** before hitting **Valle di Campoloro** and Cervione.

CERVIONE

pop 1200 / elevation 350m
Come here on a sunny day in autumn, and you'll fall in love with this diamond of a town. The liveliest village of the Costa Verde (bar Moriani-Plage), Cervione is clearly special: the setting is enchanting, with neat stone houses that are huddled around a cathedral, a small maze of alleys and archways and a smattering of peppy cafés with terraces overlooking lush valleys.

You can't miss the blindingly yellow façade of the Baroque **Cathédrale St-Érasme**, with its majestic campanile dating from the 18th century. Spitting distance from the cathedral, the **Musée de l'Adecec** (☎ 04 95 38 12 83; place du Musée; admission €3; ☽ 9am-noon & 2-6pm Mon-Sat) occupies the former bishop's palace and houses a collection of implements and artefacts.

THE EAST

A hidden gem that is well worth a detour, the Romanesque **Chapelle Ste-Christine** harbours fabulous frescoes from the 15th century. They adorn the twin apses inside and show scenes from the life of Christ. The key should be in the door. The chapel is about 3km from Cervione (take the road to Prunete for about 500m, then follow the signs 'Cappella Santa Cristina').

Sleeping & Eating

Chambres d'Hôtes Villa A Suera (☎ 04 95 38 17 41; Sant' Andria di Cotone; d with shared bathroom €45; P ☒) If you bet this B&B has spruce rooms with seaviews, a lovely terrace shaded by pine trees and a nifty pool, you'll hit the trifecta! Bathrooms are shared, but that's our only gripe. Meals are available on request (€13). It's about 3km from Cervione.

Chambre d'Hôtes Vallée di Campoloro (☎ 04 95 38 19 79; Valle di Campoloro; d €65; ☒ May-Jul & Sep) Don't expect a whole lotta love when checking in to this B&B about 800m from the main square, just off the D71. At least it's bright and it offers plenty of space to strew your stuff around. There's one studio-style room, with its own entrance at the back.

Aux 3 Fourchettes (☎ 04 95 38 14 86; place de l'Église; mains €6-13, menu €15) This restaurant is amusingly tucked *under* the cathedral – good to know in case you need to confess your sins (of gluttony, that is). The rustic food (wild boar stew, omelettes, pork cutlet, chestnut fritters) is far from exceptional but there's a lovely shady terrace.

U Casone (☎ 04 95 38 10 47; Cervione; mains €6-17, menus €12-20; ☒ closed lunch Mon) Smack dab in the old town, this is the most agreeable place in Cervione to line the stomach without breaking the bank. The menu roves from expertly cooked pizzas (from €5!) to palate-pleasing fish and meat dishes. Hoe into a comforting grilled *côte de bœuf* (beef rib) and you'll leave with a smile on your face. Less well-known dishes, like the *terrine de sansonnet aux myrtes* (starling terrine with myrtle), beg to be tried. Sample the whole thing on the terrace in the shade of a stately lime tree.

After an hour or two's sightseeing, there's nothing better than swigging a glass of Pietra. Your best bet is to run the gauntlet of bars that line the main drag. Their terraces overlook the Tyrrhenian Sea, with views of the Tuscan islands. In season they also serve light meals.

LA CASTAGNICCIA

This is Corsica at its most rural and secretive, a tapestry of bucolic ambiances, with dense forests, rippling hills, babbling streams, placid villages, majestic mountains and lush valleys, through which narrow roads twist, duck and dive. The Castagniccia (kas-ta-neech) owes its name to the Genoese, who planted its first chestnut trees in the 16th century (see p227). This is an idiosyncratic, largely unspoilt region peppered with natural wonders and infused with blissful serenity. If you happen to be passing in September or October, you'll be mesmerised by the symphony of nature: the trees flaunt their autumnal colouring and whole valleys are saturated with gold and russet hues – a magical sight. And in wet weather, a veil of mist adds a touch of the bizarre.

But nature is not the only drawcard. The Castagniccia is also of strong historical interest, with a sprinkle of stately stone houses, resplendent Baroque churches, chapels and convents, all that testify to a rich past. Here, old traditions die hard, making it a fascinating introduction to the mentality of rural Corsica. The people residing here are an independent and unhurried lot, adamantly tied to their land.

The Castagniccia lends itself perfectly to a DIY approach, preferably with your own wheels because public transport is almost nonexistent. You never know what's around the next corner: another stunning valley perhaps, or a picture-perfect village? The flipside is that it's narrow, twisting and slow going (the average speed is about 30km/h). All you need is a good road map and a little sense of adventure. *Bon voyage*!

Information

Take note that banks and petrol stations are nonexistent in the Castagniccia. At the time of research a small tourist office was due to open in Piedicroce in 2007.

For online info, take a look at www.castagniccia.net, which has pages in English. Check out also www.corsorezza.com (in French).

PIEDICROCE & AROUND

Straddling the crossroads of the Castagniccia's principal routes, Piedicroce is a good base for exploring the area. Spread around the lower reaches of Monte San Petrone, this charming settlement proffers wonderful views of the

Zucchini + prosciutto brusk[ella]

Marjoram
Parsley
Mint
Lemon x 2
Courgettes - small x 4.
Salad.
Fruit.
Chicken

T. paper
K Roll
Corn oil.

Parmesan

Proscuitio.
Bread.

THE WATERS OF OREZZA

Orezza spring waters were discovered early on to be very rich in iron and calcium, while enthusiasts claimed that they were useful in combating a raft of ailments and in improving the digestive, circulatory and nervous systems. Pascal Paoli himself came 'to take the cure' here every year, as did much of 18th-century polite society.

In 1896 a thermal spa centre with massage rooms, showers and baths was built. Despite the competition from mainland spas, Orezza developed rapidly until 1934, at which time a violent storm destroyed the pipework. During WWII the occupying Germans came to believe in the curative properties of the water and set up a small bottling plant. After the war the property changed hands numerous times, but the little bottles with green caps continued to be sold.

Production at the plant was rudely stopped in 1995 but the spring was back in business again after a complete overhaul. Today it remains one of the most popular mineral waters in Corsica.

---

valleys and has a magnificent Baroque 17th-century church, **Église St-Pierre et St-Paul**. Take a peek inside – the restored organ is said to be the oldest in Corsica.

About 1km to the north on the D71 (towards Campana), the ruins of **Couvent d'Orezza**, a former Franciscan monastery, exude an eerie ambience. It was destroyed by German troops in 1943.

From Piedicroce, it's an easy drive downhill along the D506 to **Eaux d'Orezza** (☎ 04 95 39 10 00; www.orezza.fr; 9am-8pm daily Apr–mid-Oct, 8am-6pm Wed-Sun mid-Oct–Mar), which is famous for its naturally sparkling water. From there, you can head to **Valle d'Orezza**, where artisans perpetuate the tradition of carving pipes from chestnut wood.

Follow the D506 downhill back through Rapaggio until the junction with the D46 on the right, which leads to **Piazzole** and **Monacia d'Orezza**, where you can marvel at a lovely church with a detached bell tower. Continue uphill until you reach **Parata**, a tiny hamlet clinging like a crow's nest to the crest of a hilltop. Here, it really feels like the end of the world. Parata also boasts a stunning Baroque church.

Backtrack to the junction with the D506 and follow the D46 until **Verdèse**. One of our favourite villages in the area, it is swathed in lush chestnut forest and features a lovely *chambres d'hôtes* (see p226).

Activities

If you want to work off any extra pounds gained in the area's fine restaurants, you can tackle the **Monte San Petrone** (1767m), the highest summit of the Castagniccia. You can either start the ascent from the hamlet of Campodonico, a few kilometres north of Piedicroce,

or from Col de Prato (see p227). The second option is considered gentler and offers more shade. At the top, the panorama is impossibly beautiful. Plan on five to six hours return for either route.

There's also a web of footpaths that connect the villages. The useful *Sentiers de Pays Castagniccia* leaflet has details. It's usually available at bars or in restaurants.

Seeing the area from the saddle is highly recommended, even if you're not an experienced rider. The riding centre **À Cheval en Castagniccia** (☎ 04 95 35 88 31, 06 85 48 72 69; Pie d'Orezza) has guided trips in the Piedicroce area. Expect to pay €20 for an hour and €70 for a half-day tour.

Sleeping & Eating

Les Prairies (☎ 04 95 36 95 90; Rumitoriu; camp sites per adult/child €6/3, d €60; Jun-Sep) An ecofriendly camping ground, with lots of shade and greenery, and an impeccable ablution block. Also one small room in the owners' house, with a charming retro style. There are ewes on the property (children will love it!) and the Fiumalto River is within walking distance (read: good swimming options). Hungry? There's a pizzeria 3km away. It's on the D506, between Piedicroce and Folelli.

Le Refuge (☎ 04 95 35 82 65; Piedicroce; s €43-46, d €46-59; Apr-Oct) The austere and vaguely rosy façade of Le Refuge won't feature on the cover of *Condé Nast Traveler* but inside, it's much more appealing, with luminous rooms, virginal white walls and white-glove-test-clean bathrooms. Be sure to ask for a room at the back – the views are splendid on a sunny day! The attached restaurant (mains €8 to €15, *menu* €17) has garnered high praise for its good-value, tasty traditional specialities.

THE AUTHOR'S CHOICE

Chambres d'Hôtes La Diligence (☎ 04 95 34 26 33, 06 89 22 14 26; d €47-55; Verdèse; ✆ Apr-Oct) Enter here at your own risk: you may never feel like leaving again! This bijou *chambres d'hôtes* is set in a former coaching inn that was thoughtfully revived, right in the heart of Verdèse. The five rooms exude charm, with beamed ceilings, colourwashed walls, fireplaces, period furnishings and parquet floors. At the end of the day, treat yourself to a copious *table d'hôtes* (available five days a week), with delicious Corsican specialities made from local produce (meals €20), and you'll be in seventh heaven. Anything similar in other parts of Corsica would cost twice this much – we certainly aren't complaining. To top it off, Sophie and Dominique, your charming hosts, are a mine of local knowledge.

Sant' Andria (☎ 04 95 35 82 26; Campana; menus €18-22; ✆ May-Sep, closed dinner Sun) Hmm, the *veau Corse mijoté à l'ancienne* (Corsican veal slowly stewed) and the *terrine de courgettes* (courgette terrine) are truly finger-licking here. Almost as alluring is a pleasant (at night quite romantic) atmosphere on the verandah, with robust furnishings, from where you can soak up the lovely views over the valley (despite some ugly electric wires). Treat yourself to a glass of AOC Ajaccio and you'll leave patting your tummy contently.

PIEDICROCE TO CERVIONE

From Piedicroce, the narrow D146 winds its way through tracts of dense forests like a roller coaster (*sans* barriers) to Cervione and the Morianincu (p222) – another memorable drive.

Carcheto merits a stop for its 16th-century **Église Ste-Marguerite**, with a remarkable campanile, decorated with graceful pierced arcades. Another reason to pause in Carcheto is the lovely **waterfall** that lies a couple of hundred metres down a chestnut forest (it's signposted). There's a pool just ready for a refreshing dip.

Back in the village, the D146 wobbles slowly up to the **Col d'Arcarotta** (Arcarotta Pass; 819m), famous for its local produce market which is held every Sunday in July and August. After the pass, take the D17 which dives to the **Couvent St-François-d'Alesani**, nestled amid lush vegetation deep in the valley. The cloister should be restored in the near future. From the *couvent*, it's 4km to **Valle d'Alesani** on the D71 and another 4km before you reach **Ortale**. Past Ortale, the Morianincu beckons, with 17km of umpteen bends engineered into the mountainsides until Cervione comes into view.

Sleeping & Eating

Gîte d'Étape de Valle d'Alesani (☎ 06 32 95 39 30; Valle d'Alesani; dm incl breakfast €25, with half-board €40; ✆ Apr–mid-Nov) Hallelujah! This newish *gîte d'étape* has all the hallmarks of a great deal; modern, spotless rooms that can sleep four people, pathogen-free bathrooms, lovely vistas and an ace location. You can't miss it: it's the only building daubed a camp shade of yellow in the village. Meals are served at the nearby Restaurant San Petru.

Restaurant San Petru (☎ 04 95 35 94 74; Valle d'Alesani; mains €8-11, menus €15-20; ✆ Apr-Dec) The décor of the dining room won't start a revolution but there's outdoor seating in summer. All dishes are prepared with local produce so you can rest assured of the quality. The menu includes a delicious *salade de confit de porc aux châtaignes* (salad with pork cooked in its own fat and chestnuts) and, if you want to challenge your tastebuds, *carpaccio de museau* (pig's snout carpaccio-style).

Auberge des Deux Vallées (☎ 04 95 35 91 20; Col d'Arcarotta; mains €8-16, menus €17-26; ✆ mid-Jun–mid-Sep) A reputable inn making a brave attempt at modern-meets-traditional décor but please, dump the cheap plastic chairs on the terrace! The roasted lamb with chestnut honey was above average, but we found the chestnut mousse disappointing. Never mind, the views over Monte San Petrone never fail to impress.

LA PORTA

Another lovely settlement in the heart of Castagniccia, La Porta is a definite must-see, if only for its **Église St-Jean Baptiste**, one of the most beautiful Baroque churches in Corsica, dating from the 17th century. No doubt you will gasp at the overblown splendour of its façade and its majestic bell tower, which is 45m in height. Inside it's no less impressive, with a superb church organ and various well-preserved paintings.

If you're feeling peckish, **Chez Élisabeth – L'Ampugnani** (☎ 04 95 39 22 00; La Porta; mains €8-14, menus €10-23; ⏰ closed Mon & Jan-Feb, lunch only in low season) is the most obvious choice. Make no bones about it, this is a typically Corsican *restaurant de village* (village eatery). The menu adheres to tried-and-true classics, such as veal stew, lamb, cannelloni, pastas and salads. Pity about the generic dining room. It's popular with coach parties at lunch in summer.

You can stock up on Corsican delicacies, including charcuterie, jams and *canistrelli* (local biscuits) at **Casi di Cornu** (☎ 04 95 39 23 91; www.casadicornu.com; Stoppia Nova), a tiny produce shop in Stoppia Nova, about 5km from La Porta.

MOROSAGLIA & AROUND

For most Corsicans, Morosaglia is almost talismanic: it's revered as the birthplace of the Babbu di a Patria (father of the nation), Pascal Paoli (see p31). From La Porta, follow the D515 until the junction with the D71, then forge northwest to Morosaglia via the **Col de Prato** (Prato Pass; 985m).

In Morosaglia, the **Maison Natale de Pascal Paoli** (Birthplace of Pascal Paoli; ☎ 04 95 61 04 97; rte Principale, Morosaglia; admission €2; ⏰ 9am-6pm May-Sep, 9am-5pm Oct-Apr) offers an insight into the life of the Corsican hero. When his remains were returned to his home village on 3 September 1889, villagers lined the route to pay their respects.

On top of its aesthetic appeal and historical significance, Morosaglia is also at the nexus of several inland routes. If you drive to the north, you'll hit the Rustinu; if you follow the wild backroad D15 to the south, you'll reach the Boziu (p242); if you head west the road drops down to the main Bastia–Corte road (N193).

Sleeping & Eating

A Curbaghja (☎ 04 95 61 11 39, 06 23 17 17 78; Morosaglia; d €46; ⏰ Apr-Oct) This place is a real find – a fully-equipped, stadium-sized flat in a tastefully restored 17th-century mansion. Period furniture, hardwood floors, a terrace and squeaky-clean bathrooms are *de rigueur*, and you deserve it. Just take note that it's usually rented by the week in July and August (about €500).

Chambre d'Hôtes Petri (☎ 04 95 48 43 27; psan tori@aol.com; Borgo, Gavignano; d €52) No English is spoken at this welcoming B&B in the hamlet of Borgo, a few kilometres south of Morosaglia. Never mind, it's snug and has a likeably old-fashioned feel, with wood-panelled ceilings, parquet flooring and walls carpeted with country-style floral patterns, as well as killer views thrown in for good measure. The terrace at the rear is a treat and Monsieur Petri will be happy to explain to you everything you ever wanted to know about Corsican charcuterie (but were too afraid to ask). There's only one room, so book ahead.

Osteria di U Cunventu (☎ 04 95 47 11 79; Morosaglia; mains €9-22; ⏰ closed Tue) This charming eatery on the main street has garnered hearty recommendations, and justifiably so. It offers up a blackboard menu of seasonal delights. Regular dishes to look out for are the generous Corsican salad (€9), with a bit of everything, and *côte de vache* (rib of cow), which transcends its simple ingredients. Oh, and there's a small terrace blessed with lovely views over the rippling hills.

LE RUSTINU

Ask most Corsicans to pinpoint this rural enclave sandwiched between the N193 to the north (the Bastia–Corte highway) and

---

NUTS ABOUT CHESTNUT

Pascal Paoli said, 'As long as we have chestnuts, we'll have bread'. For Corsicans, the chestnut tree was for many long centuries 'the bread tree'. In the glory days of Corsican chestnut culture, a Corsican wedding dinner typically required 22 different chestnut delicacies. In the Castagniccia (from *castagnu*, meaning 'chestnut') a single chestnut tree kept a family for a month. The people of the Castagniccia, once the single most prosperous and most populous of the island's many regions, traded their chestnuts with the Balagne for olive oil, with the Niolo for cheese, and with Porto-Vecchio for salt.

Chestnut culture began to decline after WWI as the result of massive depopulation, fungal diseases and an infant chemical industry that used the chestnut wood, and just the wood, for the production of cellulose and tannin.

In the 1880s Corsica harvested some 150,000 tonnes of chestnuts. By 2004 the chestnut harvest was down to a mere 1200 tonnes.

Morosaglia to the south, and they would flounder. This discreet little charmer that is still overlooked by travel books retains a refreshingly humble scale, with a distinct atmosphere. It's less verdant than the rest of the Castagniccia, but it's as hilly, and the zigzagging roads are no less wonderfully scenic (be prepared for heartstopping drives). It's also completely nontouristy, so you'll probably have it all to yourself.

From Morosaglia, it's a relatively easy drive to **Valle di Rustinu**, where you can have a look at the ruined **Église Santa Maria**, accessible via a dirt track. Afterwards you could head to **Pastoreccia**, which is famous for its lovely Romanesque **Chapelle San Tumasgiu**, perched on a plateau overlooking the valley of the Golo, on the outskirts of the village. Push the door open, and you won't believe your eyes: the apse is enlivened with a series of poignant frescoes, including scenes depicting the life of Christ. The frescoes should be restored in 2008.

From Pastoreccia, you can head south to La Porta (p226) via Bisinchi, Campile and Ortiporio – almost a complete loop and a fantastic drive.

Sleeping & Eating

U Vecchju Mulinu (☎ 04 95 28 91 87; http://monsite .wanadoo.fr/vecchju-mulinu; Fornoli; d €65-72; ☒) Hide away in this refurbished *vecchju mulinu* (old mill) nestled within a lush property. This bucolic treat exudes equal parts classic and modern aesthetic, with three oh-so-inviting rooms with well thought-out decorative touches, bags of character and a common lounge. Mix in a warm welcome, a cool pool and a great location (about 4km from Ortiporio), and you've got a recipe for a restful retreat. The gracious owner, Colette Routa, is fluent in English.

U Penta Rossa (☎ 04 95 38 21 32; Ortiporio; mains €8-16, menus €16-22) Despite its fairly bland décor, this auberge is held in high esteem by locals, and it's easy to see why. It trots out hearty Corsican fare, including savoury *buglidicci* (pancakes with ewe's milk cheese) and tasty *cannelloni au brocciu* (cannelloni stuffed with *brocciu*), while the wild boar stew falls apart at the touch of the fork. Save room for desserts – the homemade *coupe Penta Rossa* (chestnut mousse) is out of this world. It also features a handful of very ordinary rooms (doubles €55 to €63).

A Stella di Rustinu (☎ 04 95 38 77 09; Valle di Rustinu; mains €9-16, menus €25-32; ☼ Apr-Oct) This country

inn offers delightful, simple and reasonably priced Corsican food, including *cabri rôti* (roasted kid's meat), which is cooked on an open fire and prepared by a husband-and-wife team. It's a jolly evening, but a touch of eccentricity in the dining room wouldn't harm.

LA COSTA SERENA & LA CÔTE DES NACRES

Look at a map of Corsica. See this flat section that stretches from Étang de Diane to Solenzara? That's the Costa Serena and the Côte des Nacres. Never a high point on the tourist trail (except, maybe, if you are a nudist), the Costa Serena and the Côte des Nacres are often merely charged through on the way to the Far South. But it's well worth slowing down and making detours from the arrow-straight N198. Pack an open mind and investigate the possibilities.

ALÉRIA
pop 2000

Though Aléria won't win the award of tourist destination of the year, this haphazard town will hold your attention for a day.

In ancient times, the region that today forms Aléria – first known as Alalia (p27) – was Corsica's capital. Today the main activity is clustered around Caterraggio, a regional hub that most travellers pass through on their way between Bastia and Porto-Vecchio on the N198.

Even if the idea of an archaeology museum usually sends you to sleep, don't miss the **Musée Archéologique Jérôme-Carpino** (☎ 04 95 57 00 92; Fort de Matra; admission €2; ☼ 8am-noon & 2-7pm mid-May–Sep, 8am-noon & 2-5pm Oct–mid-May), a few blocks south of the main intersection, following the N198. This well-organised museum is housed in the magnificent Fort de Matra. Built by the Genoese in 1484, this well-proportioned edifice towers over the Vallée du Tavignano and the Étang de Diane. It holds a hoard of finds unearthed at the former site of Alalia and testifies to the town's Etruscan, Phocaean and Roman past. The archaeological site's a 300m walk southwest of the fort. It boasts the remains of a forum, a citadel, some temples and part of the centre of the Roman town, but the largest part of the city is still to be excavated.

After visiting the museum, ponder on your new-found knowledge while working on your

LA COSTA SERENA & LA CÔTE DES NACRES

Sun in summer, 9am–noon & 2–6pm Mon-Fri in low season) is near the main intersection. There are a number of banks with ATMs on the main road.

Sleeping & Eating

Camping Marina d'Aléria (☎ 04 95 57 01 42; www .marina-aleria.com; Plage de Padulone; 2-person camp sites €17–28; ✹ mid-Apr–mid-Oct; ⌨) This four-star camping ground is the best for miles around, and features masses of amenities, spitting distance from the beach. Recommended.

Hôtel-Restaurant L'Empereur (☎ 04 95 57 02 13; www.hotel-empereur.com; N198; s €40–70, d €46–82; P ✹ ⌨) Never mind the busy thoroughfare and the somewhat generic exterior; this professionally run abode is kept in top nick, featuring a fine selection of cheerful rooms with all creature comforts. After a day of turf pounding, relax in the stress-melting pool at the back before retiring to your cosy room, which, like the rest of the place, sparkles. If you don't fancy venturing out, there's an onsite bar and restaurant.

Hôtel Les Orangers (☎ 04 95 57 00 31, fax 04 95 57 05 55; rte de la Plage; s/d €45/56) Les Orangers is not exactly decked out for honeymooners but the spare rooms are more than acceptable and the private bathrooms passed the schoolmarm's cleanliness inspection. It's on the road to the beach, about 100m from the main intersection.

Hôtel Atrachjata (☎ 04 95 57 03 93; www.hotel -atrachjata.net; N198; d €51–144; P ✹) This hulking tower with a sunflower façade on the main drag flaunts its three stars with pride. Rooms are snug and well appointed and it scores high

sun tan on the **Plage de Padulone**, about 3km east of the centre.

In the mood for a picnic? The peaceful **Étang de Diane**, a large saltwater lagoon about 3km north of Aléria, is a good spot. There's an oyster farm where you can buy oysters, mussels and *poutargue* (dried, pressed roe of mullet).

Adventurous types can try **kayaking** on the Tavignano, which flows through Aléria before debouching into the sea. Riding the river is best in high summer when the river is usually low and the descent a lazy trip over mostly calm water. The **Club Nautique d'Aléria** (☎ 06 14 23 50 93; rte de la Plage, Aléria; ✹ May-Sep) rents out kayaks (from €8 per hour) and organises guided descents of the Tavignano (€25).

If you still have some energy to burn, the **Centre de Tourisme Équestre de Bravone** (☎ 04 95 38 91 90; Bravone), about 10km north of Aléria along the N198, offers guided horse-riding trips in the maquis or on the beach for all levels of experience. A typical beach ride lasts about one hour (€18).

Aléria's **tourist office** (☎ 04 95 57 01 51; www .corsica-costaserena.com; ✹ 9am-8pm Mon-Sat, 10am-1pm

---

THE AUTHOR'S CHOICE

Aux Coquillages de Diane (☎ 04 95 57 04 55; Étang de Diane; mains €12–22; ✹ lunch & dinner Jun-Sep, lunch Oct–May, dinner Fri & Sat Oct–May, closed Jan) With eye-catching port-holes and an inviting nautical décor, this seafooder resting on the saltwater lagoon is a true winner. The obvious choice here is the fleshy oysters and the mussels straight from the *étang*, which are available in multiple combinations. All are voluptuous and positively naughty as they slither down. Other seafood delights are treated with equal respect – such as *espadon* (swordfish), *daurade* (sea bream) and *loup de mer* (sea bass). Well worth the splurge.

THE EAST

on facilities, with TV, air-con, lift and modern furnishings. Fear not, it's soundproofed.

You'll find a handful of *paillottes* and restaurants on the seafront at Plage de Padulone, including **Le Bounty** (☎ 04 95 57 00 50; Plage de Padulone; mains €8-18, menus €14-22; ☒ May-Sep), with a zany, crenellated façade, an all-wood décor and a lovely terrace overlooking the waves.

Shopping

Domaine Mavela (☎ 04 95 56 63 15; U Licettu; ☒ 9am-8pm Jun-Aug, 9am-noon & 2-6pm Mon-Sat Sep-Jan & Apr-May) Head to this store, about 5km south from Aléria, to fill your coffers with fabulous local produce. This treasure-trove is wont to overwhelm the senses: noses assail chunks of cheese and clumps of cured meats and eyes flutter at homemade jams and honey. Everything is organic. You can also buy various liqueurs (flavoured with myrtle, plum, citron or chestnut), the only Corsican whisky (yes!), and the vaulted wine cellar has an impressive selection of Corsican wines – what about a Gentile Noble, a Clos Canarelli or a Domaine Torraccia to spoil the ones left at home?

Getting There & Away

Autocars Cortenais (☎ 04 95 46 02 12) Operates a service to Aléria from Corte (€10) on Tuesday, Thursday and Saturday in July and August, and daily from Monday to Friday during the school period.

Rapides Bleus Corsicatours (☎ 04 95 31 03 79, 04 95 70 10 36) Bastia–Porto-Vecchio via Aléria (twice daily except Sunday from mid-September to mid-June, twice daily from mid-June to mid-September). Aléria–Bastia costs €11 and Aléria–Porto-Vecchio is €11.50.

Transports Tiberi (☎ 04 95 57 81 73) Solenzara–Bastia via Aléria (€11, daily except Sunday).

KIT-OFF CORSICA

If you've come to Corsica to lose your inhibitions then Aléria is a good place to start. There are 20km of naturist resorts and villas in a, ahem, strip, heading south along the N198 between the turn-off for the D71 (towards Cervione) and the tourist office at Aléria. No sniggering at the back now.

The pick of the bunch is **Riva Bella** (☎ 04 95 38 81 10; www.rivabella-corsica.com; treatments 9am-1pm & 3-8pm Apr-Oct), which has comfortable bungalows located on the beach and specialises in massage and hypoallergenic treatments.

GHISONACCIA

Let's face it: searching for a suitable adjective that's not pejorative to describe Ghisonaccia is a challenge. We'll settle for 'desultory'. Approximately halfway between Bastia and Bonifacio, this half resort-, half agro-town is strung along the monotonous N198, with no real attractions to catch the eye.

It's not all that bad, though. Due to the dynamic local tourist office, it has perked up considerably in recent years and now makes a convenient, if not glamorous, base from which to explore the coast. There are also several enticing beaches a mere 4km to the east, including **Plage de Tignale** and **Plage de Pinia**. It's also supremely well placed for forays into the hinterland, and offers lots of accommodation options for families, with a host of *résidences de vacances* and camping grounds.

For a back-to-nature experience, the **Étang d'Urbino**, which is similar to the Étang de Diane (p229) is worth checking out. About 5km north of Ghisonaccia, it's a vast saltwater lagoon where oysters and mussels are farmed.

The helpful **tourist office** (☎ 04 95 56 12 38; www.corsica-costaserena.com; rte de Ghisoni; ☒ 9am-12.30pm & 2-7.30pm Mon-Sat, 9.30am-12.30pm Sun Jul & Aug, 9am-12.30pm & 2-6pm Mon-Fri in low season) is across the street from the Casa Maria Cicilia hotel.

Sleeping

Camping Arinella Bianca (☎ 04 95 56 04 78; www.arinellabianca.com; rte de la Mer; 2-person camp sites €20-33; ☒ Apr–mid-Oct; ☒) A flashy four-star camping ground, right on Plage de Tignale, with loads of amenities, including a glistening pool and a restaurant, and plenty of shade. It's unsurprisingly packed to the gills in summer. It also rents bungalows by the week.

Casa Maria Cicilia (☎ 04 95 56 00 41; www.casamariacicilia.com; rte de Ghisoni; d €59-124; ☒ ☒) After a complete make-over in 2006, the Casa Maria Cicilia is now one of the major players in the area. Spruce rooms, shiny-clean toilets, blondwood fittings, cream bedspreads, flat-screen TVs, wi-fi, air-con and well-sprung mattresses are the order of day here. All the perks of a three-star, including a licensed bar and a restaurant. One negative: its location is dull – it lies near the main intersection.

Chambres d'Hôtes Annonciade Prieur (☎ /fax 04 95 57 43 83, 06 24 29 58 84; Villa le Cèdre Bleu, Vix-Ventiseri; d €65-85; ☒) This adorable B&B seduces all who stay. There's a fresh, modern feel and the attention to detail is impressive. The three rooms are coolly tiled and are decorated in soothing pastels with matching linens and fluttering *voiles*, nice prints on fresh walls and pale exposed beams. The hosts occupy a separate building, so if privacy is at a premium, this place is hard to beat. Breakfast is served under a gazebo-like building by the lovely pool in the garden – bliss ! Madame is intent on promoting the underrated Costa Serena, and has itineraries for your deeper discovery of secret delights. Beaches are a short drive away. A peaceful place perfect for a civilised holiday in the area. It's about 6km south of Ghisonaccia, off the N198.

Eating & Drinking

La Ferme d'Urbino (☎ 04 95 57 30 89; Étang d'Urbino; mains €8-16, menus €10-20; ☾ May-Sep) With a lovely position opening out onto the Étang d'Urbino, this sprightly eatery consistently delivers quality meals with a minimum of fuss. Its forte? Well-priced, divine pots of mussels. It also offers *friture* (deep-fried fish), oysters and grilled fish. Brilliant value.

Les Deux Magots (☎ 04 95 56 15 61; rte de la Mer; mains €19-26; ☾ Apr–mid-Oct) This chic *paillotte* slap on Plage de Tignale woos diners from afar. Nab a seat on the breezy alfresco deck and tuck into delicious fish dishes, such as tuna, sea bream or sea bass.

A Tribbieria – Pasquale Paoli (☎ 04 95 56 37 23; Casamozza; ☾ Tue-Sun) If A Tribbiera didn't exist, someone would have invented it. The closest thing eastern Corsica has to a Corsican pub, it certainly has novelty value. Here's your chance to sample unique, homemade nectars (there's an attached brewery), flavoured with arbutus berry, Corsican honey or clementines, served by the *mezzu* (25cL), *pinta* (50cL), *carafon* (1L) or *funtana* (2L). It's not all about the beer though; convivial socialising is a mainstay in the sunny courtyard or inside the big main bar. On Friday you could be entertained by live music. It's in Casamozza, about 3km south of Ghisonaccia, on the N198 – you can't miss it.

Entertainment

Le G (☎ 04 95 56 20 30; rte de la Mer, Ghisonaccia; ☾ Jul & Aug) If you want to tear it up on the dance floor, head to Le G. In high season it's usually packed to the rafters with fun-seekers of all backgrounds and nationalities, all jostling shoulders with a minimum of worries. Whether you're into electronic soundscapes or R&B, Le G has a gig for you.

Getting There & Away

Rapides Bleus Corsicatours (☎ 04 95 31 03 79, 04 95 70 10 36) Bastia–Porto-Vecchio via Ghisonaccia (twice daily except Sunday from mid-September to mid-June, twice daily from mid-June to mid-September).
Transports Tiberi (☎ 04 95 57 81 73) Solenzara–Bastia via Ghisonaccia (daily except Sunday).

LE FIUMORBU

If you need a break from the hurly-burly of the coast, here's the antidote. West of Ghisonaccia, the Fiumorbu doesn't have anything particularly fantastic to offer, but it is certainly worth a detour if the trials of the coastal cities start to overwhelm you. Because it's not promoted heavily as a tourist destination, this microregion remains largely overlooked by visitors. It is well known among walkers, though, because it's traversed by the Mare a Mare Centre trail (p76).

With its cluster of *villages perchés*, built like eagles' nests on hilltops or nestled within dense forests, you'll enjoy unparalleled views of the coast. And, man-oh-man, lots of hush and seclusion. To get there from Ghisonaccia, you could take the D145 inland and follow your nose. All you need is a good touring map (see p259). Of course, some words in French for directions always help. Head to **Pietrapola**, famous for its thermal baths, then make your way to **San Gavinu di Fiumorbu**, clinging to a hillside at the curve of the valley. You could also drive up to **Isolaccio di Fiumorbu**, the highest village of the area, at an altitude of 700m, or pull over for a gentle stroll in **Prunelli di Fiumorbu**, the most distinctive *village perché* in the area.

Horse riding in the area is available at **Ranch Évasion** (☎ 04 95 57 37 13; Ghisonaccia), based in Ghisonaccia.

Allow one or two days to soak up the atmosphere of this intriguing region.

Sleeping & Eating

Gîte d'Étape de Serra di Fiumorbu (☎ 04 95 56 75 48, 06 81 04 69 49; Serra di Fiumorbu; dm with/without half-board €28/10; ☾ mid-Apr–Sep) A night halt on the Mare a Mare Centre trail, this *gîte* is housed in a converted primary school. It's nothing fancy but will do for a night's kip, with uncluttered four- to nine-person dorms and OK shared bathrooms. There are self-catering facilities.

Gîte d'Étape de Catastaju – San Gavinu di Fiumorbu (☎ 04 95 56 70 14, 04 95 56 74 97, 06 79 74 81 58; San Gavinu di Fiumorbu; dm with/without half-board €32/12;

THE EAST

THE AUTHOR'S CHOICE

Villa Clotilde (☎ 04 95 57 93 92, 06 79 49 00 44; Prunelli di Fiumorbu; s with shared bathroom €40-50, d with shared bathroom €50-60) Swap stress for bliss at this Tuscany-style palazzo smack dab in Prunelli di Fiumorbu. The three gleaming rooms, offering a fine sense of individuality, swim in light and are designed to spoil you rotten. Expect unremitting comfort: oak parquet, period furnishings and excellent bedding – not to mention ravishing views over the valley. Bathrooms are shared but that's a minor inconvenience when you factor in all the positives. Breakfast is served in an atmospheric room or on the terrace. A dream-come-true *chambres d'hôtes* at prices that won't make you flinch.

(☽ Apr-Oct) A great place to commune with nature. Set in a converted hydroelectric station, this *gîte d'étape* on the Mare a Mare Centre trail (stage two) is tucked away 3km from San Gavinu di Fiumorbu in a glowingly verdant forest. It features well-kept four- to 10-bed dorms and prim bathrooms. Fancy a dip? The *vasques* (natural pools) of the Abatescu River are just beside the building. Top that off with the motherly welcome of Madame Paoli, who is a good cook too (mains €10 to €20) – try her simple but stupendous *gâteau du pauvre* ('poor man's cake'), flavoured with orange jam – and you have a *gîte* that beckons you to stay for a few extra days.

Caffè Buttéa (☎ 04 95 56 74 75; Prunelli di Fiumorbu; mains €8-13) An agreeable *bistrot de village*, with limited choice but excellent cuisine. Hoe into their *filet mignon de porc aux figues et pistaches* (tenderloin of pork with figs and pistachio) or the homemade vegetables terrine, all prepared with great finesse. Décorwise it's very simple, with plastic chairs on the terrace and a modest interior. A good surprise.

SOLENZARA

In the charisma stakes, Solenzara's heavily trafficked centre and bland buildings strung along the N198 come a very poor second to the picture-postcard beauties further south – Porto-Vecchio and Bonifacio. Although this seaside town is not arrestingly picturesque, it's important not to judge it too early. There have been successful efforts to smarten it up,

and it shows. The lively marina is a good place to watch the world sail by, and Solenzara is blessed with lovely beaches to the south – not to mention a good deal of outdoor activities and a hatful of well-regarded restaurants.

It's also optimally placed for explorations of the coast and forays into the Alta Rocca – via the sensational rte de Bavella (p234) that connects Solenzara with Col de Bavella.

The helpful **tourist office** (☎ 04 95 57 43 75; www .cotedesnacres.com; ☽ 9am-8pm Jul & Aug, 9am-noon & 3-7pm Jun & Sep, 9am-noon & 2-5pm Mon-Fri in low season) is on the main drag. You'll also find banks with ATMs.

Sights & Activities

Beaches are Solenzara's main *raison d'être*. The half-moon–shaped **Anse de Canella** wouldn't be out of place in the Caribbean, while the much-photographed **Anse de Fautea**, about 18km south of Solenzara, has the additional bonus of a Genoese watchtower. **Anse de Tarco** and **Anse de Favona** are also worth investigating. All are OK for swimming and sunbathing.

Renting a boat is a heavenly way to approach the beaches and explore the coast at your leisure, far from the jam-packed coastal roads. **Corse Pneu'marine** (☎ 04 95 57 10 94; www .corse-pneumarine.fr; Plage de Favona), based at Anse de Favona, rents outboard-powered boats (no boating license is required) for €100 for the full day. Petrol is extra. The boats can seat up to four passengers. Don't forget your snorkelling equipment.

Horse riding is another fun way to experience the visual appeal of the area. If you've ever fancied riding along the beach by moonlight or cantering across the sand on the edge of a turquoise sea, visit **Ranch José** (☎ 06 22 62 91 18; Pielza), 5km north of Solenzara. The place offers horseback excursions for all levels of experience (from €20 for 1½ hours to €70 for a full day). It also has trips in the hinterland, near Solaro. In the Favona area, **Ranch Bon Annu** (☎ 06 74 30 29 70; rte de Conca, Favona) has guided trips in the maquis and gallops on the beach (€16 per hour).

For Tarzan types, the **Parc Aventure de la Solenzara** (☎ 06 11 16 13 07; N198; circuit €5-22; ☽ Jun-Sep) has three adventure circuits in a eucalyptus forest, including a very secure one for the kiddies (minimum height is 1m). The most thrilling circuit boasts four tyrolean slides, including a 120m one over the Solenzara River.

THE EAST

Sleeping

Gîte d'Étape-Restaurant U Saltu (☎ 04 95 56 32 70, 06 73 37 14 87; Solaro; dm €18) This newish *gîte*, right in the centre of Solaro, 8km west of the N198 (take the D845 inland from Marine de Solaro, 3.5km north of Solenzara) has meticulously maintained four-bed rooms and boasts divine views over the coast. There's an attached restaurant, with a standard *menu Corse* (€16). Breakfast (€4) is served on a shady terrace or inside an exposed-brick dining room.

Hôtel Orsoni (☎ 04 95 57 40 25; www.hotelorsoni.com; rte Principale, Solenzara; d €42-57; ⏳ Apr–mid-Oct) The family-run Orsoni is a dandy little performer in Solenzara's accommodation scene, with 10 uncluttered but neat rooms, firm mattresses and an old-fashioned model of tiles on the floor (white with black dots). The cheaper rooms have shared bathrooms. Room 2 is cute as a button. One grumble: bathrooms are on the small side. Half-board is mandatory in August (from €110 for two people).

La Solenzara (☎ 04 95 57 42 18; www.lasolenzara .com; rte Principale, Solenzara; s incl breakfast €58-92, d incl breakfast €62-96; ⏳ mid-March–Oct; ✷ ▨) Deservedly three-star, this stately old-timer is distinguished by the elegance of its setting – it occupies an ancient Genoese villa dating from the 18th century – and mixes modern and old décors in a self-assured feast for the eyes. High ceilings, ancient tiles, exposed beams and all mod cons, including air-con. The real clincher is the kidney-shaped pool that overlooks the sea – so exotic.

Eating

RESTAURANTS

Restaurant Casa Corsa (mains €8-15, menus €20-30; ⏳ Jun-Sep) Run by a daughter of the family-run Hôtel Orsoni, this restaurant is located next to the hotel's reception. The menu focuses on grilled fish and meat dishes. The lovely tiled floor is also worth a gander.

La Fonderie (☎ 04 95 57 42 47; port de plaisance; mains €9-20, menus €15-23; ⏳ May-Sep) A fine-dining establishment serving an array of refined dishes, this is a welcoming place just perfect for that special meal. Can you resist a menu that includes *gigot d'agneau confit* (leg of lamb cooked in its own fat), *gâteau d'aubergine au brocciu* (eggplant terrine with *brocciu*) and *filet de daurade* (sea bream)? At least we couldn't. Should you still have a spare cranny to fill, the *pannacotta aux fruits rouges* (an Italian-style custard with fruits of the forest) or the chestnut flan are criminally good. You want more? Give up wanting; there's nothing more to want. On the marina.

A Mandria de Sébastien (☎ 04 95 57 41 95; mains €10-16; ⏳ Apr-Dec, closed Mon & Sun dinner) Stepping through the doorway of this converted *bergerie* (shepherd's hut) at the northern entrance to town is like zapping away a century. The walls are beguilingly adorned with ancient

---

BACKROADS: VALLÉE DU TRAVO – A HIDDEN GEM

If the Casinca or the Fiumorbu have whet your appetite for eastern Corsica's hidden splendours and you're craving another bite, then head south for 12km from Ghisonaccia along the N198 and turn right on to the D645. The village of Chisà emerges like a hamlet in a fairy tale after 15km of tight bends on a corniche along the Travo Valley. One of the most isolated villages in eastern Corsica, it offers one of the most thrilling **Via Ferrata** circuits in Corsica, U Calanconi, which includes an adrenaline-pumping 230m tyrolean slide, a 50m Himalayan bridge and various vertical ladders (for experienced climbers only). It costs €23 per person. Gear is included. Inquire at the Gîte d'Étape Bocca Bè.

In the mood for a dip? There are some enticing **vasques** (natural pools) at the foot of the bridge, at the entrance to the village. But the jewel in the crown lies about 1.4km to the east (from the bridge); a big pine tree and an electric pole to the left of the roadside, just before a small, unofficial parking area, serve as landmarks; from there, a narrow, steep path leads down through the maquis to the best *vasques* imaginable, where you can lounge in crystal-clear waters or work on your sun tan lying on perfect stone slabs… Bring a picnic!

In Chisà, you can hunker down in the ultrabasic **Pension-Restaurant U Chisà** (☎ 04 95 57 31 06; Chisà; r with shared bathroom €25; ⏳ Jul & Aug), which also serves up meals (mains €6 to €11), or in the much more appealing **Gîte d'Étape Bocca Bè** (☎ 04 95 56 36 61; Chisà; r per person with half-board €33), which lies just opposite the kiosk booth marking the start of the Via Ferrata.

For more information on this little charmer, check out the website www.villagedechisa.com.

tools and other knick-knacks. In summer, tables line up under a pergola in the garden. Bona fide carnivores will find nirvana here; meat (lamb or beef) is grilled to perfection and the local charcuterie *(panzetta, figatellu)* is faultless. Service could use a little improvement, but once you taste the food you'll forget how long it took to arrive. Credit cards are not accepted.

QUICK EATS & SELF-CATERING
Glacier du Port (☎ 04 95 57 42 21; port de Plaisance; ☺ Apr-Sep) A lighthouse for ice-cream lovers. Luscious homemade ice creams and a large terrace right on the marina.

A Buttega di A Mandria (☎ 04 95 31 59 35; rte principale; ☺ Tue-Sun Apr-Oct) A recently opened local produce store and a wine bar, on the main drag, run by Sébastien of A Mandria de Sébastien (p233).

Getting There & Around
It's worth knowing that during July and August shuttles buses ply the route between Travo and Tarco (€3, valid for one day, three times daily) and serve all the beaches in between. Other useful services:

Rapides Bleus Corsicatours (☎ 04 95 31 03 79, 04 95 70 10 36) Bastia–Porto-Vecchio via Solenzara (twice daily except Sunday from mid-September to mid-June, twice daily from mid-June to mid-September). Solenzara–Bastia costs €14.50 and Solenzara–Porto-Vecchio is €7.

Transports Tiberi (☎ 04 95 57 81 73) Bastia–Solenzara (€14, daily except Sunday).

FROM SOLENZARA TO BAVELLA
Now, take a deep breath. The D268, which connects Solenzara with the Col de Bavella, 30km to the west, ranks as one of the most dramatic mountain roads in Corsica (and this is saying a lot!). The net change of elevation is 1218m up and the surrounding grandeur is incomparable.

The first 8km are delightful. From the coast, the Solenzara River valley slithers into the mountains. The road follows the wide stony bed of the river and goes past numerous

vasques that look like something out of a tonic drink advert, with mountains rising gloriously on all sides. Immediately after Camping U Rosumarinu, the **Corsica Forest Parc Aventure** (☎ 06 25 97 27 95, 06 16 18 00 58; www.corsica-forests .com; rte de Bavella; adult/child €17/14; ☺ May-Sep) is a definite must-do for those who want to see the valley from a different perspective. With 25 fixtures, including a gut-wrenching 250m tyrolean slide over the river, it looks like something straight out of Dr Seuss. Fear not, you'll start with a 10-minute crash course. There's a 'baby parc' for the kiddies (€8). The site also comprises a superb Via Ferrata circuit, **A Buccarona** (adult/child €17/14), which is no less impressive.

The ensuing ascent is steep and steady, until you reach **Col de Larone** (608m). A 13km series of intestine-like S-curves offers an ever closer and more dramatic look at the saw-toothed Aiguilles de Bavella. The Col de Bavella (1218m) is the perfect finale to this memorable ascent (see p217).

Sleeping & Eating
Camping U Rosumarinu (☎ 04 95 57 47 66; www.rosu marinu.com; rte de Bavella; camp sites per adult/car/tent €4/2/3; ☺ May-Sep; ☒) When it comes to grandiose setting, this camping ground right by the river is hard to beat, with blissful natural pools (and beaches!) and a stunning mountain scenery. The Corsica Forest Parc Aventure is just up the road and there's an onsite restaurant. It's 7km from Solenzara.

Ferme-Auberge A Pinzutella (☎ 04 95 57 41 18; rte de Bavella; menus €24-28; ☺ Mon-Sat May-Sep) Dishes are delicious in their earthy simplicity in this middle-of-nowhere inn: wild boar stew, veal scallop with honey-flavoured wine vinegar and myrtle mousse. The food is savoury and authentic, but the generic interior borders on boring. Despite an open fireplace, its dull décor is disappointing. The terrace more than compensates, with views of the craggy summits that tower over the Solenzara River valley. It's set back from the road to Bavella (it's signposted).

The Central Mountains

You visit the Centru di Corsica, the island's physical and metaphorical heart, to walk, drive or simply savour its towering granite mountains, tucked-away villages, cool forests and crystal clear streams with their deep, inviting pools.

Corte, the only town of any size, was the capital of Pascal Paoli's short-lived Corsican nation. It's still a symbol of Corsica's distinct cultural identity, its architecturally striking Musée de la Corse the physical repository of this identity. It's a great base for exploring the twin valleys that open out at its feet. Above the wooded Vallée de la Restonica, accessible so far by car, is a pair of glorious high tarns, while the lightly tramped Vallée du Tavignano, whose former mule track leads deep into the mountains, is strictly walkers only.

Three other regions each make for a fulfilling day's driving. The Vénachese, traversed by both the railway and N193 road linking Ajaccio and Bastia, is the most accessible. Here you can plunge into cool forests of pine and beech and explore marked trails leading to gems such as the Cascades des Anglais. The Niolo, linking the centre with Porto and the west coast via the spectacular Col de Verghio, is more lightly trafficked. This stark land, traditionally the preserve of shepherds and goatherds, was for centuries all but cut off from the rest of the island. Calacuccia, beside a sparkling lake, has plenty of accommodation options. From it you can enjoy walks both gentle and demanding (including the ascent of Monte Cinto, the island's highest peak). For real solitude and a sense of being first there, Le Boziu, right on Corte's doorstep, beckons. You'll be almost alone on its narrow lanes, passing through tiny villages with well-preserved parish churches, abandoned hamlets and wooded valleys.

HIGHLIGHTS

- **Culture Time**
  Enjoy the artefacts and stylish architecture of Corte's Musée de la Corse (p239)

- **Earning the Views**
  Huff and puff up the steep trail to the Lac de Melu (p243) above Vallée de la Restonica (p241)

- **All Alone**
  Savour the solitude in the car-free Vallée du Tavignano (p243)

- **Driving Away from It All**
  Visit the little-explored hamlets of Le Boziu (p242)

- **Playing Tarzan**
  Swing through the trees with Grandeur Nature (p247) or Vizzavona Parc Aventure (p248)

- **Coffee Break**
  Sip a coffee in Corte's Le Grand Café du Cours (p241)

★ Vallée du Tavignano ★ Corte
                       ★ Le Boziu
★ Vallée de la Restonica
                ★ Grandeur Nature

        ★ Vizzavona Parc Aventure

THE CENTRAL MOUNTAINS

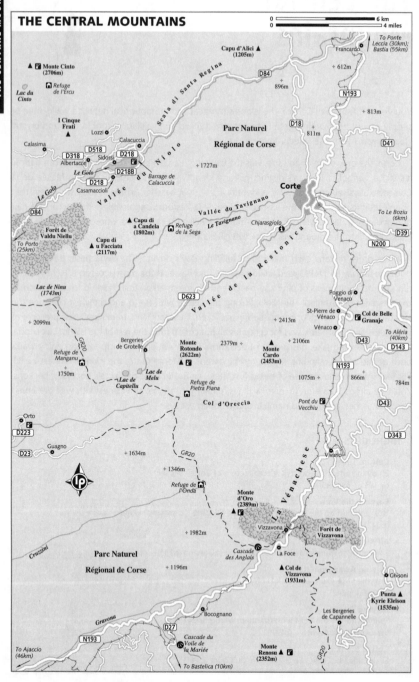

0 _____ 6 km
0 _____ 4 miles

▲ 🅿 Monte Cinto
(2706m)

🏠 Refuge
de l'Ercu

Lac du
Cinto

Capu d'Alici ▲
(1205m)

To Ponte
Leccia (30km);
Bastia (55km)

Francardo

D84

+ 612m

+ 896m

N193

+ 813m

I Cinque
Frati ▲

Lozzi

Calacuccia

Parc Naturel

D18

+ 811m

D41

Calasima

D318

D518

D218

Régional de Corse

Albertacce

Sidossi

🅿

Le Golu

D218

D218B

+ 1727m

Casamaccioli

Barrage de
Calacuccia

Corte

D84

Le Golo

Vallée du Niolo

Vallée du Tavignano

To Le Boziu
(6km)

Forêt de
Valdu Niellu

▲ Capu di
a Candela
(1802m)

🏠 Refuge
de la Sega

Le Tavignano

Chjarasgiolu

D39

To Porto
(25km)

Capu di
▲ u Facciatu
(2117m)

N200

Lac de Ninu
(1743m)

D623

Vallée de la Restonica

Poggio di
Venaco

+ 2099m

St-Pierre de
Vénaco

🅿 Col de Belle
Granaje

GR20

Bergeries
de Grotelle

Monte
Rotondo
(2622m)

2379m ✦

+ 2413m

Vénaco

D43

To Aléria
(40km)

D143

Refuge de
Manganu 🏠

▲ Monte
Cardo
(2453m)

+ 2106m

N193

+ 866m

+ 784m

1750m

Lac de
Capitellu

Lac de
Melu

🏠 Refuge de
Pietra Piana

1075m ✦

Orto

🅿

Col d'Oreccia

Pont du 🅿
Vecchiu

D43

D223

Guagno

D343

D23

+ 1634m

GR20

Vivario

+ 1346m

🏠 Refuge de
l'Onda

Monte
d'Oro
(2389m)
🅿

La Vénachese

Parc Naturel

Régional de Corse

+ 1982m

Vizzavona

Forêt de
Vizzavona

Cruzzini

Cascade
des Anglais

La Foce

+ 1196m

▲ Col de
Vizzavona
(1931m)

Ghisoni

Punta ▲
Kyrie Eleison
(1535m)

To Ajaccio
(46km)

Gravona

D27

Bocognano

N193

Cascade du
Voile de
la Mariée

Les Bergeries
de Capannelle

GR20

Monte
Renosu ▲ 🅿
(2352m)

To Bastelica (10km)

GETTING AROUND

Corte and the Vénachese are linked to Bastia, Ajaccio and Calvi by the Chemins de Fer de la Corse, Corsica's narrow-gauge, single-track railway, which winds lazily through forests and around mountains. Apart from the train, there's scant public transport – the Niolo, for example, has only a solitary summertime bus connection. So, to really get to the heart of this central, mountainous area, you're much better off with your own wheels.

CORTE (CORTI)

pop 6350 / elevation 400m

Corte, roughly midway between Bastia and Ajaccio, isn't a pretty town. In fact, with its peeling façades and tall, undistinguished buildings, it's fairly ugly. So you have to bring other senses into play to appreciate the huge significance this inland fastness holds for Corsicans. Caretaker of the island's identity, the town was, so briefly, the capital of an independent Corsica between 1755 and 1769, and remains a symbol of its people's aspirations and longings.

Memories in Corsica are long. Pascal Paoli, who established his base in Corte, deep inland, also founded a national university here in 1765. A mere four years later, it was forced to close its doors when the short-lived Corsican republic foundered. But in 1981, after strong popular and political pressure, it opened once again and the University of Corsica Pascal Paoli bears the name of its farsighted founder. With a little over 4000 students, the university is one of the driving forces behind the revival of the Corsican language.

The graffiti on the walls are evidence that Corte remains a nationalist stronghold and – biting the hand that feeds the starved Corsican economy – both the gendarmerie lodgings and tourist office were bombed in 2005. It's an undercurrent to be aware of though you'll almost certainly meet nothing but courtesy during your stay.

Students give the town a special buzz during term time. During the summer recess, it's mainly tourists who walk the streets and fill the cafés. They're supplemented by a sun-bronzed leavening of hikers, taking a break from the Mare a Mare Nord trail, which has its halfway point here, or enjoying day walks amid the soul-stirring scenery of the Restonica and Tavignano Valleys, both of which open out at the town's feet.

Haul your way up to the citadel, which seems to grow organically from the rocky pinnacle to which the town clings. At its southern tip, there's a magnificent panorama from Le Belvédère and within its ramparts is Musée de la Corse, the island's major museum.

ORIENTATION

Cours Paoli, the main street, splits the town in two. Steps to the west mount to the upper town and citadel. To the east, they descend steeply towards the train station and newer development. The citadel quarter dominates the upper town (*haute ville*), and the university district is the focus of the lower town (*basse ville*).

INFORMATION

Bookshops

Maison de la Presse (24 cours Paoli) Has a good range of guides, maps and some foreign-language newspapers.

Emergency

Police station (☎ 04 95 46 04 81; av Xavier-Zuciani) On the outskirts of town, beside the N200, direction Aléria.

Internet Access

Le Grand Café du Cours (22 cours Paoli; per hr €5; ⏲ 7am-2am) Has eight internet terminals in its back room.
Video Games (av Président Pierucci; per hr €4; ⏲ 10am-midnight)

Laundry

Speed Laverie (⏲ 8am-9pm) Behind Monsieur Bricolage, the DIY supermarket.

Medical Services

Santos Manfredi Hospital (☎ 04 95 45 05 00; allée du 9 Septembre)

Post

Main post office (av du Baron Mariani)

Tourist Information

Tourist office (☎ 04 95 46 26 70; www.corte-tourisme .com; ⏲ 10am-5pm Mon, Wed & Sat, 9am-7pm Tue, Thu & Fri Jul & Aug, 9am-noon & 2-6pm Mon-Fri Sep-Jun) In the Padoue barracks at the entrance to the citadel. Its multilingual free pamphlet *Parcours Patrimonial* describes Corte's main sites.

CORTE

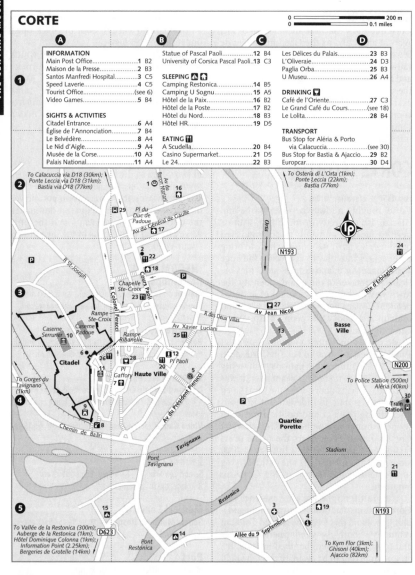

| 0 | 200 m |
| 0 | 0.1 miles |

INFORMATION
Main Post Office......................1 B2
Maison de la Presse..................2 B3
Santos Manfredi Hospital..........3 C5
Speed Laverie.........................4 C5
Tourist Office.....................(see 6)
Video Games...........................5 B4

SIGHTS & ACTIVITIES
Citadel Entrance.....................6 A4
Église de l'Annonciation..........7 B4
Le Belvédère..........................8 A4
Le Nid d'Aigle........................9 A4
Musée de la Corse..................10 A3
Palais National......................11 A4

Statue of Pascal Paoli..............12 B4
University of Corsica Pascal Paoli..13 C3

SLEEPING
Camping Restonica.................14 B5
Camping U Sognu...................15 A5
Hôtel de la Paix....................16 B2
Hôtel de la Poste...................17 B2
Hôtel du Nord.......................18 B3
Hôtel HR.............................19 D5

EATING
A Scudella...........................20 B4
Casino Supermarket................21 D5
Le 24................................22 B3

Les Délices du Palais...............23 B3
L'Oliveraie..........................24 D3
Paglia Orba..........................25 B3
U Museu.............................26 A4

DRINKING
Café de l'Oriente...................27 C3
Le Grand Café du Cours.........(see 18)
Le Lolita.............................28 B3

TRANSPORT
Bus Stop for Aléria & Porto
  via Calacuccia...................(see 30)
Bus Stop for Bastia & Ajaccio...29 B2
Europcar.............................30 D4

SIGHTS & ACTIVITIES
Citadel

Corte's high-perched, roughly triangular citadel is the island's only inland fortification. Offering great views of the Tavignano and Restonica Rivers and the cobbled alleyways of the *haute ville*, its highest point is a tower (known as the **Nid d'Aigle**, or Eagle's Nest), built in 1419

by a Corsican nobleman, Vincentello d'Istria, who rebelled against the Genoese occupiers.

The brooding barracks and outbuildings were added in the 19th century under Louis-Philippe. They also served as a prison – for the last time in WWII, when the Italians incarcerated captured *maquisards* (Corsican resistance fighters). The barracks continued to have a military purpose until 1983, as a base for the French Foreign Legion after its withdrawal from Algeria 20 years earlier.

From place Paoli (outside the citadel), climb the flight of stairs cut from Restonica marble to reach the ramparts and pass through the main gate. The two buildings facing one another are the **Caserne Serrurier** and **Caserne Padoue** (Serrurier and Padoua Barracks). Today, the Caserne Serrurier houses the Musée de la Corse. The Caserne Padoue (where the tourist office occupied a temporary corner at the time of writing) is undergoing renovation.

To reach the upper levels of the citadel and Nid d'Aigle, you have to pass through the museum. To enjoy just as impressive a panorama for free, climb the stairs outside and beneath the ramparts to the viewpoint of **Le Belvédère**.

Musée de la Corse (Museu di a Corsica)
The **Museum of Corsica** (☎ 04 95 45 25 45; adult/concession €5.30/3, audioguide €1.50; ☒ 10am-8pm daily mid-Jun–mid-Sep, 10am-6pm Tue-Sun Apr–mid-Jun & mid-Sep-Oct, 10am-5pm Tue-Sat Nov-Mar) is also (and perhaps more accurately) called the Musée Régional d'Anthropologie. From within, it's an impressive contemporary structure, designed by the Italian architect Andrea Bruno, who kept the barracks' long, brutal façade while enlarging the windows to allow more light to enter. The collection is exceptionally well displayed and lit. It's worth investing an extra €1.50 for the English audioguide – it's more stimulating than some of the didactic panels in French.

The building has two main galleries with a third space allocated to temporary exhibits. On the 1st floor, the **Galerie Doazan** exhibits a selection from the magnificent collection of around 3000 traditional Corsican craft objects amassed by Père Louis Doazan over nearly three decades, between 1951 and 1978, illustrating themes such as agriculture, pastoral life and cottage industries such as weaving.

On the next level, the **Musée en Train de se Faire** (Museum under Construction) deals with contemporary subjects such as industry, tourism and music, including a fascinating selection of publicity material for Mattei, the distiller whose original Bastia shop (p106) lives on.

Palais National (Palazzu Naziunale)
The large rectangular building to the left of the citadel entrance was once the palace of the local Genoese government: it subsequently housed Paoli's first and only independent Corsican government (p30). Paoli lived in this palace, which was simultaneously its principal university facility.

Below the palace on place Gaffory is the **Église de l'Annonciation**, built in the mid-15th century and transformed and enlarged in the 17th century.

University of Corsica Pascal Paoli
One of the demands of the nationalists in the 1960s was that Corsica should have its own institution of higher learning. In 1975 the French government acceded and in October 1981, nearly two centuries after Paoli first founded a university in Corte, doors were opened to students, establishing the town once again as the island's centre of learning. The main building of the university is on av Jean Nicoli, near the entrance to the lower town.

FESTIVALS & EVENTS
Corte is the centre for Corsica's burgeoning hiking industry and plays host each July to the gruelling **Inter-Lacs** (www.interlacs.com in French), a cross-country marathon that makes walking the GR20 seem a summer afternoon stroll in the park.

SLEEPING
As well as Corte's accommodation options, there are several charming sleeping choices in the nearby Vallée de la Restonica (p243), which are well worth considering if you are overnighting in the area.

Chambres d'Hôtes
Kyrn Flor (☎ 04 95 61 02 88; www.kyrnflor-chambresdhotes.com in French; U San Gavinu; r €55, 2-/4-person studios €65/100; ☒ year-round; Ⓟ ☲) At the right time of the year, you'll probably smell the Flower of Corsica before you reach it. The owner collects wild aromatic plants and distils their essences in his still, just opposite. Above, the pool has a magnificent view of the surrounding hills. This peaceful *chambres d'hôtes*, a 3.5km drive southwards from town along the N193, is a very tempting option, whether you opt for a room in the large stone house (look out for it on the left, driving from Corte) or a fully equipped studio.

Osteria di L'Orta (☎ 04 95 61 06 41; www.osteria-di-l-orta.com; Casa Guelfucci; s/d €60/75; year-round; Ⓟ)

Look out for a large powder-blue building with darker blue shutters, set back on the right as you leave Corte, heading northwards. Restored with great taste and restraint, it's run by a welcoming young couple. The four rooms and single suite (€100 to €120) are airy and spacious with parquet flooring and power showers. There's a kitchen for self-catering but you really ought to sign on for dinner (see opposite).

Hotels

Hôtel HR (☎ 04 95 45 11 11; www.hotel-hr.com; 6 allée du 9 Septembre; s/d with washbasin €25/29, d with bathroom €39-49; P) This hotel, Corte's best budget option, feels very institutional – not surprisingly since it was constructed in the 1960s as housing for the Foreign Legion after its withdrawal from North Africa. It's now a student residence during term time (when we last visited, it was home to several gendarmes too, whose own accommodation had recently been blown up). There are no frills, but rooms are spruce and functional; ask for one facing inwards over the garden. Its apartments (essentially two separate doubles, each with bathroom, plus cooker and fridge) are excellent value at €79. There's a sauna (€4), a fitness room (free) and a couple of washing machines (€5). Be sure to reserve, especially – and paradoxically – during the low season, when the students are in residence.

Hôtel de la Poste (☎ 04 95 46 01 37; 2 place Duc de Padoue; s/d €35/38, with bathroom €41/50; mid-Feb–Nov) On a quiet square, Hôtel de la Poste is a no-frills hotel for those who enjoy a little retro charm. Of its 11 good-sized, eccentrically furnished rooms, Nos 5 and 6 have balconies while rooms 9 and 10 share a wide terrace.

Hôtel de la Paix (☎ 04 95 46 06 72; socoget@wanadoo.fr; av du Général de Gaulle; s €38-62, d €45-62, tr €55-75; year-round) With 63 spick-and-span rooms, 12 of them with balcony, this welcoming, comfortable hotel, a favourite of passing tour groups, has been in business for over 75 years. Sitting calmly on a quiet square just off cours Paoli, it runs a more than decent restaurant from April through to mid-October.

Hôtel du Nord (☎ 04 95 46 00 68; www.hoteldunord-corte.com in French; 22 cours Paoli; s €65-75, d €78-88, tr €106-116; P) Don't be deterred by the scruffy façade of Corte's oldest hotel. Over 150 years in business and right on the main street, it remains a fine choice. Renovated throughout in 2004, this family-run place has 16 rooms, each with soaring, stuccoed ceilings, double-glazed windows and timber floors; the best rooms have mountain views. There's free parking no more than 50m away, a cosy onsite café with internet access and wi-fi in the hotel bar. Add €19 per person for half-board.

Camping

Camping U Sognu (☎ 04 95 46 09 07; camp sites per adult/tent/car €6/2.50/2.50; Apr-Sep) Within easy walking distance of town, this camping ground has splendid views of the citadel, illuminated at night. The bar and sanitary block occupy former farmhouse buildings and there's wood-fired pizza on offer in the evenings from the separate oven. The most attractive pitches, quieter and shaded by olive and oak trees, are on the upper terraces.

Camping Restonica (☎ / fax 04 95 46 11 59; camp sites per adult/tent/car €6.50/4/3.50; May-Sep) This fairly basic, shaded camping ground with its bluff owner has a café-bar with terrace. It sits right beside the river with the opportunity to dunk yourself in its shallow pools.

EATING
Restaurants

Paglia Orba (☎ 04 95 61 07 89; 5 av Xavier Luciani; salads €6-8, mains €11.50-14.50, menu Corse €14; Mon-Sat) It serves classic Corsican cuisine on its small, flower-decked terrace or in the cool of its airconditioned interior. While the food's well priced and uncomplicated, service would benefit from an extra smile or two; maybe we chose a bad day but staff were particularly glum.

U Museu (☎ 04 95 61 08 36; rampe Ribanelle; pizzas €7-8, mains €10-16, menu Corse €16; Apr-Oct) Just below the entrance to the citadel, U Museu may look like your typical tourist trap but that's deceptive. Dine on its gazebo-covered terrace and choose from its wide range of Corsican specialities (the *menu Corse* at €16 is excellent value), including *civet de sanglier aux myrtes sauvages* (wild boar with myrtle) and *tripettes à la Cortenaise* (tripe with shallots in a red-wine sauce). It doesn't take reservations and closes on Sunday in low season.

L'Oliveraie (☎ 04 95 46 06 32; rte d'Erbiagiola; mains €11-17, menus €15-24; Easter-Sep, closed dinner Mon Oct-Easter) Offering particularly friendly, attentive service, this restaurant, on the outskirts of town, serves creative family cooking (Madame up front, her son in the kitchen). Try, for example, squid stuffed with *brocciu* or the house creation, *poulet aux cèpes et pommes* (chicken with cepe mushrooms and apple). For dessert, the homemade crunchy chestnut tart contrasts wonderfully with the scoop of ice cream that's served with it.

Le 24 (☎ 04 95 46 02 90; 24 cours Paoli; mains €13-17, menus €19-25; ⊙ Mon-Fri, dinner Sat) The stylish, contemporary décor sits prettily with the exposed stone walls, a pair of sweeping stone arches and a lovely old dresser. Run by a young couple (an extra member of staff, front of house, would help; service can be slow), its innovative menu uses top-quality ingredients and changes with the seasons. Save a cranny for one of the house desserts, chalked up on the portable blackboard.

A Scudella (☎ 04 95 46 25 31; 2 place Paoli; menus €13-18; ⊙ Mon-Sat) The decision making's easy at this snug, rustic place, rich in regional produce. There's no à la carte selection to dither over – just one, simple menu, short, sweet and carefully composed, from which you can select either two or three courses. What's far from simple is their original marriage of unlikely flavour combinations and the delightful presentation.

Osteria di L'Orta (☎ 04 95 61 06 41; www.osteria-di -l-orta.com; Casa Guelfucci; menus €20-35; ⊙ dinner daily Jun–mid-Sep, dinner Sat mid-Sep–May; ℗) The restaurant of this delightful *chambres d'hôtes* is well worth a visit, even if you're not staying the night. Meals are taken in the dining room, below the main building, with its vast bay windows. The menu, based upon fresh produce, changes daily. Reservations for the restaurant are essential.

Self-Catering

Les Délices du Palais (7 cours Paoli; ⊙ Mon-Sat, Sun morning) This wonderful little patisserie bakes all sorts of tempting Corsican cakes and sweetmeats.

There's a large Casino supermarket near the train station.

DRINKING

Le Grand Café du Cours (☎ 04 95 46 00 33; 22 cours Paoli) On the ground floor of Hôtel du Nord, this stained-woodwork bar is Corte's oldest watering hole. It has a huge menu of drinks and snacks (internet too, if you fancy talking to the wider world).

Pub Le Lolita (2 place Gaffory; ⊙ 10pm-2am Tue-Sun) You'll need to look out for this place, which is squeezed between a café and a sandwich joint on the square's northern side. There's a great selection of tapas, with quality wines to help

them down, and you may be lucky enough to hit a night of live guitar music.

Café de l'Oriente (☎ 04 95 61 11 77; 5 av Jean Nicoli) Opposite the university, this is the hub of student life during the academic year. A friendly spot year-round, it also acts as an outpost of the tourist office. Claude Cesari, the owner and a keen walker, is a mine of information about hiking opportunities in the area.

GETTING THERE & AROUND
Bus

Eurocorse (☎ 04 95 46 06 83) run two services a day, Monday to Saturday, to Bastia (€10, 1¼ hours) and Ajaccio (€11, 1¾ hours). Buses stop outside Brasserie Le Majestic (19 cours Paoli).

Autocars Cortenais (☎ 04 95 46 02 12) has one bus to Bastia (€10, 1½ hours) via Ponte Leccia on Monday, Wednesday and Friday. It, too, stops outside Brasserie Le Majestic. From July to September it also runs a bus to Aléria (€10, one hour) on Tuesday, Thursday and Saturday, leaving from in front of the train station.

From July to mid-September, **Autocars Mordiconi** (☎ 04 95 48 00 04) runs one bus, Monday to Saturday, to Porto (€20, 2¾ hours) via Calacuccia (€9, one hour) and Évisa (€17, two hours). Buses leave from in front of the train station.

Taxi

For a taxi, call **Michel Balvani** (☎ 04 95 46 04 88) or **Taxi Francois** (☎ 04 95 61 01 17). A trip up the Restonica Valley (you might like to consider this option, rather than negotiating the narrow road yourself) costs about €35.

Train

From the **train station** (☎ 04 95 46 00 97) there are trains to Ajaccio (€11, two hours, up to four daily) and Bastia (€9.70, two hours, five daily). There's also a service to Calvi (€13.10, three hours, three daily) via Île Rousse (€10.40, 2¼ hours) with a change at Ponte Leccia.

AROUND CORTE

VALLÉE DE LA RESTONICA

The Vallée de la Restonica is one of the prettiest spots in all Corsica. The river, rising in the grey-green mountains, has scoured little basins in the rock, offering sheltered pinewood settings for bathing and sunbathing alike. From Corte, the D623 winds its way through the valley for 15km to the Bergeries de Grotelle. Here, a car park (€5) and a huddle of shepherds' huts (three of which offer drinks, local cheeses and snacks) mark the end of the road. From them, a rugged trail climbs up to a pair of high mountain lakes.

Sadly, here's a prime example of what happens when a blacktop road is forged deep into a narrow mountain valley. Its delights are easily – perhaps too easily – available to any-one with a vehicle. For 10 months of the year, the valley is tranquil and a mildly trafficked delight, while the mountains above it remain snowcapped well into May. In high summer the pressure is intense. Then, consider leaving your vehicle at the information point to take the hourly shuttle bus, both to avoid the slalom of a drive and so that there's one fewer vehicle adding strain to this fragile environment.

EXPLORING LE BOZIU

Overwhelmed by the hordes in the Restonica Valley? Wilting from the heat of Corte in high summer? Here's the ultimate in off-the-beaten-track driving: a route that takes you into the deepest aorta of Corsica's inland heart yet stays throughout on well-surfaced back lanes.

Set aside a whole day to explore this microregion that begins on Corte's very doorstep yet remains unknown, even to most Corsicans. As you drive the narrow, twisting roads, you'll come across drowsy hamlets, deep wooded valleys, glorious little village churches and panoramas to make the heart beat faster. Here, in the island's deepest recesses, is where the *paghjella*, perhaps the most haunting genre of polyphonic singing, was born and matured.

Follow the N193 northwards from Corte, then branch off to the right along the D41 towards **Tralonca** with its lovely parish church, painted in yellow and white. Continue towards **Santa Lucia di Mercurio**, then **Sermano**. Within Sermano's little Romanesque chapel of **San-Nicolao** are some sensitive 15th-century frescoes (the Gîte d'Étape U San Fiurenzu, see below, in Sermano will hand you the keys). Drive on as far as **Bustanico**, where there's another lovely stone church, then loop left and northwards to pass through **Carticasi** (9km) and **Cambia**, 2km beyond.

Here, take the D39, direction San Lorenzo, and turn right at a sign indicating the 13th-century **church of San Quilico**. Deep inside a little wood, this Romanesque building has some finely carved sculptures on the outside and, within, a series of frescoes depicting the Holy Trinity and the Archangel Gabriel weighing the souls of the dead (ask for the key at the last house in this hamlet).

Retrace your steps as far as Bustanico, then follow the sign for Alando (2.5km) with its **Convent of San-Francescu-di-u-Boziu**. Continue to **Favallelo** (3km) to admire the equally impressive frescoes of the **church of Santa-Maria-Assunta**. After 1km, turn left onto the D339 to arrive at the village of **Sant Andrea di Boziu** after about 9km. The hamlet of **Piedilacorte** has another beautiful **parish church**.

Head for **Erbajola**, where the lovely **church of San-Martinu** is a short 15-minute walk away along a stony track. This track also leads to the atmospheric ruined village of **Casella**, these days reclaimed by the maquis but with its church still almost intact.

From Erbajola, follow signs for **Foccichia** (6km) and **Altiani** (8km) to take the N200 Aléria–Corte road, direction Corte, at a junction 8km beyond Altiani. At this crossroads, an attractive **Genoese bridge** spans the stream. From here, Corte and the wider world once more are some 20km along the N200.

You may well be tempted to linger. Accommodation opportunities are few but here is a trio of attractive options.

Gîte d'Étape U San Fiurenzu (☎ 04 95 48 68 08; Sermano; dm with/without half-board €34/15; ☼ Apr-Sep) This modern *gîte*, clean as a new pin, has rooms accommodating four sleepers. Meals (€16) are filling and there's a pleasant terrace with striking views.

Altu Pratu (☎ 04 95 48 80 07; www.altupratu.com in French; Erbajola; d €60-70; ☼ year-round; ☒) This complex, combining a small hotel and a *ferme-auberge*, offers a superb panorama over Monte d'Oro and Monte Renoso. Its cuisine and wines are renowned hereabouts (meals €22.50, including apéritif) and the pool is a welcome add-on in summer.

Chambres d'Hôtes Casa Capellini (☎ 04 95 48 69 33; www.vallecime.com; Sant Andrea di Boziu; d from €80, with half-board €120-140; ☼ year-round). This imposing salmon-pink structure has five comfortable rooms and serves copious meals. It's prudent to reserve.

Alternatively, for a long (allow five hours) walk through shaded forest with plenty of opportunity for picnicking and swimming, take the shuttle service up the valley and follow the signed path down through a forest of pine and chestnut. It's much more gentle than the high mountain alternatives.

Information

The valley **information point** (☎ 04 95 46 33 92; ⊗ 8am-5pm Jun-Aug), 4km along the Restonica gorge from Corte, has a brochure that gives broad information about hiking opportunities.

The Corte tourist office (p237) can also advise.

Activities

Several challenging treks take off from signed points along the valley road. By far the two most popular destinations, marked with yellow blobs from the Bergeries de Grotelle car park (1375m), are a pair of glacial lakes, **Lac de Melu** (1711m) and **Lac de Capitellu** (1930m).

The path to Lac de Melu follows the left (west) bank of the Restonica for most of its way. With its inky waters, fringed by dwarf alder trees and juniper bushes, the lake's a lovely reward for a strenuous ascent. There's a short chain section and a couple of iron ladders to help you negotiate the steepest section, just before the lake. Allow a generous hour from the car park.

The waters of Lac de Melu, with a little help from the tributaries that leak from the gorge's lower flanks, supply the Restonica River below. The lake in its turn is fed by a stream that tumbles from Lac de Capitellu, a further 45 minutes' steep ascent away and even more spectacular. Allow 3½ to four hours, not counting stops, for the full extent of this out-and-back walk.

Sleeping & Eating

There are a couple of tempting sleeping choices in the early reaches of the Vallée de la Restonica. Stay here and you're well poised for an early getaway to beat the summertime hordes that throng up the valley.

Camping Tuani (☎ 04 95 46 11 65; camp sites per adult/tent/car €6.50/3/2; ⊗ Easter-Sep) Delightfully set in the Restonica Valley amid pines and with river bathing below, this camping ground has been run by the same lady for over 25 years. There's a bar, pizzeria and restaurant (and,

rare for Corsica, toilet paper's provided!). It's about 6km from Corte town centre and 9km before Parking de Grotelle at the end of the valley road.

Hôtel Dominique Colonna (☎ 04 95 45 25 65; www .dominique-colonna.com in French; r €60-165; ⊗ mid-Mar–mid-Nov; P ⊠ ⊠) Directly opposite Auberge de la Restonica (and owned by the same family), this place was constructed by the current owner's father (older readers may recall Rheims as distant European football champions: the team of Kopa, Fontaine – and Dominique Colonna). Rooms bear the names of his contemporaries and photos of the giants of the day bedeck the walls. All of the 28 agreeably furnished rooms have a small terrace or balcony overlooking the river and there's a small kidney-shaped heated pool.

Auberge de la Restonica (☎ 04 95 45 25 25; hotel restonica@hotmail.com; d €70-90; ⊗ year-round; P ⊠) Stone built and with polished wood everywhere – beams, stairs, cupboards, dining-room tables and chairs – this rustic place, barely 1.5km from Corte, speaks of the country mansion it once was. In addition to its six rooms, there's an excellent-value split-level studio apartment (€110 for two) that can accommodate up to six (€25 per extra person). You can plunge into its large swimming pool or dunk yourself in the river's natural pools just below. It also runs a first-class restaurant, along with a cosy bar with deep leather armchairs.

Getting There & Away

A **shuttle bus** (adult/child return €2/1) operates from mid-July to mid-August, starting from the information point, 2km into the valley from Corte, and running to the parking de Grotelle. It leaves on the hour from 8am to 1pm with return journeys from 2pm until 5pm. Caravans and camper vans are halted at **Tuani**, 7km from Corte (it's a wonder they're allowed this far).

If you're driving, the 30km per hour speed limit makes sound sense on this narrow road with its infinity of tight bends and few passing opportunities.

VALLÉE DU TAVIGNANO WALK

Corsica's deepest gorge makes for a classic, day-long walk from the centre of Corte. Unlike the Restonica Valley hike, however, this track has no facilities en route for walkers. Stock up on everything you will need before

THE CENTRAL MOUNTAINS

setting off and be sure to have strong shoes, a sun hat and plenty of water.

From Corte, the track climbs through the maquis and scrubland, hugging the river as it climbs deep into the mountains following an old mule track. About 5km from Corte the gorge walk really kicks in and the scenery becomes increasingly dramatic. If you're planning to push onwards towards the **Lac de Ninu** (1743m), a key point on the GR20 walking route (p56), there's a small walkers' *refuge*, **Refuge de la Sega**, roughly about halfway along the Tavignano Valley.

VALLÉE DU NIOLO

The Vallée du Niolo is the traditional sheep- and goat-herding district of Corsica, a tough place where lonely shepherds have eked out a stark, rural existence for centuries. Until the D84 was forged through the valley, the only access was over the Col de Verghio or along a precipitous mule track that threaded through the Scala di Santa Regina. Today it remains relatively isolated from the rest of the island, not helped by a solitary summer-only bus service (p246) and long, hard winters, which is no doubt why it retains its special character. Calacuccia, with plenty of accommodation options, makes a great base for getting to know this special area, sometimes known as the kernel of Corsica.

SCALA DI SANTA REGINA

This awesome mountain pass northwest of Corte was the only means of access from Corte to Calacuccia and the villages of the Niolo region until the road was constructed under Napoleon III. The deep granite gorges that plunge down to the bed of the **River Golo** make this one of the island's most dramatic mountain landscapes – and all the more so because of the rock's warm, reddish rust colour.

The narrow D84, sometimes hardly more than a ledge supported by arches, winds its way through the pass for around 20km, from the outskirts of Calacuccia close to the junction with the N193. The only blot on the landscape is the chain of rusty electricity pylons following the line of the river.

The upstream dam and hydroelectric power station, which can dramatically alter water levels without warning, make any descent into the gorges perilous.

From Corte, head north along the N193 as far as Francardo, then take the turning west onto the D84 (in the direction of Calacuccia).

CALACUCCIA

pop 350 / elevation 820m

Rising above the lake at its heart, the quiet little village of Calacuccia, a waystage on the Mare a Mare Nord trail, is a haunt for hikers. It lies in the shadow of **Monte Cinto** (2706m; see the boxed text, below) and affords good views of **I Cinque Frati** (The Five Monks), five jagged peaks that glower over the rural community below. There are plenty of opportunities for bathing in the mountain streams between Casamaccioli and Albertacce but swimming in the lake is not allowed.

The **tourist office** (☎ 04 95 48 05 22; www.asniolu .com in French; ☼ 9am-noon & 3-7pm Jul & Aug, 9am-noon

---

CLIMBING MONTE CINTO

Many summer visitors to Calacuccia come to attack Monte Cinto (2710m), Corsica's highest peak. It's a six-hour climb from Lozzi (p246), above Calacuccia and the valley bottom. Here, you can leave your car beside the pair of camp sites (if you're at the wheel of a 4WD, it can take you further up the pitted track but don't risk it in an ordinary saloon car).

If you're planning to tackle the summit and return in the same day, you'll need to make a very early start, both to enjoy the cool of the early morning and to be off the mountain before the storm clouds, frequent in summer during late afternoon, begin to build up.

From Lozzi, the trail, waymarked by bright orange markers, ascends a track, at first deceptively gently, then by a series of acute hairpin bends towards the Refuge de l'Ecru (1650m), which you reach in 2½ to three hours. From this unstaffed mountain hut (consider packing a sleeping bag, overnighting at this rudimentary accommodation and spreading the trek over two days), the climbing really starts with the summit a further three to four hours away. It's a hard slog but the truly magnificent panorama – taking in the east and west coasts, the islands of Italy's Tuscan archipelago and, if the air is very clear, the French coastline – will keep your spirits buoyant.

& 2-5pm Sep-Jun) is beside the main road, 100m east of Hôtel des Touristes. It produces a pamphlet, *Randonner dans le Niolu* (€1), which outlines five walks varying from 1½ hours to a full day. It also carries a similar Parc Naturel Régional de Corse (PNRC) pamphlet, *Sentiers de Pays: Niolu*, which gives broad details for seven walks from two to seven hours in and around the valley. You'll need to supplement both with the IGN Top 25 sheet *Corte, Monte Cristo* (4250OT).

The **Association Sportive du Niolu** (☎ 04 95 48 05 22, 06 22 50 70 29; www.asniolu.com), also called, more verbosely, the Compagnie Régionale des Guides et Accompagnateurs en Montagne de Corse, offers guided hiking, climbing, canyon descents and, in winter, cross-country ski treks throughout the valley.

Sleeping
CHAMBRES D'HÔTES
Casa Balduina (☎ 04 95 48 08 57; www.casabalduina .com; r €55-74, with half-board €117-136; ⌚ year-round; Ⓟ) This is a truly delightful seven-room boutique-style place, 1km west of Calacuccia beside the D84. There's lavender at the gate and a wonderful arbour, shaded by wisteria and honeysuckle, where breakfast is served. Rooms are decorated and furnished with flair by Jeanne Quilichini, your hostess, who speaks excellent English. Having run a restaurant in her time, she'll prepare a memorable dinner, for which you need to reserve in advance.

HOTELS
Hôtel des Touristes (☎ 04 95 48 00 04; www.hotel-des -touristes.com in French; s/d/tr with shower €40/48/58, with bathroom €48/58/68; ⌚ May–mid-Oct) The 30 rooms of this venerable old hotel, built in 1925, are spacious, comfortable and very reasonably priced. It also offers dorm beds (€15) and *gîte* rooms (€19 per person) for hikers in the nearby annexe. The owner, Monsieur Mordiconi also runs the local summer season bus service and is knowledgeable about the Niolo's walking trails.

Hôtel Acqua-Viva (☎ 04 95 48 06 90; d/tw €62/66; ⌚ year-round; Ⓟ) Friendly and family-run (they also operate the camping ground opposite), this roadside hotel has 14 fresh rooms with pleasant furnishings. All have great mountain views so choose one at the rear, away from the road and petrol station below. There's a popular bar downstairs where locals congregate to play cards.

HOSTELS
Couvent Saint François (☎ 04 95 48 00 11; dm €15, d/tr €42/56; Ⓟ ✗) The brothers have long since moved on from this converted 17th-century Franciscan monastery, opposite Casa Balduina. Still run by the church, it has rear-facing dorms. Doubles and triples, all with bathroom and balcony, overlook the lake. There's a kitchen for self-caterers.

CAMPING
Camping Acqua-Viva (☎ 04 95 47 00 39; camp sites per adult/tent/car €5/2.50/2.50; ⌚ May–mid-Oct) This relatively new camping ground has modern, impeccable facilities, wooden tables and benches beside most pitches and a large freezer for campers' use. The barbecue area is on the flagstones of what was once a grain-threshing area and reception is in a former chestnut-drying shed. Shade is in short supply (until the recently planted trees mature), except for some prime pitches with views of the lake that are shielded from the sun by giant chestnut trees.

Eating
U Valduniellu (☎ 04 95 48 06 92; pizzas €8.50-9, mains €17) Opposite Hôtel des Touristes, this place has friendly service and offers wood-fired pizzas plus a range of local specialities, inside or on its small terrace.

Restaurant du Lac (☎ 04 95 48 02 73; mains €10-16, menus €15.20-22) Located at Sidossi, 2km west of Calacuccia, this restaurant is near the lake but, despite its name, can't offer you lakeside views. No matter: you're here for the food and the chef makes good use of fresh, local produce, especially veal from the valley and free-range lamb.

PLANTING IDEAS

Those watchtowers all around the coast are the most evident and recurrent reminder of centuries of Genoese presence on the island. But Genoa left another long lasting and more significant, if less obvious, legacy. When settlers from the mainland repopulated the Corsican coast in the 16th century, with the grant of land came a strict obligation to plant vines, at least four fruit trees and one chestnut tree. To this day, you can see how this early example of enforced agricultural planning has shaped the Corsican countryside.

Getting There & Away

Autocars Mordiconi (☎ 04 95 48 00 04) runs one bus (Monday to Saturday from July to mid-September) between Corte (€9, one hour) and Porto (€15, 1½ hours) via Calacuccia.

ALBERTACCE

pop 200 / elevation 860m

The D84 leads west from Calacuccia towards the tiny hamlet of Albertacce. On the way, a couple of attractive detours beckon.

Follow a sign to the right for **Lozzi**, the trailhead for climbing Monte Cinto (see the boxed text, p244). Above the village, there's a staggering view of the valley from beside **Camping L'Arimone** (☎ 04 95 48 05 51; camp sites per adult/tent/car €5/2/2; Jun-Sep; **P**), itself an attractive option for tenters with plenty of space and shade beneath the pines. Beside it is **U Mulinu** (☎ 04 95 48 09 08; adult/child €5/free; 9am-1pm & 4-8pm Jul & Aug, 3-7pm May, Jun & Sep), a functioning chestnut flour mill.

A stirring 6.5km drive up the D318 with plunging views of the valley to the south brings you to **Calasima** (1100m), which lays claim to being Corsica's highest village. To the north, you can make out the peak of Monte Cinto, the cutaway slab of Paglia Orba and the distinctive jagged peaks of I Cinque Frati, the Five Brothers. Push on for a further 2km to the end of the blacktop road, where you can scramble over the rocks and take a dip in the inviting natural pools below.

Eating

U Cintu (Chez JoJo; ☎ 04 95 48 06 87; daily special €13, menu €20) You certainly aren't spoilt for choice

PIGS ON THE RUN

There are no longer any wild pigs (except wild boar) in Corsica: pigs seen at the sides of mountain roads are domestic animals known as *cochons coureurs* (free-ranging pigs). It is estimated that there are 15,000 free-ranging pigs in Haute-Corse and 30,000 in Corse-du-Sud.

The best of Corsican pork derives its flavour from the pigs' diet of acorns and chestnuts (supplemented with other food at certain times of the year). The charcuterie produced in Corsica is excellent – and some of the specialities sold on the island are actually made from imported pork meat.

at this modest, warmly recommended family restaurant where a huge clock is stuck permanently at 12.30 and the TV blares from the adjacent family parlour: it's the *menu* or the *plat du jour*. No prizes for the décor either, with its pink walls and floral fabric-covered lamps. But top marks for friendliness and honest, quality Niolo cooking. On the walls, family photos vie with vintage black-and-white shots of the Niolo valley as it used to be.

CASAMACCIOLI

pop 100 / elevation 860m

A drive around the southern side of the lake brings you to this sleepy hamlet. In the village church and gazing down from the chapel to the left of the main altar is the gaudy statue of the Madonna, **Santa Maria della Stella**, said to have transported herself here by mule, escaping from Turkish pirates. Each September, the Madonna is proudly paraded through the village, an event that attracts thousands of pilgrims and local émigrés who return to their roots to take part in one of Corsica's most venerated religious festivals, the **Santa di u Niolo**.

CORTE TO VIZZAVONA

Getting There & Away

The region between Corte and Vizzavona is well served by transport connections, with the N193 cutting a swathe through the mountains and trains on the Corte–Ajaccio route offering daily connections.

Eurocorse Voyages (☎ 04 95 21 06 30) runs buses twice daily between Ajaccio and Bastia, Monday to Saturday, stopping at Vizzavona, Vivario, Vénaco and Corte. Buses leave both Ajaccio and Bastia at 7.45am and 3pm (€18, three hours).

Chemins de Fer de la Corse (☎ 04 95 23 11 03) runs four trains daily from Ajaccio, stopping at Vizzavona (€8.40, 1¼ hours), Vivario (€9.20, 1½ hours), Vénaco (€10.70, 1¾ hours), Corte (€12.50, 2¼ hours), Ponte Leccia (€16.50, 2¾ hours) and Bastia (€23.50, 3¾ hours).

LA VÉNACHESE

Here, in the mountainous area to the south of Corte, you'll find cool, fresh mountain air, deep forests, spectacular scenery and abundant hiking trails.

Vénaco

pop 650 / elevation 610m

Vénaco, overlooking the Tavignano Valley, is renowned for the quality and variety of its local produce – from fresh trout to ewe's milk cheese. Like so many of Corsica's mountain hamlets, this once-bustling community is nowadays fairly subdued as its inhabitants move to the cities in search of new employment.

For a brief, attractive detour and a break from the N193, take the D143 to the right at the entrance to the village as you approach it from Ajaccio. After 5km, you reach the **Pont de Noceta**, spanning the little River Vecchio and overlooked by towering mountains. At this perfect picnic spot, there's a great view back to the village and you can steep yourself in the river.

If you fancy playing Tarzan for an afternoon, **Grandeur Nature** (☎ 06 03 83 68 36; www.grandeurnature-corse.com; St-Pierre de Venaco; ☽ 10am-7pm mid-Jun–mid-Sep) is an ecofriendly outfit that has suspended up in the trees four circuits of varying difficulty (€10 to €18). These, you complete by working your way along their ladders, ropes and nets.

SLEEPING & EATING

Camping-Auberge de la Ferme de Peridundellu (☎ / fax 04 95 47 09 89; camp sites per adult/tent/car €4.30/2.45/2.30; ☽ Easter–mid-Sep) On the D143, 3.5km from Vénaco, you'll find this small, friendly, family-run camping ground on a spur overlooking the valley. Meals are available (*menus* €15; reserve in advance). Facilities are clean and well maintained and you can't beat the farm cooking for value and flavour.

THE AUTHOR'S CHOICE

In the hamlet of St-Pierre de Venaco (Santo Pietro di Venaco), off the N193 at Vénaco's northern limit, stands a handsome stone house built by **Antoinette and Charles Hiver** (☎ 04 95 47 07 29; dm/d with half-board €32.50/71; ☽ Apr–mid-Oct; P ✗). It's a hugely welcoming place where meals are hearty: at breakfast, you can dip into Antoinette's homemade jams, which she also sells, strictly to visitors. There are three spick-and-span four-person dormitories and four delightfully decorated doubles. Antoinette runs the kitchen with panache while Charles, a mountain guide, is very knowledgeable about walks in the area. To get to this *gîte*, go to the top of the village, and follow the road behind the church for 500m. This place is justifiably popular with walkers so book well ahead in summer.

Hôtel U Frascone (☎ 04 95 47 00 85; www.ufrascone.com; s €40-48, with half-board €57-65, d €45-55, with half-board €79-89) At the southern limit of the village, this hotel has lovely views of the valley below, especially from its adjoining terrace restaurant, which offers *menus* (€14 to €23), giant salads and a wealth of local dishes. It has eight rooms, each attractively painted in pastel shades.

Vivario

pop 500 / elevation 696m

About 9km from Vénaco along the N193, Vivario nestles among the mountains alongside an alternative route for walkers undertaking the Mare a Mare Nord (p76).

DETOUR: GHISONI

Ghisoni (pop 250) is a tiny mountain hamlet on the D69, about 17km from the junction with the N197. Before WWII, this village boasted three dance halls, 12 cafés and 1800 inhabitants, but its population has since dwindled to barely a tenth of that size. It lies peacefully at the foot of Punta Kyrie Eleïson, a mountain southeast of Vivario. Robert Colonna d'Istria, in his *L'Histoire de la Corse*, explains the origin of the mountain's unusual and very un-Corsican name: in the 14th century members of the Giovannali sect, who were of Franciscan origin but equally resentful of secular and church authorities, were burnt alive on the mountain. Legend has it that, as the flames rose and the priest sang the prayer of the Kyrie Eleïson, a white dove began to wheel above the burning woodpiles.

Wandering its lanes, bordered by handsome stone houses, its not difficult to imagine the village as it was up to WWII: a thriving community, its wealth created by milling chestnut flour and selling lumber from the nearby forest of laricio pine.

Ghisoni has a small seasonal **tourist office** (☎ 04 95 62 02 27; ☽ 9am-noon & 3-7pm Mon-Sat Apr-Sep).

Precisely 4.5km north of Vivario, the handsome viaduct spanning the Vecchio River was designed by Gustave Eiffel. Carrying the Bastia–Ajaccio railway, it upstages the modern bridge that carries the N193.

SLEEPING & EATING

Camping Le Soleil (☎ 04 95 47 23 08; camp sites per adult/tent/car €6/2.50/2; 🕙 May-Oct; **P**) Halfway between Vivario and Vizzavona, 5km from each and just below Tattone station, this delightful, friendly little camping ground is installed within an orchard of apple, pear and cherry trees. Facilities are immaculate and it accepts reservations. There are also three basic chalets (€30 per person).

Le Macchje Monti (☎ 04 95 47 22 00; r €50, with half-board per person €60; 🕙 Apr-Oct) Near the church, this is the only hotel in town. Well-maintained bedrooms with washbasin have corridor bathrooms, while its restaurant, Chez Marie-Anne (mains €10 to €15), is a simple place that offers a decent *menu Corse* (€15).

VIZZAVONA

pop 100 / elevation 910m
The N193 climbs steeply in the shadow of Mont d'Oro (2389m), the fifth-highest peak on the island, before arriving at the cool mountain hamlet of Vizzavona. A mere cluster of houses and hotels around its train station and 700m from the main road, Vizzavona's

a major hub for the huge number of walkers who congregate here in high season to start, end or continue their GR20 trek.

Deep in the **Forêt de Vizzavona**, which all but surrounds this tiny halt, bandits routinely held travellers to ransom right up until the 19th century. Nowadays the forest is a peaceful haven, its 1633 hectares covered mainly by beech and laricio pine trees – some reputed to be more than 800 years old – and crisscrossed by over 25 hiking trails.

Within the forest, **Vizzavona Parc Aventure** (☎ 04 95 37 28 41; Col de Vizzavona; 🕙 10am-7pm mid-Jun–mid-Sep) has 10 ropeways and clambering nets through the trees (€10 to €20) at a variety of levels of difficulty. It's beside the N193, just before the Col de Vizzavona and near the Cascades des Anglais (below).

Sleeping & Eating

Hôtel Restaurant I Laricci (☎ 04 95 47 21 22; www .ilaricci.com in French; s/d/tr €56/74/108; 🕙 May-Sep; **P**) This large chalet-style building just above the station has 12 comfortable rooms, six with mountain views. All have parquet floors and soft beds into which many a weary trekker has sunk. The few with private bathroom cost €6 extra. Half-board is a mere €4 extra per person; folly not to take it. There's also a dormitory annexe (€27 for dormitory and dinner), which can sleep up to 18 hikers. You can choose from a range of snacks and drinks

---

WALKS AROUND VIZZAVONA

Two-and-a-half kilometres from the spot where the road from Ajaccio branches off towards the train station, a signpost indicates a short, gentle path that meanders down through a superb forest of pine and beech to **Cascades des Anglais**, a sequence of gleaming waterfalls.

After about 15 minutes on foot you intersect with the GR20 and a small refreshment stall (open in summer only). The path to the waterfalls continues to the left while the right fork leads back to Vizzavona train station (30 minutes).

In summer, there is a series of clear pools, ideal for swimming, where you can sunbathe on the smooth rocks. The falls owe their name to the wealthy British visitors in the 19th century for whom Vizzavona was a mandatory stop – especially once the railway was established – on their European grand tour.

Continuing southwest along the N193 for a few kilometres brings you to the village of **Bocognano**. From here the road to the **Cascade du Voile de la Mariée** (Bridal Veil Falls) is on the left as you leave the village.

The narrow road passes a railway bridge, then comes up on a second bridge, recognisable by its iron guard-rails, 3.5km from the main road. A small wooden ladder on the left allows you to get over the fence. Continue along the path that climbs through the undergrowth, roughly marked out with lengths of rope tied between the trees. After around 10 minutes of rather difficult terrain you come to a tall, broad waterfall. Impressively fast-flowing in winter, you may find it little more than a dribble in summer.

THE AUTHOR'S CHOICE

Hôtel & Relais Monte D'Oro (☎ 04 95 47 21 06; www.monte-oro.com in French; s/d €36/46, with bathroom €57/75, with half-board €73/120; 🗓 May-Sep; Ⓟ 🖳) Offering an attractive option for every budget, this place even has a serene little chapel in the grounds, should you need a little spiritual uplift. Le Relais, its roadside café (and formerly the local gendarmerie headquarters) serves snacks and drinks and is popular with passing hikers and motorists.

Built in 1880 to house workers on Corsica's first railway track, running from Ajaccio to Corte, the hotel has belonged to the same family, the Plaisants, since 1904. Rooms are comfy and the furniture has that early 20th-century feel. You won't find – or need – air-con and satellite TV but if you take the half-board option that includes a hearty dinner, just like your grandma used to make, it's excellent value.

The hotel was a favourite of Dorothy Carrington, the venerable grande dame who wrote *Granite Island: a Portrait of Corsica* (p22), still the best-known literary work in English about Corsica. 'Madame Carrington stayed with us for the last time in the year before she died,' recalls Madame Sicurani, the current owner. 'She was a little frail physically but still had all her mental faculties.'

In the grounds, there's also a gîte (dorm beds with/without half-board €36/17) with en suite rooms for four and a refuge (dorm beds with/without half-board €30/11), run by Madame Sicurani's nephew.

The complex is 3km south of Vizzavona in the hamlet of La Foce. A free shuttle bus will collect and drop off guests at Vizzavona train station if you call ahead.

---

on the sunny hotel terrace or in the bar, where Moroccan rugs hang from the walls – its mint tea (€2.50) slakes the thirst wonderfully after a hard day's walking.

Bar Restaurant de la Gare (☎ /fax 04 95 47 22 20; dm with/without half-board €34/15; 🗓 May–mid-Oct)

Trekkers congregate on the terrace here to exchange tales of mountain exploits. Dorms are for four or six sleepers. This friendly place also offers a small à la carte selection (€8 to €13), ample plates of pasta (€7 to €8) and a filling dinner *menu* (€12).

Directory

CONTENTS

ACCOMMODATION

We've categorised our Sleeping entries by type of accommodation; recommendations within these listings are in ascending order of price.

Given that the detailed price structure is a nightmare in Corsica – there can be up to six different prices for one given room (aaargh!!!) – we've simplified it for the sake of convenience. Thus, for each hotel and *chambres d'hôtes*, we quote a price range that reflects seasonal price variations. The lower end of the scale corresponds to the cheapest rate you can get for any given room (usually out of season); the higher end of the scale corresponds to the most expensive rate that is applied for the same type of room (in August, in most cases).

If there's no range, this means that the price stays the same year-round (sadly, this is very uncommon).

All of the rates listed are for rooms with bathrooms unless otherwise specified.

You are seriously advised to book a room in advance for July and August (the French *grandes vacances*). The whole of France and half of Italy seem to descend onto the island during the holiday period and most reasonable accommodation gets snapped up fast. If the need for a flexible itinerary prevents you from making reservations way in advance, a telephone call the day before is still better than nothing. It widens the choice enormously if you have your own transport and speak at least a little bit of French.

High-season prices in many hotels can be up to triple the prices charged in the low season.

Camping

Good news for those who want to spend their holiday under canvas: there are dozens, maybe even hundreds, of camp sites in Corsica, classified from one to five stars depending on their amenities and convenience of location. The cheapest ones, *camping à la ferme* (farm camp sites), offer only basic facilities but are good value if you factor in their scenic location. Top-quality camping grounds boast restaurants, bars, mini-golf courses and swimming pools. Most sites fall somewhere in between the two extremes.

The majority of camping grounds in Corsica open only from June to September.

In this book the price is broken down into adult/tent/car, but this does not include extras. Prices vary seasonally – they are at their

---

BOOK ACCOMMODATION ONLINE

For more accommodation reviews and recommendations by Lonely Planet authors, check out the online booking service at www.lonelyplanet.com. You'll find the true, insider lowdown on the best places to stay. Reviews are thorough and independent. Best of all, you can book online.

PRACTICALITIES

- Corsica uses the metric system for weights and measures; kilometres, kilograms, litres, and degrees in Celsius.

- Electric current is 220V, 50Hz AC; plugs have two round pins.

- Video recorders and players run on the PAL system.

- If your French is up to it, keep a finger on the pulse by reading the daily regional newspaper *Corse Matin*. Or pick up *Arriti* or *O Ribombu* (in French and in Corsican) if you want to get an idea of some Nationalist prose. The monthly magazine *Corsica* (in French) is good for the latest on Corsica's current issues.

- For French TV, try the commercial stations Tf1 and M6 or the state-owned channels France 2 and France 3.

- Tune in to *France Bleu Frequenza Mora* (www.bleurcfm.com) or *Alta Frequenza* (www.alta -frequenza.com) for local news (in French and in Corsican), reports and polyphonic singing.

---

highest in August. Charges per night range from around €3 to €8 per person, plus €2 to €4 for a tent, and from an additional €2 for a car. Make a telephone call ahead, as in the high season camps might be full, and at the start or end of the season camps may also close if demand is low or weather is poor. Credit card is accepted only at the top-end camping grounds. Some camping grounds rent bungalows and cottages by the week.

Camping sauvage (literally 'wild camping', or camping outside recognised camping grounds) is prohibited; this is largely to reduce the risks of forest fires (especially in the maquis). In remote areas, including on the GR20, walkers or hikers can pitch their tent in *refuge* (mountain shelter) grounds for a nominal fee.

Chambres d'Hôtes

Chambres d'hôtes are the French equivalent of B&Bs, where, for marginally less than the price of a two-star hotel you can stay as a paying guest in a 'host' house. They are normally tucked away in the hills or in scenic locations and offer a window into a more traditional way of life. Interestingly, *chambres d'hôtes* in Corsica, by comparison with, say, Provence or southwest France, have not really caught on and are less sophisticated than on the mainland. There's a huge potential here, though.

Some of the cheapest places aren't much to write home about, but on the whole standards are high, and rooms are generally excellent value. Options include everything from restored village houses, modern buildings or country villas to rooms in family houses. Many have separate guest entrances and most places come equipped with private bathrooms. Rates cover a wide price range, typically €50 to €90 for two people. Breakfast is always included. Bookings are essential – you're not expected to pop up at the last minute.

Many *chambres d'hôtes* also offer *table d'hôtes* (hearty evening meals) at around €17 to €23 per person (set menu), but this must be reserved in advance.

Maisons d'hôtes (boutique-style B&Bs) are the latest trend. At the time of writing, there was a dozen of them, but new places should have opened by the time you read this.

Many *chambres d'hôtes* are members of **Gîtes de France** (☎ 04 95 10 06 14; www.gites-corsica .com; 77 cours Napoléon, Ajaccio). The Ajaccio branch has a brochure listing all the *chambres d'hôtes* in Corsica (with photos and full information). They are also listed on the Gîtes de France website (www.gites-corsica.com/chambres _hotes/chambre-hotes-en-corse.html). They are graded on a scale that rises from *un épi* (one ear) to *quatre épis* (four ears). *Chambres d'hôtes* can be booked either through Gîtes de France or by phoning the owners directly.

Take note that a number of excellent *chambres d'hôtes* do not belong to any association.

Gîtes d'Étape

Gîtes d'étape (walkers' lodges) are a greatvalue accommodation option. Though they were primarily set up for walkers, they also welcome non-walkers, space permitting (whisper it softly). They're an increasingly popular option, since they are almost all accessible by road, unlike *refuges*. Guess what? They boast wonderful settings – think secluded hamlets, renovated stones houses, dense forests, gushing rivers and breathtaking views. It's also a good way to meet other travellers. Out of season, you'll have the whole place for yourself.

Most *gîtes d'étape* are located along the Mare a Mare and Mare e Monti trails (see p54); in other words, they are dotted around the island, in the hinterland. They offer dormitory accommodation in four- to eight-bed rooms with shared bathroom facilities. Some places even have doubles. *Gîtes* are not to be confused with *refuges* – they are better equipped and much more comfortable, some with impeccable facilities that would put many a hotel to shame. The *gardien* (warden) will often offer quality meals or cooking facilities.

A bunk bed in the dorm usually costs between €11 and €17 per night and about €35 with half-board. Half-board is mandatory in certain places, especially in high season. Sheets are not provided but can usually be rented (about €3), so it's a good idea to bring your own sleeping bag or sleeping sheet. *Gîtes* are generally closed from 10am to 4pm, and they can be booked in advance.

The Maison d'Information du Parc Naturel Régional de Corse in Corte and in Ajaccio provides lists of refuges and *gîtes d'étape*. You can also go to www.parc-naturel-corse.fr/randos/heberg.html.

Hostels

There aren't really any youth hostels, as we know them, in Corsica, though you'll find dorm accommodation in many *gîtes d'étapes*.

Hotels

Corsica boasts hotels of all categories that will suit all wallets. There is a great deal of small-scale, often family-run, comfortable establishments – not really the period hotel you were dreaming of, but they blend pretty well with the environment and are intimate.

Rooms are impressively clean and frequently have balconies or terraces with views of mountains or of the sea. At the budget level, Corsica's hotels are said to be more expensive than budget hotels on the mainland, but in low season they are frequently discounted.

The weak point is the lack of imaginative places to stay. Many places, including some top-drawer options, rate zero in the charm department. But the lovely views and the scenic locations offer ample compensation.

A double has one double bed, so be sure to specify if you prefer twin beds *(deux lits séparés)*.

Breakfast is not included and can add €5 to €12 per person, but it's not obligatory – you'll soon realise it's more economical to buy a Danish pastry or a croissant at the local *boulangerie-pâtisserie*.

Air-con is not as frequent as you might think, but rooms often have TV and telephone. Not all hotels accept credit cards.

In high season, consider yourself lucky if you can score a double at less than €45. For midrange ventures, prices range from around €45 to €70. Expect to pay €70 to €120 for a three-star, and up to €500 in a luxurious establishment.

Mountain Refuges

Refuges (mountain shelters), located mainly along the GR20 (p54), offer basic dormitory accommodation to walkers. They are usually manned from mid-May to late September or mid-October, depending on the weather. The price per person for an overnight stay is €9.50. Basic meals (around €14) and supplies are available in most *refuges*, and they are also equipped with self-catering facilities.

BORED OF HALF-BOARD?

In high season, half-board is mandatory in many hotels in Corsica. In theory, this practice is not legal. Should you be brave enough to ask for a room-only rate, you'll soon realise what a blunder this is – you'll see this on the face of the grumpy owner, you're definitely not welcome! Some deft hotel owners have found a device to enforce the deal in a more gentle way: they charge almost the same price for the night, which means it would be pure folly not to take half-board. Many *gîtes d'étape* also impose half-board in high season. That said, it can be a good deal if the hotel's restaurant is of gourmet standard – more often than not. But freedom of choice is invaluable, *non*?

Rental Accommodation & Gîtes Ruraux

You can enjoy anything from a bargain-basement to an ultra-luxurious Corsican holiday by renting by the week or month. Several agencies offer villas at various (but invariably expensive) rates around the island (see p261).

A more affordable option is to rent out a simple but comfortable *gîte rural* (self-catering cottage in the country). These are private houses and lodges that families can rent for self-catering holidays, normally by the week. *Gîtes ruraux* are as common as chestnut trees in Corsica and are scattered all over the island. Most offer lodging for four or more people, with facilities of varying standards. Costs vary from around €400 to €800 per week in high season and from €200 to €250 for a weekend (note that not all offer bookings for just a weekend), depending on the location. Rates are usually slashed by 50% in low season. If you average out the per-person, per-week price and factor in cooking several meals in the house, *gîte* stays can actually be quite economical. Plus, the *gîte* owner often lives nearby and can be a mine of local information.

Contact Gîtes de France (p251), local tourist offices or check out the website at www.gites-corsica.com/gites_ruraux/gites-de -france-corse.html. *Gîtes ruraux* can be booked either through Gîtes de France or by phoning the owners directly. A deposit of some sort is usually required in advance.

For summer accommodation by the week or month, in a villa or in a *gîte*, advance booking is essential.

Resorts

Holiday villages or *résidences de vacances* are dotted all around the coast. Standards and prices vary but most have bungalow-type self-catering accommodation, which you can rent on a weekly basis (from €600 to €2500 a week for two), with laundry facilities, restaurants, swimming pools and children's play areas. The best thing about these villages is that they are often located next to the beach. Tourist offices can give you details.

BUSINESS HOURS

Many businesses have continuous opening between 8am and 8pm – and sometimes even later – every day in July and August. Others, despite the once-a-year opportunity to replenish the till, continue to close for a couple of hours in the early afternoon.

In other months of the year, businesses tend to open between 8am and noon and between 2pm and 6pm Monday to Friday or Saturday. Many food businesses such as pastry shops, bakeries, butchers and greengrocers shut down between these hours as well.

Banks usually open from 8am or 9am to 11.30am or 1pm and then 1.30pm to 4.30pm or 5pm, Monday to Friday or Tuesday to Saturday. Exchange services may end half an hour before closing time.

Post offices generally open from 8.30am or 9am to 5pm or 6pm on weekdays (perhaps with a midday break) and Saturday morning from 8am to noon.

Bars open daily from 7pm to 2am or 3am the following morning. Cafés open early morning until around 10pm.

Churches are usually open all day; if not, you can ask for the key at the local *mairie* (town hall).

In summer (June to September) most restaurants open seven days for lunch and dinner. In tourist-populated areas many restaurants shut for several months in the off-season. Those that stay open all year usually close one day a week (although most open daily from June to September). Lunch is between noon and 2pm or 3pm; dinner, any time between 6.30pm and 11pm or midnight.

CHILDREN

Although purpose-made attractions are scarce, Corsica is an eminently suitable destination if you're travelling with children. With its abundance of beaches and outdoor activities, plus its healthy food, if offers plenty to do for travellers of all ages in a generally hazard-free setting. Most Corsicans are welcoming to children.

In summer, you should make sure that children are not overexposed to the sun: you should use a high-protection sunscreen and reapply it several times daily, and make sure that they wear a hat. Try to ensure that they drink lots of water as well. There are excellent medical facilities in the main cities.

Lonely Planet's *Travel with Children* by Cathy Lanigan is full of tips for keeping children and parents happy on the road.

Practicalities

If possible, families should book accommodation in advance to avoid any inconvenience. You might want to try a villa or some other self-catering accommodation so you can have your own kitchen facilities. Many hotels provide cots for free and additional beds for children at a small extra cost. Car seats can also be hired with rental car.

Many restaurants will provide high chairs and have children's menus with significantly lower prices. Nappy changing facilities are a rarity outside airports or large museums. Formula for babies up to 12 months of age, mineral water and a range of medicines are readily available at pharmacies. Disposable nappies are widely available at supermarkets. UHT milk, which does not need to be refrigerated, is sold in cartons. Of course, it's possible (and necessary with the dearth of baby-care facilities) to breastfeed anywhere in public: where and how discreetly you do it is up to your own sensitivity. Discounts for children are common at attractions and toddlers, in general, go free.

Sights & Activities

As well as the obvious attraction of the beaches, playgrounds are plentiful. Special attractions such as Parc Aventure ('adventure-course parks') are spread over the region but abound in the interior (see p247, p248 and p217). Children (and their parents!) adore them – here they can play Tarzan. The minimum height is usually 1m. The Petits Trains (tourist 'trains'), such as in Ajaccio (p169), are also a good way of entertaining the little 'uns. Armed with a picnic and plenty of sun cream, you can also enjoy a lovely afternoon with the toddlers by the *vasques* (natural pools) in the interior, far from the maddening crowds of the coast. Cruises to Réserve Naturelle de Scandola (p152) and to Îles Lavezzi (p201) are also fun.

Horse riding and diving are accessible for those over eight years old. In Balagne (p142) and Propriano (p185), donkey rides are also available – so fun! Older kids (over 12) might like to try canyoning in Bavella (p217) or windsurfing near Bonifacio (p202). More adventurous young adults can try kitesurfing in the Golfe de Figari.

See the boxed text, p22, for more ideas on the best activities for children around the island.

CLIMATE CHARTS

The Mediterranean climate, characterised by its summer droughts and abundant sunshine, gives Corsica an average annual temperature

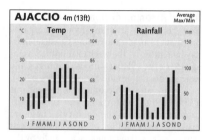

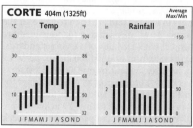

of 12°C. The mountains are cooler, however, and the temperature drops significantly as you climb. Snow can be seen above 1600m from October to June. This means that some skiing is feasible, but visitors to Corsica are usually sun- rather than snowseekers.

On average, the island has 2800 hours of sunshine each year. This is one and a half times the sun that Paris ever sees. Between June and September, average temperatures often exceed 25°C; in July and August temperatures can sizzle above 35°C. According to the French meteorological office in Ajaccio, temperatures climb over 30°C on average 12 days a year in Ajaccio and 32 days in Corte.

Spring and autumn are both fine, with average temperatures of around 15°C and maximum temperatures of around 20°C. Rainfall is highest during the last three months of the year, when there are often severe storms and flooding. In high summer, precipitation is minimal. The mountains often experience severe winters and some of the island's peaks are snowcapped year-round. Corte has, on average, 30 days of frost per year, compared with 11 in Ajaccio and three in Bastia. Corsica's climate is typically slightly warmer in the north than in the south.

The prevailing winds are the dry, gentle libeccio, especially in Haute-Corse, and the tramontane, which comes down from the north in winter. The warm, moisture-bearing sirocco occasionally blows up from the south-east. Cap Corse and the Bouches de Bonifacio are the windiest points (in 1965 wind speeds hit 288km/h).

See p20 for information on the best times to visit Corsica.

CUSTOMS

The following items can be brought into France, hence into Corsica, duty-free from non-EU countries: 200 cigarettes, 50 cigars, 1L of strong liquor or 2L of liquor which is less than 22% alcohol by volume, 2L of wine, 50g of perfume and 0.25L of *eau de toilette* and other goods up to the value of €183. Anything over the limit must be declared on arrival and the appropriate duty paid.

Note that your home country may have strict regulations regarding the import of meat, dairy products or plants.

In the unlikely event that you will be arriving on the island by boat from outside the EU – few visitors do – you must present yourself to the port authorities when you disembark. Customs authorities will usually want to board the boat.

DANGERS & ANNOYANCES

When Corsica makes the headlines, it's often because nationalist militants seeking Corsican independence have engaged in some act of violence, such as bombing a public building or robbing a bank. But the violence has never been targeted at tourists, and there's no reason for visitors to fear for their safety from this particular quarter. Muggings and overcharging in hotels are unheard of, and your stay should be trouble-free. Still, do not leave any valuables in your car.

The main peril in Corsica is the winding roads that follow narrow precipices and the sometimes blind turnings, combined with the impatience of Corsican drivers, and the tendency for livestock and other animals to appear suddenly and without warning in the right of way.

The majority of motor-vehicle accidents appear to involve local young people on their way home from clubs in the early morning. Keep your eyes on the road. If you want to admire the scenery, stop at a lay-by. And if you do happen to pass a bunch of stray wild pigs, don't try to feed them or allow children to pet them. They may be cute but they are unpredictable and may bite.

Bring repellent and antihistamine cream with you if you're prone to insect bites, particularly mosquitoes, though both are available from pharmacies here.

Take note that Corsica is far less multiracial than the mainland, and racist attitudes are not uncommon towards Arabs or Africans.

DISCOUNT CARDS
Senior Cards
Senior cards entitling those aged over 60 to 50% discount on train travel are available from Chemins de Fer de la Corse (p273).

Student & Youth cards
An International Student Identity Card (ISIC; €12) can get you discounts on things such as air tickets, sports events, concerts and movies. Many places stipulate a maximum age, usually 25.

EMBASSIES & CONSULATES
French Embassies & Consulates
Australia Canberra (☎ 02-6216 0100; www.ambafrance -au.org; 6 Perth Ave, Yarralumla, ACT 2600); Sydney Consulate (☎ 02-9261 5779; consulat@consulfrance -sydney.org; Level 26, St Martin's Tower, 31 Market St, Sydney, NSW 2000)
Canada Ottowa (☎ 613-789 1795; www.ambafrance-ca .org; 42 Sussex Dr, Ottawa, ON K1M 2C9); Toronto Consulate (☎ 416-925 8041; www.consulfrance-toronto.org; 2 Bloor St East, Ste 2200, Toronto, ON M4W 1A8)
Germany Berlin (☎ 030-590 039 000; www.botschaft -frankreich.de; Pariser Platz 5, 10117); Munich Consulate (☎ 089-419 4110; www.consulfrance-munich.de; Heimeranstrasse 31, 80339 Munich)
Ireland (☎ 01-277 5000; www.ambafrance.ie.org; 36 Ailesbury Rd, Ballsbridge, Dublin 4)
Italy (☎ 06 686 011; www.ambafrance-it.org; Piazza Farnese 67, 00186 Rome)
Netherlands Amsterdam Consulate (☎ 020-530 6969; www.consulfrance-amsterdam.org; Vijzelgracht 2, 1000 HA Amsterdam); The Hague (☎ 070-312 5800; www .ambafrance-nl.org; Smidsplein 1, 2514 BT)
New Zealand (☎ 04-384 2555; www.ambafrance -nz.org; 34-42 Manners St, Wellington)
UK London (☎ 020-7073 1000; www.ambafrance-uk.org; 58 Knightsbridge, London SW1X 7JT); Consulate (☎ 020-7073 1200; www.consulfrance-londres.org; 21 Cromwell Rd, London SW7 2EN); Visa section (☎ 020-7073 1250; 6A Cromwell Pl, London SW7 2EW); Edinburgh (☎ 0131-225 7954; 21 Randolph Cres, EH3 7TT)
USA Washington (☎ 202-944 6195; www.ambafrance -us.org; 4101 Reservoir Rd NW, Washington, DC 20007); New York Consulate (☎ 212-606 3600;

www.consulfrance-newyork.org; 934 Fifth Ave, NY 10021);
San Francisco Consulate (☎ 415-397 4330; www
.consulfrance-sanfrancisco.org; 540 Bush St, CA 94108)
Other consulates are located in Atlanta, Boston, Chicago,
Houston, Los Angeles, Miami and New Orleans.

Embassies & Consulates in France

All foreign embassies can be found in Paris,
although some countries also have consulates
in other major French cities such as Marseille
and Lyon.

Only a few countries, Italy among them,
have any kind of diplomatic representation
in Corsica.

Australia (☎ 01 40 59 33 00; www.france.embassy.gov
.au; 4 rue Jean Rey, 15e, Paris)
Canada (☎ 01 44 43 29 00; www.amb-canada.fr; 35 av
Montaigne, 8e, Paris)
Germany (☎ 01 53 83 45 00; www.amb-allemagne.fr;
13-15 av Franklin D Roosevelt, 8e, Paris)
Ireland (☎ 01 44 17 67 00; www.embassyofireland
paris.com; 12 av Foch, 16e, Paris)
Italy (☎ 04 95 34 93 93; fax 04 95 32 56 72; rue
St-François, 20200 Bastia)
Netherlands (☎ 01 40 62 33 00; www.amb-pays-bas
.fr; 7 rue Eblé, 7e, Paris)
New Zealand (☎ 01 45 01 43 43; www.nzembassy
.com; 7ter rue Léonard de Vinci, 16e, Paris)
UK (☎ 01 44 51 31 00; www.britishembassy.gov.uk; 35
rue du Faubourg St-Honoré, 8e, Paris); Consulate (☎ 01 44
51 31 02; 16 rue d'Anjou, 8e, Paris)
USA (☎ 01 43 12 22 22; www.amb-usa.fr; 2 ave Gabriel,
8e, Paris); Consulate (☎ 01 43 12 22 22; 2 rue St-Florentin,
1er, Paris)

The following countries are represented on
Corsica by honorary consulates:
Belgium & the Netherlands (☎ 04 95 20 89 99, fax
04 95 23 56 44; aéroport Campo dell'Oro, 20090 Ajaccio)
Germany (☎ 04 95 33 03 56; RN 193, zone industrielle
Furiani, 20600 Bastia)

FESTIVALS & EVENTS

Easter in Corsica is a very big deal and is
marked by solemn processions and Passion
plays all over the island. Some are more striking than others. The celebrations in Sartène
(see the boxed text, p189), Calvi, Bonifacio,
Corte, Erbalunga (see the boxed text, p110)
and Cargèse are the most evocative. They feature parades across town bearing a cross or a
statue of the Virgin or of Christ and a procession of penitents, called *granitola*, when a line
of participants forms a coiling and uncoiling
spiral as it moves through the town. Other

fervent religious festivals include the Assumption of the Virgin Mary (15 August).

Rural fairs are also hugely popular and
usually celebrate local produce (wine, cheese,
olive, chestnut). For foreigners, they offer
a chance to immerse in local culture and
buy top-quality regional specialities. Music
festivals and sporting events also feature
prominently.

See also Festivals & Events in the destination chapters. Local tourist offices also have
details.

February
Rencontres du Cinéma Italien de Bastia Classic
Italian films, concerts, exhibitions; held in the first week of
February in Bastia.
A Tumbera, Foire du Porc Coureur Pigs, pigs, pigs!
Early February, Renno celebrates a Corsican variety of
mountain pig. Cooking competitions are the star
attractions of this festival.

March/April
Fête de l'Olive, A Festa di L'Olliu Olive oil is offered
for tasting and sale. Held mid-March in Sainte-Lucie de
Tallano.
Processions de la Semaine Sainte The most famous
Easter celebrations include La Cerca in Erbalunga,
U Catenacciu in Sartène (p189), La Granitola in Calvi and
the procession of the Five Orders in Bonifacio.
Orthodox Easter Follows the Greek liturgy, Cargèse.
La Passion – A Passione A superb procession
re-enacting the Crucifixion, held every Easter in Calvi.
Traditional Corsican singing from the group A Filetta.
A Merendella in Castagniccia Celebrates local farm
products, each Easter in Piedicroce. Hmm!
Salon de la Bande Dessinée Exhibition of international
cartoon art held in early April in Bastia.
Journée du Fromage et du Vin Rural fair featuring
wine and cheese tasting held in mid-April, Cauro.
Journée du Brocciu A celebration Corsica's world-
famous cheese held in late April in Piana.

May
Procession du Christ Noir des Miracles Local Bastia
fishermen carry the 'Black Christ', which was found floating
in the sea, around Terra Nova; 3 May.
A Fiera di u Casgiu This rural fair in early May, Vénaco,
honours local cheese and features competitions and
tasting.
Festimare Celebrates the sea, with plenty of fish and
seafood specials on offer and various amusements; held
late May/early June in Île Rousse.
La Corsica Tour A three-day team cycle race around the
south of the island, ending in Ajaccio.

June

Saint-Érasme Nautically themed festivities, boat rides and blessings of fishing boats honour the patron saint of fishermen; 2 June in Ajaccio, Bastia and Calvi.

Cavall'in Festa Equestrian competitions and shows in mid-June, Corte.

Fiera di u Mare, Foire de la Mer Solenzara's sea festival in mid-June with sailing races and seafood-cooking competitions.

Fête de la Saint-Jean Fireworks and concerts are held in various venues in Corte, 24 June.

Calvi Jazz Festival Concerts and jam sessions featuring big names from the international jazz scene in Calvi, late June.

Corsica Raid Aventure A five-day adventure race in mid-June, combining canyoning, trekking, orienteering and mountain biking in the mountains.

July

Festivoce Here's your chance to listen to Corsican polyphony in early July, Pigna.

Foire du Vin de Luri A popular wine fair held in early July, Luri, where Corsican winemakers promote their wines.

A Notte di a Memoria A *reconstitution historique* (historical re-enactment) of the Genoese governor's arrival in the citadel; early July, Bastia.

Fiera di l'Alivu, Foire de l'Olivier A celebration of the olive tree and all products made from it held in mid-July, Montemaggiore.

Nuits de la Guitare One of Europe's largest guitar festivals held in mid-July, Patrimonio. Featured Joe Satriani and Gilberto Gil, among others, in 2006.

Calvi on the Rocks Three days of electronic and experimental music in Calvi, mid-July.

Santa Severa This *fête de la mer* (sea festival) is held in the Luri's harbour in late July.

Inter-Lacs An iron man two-stage running race covering 28km around the mountains near Corte.

Trophée Méditerranée This major international sailing competition for vessels greater than 9m in length is held over nine days. Starting and ending in Corsican ports, it also takes in the neighbouring island of Sardinia.

August

Pèlerinage de Notre-Dame-des-Neiges Pilgrimage to the miracle-working Madonna on Col de Bavella; 5 August, Bavella.

Foire du Pratu Animal showing, local produce competitions and traditional Corsican singing, including polyphonic songs and *Chjami e Rispondi* (vocal contests); early August, Col de Prato, Castagniccia.

Festival Européen du Film de Lama Features films set in or about the countryside and rural life; early August, Lama.

Festa Antica Locals decked out in Roman garb are joined by numerous visitors for a rollicking festival in the streets of Aléria in early August.

Fêtes Napoléoniennes A hugely popular mid-August festival in Ajaccio celebrating Napoleon's birthday. Fireworks, parades and various amusements.

Rencontres Théâtrales de Haute-Corse This well-known theatre festival is held in various villages of the Giussani Valley in early August. Amateur and professional actors.

Porto Latino Four days of live music with Cuban and Latin bands; early August, St-Florent.

Fiera di l'Amandulu, Foire de l'Amande A popular event in early August, Aregno, celebrating the almond and other local produce. Exhibitions and competitions.

September

Santa di u Niolo A hugely popular event held in early September, Casamaccioli. Thousands of pilgrims celebrate the Nativity of the Virgin. Also vocal contests.

Rencontres de Chants Polyphoniques Festival of polyphonic singing held at various venues in Calvi's citadel in mid-September.

Settembrinu di Tavagna A warm-hearted music festival in Casinca with gigs by Corsican, Italian, Spanish and Irish groups.

Mele in Festa A celebration of honey and other *produits du terroir* (local produce) held in late September, Murzo.

Les Six Jours Cyclotouristes de l'Île de Beauté A six-day, 600km cycle tour, one route in the north of the island, one in the south, with up to 100 participants, in the second half of September.

Tour de Corse Cycliste A four-day race around Corsica.

October

Festiventu, Le Festival du Vent Hundreds of kites on Calvi's beach; late October. Celebrates the role of the wind.

Les Musicales de Bastia Jazz, classical music, dance, theatrical performances held at various venues around Bastia.

Tour de Corse Automobile Souped-up rally cars roar around the island in this three-day, high-profile event, the French leg of the World Rally Championship. It celebrated its 50th anniversary in 2006. Some years it's held in May.

Tour de Corse à la Voile A four-day sailing race starting and ending in Bonifacio in mid-October.

November

Foire de la Pomme et des Produits Naturels Rural fair celebrating apple (jams, juices, jellies) and other farm produce from the Prunelli Valley; held in early November, Bastelica.

Fête du Marron Évisa's mid-November rural fair that celebrates a variety of local chestnut and mushrooms.

December

Foire à la Châtaigne One of the most famous rural fairs in Corsica, which honours the chestnut and all things made from it; held in mid-December, Bocognano.

FOOD

In this book, we usually indicate the price of mains, followed by the price of *menus* (two- or three-course set menus). Set menus include all courses but no wine, except in some *fermes-auberges*, where a bottle of wine is included. Within each eating section, restaurants appear in order of prices.

For a full, midrange restaurant meal you should expect to pay €25 to €35 per person with wine.

See the Food & Drinks chapter (p88) for plenty of succulent information about Corsican gastronomy.

GAY & LESBIAN TRAVELLERS

There is practically no open gay scene in Corsica, despite the fact that homosexuality does not seem to pose a problem to this conservative and traditional society – in theory at least. When it comes to being 'out' in public, the adage 'out of sight, out of mind' seems to apply, especially in the countryside and villages. What you do behind closed doors (or in the maquis or on deserted beaches!) may be perfectly acceptable to most Corsicans but open displays of affection, especially between men, will be frowned upon at the very least. Discretion is advisable. That said, few hoteliers will bat an eyelid if a same sex couple book into a room.

Some fairly well-known cruising spots include the Plage de la Marana and the Jardin Romieu in Bastia (daytime only), Port Tino Rossi in Ajaccio, a few areas near Ajaccio Campo dell'Oro airport (evenings only), the Tour de Capitello (daytime only), the Plage Ste-Restitude in Lumio, the northern tip of Plage d'Algajola, a section of Plage de Santa Giulia near Porto-Vecchio and the Plage du Liamone in Sagone.

Online, it's worth checking out www.gayscape.com and www.leguidegay.com (in French), even though information on Corsica is very limited.

HOLIDAYS

Most French people take their annual holiday in July or August, deserting the cities for the coastal or mountain resorts. Thus a good deal of France's vacation populace head for Corsica, along with a healthy contingent of foreigners. Corsicans have to go on holiday too, and they usually go in winter for *sports d'hiver* (skiing) on the mainland.

The following *jours fériés* (public holidays) are observed in Corsica:

New Year's Day (Jour de l'An) 1 January.
Easter Sunday & Monday (Pâques & lundi de Pâques) Late March/April.
Labour Day (Fête du Travail) 1 May.
Victoire 1945 8 May – the Allied victory in Europe that ended WWII.
Ascension Thursday (L'Ascension) May – celebrated on the 40th day after Easter.
Pentecost/Whit Sunday & Whit Monday (Pentecôte & lundi de Pentecôte) Mid-May to mid-June – celebrated on the seventh Sunday after Easter.
Bastille Day/National Day (Fête Nationale) 14 July – *the* national holiday.
Assumption Day (L'Assomption) 15 August.
All Saints' Day (La Toussaint) 1 November.
Remembrance Day (Le onze novembre) 11 November – celebrates the WWI armistice.
Christmas (Noël) 25 December.

INSURANCE

A travel-insurance policy to cover theft, loss and medical problems is a good idea. Some policies specifically exclude dangerous activities, which can include scuba diving, motorcycling, and even trekking.

You may prefer a policy that pays doctors or hospitals directly rather than you having to pay on the spot and claim later. If you have to claim later ensure you keep all documentation. Check that the policy covers ambulances or an emergency flight home. Paying for your airline ticket with a credit card often provides limited travel accident insurance. Ask your credit card–company what it's prepared to cover.

See p274 for health insurance and p270 for car insurance.

INTERNET ACCESS

Corsica is not the most internet-friendly place – probably due to the lack of international business travel to the island. Most hotel rooms are not really geared towards travellers seeking to connect to the internet and usually don't have the necessary plugs and sockets, but wi-fi access is slowly developing.

You can also try your luck with internet cafés, which are now slowly (very slowly) spreading across the island. Currently, however, cybercafés tend to be found only in bigger towns and resort areas such as Ajaccio, Bastia, Bonifacio, Calvi, Corte, Porto-Vecchio and Propriano, and consider yourself lucky if you can find more than one or two outlets in each city. In smaller towns and villages internet cafés are unheard of. The connection is generally good and rates are fairly standard at around €5 per hour.

LEGAL MATTERS

Thanks to the Napoleonic Code (on which the French legal system is based), the police can pretty much search anyone they want to at any time – whether or not there is probable cause. Foreigners must be able to prove their legal status in France (eg passport, visa, residency permit) without delay. If the police stop you for any reason, be polite and remain calm.

As elsewhere in the EU, the laws are very tough when it comes to drinking and driving. The acceptable blood-alcohol limit is 0.05%, and drivers exceeding this amount face heavy fines, plus several years in jail. Licences can also be immediately suspended. The import or export of drugs can lead to a jail sentence of up to 30 years. The fine for possession of drugs for personal use (including cannabis, amphetamines, ecstasy etc) can be as high as €3750 and a one-year jail sentence. The fine for littering starts from about €150.

Eighteen is the legal age for voting, driving and for heterosexual/homosexual sex.

MAPS

The maps available from local tourist offices are usually poor quality so a good map is an essential before-you-go purchase. The Michelin road map No 90, at a scale of 1:200,000 (1cm = 2km) and the two IGN *cartes de promenade* maps (No 73 for the north and No 74 for the south) at a scale of 1:100,000 (1cm = 1km) are excellent for motoring.

Travellers intending to do lots of hiking should consult a specialist map retailer before departure. For those planning to walk the GR20 trail, see the map information on p59. Lonely Planet's *Walking in France* is also a useful reference.

MONEY

Corsica's unit of currency is the euro (€), which is divided into 100 cents. Coin denominations are one, two, five, 10, 20 and 50 cents, €1 and €2. The notes are €5, €10, €20, €50, €100, €200 and €500.

For exchange rates, see the table inside the front cover of this guide. For information on costs, see p21.

ATMs

Known in French as Distributeurs Automatiques de Billets (DABs) or *points argent*, ATMs (Automated Teller Machines) are the easiest way to access funds while in Corsica. Visa, MasterCard and Cirrus are accepted widely. Most of the larger Corsican towns have an ATM machine and many post offices also offer ATM service. However, ATMs are still not nearly as widespread in Corsica as they are in mainland France, and are more scarce in rural areas – Cap Corse, the Alta Rocca or the Haut Taravo have only one or two ATMs each. If you're heading off into central Corsica, it's wise to stock up with euros beforehand.

Cash

Hard cash, despite its advantages, is generally not a very good way to carry money. Not only can it be stolen, but also in France you don't get an optimal exchange rate. Nevertheless, it can be a good idea to bring around €100 in low-denomination notes to get you started upon arrival.

Credit Cards

Despite some shortcomings (see the boxed text, below), credit cards will prove the cheapest and easiest way to pay for major purchases in Corsica. On the island, as throughout mainland France, Visa (Carte Bleue) and MasterCard (Eurocard) are the cards most widely accepted by hotels, supermarkets, major petrol stations and stores. Both can be used to pay for air, train and ferry travel, as well as car rentals. Credit cards are mandatory if you want to rent a car, as they'll be used as a form of *caution* (deposit).

It's a good idea to check with your credit card–company about charges on international transactions before leaving home.

LOST IN TRANSACTION

Be warned: surprisingly, many restaurants and hotels in Corsica don't accept plastic, and it's very rare for *chambres d'hôtes* and *gîtes d'étape* to take credit cards. Some places refuse cards for small amounts (typically under €15). And it's common to come across a reputable restaurant where the credit card machine has been *en panne* (out of order) for several weeks. Always inquire first.

Moneychangers

The number of banks that do change cash has been dramatically dwindling over the last few years – the moneychanging service seems to have been superseded in favour of ATMs. 'Bring a credit card and use ATMs,' say most staff at the banks. Consider yourself very lucky if you find a bank that will change foreign currencies in Bastia or in Ajaccio.

Travellers Cheques

If you don't want to carry large amounts of cash, and if plastic isn't the right solution for you either, you may want to carry at least some of your money in the form of euro-denominated travellers cheques. But most banks are reluctant to cash them.

PHOTOGRAPHY & VIDEO

Generally print film is both more widely available and cheaper to develop in Corsica, while both buying and developing slide film is a more expensive and time-consuming business – the film is usually sent off to mainland France for processing.

Professional snappers arriving armed with a ready supply of film will not be disappointed: Corsica is exceptionally photogenic, with lots of subject matters such as beaches, festivals, mountainscapes, forests… However strong light can present a problem in summer and, as such, it's pointless to use very sensitive film. Films with an ISO rating of 100 should do in most situations, and a polarising filter may prove a useful purchase.

There are no major restrictions on photography in Corsica, except in museums and art galleries. And, when photographing people, it is basic courtesy to ask their permission first.

Lonely Planet's full-colour *Travel Photography: A Guide to Taking Better Pictures*, written by internationally renowned travel photographer Richard I'Anson, is full of handy hints and is designed to take on the road.

Both VHS and Hi-8 video film are available in major cities. You'll also find memory cards and other accessories for digital and DV cameras, but prices are usually higher than on the continent.

POST

Post offices are widespread across the island and, in some rural hamlets, often provide a community focus as they are housed alongside the *mairie* and the local administrative offices. In addition to providing the customary mail services, some will also send and receive faxes, and offer a photocopying or mail-holding service. Some larger branches also cash travellers cheques and perform other modest banking services. Public telephones are either in or near the post office.

Domestic letters weighing up to 20g cost €0.54; postcards and letters up to 20g cost €0.60 within the EU, €0.90 to most of the rest of the world.

SOLO TRAVELLERS

Generally Corsica is a poor destination choice for solo travellers, except if you are a walker and stay in *gîtes d'étape*. The mainstay of the tourist season comprises families or couples so lone travellers might face a feeling of isolation. They are also hard hit, with single rooms disproportionately expensive compared to double or triple rooms. Worse still, some restaurateurs are rather hostile to single diners taking a table with two covers.

For single women the macho nature of Corsican society could be an issue, although physical attacks on women are relatively rare. They could, however, be made to feel uncomfortable – especially if they stray off the tourist beat into some of the more traditional rural communities. See p263 for more information.

TELEPHONE & FAX
Mobile Phones

Corsica uses the GSM 900/1800 system for mobile phones, which is compatible with the rest of Europe and Australia but not with the North American GSM 1900 system or the totally different system in Japan. If you have a GSM phone, check with your service provider at home about using your mobile phone in Corsica. Beware in particular of calls being routed internationally – this ends up proving a very expensive way of making a supposedly 'local' call. Ask your service provider about international roaming agreements and the charges involved.

The network covers most towns and villages throughout the island, even in the interior.

Fax

To send or receive a fax the best option is to pop into the nearest post office. Some *tabacs* (tobacconists) also offer a fax service. Expect to pay the usual international rates for faxes, plus some nominal fee for the service.

Phonecards

Most public telephones in Corsica require a *télécarte* (telephone card), which can be purchased at post offices, *tabacs*, supermarket check-out counters and anywhere you see a blue sticker reading *télécarte en vente ici*. Cards worth 50/120 units cost €7.50/15.

To make a domestic or international phone call with a *télécarte*, follow the instructions on the LCD display.

Phone Codes

The country code for France is 33 and the international access code is 00. All telephone numbers throughout Corsica consist of eight digits and start with the prefix '04'. If calling Corsica from overseas, you would drop the first '0', that is, dial '00 33 4' then six digits. All mobile phone numbers start with the prefix '06'. If calling a Corsican mobile number from overseas, you would drop the first '0', that is, dial '00 33 6' then six digits. International Direct Dial (IDD) calls to almost anywhere in the world can be made from public telephones, of which there are a reasonable number on the island. But for most you will need a *télécarte* (phonecard).

TIME

Corsica uses the 24-hour clock, with hours separated from minutes by a lower-case 'h'. Thus, 15h30 is 3.30pm, 21h50 is 9.50pm, 00h30 is 12.30am, and so on.

Corsica is on the same time as the rest of France, that is, on Central European Time, which is one hour ahead of (later than) GMT/UTC. During daylight-saving time, which runs from the last Sunday in March to the last Sunday in October, France is two hours ahead of GMT/UTC. Without taking daylight-saving time into account, when it's noon in Paris it's 3am in San Francisco, 6am in New York, 11am in London, 8pm in Tokyo, 9pm in Sydney and 11pm in Auckland.

TOILETS

Public toilets, signposted *toilettes* or WC, are rare on the island so most people tend to stop at a café, have a quick coffee and then use the toilets on the premises. Simply ask, *Est-ce que je peux utiliser les toilettes, s'il vous plaît?*

WHERE THERE'S NO TAP

Not least of the many Italianate influences and importations on Corsica is the wash-basin bereft of any tap that you sometimes find in cafés and restaurants. Just press your foot on the knob below or pull the lever at the side of the basin and, as for Moses, the water will flow.

Frustratingly, travellers often find there are no toilet or washing facilities at beaches, and obviously the more remote the beach the greater the likelihood that there will be no toilet facilities at all. Hikers will find a few chemical toilets near PNRC *refuges* but none, of course, along the hiking trails. Be prepared to go back to nature at times.

You may find that carrying a small supply of paper tissue or medicated wipes in lieu of toilet paper would be a smart move.

TOURIST INFORMATION

There are generally tourist information offices in most main towns across the island. Increasingly there is also some sort of small tourist information kiosk or centre in the more rural areas. Indeed, new branch offices are opening all the time.

The quality of tourist offices in Corsica varies hugely. One office might have enthusiastic and competent staff (Calvi, Bastia, Bonifacio), while others are largely indifferent and devoid of any useful information.

L'Agence du Tourisme de la Corse (ATC; ☎ 04 95 51 00 00; www.visit-corsica.com; 17 blvd du Roi Jérôme BP 19, 20180 Ajaccio) is Corsica's regional tourist office.

Tourist offices are generally open 8am to 12.30pm or 1pm and 2pm to 5pm Monday to Friday. Hours are extended in summer, when most offices open seven days a week.

French government tourist offices abroad, usually called Maisons de la France, can provide every imaginable sort of tourist information. The general website www.franceguide .com lets you access the site for your home country.

TOURS

Options for organised travel to Corsica are increasing all the time. Established specialists in the UK and North America:

Adventure Center (www.adventure-center.com) Based in the USA. Offers Corsican village treks.

ATG (www.atg-oxford.co.uk) Has an eight-day itinerary from Bavella to Propriano.

Breakaway Adventures (www.breakaway-adventures .com) Based in the USA. Walking trips in Corsica.

Corsican Places (www.corsica.co.uk) Handpicked collection of villas, apartments and hotels.

Direct Corsica (www.directcorsica.com) Discounted flights and a wide range of accommodation options.

Holiday Options (www.holidayoptions.co.uk) Flights and various package holidays.

Kalliste Tours (www.kallistetours.com) Based in the USA. Heritage and cultural ecotours.

Saddle Skedaddle (www.skedaddle.co.uk) Cycling holidays in Corsica.

Simply Corsica (www.simplytravel.co.uk) Hotels, villas and cottages.

VFB Holidays (www.vfbholidays.co.uk) Villas, hotels and seaside apartments.

VillaFinders.com (www.villafinders.com) Provides package holidays in over 300 quality properties, cottages, village apartments and family residences.

Voyages Ilena (www.voyagesilena.co.ok) Hotels, cottages and self-catering accommodation.

TRAVELLERS WITH DISABILITIES

France and especially Corsica could not be considered progressive in terms of its facilities for people with disabilities. However, the situation is changing, albeit slowly. Hotels and restaurants are modernising and adding wheelchair-accessible rooms and toilet facilities. The Ajaccio branch of the **Association des Paralysés de France** (☎ /fax 04 95 20 75 33; 18 rue du Colonel d'Ornano, 20000 Ajaccio) publishes the details of places in Corsica (hotels, restaurants, cultural sites and so on) that are accessible to disabled people. These details can also be obtained from Ajaccio's tourist office.

Airlines ensure that there are no access problems for travellers with disabilities on aeroplanes or at the airports. The traditional ferries *Napoléon Bonaparte, Île-de-Beauté, Danièle Casanova, Monte d'Oro* and *Paglia Orba* all have some cabins that are accessible to wheelchair users, as do the NGVs (high-speed ferries). However, in all cases you must contact the companies in question before travelling; see p267.

VISAS

By law, everyone in France, including tourists, must carry some sort of ID on them at all times. For foreign visitors, this means a passport (if you don't want to carry your passport for security reasons a photocopy should

do, although you may be required to verify your identity later) or, for citizens of those European Union (EU) countries that issue them, a national ID card.

EU nationals have no entry requirements, and citizens of Australia, the USA, Canada, New Zealand and Israel do not need visas to visit France as tourists for up to three months. Others will need a Schengen visa, named after the Schengen Agreement that abolished passport controls between Austria, Belgium, Denmark, Finland, France, Germany, Greece, Italy, Luxembourg, the Netherlands, Norway, Portugal, Spain and Sweden. A Schengen visa allows unlimited travel throughout the entire zone within a 90-day period.

When you apply, you will need your passport (valid for a period of three months beyond the date of your anticipated departure from France), a return ticket, proof of sufficient funds to support yourself, two passport-size photos and the visa fee in cash. You may also be asked for proof of pre-arranged accommodation.

If all the forms are in order, your visa will be issued on the spot at the French consulate closest to you in your home country. You can also apply for a French visa after arriving in Europe – the fee is the same, but you may not have to produce a return ticket. If you enter France overland, your passport may not be checked for a visa at the border, but, if you don't have one, major problems can arise later on (for example, at the airport as you leave the country).

Citizens of EU countries and Switzerland wishing to stay in Corsica for longer than 90 days must apply for a residence permit from the nearest town hall or from the *service des étrangers* (foreigners' department) of the Corsican prefecture. Citizens of Australia, Canada and the USA are limited to two stays of 90 days each per year. Those wishing to extend their stay must apply for an extended residence permit from the French embassy or consulate in their own country.

Non-EU nationals wanting to work or study in France or stay for over three months should apply to their nearest French embassy or consulate for the appropriate *long séjour* (long-stay) visa. Unless you live in the EU, it is extremely difficult to get a visa allowing you to work in France.

For up-to-date information on visa requirements, see the Foreign Affairs Ministry site, www.diplomatie.gouv.fr under 'Entering France'.

WOMEN TRAVELLERS

Women travelling solo, or with one or more other women, should experience no problems in Corsica, and physical attack is rare. Corsicans are almost universally polite to women, and it is very unlikely that you will be subjected to the catcalls you may encounter in big cities on the mainland. As in any country, however, women should use their common sense and remain conscious of their surroundings. If you find yourself the recipient of unwanted male attention it's best to ignore it.

It's wise to dress modestly in the towns of inland Corsica, where communities are more conservative than in coastal cities. Skimpy clothing in such a context is both shocking and inconsiderate.

France's national **rape-crisis hotline** (☎ 0800 059 595) can be reached toll-free from any telephone without using a phonecard. It's run by a women's organisation.

In an emergency, you can also call the police ☎ 17.

WORK

The tourist season generates thousands of seasonal jobs. If you can speak French, it's fairly easy to get a job in hotels, bars and restaurants catering to visitors.

EU nationals have an automatic right to work in France. Non-EU citizens will need to apply for a work permit, for which they first need a *carte de séjour* or a Working Holiday Visa for citizens of Australia, Canada, Japan and New Zealand aged between 18 and 29 years, as well as a written promise of employment. Working permits may well be refused on the grounds of high local unemployment.

Working 'in the black' (that is, without documents) is difficult and risky for non-EU travellers. The only instance in which the government turns a blind eye to undocumented workers is for agricultural works, including fruit harvests in summer.

Transport

CONTENTS

By far the best way to get around Corsica is by car, whether hired or brought from home. Bus services, especially and paradoxically during the tourist season (most are geared to getting children and workers between home and school or the nearest town) are lean. The train is an attractive option in itself, running through stunning countryside between Bastia and Ajaccio, with a branch route to Calvi. For the superfit, or those who aim to head home that way, Corsica's little-travelled, twisting, climbing roads make for hugely satisfying, if gruelling, cycling.

GETTING THERE & AWAY

AIR
Airports & Airlines
Corsica has four airports: Ajaccio, Bastia, Calvi and Figari. The main hub is Ajaccio's Campo dell'Oro airport, which is where the bulk of European scheduled and charter flights land. Figari-Sud airport is the handiest landing point for access to Porto-Vecchio, Bonifacio and Propriano in southern Corsica.

Direct international flights are few and far between, with the exception of flights to/from mainland France operated by Air France and the Corsican home-grown CCM Airlines (Compagnie Corse Méditerranée), also known as Air Corsica.

Many non-French carriers, including budget airlines, fly into Nice and Marseille in mainland France, and into Genoa, on the Italian coast. From each of these port cities, there are regular ferries to Corsica.

Some airports serving the region:
Ajaccio Campo dell'Oro (code AJA; www.ajaccio.aeroport.fr in French)
Bastia Poretta (code BIA; www.bastia.aeroport.fr)
Calvi Ste-Catherine (code CLY; www.calvi.aeroport.fr)
Figari Sud Corse (code FSC; www.figari.aeroport.fr)
Genoa Cristoforo Colombo (code GOA; www.airport.genova.it)
Marseille Provence (code MRS; www.mrsairport.com)
Nice Côte d'Azur (code NCE; www.nice.aeroport.fr)
Pisa Galileo Galilei (code PSA; www.pisa-airport.com)

Some airlines flying into these airports:
Air Corsica (CCM airlines; code XK; ☎ 08 20 82 08 20; www.aircorsica.com; hub Ajaccio)
Air France (code AF; ☎ 08 20 82 08 20; www.airfrance.com; hub Paris)
BMI Baby (code WW; ☎ 08 90 71 00 81; www.bmibaby.com; hub East Midlands, UK)
British Airways (code BA; ☎ 08 25 82 54 00; www.britishairways.com; hub London Heathrow)
CCM Airlines (Air Corsica; code XK; ☎ 08 20 82 08 20; www.ccm-airlines.com; hub Ajaccio)
Crossair (code QE; ☎ 08 20 04 05 06; www.swiss.com; hub Basel-Mulhouse)
EasyJet (code U2; ☎ 08 25 08 25 08; www.easyjet.com; hub London Stansted)
Luxair (code LG; ☎ 08 20 82 08 20; www.luxair.lu; hub Luxembourg airport)
Ryanair (code FR; ☎ 08 99 70 00 07; www.ryanair.com; hub London Stansted)
Virgin Express (code TV; ☎ 08 00 52 85 28; www.virgin-express.com; hub Brussels)

THINGS CHANGE...

The information in this chapter is particularly vulnerable to change. Check directly with the airline or a travel agent to make sure you understand how a fare (and ticket you may buy) works and be aware of the security requirements for international travel. Shop carefully. The details given in this chapter should be regarded as pointers and are not a substitute for your own careful, up-to-date research.

Tickets

Air travel has never been better value – assuming you've researched the options carefully to get the best deal. Full-time students and those aged under 26 (under 30 in some countries) occasionally have access to better deals than other travellers.

Checking fares and buying tickets on the internet can be a good way to find the best deals; try the web-based budget carriers that only sell direct to travellers (mainly online), airline websites and the ever- increasing number of online agents. Reliable online agencies:

Cheap Tickets (www.cheap tickets.com)

Deckchair (www.deckchair.com)

Expedia (www.expedia.com)

Last Minute (www.lastminute.com)

Priceline (www.priceline.com) With this US-based site you can bid for a ticket online.

Travel Cuts (www.travelcuts.com)

Travelocity (www.travelocity.com)

Be aware, however, especially if you're travelling to Corsica from a considerable distance, that online super-fast fare generators are not necessarily a substitute for an old-fashioned travel agent behind a desk, who can take into account your personal requirements.

Paying by credit card can offer protection; most card issuers will provide refunds if you can prove that you didn't get what you paid for. Similar consumer protection can be obtained by purchasing a ticket from a bonded agent, such as one covered by the UK's Air Travel Organiser's Licence (ATOL) scheme.

From Australia

STA Travel (☎ 1300 733 035; www.statravel.com.au), **Flight Centre** (☎ 133 133; www.flightcentre.com.au) and **Zuji** (☎ 1300 888 180; www.zuji.com.au) all have offices countrywide. For online bookings, try www.travel.com.au.

Qantas and Air France fly from Australia to Ajaccio, via Paris.

From Continental Europe

The following are among the many travel agents with proven track records.

ITALY

CTS Viaggi (☎ 02 584 751; www.cts.it) A recommended student- and youth-travel specialist.

SPAIN

Barcelo Viajes (☎ 902 116 226; www.barceloviajes.com)

GERMANY

Just Travel (☎ 089 747 3330; www.justtravel.de)

STA Travel (☎ 01803 100 040; www.statravel.de) For travellers under the age of 26.

CLIMATE CHANGE & TRAVEL

Climate change is a serious threat to the ecosystems that humans rely upon, and air travel is the fastest-growing contributor to the problem. Lonely Planet regards travel, overall, as a global benefit, but believes we all have a responsibility to limit our personal impact on global warming.

Flying & Climate Change

Pretty much every form of motor transport generates CO_2 (the main cause of human-induced climate change) but planes are far and away the worst offenders, not just because of the sheer distances they allow us to travel, but because they release greenhouse gases high into the atmosphere. The statistics are frightening: two people taking a return flight between Europe and the US will contribute as much to climate change as an average household's gas and electricity consumption over a whole year.

Carbon Offset Schemes

Climatecare.org and other websites use 'carbon calculators' that allow travellers to offset the greenhouse gases they are responsible for with contributions to energy-saving projects and other climate-friendly initiatives in the developing world – including projects in India, Honduras, Kazakhstan and Uganda.

Lonely Planet, together with Rough Guides and other concerned partners in the travel industry, supports the carbon offset scheme run by climatecare.org. Lonely Planet offsets all of its staff and author travel.

For more information check out our website: www.lonelyplanet.com.

MAINLAND FRANCE
Anyway (☎ 08 92 89 38 92; www.anyway.fr)
Nouvelles Frontières (☎ 08 25 00 07 47; www
.nouvelles-frontieres.fr)
OTU Voyages (www.otu.fr) Student and youth specialists.
Voyageurs du Monde (☎ 01 40 15 11 15; www.vdm
.com) Student- and youth-travel specialist.
Voyages Wasteels (☎ 01 42 61 69 87; www.wasteels.fr)

NETHERLANDS
ISSTA (☎ 020 618 8031; www.issta.nl)

Any continental European carrier – for example **Lufthansa** (www.lufthansa.com), **KLM** (www.klm.nl), **SAS** (www.scandinavian.net), **CSA Czech Airlines** (www.csa.cz) or **Lot Polish Airlines** (www.lot.com) – will sell you a through ticket to Corsican airports. This will mean a change of planes in mainland France to link up with a flight operated by French national carrier Air France or Corsica's Air Corsica/CCM Airlines. These two airlines operate direct flights from several airports in France, including Clermont Ferrand, Lyon and Paris (Orly).

Between April and October and during the Christmas and New Year holidays, a couple of companies operate cheap charter flights from major French cities to Corsica. **Corsair** (www.corsair.fr), an affiliate of France's leading budget-minded travel agency, **Nouvelles Frontières** (☎ 08 25 00 08 25; www.nouvelles-frontieres.fr), runs up to 10 Corsica-bound flights a week from Paris and other French regional airports. **Ollandini Charter** (☎ 04 95 23 92 40; www.ollandini-voyages.fr) does likewise, flying mainly into Ajaccio.

No-frills operator Luxair flies seasonally from between Luxembourg and Brussels to Ajaccio and Bastia (once weekly May to September).

Budget airline easyJet flies to Nice from Paris (Charles de Gaulle and Orly), Geneva, Berlin and Dortmund. Ryanair flies to Marseille from Dublin, Brussels and Frankfurt and Virgin Express links Brussels with Nice.

There are plenty of daily flights to the island from both Nice and Marseille, shortest of the aerial hops.

From the UK
Discount air travel is big business in London. Advertisements for many travel agencies appear in the travel pages of the weekend broadsheet newspapers, in *Time Out*, the *Evening Standard* and the free magazine *TNT*.

> **DEPARTURE TAX**
>
> Airport taxes in Corsica vary slightly from airport to airport and can add up to around €35. They are almost always included in the price of an air ticket.

Good travel agencies and online ticket sites include the following:
Cheap Flights (www.cheapflights.co.uk)
Cheapest Flights (www.cheapestflights.co.uk)
Flight Centre (☎ 0870 890 8099; www.flightcentre.co.uk)
Online Travel (www.onlinetravel.com)
STA Travel (☎ 0870 162 7551; www.statravel.co.uk) Primarily for travellers under the age of 26.
Trailfinders (www.trailfinders.com)
Travel Bag (☎ 0870 814 441; www.travelbag.co.uk)

Excel Airways (www.xl.com) flies between London (Gatwick) and Bastia once a week from mid-May to September.

Plenty of charters (flying between May and October) are sold via UK-based tour operators such as **Corsican Places** (☎ 0845 330 2059; www.corsica.co.uk), **Simply Travel** (☎ 0870 405 5005; www.simplytravel.co.uk), **VFB Holidays** (www.vfbholidays.co.uk) and **Voyages Ilena** (☎ 020 7924 4440; www.voyagesilena.co.uk). You may find that flights are only sold as part of a package together with accommodation. **Direct Corsica** (www.directcorsica.com) and **Holiday Options** (☎ 0870 420 8386; www.holidayoptions.co.uk) are two operators that also offer complete packages but will sell flights only to/from London and regional airports such as Birmingham, Newcastle, Edinburgh and Manchester.

A sensible, cost-effective alternative for travel from the UK is to fly as far as Nice, Marseille, Genoa or Pisa (for Livorno) and to catch a ferry for the last leg of the journey to Corsica. British Airways flies to all four port cities from London. There is also a rapidly multiplying range of cheaper airline routes you can pick from. Ryanair flies from London (Stansted) to Marseille and Genoa, from Glasgow to Marseille and to Pisa from London (Stansted), plus several UK regional airports. EasyJet flies to Nice from London (Gatwick, Luton and Stansted), as well as several UK regional airports, and also links Bristol and Pisa. BMI Baby also flies to Nice from London (Heathrow) and Birmingham.

TRANSPORT

BY LAND & SEA FROM THE UK

Corsica is a hop across the Channel, a skip (albeit a mighty big one) over mainland France and a jump across the Med for Brits with time and a sense of adventure on their hands.

If you've time (read: 23 hours) on your hands, one possibility is to bus it with **National Express** (☎ 0870 580 8080; www.nationalexpress.com) from London to Nice (via Lyon; around UK£110 return), then pick up a Corsica-bound ferry independently.

Travellers able to plan their journey to Corsica well in advance would do just as well to travel by train: 2nd-class London–Nice or London–Marseille return fares with a change of train from the cross-Channel **Eurostar** (☎ 0870 518 6186; www.eurostar.com) to a high-speed French **TGV** (www.tgv.com) in Paris or Lille start at around UK£129. The tickets are nonrefundable and nonchangeable, and can be booked up to 60 days in advance through **Rail Europe** (☎ 0870 584 8848; www.raileurope.com).

Rail enthusiasts with a penchant for experiencing (rather than vaporising) distance can ride a regular British train to Dover or Folkestone, take a cheap ferry across the Channel to the French mainland ports of Calais or Boulogne respectively, then connect with the French rail network to reach the port of Nice or Marseille. Longer channel crossings (with less competitive fares) include Newhaven–Dieppe, Poole–Cherbourg, and Portsmouth–Cherbourg/Le Havre. Ferries are run by several cross-Channel companies; updated schedules and fares can be found on the web. Motorists can cross the Channel by ferry, or aboard a high-speed **Eurotunnel** (☎ 0870 535 3535; www.eurotunnel.com) train which takes 35 minutes.

Crossing mainland France by train, super-sleek **TGVs** (www.tgv.com) purr along at 310km/h, serving a highly efficient network operated by the state-owned **SNCF** (Société Nationale des Chemins de Fer; ☎ 08 36 35 35 39; www.sncf.com). Ticket reservations can be made in France by telephone, internet or at any SNCF train station. Marseille is three hours from Paris.

From the USA

The North Atlantic is the world's busiest long-haul air corridor and the flight options are bewildering. Flights from the USA to Corsica require a change of aircraft in Paris. Discount travel agencies in the USA are known as consolidators (although you won't see a sign on the door saying 'Consolidator'). San Francisco is the ticket consolidator capital of America, although some good deals can also be found in Los Angeles, New York and other big cities. The following agencies are recommended for their online booking service:

Air Brokers International (☎ 1 800 883 3273; www.airbrokers.com)

STA Travel (☎ 1 800 781 4040; www.sta.com) Mainly for travellers under the age of 26.

Travelocity (☎ 888 872 8356; www.travelocity.com)

SEA

Approaching Corsica by sea is an experience. Whether you do it aboard a nippy NGV (*navire à grande vitesse*; high-speed vessel) or a romantic, slow ferry, afloat a luxury palace or a private yacht, any sea voyage reveals just how remote and isolated from the continent the island really is.

Ferry

Corsica has seven ferry ports: Bastia, Île Rousse, Calvi, Ajaccio, Propriano, Bonifacio and Porto-Vecchio. By sea, the island can be reached from the ports of Nice, Marseille and Toulon in mainland France; and from Genoa, Livorno and Savona in Italy. Ferries also link Corsica with the Italian island of Sardinia.

Advance reservations are essential in high season, especially for motorists planning to take a vehicle. Students under 27, seniors aged over 60 and families get reduced rates with most ferry companies; children aged four to 12 years usually pay 50% or two-thirds of an adult fare, and children aged under four sail for free. Most companies also offers packages of, for example, car plus two adults or car plus two adults and two children. Taking a bicycle on board costs around €3 one-way.

FROM MAINLAND FRANCE

Nice, Marseille and Toulon are linked year-round by ferry to Corsica.

In high season, **Société Nationale Corse Méditerranée** (SNCM; ☎ in France 08 91 70 18 01, in Italy 02 66 117 104, in the UK 020 7491 49 68; www.sncm.fr) operates speedy NGVs between Nice and both Île Rousse and Ajaccio. Normal ferries run between Marseille and the island ports of Ajaccio, Bastia, Île Rousse, Porto-Vecchio and Propriano. There are also a couple of less regular overnight ferries in July and August between Toulon and Ajaccio and Propriano. In winter, services are reduced to just a handful of weekly sailings to/from Nice and Marseille.

CMN/La Méridionale (☎ 08 10 20 13 20; www.cmn .fr) shares routes with SNCM and has sailings from Marseille to Ajaccio, Bastia, Porto-Vecchio, Île Rousse and Propriano. It also sails between Nice and Calvi, Ajaccio and Île Rousse.

Corsica Ferries (☎ 08 25 09 50 95; www.corsicaferries .com) runs high-speed boats from Nice to Ajaccio, Bastia, Calvi and Île Rousse and regular ferries to these last three. It also has a NGV service from Toulon to Ajaccio and a normal ferry to/from Bastia and, less frequently, Île Rousse.

From Nice (the closest French port to Corsica), you can nip across by NGV to Île Rousse in three hours (the regular ferry takes four to 5½ hours to Île Rousse and four hours to Ajaccio). CMN operates mostly 10-hour night crossings.

One-way CMN fares between the French mainland and Corsica are €35/7 (low season) to €56/22 (high season) per adult/child, plus €37 to €93 for a cabin. Transporting a small family car one-way costs €40 to €102 depending upon the season. Tariffs charged by SNCM and Corsica Ferries are much the same.

Quoted fares do not include port tax. Count on an additional €7.45 to €11.20 per passenger, plus €5.50 to €8.50 per vehicle.

FROM ITALY

Between April and September, scheduled ferry boats run by Corsica Ferries and Moby Lines link Corsica with the Italian mainland ports of Genoa, Livorno and Savona.

Between April and October, **Corsica Ferries** (☎ in France 08 25 09 50 95, in Livorno, Italy 0586 88 13 80, in Savona, Italy 019 215 62 47; www.corsicaferries .com) runs to Bastia from both Livorno and Savona. In high summer, it also has a less-frequent service from Savona to Île Rousse (June to mid-August) and Calvi (mid-June to August).

Moby Lines (☎ in Corsica 04 95 34 84 94, in Genoa, Italy 010 254 15 13, in Livorno, Italy 0565 93 61; www.mobylines .it) runs seasonal ferry services (mid-April

to September) from Genoa and Livorno to Bastia.

From Livorno (easily accessible from Pisa airport) it's a four-hour voyage to Bastia; Genoa to Bastia takes 3¾ hours. It's six hours from Savona to each of Bastia, Calvi and Île Rousse.

Fares from mainland Italy are lower than from mainland France. Corsica Ferries charges €32 to €90 to transport a small car one-way and €16 to €31 per person (€25 to €33 on a night crossing) from Savona to Bastia, Calvi or Île Rousse. For port taxes, add about €6 per passenger and €5 per car.

FROM SARDINIA

Many holidaymakers, especially ones from Italy, combine a driving holiday with a visit to the neighbouring Italian island of Sardinia.

The crossing between Bonifacio and Sardinia's Santa Teresa di Gallura takes about one hour. **Saremar** (Sardegna Regionale Marittima; ☎ in Corsica 04 95 73 00 96, in Sardinia 0565 90 89 33; www.saremar .it in Italian), Sardinia's public ferry line, has up to six sailings daily, in conjunction with Corsica Ferries, from April to September. Fares are €10/5 per adult/child. The tariff for a small car is €21 to €37, according to season. During these same months, **Moby Lines** (☎ 04 95 34 84 94; www.mobylines.it) also serves this route. The passenger tariff is €8 to €12, while for a small car it's €26 to €43, each according to season. To these rates, add port tax of €4.10 per passenger and €2.50 per car.

CMN (La Méridionale; ☎ 08 10 20 13 20; www.cmn.fr) has seasonal ferries (April to October) between Porto Torres (Sardinia) and Propriano (three hours) and Ajaccio (four hours). Tariffs are €19/11 per adult/child, while a small family car costs €35. To this, add on €7.75 to €12.45 for port taxes.

Under Your Own Sail/Steam

Corsica has some 16 marinas (ports de plaisance) and is a yachters' paradise. Yachts can be hired with or without a crew at most marinas along the coast; the various tourist offices have lists.

Up-to-date marina and harbour master information is available from the **Fédération Française des Ports de Plaisance** (FFPP; www.ffports -plaisance.com in French). Follow the 'Ports de Plaisance Corses' link online to get a full listing of Corsican ports.

GETTING AROUND

BICYCLE

Corsica, with its dramatic mountain passes and stunning coast, is superb cycling terrain – for experienced cyclists.

By law, bicycles must have two functioning brakes, a bell, a red reflector on the back and yellow reflectors on the pedals. After sunset and when visibility is poor, road cyclists must turn on a white light in front and a red one at the rear. If you're hiring to cycletour, check that your machine's fully equipped before leaping into the saddle. Marked cycling lanes (on roads) or trails (for mountain bikers) are practically nonexistent, except for a kilometre or two in Bastia and Ajaccio. Cycling in the Parc Régional Naturel de Corse is not forbidden, but there are few trails suitable for cyclists and you'll need a sturdy mountain bike.

For information on travelling by train with your bike, see p273.

Hire

For information about hiring bikes, see the Great Outdoors chapter, p84.

Bike Organisations

The volunteer-run **Fédération Française de Cyclotourisme** (FFCT; www.ffct.org in French) liaises between 3100-odd cycling clubs in mainland France and Corsica, and can send you a free information pack in English. It also sells touring itineraries, cycling maps and topoguides for cyclists, and organises bicycle trips, tours and races.

Local cycling association La Roue d'Or Ajaccienne, in cooperation with the Comité Régional de Corse, the local government, organises Corsica's legendary Tour de Corse Cycliste, a four-day, 400km race in May that has sped around the island since 1920.

Corsica Bike (www.corsicabike.com) is the force behind Corsica Bik'Up, an event for mountain bikers in late June with five stages of 40km to 100km (there's also the less demanding Bik'Up Light, where each stage is 30km to 80km).

Lastly, the **Six Jours Cyclotouristes de l'Île de Beauté** (☎ 04 95 21 96 94) is a six-day, 600km participatory event in the second half of September, aimed at revealing the island's beauty spots by pedal power.

For its members, the UK-based **Cyclists' Touring Club** (CTC; ☎ 0870 873 0060; www.ctc.org.uk) publishes a free information sheet on cycling in France, as well as touring notes and itineraries for several routes in Corsica. The CTC also offers tips on bikes, spares and insurance; it sells maps and topoguides by mail order.

BOAT

There is no scheduled commercial boat service between any two Corsican ports. This said, one of the tour-boat companies making daily excursions from one Corsican port to another and back might sell you a one-way ticket – and might also be willing to let you go out one day and back another.

Tourist boats ply the waters between Calvi and Girolata, Calvi and Ajaccio, Ajaccio and Bonifacio and, the weather permitting, Bonifacio and Porto-Vecchio.

BUS

Corsica's major towns and many of the little ones in between are linked by bus, as are the airports of Ajaccio and Bastia with town centres. In remoter areas services are scarce or quite simply nonexistent.

Bus services are geared to local inhabitants rather than tourists, meaning that many services are less frequent during the height of the tourist season when school children are on holiday. In July and August there is often only one departure a day and no departure at all on Sunday and public holidays. Secondary routes often only have service on alternate days or once or twice a week. Many passenger routes year-round are combined with school and/or postal services.

By contrast, there are a trio of summer-only bus services that manage to sustain themselves precisely because of the tourist trade. Between July and mid-September **Autocars Mordiconi** (☎ 04 95 48 00 04) runs one bus daily along the spectacular route between Porto and Corte, via Évisa and Calacuccia. Similarly, in July and August Autocars Santini has a twice daily run, Monday to Saturday, between the coastal resorts of to Île Rousse and St-Florent, while Les Beaux Voyages runs between Calvi and the fascinating coastal hamlet of Galéria.

Autocars (regional buses) are operated by a range of different bus companies, some of whom might have an office at the bus station *(gare routière)* of the towns they serve. Often one company sells tickets for all the bus companies operating from the same station, although passengers, as a rule, do not need to worry about buying tickets in advance. You

TRANSPORT

can buy your ticket on any particular route, or leg of a route, from the driver – fares average around €13 per 100km. Minibuses serve many bus routes.

The island's two main towns, Ajaccio and Bastia, have the largest bus stations. In smaller places, where a bus stop can constitute a 'station', bus schedules are invariably pinned up in the window of the local tourist office or in the nearest bar to the bus stop (if there's no printed schedule, just ask the bar owner). Bus stations do not have left-luggage facilities.

Primary bus routes and bus-travel companies include the following:

Autocars Ceccaldi (☎ 04 95 22 41 99) Ajaccio–Sagone–Porto–Évisa.

Autocars Cortenais (☎ 04 95 46 02 12) Bastia–Corte; Corte–Aléria.

Autocars Ricci (☎ 04 95 76 25 59) Ajaccio–Propriano–Sartène–Lévie–Zonza–Bavella.

Autocars Santini (☎ 04 95 37 04 01) Bastia–St-Florent.

Autocars Santoni (☎ 04 95 22 64 44; www.autocars-santoni.com) Ajaccio–Zicavo.

Eurocorse Voyages (☎ 04 95 21 06 30; www.eurocorse.com) Ajaccio–Corte–Bastia; Ajaccio–Propriano–Sartène–Porto-Vecchio and Ajaccio–Propriano–Sartène–Bonifacio; Porto-Vecchio–Bonifacio; Ajaccio–Sartène–Zonza.

Les Beaux Voyages (☎ 04 95 65 11 36; www.lesbeauxvoyagesencorse.com in French) Bastia–Île Rousse–Ponte Leccia–Calvi.

Rapides Bleus (☎ 04 95 31 03 79) Bastia–Porto-Vecchio.

See the Getting There & Away sections of the respective regional chapters for more information.

CAR & MOTORCYCLE

To really enjoy Corsica, we strongly recommend hiring a vehicle. No other form of transport lets you explore the island's secret backwaters and enjoy as much freedom as a set of motorised wheels. There are some gorgeous runs, cruising along the island's beautiful, dramatic roads – the D81 linking Calvi and Porto, the D84 between Porto and Francardo (via Évisa, the Forêt d'Aïtone and the Scala di Santa Regina), and the D69 from just below Vivario to Ghisoni are but a sample of the memorable drives you can undertake – in a car, aboard an open-top 4WD or purring along on a motorbike.

Here is a list of distances and approximate driving times between major towns.

Towns	Distance (km)	Driving time (hr)
Bastia–Ajaccio	153	2¼
Bastia–Bonifacio	171	2½
Bastia–Porto-Vecchio	143	2
Bastia–Calvi	92	1¾
Bastia–Corte	70	1
Ajaccio–Bonifacio	132	2
Ajaccio–Porto-Vecchio	140	2¼
Ajaccio–Calvi	164	2½
Ajaccio–Corte	80	1¼

Exhilarating views aside, motoring around Corsica can be fairly hair-raising on occasion. Roads are narrow; hairpin bends (*lacets*) are torturous and blind; and rocky outcrops often prevent you spotting oncoming traffic (or the menagerie of livestock that wanders freely over mountain roads) until it's bang on top of you, or you're on top of it. Use your horn to announce your presence. Drops either side of the road may be sheer and guard rails are a luxury. Visitors tend to drive timidly; the locals with a panache that verges on the irresponsible.

Corsica has no motorway (*autoroute*). The largest roads are called *routes nationales*, such as the N198, which skirts the flat eastern coast from Bastia to Bonifacio, or the N193, running through the dramatic relief between Bastia, Corte and Ajaccio. *Routes départementales*, whose names begin with the letter D, are tertiary local roads, many of them potholed and far from silky smooth. *Routes communales*, whose names begin with the letter C (or nothing at all), are rural roads best suited to off-road vehicles and mountain bikes.

Corsican towns are small by any standard and were not designed with cars in mind so

---

2B OR NOT 2B?

Driving? Let's just say that Corsica is close to Italy geographically, culturally – and in the way its citizens drive. Check in your mirror for a numberplate ending in 2A or 2B (the *départements* of Corse du Sud and Haute-Corse; if it's being driven prudently, it's probably a hired car). Too many locals at the wheel have a tendency to drive halfway up your backside before pulling out abruptly, then overtaking in situations where responsible drivers would hold back.

parking can be frustrating. On town maps within destination chapters, we indicate public parking, usually paying, with a small 'P'. *Défense de stationner* means 'No Parking' and you'd be wise to respect the injunction; fines can be harsh.

Michelin's *Cors-du-Sud, Haut-Corse* map 345 (scale 1:150,000) is reliable and invaluable for getting around.

Bring Your Own Vehicle

The fleet of car ferries that ply regularly to Corsica from French and Italian ports makes bringing your own vehicle onto the island simplicity itself. A right-hand drive vehicle brought to France from the UK or Ireland should have deflectors clipped to the headlights to avoid dazzling oncoming traffic.

By law, motorists (driving their own car or a rented vehicle) need to carry a national ID card or passport; a valid driving permit or licence *(permis de conduire)*; car ownership papers, known as a *carte grise* (grey card); and proof of insurance (the *carte verte* or green card). If you're stopped by the police and don't have one or more of these documents, you risk a hefty on-the-spot fine. Never leave your car ownership or insurance papers in the vehicle.

By law, all vehicles must carry a reflective warning triangle, to be used in the event of a breakdown. Recommended accessories include a first-aid kit, spare bulb kit and fire extinguisher. These are normally standard extras if you hire a vehicle but do peer into the boot/trunk to ensure they're there.

If you're involved in a minor traffic incident with no injuries, the easiest way for drivers to sort things out with their insurance companies is to fill out a *Constat Aimable d'Accident Automobile* (jointly agreed accident report), known in English as a European Accident Statement. Make sure the report includes any details that will help you prove that the accident was not your fault, if you feel that the other party was in the wrong. If problems arise, alert the police.

In the UK, the **RAC** (☎ 0870 010 6382; www.rac .co.uk) or the **AA** (☎ 0870 600 0371; www.theaa.com) can give you more advice.

Petrol *(essence),* also called *carburant* (fuel), costs around €1.10 per litre (unleaded, 95 or 98 octane). Outside main towns, petrol stations are few and far between so keep an eye on the fuel gauge.

Rental

You can rent a car when you arrive in Corsica, be it at an airport or in town. Most companies require the driver to be at least 21 years old (23 for some categories of car) and to have had a driving licence for at least one year.

Although multinational rental agencies such as Avis, Budget, Hertz and Europcar (Europe's largest) can be expensive for on-the-spot rental, their prepaid promotional rates are usually more reasonable. Fly-drive deals offered by Avis and Europcar are also worth looking into. For quick, walk-in rental, domestic firms such as ADA sometimes offer better rates. All major firms have a desk at the airports in Corsica. Most companies charge an airport pick-up or drop-off surcharge of around €20.

Most companies require a credit card, primarily so that you can leave a deposit *(caution).* They'll probably ask you to leave a signed credit card slip without a sum written on it as a deposit. If you don't like this arrangement, ask them to make out two credit card slips: one for the sum of the rental, the other for the sum of the excess. Make sure to have the latter destroyed when you return the car.

Insurance *(assurance)* for damage or injury you cause to other people is mandatory, but collision damage waivers vary. If you're in an accident where you are at fault, or the car is damaged and the party at fault is unknown (as, for example, if someone dents your car while it's parked), or the car is stolen, the *franchise* (excess/deductible) is the amount you are liable for before the policy kicks in. When signing the rental agreement, you can agree to pay an extra daily fee (anything from to €15 to €50 per day) to reduce the excess (usually €350 to €800 depending on the vehicle size) to either zero or a minimal amount.

The packet of documents you get when hiring a car includes a 24-hour number to call in case of breakdown and a European Accident Statement (see the previous section). Check how many 'free' kilometres are in the deal you're offered; *kilométrage illimité* (unlimited mileage) means you can drive to your heart's content.

To rent a scooter or *moto* (motorcycle), you will probably also have to leave a deposit (of several hundred euro), which you forfeit (up to the value of the damage) if you're in an accident and it's your fault. Since insurance

TRANSPORT

companies won't cover theft, you'll also lose the deposit if the bike is stolen. Expect to pay about €60/350 per day/week for a 125cc motorbike. Rates usually include helmet hire.

A complete list of car- and motorcycle-rental companies is online at www.visit-corsica.com. Go to 'plan your stay/how to get around', then click on 'type of transport' and 'car rental'. Some of the major operators in Corsica:

Ada (www.ada-en-corse.com in French)
Avis (www.avis.fr)
Budget (www.budget-en-corse.com in French)
Europcar (www.europcar.fr in French)
Hertz (www.hertz-en-corse.com)
National-Citer (www.corse-auto-rent.fr)
Rent a Car (☎ 04 95 23 56 26; www.rent-car-corsica .com in French)
Sixt (www.sixt.fr in French)

Road Rules

In Corsica, as throughout continental Europe, people drive on the right side of the road and overtake on the left. Unless otherwise indicated, you must give way to cars coming from the right. North American drivers should remember that turning right on a red light is illegal.

A speed limit of 50km/h applies in built-up areas. On intercity roads you must slow to 50km/h the moment you pass a white sign with red borders on which a place name is written in black or blue letters. This limit remains in force until you arrive at the other side of the town or village, where you'll pass an identical sign with a red diagonal bar across the name, indicating that you're leaving the built-up area.

Outside towns and villages, speed limits are 90km/h (80km/h if it's raining) on single carriageway N and D roads and 110km/h (100km/h if it's raining) on the few stretches of four-lane highway. This said, you're more likely in Corsica to fall short of the speed limit than to exceed it.

French law is tough on drunk drivers and police conduct random breathalyser tests to weed out drivers whose blood-alcohol concentration (BAC) is over 0.05% (0.50g per litre of blood) – two glasses of wine for a 75kg adult. Licences can be suspended.

Helmets (*casques*) are compulsory for motorcyclists and moped riders. Bikes of more than 125cc must have their headlights on during the day. No special licence is required to ride a scooter with an engine capacity of 50cc or less.

HITCHING

Hitching is never entirely safe in any country. Travellers who decide to hitch should understand that they are taking a small but potentially serious risk. This said, if you're trekking, an outstretched thumb may be the only way to or from the trail. As a driver, you'll be doing a huge favour to a weary walker if you can squeeze them and their backpack in. Hitchers will be safer if they travel in pairs and let someone know where they are planning to go.

LOCAL TRANSPORT

All Corsican towns are small enough to get around on foot. Ajaccio and Bastia both have local bus services. Elsewhere, you may find yourself dependent to some degree on taxis.

Taxis in Corsica have a 'Taxi' sign on the roof; the cars can be any colour. Look for phone numbers of taxi companies in the Getting Around section of individual towns.

TRAIN

Travelling by train in Corsica – a fun experience in its own right – is much more than simply a means of getting from A to B. Dubbed *U trinighellu* (literally 'the trembler'), the 110-seat train trundles along a remarkable railway line constructed in the 1880s and 1890s. With 38 tunnels (the longest is 4km), 34 viaducts and 12 bridges (one designed by Gustave Eiffel no less), it represents one of the great triumphs of man over topography and ranks among the world's great scenic railways.

Corsica's two lines are operated by **Chemins de Fer de la Corse** (CFC; ☎ in Bastia 04 95 32 80 61, in Corte 04 95 46 00 97, in Ajaccio 04 95 23 11 03, in Calvi 04 95 65 00 61, in Île Rousse 04 95 60 00 50; www.ter-sncf.com/corse in French).

The main, north–south line runs between Bastia and Ajaccio. From the Ponte Leccia junction between Bastia and Corte, a spur runs to the Balagne towns of Île Rousse and Calvi. There was once a third line, connecting Bastia and Porto-Vecchio along the flat east coast of the island but it was badly damaged by German bombing raids in 1943. There's talk of restoring it but no-one has yet lifted a hammer.

Travelling by train is slower than a bus ride – a factor not helped by the occasional wild goat that wanders on the track. There's only one class and there's no system of advance reservations.

TRANSPORT

GREAT GREEN RAIL ESCAPE

In July and August nature-loving railway buffs can ride the mountain railway as far as Vizzavona (2¾ hours from Bastia, one hour from Ajaccio) then delve deep into the heart of the Forêt de Vizzavona – a fairy-tale forest of beech and laricio pines – with the help of an experienced guide from the Office National des Forêts (ONF; National Forestry Office).

The two-hour forest discovery walk leads nature lovers to the Cascade des Anglais, impressive winter-time waterfalls which melt into a picture-postcard set of serene pools (to swim in) in summer. The GR20 links the latter with Vizzavona train station.

Tickets covering the return train trip and forest guide cost €48/35 per adult/child from either Bastia or Ajaccio and are available from CFC train stations. The **ONF office** (☎ 04 95 32 81 90) in Bastia also has details.

At the train station *(gare)*, you can get updated train timetables and information, which also feature on the website (www.ter -sncf.com/corse in French). There are no left-luggage facilities at any station.

The train routes are:

Bastia–Ponte Leccia–Corte–Ajaccio Corsica's primary north–south rail route, with dozens of stops in smaller stations, including Furiani, Biguglia, Casamozza, Ponte Novu, Francardo, Vénaco, Vivario, Vizzavona and Bocognano. Trains run year-round in each direction four times daily. It takes four hours to travel the length of the line from Bastia to Ajaccio.

Bastia–Casamozza Up to 13 trains daily make the short 30-minute journey from Bastia to Casamozza, Monday to Saturday, stopping approximately every two minutes at every local station along the way.

Bastia–Ponte Leccia–Calvi Corsica's east–west link, this line follows the Bastia–Ajaccio line south to Ponte Leccia, then curves west towards the coast, stopping en route in Île Rousse. There are two trains daily, both requiring a change in Ponte Leccia.

Île Rousse–Calvi On the same track that the CFC uses, runs the Tramway de Balagne (p133) – little two-car trains that shuttle back and forth up to nine times daily between April and October along the spectacular coastline between Calvi and Île Rousse. With 15 intermediate stops, including Lumio, Sant'Ambrogio, Algajola and Davia, the full journey takes 45 minutes. Wherever you happen to be along the line, a train will pass in each direction approximately once an hour.

Costs

Train fares are reasonable, averaging around €15 per 100km. Children aged under four travel for free and those aged four to 12 years pay 50% of the adult fare.

Cyclists can take their bicycles aboard for a €12.50 fee, but there is only space for four or five bikes on each train, and places cannot be reserved in advance.

Train Passes

Senior travellers with a one-year Carte Sénior issued by the French national rail line, the SNCF, can use it on CFC trains to get a 50% reduction. SNCF's Carte Famille Nombreuse, which gives families with three or four children aged under 18 discounts of at least 30%, is likewise valid in Corsica. More information on both annual travel passes is online at www.sncf.com.

The CFC also sells its own rail pass, the Carte Zoom, valid for seven consecutive days of unlimited travel throughout the CFC network. It costs €48 and is sold at all staffed CFC stations. None of the major European rail passes – InterRail, Eurail, Eurorail or even the France Railpass – provides for unlimited free travel on the CFC system. The major rail passes do, however, yield a 50% discount on CFC fares between Bastia and Ajaccio (but not on the Tramway de Balagne between Calvi and Île Rousse).

Health

CONTENTS

Corsica is a healthy place to travel. Hygiene standards are high and there are no unusual diseases to worry about.

BEFORE YOU GO

A little planning before departure, particularly for pre-existing illnesses, will save trouble later: pack a spare pair of contact lenses and glasses, if you use them, and take your optical prescription with you. Bring any medicines in their original, clearly labelled, containers. A signed and dated letter from your physician describing your medical conditions and medications, including generic names, might be worthwhile. If you're carrying syringes or needles, a doctor's letter saying you need them should satisfy any querulous customs official.

INSURANCE

EU nationals and citizens of Switzerland, Iceland and Norway need to carry a European Health Insurance Card (EHIC) in order to qualify for abated medical treatment in Corsica. Consult your local Ministry of Health. UK nationals, for example, can go www.dh.gov.uk, follow the leads and apply on line.

In Corsica, as elsewhere in France, you'll need to pay for medicines and medical care upfront. The French health system, which subsidises medical care rather than offering a free system, will reimburse you a good proportion, but not all, of your outlay.

Travel insurance is all but essential for other nationalities and strongly recommended as a fallback for EU citizens too since the EHIC doesn't cover you for non-urgent treatment or emergency repatriation.

If you're from outside the EU, you might want to check if there's a reciprocal arrangement for free medical care between France and your country.

If you take out health insurance, make sure you get a policy that covers you for the worst possible scenario, such as an accident requiring an emergency flight home. Find out in advance if your insurance plan will make payments directly to providers or reimburse you later for overseas health expenditures.

RECOMMENDED VACCINATIONS

You don't need any vaccinations to visit Corsica. The World Health Organisation (WHO) recommends that all travellers, wherever they're heading, should be covered for diphtheria, tetanus, measles, mumps, rubella and polio, as well as Hepatitis B. Since most vaccines don't produce immunity until at least two weeks after they're given, get pumped at least six weeks before departure. Then again, the chances of you picking up any of these diseases on the island are really very remote.

ONLINE RESOURCES

The WHO publication *International Travel and Health* is revised annually and is available online at www.who.int/ith. Other useful websites include www.mdtravelhealth.com (travel health recommendations for every country; updated daily), www.fitfortravel.scot.nhs.uk (general travel advice for the layman), www.ageconcern.org.uk (advice on travel for the elderly) and www.mariestopes.org.uk (information on women's health and contraception).

IN CORSICA

AVAILABILITY & COST OF HEALTH CARE

Good health care is readily available in Corsica. For minor illnesses, pharmacists *(pharmaciens)* can give valuable advice and sell over-the-counter medicines. If you need a doctor, any *pharmacie* can provide you with the name and address of a local practitioner and point you in the right direction. The sign for a *pharmacie* is a green neon cross. If it's closed, the address of the nearest open alternative will be posted, together with its hours.

There are hospitals in Ajaccio, Bastia, Bonifacio, Corte and Sartène.

Dental care is usually good, should you need emergency treatment, though there may be a language problem.

TRAVELLERS' DIARRHOEA

Should you develop diarrhoea, drink plenty of fluids, maybe supplemented by an oral rehydration solution such as Dioralyte. A few loose motions are almost part of the holiday experience for lots of travellers and don't need treatment. But if you're making more than four or five trips to the toilet a day, you should start taking an antibiotic (usually a quinolone drug) and an antidiarrhoeal agent (such as Loperamide). If diarrhoea is bloody, persists for more than 72 hours or is accompanied by fever, shaking, chills or severe abdominal pain, consult a doctor.

ENVIRONMENTAL HAZARDS
Bites & Stings

Jellyfish stings are generally just rather painful. Antihistamines and analgesics may reduce the reaction and relieve the pain. There are no poisonous snakes on Corsica.

Decompression Sickness

Corsica is perfect for two activities that should *not* be tried on the same day: diving and mountain walking. Always avoid climbing at altitude straight after diving; this will allow your body to get rid of the residual nitrogen that it has stored up. Climbing only up to 1500m can prove dangerous if you have been diving only a few hours earlier. So too can air travel, so build in a rest day after that last dive before you fly home. As a rule of thumb, wait at least 24 hours after resurfacing for either.

The **Ajaccio hospital** (☎ 04 95 29 90 90; 27 av de l'Impératrice Eugénie) has a decompression chamber.

Heatstroke

Corsica gets seriously hot in summer and you'll need to constantly top up your fluids. Heat exhaustion happens after excessive fluid loss (though peeing and sweating) if you don't compensate for the liquid lost – and replace the salt of your sweat too. Symptoms include headache, dizziness and tiredness. Dehydration is already happening by the time you feel thirsty – if your pee's dark yellow, you need to be drinking more. To treat heat exhaustion, replace fluids with water and/or fruit juice, and cool the body with cold water and fans. Treat salt loss with fluids topped up with salt or sprinkle a little more table salt than you'd normally do onto foods.

Heatstroke is much more serious, resulting in irrational and hyperactive behaviour and eventually loss of consciousness, even death. Rapid cooling by spraying the body with water and fanning is ideal. Emergency fluid and electrolyte replacement by intravenous drip is recommended.

Hypothermia

If you're trekking the central mountains of Corsica on a hot summer's day, the weather may change in the blink of an eye in the late afternoon, when storms can rage. So pack your waterproofs, add an extra warm layer to your pack – and make sure that someone else knows where you're heading. You're most unlikely to suffer from hypothermia; just be aware of the symptoms. They start with shivering, loss of judgement and clumsiness. Prevent further heat loss by seeking shelter, warm dry clothing, hot sweet drinks and shared bodily warmth.

Sunburn

The sun can be deceptively strong, especially in the mountains, so slap on plenty of high-factor sun block. On the beach, use a waterproof kind, especially with children who may be dashing in and out of the waves.

Water

Tap water in Corsica is generally safe to drink. Some springs and fountains have a sign, *eau non potable* (water not suitable for drinking). Often, this is because the water hasn't been formally tested, yet generations of locals have drunk deep from them and lived to tell the tale.

Many people happily drink water from streams during their walks. However, given all the free-ranging livestock and other animals, you can't be sure that this water is safe. On the classic GR20 long-distance trail, we indicate springs and fountains that are reliable.

HEALTH

TRAVELLING WITH CHILDREN

Lonely Planet's *Travel with Children* has lots of advice on travel health for younger children.

WOMEN'S HEALTH

Careful, if you're on the pill: some antibiotics, diarrhoea and vomiting can stop it from working so pack those condoms, just in case. Gastrointestinal upsets and antibiotics don't affect injectable contraception.

Just because you're pregnant doesn't mean you have to stay at home. Travelling during pregnancy is usually quite possible. The most risky times are during the first 12 weeks and after 30 weeks.

HEALTH

Language

French is Corsica's official and working language and the language in which Corsicans express themselves most of the time. Corsica is nevertheless impressively bilingual and even trilingual. Many older Corsicans, and even some younger ones, express themselves quite eloquently in Corsican (*Corsu*) and even in Italian – not that the differences between the two are all that vast.

Spontaneous use of Corsican by the native inhabitants has been on the decline, but it has benefited from various forms of life support. It's now even part of the curriculum for the primary and secondary schools on the island. This is a significant turnaround from the days when signs posted in Corsican village schools read: *Il est interdit de cracher par terre et de parler corse* (Spitting on the floor and talking in Corsican are forbidden). Moreover, young people can now study Corsican at the university in Corte. Politicians have seen to it that Corsican enjoys equal status with French on road signs, although the French will often have been edited out with a spray of paint or bullets!

For more information on Corsican, see the 'Corsican' boxed text on the following page. For a more comprehensive guide to the French language, pick up a copy of Lonely Planet's *French Phrasebook*.

PRONUNCIATION

The pronunciation guides included with each French phrase should help you in getting your message across. Here are a few of the letters in written French that may cause confusion:

j	as the 's' in 'leisure', eg *jour* (day)
c	before **e** and **i**, as the 's' in 'sit'; before **a**, **o** and **u** it's pronounced as English 'k'. When undescored with a 'cedilla' (**ç**) it's always pronounced as the 's' in 'sit'.
r	pronounced from the back of the throat while constricting the muscles to restrict the flow of air
n, m	where a syllable ends in a single **n** or **m**, these letters are not pronounced, but the vowel is given a nasal pronunciation

BE POLITE!

An important distinction is made in French between *tu* and *vous*, which both mean 'you'; *tu* is only used when addressing people you know well, children or animals. If you're addressing an adult who isn't a personal friend, *vous* should be used unless the person invites you to use *tu*. In general, younger people insist less on this distinction between polite and informal, and you will find that in many cases they use *tu* from the beginning of an acquaintance.

GENDER

All nouns in French are either masculine or feminine and adjectives reflect the gender of the noun they modify. The feminine form of many nouns and adjectives is indicated by a silent **e** added to the masculine form, as in *ami* and *amie* (the masculine and feminine for 'friend').

In the following phrases both masculine and feminine forms have been indicated where necessary. The masculine form comes first and is separated from the feminine by a slash. The gender of a noun is often indicated by a preceding article: 'the/

LANGUAGE

CORSICAN

'Good day' in the Corsican language is *bunghjornu*. 'Thank you' is *grazie*. Bread is *pane*. Dog is *cane*. 'Best wishes!' is *pace i salute*! If this all sounds suspiciously like Italian to you, you're not off the mark. The Corsican language – Corsu in Corsican – is descended from, and still related to the Tuscan language that formed the basis of standard Italian. If you think Corsican is Italian or a dialect of Italian, you might nevertheless do well to keep this view to yourself. Though Corsicans are too good-natured to want to punish innocent foreigners for the hasty conclusions they draw on only partial evidence, many Corsicans are committed to the view that Corsican is not a dialect, and still less Italian itself, but a distinct language.

It's not recommended that you make any effort to communicate with Corsicans in Corsican. As Alexandra Jaffe says in her excellent *Ideologies in Action: Language Politics in Corsica*, Corsican is the language of the Corsican heart and hearth. French 'commands the domain of the formal, the authoritative, the instrumental and intellectual'. You may think you are being ingratiating if you attempt a few words of Corsican. More likely, however, you'll be perceived as patronising or condescending, as if the person you are addressing didn't speak French perfectly well. You may be perceived to be baiting the person you are addressing on what is in Corsica a heavily charged political issue. Finally, again Corsican being the language of the Corsican heart and hearth, you may be perceived as intruding on personal and private space – as if, invited into a stranger's living room, you proceeded immediately into their bedroom. Another way to put it is that presuming to address a stranger in Corsican is akin to the liberty you take in addressing a stranger in the familiar pan-Mediterranean 'tu' form rather than in the more respectful 'vous', 'lei' or 'usted' form.

If you speak French or Italian, stick with that. Dedicated Corsophiles can enrol in language courses at the Università di Corsica Pasqual Paoli in Corte or those offered by the association **Esse** (☎ 04 95 33 12 00) in Bastia.

---

a/some', *le/un/du* (m), *la/une/de la* (f); or one of the possessive adjectives, 'my/your/his/her', *mon/ton/son* (m), *ma/ta/sa* (f). With French, unlike English, the possessive adjective agrees in number and gender with the thing in question: 'his/her mother', *sa mère*.

ACCOMMODATION

I'm looking for a ...	Je cherche ...	zher shersh ...
campground	un camping	un kom·peeng
guesthouse	une pension (de famille)	ewn pon·syon (der fa·mee·ler)
hotel	un hôtel	un o·tel
youth hostel	une auberge de jeunesse	ewn o·berzh der zher·nes

Where is a cheap hotel?
Où est-ce qu'on peut trouver un hôtel pas cher?
oo es·kon per troo·vay un o·tel pa shair

What is the address?
Quelle est l'adresse?
kel e la·dres

Could you write it down, please?
Est-ce que vous pourriez l'écrire, s'il vous plaît?
e·sker voo poo·ryay lay·kreer seel voo play

Do you have any rooms available?
Est-ce que vous avez des chambres libres?
e·sker voo·za·vay day shom·brer lee·brer

I'd like (a) ...	Je voudrais ...	zher voo·dray ...
single room	une chambre à un lit	ewn shom·brer a un lee
double-bed room	une chambre avec un grand lit	ewn shom·brer a·vek un gron lee
twin room with two beds	une chambre avec des lits jumeaux	ewn shom·brer a·vek day lee zhew·mo
room with a bathroom	une chambre avec une salle de bains	ewn shom·brer a·vek ewn sal der bun
to share a dorm	coucher dans un dortoir	koo·sher don zun dor·twa

How much is it ...?	Quel est le prix ...?	kel e ler pree ...
per night	par nuit	par nwee
per person	par personne	par per·son

May I see it?
Est-ce que je peux voir la chambre?
es·ker zher per vwa la shom·brer

Where is the bathroom?
Où est la salle de bains? oo e la sal der bun

MAKING A RESERVATION

(for phone or written requests)

To ...	A l'attention de ...
From ...	De la part de ...
Date	Date
I'd like to book ...	Je voudrais réserver ... (see the list under 'Accommodation' for bed and room options)
in the name of ...	au nom de ...
from ... (date) **to ...**	du ... au ...
credit card	carte de crédit
number	numéro
expiry date	date d'expiration
Please confirm availability and price.	Veuillez confirmer la disponibilité et le prix.

Where is the toilet?
Où sont les toilettes? oo·son lay twa·let
I'm leaving today.
Je pars aujourd'hui. zher par o·zhoor·dwee
We're leaving today.
Nous partons aujourd'hui. noo par·ton o·zhoor·dwee

CONVERSATION & ESSENTIALS

Hello.	Bonjour.	bon·zhoor
Goodbye.	Au revoir.	o·rer·vwa
Yes.	Oui.	wee
No.	Non.	no
Please.	S'il vous plaît.	seel voo play
Thank you.	Merci.	mair·see
You're welcome.	Je vous en prie.	zher voo·zon pree
	De rien. (inf)	der ree·en
Excuse me.	Excuse-moi.	ek·skew·zay·mwa
Sorry. (forgive me)	Pardon.	par·don

What's your name?
Comment vous appelez-vous? (pol) ko·mon voo·za·pay·lay voo
Comment tu t'appelles? (inf) ko·mon tew ta·pel
My name is ...
Je m'appelle ... zher ma·pel ...
Where are you from?
De quel pays êtes-vous? der kel pay·ee et·voo
De quel pays es-tu? (inf) der kel pay·ee e·tew
I'm from ...
Je viens de ... zher vyen der ...
I like ...
J'aime ... zhem ...

SIGNS

Entrée	Entrance
Sortie	Exit
Renseignements	Information
Ouvert	Open
Fermé	Closed
Interdit	Prohibited
Chambres Libres	Rooms Available
Complet	Full/No Vacancies
(Commissariat de) Police	Police Station
Toilettes/WC	Toilets
Hommes	Men
Femmes	Women

I don't like ...
Je n'aime pas ... zher nem pa ...
Just a minute.
Une minute. ewn mee·newt

DIRECTIONS

Where is ...?
Où est ...? oo e ...
Go straight ahead.
Continuez tout droit. kon·teen·way too drwa
Turn left.
Tournez à gauche. toor·nay a gosh
Turn right.
Tournez à droite. toor·nay a drwa
at the corner
au coin o kwun
at the traffic lights
aux feux o fer

behind	derrière	dair·ryair
in front of	devant	der·von
far (from)	loin (de)	lwun (der)
near (to)	près (de)	pray (der)
opposite	en face de	on fas der

beach	la plage	la plazh
castle	le château	ler sha·to
church	l'église	lay·gleez
island	l'île	leel
main square	la place centrale	la plas son·tral
museum	le musée	ler mew·zay
old city (town)	la vieille ville	la vyay veel
quay	le quai	ler kay
ruins	les ruines	lay rween
sea	la mer	la mair
tourist office	l'office de tourisme	lo·fees der too·rees·mer
tower	la tour	la toor

EMERGENCIES

Help!
Au secours!   o skoor
There's been an accident!
Il y a eu un accident!   eel ya ew un ak·see·don
I'm lost.
Je me suis égaré/e. (m/f)   zhe me swee·zay·ga·ray
Leave me alone!
Fichez-moi la paix!   fee·shay·mwa la pay

Call ...!	*Appelez ...!*	a·play ...
a doctor	*un médecin*	un mayd·sun
the police	*la police*	la po·lees

HEALTH

I'm ill.	*Je suis malade.*	zher swee ma·lad
It hurts here.	*J'ai une douleur ici.*	zhay ewn doo·ler ee·see

I'm ...	*Je suis ...*	zher swee ...
asthmatic	*asthmatique*	(z)as·ma·teek
diabetic	*diabétique*	dee·a·bay·teek
epileptic	*épileptique*	(z)ay·pee·lep·teek

I'm allergic to ...	*Je suis allergique ...*	zher swee za·lair·zheek ...
antibiotics	*aux antibiotiques*	o zon·tee·byo·teek
aspirin	*à l'aspirine*	a las·pee·reen
bees	*aux abeilles*	o za·bay·yer
nuts	*aux noix*	o nwa
peanuts	*aux cacahuètes*	o ka·ka·wet
penicillin	*à la pénicilline*	a la pay·nee·see·leen

antiseptic	*l'antiseptique*	lon·tee·sep·teek
aspirin	*l'aspirine*	las·pee·reen
condoms	*des préservatifs*	day pray·zair·va·teef
contraceptive	*le contraceptif*	ler kon·tra·sep·teef
diarrhoea	*la diarrhée*	la dya·ray
medicine	*le médicament*	ler may·dee·ka·mon
nausea	*la nausée*	la no·zay
sunblock cream	*la crème solaire*	la krem so·lair
tampons	*des tampons hygiéniques*	day tom·pon ee·zhen·eek

LANGUAGE DIFFICULTIES

Do you speak English?
Parlez-vous anglais?   par·lay·voo ong·lay
Does anyone here speak English?
Y a-t-il quelqu'un qui parle anglais?   ya·teel kel·kung kee par long·glay
How do you say ... in French?
Comment est-ce qu'on dit ... en français?   ko·mon es·kon dee ... on fron·say

What does ... mean?
Que veut dire ...?   ker ver deer ...
I understand.
Je comprends.   zher kom·pron
I don't understand.
Je ne comprends pas.   zher ner kom·pron pa
Could you write it down, please?
Est-ce que vous pouvez l'écrire?   es·ker voo poo·vay lay·kreer
Can you show me (on the map)?
Pouvez-vous m'indiquer (sur la carte)?   poo·vay·voo mun·dee·kay (sewr la kart)

NUMBERS

0	*zero*	zay·ro
1	*un*	un
2	*deux*	der
3	*trois*	trwa
4	*quatre*	ka·trer
5	*cinq*	sungk
6	*six*	sees
7	*sept*	set
8	*huit*	weet
9	*neuf*	nerf
10	*dix*	dees
11	*onze*	onz
12	*douze*	dooz
13	*treize*	trez
14	*quatorze*	ka·torz
15	*quinze*	kunz
16	*seize*	sez
17	*dix-sept*	dee·set
18	*dix-huit*	dee·zweet
19	*dix-neuf*	deez·nerf
20	*vingt*	vung
21	*vingt et un*	vung tay un
22	*vingt-deux*	vung·der
30	*trente*	tront
40	*quarante*	ka·ront
50	*cinquante*	sung·kont
60	*soixante*	swa·sont
70	*soixante-dix*	swa·son·dees
80	*quatre-vingts*	ka·trer·vung
90	*quatre-vingt-dix*	ka·trer·vung·dees
100	*cent*	son
1000	*mille*	meel

PAPERWORK

name	*nom*	nom
nationality	*nationalité*	na·syo·na·lee·tay
date/place of birth	*date/place de naissance*	dat/plas der nay·sons
sex/gender	*sexe*	seks
passport	*passeport*	pas·por
visa	*visa*	vee·za

QUESTION WORDS

Who?	*Qui?*	kee
What?	*Quoi?*	kwa
What is it?	*Qu'est-ce que c'est?*	kes·ker say
When?	*Quand?*	kon
Where?	*Où?*	oo
Which?	*Quel/Quelle?*	kel
Why?	*Pourquoi?*	poor·kwa
How?	*Comment?*	ko·mon

SHOPPING & SERVICES

I'd like to buy ...
Je voudrais acheter ...   zher voo·dray ash·tay ...
How much is it?
C'est combien?   say kom·byun
I don't like it.
Cela ne me plaît pas.   ser·la ner mer play pa
May I look at it?
Est-ce que je peux le voir? es·ker zher per ler vwar
I'm just looking.
Je regarde.   zher rer·gard
It's cheap.
Ce n'est pas cher.   ser nay pa shair
It's too expensive.
C'est trop cher.   say tro shair
I'll take it.
Je le prends.   zher ler pron

Can I pay by ...?	*Est-ce que je peux payer avec ...?*	es·ker zher per pay·yay a·vek ...
credit card	*ma carte de crédit*	ma kart der kray·dee
travellers cheques	*des chèques de voyage*	day shek der vwa·yazh

more	*plus*	plew
less	*moins*	mwa
smaller	*plus petit*	plew per·tee
bigger	*plus grand*	plew gron

I'm looking for ...	*Je cherche ...*	zhe shersh ...
a bank	*une banque*	ewn bonk
the ... embassy	*l'ambassade de ...*	lam·ba·sahd der ...
the hospital	*l'hôpital*	lo·pee·tal
the market	*le marché*	ler mar·shay
the police	*la police*	la po·lees
the post office	*le bureau de poste*	ler bew·ro der post
a public phone	*une cabine téléphonique*	ewn ka·been tay·lay·fo·neek
a public toilet	*les toilettes*	lay twa·let

TIME & DATES

What time is it? *Quelle heure est-il?* kel er e til
It's (8) o'clock. *Il est (huit) heures.* il e (weet) er
It's half past ... *Il est (...) heures et demie.* il e (...) er e day·mee

in the morning	*du matin*	dew ma·tun
in the afternoon	*de l'après-midi*	der la·pray·mee·dee
in the evening	*du soir*	dew swar
today	*aujourd'hui*	o·zhoor·dwee
tomorrow	*demain*	der·mun
yesterday	*hier*	yair

Monday	*lundi*	lun·dee
Tuesday	*mardi*	mar·dee
Wednesday	*mercredi*	mair·krer·dee
Thursday	*jeudi*	zher·dee
Friday	*vendredi*	von·drer·dee
Saturday	*samedi*	sam·dee
Sunday	*dimanche*	dee·monsh

January	*janvier*	zhon·vyay
February	*février*	fayv·ryay
March	*mars*	mars
April	*avril*	a·vreel
May	*mai*	may
June	*juin*	zhwun
July	*juillet*	zhwee·yay
August	*août*	oot
September	*septembre*	sep·tom·brer
October	*octobre*	ok·to·brer
November	*novembre*	no·vom·brer
December	*décembre*	day·som·brer

TRANSPORT
Public Transport

What time does ... leave/arrive?	*À quelle heure part/arrive ...?*	a kel er par/a·reev ...
boat	*le bateau*	ler ba·to
bus	*le bus*	ler bews
plane	*l'avion*	la·vyon
train	*le train*	ler trun

I'd like a ... ticket.	*Je voudrais un billet ...*	zher voo·dray un bee·yay ...
one·way	*simple*	sum·pler
return	*aller et retour*	a·lay ay rer·toor
1st class	*de première classe*	der prem·yair klas
2nd class	*de deuxième classe*	der der·zyem klas

I want to go to ...
Je voudrais aller à ...   zher voo·dray a·lay a ...
The train has been delayed.
Le train est en retard.   ler trun e ton rer·tar
The train has been cancelled.
Le train a été annulé.   ler trun a ay·tay a·new·lay

ROAD SIGNS

Cédez la Priorité	Give Way
Danger	Danger
Défense de Stationner	No Parking
Entrée	Entrance
Interdiction de Doubler	No Overtaking
Péage	Toll
Ralentissez	Slow Down
Sens Interdit	No Entry
Sens unique	One-way
Sortie	Exit

the first	*le premier* (m)	ler prer·myay
	la première (f)	la prer·myair
the last	*le dernier* (m)	ler dair·nyay
	la dernière (f)	la dair·nyair
platform number	*le numéro de quai*	ler new·may·ro der kay
ticket office	*le guichet*	ler gee·shay
timetable	*l'horaire*	lo·rair
train station	*la gare*	la gar

Private Transport

I'd like to hire a/an...	*Je voudrais louer ...*	zher voo·dray loo·way ...
car	*une voiture*	ewn vwa·tewr
4WD	*un quatre-quatre*	un kat·kat
motorbike	*une moto*	ewn mo·to
bicycle	*un vélo*	un vay·lo

Is this the road to ...?
C'est la route pour ...?   say la root poor ...
Where's a service station?
Où est-ce qu'il y a une station-service?   oo es·keel ya ewn sta·syon·ser·vees
Please fill it up.
Le plein, s'il vous plaît.   ler plun seel voo play
I'd like ... litres.
Je voudrais ... litres.   zher voo·dray ... lee·trer

| petrol/gas | *essence* | ay·sons |
| diesel | *diesel* | dyay·zel |

(How long) Can I park here?
(Combien de temps) Est-ce que je peux stationner ici?   (kom·byun der tom) es·ker zher per sta·syo·nay ee·see?
Where do I pay?
Où est-ce que je paie?   oo es·ker zher pay?
I need a mechanic.
J'ai besoin d'un mécanicien.   zhay ber·zwun dun may·ka·nee·syun

The car/motorbike has broken down (at ...)
La voiture moto est tombée en panne (à ...)   la vwa·tewr/mo·to ay tom·bay on pan (a ...)
The car/motorbike won't start.
La voiture/moto ne veut pas démarrer.   la vwa·tewr/mo·to ner ver pa day·ma·ray
I have a flat tyre.
Mon pneu est à plat.   mom pner ay ta pla
I've run out of petrol.
Je suis en panne d'essence.   zher swee zon pan day·sons
I had an accident.
J'ai eu un accident.   zhay ew un ak·see·don

TRAVEL WITH CHILDREN

Is there a/an ...?	*Y a-t-il ...?*	ya teel ...
I need a/an ...	*J'ai besoin ...*	zhay ber·zwun ...
car baby seat	*d'un siège-enfant*	dun syezh·on·fon
child-minding service	*d'une garderie*	dewn gar·dree
children's menu	*d'un menu pour enfant*	dun mer·new poor on·fon
disposable nappies/diapers	*de couches-culottes*	der koosh·kew·lot
infant milk formula	*de lait maternisé*	de lay ma·ter·nee·zay
(English-speaking) babysitter	*d'une baby-sitter (qui parle anglais)*	dewn ba·bee·see·ter (kee parl ong·glay)
highchair	*d'une chaise haute*	dewn shay zot
potty	*d'un pot de bébé*	dun po der bay·bay
stroller	*d'une poussette*	dewn poo·set

Do you mind if I breastfeed here?
Cela vous dérange si j'allaite mon bébé ici?   ser·la voo day·ron·zhe see zha·lay·ter mon bay·bay ee·see
Are children allowed?
Les enfants sont permis?   lay zon·fon son pair·mee

Also available from Lonely Planet:
French Phrasebook

Glossary

For terms for food and drinks and other culinary vocabulary, see p96.

French (F) Corsican (C)

AGENC – Agence pour la Gestion des Espaces Naturels de Corse; Office for the Management of the Natural Areas of Corsica
aiguille (F) – rock mass or mountain peak shaped like a needle
anse (F) – cove
AOC – Appellation d'Origine Contrôlée; mark of quality for wines and cheeses
ATM – automated teller machine; cashpoint
auberge (F) – inn
auberge de jeunesse (F) – youth hostel

baie (F) – bay
bain (F) – bath
barrage (F) – dam
bastiglia (C) – fortress
bergerie (F) – shepherd's hut, often used as accommodation for walkers
bocca (C) – mountain pass
bouches (F) – straits
brèche (F) – breach, gap
brocciu/bruccio (C) – Corsican goat's or ewe's milk cheese
bruschetta – toasted bread rubbed with garlic and topped with any of a number of salads, roasted vegetables or other treats

calanques (F)/**calanche** (C) – rocky inlets
cap (F)/**capu/capo** (C) – cape
carrefour (F) – crossroads, intersection
cascade (F) – waterfall
casgili (C) – cheese cellar
castagnu (C) – chestnut
castellu (C) – castle
chambre d'hôte (F) – French equivalent of a B&B
chapelle (F) – chapel
charcuterie (F) – cured pork meats
cignale (C) – wild boar
cirque (F) – a semicircular or crescent-shaped basin with steep sides and a gently sloping floor, formed by the erosive action of ice
clos (F) – vineyard
cochon coureur (F) – free-ranging pig
col (F) – mountain pass
commune (F) – smallest unit of local government in rural areas/districts

Conseil Général (F) – General Council; implements legislation at local level
Conservatoire du Littoral (F) – Conservatoire de l'Espace Littoral et des Rivages Lacustres; Organisation for the Conservation of Coastal Areas and Lakeshores
Corse (F), **Corsu** (C) – Corsican language
couloir (F) – deep gully on a mountain side
couvent (F) – convent
crête (F) – ridge

défilé (F) – gorge, narrow pass
démaquisage (F) – scrub clearance
département (F) – unit of French regional administration
désert (F) – desert
dolmen – megalithic standing stones capped by a horizontal stone, thought to be tombs
domaine (F) – estate, especially one that produces wine

écobuage (F) – cultivation on burnt stubble
église (F) – church
étang (F) – lake, pond

fiadone (C) – flan made with *brocciu*, lemon and eggs
figatellu (C) – type of liver sausage
fola (C) – folk tale
forêt (F) – forest
FLNC – Front de Libération Nationale de la Corse; Corsican National Liberation Front

gîte d'étape (F) – mountain lodge, more comfortable than the basic *refuge*
golfe (F) – bay, gulf
goulet (F) – narrows; bottleneck at entrance to a harbour

half-board – bed, breakfast and one main meal

île (F) – isle, island

lac (F) – lake
laricio – type of pine native to Corsica
lauze (F) – type of stone found only in the area around Bastia
libeccio – southwesterly wind

magmatic rock – igneous rock, including granite, formed by magma rising within the earth's crust, which slowly crystallised as it rose
mairie (F) – town hall
maison (F) – office, house

maquis (F) – scrub vegetation
marché (F) – market
menhir – single standing stone, often carved, dating from the megalithic era
mouflon (F) – wild sheep native to Corsica

névé (F) – mass of porous ice; also known as a firn

ONF – Office National des Forêts; National Office for Forests
Optimist (F) – coracle

paillotte (F) – beach restaurant
panini – filled bread rolls
phare (F) – lighthouse
pieve (C) – small region; parish
pinzutti (C) – settlers from the French mainland
place (F) – square
plage (F) – beach
plongée (F) – diving
PNRC – Parc Naturel Régional de Corse; Corsican Nature Reserve
port de plaisance (F) – marina
pozzi (C) – pits
pozzines (C) – interlinked water holes
préfecture (F) – unit of regional administration in France

priorité à droite (F) – give way to the right
prisuttu (C) – Corsican raw ham
pointe (F), **punta** (C) – point; headland

randonnée (F) – walk
refuge (F) – mountain accommodation, from a basic hut to a simple hostel

sanglier (C) – wild boar
Saracen – Moor; Moorish
sec (F) – shallow (diving); dry (climate, wine, etc)
Sécurité Civile (F) – civil defence department
sémaphore (F) – coastal signal station
Shardanes – 'sea people'; ancient nautical race
son et lumière (F) – night-time presentation at a historic site using lighting, sound effects and narration
source (F) – spring

tafoni/taffoni (C) – cavities (geology)
torre (C) – circular stone formation or tower; plural *torri*
Torréens – invaders who conquered Corsica around 1100 BC; possibly the Shardanes
tour (F) – tower

vallée (F) – valley
vasques (F) – natural pools
vendetta – blood feud

The Authors

JEAN-BERNARD CARILLET   Coordinating author

A Paris-based journalist and photographer, Jean-Bernard has written extensively about Corsica, including Lonely Planet's *Corse* (in French) and several
features for French magazines. As an incorrigible Frenchman and foodie, he
confesses a pronounced penchant for the robust Corsican cuisine. When
he's not sampling charcuterie and pungent cheeses in the Castagniccia or
the Haut Taravo, or sipping a glass (or two) of a fruity Saparale, he burns
off the calories by meandering along hiking trails or diving in the Med (or
in other exotic locations). For this edition, he was all too happy to travel
the length and breadth of eastern and southern Corsica – an epic 5000km
journey along twisting roads in the most and least visited corners of the
island. For this edition he wrote the Introduction, Highlights, Getting Started, Snapshot, Walking & the
GR20, The Great Outdoors, Food & Drink, The East, The South and the Directory chapters.

MILES RODDIS

Miles, who lives beside the Mediterranean in Valencia, Spain, has hiked the
island of Mallorca for Lonely Planet's *Walking in Spain*, explored the island
of Elba, visible across the water from Corsica, for the *Italy* guide, and lazed
on the beaches of Sardinia, Corsica's southern neighbour, for sheer fun. He's
written or contributed to over 25 Lonely Planet titles including, on the French
mainland, *France*, *Brittany & Normandy* and – perhaps most enjoyably of
all – *Walking in France*. But this is the first, hugely satisfying time he has
married these two strands by exploring Corsica – Mediterranean, French,
yet in so many ways not completely French.

For this edition he wrote the History, The Culture, Environment, Walking
& the GR20, Bastia & the Far North, Calvi & La Balagne, The West Coast, The Central Mountains and
Transport chapters.

Behind the Scenes

THIS BOOK

This is the 4th edition of Lonely Planet's *Corsica* and was written by Jean-Bernard Carillet and Miles Roddis. The 1st French-language edition of *Corse* was written by Olivier Cirendini, Jean-Bernard Carillet, Christophe Corbel, Laurence Billiet and Tony Wheeler, and was translated into English as *Corsica* by Atlas Translations in London. The 2nd edition of *Corse* was updated by Olivier and Julien Fouin. The 2nd English-language version was revised and updated by Mark Zussman. The 3rd edition was revised and updated independently of the French-language edition by Oda O'Carroll and David Atkinson; the GR20 chapter was updated by Adrienne Costanzo using material written by Olivier Cirendini and Arno Lebonnois from the 3rd edition of *Corse*. The Health chapter is based on text by Dr Caroline Evans. This guidebook was commissioned in Lonely Planet's London office, and produced by the following:

Commissioning Editor Judith Bamber, Ella O'Donnell, Sally Schafer
Coordinating Editor Rosie Nicholson
Coordinating Cartographer Anita Banh
Coordinating Layout Designer Margaret Jung
Managing Editor Bruce Evans
Managing Cartographer Mark Griffiths
Assisting Editors Yvonne Byron, Sally O'Brien, Kyla Gillzan
Assisting Cartographers Erin McManus, Andy Rojas
Cover Designer Pepi Bluck
Project Manager Glenn van der Knijff, Sarah Sloane
Language Content Coordinator Quentin Frayne

Thanks to Sally Darmody, Fayette Fox, Trent Paton, Stephanie Pearson, Wibowo Rusli, Tamsin Wilson, Celia Wood

THANKS
JEAN-BERNARD CARILLET

Heaps of thanks to Lonely Planet's Ella, Judith and Sally for their trust and encouragement since the beginning of this fantastic Corsican experience. In the production department, I'd like to say a *'merci énormément'* to Rosie Nicholson who worked so hard on this book – thanks for your enthusiasm, cooperation and constant support. I'd also like to express my gratitude to Miles, whose flexibility was much appreciated, not to mention his *bonne humeur*. A big thanks also to the cartos, especially Anita, for their patience and cooperation. At home, tons of *gros bisous* to my daughter Eva, who shared some of my Corsican adventures some years ago and gives a meaning to my otherwise gypsy life. Lastly, to all the Corsicans I met and interviewed while on the road – thanks for having shared your passion and opened doors.

MILES RODDIS

Huge thanks, as always, to Ingrid for so much – especially her girl-racer rally driving around the tight bends and ribbon-narrow country roads of Corsica. A very special thank you too to Jean-Bernard, for his infectious enthusiasm and generous sharing of information. Also to Lonely Planet France colleague Olivier Cirendini for tips passed on and information shared. Claire Hall of Direct Corsica Travel kindly gave me some much appreciated leads and reader Marnix Koets alerted me to the Argentella silver mine. So

---

THE LONELY PLANET STORY

The story begins with a classic travel adventure: Tony and Maureen Wheeler's 1972 journey across Europe and Asia to Australia. There was no useful information about the overland trail then, so Tony and Maureen published the first Lonely Planet guidebook to meet a growing need.

From a kitchen table, Lonely Planet has grown to become the largest independent travel publisher in the world, with offices in Melbourne (Australia), Oakland (USA) and London (UK). Today Lonely Planet guidebooks cover the globe. There is an ever-growing list of books and information in a variety of media. Some things haven't changed. The main aim is still to make it possible for adventurous travellers to get out there – to explore and better understand the world.

At Lonely Planet we believe travellers can make a positive contribution to the countries they visit – if they respect their host communities and spend their money wisely. Every year 5% of company profit is donated to charities around the world.

SEND US YOUR FEEDBACK

We love to hear from travellers – your comments keep us on our toes and help make our books better. Our well-travelled team reads every word on what you loved or loathed about this book. Although we cannot reply individually to postal submissions, we always guarantee that your feedback goes straight to the appropriate authors, in time for the next edition. Each person who sends us information is thanked in the next edition – and the most useful submissions are rewarded with a free book. See the Behind the Scenes section.

To send us your updates – and find out about Lonely Planet events, newsletters and travel news – visit our award-winning website: **www.lonelyplanet.com/contact**.

Note: we may edit, reproduce and incorporate your comments in Lonely Planet products such as guidebooks, websites and digital products, so let us know if you don't want your comments reproduced or your name acknowledged. For a copy of our privacy policy, go to www.lonelyplanet .com/privacy.

many tourist office staff went out of their way to be helpful. Thank you, once again, to Anne-Marie Piazzoli (Calvi), Marie-Jo Corombani (Île Rousse), Sylvie (Olmi-Cappella), hyper-efficient Rose-Marie Marchioni (Bastia), Stéphanie Saladini (Maison de Cap Corse, Bastia), Sandrine Ohresser (Cargèse), Josette Leca (Porto) and Marie-Dominique (Corte). My chapters are all for Finley, hoping that he'll come to love mountains and wildness as much as his Yayo does.

OUR READERS

Many thanks to the travellers who used the last edition and wrote to us with helpful hints, useful advice and interesting anecdotes:

Anne Brasier, Major Chris Crowther, Quentin Curran, George Dehnel, Fionnuala Hoffmann, Tina Hough, Klaus & Gerdy Kelson, John Langbein, Mauro Leoni, Toby Manhire, Michael Marcus, Alain Paillard, Tanya Pankhurst, Mike Robinson, Sue Royal, Stephanie Rubec, Anne Slump, Victoria Szwec, Esther van den Reek, Sofie Vanhoutte, Andrea Weyand, Marvin Wiehe

ACKNOWLEDGMENTS

Many thanks to the following for the use of their content:

Index

| 12am | 1am | 2am | 3am | 4am | 5am | 6am | 7am | 8am | 9am | 10am | 11am | 12pm |